# World Revolutionary Elites
*Studies in Coercive Ideological Movements*

# World Revolutionary Elites
## Studies in Coercive Ideological Movements

*edited by*
*HAROLD D. LASSWELL*
*and*
*DANIEL LERNER*

The M.I.T. Press
*Massachusetts Institute of Technology*
*Cambridge, Massachusetts*

# Foreword

THIS VOLUME brings together a group of studies that broke new ground for modern political science, notably in the effort to formulate and further the "policy sciences of democracy." The scientific study of politics serves public policy when it describes past trends and the conditions of their occurrence so as to project the probable course of future events. It thereby teaches policy makers where they must intervene to reshape the projected course of future history in directions closer to the objectives they serve. The policy sciences serve democratic objectives when they clarify the policy alternatives available, in terms of democratic values, at any given time and place.

How do elite studies serve democratic objectives? First, they do so by correcting the "democratic fallacy" that governments are run *by* the governed. Governments are run by the governors who, in our preferred democratic polity, *represent* the governed and can be turned out of office upon failure to perform this function adequately. Second, they correct the "pathetic fallacy" that assumes, in politics as in all creative arts, that the object of one's attention is necessarily also the object of one's affection. In political science, as in all science, the case is usually the reverse. One pays attention to a process one does not understand, an assumption one questions, a conclusion one doubts.

In precisely this sense, elite studies are not "elitist." Quite the contrary! Those who celebrate elites do so by dedicating their poems, their music, and even their lives. Those who *study* elites question their assumptions and doubt their conclusions—thereby inducing better understanding of elite functions in a democratic society. The ultimate objective of elite studies in the description of past trends, in the analysis of conditions, and in the projection of future sequences is to put policy on a more deliberately ethical basis by clarifying goals and on a more deliberately rational basis by evaluating options.

This, clearly, is not the political methodology practiced by the world revolutionary elites that we have studied in the volume at hand. Despite the intense moral indignation of their utterances, the totalitarians were not deliberately ethical. Despite their intense intellectuality, notably the revolutionary generation of Communists in Russia and China, they were not deliberately rational. Coercive ideology, the common denominator of the totalitarian movements and their regimes, is the polar opposite of ethical rationality as historically understood. The "purges" by the Communists, the genocidal *Judenreinigung* practiced by the Nazis, the castor oil administered by the Fascists—all these horrors, by their nomenclature as by their practice, indicate a constriction of spirit far removed from ethical refinement. That such practices were rationalized by symbols of righteous self-justification indicates that ideology can work many variations upon rationality without concern for its basic laws of objectivity and verifiability.[1]

The coercive ideologues thus confronted the complacent Western assumption of inevitable democratic progress based upon ethical rationality with the counterformation of totalitarian regress based upon coercive ideology. As a result, the West erupted in total war demanding unconditional surrender. But World War II only stilled the most urgent threat without transforming the underlying social process that gives birth to coercive ideologues. The U.S.S.R. survived World War II and took charge of Eastern Europe. Shortly thereafter, the political methodology of coercive ideology was introduced into Asia by the Communization of China. Today, China vies with Russia for pre-eminence in the global spread of coercive ideology as the political mode of the future. It is this which gives point and poignancy to the republication of studies made a decade and longer ago.

With the exception of the opening and closing chapters, and much of Chapter 2, the original text is reproduced. This policy is adopted with several considerations in mind. Full-scale studies will eventually appear in the present series that carry the analyses to date and intensify the initial coverage. We are greatly interested in improving the technique of projecting future developments. Many formulations that were made a few years ago have been partially fulfilled (or falsified) by intervening events. How can these successes or failures be accounted for? Was it a matter of insufficient access to significant facts; or was it mainly a question of appropriate or inappropriate inferences drawn

[1] For the philosophic analysis of this aspect of totalitarian thinking, see the remarkable little book by Svend Ranulf, *Hitlers Kampf Gegen Die Objektivität* (Copenhagen: Universitets Vorlaget i Aarhus, Ejnar Munksgaard, 1946).

from available information? Surely the growth of the policy sciences depends on the continuing reappraisal of findings and techniques.

These researches evolved as part of a program initiated at the Hoover Institute of Stanford University by Harold H. Fisher and C. Easton Rothwell, chairman and vice-chairman of the Institute. Funds were supplied by Stanford University and a grant from the Carnegie Foundation of New York.

HAROLD D. LASSWELL
DANIEL LERNER

# Acknowledgments

The following have been reprinted with permission of the authors and publishers:

HAROLD D. LASSWELL, *The World Revolution of Our Time: A Framework for Basic Policy Research*, Parts I-III. Originally published by the Stanford University Press in 1951. Series A: General Studies, No. 1, of the Hoover Institute Studies.

GEORGE K. SCHUELLER, *The Politburo*. Originally published by the Stanford University Press in 1951. Series B: Elite Studies, No. 2, of the Hoover Institute Studies.

HAROLD D. LASSWELL with RENZO SERENO, "The Fascists: The Changing Italian Elite." Originally published in the *American Political Science Review*, Vol. XXXI, pp. 914-929.

DANIEL LERNER with ITHIEL DE SOLA POOL and GEORGE K. SCHUELLER, *The Nazi Elite*. Originally published in 1951 by the Stanford University Press. Series B: Elite Studies, No. 3, of the Hoover Institute Studies.

ROBERT C. NORTH with ITHIEL DE SOLA POOL, *Kuomintang and Chinese Communist Elites*. Originally published by the Stanford University Press in 1952. Series B: Elite Studies, No. 8, of the Hoover Institute Studies.

# Contents

CHAPTER THREE

## The Politburo                                                     97

*George K. Schueller*

CHAPTER FOUR

## The Fascists: The Changing Elite                                 179

*Harold D. Lasswell* with *Renzo Sereno*

CHAPTER FIVE

## The Nazi Elite                                                   194

*Daniel Lerner* with *Ithiel de Sola Pool* and *George K. Schueller*

CHAPTER SIX

## Kuomintang and Chinese Communist Elites   319

Robert C. *North* with Ithiel de Sola *Pool*

CHAPTER SEVEN

## The Coercive Ideologists in Perspective   456

Daniel *Lerner*

## Index   469

# World Revolutionary Elites
*Studies in Coercive Ideological Movements*

## CHAPTER ONE

HAROLD D. LASSWELL

# Introduction:
# The Study of Political Elites

IN RECENT YEARS the study of elites has come to occupy a prominent position on the research agenda of political scientists, historians, and other scholars in the social and behavioral fields.[1] The theoretical framework originally developed beyond its sources in the classical literature of the Greeks by Gaetano Mosca, Vilfredo Pareto, and Robert Michels has been progressively reassessed in the light of contemporary inquiries.[2] In the early nineteen-fifties when the first version of the elite studies was published, it was possible to call attention to only a few monographs on political elites outside Europe and the United States.[3] Today we have at hand or in preparation a number of studies on Asia, Africa, and Latin America.

Thus we shall restate the approach, dealing first with general questions, and eventually examining the significance of the data reported in the current volume for elite analysis. We shall also reissue the original essay on "The World Revolution of Our Time," augmented by

[1] Bibliographic guides can be found in Dwaine Marvick (ed.), *Political Decision-Makers* (New York: The Free Press of Glencoe, 1961). The editors of the present series plan to include an annotated and selective bibliography at an early date.

[2] See J. H. Meisel's *The Myth of the Ruling Class: Gaetano Mosca and the "Elite"* (Ann Arbor: University of Michigan Press, 1958), R. Sereno, *The Rulers* (New York: Praeger, 1962), and the voluminous recent publications on the theory of power.

[3] In H. D. Lasswell, D. Lerner, and C. E. Rothwell, *The Comparative Study of Elites: An Introduction and Bibliography*, Hoover Institute Studies (Stanford: Stanford University Press, 1952).

a section that embellishes the fundamental construct. As the volumes appear in the present series, we propose to reappraise the theoretical models and the methodology outlined in these introductory pages. Since our approach is explicitly contextual, it is open to orderly revision as the curtain rises on future events.

By this time recognition is widespread that the world-inclusive study of power elites is indispensable to all serious inquiry into political processes. If inquiry is directed toward the past, to retrace the sequence of change, the omission of elite data is unthinkable. If the principal aim is to uncover key factors in the arena of power, there is no avoiding the study of elites. The inquirer who faces the future, seeking to estimate the locus and speed of political encounters, must perceive the salience of elite data. If the task is to clarify value goals for the political process, it is essential to consider the issues that arise in the relations of elites with one another and with nonelites. Inseparable from every policy option is the weighing of costs and benefits to elites who are in potential conflict or cooperation. Whatever the intellectual task in the total problem-solving process — whether it is chiefly a question of trend, condition, projection, goal, or alternative — the elite dimension is always pertinent.

## PRELIMINARY DEFINITION

A great variety of definitions — contemplative, manipulative, conceptual, and operational — have been and doubtless will be given to the elite category. By this time most scientific observers realize that any single definition for such a key term as "elite" is inadequate. Too many objectives of science and policy are at stake. The scholar's obligation is discharged when he gives his definition in general terms and shows by specific indices what is intended in concrete situations. Any competent theorist can match the definition with his preferred systematics.

Most simply, the elite are the influential. The following sentences provide illustration of common usages that refer to elites: "The Democratic Party has dominated the South for many years"; "The Italians continue to control the College of Cardinals and the Papacy"; "In scientific societies the biologists and the social scientists carry less weight than the physicists, chemists, astronomers, and mathematicians"; "Great family fortunes continue to affect investments"; "The influence of religion on the birth rate is paramount in preindustrial societies"; "The standards of education are set largely by the college entrance boards"; "The influence of parents on the choice of marriage partners is declining everywhere"; "The films have more impact upon the individual's sense of responsibility than churches."

For the moment we do not concern ourselves with the truth or falsity of these propositions. The immediate point is solely the manifest content of what is asserted, and the questions that arise in connection with the elite concept. Obviously, most if not all of the quoted statements assume that influence is unequal. And all students of politics and society are well aware of the enormous number of cases in which inequalities do in fact exist. The interesting question is whether the term "elite" is to be applied to concrete situations, if any, in which influence is equal.

Since our purpose is to provide a conceptual tool for designating configurations of influence disclosed by empirical research, it is inappropriate to exclude hypothetical contingencies in advance. If influence is equally shared, every participant in the situation belongs to the elite. If sharing is unequal, the most influential are called elite; others are mid-elite and rank-and-file.

Elite analysis distinguishes between members and nonmembers of a group in the context under study. The former are self-identified, or identified by knowledgeable observers, as participants in the formation and execution of policy. Influence on group policy is also exercised by nonmembers. The allusion in a previous paragraph to family fortunes and the investment market is a convenient instance. The American investment market is affected not only by American families but by families other than American nationals. If a given elite study is restricted to comparing the influence of the nationals of a state, the assets (and liabilities) of foreign support are properly described as among the base values of those nationals who are able to use foreign influence.

The investment example is useful in bringing out the distinction between collectivities, which are groups, and aggregates. On the one hand, families are identifiable entities, possessing symbols of common identity, value demands, and expectations. We can ascertain family names and expectations about the family's past, present, and future. An investment market, on the other hand, may not be comprehensively organized; nor may its limits be generally understood. Unreported transactions may occur that stretch the actual dimensions of the market well beyond prevailing public expectations. In the postwar world the foreign-investing role of socialist economies, and of many individual operators, has often been elusive. The distinctions to be insisted upon for analytic purposes hold that a group is a collectivity with at least a specified frequency of shared symbols of identity, demand, and expectation; aggregates fall below these critical frequencies.

The difference between organized and unorganized groups deserves explicit mention. Some of the most widely acknowledged entities in the world social process, such as civilizations, are only partially organized. For example, the carriers of Western European civilization have long been divided into separate states. Religions, languages, and markets are, in varying degree, transnational. "Races" too are not always neatly distributed in organized domains. When we examine the participants in the world arena from the legal perspective, we find that only *individuals* and *organized groups* are sufficiently responsible to be recognized as entities. The organized groups are nation-states, transnational intergovernmental organizations, transnational political parties and pressure groups, and other transnational private associations.[4]

## THE CONTEXTUAL APPROACH

Our discussion has laid the foundation for a fundamental principle of inquiry into power elites. The approach must be contextual; if arbitrary characterizations are to be avoided, it must locate power elites in the context of the relevant process. And the "relevant" social process depends on intensity of interaction. For many centuries the peoples of the Americas had only intermittent, sporadic, and minuscule contact with Afro-Asian or island peoples in the the world environment. *Some* interactions were taking place,[5] but so infrequently that the social process of the globe as a whole constituted a very thin aggregate indeed. It is increasingly plausible to select as a major turning point in human affairs the emergence of urban civilizations from the previously existing folk societies. It appears that urban civilizations arose concurrently in at least three river valleys: the Nile, the Tigris-Euphrates, and the Indus. The time was about the fourth millennium B.C.[6]

The complex division of labor that deserves to be called a civilized society brought with it, and perpetually interacted with, many novel

[4] See the systematic contributions to international law that are in the course of publication by The Yale University Press under the leadership of Myres S. McDougal. The most recent title is *The Public Order of Space*, by M. S. McDougal, H. D. Lasswell, and I. Vlasic (1963).

[5] On prehistoric migration and travel, see the various clues referred to in Stuart Piggott (ed.), *The Dawn of Civilization: The First World Survey of Human Cultures in Early Times* (New York: McGraw-Hill, 1961), and Edward Bacon (ed.), *Vanished Civilizations of the Ancient World* (New York: McGraw-Hill, 1963).

[6] Consult V. Gordon Childe, *What Happened in History* (Baltimore: Pelican Books, 1954).

institutions. Outstanding was literacy, which fostered the cumulative increase of social capital in the form of enlightenment. Conspicuous, likewise, was law in the form of deliberately codified prescriptions to be applied throughout a territorial jurisdiction almost without regard to traditional ties of kinship. The production and distribution of wealth were accelerated by the expansion of commerce, manufacturing, money, and credit. Sanitary engineering and economic opportunity contributed to population growth. Local religious faiths were either superseded or fused with more comprehensive theologies and rites. Traditional respect orders and ranks were modified to fit the pretensions of the rich, the holy, the powerful, the learned, the skillful, the popular, the energetic.

Since the invention of civilization the history of man can be meaningfully written in terms of the spread and restriction of civilizations in competition and conflict with one another, and with folk societies.[7] In modern times we are acutely conscious of the spread of the Western European pattern of civilization, which is rapidly becoming the universal culture of mankind. The power elites that function inside civilized societies differ in profound ways from the top power components of folk societies, whether the latter are wandering bands of hunters, fishers, and gatherers, or sessile agriculturists. The power elites reflect and reshape the relations internal to every body politic organized within civilizations or folk communities; they interact with every external threat and opportunity.

## THE SOCIAL PROCESS

If we are to subject these intricate developments to scholarly, scientific, and policy-oriented discipline, we must operate with a comprehensive scheme or model of the social process and give particular prominence to the role of power. The most general way to think of social process is as "people" who are "interacting" with one another and with their "resource environment." The people may be classified as "individuals" or "collectivities"; and the collectivities are "organized" and "unorganized." To interact is to affect others and, in turn, to be affected. The resource environment includes the Earth and the configurations of inner and outer space, and all biological forms.[8]

Since man is a living form, we adopt the maximization postulate as

[7] Robert Redfield, *The Primitive World and Its Transformations* (Ithaca: Cornell University Press, 1953).

[8] The categories employed here are elaborated in more detail in H. D. Lasswell and A. Kaplan, *Power and Society* (New Haven: Yale University Press, 1950).

a guide to stating hypotheses for the study of his interactions. According to the postulate, man seeks to maximize valued outcomes; he does something in the expectation of being better off than if he did something else. We remark in passing that this is intuitively plausible, especially since the postulate holds even when human beings make erroneous calculations and in retrospect wish they had acted differently.

For the analysis of social process we now introduce a further elaboration of our preliminary outline. Man seeks to maximize "valued outcomes" by adopting "institutional practices" that also affect the "resource environment." We adopt eight categories of reference to outcome events, which will be illustrated presently. Why eight categories? The answer is that it is convenient to think in terms of a short list, and to use a list that roughly approximates the categories by which data are obtained and processed in the historical and social sciences. In scanning a social process it is important to identify as "outcomes" the interactions that are often perceived as culminating events in a sequence of planning and striving.

The following comments relate explicitly to the eight valued outcomes and institutions: (1) "Power" outcomes include such a final decision as winning or losing an election or a war; and the relevant institutions are specialized as government, law, and politics. (2) "Enlightenment" outcomes are the giving and receiving of information, as in disseminating or reading books; the institutions include mass media and research agencies. (3) "Wealth" outcomes are, for example, trading, borrowing, and lending; the institutions are units of production and markets. (4) "Well-being" outcomes directly involve safety, health, and comfort; the institutions include patterns specialized to medical care. (5) "Skill" outcomes are demonstrations of excellence in arts, crafts, and professions; the institutions include the procedures of training. (6) "Affection" outcomes are the giving and receiving of love and intimacy; the institutions are the practices of family and friendship. (7) "Respect" outcomes are the giving and receiving of honor and consideration; the relevant institutions include the practices of discrimination and distinction. (8) "Rectitude" outcomes are, for example, mutual characterizations as "righteous" or "sinful," "ethically upright," or "immoral"; the rectitude institutions are the ecclesiastical or secular specializations in articulating and applying standards.

Employing the definition of "elite" as the influential, we distinguish eight elite levels in a social process. Where influence is unequal, the elite class with respect to each value outcome may be occupied by few or many. Obviously, the distribution pattern of influence for each value may approximate many different geometrical figures, notably the pyramid or the "onion tower." It is clear on reflection that the specific persons who occupy a top position with respect to one value are likely to hold correspondingly favorable positions with respect to other values; in fact, this possibility is the "agglutination hypothesis."[9] The social context as a whole can be characterized according to each value or all values aggregatively.

In order to fit a model to concrete circumstances, one must distinguish between the "conventional" and the "functional" meaning of key categories, such as elite or power. If we sift the vocabulary of a given community, it is often easy to discover words that closely approximate the definitions that a scientific observer uses for comprehensive analytic and comparative purposes. In Italian, for instance, there are "the fat" and "the thin"; and the connotations are wider than any particular value. If the scientist is beginning the study of a little-known society, he can plan his research in ways that disclose more and more information about the context and enable him progressively to reorganize the data in closer accord with basic functional definitions.

Consider in this connection the anthropologist who begins his work on a poorly described tribe or village. Whatever information can be scraped together at the start can be employed to make a preliminary assignment of situations to each value-institution category. Perhaps he has evidence of disputes between one tribe or village and another. Obviously, he can assign this to the power outcomes. He may learn of a steady flow of decisions taken within the community by a council of elders. Clearly, this is an institutional power practice. He learns of marriages (initially allocated to affection outcomes), of deaths (well-being), of a new radio (enlightenment), of harvesting (wealth), of a religious fiesta (rectitude), of concerts by musicians (skill), of a memorial ceremony for a dead hero (respect). The value-institution map serves as a comprehensive reminder of the total design of the community process.

Of course, the initial assignments may be vastly changed before research is concluded. Wholly new participants may be discovered, such as secret societies, whose conclaves are the most important occasions of decision. Research may indicate that while various fiestas or memorial ceremonies do in fact make use of religious symbolism and give respect to heroic figures, they are more adequately classified as

---

[9] "Forms of power and influence are agglutinative: Those with some forms tend to acquire other forms also," *ibid.*, p. 97. This proposition is especially helpful in drawing research attention to factors that account for seeming deviation from the predicted relationship. A corroborating study is G. W. Skinner, *Leadership and Power in the Chinese Community of Thailand* (Ithaca: Cornell University Press, 1958).

acts of political defiance against alleged exploitation by a "colonial" power. Family institutions may eventually figure but mildly in the list of important occasions for the expression of affection. Instead, kinship institutions may be the principal apportioners of power, wealth, and respect. Since all acts involve all values in some degree, the significance of particular practices will presumably shift as the context comes into view.[10]

Before these conclusions can be supported by data of observation, the preoutcome, outcome, and postoutcome events of every category must be systematically traced. For this purpose it is necessary to describe the participants, perspectives, situations, base values, and strategies that lead up to the outcomes, and to follow through to post-outcome effects. Briefly defined, the participants are the individuals and groups who are relatively active in pursuing a value outcome and effect. The perspectives are the demands and expectations associated with the "primary ego" and the "total self." The situations are the organized and unorganized settings created by the flow of interactions relating to a particular value process. The base values are the assets and liabilities available at any time to participants; and the strategies are the ways in which base values are managed to affect outcomes and effects. In the course of these operations it becomes more evident who participates how often and with what weight in decisions and choices.

## THE DECISION PROCESS

The distinction between decisions and choices is critical for the identification of power elites. We have cited as examples of decision outcomes the final votes taken by electorates, legislatures, cabinets, administrative agencies, or courts; and we might add final victories or defeats in combat. The common features are that the outcome involves the whole context to a significant degree; severe coercive measures are actually employed, or expected to be employed with success, against challengers of the result.

Not all the occasions called "voting," in the conventional sense of casting a ballot, are decisions in the functional sense. They are choices. Stock instances are statutes that are voted by a majority, yet are expected by very few legislators to be enforced, or even to affect community conduct. They may be token reaffirmations of almost obsolete ethical norms—for instance, Puritan norms of Sabbath observance or

---

[10] A detailed exemplification of "systematic functionalism" will be presented in the forthcoming analysis of Vicos, Peru, by Allan Holmberg, H. D. Lasswell, and others.

sumptuary prohibitions of the manufacture and sale of alcoholic beverages. Such legislation may be passed in response to lobbies on the eve of elections; but the lobbies may be discounted by competent observers as effective influences on community behavior. Influences are factors that affect "commitments"; unless the commitments are sustained by expectations (subsequently verified) of enforcement by the use of severe sanctions, they are choices, not decisions.

If the relevant context is to be brought into the open for scientific purposes, distinctions must be made between "public order" and "civic order," which are the components of "social order."[11] The public order embraces the value patterns and institutions of the power process, as well as the distinctive values, patterns, and institutions of the whole society which are protected and fulfilled by the process of decision. Political institutions defend themselves; they likewise sustain the fundamental patterns of the market, the family system, and other components of the culture. The scope of the civic order is no less inclusive; but civic order employs mild, not severe, sanctions. In a stable body politic the power elite has the role of mobilizing the predispositions of the community to adopt and execute policies consistent with its basic goals. Where human dignity is taken seriously, a long-run objective is to allow the civic order to expand as public order recedes, since persuasion, and not coercion, is the strategy most consistent with the long-range goal. The power elite, in common with all elites, is influential; it differs in having severe sanctions at its disposal. Thanks to the interdependent character of the social process, conventional institutions involve all values to some extent. The wealth elite, for instance, typically exercises some degree of effective power besides operating in a free market.

The exploration of elites is furthered by examining the several outcomes that specifically relate to decision. We can identify the elite of overt and covert services of intelligence and planning; the elite of political parties and pressure associations, who exercise the promoting function; the elite of legislatures and related agencies of prescription; the elite of police and prosecutors, who specialize in invocation; the elite of administrative organs and judicial tribunals of application; the elites of appraisal and termination.[12] Because of the need for active consent in popular government, the top figures in every outcome phase are likely to have strong party connections. However, attempts

---

[11] See H. D. Lasswell in C. J. Friedrich (ed.), *The Public Interest*, "Nomos," Vol. 5 (New York: Atherton Press, 1962), especially pp. 66-67.

[12] On the seven decision-outcome categories, consult H. D. Laswell, *The Future of Political Science* (New York: Atherton Press, 1963), Chs. 3 and 4.

are usually made to nullify party influence in the invocation and application stages of decision.

Another major point remains to be clarified regarding the scope of
the elite concept. A term like "leaders" or "leadership" carries the
connotation of persons who are affirmatively engaged in politics; and
this connotation is convenient. The political elite, on the contrary, are
not necessarily active participants at a given moment. We think of the
power elite as the collectivity from which active decision makers are
drawn during particular periods in the life of a body politic. Not all
members of a "ruling family" try to rule; nor do they necessarily rule
all the time.[13]

## POWER ELITES

Research on power elites must raise the questions common to the
study of any participant in the political process. Who are they? What
are their perspectives? In what arenas do they function? What base
values are at their disposal? What strategies do they use? How successful are they in influencing outcomes and effects?

These questions require answers that identify the power elite in a
given context, and permit the investigator to turn to the task of scientific explanation. Under what conditions do elites exhibit a given pattern of composition, of perspective, of arena activity, of base values,
of strategies, or of impact?

### Participants

We shall comment upon some of the problems that face an investigator who seeks to identify and explain elite phenomena. The first
issue is: What categories are useful in describing elite composition?
Clearly, the general answer includes whatever factors are important
determiners of behavior. As the social and behavioral sciences evolve,
investigators attach importance to factors that have previously been
neglected, and de-emphasize factors that were formerly judged to be
significant. For purposes of identifying elite members the following
general categories are unmistakably relevant.

*Community.* By this term is meant the territorially oriented settings

---

[13] An analysis of a sample of one hundred families of the British peerage in
which the title has descended without interruption between 1800 and 1900 shows
that less than thirty-one of these elite families engaged in known political activity. In
thirty-four families two thirds or more of the members were active in politics. If
we limit the term "leadership" to persons who exhibit a high degree of public
activity in the decision process, only a few of the latter would qualify. W. L. Gutts-
man, "The Changing Social Structure of the British Political Elite, 1886–1935,"
*British Journal of Sociology,* II (1951), pp. 122–134.

to which individuals have been, or are currently, exposed. It is particularly important to inquire into the culture, using the term "culture" to designate distinctive and comprehensive patterns of life. Judgments of distinctiveness are made with the panorama of history and pre-history in view. Less distinctive patterns are subcultures. If we take "Western European civilization" as a culture, it is possible to identify an "American" subculture, and below that, to take note of regional and local variations. Nobody doubts the relevancy of such information to elite study, since a fundamental theory is that young people introject the culture in which they are reared, and many predispositions of an elite are presumably to be accounted for in such terms. The truth is, of course, that it is more common to assume than to demonstrate that culture counts. We know that under various circumstances the culture of one's early years is rejected in whole or part, especially if it is perceived as a handicap to a successful career in politics. Individuals reared in minority cultures not infrequently break away and acquire the majority way of life; and local or regional figures reach out to achieve enough sophistication to pave the way to the playing of an active part in the larger national or transnational arena. There are cases of shift in the opposite direction, as when persons of cosmopolitan upbringing settle down to identify themselves as fully as possible with a parochial community.[14]

*Class.* A frequent finding in elite analysis is that the top office-holders and public leaders of a given time were exposed in formative years to the class culture of the power elite. They were not necessarily members of elite families; even in the role of servants, dependents, assistants, or acquaintances they were in a position to see and partially to acquire outlook and style "to the manner born."

It is generally believed that if early years are spent in penury or opulence, a permanent mark is left upon the politician. Given the acute economic differentiations current in contemporary culture, no elite analyst is likely to overlook this factor.

Research on social classes has emphasized the role of the respect position of the family. The "old family" is not necessarily the rich family; in fact, there are many active political leaders whose ambition was presumably fired by the discrepancy between their status as a member of a noble, though impoverished, family and the economic freedom of others.

The power elite is differentially recruited in many communities from

[14] The significance of cross-cultural exposure is confirmed by the studies that appear in this series. The occasion may be a parental environment with cross-cultural kin, friends, or servants; or early travel and study. Absence of primary exposure may be supplemented by secondary exposure to books and other media.

those who have acquired or exercised particular skills. Legal and military training often come in this category.

The enlightenment resulting from foreign travel or from study has provided an advantageous background for entry into active public life.

The significance of love and friendship as a steppingstone to power is obvious in the case of many mistresses and former playmates or schoolmates who have been elevated by their powerful friends.

Similarly, political elites may be refreshed by an infusion of exceptionally strong, healthy, and mentally alert individuals whose traits were allowed to exhibit themselves in the early years of life.

Holiness or uprightness, also cultivated in formative years, may lead to political preferment.[15]

*Interest.* Power elites are recruited from a vast range of exposure to interest groups; and political scientists are especially keen in detecting interests. We define "interest groups" as other than community and class formations, since a term is needed to designate groups that cut across such lines, or are too small to qualify as communities or classes. Interest groups are noncommunity or nonclass groups sharing expectations of common advantages (or perceived by scientific observers as actual or potential possessors of common advantages).

Interest groups that are primarily specialized to the power process, and that contribute to the elite class, include political parties, pressure groups, and civil and military organizations. Economic distinctions can be recognized among fishing, hunting, mining, agriculture, manufacture, trade, finance, transportation, and the like. Respect interests vary by social rank and according to identifiable kin group. Interests divide by levels of excellence in acquiring and exercising artistic, occupational, and professional skills. Often the poor performers in these categories turn to politics and find a congenial ladder. Enlightenment interests divide according to school of thought, including the traditional theorists and traditions of strong or weak government, militant or pacific foreign policy, "East" or "West" orientation, and the like. Every pair or circle of friends becomes an interest group, as does every loyalty to extended social formations, such as cultures or ethnic entities. Religious faiths and diverse ethical positions also affect the recruitment of political elites.[16]

[15] Consult H. D. Lasswell, *Power and Personality* (New York: Norton, 1948), and this series.
[16] What is frequently called "interest group theory" presumably stresses the role of collectivities rather than personalities in the political process. Most of the research tools employed by "interest group" investigators do not include the techniques by which the interplay between personality and collectivity can be studied. Albion W. Small introduced the group theories of Gumplowicz and other

*Personality.* The role of personality in elite composition is a topic of lively concern in this psychological age. There are many indications that the pursuit of power rather than other value outcomes is to be understood by examining the vicissitudes of early experience in the family or intimate circle, and that predispositions favoring the easy acquisition and performance of particular roles are likewise organized.

Besides the value preferences of the power-oriented personality it is important to recognize the selective effect of the mechanisms upon which the individual relies in coping with internal conflicts. Obsessionality, for instance, can encourage rigidity of outlook and place obstacles in the way of perceiving new developments.[17]

*Crisis.* The relative importance of various factors in the formation and re-formation of power elites varies according to the level of crisis. The most comprehensive conception of crisis emphasizes intensity of stress toward action. If a creditable report asserts that a flood is approaching, there may be little divergence among the inhabitants of a community about getting to high land as quickly as possible. There are, of course, crises of conflict within or between groups, which depend upon different value demands, identities, and loyalties.

The category of crisis level can be defined to reclassify the previously introduced distinctions regarding communities, classes, interests, and personalities. Levels may vary from low to high. The term "crisis" can be regarded as a fifth category if the previous classification is defined to apply to low or mid-range levels of stress toward action, which leaves "high-level" situations to be dealt with here.

High-level community crises have profound implications for elites. In such power crises as wars or revolutions the composition of elites may undergo drastic change. It is also true that crises may themselves be precipitated by conflicts among or within the power elites.

Class crises occur, for instance, when the unity of the class is perceived to be in danger. As implied earlier, the conflicts generated within top elite elements may make it possible for new elements to

---

Continental writers at the University of Chicago, and influenced such books as A. F. Bentley, *The Process of Government* (Chicago: University of Chicago Press, 1908), and more recently, D. B. Truman, *The Governmental Process* (New York: Knopf, 1951).

[17] The complex interaction between culture and personality is illuminated by contemporary research on modernizing societies. See especially the role attributed to empathy in D. Lerner, *The Passing of Traditional Society* (Glencoe, Ill.: The Free Press, 1958); Marvin K. Opler (ed.), *Culture and Mental Health* (New York: Macmillan, 1959); Francis L. K. Hsu, *Psychological Anthropology: Approaches to Culture and Personality* (Homewood, Ill.: Dorsey, 1961), especially Alex Inkeles's discussion, pp. 172–208; Lucian W. Pye, *Politics, Personality, and Nation Building: Burma's Search for Identity* (New Haven: Yale University Press, 1962).

ally themselves with one side or another, and this alignment may transform the public order.

Interest crises depend likewise upon perceptions of common threat or of heightened opportunity. Clashing leadership in one party can open the door to a permanent realignment based upon recruitment from hitherto excluded social formations.

Personality crises are sometimes synchronized with an ideology or a conception of strategy that reverberates in the lives of other disturbed persons and affects the composition and policy of power elites.[18]

*Perspectives*

The task of research on elite perspectives is to uncover the demands, expectations, and identities of power elites, and to see to what extent they can be accounted for in terms of the predispositions formed during pre-elite or preactive years.

The latter distinction — between eliteness and active political role — is necessary if we are to take account of variations within the elite class, and of the emergence of newcomers (and the disappearance of some older members). At any time we may regard as members of the power elite class of a body politic the following: (*a*) all individuals who occupy high office during the period; (*b*) all individuals who have occupied high office in previous periods and who regard themselves, and are regarded by others, as continuing to be in harmony with the established order; (*c*) all individuals who, though holding no high office, or any office, are perceived as highly influential in important decisions; (*d*) all individuals who, though perceived as adherents of a counterideology, are recognized as exercising a significant influence over important decisions; (*e*) close family members. The foregoing categories allow for the inclusion of newcomers into the power elite class and likewise render it feasible to identify individuals who, though enjoying an elite status, refrain from playing an official or unofficial role in decision.

Note that the power elite is defined in the previous paragraph to exclude participants who are not identified as members of the community. The result of this choice is to classify influential nonmembers as base values of the members for whom they provide assets (or liabilities). If a nonnational occupies an office in the formal power

[18] The synchronization of personality crisis levels with the opportunities presented in a given time-place context is a major problem of elite analysis. See Erik H. Erikson's *Young Man Luther: A Study in Psychoanalysis and History* (New York: Norton, 1958).

structure, he qualifies. We include counterelite figures (d) when they inhibit, or otherwise modify, the established elite. Officeholders or holders of effective unofficial control during previous periods are excluded unless they are identified with the established order (b). The point of including close family members (e) is that even in societies where power is not formally inherited there is usually a sense of obligation to perpetuate the kin in an influential role; and the community ascribes importance to the supposed influence that such individuals may exert.

As in all social research the foregoing specifications are of varying definiteness in different contexts. We have called attention to the fact that conventional usage may identify "offices" in "government," "party," or "pressure group"; and further research may reveal that the office is inconsequential, having declined to a respect-laden emblem occasionally expected to perform rubber-stamp (that is, nondiscretionary) ministerial functions. Category (c) allows for the inclusion of individuals who are potent despite their lack of official position (or occupancy of a modest office). Where field research is practicable, it is possible to choose a panel of insiders, or to conduct random-sample interviews of the population, in order to obtain information about how individuals are perceived in power terms. Even these results are open to supplementation, as data are kept about actual decisions.[19]

The most inclusive category for the stable patterns of elite perspective is "political myth." We distinguish three principal subdivisions: the "doctrine," or assumption about political goals and fundamental justifications of public policy; the "formula," or expectations about the prescriptions that are authoritatively enforced; and the "miranda" (or "lore"), which comprehend the popular images of the body politic. As indicated earlier, the myth according to which the top decision makers justify their decisions is "ideology." A "counterideology" rejects the established perspectives. Counterideologies are shared in some instances across community lines; sometimes they are unique.

How intensely are ideologies held? In answering this query, we are reminded of the task of measuring degrees of commitment to doctrines, formulas, and miranda. Plainly, it is not enough to demonstrate that specific words or statements occur — in the official utterances of power elite figures, in unofficial public utterances, or in private mes-

[19] A useful guide is R. C. Snyder, "Some Recent Trends in International Relations Theory and Research," in A. Ranney (ed.), *Essays on the Behavioral Study of Politics* (Urbana: University of Illinois, 1962). See Karl W. Deutsch, *The Nerves of Government* (New York: The Free Press of Glencoe, 1963).

sages. How can we compare the relevant context in which the utterance takes place in ways that show degrees of commitment? One simple and partial measure is repetition. Whatever objections can be raised to frequency of iteration, the fact remains that every critic must agree that this raises a presumption of commitment.

Even such a simple criterion as repetition makes it possible to describe roughly the variations among elite elements, and to evaluate hypotheses about the impact of predispositions upon perspectives. First of all, the technique makes it possible to distinguish trends among elite elements that give elaborate or meager deference to the myth. Compare, for example, the utterances of responsible decision makers with systematic theorists or with the rank and file of laymen. The language may move toward or away from the theorists or the rank and file. A trained elite — professionally competent in philosophy, jurisprudence, and the social sciences — may adhere to relatively complex statements if it expects to obtain the support of the rank and file. An untrained elite — especially after a seizure of power — may use the gruff vocabulary of the outlaw camp until it has been impressed into using scholarly speech.

The implication in the foregoing discussion has been that elite perspectives can be accounted for, in significant measure, by exploring the perspectives that were incorporated on the road toward active power or at least toward an adult status. It is necessary to introduce a major reservation to this approach. Not only predispositions but environments count; if environments are full of important challenges and opportunities, these environing changes may override most of the predispositional differences of elite members. All political responses $(R)$ can be explained in terms of current environmental factors $(E)$ acting on predispositional factors $(P)$.

Striking examples of elite responses that owe little to most predispositions are the unified front with which the top decision makers of a nation-state may respond to an external threat. Differences of culture, class, interest, personality, and crisis conditioning may vanish; the elite acts as one. There may be exceptions to the generalization that testify to the intensity with which various antiwar perspectives are held at the outset. Religious sects, for instance, may eschew violence, and hence refuse to become infected by the collective steamroller — the crowd state — that initiates national defense.

In this context the scientific problem is to devise procedures that can be applied immediately before the crisis to ascertain the predispositions of individuals and groups to respond to such hypothetical contingencies as crises. Such procedures, if developed, can be applied through time until appropriate circumstances arise in which the "tests" can be validated by recording performance under stress.[20]

Perhaps the most tantalizing question about elite perspectives arises when myths that were once accepted without doubt are weakened as effective claims on faith, belief, and loyalty. The most searching questions refer to the modern, largely urban, division of experience, which rests upon a subdivision of task. The gist of the interrogation concerns involvement. As society multiplies unique action environments, does it not multiply perspectives? More concretely, does it not multiply foci of attention, expectations regarding past and future reality, values, demands, and identities? Is not the upshot a fantastic proliferation of individual and small-group perspectives that dilute the guiding impact of "large-group" myths?[21]

*Arenas*

An arena is established whenever interactions affecting power outcomes and effects become stabilized. If the frequency is below a minimum critical number chosen by the scientific observer, the "aggregate" may not be sufficiently interactive to deserve attention. Levels must also be selected to identify a "group," and groups are "unorganized" or "organized."

The world arena of power has never been sufficiently well organized to justify referring to a "world state" or "comprehensive public order." The "universal states" of history have been the dominant body politic in a regional area, as in the case of the Chinese Empire, the empires of the Near and Middle East, or the Roman Empire. Active power elites have often played a crucial role in enlarging the boundaries of the "known world," as Ferdinand and Isabella did in supporting the voyages of Columbus. More commonly the power elites have consolidated or rearranged the arenas within the "known world." In this historically illustrious company modern scholarship agrees in recog-

[20] The continuing institutions of self-observation that are currently in the course of development are beginning to provide data of the kind required. Reinterviewing was effectively used by Daniel Lerner, for instance, in *The Passing of Traditional Society, op. cit.*

[21] These issues are more fully considered in the Hoover Institute Studies that focus upon symbols. See the original publication, Harold D. Lasswell, Ithiel de Sola Pool, and Daniel Lerner, *The Comparative Study of Symbols* (Stanford: Stanford University Press, 1952), which, with accompanying reports, will be restated and amplified here. See Gabriel A. Almond and Sidney Verba, *The Civic Culture: Political Attitudes and Democracy in Five Nations* (Princeton: Princeton University Press, 1963); R. A. Bauer, I. de Sola Pool, and L. A. Dexter, *American Business and Public Policy: The Politics of Foreign Trade* (New York: Atherton Press, 1963); Lucian W. Pye (ed.), *Communications and Political Development* (Princeton: Princeton University Press, 1963).

nizing, among others, Darius I, Han Wu-Ti, Genghis Khan, Timur-I-Leng (Tamerlane), Alexander the Great, Julius Caesar, and Charlemagne, all of whom were consolidators, as well as George Washington and similar nation founders, who were dividers or rearrangers.

Power elites usually work within the territorial limits of a nation-state, often taking the initiative to modify the structures specializing in decision. In nation-states, for instance, the formal and informal arenas may become more or less centralized, as when unitary government takes the place of federal or confederate forms. Arenas may become more or less concentrated at a given level, as when hitherto independent departments and commissions are consolidated, or legislative and judicial organs achieve positions coequal to the executive. Many of these changes reflect the territorial readjustment of traditional units to fit the perspectives generated by urbanization and the dispersal or focalizing of production units. Power elites may multiply the number of organized activities that grow up outside government and limit its scope, or, conversely, extend the enterprisory and regulatory functions of government. Elites also adapt to, and in turn influence, the balance between regimentation and individual freedom of choice.

An examination of the identity of elite participants and of elite perspectives is helpful in exposing the factors that influence power elites in relation to arenas. The great empires of the past were dependent upon the prowess of ambitious soldiers. Commercial cities, on the other hand, fostered power elites concerned with the economic consequences of trade routes, sources of exchangeable commodities, and customers. Industrialization favored more permanent and massive penetrations of economies, appropriate to the sharply rising productivity made possible by improved technology.

The role of intellectuals in shaping the perspectives of the nation-state is a matter of enormous importance, since the loyalties, expectations, and demands that are called nationalism are among the potent elements in the reconstitution of arenas in world politics. Sometimes the influence of intellectual specialization is exceedingly indirect, as when scientists develop new energies, materials, and techniques as by-products of the quest for enlightenment and skill. The influence is very direct when students or professors find themselves exposed to derision as members of "primitive societies" or weak nations. It may be obvious to them that knowledge is transferable, and that when their local communities develop more science and technology, they may consolidate effective arenas of power. If traditional elites are indifferent or hostile (as in China), the intellectuals may become alienated and radicalized to a degree that largely determines the course of politics.

Where the elite is less indifferent or even supportive (as in Meiji Japan), the changes, though great, may be smoother.[22]

### Base Values

What base values are used by elite or pre-elite members at different stages of their careers? To what extent are these bases determined by the factors mentioned earlier in connection with participants, perspectives, and arenas?

Elite members who prepare to play active political roles usually become differentiated at an early age from their more passive contemporaries. Such differences of perspective affect motivation to acquire the base values appropriate to politics, notably the skills essential to leadership or to more anonymous roles. The typical preparation of nonelite persons differs greatly from youths and young people of elite origin. Among the nonelite we are able to identify individuals who will later become elite, or who seem destined to enter the elite class. We speak of these as pre-elite. Although established training courses may include military, diplomatic, and civil posts for everyone, the pre-elite person can usually expect to spend much longer periods of time at each level, and to qualify for admission to top positions much later in life than individuals of elite origin. In periods of great instability the emerging elite may come largely from pre-elite sources. The Chinese Emperor Han Wu-Ti, for instance, was the most conspicuous early example of a peasant rebel who received a mandate from Heaven to rule China. Genghis Khan was the orphaned son of the leader of a small band of nomads who reconstituted an independent band and used this as a base for his subsequent career. Napoleon's rise is classical for the young and obscure officer who moves to the top in modern civil wars.[23]

At any given moment it is far from simple to summarize realistically the relative importance of values as bases of power. It is always possible to describe the sequence in which yesterday's elite acquired power,

---

[22] On the consequences of the division of labor for society, the writings of Saint-Simon and Marx are of particular importance. For the explicit introduction of "attention focus" and "perspectives" into the analysis (and of procedures appropriate to quantification), see H. D. Lasswell, *World Politics and Personal Insecurity* (New York: McGraw-Hill, 1935); republished in *A Study of Power* (Glencoe, Ill.: The Free Press, 1950). See also D. Lerner (ed.), *Quantity and Quality* (Glencoe, Ill.: The Free Press, 1961), pp. 103–116.

[23] See the enlarging literature on socialization: H. Hyman, *Political Socialization* (Glencoe, Ill.: The Free Press, 1959); R. E. Lane, *Political Life* (Glencoe, Ill.: The Free Press, 1959); R. E. Lane, *Political Ideology* (New York: The Free Press of Glencoe, 1962). Among older studies is C. E. Merriam, *The Making of Citizens* (Chicago: University of Chicago Press, 1931).

wealth, respect, and other assets; but the evaluation of a present base is contingent upon future combinations of circumstances. The scientific observer can always extrapolate recent trends, of course, by assuming that the factors which have strengthened such trends will continue. In the United States today such extrapolations as the following can be made: Nonwhite physical characteristics will be of increasing advantage; females will rise in importance relative to males; scientific and technical training will be more of an asset; skill in projecting charm and sincerity over mass media will grow in usefulness. It is not difficult to imagine disasters whose impact will block or reverse these trends. In any case, when base values are described, it must be clear what assumptions are made about the constellation of surrounding factors.

The base values of greatest import for active power figures are positively related to the perceived policy problems of the body politic. The spectacular ascension of political police is obviously connected with apprehensions about counterrevolutionary elements at home and subversion from abroad.[24]

### Strategies

The strategies relied upon by elites in the external arena of a body politic are the management of diplomatic, informational, economic, and military instruments. Parallel distinctions apply to intraelite relations; military (police) weapons, however, are missing from the scene unless coercive levels are high. Where official and unofficial organizations are continually in touch concerning a wide range of problems, the diplomat ("fixer," or "negotiator") comes to play a major role.

The management of any value or instrument for power purposes calls for degrees of indulgence or deprivation of allies, enemies, and uncommitted participants. In civil arenas the tendency is to depend on positive inducements more than deprivations, and to rely on persuasion in preference to coercion. Strategies of isolated rather than concerted action are usually available to elites on both domestic and foreign issues.

Perhaps it is in the sphere of strategy that power elites exhibit the most obvious signs of competence or incompetence. Although the British Empire has been a declining power for some decades, the flexibility of the power elite has not been wholly lost. The retreat from India, for example, was executed in a way that kept many of the assets of Britain comparatively intact. The obstinacy of elites of big landlords

[24] See S. M. Lipset, *Political Man: The Social Bases of Politics in the Modern World* (Garden City, N.Y.: Doubleday, 1960).

(with relics of feudal arrogance) is notorious. Witness the provocative behavior of old French, Russian, and many contemporary Latin-American ruling classes. Revolutionary elites usually perseverate by continuing the ruthless tactics appropriate to the seizure of power into the period of consolidation and construction.

Many difficulties are present in devising common strategies of action against common threats, partly because of lagging perceptions of the magnitude of the danger, and partly because of differing estimates of its duration. The insiders' view of coalition warfare is full of evidence of flagrant misjudgment as well as sound realism, and of the heights and depths of mutual distrust.

Through the generations the most impressive chronic example of noncooperation is the world arena. It is generally recognized that the consequences of an anarchic world arena are destructive of man's latent potential. Yet the responsible elites of a modern nation-state find it beyond their capability to agree to an effective minimum world order. No head of state, prime minister, secretary of state, or chief of staff can show his willingness to risk some national independence in strengthening international bodies without taking chances that may put an end to his career. Colleagues and opposing factions in agencies or parties are almost sure to see the immediate political advantage to themselves of blocking such initiatives. This play of the power-balancing process has thus far been enough to maintain the status quo of division — though not a particular division — in the world arena.

Separatist forces are particularly easy to mobilize when elites who appear in the world arena are recruited from ideologies favoring world domination. The manifest content of such ideologies will not be taken at face value by the experienced political analyst, who is well aware of the frequent tendency of ideology to become phraseology. However, experience and sophistication are not to be taken for granted as applicable to a specific situation without adequate inquiry. It is also true that ideologies tend to be revalidated from time to time by rebirths of faith, loyalty, and belief.[25]

### Outcomes

All hypotheses about power depend for confirmation upon the results of research upon final outcomes. When votes are formally registered and the outcome is expected to be enforced, the task of

---

[25] Elite strategies can be accounted for in terms of predisposing and environmental factors (community, class, interest, personality, crisis). Studies of elite strategy include N. Leites, *On the Game of Politics in France* (Stanford: Stanford University Press, 1959); N. Leites and E. Bernaut, *The Ritual of Liquidation: The Case of the Moscow Trials* (Glencoe, Ill.: The Free Press, 1954).

summarizing wins, losses, and noncommitment is comparatively simple. The task is more complex if the scientific analyst probes more deeply into the prehistory of final alignments. Some participants play an "initiating" role more often than others and thereby influence the terms in which a problem is formulated. Participants also differ in the frequency with which they play a "pivotal" role in precipitating the final alignments.[26]

Detailed investigation of any decision process calls for the analysis of every type of commitment: intelligence, promotion, prescription, invocation, application, appraisal, and termination.

In complex societies at least, the study of each type of commitment usually leads to the discovery of a component elite which is relatively specialized with regard to the function involved. The covert intelligence services have produced many notable figures in history, among whom the durable Joseph Fouché, who survived during the turmoil of revolutionary France, is among the most phenomenal. The characteristics of spies and double agents are especially puzzling to more conventional minds. Specialists in open intelligence include prosaic census takers and glamorous newshawks. Since intelligence takes in predictions and planning activities, some of the most influential — if dangerous — elites have specialized as seers and prophets, notably in the "Asiatic autocracies."

Exhaustive research upon official and unofficial intelligence activity must bring into the picture all features of the interactions involved (participants, perspectives, arenas, base values, strategies, outcomes, and effects).

The elites who specialize in promotional activity include the great agitators who flourish in periods of community crisis. The international arena provides occasions on which an orator like Demosthenes may consolidate his fame by mobilizing his fellow citizens against a foreign enemy like King Philip of Macedon. Peasant risings in agrarian and feudal societies, slave revolts in cosmopolitan centers of empire, factory workers' revolutions in industrializing societies — all such movements leave their memorial shelf of promotional heroes.

When crisis levels in the body politic are less high, the promotional function is usually conducted by diplomatic rather than agitational strategies. The officials of political parties and pressure organizations, which are the promotional structures most characteristic of contem-

---

[26] See M. Kaplan, *System and Process in International Relations* (New York: Wiley, 1957); G. Liska, *International Equilibrium* (Cambridge: Harvard University Press, 1957); T. C. Schelling, *The Strategy of Conflict* (Cambridge: Harvard University Press, 1960); W. H. Riker, *The Theory of Political Coalitions* (New Haven: Yale University Press, 1962).

porary industrial nations, become highly bureaucratic in style. However, they are only beginning to develop professional services of selection and training. As in the case of intelligence — or of any other functions — detailed researches on promotion call for the use of the basic categories of process analysis.

Legislatures are the most prominent organs of government largely specialized with regard to the prescriptive function. Besides providing an arena in which promotional activities are also carried on, they afford an opportunity for new skills to arise and to establish an important claim to participate in the power process. Knowledge of parliamentary rules of procedure, adroitness in negotiating agreements, and precision in timing are among the principal strategies of success.

In folk societies the legislative function is not usually acknowledged, since the prevailing myth assumes that all general prescriptions are already in existence. The elders or the heads of ceremonial societies may actually perform a lawmaking role simply by alleging that a norm exists. The key base value, obviously, is expectation by the community that an individual is a repository of enlightenment, or at least of the rites by which crucial knowledge can be obtained.

The act of invocation is a preliminary characterization of concrete cases in terms of prescriptions. A violation is alleged. The explicit basis of most quarrels in every society, civilized or not, is conflict over the appropriateness of such characterizations. Police officials, prosecuting attorneys, and similar specialists perform the official role of invokers in urbanized nations. Since common experience recognizes the gravity of public accusations, an elite of initial and private mediation and conciliation is usually found in every community. Its task is to persuade disgruntled individuals to refrain from acts that enlarge the dispute and make the parties more rigid. If a quarrel reaches the level of formal visibility, the merits of the issue are diluted by perspectives of system maintenance. Each participant must pay attention to the value indulgences or deprivations that are at stake for his political party, pressure organization, official agency, or other affiliations. Thus far, relatively little study has been directed to the preventive role of invokers.

Final appliers of power exist in great numbers in large-scale bodies politic. Hence, the top or near-top elite of power usually includes judges, civil, military, and diplomatic administrators. Chief executives combine so many major decision functions that there is constant pressure to subdivide the executive office along clearer lines. Thus the roots of many application structures in modern government are found in the immediate secretariat of a pope or prince.

The principal question that appraisers try to answer is whether officials are accomplishing the policy goals set for them, and if not, why not. Although the appraisers, strictly speaking, are not empowered to invoke prosecution or to apply sanctions to unlawful or inefficient behavior, their word is almost sure to set such activities in motion. Hence, the function of appraisal is of obvious importance to all top power figures, and a specialized elite is not always allowed to perform this role. The classical model for the function is the office of censor in ancient Rome. In contemporary industrial societies the professional economist has sometimes achieved enough acceptance to establish official bodies that will report upon the state of the economy in terms of high levels of productive employment, and to identify factors that interfere with its functioning.

The terminating function gains visibility in communities where policy changes are frequent and high deference is given to individual rights. For example, when public policy permits private houses to be built, legitimate expectations are established that may be frustrated if the community shifts to public housing. Provision for proper compensation is part of the terminating process and becomes more technical and specialized with the years.

### Effects

A relevant part of summing up the aggregate effects of politics during a given period is to describe changes in elite impact and composition. Theoretical models of political equilibrium can be constructed to account for elite continuity, or for degrees of change ranging from the trivial to the important.

In constructing models of elite continuity, the maximization postulate is a selective guide. This postulate, it will be recalled, assumes that people act as they do because they expect to be better off than by acting any other way. The postulate allows for error and for unconscious factors to be included as conditioning factors.

By emphasizing the perspectives of individuals, we give full emphasis to the complexity of politics. The implication is that all component arenas, organized or unorganized, are set up so that the policies made effective in these situations are meshed together in sequences that sustain elite stability. The same comment applies to the recruitment and training of elites, to the availability of base values, to the selection of strategies, and to the ultimate alignments at the outcome phase. It is also relevant to the details of perspective since a particular surge of conviction, loyalty, or belief is analyzable in maximization terms.

Ideologies rise or fall to the extent that they are expected to yield better value consequences than their rivals.

By phrasing the postulate in terms of subjective events, we indicate relevant lines of elite research. Elite subjectivities include the perspectives of identity, demand, and expectation characteristic of the group. Hence, it also can be described according to the category of myth, and the component doctrine, formula, and miranda. These subjectivities can be rather directly inferred by obtaining interviews from representative individuals under conditions of mutual confidence. Such findings can be used with caution to interpret historical personages. Elite subjectivities can also be explored by less intensive methods, as when brief interviews or questionnaires are used, or when intimate material — diaries, or personal correspondence — are scrutinized analytically.

Subjectivities are immediately influenced by the environments to which individuals are exposed, especially by the content of primary and secondary communication media. We have drawn attention to the intelligence function that supplies the information and estimates of the future to participants in all political arenas, formal and informal.

The content of communication media can in part be explained by examining the value predispositions of those who influence the selection and dissemination of intelligence. Presumably, the choices will be made to further the perceived value advantage of the media controllers.

The foregoing comments upon elite models indicate many of the complications that arise in concrete research. There are, of course, many general hypotheses that call attention to some of the major factors in elite stability. Slow rather than rapid social change fosters elite stability; homogeneous rather than heterogeneous structure in terms of culture, class, interest, and personality contributes to the same effect. Among the factors that increase the likelihood of realistic rather than fantastic response to moderately changed circumstances are institutions organized to favor definite elite action rather than indecisiveness.

By focusing more narrowly upon elite recruitment, it is possible to draw attention to some factors that favor a positive problem-solving result. The demand to take responsibility in the common interest is transmitted when doctrines of inclusive and exclusive, rather than special, interest are exemplified in the conduct of teachers, parents, public leaders, and similarly influential persons. Models speak louder than maxims, but maxims provide guides to individual and concerted action. Disturbing to responsible elite formation is the spectacle in public or private of irresponsible conduct by the older generation. It is also true that codes of responsibility can be interpreted in ways that arouse resentment and encourage the rejection of the demand to serve the common good. Extremes of seeming conformity constitute innovations of as much danger to sound elite formation as deviations in an obviously nonconformist direction.

More formally, the relevant hypotheses can be phrased as follows: If the preoccupation of an elite generation with rectitude values leads to an increase in austerity (and severity), the younger generation, exposed to more requirements and negative sanctions, is predisposed to reject the rectitude code. Extremism can be justified in terms of any value. Recent sacrifices on behalf of power, wealth, or honor may have a cumulative impact of the same kind, generating demands for individual enjoyment rather than accumulation of collective advantage. Even an easygoing code of satisfaction in collective sociability and well-being can provoke countertendencies, possibly in the direction of challenge and sacrifice, or toward the cultivation of competitive skills and knowledge. All these responses are given an additional dimension of complexity by conflicts that may be generated between the primary ego, the community self, and other collective self-components. For example, the rejection of additional demands for capital formation on community-wide projects can be accompanied by demands to accumulate family wealth, or to augment the wealth of some other private association. The withdrawal of support for expansionist designs in the world arena of power may strengthen the demand of internal revolutionary elements for an improved power position.

Innovations may be along lines of conflicting expectation rather than value demand or identity. Even within the same frame of value reference, for example, an exaggeratedly sanguine outlook may bring its antithesis into vogue. Changes in the opposite direction also occur, such as seizures of optimism following doubt and uncertainty about the prospects of nation, party, or other political identity.

Hypotheses of this kind are far from the dogmatic affirmations of Hegel about the grand design of history. These propositions are generalized from concrete circumstances according to theoretical postulates and principles whose aim is to provide guidance for the skeptical yet industrious enterprise of empirical inquiry. As our data-gathering and data-processing procedures improve, and institutions of social intelligence and appraisal become more comprehensive, eventually the sequence of changes in individual and collective predisposition will be illuminated in preparation for the determination of public policy.

## CHAPTER TWO

HAROLD D. LASSWELL

# The World Revolution of Our Time: A Framework for Basic Policy Research*

## I

THAT OUR EPOCH is a time of revolutionary change on a global scale is no longer in dispute. We disagree only when the issue is the specific nature of the revolution. From the Communist standpoint there is no doubt about the truth: we are moving from capitalism to socialism, from the primacy of the bourgeoisie to the supremacy of the proletariat. However, the Marxist tradition is interpreted in many different ways. Machajski suggested that the most important development of our epoch is the rise to power, not of the working class as a whole, but rather of the intellectual worker, whose capital is his knowledge. Relying upon the superiority of knowledge, the intellectual wins the support of the manual workers, whom he exploits mainly for his own benefit. Of all theories of the place of the intellectual in history this is the most uncongenial to those who claim to speak in the name of the masses.[1]

Until recently the spokesmen of liberal capitalism were riding the tide of success, confident that the business revolution was carrying all

---

* Parts I through III of this essay were originally published in 1951 by the Stanford University Press as Series A: General Studies, No. 1, of the Hoover Institute Studies. Reprinted with permission of the author and publisher. Minor changes in the text and footnotes have been made.

[1] See the brief account in Max Nomad, *Rebels and Renegades* (New York: Macmillan, 1932), pp. 206 ff. The pen-name of Waclaw Machajski was A. Wolski.

before it. The sobering impact of recent events has done more than to undermine faith in business, science, and technology. It has brought about a revival of man's mistrust in himself. The "new pessimism" calls into question the "cult of progress" and challenges the "myth of man's perfectibility." Several names symbolize the deflation of progress: there is Spengler; there is Toynbee; there is Berdyaev. Eric Voegelin argues that we have been suffering from the rise of Gnostic politics since the ninth century.[2] From this standpoint man is plunged in bitterness at his failure to attain the perfection that he has arrogantly proclaimed himself capable of achieving. Holding himself responsible for every discrepancy between fact and aspiration, man turns against himself as the author of his own betrayal.

## THE "POPULATION" OF HUMAN HISTORY

If we were making a complete classification of theories about the present epoch, we would identify all the entities that have been named as the true "population" of human history. Often the significant entity is the "empire" (or alternatively, the "state" or "power"); and the major transformation is said to be the emerging "world (or universal) state." There have, of course, been "universal" states embracing the "known world." Since less than the globe was known, the universal states of the past spread their tent of authority from some dominant center to a dim periphery of "savage tribes" wandering at the edge of geographical knowledge. Today for the first time in all history, a technology has been devised capable of encompassing the globe in a durably interdependent community.

The true units of human history have often been conceived as "races." In "racial" terms we are told that our epoch marks the passing of supremacy from the "white" to the "colored" races, or, according to the abortive myth of the Nazis, from the "Jews" (and their allies) to the "Aryans."

Under the influence of modern historical and anthropological sciences the proper entities of history are often taken to be persons sharing a distinctive way of life. Hence Toynbee studies "civilizations." Since today the scope of a dominant civilization is worldwide, interpretations of this type merge with theories of history that include the whole of mankind (after the manner of Spencer and Comte).

History is also interpreted as the story of "classes." Since a class is defined according to the manner in which values are shaped and

[2] Eric Voegelin developed the theme in a series of lectures at the University of Chicago in 1951.

shared within a community, corresponding classes may be found at the same or different times among various states, "races," or cultures. Class theories are usually phrased in terms of economic relations. But classes are also recognizable in terms of power, respect, and other values. The greatest flowering of class interpretations can be traced to the impact of Marxism. A variant upon the "bourgeois-to-proletariat" theme, for instance, is James Burnham's hypothesis concerning the "managerial class." The managers are described as technical integrators of production.[3]

Whatever group is assumed to be the true entity of history, group theories imply or make articulate assumptions about social institutions. Saint-Simon and Marx were highly explicit when they characterized a supposed sequence of myth and technique (social institutions). But when interpreters begin with groups, they often discuss institutional details in casual and unsystematic fashion. If, on the other hand, they start with institutions, they fail to spell out group implications. For example, when Albert V. Dicey considered the main currents of public opinion in the nineteenth century (with some extensions into the twentieth), he spoke of "collectivism" as rising at the expense of "individualism."[4] However, Dicey gave cursory treatment to the impact on states, "races," civilizations, or classes.

Many interpreters of man and his institutions place these developments in a vast panorama in which man is seen as one among many energy transformations in nature. A cryptic and imaginative theory of this type, propounded by Friedrich Jünger, described the predicament of modern man as the inevitable result of a "technical man" who is, in effect, compelling reprisals from an outraged physical nature.[5]

## TRANSCENDENCE

Theories of man in nature (or during any epoch) often speak in the name of a "higher" truth than the truth of actual or potential observation. A comprehensive classification of theories of history would

[3] "I mean by managers, in short, those who already for the most part in contemporary society are actually managing, on its technical side, the actual process of production, no matter what the legal and financial form — individual, corporate, governmental — of the process." *The Managerial Revolution* (New York: John Day, 1941), p. 80. Thorstein Veblen laid the basis for this type of interpretation in the United States.

[4] *Lectures on the Relation between Law and Public Opinion in England in the Nineteenth Century* (New York: Macmillan, 1905).

[5] Friedrich Georg Jünger, *The Failure of Technology: Perfection without Purpose* (Hinsdale, Ill.: H. Regnery Co., 1949).

therefore note the presence or absence of claims to transcendence. The symbols employed in claiming transcendence are either theological or metaphysical. Theological conceptions typically invoke "God" as the key symbol. In classifying a specific interpretation we ask: Is "God" invoked to support the statement that the proper units of history are states or "races" or cultures or classes, and that the world is so designed that all such entities vanish and decline, leaving no increment of advance for humanity as a whole? Or, on the contrary, is "God" invoked to affirm the view that Divine Plan includes human "perfectibility"? Or that since the Will of God is not vouchsafed to the fallible mind of man, God may, or may not, intend to permit progress?

When key symbols are metaphysical, transcendence is phrased in terms of "Nature." If God is dead, as Nietzsche would have it, it may be alleged that cosmic evolution is to culminate in an all-inclusive, or a highly exclusive, society of supermen. Or the assertion may be that only the indifference of an unplanned concatenation of cosmic circumstances provides man with his precarious perch on a doomed speck of dust.

It is evident that rational minds may come to conflicting estimates of the many interpretations of our epoch. We may properly debate whether history is a movement of all men toward a common destiny, or only of special categories of men; or whether the future spells perfection, fluctuation, or degradation for the entities of history; or whether it is most appropriate to invoke the categories of theology, metaphysics, or descriptive science.

We do not expect to bring this debate to a close. We do, however, suggest that it is possible to narrow the range of choice and therefore to enlarge the area of possible agreement.[6]

## THE CRITERIA OF JUDGMENT

It is not the purpose of the present inquiry to arbitrate among metaphysical or theological beliefs. Rather, the intention is to work with conceptions of human affairs that are both tentative and amenable to revision in the light of empirical inquiry. Of course, from the standpoint of any system of theology or metaphysics, failure to take a position is construed as implying a position. But we are willing to leave this aspect of our undertaking to others and to introduce state-

[6] A convenient summary and evaluation of all theories in terms of one system is offered by P. A. Sorokin in *Social Philosophies of an Age of Crisis* (Boston: Beacon Press, 1950).

ments of theological or metaphysical position solely as data to be described, not as beliefs to be confessed or rejected.

If we reserve the term "knowledge" for what is observed, the word does not properly apply to statements about future events. This raises the question whether any rational criteria are available for choosing among the diverse interpretations of our period, since these interpretations necessarily refer to the future as well as the past.

Our position is that criteria can be clarified and that under certain restrictions it is reasonable to extend our knowledge of the past into the future. In extending the past, two operations are involved: the extrapolation of trend and the extrapolation of conditions. When we extend the curve of population growth, we are extrapolating a trend. When we postulate the continuation of a relationship between population change and some factor that has affected it, we are extrapolating a condition (a conditioning relationship).

We are moderately well equipped with information about current trends. This is true of population, even after the usual reservations have been made about the figures for China, for instance. It is also true about resource reserves and rates of exhaustion. There are grounds for projecting per capita military expenditures. Future capital formation and standards of living can also be estimated. We can also extrapolate trends in the reduction of the respect deprivations to which women, children, and ethnic groups have been subjected. We estimate the future of infant mortality and of life expectancy. It is practicable to extrapolate curves showing the decline of illiteracy and the behavior of other criteria of enlightenment. We gauge future frequencies of "crimes against persons and property." The future of congenial relations among primary groups (families and cliques, for example) can be estimated to some extent in the light of the "broken family" curve.

As we extend curves into the future, we usually uncover incipient conflict. Which trend is likely to win out? In answering this question, we must mobilize available knowledge of conditioning relationships that have held true in the past. In extending a line, such as population, the postulate is that the factors conditioning the past will operate in the future. Perhaps our studies have established a connection between changes in population and factors such as "pessimistic expectations about world politics." If we assume that in a prolonged crisis of insecurity the factor of pessimism will have greater influence, it will be necessary to modify the future projection accordingly.

In forecasting human affairs a factor enters which is absent from predictions about nonhuman relations. Human beings may alter their conduct when they are told how they have acted in the past. A subjective event, namely awareness (insight), has changed the context by altering the current meaning. Since the laws of social relations are about meanings, they are subject to change *with* notice (with insight). An element of free choice is thereby introduced that reduces our reliance upon prediction.

## THE DEVELOPMENTAL CONSTRUCT

As a means of improving judgments of the future such special tools as the "developmental construct" have been invented. A developmental construct characterizes a possible sequence of events running from a selected cross section of the past to a cross section of the future.[7] Taken critically, all interpretations of our epoch are developmental constructs (such as the alleged passage from "nineteenth-century capitalism" to "twentieth-century socialism"). However, these constructs are often put forward as though they were "scientific" and "inevitable." If we strip such self-serving declarations from a theory of history and lay bare the developmental picture, what remains is the statement of hypotheses that may prove to be helpful guides to judging the period.

By emphasizing that developmental constructs are not scientific propositions, we do not imply that available scientific knowledge is irrelevant. On the contrary, a disciplined use of developmental constructs calls for the study of both trends and conditions. Strictly, we might demonstrate that a given construct can be derived from accepted scientific generalizations. For expository purposes the alleged passage from "capitalism" to "socialism," for example, may be connected with many propositions that are basic to psychology and social science. But the complexity of such a demonstration would do away with one of the chief advantages of the construct, which is the succinct, stimulating contribution that it makes to an inquiring mind. The construct is a tool for sketching the plains, plateaus, and mountain chains of the continent of events comprising past, present, and future. The developmental pattern throws the time axis — the "from what, toward what" — into relief.

The task of thinking responsibly and critically about the future has ramifications that have been insufficiently explored even in this method-

---

[7] This tool was proposed in H. D. Lasswell, *World Politics and Personal Insecurity* (New York: McGraw-Hill, 1935), Chapter 1. The volume is reprinted in *A Study of Power*, by Lasswell, C. E. Merriam, and T. V. Smith (Glencoe, Ill.: The Free Press, 1950).

conscious era. The burden is especially heavy since some of the most reliable guides are able to make only limited contributions to the undertaking. For example, we cannot depend upon the future to conform to the ordinary postulates of probability theory, such as that a series of uniform events is in prospect (as in the tossing of the same penny to show "heads" or "tails"). In estimating the future, part of the problem is the likelihood that future events will be uniform; or, in other words, it is necessary to appraise the degree to which the more familiar probability postulates will apply.[8]

Because technical issues have been little discussed, it is not inappropriate to consider at greater length the postulation of goal values, the choice of time period, and the weighing of conditioning factors.

## THE STARTING POINT: GOAL VALUES

How do we go about inventing and evaluating hypothetical constructs about our epoch? Our reply: select according to goal values.

The grounds of this advice are the characteristics of rational thought. Rational thinking takes the consequences of its own exercise into account. Among the factors molding the future are interpretations of the future. Since expectations have an impact, however modest, upon policy, we proceed rationally when we operate with a clear conception of our possible effect upon the shape of things to come. Since the function of policy is to achieve goal values, our initial step is the clarification of these values.

Without introducing an extensive treatment of our values at this point, we submit the following anticipatory comment: we are concerned with the dignity of man. We want to participate in the realization of human dignity on the grandest possible scale. Hence we are opposed to the prevalence of caste in human society and in favor of mobile societies in which the rule is individual merit rather than family privilege. This is equivalent to saying that we are in favor of shaping and sharing values on a wide rather than a narrow basis. (We use the eight terms enumerated in the discussion of "social process" in the Introduction to the present book: power, wealth, well-being, skill, enlightenment, affection, rectitude, respect.) The

---

[8] The mathematical analysis of choice has been sharpened by the work of John von Neumann and Oskar Morgenstern in the *Theory of Games and Economic Behavior* (Princeton: Princeton University Press, 1947); N. Rashevsky, *Mathematical Biophysics* (Chicago: University of Chicago Press, 1948); Norbert Wiener, *Cybernetics* (New York: Wiley, 1948). See the discussion of the use of mathematical models in the social sciences by Kenneth Arrow in D. Lerner and H. D. Lasswell (eds.), *The Policy Sciences* (Stanford: Stanford University Press, 1951).

order of mention does not constitute a rank order, but a random sequence. The relative significance of values for persons and groups is to be discovered by inquiry and not settled by definition.[9]

By taking human dignity as our central focus, we are in step with ideal values of the American tradition, and with the progressive ideologies of our epoch. Liberalism and socialism are united in affirming the free man's commonwealth as a goal of human society. That man's dignity is not to be realized in this world is the principal forecast of whoever takes a dim view of human perfectibility.

## ALTERNATE CONSTRUCTS

Until recently it was not fantastic to imagine that the next few decades would mark the triumph of free societies throughout the globe. Today it must be conceded that antiprogressive tendencies may win out. In a crisis of such serious proportions, we may be disposed to cramp our interpretations into a single mold. As a precaution against the warping effect of these factors, we use more than one construct, and continually weigh these alternatives against one another.

### Alternative One

The historic trend away from caste societies will continue until the free man's commonwealth is achieved on a global stage. A commonwealth is free to the extent that values are widely rather than narrowly shared: power, respect, rectitude, affection, wealth, well-being, skill, enlightenment.

### Alternative Two

The direction of history is reversing itself, and moves toward the restoring of caste. More specifically: Assuming that the world crisis of insecurity continues, power and other values will be further concentrated in a few hands in the name of providing for the common

---

[9] A systematic theory of "law, science, and policy" has been in the course of development at the Yale Law School by the present writer and Myres S. McDougal. See the programmatic statement, "Legal Education and Public Policy: Professional Training in the Public Interest," *Yale Law Journal*, LII (1943), pp. 203-295 (reprinted in somewhat condensed form in H. D. Lasswell, *The Analysis of Political Behaviour: An Empirical Approach* [New York: Oxford University Press, 1947]). See further McDougal, "The Role of Law in World Politics," *University of Mississippi Law Journal*, XX (1949); and McDougal and Gertrude C. K. Leighton, "The Rights of Man in the World Community: Constitutional Illusions versus Rational Action," *Yale Law Journal*, LIX (1949). The eight value terms are developed in Lasswell and Abraham Kaplan, *Power and Society: A Framework for Political Inquiry* (New Haven: Yale University Press, 1950).

defense. As the world is bipolarized between the United States and the Soviet Union, perpetual crisis favors the loss of freedom, and the eventual consolidation of garrison-police states. As power and influence concentrate in the hands of the soldier and political policeman, other groups decline in weight, perhaps disappearing entirely (such as the businessman and the free professional man in the Soviet Union). In the end, if the process is carried to the logical (thinkable) conclusion, the leaders of the garrison-police state will constitute the top layer of the new caste system.

## THE TIME PERIOD: 1890——

For what time period are we making our construct; and for what decades are we organizing data on a rather intensive scale? The first alternative generalizes the course of history since, let us say, the eighteenth century; the second alternative — concerning the return to caste — may be roughly dated from the nineteen-thirties to the decades immediately ahead. The former alternative is substantially the forecast of liberals and socialists after the "bourgeois revolution" ran its course. The Marxists began to predict the imminence of freedom through social revolution about the middle of the nineteenth century; and the liberals, in return, proclaimed the coming of freedom by evolution.

There can be no uniform time-period appropriate to all constructs, since meaning in history depends upon context, and significant contexts can be identified in unlimited profusion.[10] We have already referred to ideas that take vast time spans into consideration, such as the hypothesis that "Gnostic politics" got under way in the ninth century. At the moment it is unnecessary to evaluate the utility of these comprehensive conceptions.

Whatever misgivings there may have been current among occasional observers during the latter years of the nineteenth century, the most disturbing events began in the thirties with the rise of the Nazis in Germany and the remilitarization of Japan. By the mid-thirties it became rather apparent that the ideal promises of the Soviet world were far from being realized, and that the regime was becoming stable at a level far out of line with the early hopes and promises of the Revolution. Nazi racialism, in particular, was a shocking eruption of antihumanistic conceptions and methods.

As a means of placing these occurrences deeper in perspective, it

[10] This is indicated not only by the endless literature of "periodization" but by theories of historical "cycles." A compendium of the latter is in P. A. Sorokin, *Contemporary Sociological Theories* (New York: Harpers, 1928).

was decided to organize a series of researches beginning about 1890. The eighteen-nineties saw the emergence of great powers and of patterns of activity that gave distinctiveness to the twentieth century. With the defeat of China by Japan, decisive shifts were registered in Far Eastern affairs. The war with Spain brought the United States outside the Western Hemisphere as an "imperial" power. Britain's clash with the Boers provided Germany with an opportunity to play a strong hand against Britain, and accelerated the formation of the grand alliances that dominated the diplomacy of the first decades of the new century. Alongside and interacting with these changes went profound shifts in the internal balance of power of many countries, and in the scope of modern industrial civilization.

## THE CHOICE OF DATA

There are several advantages to be gained from concentrating upon the study of a comparatively short span of recent history. We take it for granted that monographs will continue to appear that deal in detail with episodes in the official relations among the powers. We assume, furthermore, that interpretative essays will continue to be written in which scholars present the fruits of their experiences with the sources, though without presenting the supporting data. Our purpose is to contribute something comparatively new. By choosing a "turning point" in 1890, we are able to apply some of the procedures that have been developed by the psychological and social sciences in recent times, but that have not as yet been applied in a comprehensive program of research.

It is possible to do for certain branches of history what has already been done in the study of changes in population, production, consumption, and price. In the writing of history it is now commonplace to enlist the collaboration of specialists upon shifts of population and changes in economic relations (or to incorporate the results of specialized investigation of these topics). Our aim is to make available to historical scholars a body of trend data concerning what is variously called "ideology," "public opinion," "Zeitgeist," "public attention," "public attitudes," "cultural perspectives," "political myths," "class attitudes," "class analysis," "elite analysis," "social affiliations," and the like. We speak of "symbol" trends and "elite" trends in referring to these developments.

What can be expected from work of this kind can be inferred by examining the interplay between economists and historians. As economists improved their methods of describing the history of "business cycles," for instance, these results were incorporated by historians of the whole period.[11] Typically, the historical scholar provided intimate knowledge of sources. Sometimes the historian became proficient in economic research on his own account and directly studied his sources by the new procedures. Historians and economists acted together in order to plan for the keeping of better records of the present and the future. Our prophecy is that historians will evolve a similar working relationship to those who specialize on the study of symbols and elites.[12] Historians will absorb the new results in general histories; they will recommend sources for the study of new periods. Occasionally the historian will acquire the methods of symbol and elite analysis, and put them to work on his period. Historians and specialists on symbols and social structure will evolve improved methods of recording the present and future for scholarly use.

## THE ANALYSIS OF CONDITIONS

The growth of modern methods of studying economic change has profoundly affected the interpretation of history. All sorts of hypotheses could be entertained until the data provided by the National Bureau of Economic Research, for example, settled certain questions and cleared the ground for more refined and sophisticated inquiries. These impacts on general history were by-products of the scientific and policy problems that led economists to invent and improve their procedures of investigation. Why did the economists invent "index numbers" of the "general price level"? The original scientific incentive was to provide data of sufficient scope, range, and comparability to allow for the verification of theories of the economic process.[13] From a policy point of view the economists were under pressure to improve their forecasts of general business conditions. In prosperity they were asked how to curb inflation, and in depression how to restore high levels of productive employment at rising standards of living. With the expansion of empirical research there occurred a tremendous advance in economic analysis. As concepts grow clearer, the demand for

[11] A detailed study of the diffusion of the research studies of the National Bureau of Economic Research into the history books would be worth making, for example.

[12] I shall make no further reference to the introductions prepared by the present writer for the elite and symbol studies of the Hoover Institute and Library publications, where certain possibilities are referred to in more detail.

[13] It is of interest that Irving Fisher's monumental work on index numbers was conceived and evolved in a seminar at Yale conducted by William G. Sumner, who was interested in a comprehensive theory of the social process.

more precise data is more insistent; and precise data usually call for some remodeling of economic generalizations.

The modern study of the social process is converging upon one of the most ambiguous aspects of society: namely, communication. As with the inception of research on economic relations, scientific and policy considerations have been intermingled. The problem of the interplay of "material" and "ideological" factors was given great currency by the political resonance of Marxist socialism. Marx spoke of established perspectives as "ideology"; but he did not include his own doctrines. It was Sorel who took the step of treating the revolutionary view as "myth," which stimulated further probing into the impact of "myth" upon "myth," and of "material" upon "material" patterns in society. But great ambiguities continued to lurk in the treatment of a given set of relations as "material." For instance, it was not vague to speak of "horsepower per capita" as an index of "industrialization." But by what intermediate steps did "horsepower" affect minds? This question led to the gradual clarifying of the "attention frame" to which workers and other groups cooperating in production were exposed. The "attention frames" were not simply "sensations," but "perceptual screens," and the screening process involved conceptions of the self, of value demands, and of expectations. But does there exist a precise "one-to-one" correspondence between horsepower exposure and the emerging perspectives of a given culture? Are there reciprocal impacts of perspectives upon the future of horsepower?

For example, the initiative for electrification may be taken by a government adviser who argues that, unless there is a wider energy base, the defense of the state will be undermined. After inquiry and discussion the decision-making elite of the state may vote public funds for purposes of energy development, claiming that national security and prosperity are at stake. Between the statute of authorization and final execution many intervening steps may be taken. It is possible to follow the stream of official orders, and to explore the accompanying flow of formal and informal communication up and down the hierarchy. At every link the inquirer can pose the important question: Who was told what when? On the basis of what predispositions did the officials interpret what they heard, saw, or read? What communications did they direct to what other persons (including large group-publics) and with what effect? The attempt to cope with such issues provided a scientific background for the growth of empirical studies of social psychology. These studies yielded useful results for the "politics of persuasion." The propagandists of politics, religion, commerce, charity, and health saw how studies of information, opinion, and attitude put useful data at their disposal.

Even as the myriad of changes constituting a general price rise or fall can be described in ways that bring clarity into a fog of detail, the methods now available for studying communication can summarize in precise and comprehensive fashion "public attention" (or "perception") and "public opinion."

It is sometimes falsely assumed that statistical modes of description and correlation are supposed to eliminate other ways of characterizing current or historic happenings, such as the interpretative essay. We have suggested that this assumption is mistaken, as indicated by the impact of economic analysis upon history. It is a question not of eliminating significance but of enlarging relevance. Very likely, symbol research will have the same effect upon "intellectual" or "ideological" history that mathematical and statistical research have had upon economic history. The study of "intellectual" history has been handicapped by the lack of usable tools by means of which controversial interpretations can be disciplined. Much the same limitation plagued the field of economic history before the advent of modern methods. By describing typical "contents of communication" we can summarize the changes of absolute and relative emphasis put upon different themes. Hence we are able to study social perspectives with the same precision that we can use in describing "material culture" or "culture materials." Some controversies can be resolved, and many issues can be refined for more rewarding study, as results are made available.

The more precise ordering of symbol data to illuminate social perspectives will put us in a better position to relate perspectives and practices within the more general process of social change. The interplay of "material" and "ideological" factors, to which we have referred, can be handled systematically when to the available techniques for dealing with the material culture (such as economic analysis) we add the newer techniques for dealing precisely with symbolic behavior. Accordingly we have studied, as aspects of the total process of world change in our time, trends in the behavior of both "elites" and "symbols."

The principal emphasis in the present research is upon the period since 1890; and we are interested in stimulating scholars to fill in the gaps which are left in this cross section. We are equally concerned with inducing research workers to apply modern methods to earlier periods. It is partly a matter of extending the data series backward through the nineteenth century, and before. But we also recognize that it is important to reassess the history of periods where the sources may not lend themselves to quantification, but which are capable of being compared with significant features of our own time. It may be possible to learn about the nature of bipolar conflict by re-examining the First Crusade, or the breakdown of the diplomatic unity of Christendom at the end of the fifteenth century. It will be rewarding to concentrate upon the years in which a nominally united Chinese Empire was, in fact, rent asunder between two (or more) poles (Northern and Southern). In the history of Egypt there were moments of acute tension between two rallying points; similarly in the classical world when Athens stood over against Sparta and Rome faced Carthage.

## II

### *THE CRITIQUE OF VALUES*

We now consider in further detail the specific framework of values that are postulated in the present inquiry. We associate ourselves with the dignity of man, the ideal aim of American policy. Our list of eight values can be directly related to the "life, liberty, and pursuit of happiness" of the Declaration of Independence. For "life" we read "well-being." Liberty includes the ideal of shared "power," and "enlightenment"; and since liberty is not license, it includes shared "rectitude" in the sense of a responsible attitude toward the fundamental goals of a free society. The pursuit of happiness is the pursuit of property ("wealth") and "respect" and of opportunity for the acquisition and exercise of "skill." It is also congenial intimate relations, and devotion to the larger group ("affection").

The categories are influenced by the division of academic labor in the United States and in Western Europe. Each of our value-institution relations is the subject of specialized research and teaching in the social and psychological sciences. Power and government are studied by political scientists, lawyers, and specialists on international politics; wealth and economic institutions come within the province of economists; respect and social class institutions are the concern of sociologists and anthropologists who are specialized on the study of social structure; well-being comes within the scope of social medicine; enlightenment is the subject matter of specialists on mass media and public instruction; affection and the institutions of family, friendship, and large-group loyalty fall mainly within the field of sociology, social

psychology, and anthropology; rectitude and the institutions of morality concern students of comparative religious and moral standards;
skill and the institutions of skill are the field of specialists in professions and vocations (and include aesthetic creation and criticism).[14]

We do not assume that the values are embedded in genes and chro-
mosomes; rather, it is to be discovered by empirical study whether any
clear line of development connects the genetic predispositions of original nature with the ultimate choice of roles in any given society.

Although we do not assume that the eight values are definitive, we
have found no difficulty in classifying the institutional detail from societies of widely contrasting culture. (Perhaps it is worth repeating
that the rank enjoyed by one value in relation to another is to be ascertained by empirical investigation, whether we are considering the
personality as a whole or as a culture.)

No amount of empirical research can be expected to alter our basic
preference for human dignity, rather than the indignity of man. If
other cultures, or if parts of our own culture, do not share our fundamental standard of judgment, we want to know it, partly as a matter
of scientific curiosity, and partly for the purpose of discovering the
courses of action by which destructive discrepancies between goals
and acts can be overcome (at least sacrifice of values).

To say that we do not intend to change our basic values in the light
of more facts does not mean that we are determined to be unaffected
by the facts revealed by research. Although our attachment to human
dignity is an absolute of intention, we do not know how to recognize
all the institutional means by which human dignity can be made explicit in all conceivable circumstances. Perhaps the principal function
of a comprehensive program of global and historical inquiry is that
of assisting in the discovery of which institutional patterns exemplify
our goal values in various contexts, and which ones condition the realization of these goals in concrete circumstances.

In recent years it has become increasingly apparent how complex is
the conception of human dignity. It is not within the scope of the
present discussion to celebrate or to justify the dignity of man, rewarding as such an enterprise may be. The special problem at hand
is that of amplifying our brief definitions of human dignity in more
specific ("operational") terms. The moment anyone tries to pass from
the "ambiguous" to the "operational," empirical questions arise. For
example: How many members of the adult population, participating

[14] For operational indices of value categories consult Bruce M. Russett, Hay-
ward Alker, Karl Deutsch, and Harold Lasswell, *World Handbook of Political and
Social Indicators* (New Haven: Yale University Press, 1964).

how often in the election of official personnel, enable us to classify a given institution as "democratic" (power-sharing)?

Fortunately, it is seldom useful to distinguish the "either" from the "or." For comparative purposes it is more fruitful to describe the full pattern of an election (in its community context) than to evolve and apply superprecise definitions in a pedantic and routine way. We shall therefore seldom classify specific details as "X" or "not X" ("democratic" or "nondemocratic," for instance). By describing the practices that are relevant to the making of an ultimate judgment of the context, we defer the classification of concrete patterns until the whole has been described.

In this way we soften the difficulties that arise in cross-cultural or cross-period research. The experts on any period, or culture, know the connection between each detail and the whole. Although our value categories facilitate the ultimate comparison of one total context with another, we do not *begin* by making these comparisons. On the contrary, we encourage the specialist to use his customary habits of work, and to start by assuming the frame of mind of the participants in the culture or period under consideration. Then he is able to decide whether the participants recognize a cluster of patterns called "governmental" or "economic" as constituting an identifiable entity. (And so on, through the value-institution list.) "Functional" classifications are made when "conventional" data are available for the entire context.

## SELECTING OPERATIONAL INDEXES

Two types of patterns are involved in every institutional practice. Recurring ideas and sentiments constitute distinguishable "perspectives"; recurring ways of doing things are "operations." The ways in which a given perspective, such as love of country, is made articulate is an operation (such as the act of singing at patriotic ceremonies). We speak of a closely knit pattern of perspective and operation as a "practice" (for example, the practice of expressing patriotic devotion). We have already introduced the term "institution" to designate all the practices found in a community, or specializing in one value. A synoptic word for all the perspectives is "myth." The corresponding label for operations is "technique."

Because of our great interest in political relations, it will be convenient to make a relatively detailed classification of the "power myth." We speak of political "doctrine," "formula," and "miranda" (political philosophy, public law, folklore). Political technique includes the ways in which myth patterns are actually used. For instance, if the statutes prescribe a secret ballot, studies of "law in action" may show that the ballot is in fact open. (We do not speak of a "law" unless there is both "authority," in the sense of formal doctrine, and "control," in the sense of a certain minimum frequency of observance when the opportunity is offered.)

No scholar is surprised to find that it is easier to describe the myth of a society than to give a satisfactory account of its technique. The myth is usually frozen into documents or agreed-upon statements. Even in nations of the West it is not easy to fill in the operations, and when we move farther afield or back through time, the materials for such an appraisal are often entirely gone. It is not unusual to discover that the most adequate account of a community is the report by a cultural anthropologist concerning a tiny village inhabited by vanishing primitives.

It is evident that we must rely upon interdisciplinary cooperation to arrive at a comprehensive grasp of the world revolution of our time. In addition to the data about folk societies, which come almost exclusively from anthropologists, we depend upon the historian for the earlier years of our own and other civilizations. The value-institution patterns of our civilization are known in great detail by political scientists, economists, sociologists, and related specialists; it is imperative, therefore, to draw them into the enterprise. Because of the statistical problems involved, intimate collaboration is necessary with mathematical statisticians, especially in the handling of the newer time series (of symbol-elite data, for example) that involve the association of trends with conditions.

One of the principal reasons for presenting the findings of the present research in a series of pamphlets is to stimulate active interest and paralleling of effort on the part of specialists in every related area and function.

## DEMOCRACY (SHARED POWER)

The first value mentioned in our list is power, and the first goal value specifies our preference for the wide sharing of power in the community, hence ultimately in the world community. The short definition of power is "decision making," a definition that is intended to distinguish decisions from other acts of choice, such as buying or selling in a competitive market. The distinction is made by stipulating the nature of the perspectives that must be realized in the concrete situation. We specify that a decision is the culminating point of a situation in which the participants entertain certain "expectations" and "demands." The expectation is that the choice to be made will be defended against any challenger (present or prospective) by inflicting extreme deprivations upon him. The demand is for a share in making the choice. We can therefore speak of the passing of a statute by a legislature as constituting a decision if it is assumed by the legislators that the statute will be enforced against any challenger, and if the members of the legislature demand a voice in passing the statute. In many situations it is obvious that the demand to participate is restricted to a few, even though the expectation is widely entertained that the choice is enforceable. Even where the demand to participate is widely shared, there may be denial in fact.

When severe deprivation is taken as a defining characteristic of a decision, we do not limit the deprivation to the well-being value, such as the imposition of capital punishment. Any value may be at stake, as when a business is confiscated (wealth deprivation), or reputations are ruined (respect deprivation).

We assess power according to the degree of influence exerted over decisions, which is a matter of position in the final outcome (vote or military victory, for instance), and also of impact upon preoutcome activities.

In the empirical study of power it is a matter of research convenience to begin with indexes of "conventionally" defined institutions of "government." We then consider whatever institutions are locally assumed to specialize in the "influencing" of government, such as "political parties" and "pressure groups." Before the final inventory of power relations, functionally defined, the entire network of community institutions must be surveyed (since it may be true that severe deprivations are in fact not limited to the "conventional" institutions of government).

### "Government"

When we begin with what is locally known as "government," the first step is to describe the prevailing myth. We therefore look for the doctrines pertaining to power that embody the "high-level abstractions" on the subject, and endorse or condemn power sharing. We examine the formulations made in fundamental documents, or in declarations by prominent figures (as in the Declaration of Independence and Lincoln's Gettysburg Address).[15]

---

[15] Many of the documents reprinted in the handbooks on the history of political theory are relevant, such as Francis W. Coker (ed.), *Democracy, Liberty and Property: Readings in the American Political Tradition* (New York: Macmillan, 1942).

Since doctrinal statements are not necessarily binding, they may not be part of the formulas, which are the authoritative prescriptions of the community. The "law" of a given body politic prescribes "who" is authorized to decide "what." If the authority to change the constitution is vested in the people as a whole, acting directly by referendum or indirectly through elected officials, the state is democratically organized (to this extent). The same criteria apply to decisions that are less comprehensive in scope than constitutional questions. In a democratic formula, referenda or elections must be prescribed at frequent intervals, and the freedom of choice on the part of voters must be safeguarded.[16]

The miranda of a body politic are democratic when the popular version of history and destiny assume that decisions are properly in the hands of the people. In a full democracy the songs, poetry, anecdotes, and dramas portray and reinforce the democratic ideal.[17]

After describing the myth of a given body politic, we turn to the myth in action (the technique of power). We look first at the outcomes of decision-making situations. Even though the constitutional document calls for regular and popular elections, we may learn that no elections are actually held or that, if held, they are participated in by a minute fraction of the people. Unless elections are frequent and participation is general, we cannot regard power as shared.[18]

Even when elections are frequent and nonvoting is rare, we cannot be sure that democracy prevails unless coercion is at a minimum. In the absence of further information, the absence of a minority (opposition) vote is a suspicious sign (in large industrial states). In a large state, when minorities are constantly crossing from the victory to the loss column, and back again, power is shared. The presence of a chronic minority (composed of the same members) does not necessarily contradict the requirements of a democratic polity, since nothing in democratic theory says that every individual must want what the

[16] Standard collections of public law documents have been made by Joseph Delpech and Julien Laferrière (revising Dareste), Bodo Dennewitz, Walter F. Dodd, B. S. Mirkin-Getsevich, and others.

[17] Studies of "public opinion," "national character," and kindred concepts rely upon other sources than systematic statements of political doctrine and formula. For example, Gabriel Almond, *The American People and Foreign Policy* (New York: Harcourt, Brace, 1950); Robin M. Williams, Jr., *American Society: A Sociological Interpretation* (New York: Knopf, 1951).

[18] H. Tingsten, *Political Behavior* (London: King, 1937); Kaul Braunias, *Das parlamentarische Wahlrecht; ein handbuch ueber die Bildung der gesetzgebenden Koerperschaeften in Europa*, 2 vols. (Berlin and Leipzig: de Gruyter, 1932); Harold F. Gosnell, *Democracy: The Threshold of Freedom* (New York: Ronald, 1948).

majority wants when the majority wants it. This is true, even when it is admitted that deeply entrenched differences may compromise the unity and security of the commonwealth. (But this refers to a conditioning and not a defining factor.)[19]

Another partial index of democracy is the turnover of elected officials, which indicates something of the responsiveness of leadership. If there is little change in personnel, common sense tells us that this may be because the leaders know how to entrench themselves against shifting sentiments among the rank and file. This presumption can be refuted under special circumstances, as in Britain, where Parliament dispenses with general elections during war, and resumes the practice once fighting stops.[20]

It is also true that rapid official turnover is not invariably a sign of effective control by the rank and file. The French Chamber can overturn the Cabinet without running the risk of a general election, which puts a premium on personal and factional maneuvers to reorganize the Cabinet. The no-confidence vote is not used for the purpose of forging a general working agreement on policy.

A partial index of sharing is afforded by the affiliation of decision makers with the social structure. Few would doubt that people are likely to be more powerful when they are represented among decision makers than when they are not. The simple fact of representation does not ensure that the viewpoint of a person or a group will be considered, much less that it will prevail; but to say the least, representation is rarely a handicap. We take the weight of representation as indicating something of the existing distribution of power.[21]

While diversity of affiliation with all parts of the community is a plausible index of representation, such an index may be falsified by such practices as separation from the home and neighborhood, as in the civil service of Byzantium.[22]

The preceding indexes have referred to the line-up at the terminal phase of decision making. It is important to consider the earlier phases

---

[19] Voting studies can rarely report how individuals act at the polls because of the secrecy of the ballot. Only aggregate results (or the breakdown into "men" and "women") are common. Attempts have been made by researchers on the opinion-forming process to overcome these restrictions. See Paul F. Lazarsfeld, Bernard Berelson, and Hazel Gaudet, *The People's Choice: How the Voter Makes Up His Mind in a Presidential Campaign*, 2d ed. (New York: Columbia University Press, 1948).

[20] J. F. S. Ross, *Parliamentary Representation* (London: Eyre and Spottiswoode, 1943).

[21] *Ibid.*, Part I.

[22] See Bernette Miller, *The Palace School of Muhammad the Conqueror* (Cambridge: Harvard University Press, 1941).

of the process. Investigation may show that terror is used to shape the final consensus, or that bribery and favoritism may be decisive. We know that every conceivable gradation exists between power as physical intimidation and as a persuasion technique. When we are examining the values by means of which decisions are affected, we are studying the "base" values by which "scope" values are affected. Power may be a base for protecting and expanding power — as indeed may every value.

Any systematic study of base values calls for the surveying of routes along which policies are whipped into shape. No completely systematic research of this kind has been published, although case studies give ample indication of the routes prevailing now or in the past in the United States, for example. Initiative often lies with the executive departments and agencies, rather than with the Congress; also, legislative and administrative ideas often germinate in the minds of individuals connected with the numerous pressure organizations.[23]

The analyst of politics must go further than the simple recording of routes along which specific decisions are formulated. Part of his problem is the study of *potential* as well as actual power. What *might* happen under various conditions of changes in the environment or in the internal equilibrium of a specific body politic? Since many thinkable contingencies have been but partially approximated in any known historical situation, analytic work is essential to the setting up of hypotheses that may be verified only under future circumstances.

When we analyze the past as a guide to the future, it is important to keep two "yardsticks" distinct from each other. A decision may be classified according to a standard that is satisfactory to a historian or political scientist. But the decision may also be described from the point of view of the decision maker. To some observers, a big frog in a small pool is nevertheless a very little frog. But the little frog may think that he "does all right." The present question refers to whether little frogs are satisfied to croak where they are, or whether they want to move along. And it is obvious that with unrealized aspirations, tension may continue to be stirred up despite apparent success.

As a means of estimating political conduct, it is useful to reclassify the decisions made during a given period according to the intensity of the conflict involved. The assumption is that a gauge of intensity is the degree to which a participant is willing to sacrifice or to imperil his value position.

It is often possible to discover which values are close to the core of

[23] Stephen K. Bailey, *Congress Makes a Law: The Story Behind the Employment Act of 1946* (New York: Columbia University Press, 1950).

the value system of an individual or group. This particularly is important in the study of international politics, for instance, since a major question is: Under what circumstances will a nation believe that it is in serious danger? The people of the United States were far from united in perceiving the magnitude of the threat represented by certain countries in 1914 and 1939. The technical question may be stated in these terms: What communications or overt events will be interpreted as threatening when brought to the focus of attention? Manifestly, such responses will depend upon the predispositions of the official or unofficial persons who are exposed to the reports or incidents. In estimating potential acts in the arena of politics it is necessary to make an inventory of probable environing changes, and of probable levels of predisposition.

### "Political Parties and Pressure Groups"

From the study of "government" a comprehensive inquiry will turn to the examination of associations that are conventionally assumed to affect official acts.

For many purposes it is enough to define a political party as an organization specialized with regard to presenting candidates and issues under its own name in elections. (Elections are defined so that any significant use of coercion is excluded.) So conceived, the term "party" does not apply to the so-called "single parties" of the totalitarian regimes, since no true elections occur. We speak of Communist, Nazi, and Fascist organizations as "political orders" rather than true parties (when it is useful to be precise).[24]

Often it is convenient to restrict the definition of a political party in another direction. If a "party" sticks to one issue, and refrains from offering a comprehensive program, it is a different kind of organization from the party with a comprehensive program. Single-issue parties have more in common with pressure groups than the true party. The following definitions exclude Prohibition pressure groups as "parties": Political parties are organizations that put forward candidates and comprehensive programs under their own names in elections; pressure groups specialize in bringing the influence of the electorate to bear upon governments and political parties, without organizing as a party.

In a comprehensive study of any party or pressure group, the same categories apply as in describing the decision-making process in "government," including myth and technique.[25]

[24] On the political order, see William Ebenstein, *The Nazi State* (New York: Farrar & Rinehart, 1943).

[25] Consult Roberto Michels, *Political Parties* (reprinted: Glencoe, Ill.: The

*Unorganized Arenas of Power: Intergovernmental*

We have been considering organized institutions specialized to the power process, conventionally conceived. The next step is to examine the arena in which unorganized, or partly organized, decisions are made. The foremost example is the world political arena itself. It is true that there is a United Nations, and there was a League of Nations. But it is generally understood that these bodies are not effective world governments, since the expectation of violence is a dominating influence in world affairs. The world arena must be classified among the military rather than the civil arenas.

In world politics the balance of power is one means of sharing power among participating entities. It is well known that, owing to the expectation of violence, states combine into opposing groups of approximately equal fighting potential. (Under acute crises, the pattern tends to be rigid; crossing from one camp to the other is at a minimum.) The balance of power operates to prevent any one power (or combination) from dominating the globe, and to this extent preserves a pattern in which there is some degree of sharing.

Balancing is least flexible when there are two giant powers, which has been true since the end of World War II. There is somewhat more flexibility when there are three superpowers; and there is even greater flexibility of coalition when several powers possess about equal strength. The latter (or plural-power pattern) was characteristic of world politics during the decades preceding the bipolar opposition of the United States and the Soviet Union. During the Middle Ages in Western Europe the effective (though not the nominal) power pattern was multipolar, since hundreds of micropowers were in perpetually interacting arenas.[26]

Perhaps the best indicator of shared power is the frequency of coalition changes through time (assuming that the shifting of partners provides the maximum opportunity for policy differences to be bargained away). A comprehensive survey of world politics calls for a full geography of myth and technique.

*Unorganized Arenas: Interparty and Interpressure*

As in the study of intergovernmental relations, a convenient index of power sharing among the members of a party system is the crossing

Free Press, 1949). Empirical data are in the *Trade Association Survey* (Washington, D.C., Temporary National Economic Committee, Monograph No. 18, 1941).
[26] See William T. R. Fox, *The Super-Powers* (New York: Harcourt, Brace, 1944); Robert Strausz-Hupé and Stefan T. Possony, *International Relations* (New York: McGraw-Hill, 1950), pp. 177 ff.

of parties from one coalition to another. But this measure is of more limited application to parties than to nations. Since it is, as a rule, much easier for individuals to cross from one political party to another than from one nation to another, party coalitions are less essential in domestic politics as a means of obtaining flexibility than in the world arena. It is when parties *with the same personnel* are continually in the minority that danger exists for the democratic system (even though the persistence of the minority may be voluntary).

So far as pressure group systems are concerned, myth and technique can be examined in much the manner described for other institutions. Since individuals (or subgroups) are often able to pass from one organization to another, or to start new associations, the sharing of power calls for more than the study of coalitions. But pressure leaders may enforce severe deprivations against those who refuse to go along with top policy.

### "Nonpolitical Institutions"

After an examination of governmental, party, and pressure institutions (organized and unorganized), the next step in a survey of power is to inquire into the policy processes of all remaining institutions in the community. We first consider economic institutions (as conventionally conceived). One of the most distinctive institutions of modern industrial societies is the corporation organized for profit.

In countries where private capitalism is the prevailing system, the myth will have something to say about such corporations. The accepted doctrine is that resources are most efficiently used if production is organized by owners seeking profit.

In ascertaining the formula of the corporation system, we must look into constitutions and by-laws. So far as the miranda are concerned, it is not difficult to find examples of the glorifying or denigration of corporations.

When we look into the making of corporate decisions, we may learn that the facts of control are at variance with the myth. (Analysis has often shown that minority stockholders can control assets far in excess of their investment, thus violating the doctrine of owner control.)[27]

Besides the industrial corporation, other economic institutions need to be studied, such as trade-unions and cooperatives.[28]

[27] See A. A. Berle, Jr., and Gardiner C. Means, *The Modern Corporation and Private Property* (New York: Macmillan, 1939); R. A. Gordon, *Business Leadership in the Large Corporation* (Washington, D.C.: The Brookings Institution, 1945); John C. Baker, *Directors and Their Functions* (Cambridge: Harvard University, 1945).

[28] The policy-forming process in trade-unions and cooperatives has been studied less often than in industrial corporations.

No survey of power sharing is adequate that fails to explore the external and presumably unorganized relations of the firms in any given line of industry or finance. Factual situations vary along a continuum of "perfect competition" and "perfect monopoly." When the market is highly competitive, the influence that competitors exert upon one another is unorganized. It is customary for economists to speak of "perfect competition" in a market where a change in price initiated by one participant does not appreciably affect the general level of prices. Where thousands of small traders are actively transacting business with one another, perfect competition can be approximated. However, studies of modern industry in England and America have indicated that the most typical pattern is neither perfect competition nor complete monopoly, but "monopolistic competition," in which there is no single monopolist; those who occupy a dominant position are not numerous. Under these circumstances the prices set by one competitor exert a profound effect upon the level of prices in the whole market.

The task of estimating the degree of competition or monopoly in a given situation is a complex act of inquiry and judgment. There are, of course, some indexes that economists have devised over many years of study. (For example, monopoly is indicated when prices remain steady despite great fluctuations in demand and in cost of production.)

How do we relate the conception of shared power to market structure? "Monopoly power" is likely to be political power, in our functional sense of the word, since monopolists are often in an advantageous position to impose severe handicaps upon new business enterprise. In the case of industries that employ but few workers and produce luxury goods, this is a comparatively trivial matter from the standpoint of the whole community. However, when mass employment industries that produce "necessities" are involved, it is impossible to overlook the gravity of the deprivations that may be imposed under various circumstances. Provisionally, we may assert that political control accelerates with the degree of monopoly. Since simple bigness is not necessarily fatal to democracy, private monopolies may be kept within the framework of a democratic order when suitably regulated.[29]

A comprehensive survey of the market will devote special attention to labor-management relations, and to the amount of coercion employed on all sides.[30]

---

[29] Current professional thought is summed up in the papers on "capitalism and monopolistic competition" presented before the annual meeting of the American Economic Association, *American Economic Review*, XL, No. 2 (1950).

[30] See *How Collective Bargaining Works* (New York: Twentieth Century Fund, 1942); Benjamin M. Selekman, *Labor Relations and Human Relations* (New York: McGraw-Hill, 1947).

When we have exhausted the economic institutions, the policy-making process in all remaining institutions must be scrutinized in order to ascertain the presence or absence of the true decision, as functionally defined at the beginning of our analysis.

## FRATERNITY

The next step is to consider the values connected with "fraternity": to wit, the sharing of respect, rectitude, affection, and enlightenment. We deal first with respect, enlarging first upon the functional definition of the term.

### Shared Respect

What are the "outcomes" of a situation relatively specialized with regard to respect? We speak of "prestige," the giving and receiving of affirmations or denials of one's worth as a human being, and of one's individual merit. An elementary example of giving and receiving prestige is a testimonial dinner, or the conferring of a decoration. More complex examples are the inclusion or exclusion of persons from access to any value on grounds irrelevant to merit. We speak of respect as shared in a community where the prevailing myth declares that individuals are worthy of respect because they are human, and also because of personal merit. "Careers open to talent" sloganizes one of the great doctrines of respect; and when this is a rule laid down by public or private associations, the slogan is also part of the formula. If the slogan is disseminated in the folklore, it is also part of the miranda.[31]

The most direct method of ascertaining the relation between myth and technique is to examine the operative facts at first hand. In communities where the myth does not provide for a rigid class and rank system (and indeed may expressly repudiate such a structure), research may demonstrate that respect groups do in fact exist, though perhaps not strictly "ascriptive." In the United States, studies have been made during recent decades of the class pattern of several cities and towns. One procedure is to induce everyone to classify everyone else. Such testimony is the most advantageous index of prestige distinctions. (Other indexes may be used, but they are most satisfactory when they can be calibrated with direct testimony.) Community members are continually classifying one another according to social class, a category which can be defined as the largest group demanding and obtaining the same distinctions.

---

31 Note, for example, the perspective on equality among early settlers expressed in these lines from the operetta *Oklahoma!* by Rodgers and Hammerstein: "I don't claim that I'm better than anybody else, but I'll be damned if I ain't just as good!"

The prestige pattern of any community can be most successfully described by qualified persons who participate intimately in local life. In one inquiry into the working of caste and class in a southern town, three field workers spent eighteen months on the spot. The observers entered the situation as "adopted" classmates of individuals occupying high positions in the Negro and white caste strata. While they were learning how to act toward the other castes, they were also being inducted into the stratification internal to each caste.[32]

Since respect is shared only when it is given and received on the basis of personal merit, it is necessary to go beyond the static distribution of respect, and to discover how these distributions are related to merit. Although the individual may be a reliable source of knowledge on how he classifies other persons, he is not a reliable source for the bases of prestige, or for estimating the degree to which the values affecting prestige are accessible. Comparative knowledge of culture is indispensable to the making of such appraisals.

It is possible to obtain a rough guide to the facts in a given community by constructing an index of aggregate mobility among prestige positions. If there is little shift from one generation to another, so that families neither rise nor fall, it is reasonable to infer that a *de facto* set of castes exists, and that respect standards are violated.

Even where the aggregate index of mobility from one prestige position to another shows that there has been active interchange, the results cannot be taken without further study as a satisfactory index of shared respect, since comparable access to the values on the basis of which individuals rose or fell may not have been provided.

Light can be thrown upon the openness of access to base values by case studies of rising and falling persons and families.

Since respect outcomes are often unorganized (though not unstructured), scholars have less experience in gathering indices of respect than of power.

### Shared Rectitude

We speak of a "rectitude outcome" when the participants are making evaluations of goodness or badness. More generally, a rectitude evaluation is in terms of responsibility or irresponsibility. Such judgments are prevailingly serious, sober, insistent. Indeed, a typical response to violation of a positive standard is moral indignation.

In a civilized society, there is little difficulty in finding doctrinal statements about power. Doctrines relating to rectitude, however, are

[32] A. Davis, B. B. Gardner, and M. R. Gardner, *Deep South: A Social Anthropological Study of Caste and Class* (Chicago: University of Chicago Press, 1941).

likely to be less comprehensive. In Western culture, however, general rules of ethics do exist: "Do unto others as ye would they do unto you," "Honor thy father and thy mother," and so on.

Apparently some cultures have few if any general propositions about ethics. It is reported that the "good-bad" dichotomy is entirely absent from some cultures. Rules for the guidance of conduct may be found in profusion, but phrased as imperatives. In terms of content, such rules are commands sanctioned by threat of deprivations said to emanate from natural or supernatural forces. The conception of "ought" as a value (distinguished from a "must" supported by fear of annihilation by supernatural powers) is what we define as rectitude. It is not a question of terror-stricken conformity, but of perspectives in which the "self" demands that the "self" adhere to norms in harmony with, and contributory to, interpersonal relations.

Our doctrinal postulate is that each person ought to feel, think, and act responsibly for the purpose of perfecting the good society (defined as the maximum sharing of all values). We have in mind personalities who demand (of themselves and others) the bringing of conduct into harmony with the goal values of a free society. A responsible person chides himself for any failure to live up to the norm, and tries to do better next time. The point can be phrased by saying that we want a sense of impulsion to act for the common good; and we want this sense free of compulsiveness. ("Compulsiveness" is an imperious impulse not open to insight, that is, to self-knowledge.) We are speaking of seriousness without solemnity, earnestness without morbidity, persistence without flagellation. The sense of responsibility, as we understand it, is serenity of mind, not a neurotic symptom of dissociation or of obsession. We are recommending that human beings respect one another. We are also saying that it is right for human beings to do so; and that it is right to share power, wealth, and other values.

In estimating the degree to which common standards of rectitude prevail in a given society, it is illuminating to go beyond doctrine to the formula, and to study the criminal codes. Criminal codes are not necessarily phrased in the language of rectitude. Statements that unambiguously express an ethical demand use terms like "ought." Strictly speaking, the statement, "If you hurt him, we'll hurt you" is no assertion of rectitude. "You ought not hurt him; if you do, we'll hurt you" includes one rectitude statement. It is more complete when amplified: "You ought not hurt him; but if you do, I ought to hurt you, and I will." In practice, statements found in social formulas are often condensed and elliptical. (Obviously, words like "criminal," "immoral," "vicious," and "unethical" are synonyms in English for "ought not" in describing a pattern of conduct.)

Besides the criminal codes of the state, there are disciplinary provisions in most organizations, regardless of what value or values are their specialty. In our civilization the church is conventionally regarded as specialized to rectitude; and systems of canon law are worked out in detail.

In our civilization, as in others, a vast miranda exists for the moral guidance of young and old.

It is desirable to use field research in attempting to connect the rectitude myth of a given society with the facts of overt conduct. In probing into respect, we noted the usefulness of having the members of a community classify one another. In studying rectitude, such a procedure is less helpful, since in complex societies only extremes of "good" or "bad" are clearly recognized. In studying rectitude-in-action it is expedient to begin with organized, and then to investigate unorganized, activity.[33]

If we start with churches, we look for the occasions when evaluations of rectitude are made. When we analyze the rules invoked in condemning unruly members, it may appear that some rules are never, or almost never, invoked, which points to a probable discrepancy between standard and conduct. (Final judgment will depend upon studying circumstances in which it would be appropriate for the rule, taken textually, to be invoked.) By comparing the record of one church with all the churches in the society, we learn something of the degree of consensus in interpreting rectitude.

Besides noting which rules are invoked for the purpose of stigmatizing offenders, we see in what terms favorable judgments are expressed. If there are numerous citations for morality in the name of a standard which is actively invoked at the same time in disciplinary cases, there is evidence of conflict over the standard, either because it is questioned, or because inducements to violations are great.

### Shared Affection

Turning briefly to indexes of affection, we note that in some societies doctrine emphasizes the significance of affection in human nature, and glorifies the ideal of congenial human relations (the family circle, and ever-enlarging circles, until the world community is itself included). On the other hand, doctrines may portray man as a predatory rather than a loving animal. Between these extremes lie doctrines which teach that human nature is partly lovable, partly unlovable.

Some doctrines that support loyalty to the largest social groups find

[33] The contextual view of a "rule" is described with characteristic clarity and vigor in Bronislaw Malinowski, *Crime and Custom in Savage Society* (New York: Harcourt, Brace, 1926).

no place for love. The accent may be on rectitude ("ought, ought, ought"), or on power (legal obligations and liabilities).

In our society, at least, doctrines about affection undertake to affect the context in which sexual activities are carried on. From a physical standpoint, sexual activity between two individuals can be viewed as a joint means of disposing of recurring glandular products. The doctrine that sexual acts should be performed in a perspective of affection for the partner introduces a more complex context. If the partner is loved, the partner's attitude receives the same weight as one's own, and sexuality always depends on consent.

Love is sometimes made a matter of obligation and comes within the formula. Folklore is usually full of allusions to the place of love in human affairs.

In order to study the distribution of affection, special techniques have been invented by social scientists and psychologists. As in the assessment of respect, the statements made by the giver of affection provide the most satisfactory data about the fact of a relationship.[34] (Other indexes can be appraised in terms of the results of such direct testimony taken under appropriate conditions.) One method is to ask every member of a group to make a confidential ranking of all other members according to congeniality. The question can be posed in reference to some concrete possibility, such as working or living together.

Rough estimates of congeniality can often be made on the basis of such relatively crude indexes as conspicuous failures of congeniality (divorce, for instance).

### Shared Enlightenment

When we study the shaping and sharing of enlightenment, we are reminded of the high importance attributed to enlightenment in the doctrinal tradition of the Western world. In many communities, however, we find that doctrine and formula are united in opposition to the idea that there should be wide access to available knowledge on matters of important public policy. Measures hostile to enlightenment may be negative (censorship) or positive (as when propaganda is deceptive or distractive). In the West the miranda typically include the demand to give currency to the doings of public officials, at least.

The giving and receiving of knowledge is the culminating relationship in an enlightenment situation. A direct index of sharing is the

[34] J. L. Moreno, *Who Shall Survive? A New Approach to the Problem of Human Interrelations* (Washington, D.C.: Nervous and Mental Disease Monograph Series, No. 58, Nervous and Mental Disease Publishing Co., 1934)—the first lengthy report on "Sociometry."

state of public information on significant questions of policy. It is also possible to describe the contents of the media of communication in order to discover their degree of conformity to such standards of sharing as the following:

Everyone has access to media of communication in which news of current developments is reported; the media provide interpretations of the news that place them in relationship to a comprehensive context in which goals, alternatives, trends, factors, and projections are included; members of the community have access to media for the dissemination of facts and interpretations; the sources of statements are disclosed on which policy judgments depend; there is a presumption against lying; there is a presumption against the nonrational statement (the irrelevant, for example); there is a presumption in favor of statements from a competent source; there is a presumption against advocacy or neutrality, and in favor of inquiry.[35]

## SECURITY

By the term "security" we mean the sharing of the values of well-being, wealth, and skill.

### Shared Well-Being

The culminating moment in well-being, positively conceived, is an interpersonal relationship in which the psychic and somatic potentials of the participants are at their highest. Without going into detail, we think of well-being as shared under these conditions:

The myth emphasizes the importance of somatic and psychic well-being and interprets the ideal in a scientifically acceptable manner; there is adequate treatment of the diseased, injured, and handicapped; there are deliberate and successful efforts to prevent disease, injury, and handicap; progress is being made toward optimum psychic and somatic activity throughout life; the motives and circumstances leading to suicide, murder, war, and civil violence are reduced or eliminated; progress is made toward the lengthening of life.

Because of our great concern for ultimate freedom from deprivations of well-being imposed in the name of social groups (like belligerent nations) indexes of the following type are of particular interest to us (in addition to general information about the incidence of mortality and morbidity):

[35] Criteria elaborated from the recommendations of the Commission on Freedom of the Press, *A Free and Responsible Press: A General Report on Mass Communication* (Chicago: University of Chicago Press, 1947).

Number of casualties by years in war

Casualties by years in revolutions, revolts, and rebellions

Casualties in other group conflicts (labor-management, ethnic, religious, etc.)

Proportion of civilian and military casualties in war

Proportion of women and children casualties in war

Position in the social structure of war casualties (affiliations in terms of power, wealth, etc.)

(Maps) Where casualties occurred in wars; revolutions, revolts, and rebellions; other group conflicts; in relation to origin of the victim (e.g., American casualties in World War II inside and outside continental United States)

Changes of government by violence

War scares among the powers (periods of intense expectation relating to war)

Scares concerning other forms of group violence (revolution, revolt, rebellion, other group conflicts)

Peace demands (intense activity demanding an end to specific wars or to wars in general; demands for civic concord)

Conflict demands (support of war in general or specific wars; other forms of violent clash)

Proportion of national income spent on armament, police, and informal violence (or violence preparation)

Number under arms by years in various branches

Length of military experience among citizens of a power

(Map) Most important permanent military installations

Policemen in government service

Policemen in private and quasi-private military formations[36]

## Shared Wealth

We speak of wealth as shared under the following broad conditions:

The myth emphasizes the importance of expanding production in order to have the possibility of expanding the standard of living; the myth stresses the importance of a balanced (graduated) distribution rather than a division of the community into "rich" and "poor"; a progressively larger aggregate income is available for distribution; the pattern of income distribution is in fact balanced (graduated) rather than dichotomous; security of basic income is guaranteed in theory and fact; opportunities are open to every capable person to earn more than the basic income; opportunities are provided to develop potential capacities as producers and consumers.

[36] A convenient beginning is in Quincy Wright, *A Study of War*, 2 vols. (Chicago: University of Chicago Press, 1942).

Because of the great importance of economic changes in modern times it is possible to present a rather comprehensive picture of the economic relations called for in the previous paragraph.[37]

### Shared Skill

We speak of skill as a distinct value and take as the culminating moment in a skill situation the "performance," since a performance provides both the exerciser of the skill with an outlet and the audience with an occasion for the exercise of taste. Many doctrines endorse skill. But skill may also be de-emphasized, not only when there is neglect, but through the endorsement of attitudes that minimize incentives for skill. Indolence and casualness, for example, may be "aristocratic," and "luck" may lead to the disregarding of skill. Skills are intimately interwoven with all values, since the processes of creation are usually capable of being thought about separately and made the subject of deliberate efforts at the improvement of performance. Thus in some societies the base value for power, prosperity, health, and holiness (rectitude) may be the skillful conduct of rituals and ceremonies.

The formula in a given culture may prescribe tournaments of skill. In industrial societies the requirement of full employment is often justified as a means of preventing the skill deterioration of the working and managerial force. Provision is usually made for discovering and developing talent, notably by the system of instruction. Among prescribed arrangements designed to encourage skill may be cited the laws of patent and copyright.

Folklore, of course, is saturated with references to skill. Some legends appear to work against the cultivation of skill by stressing the degree to which it is a matter of inborn "genius."

When we look into the actual practices of a society, we discover that the level of performance is constantly being appraised as high, mediocre, or low; and that performers are classified accordingly. The degree of skill mastery can be aproximately ascertained from the systems of examination and certification in vogue in some societies. Sometimes a register of professional and nonprofessional skills exists.

We speak of a community as exhibiting a high level of shared skill when the following conditions occur:

The myth attaches importance to the maturing of latent talent into

---

[37] See *Readings in the Theory of Income Distribution*, selected by a committee of the American Economic Association, Philadelphia, 1946; H. G. Moulton, *Controlling Factors in Economic Development* (Washington, D.C.: The Brookings Institution, 1949); J. M. Clark, *Alternative to Serfdom* (New York: Knopf, 1948). A list of indicators of shared wealth and closely related values was published in *Essentials of Rural Welfare: An Approach to the Improvement of Rural Well-Being* (Food and Agriculture Organization, 1949).

socially acceptable skills and encourages excellence of performance; opportunities are provided for the full exercise of skills (full employment); opportunities are made available for the discovery of latent capacity and for its development; the base values upon which the acquisition and exercise of skill depend are accessible according to merit.

This emphasis upon skill as a value comes in part from the psychological study of individuals, which underlines the fact that among the deepest sources of human gratification are the maturing of latent capacities, including the tastes. Every form of expression develops perceptions of style that characterize the arrangement of the elements of which the entire performance is composed. These criteria are "intrinsic" and have no necessary reference to the "extrinsic" ends for which the operation may be carried out.[38]

## INTERRELATED VALUES AND INDEXES

We have been discussing goal values up to the present point as though they were capable of being segregated into separate compartments for which distinct indexes can be obtained. For purposes of analysis this is a convenient introduction. But once certain differentiations have been made, it is important to underline the extent to which any sequence of human activity involves all values in varying degree. Consider what goes on in a legislative session: From the standpoint of power, we may identify certain power culminations, like the final vote on a controversial bill. We also identify respect culminations, since the legislators may make laudatory or contemptuous remarks about one another (and others). It is possible to detect enlightenment culminations, as when pertinent information is presented for the consideration of the group. Affection culminations are involved, as when friendly jokes and allusions are made. Rectitude culminations take the form of denunciations. Skill may be exemplified in the adroitness of the presiding officer. Wealth may be transferred as a reward for successful manipulation of the legislature and the public. The stress and strain of the session may take its toll in the health of members. To some extent these culminations occupy a "base-scope" relationship.

Each index presupposes a procedure by the use of which the scientific observer relates himself to the context which he is to describe. It has been implied, though not made explicit, that the procedures vary

---

[38] The importance of allowing latent talent to mature into socially useful skills is a major theme in the psychology of education and of industrial employment, in particular.

in the intensiveness of the orientation required of the scientific observer toward the situation. Intensiveness is partly a question of time,
since the participant-observer who spends several weeks with a legislature may be expected to arrive at a more penetrating characterization
of the situation than a more cursory observer. Intensiveness is partly
a question of the use of special or laymanlike methods. Among the
special methods may be the use of tests (such as projective tests) or
psychiatric interviews. Systematic content analyses may be applied to
the speeches on the floor and the conversations in the anteroom.

## III

### THE CRITIQUE OF CONSTRUCTS

The foregoing pages have been concerned with one of the many
problems that arise in disciplined thinking about the structure of this,
or any, epoch in which the future enters into the reckoning. We have
elaborated upon the conception of human dignity (shared values)
and indicated the steps involved in relating such comprehensive categories to concrete circumstances. We turn now to the problem of
making a critical evaluation of a developmental construct.

We have said before that projections of trend into the future do
not have the status of scientific generalizations. It is, however, important to appraise them in a scientific frame of reference. In this
perspective any future trend will register (and interact with) the
equilibrium of factors that condition one another in the world community. We therefore examine the major trends postulated in the developmental constructs, and take stock of what we know about the
equilibrium that would account for them.

Another way to state the same approach is to say that the shaping
and sharing of values is a changing equilibrium in which changes in
one factor (or cluster of factors) bring about changes in other factors
in accordance with fixed routines. The fixed routines are the relations
that it is the province of scientific laws to describe. Such laws take the
following general form: If the magnitude of $V^1$ varies, then the magnitude of $V^2$, $V^3$ . . . will vary (as follows). If we had a complete body
of established scientific generalizations, we could answer such questions as these: Specified changes in the democratic variable (or variables) will affect security and fraternity as follows; changes in the
security variables will affect democracy and fraternity as follows;
changes in the variables of fraternity will affect democracy and security as follows. The most general postulate underlying present scientific

laws is the maximization postulate, according to which human acts are a function (in the mathematical sense) of expected indulgence over deprivation. More loosely formulated, this means that one act is preferred above another if it is expected (by the chooser) to result in leaving him better off than the alternative act. To be better off is appraised in terms of net gain of such values as power, wealth, and the other values that we have introduced.

In any concrete setting the values are construed by the participants in "practice" terms. That is, when we describe the value demands of an individual or a nation, it is necessary to specify the patterns that are assumed by the individual or the nation to constitute these values. This is the "perception pattern" of a value. Our operational indexes are chosen as a means of making precise descriptions of this kind. They point the way toward the sort of detail that must be considered if we are eventually able to make accurate and relevant descriptions of how human beings interact. All the variety of patterns called myth or technique (perspective, operation) are capable of being described as patterns of perception as well as sensation, the perception being the relation viewed from the inner standpoint of a participant, and the sensation being the impact upon the participant seen from outside.

## SAMPLE DEVELOPMENTAL CONSTRUCTS

Let us proceed by stating a few general propositions about the trends for the future which are asserted in some developmental constructs: In the next few years the trend toward interaction throughout the world community will continue; the arena of world politics will be bipolarized; the trend toward militarization will be maintained at a high level; internal structures will become more totalitarianized. These projections may be summed up in the terms interdetermination, bipolarization, militarization, and totalitarianization.

### Interdetermination

We consider first the trend toward interdetermination throughout the world community. This is equivalent to saying that human beings will continue to be affected, and affected to an increasing extent, by one another. To some extent this trend will be registered in the form of increasing awareness of the necessity of taking individuals throughout the globe into account in making choices. It is not necessarily assumed that this "taking into account" will be accompanied by greater flows of communication, goods, or people across all frontiers. The "expectation system" is what is being talked about, and this term refers to the subjective activity of making assumptions about past, present, and future events. In the present context, the reference is to the subjective event of thinking about individuals (and groups) throughout the globe. Such "interior events" can be indexed by the scientific observer, in many cases, by taking note of the stream of intelligence incoming to those who make choices. The inflow of news through open or secret channels to governments, corporations, and other institutional groups will — if the trend forecast is correct — report or speculate about the activities of key persons and institutional groups around the globe. The "attention area" of such choosers will be globally comprehensive, whether reliable or not.

I suppose no one would deny that the growth of interdetermination has been one of the principal features of recent times, if not, indeed, of human history seen as a whole.[39] This trend can be expected to reverse only if it becomes possible to reinstate barriers capable of operating as effectively in our time as the oceans once did in keeping the "New World" from the "Old." It would be necessary to imagine a catastrophe of such dimensions that only remnants of the human race would survive. Under these conditions, global contact would be deferred until population and transportation problems had been restored.

Although the trend has been to an overwhelming degree toward a world community, there are local trends of an opposite sort that repay investigation. After periods of increasing interest in the world outside, individuals have often withdrawn attention to events nearer home. This is one aspect of the complex phenomenon of "isolationism." But we speak only of the "parochialization" of attention; political withdrawal may be associated with even more active efforts to keep informed about changes in the military environment. Elites who turn from international cooperation may redouble their attention to the reports of intelligence agents operating abroad. The parochializing of attention occurs when elites feel threatened, and seek to deny the threat by refusing to have anything to do with it. Such responses have been reported among sectors of the elites of China, Japan, India, and other societies made insecure by the pressures generated by the carriers of Western civilization.

More significant than the "ostrich" response of petulant elites of old societies are the withdrawal efforts on the part of some members of Western civilization. The attempt to ignore the news of the world

[39] Hornell Hart summarized past trends in "Technology and the Growth of Political Areas" in *Technology and International Relations*, edited by W. F. Ogburn (Chicago: University of Chicago Press, 1949), pp. 28–57.

has been made with some fanfare by small bands of sectarians seeking solitude in deserts, mountains, islands, jungles, or caves; or by aesthetes who live in New York but profess to overlook Washington, Moscow, or other "merely political" centers. More significant than the cultists are the individuals who quietly "privatize" their preoccupations, and ignore larger circles of human activity as completely as possible, often devoting themselves to home, family, and friends. One form of privatization is the cultivating of skills which are used to divert attention from symbols of the globe as a whole, or the political currents and issues of the time. This is withdrawal by "technicalization," and covers a variety of activities from chess through other games and arts. Another common form of privatization has grown up in response to the penetrative strength of mass media of communication. I speak of "defense by diffuse attention," which is one of the principal means by which human beings defend themselves from psychic rape by print and broadcast. In recent times the sensational debut of television has brought at least a momentary restoration of "concentrated attention" among urban adults who had dulled themselves to radio and newsprint. Millions of persons have learned how to continue their interior fantasies in the presence of a muttering radio and a talking film. (Indeed, the task of "breaking the stream of fantasy" and riveting attention upon an exterior channel of communication is no small problem for the media manipulators.)

The significant generalization appears to be that, with increasing technical facilities for contact, the "nuclear" patterns of the self are strengthened more than the "peripheral." This means, for instance, that as the automobile comes into use, the number of long trips becomes more frequent than in horse-and-buggy days, but the number of short trips multiplies in even greater proportion. Hence the persons and physical objects in the vicinity are more frequently seen, and better known. The newspaper and the radio report remote events; but they expand the local listening public by referring more often to local affairs. It is not being denied that larger "attention" areas arise as new "activity" areas expand. We are directing notice to the distinctive manner in which this comes about. Attention to the "periphery" does not expand as fast as the "nuclear" zones of news and opinion.[40]

The point appears to be that when the zone of interaction enlarges, and the focus of attention is to some extent captured by the new context, there is active reconsideration of the self. One looks again at

[40] See Malcolm M. Willey and Stuart A. Rice, *Communication Agencies and Social Life* (New York: McGraw-Hill, 1933). This was a monograph prepared for the President's Research Committee on Social Trends.

one's body, clothes, manners, and general mode of life. The primary ego (the "I," "me") is more frequently thought of, which is another way of saying that self-consciousness increases (in the sense of self-reference). Hence the more intimate and local components of the self are elaborated before wider exposure can be tolerated. The ego sustains a sense of security by filling in the imperfectly known lineaments of the moat separating the ego from the new congregation of egos which have been introduced into the environment.

Intense self-reference appears to be a means by which the individual overcomes the uncertainties and the anxieties that arise in the presence of the unknown. We speak of the unknown "person," rather than the unknown "thing"; in general, the person is responded to as a more potential source of deprivation or indulgence than the "thing." There is pause for further enlightenment about the nature of the self, and of the environment that separates the more intimate and immediate parts of the self from newcomers. After the ego has evolved a conception of its role in the enlarged configuration, there can be a more abiding surge of interest in the "remote other." Hence, self-reference is a function of other-reference in the sense that a comparatively small exposure to new figures brings about a relatively large preoccupation with the self. The symbols referring to new figures are embellished after a considerable enrichment has occurred in the symbol of the primary ego and of the more intimate features of the self. (In this analysis we speak of the "self" as comprising all ego symbols included with the primary ego; i.e., the self typically includes the images of family, friends, and country.)

The "pause for ego examination" is an adjustment effect with large repercussions in world politics. It implies that every extension of the zone of interaction is immediately followed by intense preoccupation with a somewhat enlarged image of the self-in-situation, rather than with an image that includes even the peripheral members of the new situation. Hence the growth of regional transportation and communication induced a wave of intensified localism; expanded interregional transportation and communication induced a wave of regionalism; expanded intercultural transport and communication brought a wave of culturalism (nationalism). These are instances of the proposition that increased exposure to individuals with whom one is not already identified brings about more intense preoccupation with those with whom one is previously identified (including the primary ego).

This is by no means the same as saying that individuals are invariably hostile to strangers, or that there will always be strangers. Here it is simply a question of the way that human beings adjust to new experience. Confronted by the new, the frame of reference is relatively meager, and the situation is viewed as one of uncertainty. To some extent, uncertainty can be overcome by actively re-examining the features of the situation that are already partly known, and that can now be filled in with more detail. These features are the patterns constituting the "old" self, which are highlighted by contrast and comparison with the initial image of the new. The scrutiny of the "self-in-situation" occurs in a context in which, as usual, all values may be perceived to be at stake. Hence the self is examined in a context of possible action toward the new. If they are potential customers, competitors, allies, enemies, physicians, or teachers, for example, the self will be explored in relation to one's instrumental role in relation to customers, competitors, and the like. The new may be seen as possible "sights" for tourism; and this leads to exploring the self-image as a "sight."

The enlarging of identifications proceeds in a manner dictated by the predispositions of the personality to maximize values, and to explore a new frame of reference before arriving at new commitments. The process of self-reference permits indulgences to be given "to the self by the self," such as new increments of enlightenment in the place of confused uncertainty or even anxiety. If the self is basically benevolent rather than hostile toward the self, the act of scrutinizing one's own image provides an outlet for affectional energies.

What we have had to say about the "self-reference effect" indicates why "parochialization" is so prominent at the very moment that greater zones of human interaction are coming into existence. Each wave of new exposure induces a wave of self-reference; and those who control or explain interaction effects need to take this into account in foreseeing the psychological mechanisms by which men become accustomed to new identifications with their fellows. It suggests, too, how tendencies incompatible with the making of new and more inclusive identifications can be held in check by elites that are strategically situated to control mass media or geographical mobility. But those who favor expanded identifications need not be discouraged at the upsurge of parochialism that accompanies enlarging contact, since self-reference is an indispensable part of the broadening of identifications.[41]

### Bipolarization

A second trend that we shall consider is the bipolarization of the arena of world politics between the Soviet-centered and the America-

[41] Outstanding contributions to the theory of the self have been made by Sigmund Freud, Charles Horton Cooley, and George Herbert Mead.

centered world. Bipolarizing tendencies are visible in global affairs since the end of World War II, and for the next few years, at least, bipolarity is likely to predominate over rival patterns of alignment. One alternative is unipolarity, or the consolidation of a universal state comprehending all mankind. Another alternative is the return to a small number of powers of approximately equal strength (pluripolarity), or even a great number of small powers (multipolarity). The forecast of bipolarity does not necessarily carry with it the prediction of a third world war, since conceivably the equilibrium of world politics may eventually favor the resumption of cooperation on an enlarging and pacific basis. Part of our problem, as new insights are obtained, is to estimate the likelihood of these outcomes.

If we ask under what conditions bipolarity has succeeded pluripolarity (or some other pattern of world politics), at least partial answers can be given. Bipolarity is a function of a continuing high level of expected war. One basic characteristic of world culture is the expectation of violence, defined as the expectation that, whether one likes it or not, wars are viewed as likely. The very existence of this expectation favors the perpetuation of war, since even those who hate war may be prepared to run the risk of war rather than to make the sacrifices required by the policies through which war might be avoided. To put the matter as sharply as possible: War can always be avoided by surrender in advance of combat. The alternative to surrender is not necessarily combat; but it necessarily includes preparation for possible combat.

In concrete situations the expectation of violence has often been overcome by the expectations of peaceful agreement; and if the bipolar world is to become a world society where amicable agreements are made and lived up to, the expectation of violence must be overcome by strengthening other factors. Without going into detail, we can at least state one hypothesis, founded upon experience: The expectation of violence is not reduced by stressing the horror of war, or by urging people to stop thinking of war as inevitable. A study of the growth of "a more perfect union" in such cases as the thirteen American colonies, or the fragmented states of the Italian peninsula, suggests that changes in the expectation of violence are by-products of changes in other expectations, demands, and identifications. Some perceptions are especially significant, such as the perception of a common threat to existing values or of a common obstacle to enhancing values. If we apply these categories to the bipolar situation, we find that the ruling elite of the Soviet world has the problem common to dictatorship of "externalizing hostility" against the outside environment. Hence the ruling elite enjoys a continuing gain in internal power by sustaining a perpetual crisis. During the phase of uniting against the Soviet threat, the leaders of the non-Soviet world realize similar gains by stressing the war aims and preparations of the Soviets. By enhancing the perception of common threat, the non-Soviet world may succeed in adopting policies that deter the leaders of the Soviet bloc from initiating full-scale war. But if the non-Soviet world is not to become the initiator of hostilities, ruling elites must continue to expect to be better off by not attacking than by attacking the Soviets. In a word, the prospects of continued peace depend upon maintaining the expectation among the elites of both camps that they have more to gain by continued peace than by any alternative policy, and eventually that they will gain more by extending the area of peaceful cooperation on a global scale than by war preparation.

To some extent it is possible to relate some of the hypotheses that have just been stated to past experience. We need more critical and comparative studies of the past. There have been "more perfect unions." Under what conditions? Also, unions have split. Why? There have been periods relatively free from crisis among all the major powers. What equilibrium permitted this? There have also been periods of relatively acute crisis (with or without war). What were the significant features of the then prevailing equilibrium?

It seems apparent that one of the fundamental factors sustaining crisis and bringing the bipolar world into existence is the growth of modern industry. When we speak of "modern industry," we are referring to an extraordinarily complex pattern. For instance, we have in mind the physical facilities existing at any given place and time for the purposes of machine production. These facilities include the special equipment for mining, manufacture, transport, communication, wholesaling, and retailing. We also include "resources" in the concept of modern industry (the objects and energies expected to be utilized in production). Before a "thing" can become a resource, there must be a relationship to human expectations. This permits the often astounding leap to wealth of localities previously devoid of human significance. In addition to facilities and resources, we include in "modern industry" the perspectives and operations of science and engineering. Modern industry also refers to the human energies and skills available for production and consumption, and the policy-making arrangements by which facilities, resources, knowledge, and labor are apportioned. It may be that these arrangements are concentrated in the hands of "owners" or "managers." Or the decisive decision-makers may include government "regulators" and "planners." In varying degree, choices depend upon the result of bargaining in a truly competitive market, or upon allocation and rationing: and the latter terms may be set either by arbitrary or responsible power. These arrangements are often the outcome of traditional adjustments that nobody thinks about, but in typical modern communities the rapid rate of change has produced acute awareness of the process by which decisions are made.

When modern industry made its halting appearance in the Western world, it was pressed into the service of the existing structure of power and sentiment. When Marx wrote his epoch-making interpretation of the significance of the factory system, his synthesizing mind jumped to the prediction that the machine would promptly do away with national identifications and transform the West into two hostile, international classes. Marx wrote of the common, universal elements in receiving money rather than payment in kind. He prophesized the standardizing effect of having the same income, expressed in money, and of the diversifying effect of differences in money income. Marx described some of the common factors in having a factory job, and in managing or owning the instruments of production. What this remarkable thinker missed was the strength of the parochializing tendencies that have been discussed in connection with the "self-reference effect." When human beings are exposed to a widened frame of experience, only a few leap beyond the immediate and grasp the larger significance of the whole.

The piecemeal introduction of modern industry favored parochialism. Innovations that appeared in a given locality were perceived as part of a context that was much less than universal. The new factory was in "our town"; it gave employment to local people; it was often financed by local money; it was frequently managed by a local man; it not infrequently manufactured a local device invented by a local genius. Even when the market or source of material was not local, the nonlocal aspects of the relationship were assimilated to the locality by local representatives and interpreters of the transportation, wholesaling, and other operations at a distance. When resources of men and material were brought in, they frequently came from the vicinity, or by ever-enlarging circles involving the region and the nation.

The strength of the parochial context was so great that the new industrialism was first adapted to the nation rather than to the globe as a whole. By far the largest percentage of national savings and investment was made at home rather than abroad. When capital flowed across frontiers, it tended to conform to the national interest in the current balance of power. British capital thus went in relative abundance to the United States and to Canada and other parts of the

Empire. When states began to industrialize later than Britain, barriers were raised against foreign goods, even though Britain felt secure enough economically to allow foreign competition in British-controlled markets. The initiatives for restriction were typically taken by local businessmen who fanned the nascent national sentiment. Owing to the spread of literacy, the press, and popular government, economic processes were perceived as part of the national context rather than the world community.

Although the new industry was at first subordinated to the pluri-polar system of world politics, it presently became a dynamic factor in transforming the system. The capital sums, markets, and resources needed by modern technology provided a strong set of incentives for widening by force if necessary whatever areas could be legally in-corporated into, or effectively subordinated to, an existing big state. The new advances in military technology, psychological warfare, and central-planning technique provided the means for the implementation of these incentives. Hence the outcome of the intermittent crises of recent years has been to reorganize the frame of world politics into the mold of a bipolar system.

The relative eclipse of the smaller states has led to no leaping development toward a one-state world. On the contrary, the drag of parochializing factors has been too strong. The sequence has been from small-state identifications to identifications with giant states and giant interstate combinations. The demand for security has not meant, and does not mean today, that peace is sought at any price, but rather that peace is sacrificed if necessary in order to resist outside dictation of the policies to be followed by the largest effective state (or state coalition) with which one is affiliated. The world has not split, irre-spective of geographical lines and territorially limited loyalties, into a biclass polarization. It is divided into bizonal polarity. This gives more weight to the interplay of psychological factors than was fore-seen by Marx or by most Marxists. Bipolarization is in space; it is not dispersed according to the theory of bipolarization by class.[42]

---

[42] The present writer proposed the garrison state construct some years ago. See "Sino-Japanese Crisis: The Garrison State versus the Civilian State," *China Quarterly*, XI (1937); "The Garrison State," *American Journal of Sociology*, XLVI (1941), reprinted in *The Analysis of Political Behaviour: An Empirical Approach* (New York: Oxford University Press, 1947); *World Politics Faces Economics* (New York: McGraw-Hill, 1945, Committee for Economic Develop-ment Research Study); "The Interrelations of World Organization and Society," *Yale Law Journal*, LV (1946); "The Prospects of Cooperation in a Bipolar World," *University of Chicago Law Review*, XV (1948); " 'Inevitable' War: A Problem in the Control of Long-Range Expectations," *World Politics*, II (1949).

*Militarization*

The third trend is closely associated with the foregoing: It is the projected increase of militarization. If the trend culminates in war, it may end by transforming the bipolar world into a one-state world (if any world remains), or even into a new plural or multiple system of states (assuming, for instance, that the leading giants of the bipolar coalitions ruin each other for the benefit of third parties).

The trend toward militarization affords another example of false analysis by Marx in the early days of modern industrial innovation. The psychological and material factors connected with the processes of power were grossly misunderstood. The expectation of violence (and all institutions sustaining this expectation) was more important than originally foreseen. Hence the "inevitable collapse of capitalism" was incorrectly predicted. Continuing military crisis creates a situation in which "collapse" can be avoided. It is possible to make a relatively easy transition toward the new "mixed forms," which are continually arising to confound the prophets of "collapse." The recent bipolarization of world politics has emphasized the point that no large modern community can permit mass unemployment without courting political and military disaster.

The power structure of the modern world has exercised a decisive effect upon the growth of industrialism, and falsified many predictions that saw only the opposition of private owners and private wage workers, the latter suffering from progressive degradation and desperation. The future historians of our industrial society will undoubtedly put more emphasis than has usually been done in the past upon the influence of power classes and ideologies persisting from the preindustrial age. Why, for instance, did Germany try on two desperate occasions to force the pace of German expansion? It was obvious to many industrialists and economists that Germany was the most rapidly rising counterweight, not only to Britain and France, but to the still largely latent potentialities of the United States. Was it the power perspectives of the dynastic, feudal, diplomatic elements in Prussia that interrupted the seemingly assured victory of German industry, and lost the great gamble of 1914? In 1939 the power elements involved in making the lunge into Poland were invisible to no qualified observer.

Does militarization invariably mean war? Although this terse hypothesis has often been affirmed, and frequently confirmed, there are examples of relaxed tension among major powers (not only in the immediate aftermath of victory, and before coalitions have broken up). However, a disturbing fact has been noted by Hans Speier and some other students of the long-range movements of modern civilization.[43] Militarization is a more fundamental feature of modern times than is usually acknowledged. Not the least significant development is the removal of restrictions upon all-out war. We have witnessed the totalization of warfare, so that no one is exempt from its impact; limitations sanctified by custom and agreement have worn thinner and thinner. Gone are the days when war was an affair of the few; modern democratization and industrialization have socialized the risk for men, women, and children, whether in or out of uniform.

In power terms, the history of Western Europe in modern times has been a record of neglected opportunity, either for the cementing of pacific relations throughout the continent (and the world community as a whole), or for defending the primacy of the Western powers. The first course — toward a fully developed world society — was not taken, and the peoples of Europe share with all men everywhere the fratricidal crisis in which humanity lives today. The second course — toward safeguarding the primacy of Europe — was not taken, with the result that Western Europe is caught between the two giants who are dominating history, one rooted in Eastern Europe and Asia, the other in North America. Failure to adopt the first course was a continuing error of omission. Failure to defend the primacy of Europe was dramatized in a few striking episodes of lost opportunity.

For example, the elites of Europe were unable to unite during the Civil War in the United States for the purpose of weakening the United States by dividing the North American continent. In their wars the elites of Germany sought to conquer rather than to affiliate other peoples, and created political situations in which France could not go along with her Rhine neighbor. Hence France, Britain, and Russia were joined by the United States in 1914 to defeat Germany, with the result that a weakened Europe remained divided. In 1939 the domineering policy of Germany led to disaster on a far greater scale. Thus Germany lost two bids to become the giant industrial pole unifying the productivity of Eur-Afro-Asia against the emerging industrial giant of North America. In Asia, Soviet Russia became the beneficiary of the suicide of Europe. But the neglected opportunities of Britain were more spectacular, if possible, than those of Germany; after all, it was Britain who held the primacy among the industrial powers, and failed to hold it, either by integrating the Empire or Western Europe.

---

[43] Hans Speier, "Militarism in the Eighteenth Century," *Social Research*, III (1936); "Class Structure and 'Total War,'" *American Sociological Review*, IV (1939); "The Social Types of War," *American Journal of Sociology*, XLVII (1941).

The elite of Britain were drawn hither and yon by the attraction of the Empire on the one hand and of the Continent on the other. Having paused irresolutely for too long, Britain subsided into a secondary position.

It is not enough for the analyst of world affairs to establish that political and industrial factors contributed to militarization and bipolarization. A more subtle question is how to account for the specific poles and the actual levels of militarization. Why, after all, did Germany fail, not once, but twice? Why did Britain fail? Why did France gradually drop out of competition? Why did Germany and France fail to merge and to rise together? Why did all of Western Europe (including prewar Russia) fail to act as a unit in conquering the potential dangers and opportunities of the new technology? Why did the United States succeed, in spite of the enormous strength of centrifugal forces? Why did Soviet Russia succeed? Why did the Japanese try and fail, while both India and China lagged?

It is beyond the scope of the present discussion to propose a detailed theoretical model of the vast equilibrium of world power since the eighteenth century, or even in the period since 1890. We venture one remark that appears to be in harmony with what we know at present: Industrialization rose piecemeal, which may go far to explain why preindustrial elites persistently failed to see the world revolutionary significance of the process in which they were caught. Every enlarged circle of interaction produced an accentuation of the parochial, in accord with the "self-reference effect" explained earlier. Value adjustments were made on the basis of immediate and local advantage, with little regard to long-range effects. Even those who spoke of the modern world as an interrelated unit and celebrated the formative role of the machine on a universal scale applied their insight, for the most part, to the compounding of confusion for the sake of local and immediate gain.

Perhaps the most striking exemplification of the parochializing process is afforded by the spread and restriction of the world revolutionary symbols in the name of which the revolutionary elite seized power in Moscow in late 1917. At once there began the process by which the universal demands, expectations, and identifications contained in the new ideology were denied the universality which they proclaimed. The simplest restrictive mechanism was *total rejection*; but the most successful combined *partial rejection* with *partial incorporation*. The political ascendancy of the new Moscow elite was often rejected at the same time that part of the Moscow pattern was adopted. The original revolutionary pattern was *restricted from without* by the play of a hostile balance of power. The pattern was *restricted from within*, often by the revival of practices shaped in the course of Russian history.

The universalizing factors in the world equilibrium have thus far been held in check by active factors in which "the attention frames" of rulers and ruled may occupy a decisive place. The attention frame is not only influenced by the stimuli arising in the environment — from communications originating with others, or from visible acts and objects shaped by other persons. The attention frame is also governed by the predispositions with which an individual enters a given environmental situation. Predispositions supply not only the frame of conscious and unconscious demands, identifications, and expectations, but — and this is of great importance for the present analysis — the specific criteria by which these perspectives are applied. This means that the pattern of perception can be described as influenced by the demand for respect; it can also be described in terms of the specific patterns interpreted to evidence respect. The predispositions thus include the modes of inferring the value-significance of concrete circumstances. Hence the perceptions may, or may not, match the cues that are offered by others. (Unless there is such concordance, differences of interpretation are bound to arise.)

Such gross categories as "exposure to the machine" or "membership in the ruling elite" are not enough to provide the information that we require in order to have a comprehensive grasp of the historical process. We need operational specifications that will enable us to describe the "attention frames" that mediate between "environing stimuli" and "predisposition." It is probable that the study of attention frames will occupy the crucial position in accounting for social development. Persons of the "same" culture, the "same" position in the social structure, or the "same" exposure to technology usually are found to vary greatly when made the objects of intensive study. Such variations not only modify the "time lag" by which a "material" feature in the environment "imprints" itself upon attention and predisposition. These variations provide new contexts for perceiving details in new ways; the outcome lends diversity to the social process. Even "universal" elements are not static details of unchanging configurations. Rather, they are details of ever-changing contexts. Probably the act of perceiving new configurations is the most formative act in the process of shaping human history.[44]

---

[44] In *World Politics and Personal Insecurity*, I dealt in Chapter IX with the "milieu" and the "environment." One of the factors leading to the development of the "content analysis" of communication was the desire to describe such funda-

With this in mind, we revert to the contribution that can be made to anticipations of the future by the use of scientific theory and data. Scientific ways of thinking sum up past routines. When the interactions of people are described, the description may be brought to the attention of the individuals involved, who may modify their future conduct in order to take advantage of added insight. Insight is a potential base value for all value choices; this is the fundamental significance of science for freedom.

### Totalitarianization

Finally, we refer briefly to the trend toward *totalitarianization*. This term obviously alludes to the subordinating of society to government, and the concentration of all governmental power into a few hands, perhaps ultimately in the hands of a self-perpetuating caste of police officers. So far as scientific knowledge is concerned, we refer to a general proposition that has often been corroborated: *Centralization is a function of (perceived) common threat.* Perhaps the most important technical developments in this connection are the devices for abolishing privacy. It is a question of applying hypnosis, and, beyond hypnosis, of memory-reviving drugs. Apparently the "know-how" for bringing about the abolition of privacy, including the privacy of the unconscious (hence the forgotten), is "just around the corner," if indeed the corner has not been turned. An ever-present aim of a ruling elite is to discover the secrets of others in order to perceive common threats in time for defensive action. The future of freedom may again depend, as so often in the past, upon the propensity of tyrants to fall out among themselves, and to enlarge the share of the community in the making of decisions.

## IV

## THE BOURGEOIS REVOLUTION

As a means of presenting in more detail a construct of the present epoch, we begin by analyzing the revolutionary movement that is often characterized by Marxist and non-Marxist scholars alike as the period during which the ascendancy of the bourgeois classes was established in Western European civilization.

---

mental patterns in more precise, inclusive, and comparable ways. "Social perception" is receiving more research attention today. See Jerome S. Bruner and Leo Postman, "An Approach to Social Perception" in *Current Trends in Social Psychology* (Pittsburgh: University of Pittsburgh Press, 1948).

There is ample justification for asserting that a revolutionary transformation took place, or at least culminated, during the eighteenth and early-to-middle nineteenth centuries. Many traditional barriers to the sharing of values were removed, often by violence. All the values of democracy, fraternity, and security were affected; many limitations on the sharing of power, on individual mobility, and on education were obliterated or weakened. The symbols of the dominant political myth were profoundly changed; so, too, were the political elite.

When we refer to active *participants* in the political arena, the innovations stand out with great clarity. Social castes disappeared as formal entities and often as effective groups. Social mobility increased; hence classes superseded castes.

The *perspectives* of all participants were altered in terms of fundamental identity, value demands, and expectations. New national identities appeared in the world arena, often coinciding with, often ignoring, established boundaries. The demand for human dignity was expressed in terms of every value, in insistence upon widespread rather than narrow participation in power, fraternity, and security. The spectacle of sweeping change nourished a set of sanguine expectations about closing the gap between ideal aspiration and achievement.

Organized and unorganized *arenas* of decision were modified to accommodate democracy and nationalism. Executive institutions were usually subordinated by legislatures, and both were made accountable to an electorate that was widely recruited from the population. New institutions — notably political parties and the private press — arose to give effect to popular demands and to maintain competition among all who sought to control public demands. The jurisdiction of government was formally and effectively limited in regard to private associations, also in reference to individuals. The role of government was perceived as supervisory in dealing with private controversies; only with reluctance was it regulatory or enterprisory. In the world arena the initial demand for a federal union of free peoples perished when it became evident that many peoples remained unfree. Hence traditional expectations of violence persisted, and minimum public order was unattained.

An inventory of the *base values* at the disposal of participants in the power process calls attention to far-reaching shifts. The control of agricultural land was an asset of diminished importance. Commerce, industry, and banking produced the forms of wealth that enabled new groups of individuals and new organizations to improve their power position. As the private sector of the economy expanded, the role of agreements (contracts) rose in importance, which favored the growth of the legal profession. The lawyers also benefited from the role of written constitutions, published statutes, and opinions. Journalists and teachers took advantage of the demand for more literate managers, workers, and customers, and began to multiply in numbers and political influence. Ecclesiastical institutions had been so intimately intertwined with feudality and monarchy that when these structures were swept away or attenuated, churchmen were put at a political disadvantage. In many Protestant countries, however, they were able to play a stronger public role. Despite policies designed to separate church and state, social movements rooted in middle-class morality provided opportunities for popular leadership. Scientific and technological expansion furthered profit-seeking activities or the direct pursuit of power, and originated ever-new modes of producing capital or weapons.

The *strategies* employed in the power process reflected the new distribution of base values. The franchise — a power base of formal authority — brought large numbers of new voters into the domestic arena. The growth of literacy and the press coincided with the dissolution of ancient ties of obligation and response to the nobility, and created a competitive forum of public opinion. Competition for the support of large numbers led to the extensive use of wealth, partly in the form of contributions to political parties, partly in owning or influencing the press. Diplomatic negotiations among the elite of rival organizations were important, though these agreements might be swept aside as a result of propaganda appeals to the general public. Although violent coercion did not disappear in the internal arena of European states, it dropped to one side. The power-balancing process among parties, factions, and leaders exhibited many of the features common to the world arena itself, where great differences in effective control were modified by deference to equality of formal authority.

Intensive study of the flow of decision outcomes — in internal or external arenas — confirms the impression of very considerable freedom of choice. Governments debated and voted on statutes; heads of states negotiated and concluded international agreements. Voting and negotiating alignments gave expression to substantial freedom of coalition in the prevailing political system.

In summarizing the effects of the decision process introduced by the bourgeois revolution, it can be said that in elite terms the chief impact was the decline of feudal aristocracy and the rise of the businessman. The ideology as well as the operational techniques of caste were superseded, giving way to the doctrines, formulas, and mirandas of human dignity. Although many areas of the social process were regarded as inappropriate to government, the lesser bourgeoisie insisted upon a positive role in "legislating morals." Their rectitude norms led to an image of government as custodian of sexual ethics, teacher of thrift, and tutor of good manners. "Criminal" sanctions were actively directed against violators of prohibitions against prostitution, gambling, and brawling.

V

## THE UNNAMED REVOLUTION (THE PERMANENT REVOLUTION OF MODERNIZING INTELLECTUALS)

At this point let us shift attention to what can be characterized as the postbourgeois revolution, or the world revolution of the recent past and the immediate future. It was in postrevolutionary years, in fact, that the designation "bourgeois" was gradually adopted to refer to the earlier movement. During the decades of most active change the participants used many symbols to designate the events of the day. No doubt, the emergence of a considerable measure of consensus signified the ebbing of the wave and the gathering strength of a challenging movement.

The bourgeois revolution, though moving toward universality, fell short of inaugurating a unified public order. The proclaimed ideology at the most prominent center of origin of the revolution, Paris, was drastically modified in application. The revolutionary demand for a pacific world commonwealth of free men was partially expressed in the operational patterns of the globe.

If we investigate events in detail, beginning with the innovative center, Paris, it is necessary to describe both diffusion and restriction. If total diffusion had occurred, the peoples of the world would everywhere have risen in revolt against the established order and inaugurated a system of public order in harmony with the proclaimed ideal. Total diffusion did not take place, although a few mighty movements of protest did arise outside France that followed the revolutionary script. However universal the vocabulary of the revolutionaries — their universalizing demands, expectations, and identities — the new patterns were, in fact, parochially introduced and promptly restricted.

To emphasize the parochial character of innovation is to imply more than the obvious fact that the elite who originally seized power did so at a circumscribed site. The principal point is that participants in the immediate social context instantly perceived that their value position was affected by the change. Those who perceived themselves as value-indulged if they affiliated with the new revolutionary center proceeded to do so — in this way contributing to diffusion. Those who perceived themselves as value-deprived by joining the revolution rejected this option and acted to restrict diffusion. Hence the social environment responded as a power-balancing arena whose net result was to block total diffusion, while permitting a degree of restriction by partial incorporation (concurrently with partial rejection).

Consider a theoretical model of total diffusion. If diffusion were total, the effective elite of France's neighbors would transform their ideologies to conform to the new myth, and change their operating techniques accordingly. If the effective elite in control at the time of the innovation were opposed, a new elite would promptly arise in furtherance of revolution.

A theoretical model of this generality brings to mind the many factors that usually stand in the path of total diffusion. The elites outside Paris were, for the most part, recruited from the same social strata, and benefited from the same social institutions, as the defeated elite in France. Presumably, they perceived the innovation as a stupendous threat to their position and way of life and mobilized the base values and strategies open to them to protect themselves, in many cases seeking to liquidate the upstarts by violence. Not only was the threat evaluated as an external threat, but older elites assessed the repercussions of the new developments on the internal balance that sustained their power. In the extreme case they might at once be swept aside; in other cases they could adopt strategies that were intended to limit the appeal of the foreign center.

The analysis suggests that, in general, older elites will seek to limit the influence of the elite of the revolutionary center by "geographical differentiation," that is, by emphasizing foreignness. In reference to the French revolution, this was fused with "restriction by partial incorporation" to the extent that it stressed the national identity of all social classes in relation to "foreigners."

But restriction by partial incorporation can go much farther. An elite may modify itself by sharing authority and control with social formations that correspond to new strata at the revolutionary center. Doctrinal propositions from the new myth can be incorporated in the local ideology, and various operational arrangements adopted, such as the breaking up of large estates, the inauguration of parliaments, and the broadening of the franchise. These incorporations go beyond "geographical differentiation" to "restriction by partial incorporation," since perspectives and operations are taken over from the originating center.

While the French elite was being restricted from outside, it was undergoing internal restriction. At the phase of active power transfer, radical revolutionary demands were heartily endorsed and partially inaugurated. But these developments soon brought to the surface the conflicts latent among elite elements in the revolutionary coalition. Some groups that were obtaining immediate benefits from innovation were fearful of losing their gains if the most sweeping revolutionary demands were put into effect. Searching for allies to put a brake on revolution, these moderate elements turned to more conservative groups, hence precipitating a revival of older practices. "Restriction by revival" opened the road to the forming of coalitions with foreign groups, which widened the arena of action against revolutionary extremism.

These summary comments about the restriction of the bourgeois revolution prepare the ground for assessing future developments. Our contemporaries are in understandable doubt about the functional character of the political structure of the present epoch. The doubt is focused around the universal claims of the political movement that is variously called the "world revolution of the proletariat," of "socialism," of "communism," or of the "workers."

It is justifiable to accept Moscow as the eruptive center of a world revolutionary movement. Ambiguity and uncertainty arise when one seeks to describe its functional rather than its self-described characteristics. The following generalization is highly probable: Whatever functional characteristics are eventually recognized, they will not coincide with the ideology in the name of which power was seized in 1917. The dynamics of restriction are too deeply embedded in the world social process to admit of total diffusion, especially of the practices that conform to the early ardors of the take-over period.

We terminated our brief summary of the bourgeois revolution without referring to the gradual appearance of revolutionary Marxism. In the perspective of events it can be said that Marx and Engels initiated more than "restriction by partial incorporation" and "selective rejection." Theirs was a radical new differentiation that marked the emergence of an alternative pattern of world revolution, part of whose potential strength was the distinction that was drawn between the self-proclaimed ideology of the previous revolution, and the actual beneficiaries. Marx and Engels alleged that the revolution in the name of human dignity, of the classless society, had been perverted into a tool used to mask the rise to power of another small ruling class, the owning class, which was brought into being by emerging industrialism. Projecting this development into the future, they asserted that the dynamics of history were such that the owners of private capital would in turn be pressed aside by a novel social formation created by the new division of labor, namely the factory workers, the nonowning proletariat. But instead of installing one class in the shoes of another, the proletariat would achieve the final revolution, raising the curtain on the culminating moment of human development, the classless society.

In the decades that intervened between the *Communist Manifesto* and the later publications of Marx and Engels, the principal institutions of self-described Marxists were revolutionary in word and moderate in strategy. In industrially developed nations they were well on the way to becoming part of the loyal opposition to capitalistic societies. The typical exceptions were some nonindustrial nations where, nevertheless, a few supermodern features had been added to an institutional pattern much like prerevolutionary France. It was in the wake of external defeat and internal disorganization that a radical unit of the Marxist movement succeeded in grasping and holding power.

As usual, the mechanisms of restriction operated with prompt and potent effectiveness in widening the gap between the proclamations of a new elite and the facts of politics. The expectation that the Russian initiative would sweep the industrial countries and achieve the long-sought revolution on a world scale was promptly frustrated in Germany, and also among the trade-unionists and labor politicians of the victorious powers. Marxist and democratic predispositions in favor of the Russian revolution were, however, strong enough to handicap the elites of hostile foreign powers in conducting military operations against Moscow. Although intellectually unprepared to seize power in a nonindustrial country, the new elites adapted themselves to the situation by embarking upon vast programs of compulsory modernization and militarization. The industrial collapse of the nineteen-thirties in Europe and the United States took the Moscow leadership by surprise; their delayed and abortive strategies, which concentrated upon "social democratic" rivals, actually contributed to the success of the most dramatic and dangerous movement aimed against them. The Nazis were "national," not "international"; "socialist," not "Marxist"; "labor," not "proletarian." In ruthlessness and scope the Nazis speedily incorporated many of the strategies that had been tested in Moscow.

The Moscow elite, caught in a desperate position by the Second

World War, found it necessary to depend upon the United States and other states for the assistance in order to wage a successful struggle. Appeals to world revolution were played down as an expedient concession to the susceptibilities of the coalition. At the close of the war they were once more faced with a huge task of national reconstruction and, in addition, by the atomic technology of the United States. Again they were unable fully to exploit the disorganization of a defeated Germany, or to make decisive headway in industrial nations. Meanwhile, years of conspicuous absorption with internal problems led the Moscow elite to make repeated and sensational sacrifices of international Communist organizations on behalf of its parochial (national) expediencies. It became less and less easy to keep alive the image of a truly international movement. The spectacle of internal police control militated against the image of a genuinely democratic state. The policies of forced industrial and agricultural transformation indicated that the movement was "voluntaristic" on the part of a small elite rather than an expression of historic "inevitability." The Marxist timetable had already been disregarded; the original analysis asserted that industrialization, followed by ripening class-consciousness and political maturity of the factory proletariat, would inaugurate revolution. It became increasingly apparent that the initiative rested with a few highly politicized semi-intellectuals who used their skills of symbol management and organization to seize power in a backward country and to hammer it into modernization. The demand to collectivize productive resources was utilized as a means of concentrating the instruments of power in the hands of the party (and official) elite, and to liquidate the landed nobility and the small but strong urban plutocracy, without creating a nation of small-propertied farmers, of small or middle-sized business, or of independent professionals. The effective aim was to streamline all production into national organizations administered by a relatively small but widely recruited political elite. Values were widely shared in a pattern of unequal though graduated distribution.

The significance of the Russian innovation was gradually brought into clear perspective by developments in China and other little-industrialized countries. The extension of the revolution to China was severely handicapped by the stereotyped character of the strategy that Moscow sought to impose on the movement. Under the influence of their experience in seizing power in the cities where, conforming to the principle of uneven development, the most advanced pockets of the proletariat were to be found, Moscow was early convinced of the crucial role of urban centers. Recognizing the weakness of the proletariat, the leaders reverted to various traditional Marxist interpretations and sought to ally Communist organizations with liberal (national) business and political elements. The Communists lost this gambit, since Chiang Kai-shek and his associates promptly used all the violence necessary to keep control of their own movement and to liquidate Communist challengers. Exiled to the countryside, the Communists slowly adapted to new circumstances and consolidated their separate organization in the long march, eventually seizing key urban centers. The novel features of the situation, so successfully exploited by Mao and his associates, gradually brought the various contradictions in the Moscow-led movement to the surface, helping to exhibit the fundamental features of the political changes that have been and are being propagated in our time in the name of socialism, communism, or bolshevism and related symbols. Recent upheavals in southern Asia, Africa, and Latin America provide further evidence, as do the internal transformations in the industrial powers themselves.

We have deliberately spoken of "the unnamed revolution" as a means of emphasizing the tentative character of the constructs put forward here. However, there are many indications that a "functional differentiation" is under way. This is suggested by the growth of a strong current of consensus among observers of the contemporary scene whose starting points are in notable contrast to one another. Our analysis of the bourgeois revolution indicates that functional differentiation occurs when it is generally perceived that the universalistic ideology in the name of which power was seized at a revolutionary center has had the effect of conferring relative and circumscribed advantages on a few — in a word, on a new and circumscribed elite. It is not necessarily denied that some value advantages are more widely distributed in consequence of the movement as a whole. The essential point is the identity of the power class, if any, that enjoys a relatively favorable position.

We join with those who formulate "the world revolution of the epoch" (rather than of the "geographical center" of initial radical innovation) as follows: The major transformation is the decline of business (and of earlier social formations) and the rise of intellectuals and semi-intellectuals to effective power. In comparatively nonindustrialized countries the principal ideologies, though initially "international" and "proletarian," are chiefly "national," "socialist," pro-"modernization" and pro-"industrialization."

In relatively advanced countries the principal ideology accepts a permanent revolution of scientific and technological change. "A world revolution of permanent modernization" under the leadership of "symbol specialists" ("intellectuals") is perhaps the appropriate description. More tersely, a "permanent revolution of modernizing intellectuals" is under way. This is a more specialized version of the broad transformation that we have characterized as "the world revolution of middle-income skill groups."

The interpretation outlined in this construct was originally formulated in the Marxist movement itself.[45] It is attributed to a Polish revolutionary who applied the fundamental insight of Marx with freshness and candor. He declared that the rising social class was the intellectuals, whose capital was their knowledge, and whose strategy was to exploit the discontent of workers and peasants. It need not be emphasized how shocking this was to the orthodox, who denounced or ignored such heresy. There are no grounds for asserting that the Marxists, including Lenin, knew what they were doing when they tried to identify themselves with the "proletariat." Today this seems to be an example of temporary "false class-consciousness" on the part of intellectuals that nevertheless served the power interests of the rising intellectual class. By deceiving themselves they were better able to deceive others. One of the fascinating and little-studied problems of the movement is the strength of the value aspirations that made it intolerable for leading figures to view themselves, not as in the vanguard of the proletariat, but of the rising intellectual class. The vehemence with which it was necessary to insist upon the "parasitism" of intellectuals upon "true" social classes is a symptom of the strength of the propensities within themselves against which they were struggling. Even in quite recent times it is possible for a Communist theoretician to create a scandal by acknowledging "The New Class."[46]

Let us examine the construct in more detail. In the countries that set the modernizing pace the paths to power, wealth, respect, and other values were sufficiently open to intellectuals to render it unnecessary to rely upon affiliation with a revolutionary party to advance their fortunes. Opportunities for skill and enlightenment were made relatively abundant as educational institutions multiplied and as industrial invention and investment provided jobs. The workers in England, for instance, were originally led in movements to improve their

---

[45] See the allusion to Waclaw Machajski in H. D. Lasswell, *World Politics and Personal Insecurity* (New York: McGraw-Hill, 1935), included in *A Study of Power* (Glencoe, Ill.: The Free Press, 1950), pp. 112 ff., and the writings of Max Nomad. On symbol specialists consult H. D. Lasswell, *Politics: Who Gets What, When, How* (New York: McGraw-Hill, 1936), Chapters 2 and 6, or new edition with "postscript" (New York: Meridian Books, 1958).

[46] In Yugoslavia, for instance. See Milovan Djilas, *The New Class* (New York: Praeger, 1957).

lot by individuals from other social classes. Eventually the wage earn-
ers in mining, shipbuilding, textiles, and other forms of manufacturing
began to supply their own trade-union and party officials. But the sons
of such officials, especially at the national level, were typically raised
as members of the intellectual classes. In Russia, a nonindustrial country, significant components of the intellectual classes, frustrated by
lack of opportunity, turned to revolutionary violence with ultimate
success.[47] The most novel result was to eliminate the businessmen;
otherwise, the principal targets were typical of bourgeois revolutions.
China provides the only major example of a revolutionary movement
that closely resembles the Russian in the simultaneous liquidation of
modern business and of ancient classes based on the land. The internal cleavages among intellectuals are made particularly manifest
in the coalitions with other formations that are made in many countries or across national lines. We presently consider some of these
contingencies.

Intellectuals have been so concerned with their occupational, professional, and artistic colleagues and rivals that they are not fully
conscious of a distinct identity. However, the legacies from ancient
civilizations contain ready-made images of men of knowledge, especially of policy advisors. The Confucian scholar of China or the
philosopher-king of Plato strikingly exemplify this role. Western European civilization affords greater prominence to scientists and technologists than did previous cultures, and the division of labor among
intellectuals has become progressively refined. As each specialization
achieves an identity, clarifies values and expectations, and perfects its
operational technique, a subgroup emerges to perform the task of
relating the new skill group to the environment. The chairmen and
deans of universities, as well as the heads of bureaus and research
staffs in governmental or private organizations, have, for example,
taken over these responsibilities. They often become consultants of
public official and private associations on public policy, the assumption being that they can assist in evaluating the significance of spe-

---

[47] The fact that Russia was industrially underdeveloped immediately cast doubt
on the validity of Marxist expectations and laid the foundation for general awareness of the "intellectual" and "modernizing" character of contemporary world
political evolution. For example, see Hugh Seton-Watson, *Neither War nor Peace:
The Struggle for Power in the Postwar World* (New York: Praeger, 1960); J. H.
Kautsky (ed.), *Political Change in Underdeveloped Countries* (New York: Wiley,
1962), especially the author's introduction, pp. 3–119. Other contributors are
Merle Kling, George I. Blanksten, James S. Coleman, Edward Shils, Harry J.
Benda, Mary Matossian, George E. Lichtbau, Bernard S. Morris, Morris Watnik,
Joel Carmichael, and Richard Lowenthal.

cialized knowledge for the options open to decision makers in the public and the civic orders.

Concurrently the expansion of the social and behavioral sciences has led to detailed study of the decision process itself. Our civilization is generating the "policy sciences," which include knowledge of the decision process, and also of the policy relevance of all specialized fields.[48] Both the intelligence and appraisal phases of decision are heavily influenced by these emergents; so, too, is the recruitment of personnel for other decision functions.

In industrial societies the various strata of intellectuals are widely recruited from within the local context of community, class, interest, and personality. The symbol specialists are so broadly distributed that they share many of the parochial perspectives of the social context, despite the characteristic impersonality and latent universality implicit in the pursuit and recognition of empirical truth. The latent transnational identity appears under circumstances that have hitherto proved exceptional. Only a few of the intellectuals in any large industrial nation perceive themselves as directly dependent for security or for fraternal values upon the world community. Rather, their attention is typically focused upon sources of value indulgence or deprivation in the home locality, region, or nation.

In relatively nonindustrial countries the initial recruitment of intellectuals for the acquisition and exercise of modern skills may be remarkably unrepresentative of the older culture. The situation varies from the elite origins of scholars sent abroad at various times by some countries to acquire modern enlightenment and know-how (Japan, for example) to the lower-class provenience in many cases of the janitors, houseboys, or slaves who obtained some command of foreign languages. The perspectives of native intellectuals vary in response to changing combinations of predisposing and environing factors that combine to mold new social classes. A typical sequence is this: initial rejection of foreign models; attempts at near-total incorporation of foreign models, including national or international symbols of identity; partial rejection of foreign models and emphasis upon distinctiveness.

When we examine the organizations that have been launched to serve the interests of intellectuals, we are impressed by the degree to which these institutions reflect the decisions and conflicts of the whole world arena. Educational establishments are typically perceived as symptoms of modernization; it is not unusual therefore for emerging

[48] "The Policy Orientation," Chapter 1, in D. Lerner and H. D. Lasswell, *The Policy Sciences: Recent Developments in Scope and Method* (Stanford, Calif.: Stanford University Press, 1951).

bodies politic to insist on extending advanced educational opportunity at a rate far in excess of the capacity of official or private sectors to absorb personnel. The accelerated and unbalanced production of new-style intellectuals creates a disaffected element that is strongly disposed to demand prompt and radical means of revolutionizing the community in ways that assure them of respected, potent, and secure careers.[49]

It is important to inquire into the significance of occupational, professional, and artistic specialties considered as base values for power. In the political system of the later bourgeois period a self-recruited subelite of intellectuals formulated and applied the counterideology of Marxism (the principal early doctrine). Skills of spoken and written agitation were parallel to the skills necessary for the leadership of all political parties. Skills of party and trade-union organization, though somewhat distinctive in content, were functionally similar to the skills required to launch and sustain private associations of any kind, whether parties, pressure groups, or other voluntary associations devoted to wealth, well-being, rectitude, or other values. The skill groups utilized in many official organizations were sometimes recruited from older social formations (notably diplomatic services, and the higher echelons of judicial and other civil administration; the higher military posts were likewise kept in relatively elite circles, which often represented family fusions of businessmen and ancient aristocracy). With the multiplication of middle posts the pressure from educated persons recruited from lower social strata was partially relieved by opening the lesser grades of public and private administrative structures to merit. Wherever this process was held back, as in Germany, the accumulated resentment of old and new formations at middle and lower levels was explosive; and in times of national defeat and demoralization it provided the setting in which radical revolutionary movements could proceed.

The rapid rise of science and engineering has thus far altered the composition of active political elites to a remarkably modest extent. This comes about partly because intense specialization and dedication are required to achieve professional distinction. Specialties whose practitioners are in frequent contact with their fellow men are favorable to active politics: witness the doctors, dentists, and pharmacists who, in addition to teachers and lawyers, often make the transition. Laboratory specialties, and skills that depend on isolation in the field, are at a disadvantage.

[49] See Edward Shils, "The Intellectuals in the Political Development of the New States," World Politics, XII (1960), pp. 329–368.

My brief comment on the base values at the disposal of intellectuals has anticipated some points that are pertinent to the way in which various assets (or liabilities) can be managed for power purposes. At first glance, it might seem that the emergence of symbol specialists would inaugurate an era of persuasion in the political arena, and that coercion — which is presumably antithetical to the life of the mind — would wither away. To some extent the rise of educated politicians has indeed contributed to the life of civility. The brawls of yesteryear are no more in many communities where personal fisticuffs were formerly a measure of masculinity.[50] The decorum of the urban middle classes has altered the tone of human intercourse and greatly subdued the lusty peasant, hunter, rancher, seaman, and soldier.

It cannot, however, be successfully maintained that the larger strategy of nations and subnational groups has forsworn the use or the threat of violence. As modern science and engineering transform technology, the means of destruction — and production — facilitate action at a distance. Man-to-man combat, though far from obsolete, is a rivulet in the torrent of fire power released by remote control. This distanciation of the human planner and technician from the human consequences of his act favors the intellectual, de-emphasizes personal combat, and underplays vehement emotional expression. Technology fosters calculated risk — risk-taking that is cool, not hot.

At the same time it is evident to students of man that human beings are equipped with organic systems built for fleeing and fighting — perhaps much more for the security of "cowardice" than for the hazards of "heroism."[51] The inner signal system is sensitive to deprivations of all kinds, and slams into action with glandular accelerators of internal processes. In a symbol-rich and action-poor environment human beings become the scene of internal conflict whose details are both symbolic and physiological. The resulting tensions are among the largely hidden factors that add an explosive potential to weapon systems. They affect diplomacy and mass communication; they chronically influence the use of economic as of all other instruments of policy.

[50] See David Riesman's perceptive hypothesis in his Introduction to D. Lerner's *The Passing of Traditional Society, op. cit.,* pp. 7–8: ". . . the ingenuity needed to escape the all-too-evident impasses in the Middle East can neither be imported nor be locally engendered without a lessening of the dominant male values, what the Spaniards term 'machismo.' A greater equality between the sexes would seem to be requisite before many of the approaches toward modernization can make sense. Thus, for men to cooperate with each other outside of kin connections, they must not see each other merely as sexual rivals."

[51] The point is central to A. I. W. Simeons, *Man's Presumptuous Brain: An Evolutionary Interpretation of Psychosomatic Disease,* with a Foreword by Joost A. M. Meerloo (New York: Dutton, 1962).

Intellectuals perform for the collectivity much the function that fantasies and imaginings play in the lives of individuals. Acts that are uncompleted or in contemplation can be envisaged in individual imagination. Policy alternatives that face the collectivity can be dramatized in advance in the outpourings of intellectuals, some of whom may succeed in giving articulate form to nearly every conceivable possibility, from the weirdest to the most banal. As with individuals the exercise of fantasy and verbalization may be broken off at any time and discharged into action. With individuals this depends in large measure on the level of crisis (stress toward act completion). When individuals in the active elite are crisis-oriented, processes of deliberation can be broken off momentarily as the decision process swings toward commitment.

Among intellectuals the level of crisis may be permanently high, particularly in those who, during early years of socialization, have incompletely repressed their rebellious tendencies. In modern industrial societies we are aware of many social circumstances in which personality systems are especially likely to be shaped into perpetual lability. From such conflictful formations come agitational propensities; and among agitators are persons who are disposed to incite toward destructive action.[52] When the social process creates an unbalanced supply of symbol manipulators, it prepares more than an excess of symbolic expression; it disposes toward *destructive* expression.

Beyond personality factors that predispose intellectuals toward coercive strategy, we must not overlook the obvious advantage of entering into coalition with groups and individuals who expect to benefit from the fact or prospect of destructiveness. As we have emphasized before, militarization is built into the world arena; the expectation of violence continues — the expectation that, whether regarded as desirable or not, armed conflicts will probably continue to take place. By and large, scientists and engineers are subjectively sincere in paying tribute to the ideal of a world fraternity of science.[53] But it is rare that there is any significant degree of abstinence from accepting jobs or assistance from the defense departments of government or from private subcontractors. So long as enlightenment and skill continue to depend upon political power for values of any kind — and it is not easy to imagine a world free of politics — intellectuals will find themselves caught in the net of interlocking interests. Today this implies

[52] Richard Christie and Marie Jahoda (eds.), *Studies in the Scope and Method of the "Authoritarian Personality"* (Glencoe, Ill.: The Free Press, 1954). See Walter O. Weyrauch, *The Personality of Lawyers* (New Haven, Conn.: Yale University Press, 1964).

[53] Representative expressions are in World Academy of Art and Science, *Science and the Future of Mankind* (The Hague: Junk, 1961).

support of the prevailing structure of mutual insecurity. The structure of science becomes as warped as the structure of production at times when an important sector of the economy depends on arms and arms production for successful operation. This is true whether success is judged by the criteria of socialist or capitalist management.

In characterizing the outcomes and effects of an intellectually dominated world, it is possible to offer at least one major generalization: The trend of policy will express a balance of power favorable to more and more intellectual activity, supported by more and more utilization of social resources.

From the standpoint of human dignity the probable result cannot be foretold with confidence. Conflicting demands will continue to be put forward in terms of the common good; and there may in fact be widespread sharing of more abundant health and wealth, more freedom from discrimination, wider ranges of choice for affectionate expression, more responsible conduct — besides ever-widening enlightenment and skill.

The institutional structures inside the body politic that conform to the changing power requirements of the intellectual elite range from bureaucracies to competitive arrangements. Bureaucracies may be highly centralized at the national level, highly concentrated in a few organs at every level, strictly governmentalized in the absorption of organized activities, and regimented in the detailed direction of individual lives. Analysis may show that the bureaucratic pattern, though formally hierarchical, is effectively co-archical at many levels or on particular problems. The bureaucracies may be duplicated, one composed of party members who formulate and appraise basic policy, the other constituting the explicit officials of government. To the extent that formal relations are competitive, inquiry may show that effective and formal power coincide or diverge in many combinations.[54]

The system may be perpetually mobilized against external and internal enemies, dominated by the expectation of violence. Under these circumstances the military and political police exert a decisive influence, creating the early stages of a bureaucratized and probably despotic garrison-police state. In the Soviet Union the political police were able to express themselves through the party; hence, they kept

[54] Consult Joseph LaPolombara (ed.), *Bureaucracy and Political Development* (Princeton: Princeton University Press, 1963). The authors include Carl Beck, Ralph Braibanti, John T. Dorsey, S. N. Eisenstadt, Merle Fainsod, Bert F. Hoselitz, J. Donald Kingsley, Fritz Morstein Marx, Fred W. Riggs, Walter R. Sharp, and Joseph J. Spengler.

the upper hand over the military forces. During the Stalinist period of personal tyranny effective power was overwhelmingly focused on Stalin and his immediate lieutenants, whose principal problems were characteristic of a political police force. A possible line of evolution of garrison-prison states is the consolidation of a self-perpetuating caste dominated by military and police elements. This depends upon the relative strength of anticaste predispositions in a body politic, and the impact of such environing factors as the use and threat of violence.

A garrison-police state does not necessarily culminate in an elite caste of intellectuals who specialize in military and political police problems and methods. As implied earlier, there may be periods of relative exemption from environing threats; and there may be predispositions firmly established of democratic sharing of power, save in acute crises that are met by brief dictatorial measures. The history of small frontier communities shows that it is possible for democratic garrison states to exist on a miniature scale. The history of large industrialized states is less conclusive since they have a short history of exposure to the crises of the atomic age.[55]

We have indicated the many factors, however, that keep alive the possibility of regression from the search for human dignity. In addition to militarization many factors contribute to a constellation of conditions that may culminate in a public order of caste rather than of classes based on individual merit and common humanity. A major ideological element, already actively present in the world community, is the ideology of racial supremacy.

The Nazis of Germany went beyond restriction by geographical differentiation and partial incorporation in meeting the threat of Moscow. The Marxists, it will be recalled, counterposed the diagnostic label of the "bourgeois revolution" to the universal claim of Paris to speak for the "rights of man"; they opposed "economic" demands to "legalistic and ethical" declarations. The Nazis treated Moscow as part of a racist conspiracy — a Jewish conspiracy — against "Aryans"; hence, to the doctrines in the name of ethics, morality, and economics they replied in the language of "race."

[55] See S. P. Hutington (ed.), *Changing Patterns of Military Politics* (Glencoe, Ill.: The Free Press, 1962); authors include Philip Abrams, Martha Detrick, Raoul Girardet, H. D. Lasswell, Lawrence I. Radway, and David C. Rapoport. See also John J. Johnson (ed.), *The Role of the Military in Underdeveloped Countries* (Princeton: Princeton University Press, 1962); authors include Edward Shils, Lucian W. Pye, Edwin Lieuwen, Victor Alba, Guy J. Pauker, David A. Wilson, Manfred Halpern, Ben Halpern, James S. Coleman, and Belmont Price, Jr.. See also Robert C. Tucker, *The Soviet Political Mind, Studies in Stalinism and Post-Stalin Change* (New York: Praeger, 1963); Victor Zitta, *George Lukács' Marxism: Alienation, Dialectics, Revolution* (The Hague: Martinus Nijhoff, 1964).

True, the racist category is an intellectual monstrosity; so, for that matter, was the fiction of a proletariat. But the racist symbol has the superficial plausibility of common-sense observation — everybody admits that people differ in certain obvious physical characteristics. In the immediate future there may be little opportunity for massive re-education of the world community, disseminating the best scientific evidence of factors that truly affect human capacities and patterns of conduct. Hence, predispositions exist on a gigantic scale for the mobilization of political perspectives along lines of racist identity; and these identities may be associated with assertions of superiority and demands for supremacy. The identification of "colonialism" with the white race may be turned against the Russians in the internecine struggles among Communists, leading to an antiwhite, anticolonial, anti-imperialist, antiexploiter ideology that seeks the encirclement of Western Europe and North America.

The rebirth of caste as an organizing principle may be favored by the rapid growth of automation, and the reduced significance of individuals as producers. It can, of course, be urged that every population is a great gene pool of hidden talent, and that absence of discrimination favors the revelation and cultivation of aptitude into socially contributory skill. But the most manifest role of the individual under automation is as consumer, at least until non-income-generating specializations receive more deference than they have obtained hitherto.

If we assume that all the scientific and technological advances suggested by "automation" are rapidly introduced in both industrial and nonindustrial countries, a remarkable choice may face elites. Assume that traditional agriculture, for example, is no longer necessary and that basic foods can be prepared by automated biochemical installations. Will it not be simpler for the power elite of nation-states with folk societies and peasant cultures to leave the traditional elements undisturbed? Or at least to consolidate a dominant class (which may coalesce into a dominant caste) whose members are chosen on the basis of capability and cultivated to the limit of their potential?

VI

*THE UNSPEAKABLE REVOLUTION (TRANSHUMANITY)*

We have implied that the emergence of racist ideology in Germany may mark an ideological step toward a new world revolutionary emergent whose potentialities for caste may bring about a reversal in the long-range trends toward the realization of human dignity in highly mobile societies.

Among the relevant factors to be assessed is the future of computers. We have in mind the possibility that computers can be developed to a level at which it is impracticable to distinguish machines from men. If we speak of subjectivity as exhibiting moods and images, and define the latter to include abstract as well as concrete references, the creative prowess of computers has been sufficiently demonstrated to suggest that they have a brilliant future. Machines seem to depart from humanity in the realm of mood, which covers such swings as from euphoria to melancholy, anxiety to serenity, rage to fright. Guilt, humiliation, love, curiosity, and cupidity, for instance, are moods; they are not unanalyzable, nor is it necessary to suppose that equivalent internal sequences cannot be built in.

We may, of course, consider the possibility of supermachines; and, if so, the question is whether they will be constructed in ways that prevent them from constituting a superior caste that relegates man to a subordinate role.

In the world of contingency it is inappropriate to overlook the future of biological research and the development of new and possibly superior species of life. The recent decoding of the information system that controls the mechanisms of inheritance and development has brought a multitude of new emergents into the foreground.

Parallel with these events is the perfecting of conditioning procedures, with or without the aid of drugs and hypnosis. The abolition of privacy — already well along in our day — is placing potent instruments of control in the hands of elites who may see an opportunity to consolidate their position by policing the population medically. The "paralysis bomb" and its derivatives can make large-scale coercion truly obsolete.

We are on the threshold of the era of astropolitics, and we perceive even now that the elites of the Earth may encounter higher forms of life in space.[56]

In addition to these contingencies we do not overlook the abolition of death by the technique of detecting worn-out molecules and making suitable replacements. Nor is it sensible to ignore the chance that new factors (for instance, parapsychological processes) may further complicate the future of man's politics.

[56] A chapter is devoted to the consideration of such contingencies in M. S. McDougal, H. D. Lasswell, and I. A. Vlasic, *The Public Order of Space* (New Haven, Conn.: Yale University Press, 1963).

When I referred to the "unspeakable revolution," I had in mind the disturbing contingencies that follow if man's knowledge continues to be poorly translated into policies that harmonize with his professed aspirations. If we are in the midst of a permanent revolution of modernizing intellectuals, the succeeding phase obviously depends in no small degree on perfecting the policy sciences that aid in forestalling the unspeakable contingencies latent in tendencies already more than faintly discernible.

## CHAPTER THREE

GEORGE K. SCHUELLER

# The Politburo*

## I. WHO AND WHAT IS THE POLITBURO?

### The Politburo: A Sketch

SHORTLY BEFORE the outbreak of the revolution in Russia, the Central Committee of the Bolshevik Party elected from its midst a Political Bureau, which was supposed to prepare and direct the revolution. It was first organized on October 23 (10), 1917, and consisted of Lenin, Trotsky, Stalin, Kamenev, Zinoviev, Sokolnikov, and Bubnov.[1]

This was not a permanent committee with permanent functions. At that moment it had only one function: to ensure the success of the impending revolution. After the successful accomplishment of the revolution, this body was dissolved, and its powers reverted to the Central Committee, which had originally elected the Politburo.

Soon thereafter, as a measure to centralize and expedite the general direction of policy, both domestic and foreign, the Politburo was revived as a small, compact group, capable of making prompt decisions on all matters of general policy. The Politburo, as it functioned in these years, was later described as the "directing collective" or the "leading

* Originally published in 1951 by the Stanford University Press as Series B: Elite Studies, No. 2, of the Hoover Institute Studies. Reprinted with permission of the author and publisher. Minor changes and additions have been made in the text.

The author wishes to thank Boris Nicolaevsky and Nathan Leites for their criticisms and suggestions. Others who generously took time to comment and make suggestions include Clyde Kluckhohn, George F. Kennan, and Fritz Epstein.

[1] *Vsesoiuznaia Kommunisticheskaia Partiia (b) v rezoliutsiiakh i resheniiakh s"ezdov, konferentsii i plenumov TsK (1898–1932)*, Part I, *1898–1924* (4th ed.; Moscow, MEL Institute publication, 1932), p. 315.

organ" of the Central Committee. The members were Lenin, Trotsky, Stalin, and Sverdlov (the last-named died in 1919).[2] The Eighth Party Congress, in March 1919, made the Politburo a permanent organ of the party apparatus. The Central Committee elected Lenin, Trotsky, Stalin, Kamenev, and Krestinsky as members, with Bukharin, Zinoviev, and Kalinin as alternates.[3] The resolution adopted at this session read as follows:

> The Central Committee organizes: first, the *Political Bureau*, second, the *Organizational Bureau*, and third, the *Secretariat*. The Political Bureau consists of five members of the Central Committee. All other members of the Central Committee who have the opportunity to attend this or the other meeting of the Political Bureau have only a consultative vote at the Political Bureau meetings. The Political Bureau adopts resolutions on questions which cannot be postponed and makes biweekly reports on its work before the regular plenary session of the Central Committee.[4]

Since March 1919, the Politburo has been one of the three standing committees of the Central Committee. Inasmuch as this study is concerned with the Politburo as a permanent institution, the Politburo of the years of revolution and civil war before 1919 is not examined here.

From its inception after the revolution, the Politburo has been a small committee, varying in membership between five and twelve. It is nominally elected by and from the membership of the Central Committee. Usually it meets several times a week, and it has become the most important committee of all those elected by the Central Committee. The pre-eminent importance of the Politburo is revealed by a resolution adopted in 1923 to the effect that decisions of the Secretariat can be appealed to the Orgburo, while those of the Orgburo can be appealed to the Politburo.[5]

Today the Politburo is the highest policy-making and decision-making organ of the Soviet Union, despite the fact that it is not once mentioned in the Soviet Constitution. Quotations from speeches by Soviet leaders will serve to illustrate this point. Stalin said, in 1925:

> The Politburo is the highest organ not of the state but of the party and the party is the highest directing force of the state.[6]

[2] Boris Souvarine, *Stalin* (New York: Longmans, Green & Co., Inc., 1939), p. 265.

[3] V. I. Lenin, *Sochineniia*, XXV (2nd. ed.; Moscow, Gos. sots. ekon. izd., 1931), p. 604.

[4] Cf. p. 353 of the reference cited in note 1.

[5] Julian Towster, *Political Power in the USSR, 1917–47* (New York: Oxford University Press, 1948), p. 160.

[6] *Ibid.*, footnote.

Kaganovich said, in February 1934:

> The Politburo of the Central Committee is the organ of operative direction of all branches of socialist construction.[7]

The scope of the Politburo's decision-making power is evidenced by the work plans published in 1926 and 1928. The minutes of the meetings of the Politburo are always kept secret, but the work plans were published in the Soviet press. These plans showed that the following agencies, among others, had to report on their work to the Politburo:

| | |
|---|---|
| State Planning Board | Commissariat of Agriculture |
| Supreme Council of | Commissariat of Communication |
|    National Economy | Central Council of the Trade-Unions |
| Commissariat of Finance | State Political Administration |
| Commissariat of Trade | Revolutionary War Council |
| Commissariat of Justice | Several other government and party com- |
| Commissariat of Labor |    missions[8] |

In theory, the Politburo is elected by the Central Committee of the Communist Party and is accountable to that body. It is not strictly limited as to the number of members and alternates, but today the membership usually is kept at nine, and there are about three or four alternates. In 1919 the resolution stated there were to be five members. Alternates were not mentioned at the time. In 1923 the membership was increased to not more than seven members and four alternates. By 1926 the Politburo had nine members, and from then on it remained at approximately that figure, with an additional three to six alternates.

Usually a future member of the Politburo must first serve as an alternate member. Alternate members attend all meetings of the Politburo and have a consultative, but not a decisive, vote. Since 1923, all members have gone through this stage before advancing to full membership. Because the alternates have only a consultative vote, they will not be considered in this study.

*Preliminary Summary of the Findings*

From 1917 until the present time, there have been twenty-seven members of the Politburo. These are the ones with whom this study will deal. Because the number is small, most of our results are presented in whole figures. The main purpose of this study is to show who these twenty-seven were and how they achieved their exalted positions. The findings will be arranged under the following headings: Social

[7] *Ibid.*, footnote.
[8] *Ibid.*, p. 161.

Class, Geographic Origins and Movements, Personal History, Occupational History, Political History, and Miscellaneous Characteristics.

A look at the data presented in the main body of this study will make it clear there are three distinct periods that can be observed in the development of the Politburo. The first period runs from the revolution to Lenin's death in 1924; the second period runs from 1924 to 1938 (the end of the last big purge trial); and the third period runs from 1938 to the present (the time when Stalin had eliminated the last remnants of the opposition).

In the first period, and to a lesser degree in the second, the theoretician of middle-class origin — comparatively well educated, well traveled, cosmopolitan — predominates. These are the times when the colorful personality of the political orator and revolutionary is in the focus of attention. In the second period, when the initial phase of the revolution is over, and when the party settles down to consolidate its victory, the need for such men, and indeed the possibility to use them, is lessened; they inevitably come into conflict with the rising tide of bureaucratization and impersonality. Finally, in the third period, the theoreticians are gradually pushed out of the way by the emerging class of organizers and administrators, who now take over and occupy the whole stage. The oppositionists, in fact, were ousted from the leading party and state organs between 1926 and 1930, and their liquidation was preceded by removal from power for a considerable period of time.

Today, membership in the Politburo — and indeed in the whole of the Soviet hierarchy — is no longer won by those who are brilliant theoreticians and orators, but by those who are administrators and who do not question the decisions of Stalin (not publicly, at least). Undoubtedly, only a major upheaval, internal or external, could change this situation; but there are no signs, at least at the moment, that would make this seem probable.

Membership in the Politburo seems to have become more and more the reward for outstanding and long party work. The ladder of success has been fairly well standardized and runs:

Membership in the Politburo
↗
Candidacy in the Politburo
↗
Secretariat
↗
Central Committee
↗
Party work

In the early days it was possible to take a man like Trotsky into the Politburo despite the fact he had just become a member of the Bolshevik Party; today, this would be impossible. Since the early days of the revolution, no outsider has been taken into the Politburo.

While the members today are all experienced administrators and are long schooled in party work, they cannot be regarded as specialists in any particular field. Their value, rather, lies in their organizing and administrative talents, which are utilized to the fullest. In 1947 a brilliant young economist, Voznesensky, was taken into the Politburo, but did not keep his position very long — in 1949 he was ousted. Until 1929 the Politburo included many who could be called specialists in propaganda (Bukharin, Zinoviev, Kamenev), but by 1929 they had all been ousted.

In addition to party work, the present-day Politburo member is also required to have a certain amount of experience in police functions. In keeping with the personality of the impersonal administrator, the members of the Politburo exhibit what could be called a passion for anonymity. No book-size biographies of Politburo members have been published in Russia, with the exception of Lenin and Stalin.

In other ways, too, the Politburo is remote. There is no personal contact between the members of the Politburo and the population. They are not accountable to the people. Large sections of the Soviet Union and large national groups are unrepresented in the Politburo. Furthermore, there does not seem to be a genuine popular leader among the Politburo members. Stalin himself is a deified rather than a popular leader. The other members of the Politburo are completely overshadowed by Stalin, and their popular appeal is probably very limited.

Most of the members of the Politburo have had extensive party work in one of three specified geographic areas, almost to the complete exclusion of any other part of the Soviet Union. No information could be found, for instance, to indicate that any member of the Politburo has spent any length of time at all in the Soviet Far East. The same could be said of other large areas such as Uzbekistan or Kazakhestan.

If this information is combined with the fact that the Russian nationality is still by far the predominant one on the Politburo, it would seem to indicate that despite the federal structure of the Soviet Union, the leadership is still firmly, if not exclusively, in the hands of the Russians and certain non-Russians who have been Russified to a large extent. This lack of national representation could be one of the factors to produce such deviations as "Titoism" in Yugoslavia, where a nationalist Communist Party refused to bow to the dictates of the Kremlin and rebelled against what they considered a one-sided and selfish policy.

The remoteness of the Politburo from the general population will intensify the difficulties inherent in a dictatorship with regard to succession. Sigmund Neumann has suggested there are two conditions indispensable to the perpetuation of the dictatorship: (1) the establishment of a well-functioning party machine, and (2) the absorption or destruction of traditional institutions.[9]

It can hardly be denied that the Soviet Union has fulfilled the first prerequisite. The party organization is established and appears to function quite well. There are some doubts, however, as to whether the second condition has been fulfilled in the Soviet Union. While such traditional institutions as the Church and the Army (Czarist) were severely repressed in the beginning of the Bolshevik rule, they have since then staged a remarkable comeback. Outwardly, at least, they both seem controlled firmly by the party, and it may well be that they have no effective political personality of their own; but alternatively, it is not inconceivable that the Army that followed Stalin might refuse to follow the drab Malenkov or Molotov.

About the successor of Stalin, nothing but speculation is possible. Because of the importance of the party it might be assumed that the man who had the tightest control over the party machinery would be the successor. This would point to Malenkov. On the other hand, Molotov is generally regarded the number two man, but as will be pointed out, there are some aspects of Molotov's past that might make him unacceptable as a sole successor to Stalin. A third possibility is that a representative figurehead would be picked because the real powers behind the throne could not agree on a choice. In such a case Voroshilov might be the successor.

Whether one of the candidates above is going to succeed Stalin or whether the succession will be taken over by a directorate of two or more, it seems fairly certain that the whole governmental and party systems will be strained to the utmost, if not to the breaking point, when this occurs.

The new leader would be a comparatively unknown man, as Stalin was in 1924 when Lenin died, and he would have to rule in the name of the deceased master. Only slowly could he become ruler in his own right. How difficult that is, is demonstrated in the long and arduous road to power that Stalin himself had to take. It takes a masterful politician, who can play one faction against the other, to accomplish such a feat. Whether any of the present Politburo members will be able to do that, only the future can tell.

[9] Sigmund Neumann, *Permanent Revolution* (New York: Harper & Bros., 1942), pp. 93–94.

*Table 1*
MEMBERS OF THE POLITBURO

| Members of the Politburo | Date of Accession | Date of Removal | Death |
|---|---|---|---|
| Lenin, Vladimir I. | 1917 | 1924 | Died |
| Stalin, Josef V.° | 1917 | | |
| Sverdlov, Yakov M. | 1917 | 1919 | Died |
| Trotsky, Lev D. | 1917 | 1926 | Murdered 1940 |
| Bukharin, Nikolai I. | 1918 | 1929 | Executed 1938 |
| Kamenev, Lev B. | 1919 | 1926 | Executed 1936 |
| Krestinsky, Nikolai N. | 1919 | 1921 | Executed 1938 |
| Rykov, Alexei I. | 1919 | 1929 | Executed 1938 |
| Tomsky, Mikhail P. | 1919 | 1929 | Suicide 1936 |
| Zinoviev, Grigorii | 1923 | 1926 | Executed 1936 |
| Molotov, Viacheslav M.° | 1925 | | |
| Voroshilov, Kliment E.° | 1925 | | |
| Kalinin, Mikhail I. | 1926 | 1946 | Died 1946 |
| Kuibyshev, Valerian V. | 1927 | 1935 | Died 1935 |
| Rudzutak, Jan E. | 1927 | 1931 | Disappeared 1938 |
| Kaganovich, Lazar M.° | 1930 | | |
| Kirov, Sergei M. | 1930 | 1934 | Murdered 1934 |
| Kossior, Stanislav V. | 1930 | 1938 | Disappeared |
| Ordjonikidze, Grigorii K. | 1930 | 1937 | Died 1937 |
| Andreyev, Andrei A.° | 1932 | | |
| Chubar, Vlas Y. | 1935 | 1938 | Disappeared |
| Mikoyan, Anastas I.° | 1935 | | |
| Zhdanov, Andrei A. | 1939 | 1948 | Died 1948 |
| Khrushchev, Nikita S.° | 1939 | | |
| Beria, Lavrentii P.° | 1946 | | |
| Malenkov, Georgii M. | 1946 | | |
| Voznesensky, Nikolai A. | 1947 | 1949 | Dropped |

° These are the members of the present (February 1951) Politburo.

## II. SOCIAL CLASS

### Social Class of Family

The material obtained on the social class of the family comes mainly from Soviet sources and is not necessarily correct. In the Soviet Union it has been and still is regarded as valuable to have a proletarian background; and it may well be that some of the members have given their

social-class origin as "low," although this information does not happen
to be correct. For the same reason some others might give no information about their social backgrounds. An example of this latter category
is Malenkov, about whose family no information could be found. On
the basis of the information obtained, the breakdown is as follows:

| | |
|---|---|
| Low | 16 |
| Middle | 9 |
| Unknown | 2 |
| | — |
| | 27 |

What is meant by middle-class background is best explained by
giving the positions held by the fathers of the nine in this category:

| | |
|---|---|
| Bukharin | Teacher |
| Kamenev | Engineer |
| Krestinsky | Teacher |
| Lenin | School inspector |
| Molotov | Salesman |
| Trotsky | Rich tenant farmer |
| Voznesensky | White-collar worker |
| Zhdanov | Teacher |
| Zinoviev | Unknown[10] |

The one striking thing that appears from this evidence is that the
fate of the members of the middle class, in the majority of cases, has not
been a happy one. Of the nine members of the middle class, four have
been executed (Bukharin, Kamenev, Krestinsky, and Zinoviev), one
has been exiled and later murdered (Trotsky), and one has been
dropped from membership in the Politburo (Voznesensky).

It seems, therefore, that out of nine members of the middle class, six
lost favor with the rulers of the Soviet Union. On the other hand, the
remaining three members of the middle class were such highly respected Bolsheviks as Lenin, Zhdanov, and Molotov. Of these three,
today, only Molotov remains.

### Occupation of Father

The occupations of the fathers of the Politburo members show clearly
the "revolutionary" character of this new elite. Such a breakdown for
the fathers of the prerevolutionary Council of Ministers would tell a

---

[10] Since Zinoviev was born in a town, and went to a gymnasium, and later
studied chemistry in Bern, it is assumed that he came from a middle-class family.
See Boris Voline, 12 *Militants Russes* (Paris: Librairie de l'Humanité, 1925),
pp. 60 ff.

far different story. The majority of the fathers of Politburo members were workers and peasants:

| | |
|---|---|
| Worker | 8 |
| Peasant | 7 |
| Teacher | 4 |
| Engineer | 1 |
| White-collar worker | 1 |
| Salesman | 1 |
| Unknown | 5 |
| | 27 |

These figures tend to confirm the reliability of the estimate of social class, where we reported that sixteen came from a low-class background. The data are probably correct despite doubts as to the reliability of the biographies, which probably were supplied in many cases by the members themselves.

## III. GEOGRAPHIC ORIGINS AND MOVEMENTS

### Province of Origin

The birthplaces of the Politburo members are concentrated in a relatively small section of the vast expanse of the Soviet Union. While the territory of the Soviet Union stretches from longitude 25° to 180° east and from latitude 35° to 80° north, the Politburo members were all born between longitude 25° and 75° east and latitude 40° and 60° north.

The Soviet Union consists of sixteen Union Republics, of which only five had a native son on the Politburo:

| | |
|---|---|
| R.S.F.S.R. | 14 |
| Ukraine | 6 |
| Georgia | 4 |
| Byelo-Russia | 2 |
| Latvia | 1 |
| | 27 |

These five republics make up more than 80 per cent of the territory of the Soviet Union and contain about 85 per cent of its population.[11]

Table 2 gives a picture of the geographic distribution of Politburo members. The table shows that the Politburo, on the whole, is repre-

[11] George B. Cressey, *The Basis of Soviet Strength* (New York: McGraw-Hill Book Company, Inc., 1945), pp. 13–14.

sentative of the population of the sixteen Union Republics — at least insofar as such a small body can be said to be representative of sixteen large, more or less populous areas. The Georgian Republic, however, is overrepresented to a fairly large degree. This can probably be explained by the fact that Stalin is a Georgian and shows a certain amount of preference for people from his native republic.

*Table 2*

GEOGRAPHIC DISTRIBUTION OF POLITBURO MEMBERS

| Republic | Population in Millions 1940* | Percentage of Total Population* | Number of Politburo Members | Percentage of Politburo Members |
|---|---|---|---|---|
| Russian Socialist Federated Soviet Republic | 109 | 57 | 14 | 52 |
| Ukrainian S.S.R. | 39 | 20 | 6 | 22 |
| Georgian S.S.R. | 4 | 2 | 4 | 15 |
| Byelo-Russian S.S.R | 10 | 5 | 2 | 7 |
| Latvian S.S.R. | 2 | 1 | 1 | 4 |
| Azerbaijan S.S.R. | 3 | 2 | 0 | 0 |
| Armenian S.S.R. | 1 | 1 | 0 | 0 |
| Kazakh S.S.R. | 6 | 3 | 0 | 0 |
| Turkomen S.S.R. | 1 | 1 | 0 | 0 |
| Uzbek S.S.R. | 6 | 3 | 0 | 0 |
| Tajik S.S.R. | 1 | 1 | 0 | 0 |
| Kirghiz S.S.R. | 1 | 1 | 0 | 0 |
| Karelo-Finnish S.S.R. | 0.5 | 0.3 | 0 | 0 |
| Estonian S.S.R. | 1 | 1 | 0 | 0 |
| Lithuanian S.S.R. | 3 | 2 | 0 | 0 |
| Moldavian S.S.R. | 4 | 2 | 0 | 0 |

*The population figures are from George B. Cressey, *The Basis of Soviet Strength* (New York: McGraw-Hill Book Co., Inc., 1945), pp. 13 f.

It is recognized that the Politburo was not created with the ideal of representativeness in mind. The members are chosen as individuals, and not as group spokesmen. Nevertheless, it is of sociological interest to note how its composition parallels or deviates from that of the population.

The problem of representativeness can also be approached from the point of view of the nationalities that compose the Soviet Union. There are about 175 different and distinct nationalities in the Soviet Union. Of these, only seven have had any representation on the Politburo:

| Great Russians | 12 |
|---|---|
| Jews | 5 |
| Ukrainians | 4 |
| Georgians | 3 |
| Poles | 1 |
| Armenians | 1 |
| Latvians | 1 |
| | 27 |

Table 3 shows how far this distribution is representative of the whole. The picture obtained from this table does not materially differ from that given in Table 2. Strictly speaking, the Jews are not a nationality. Some of them were born and brought up among Great Russians, White Russians, or Ukrainians, and for some purposes could be added to these groups. Still it is interesting to note that the Jews were somewhat overrepresented and the Great Russians somewhat underrepresented in the Politburo. Jews, however, were overrepresented mainly in the period when urban intellectuals predominated in the Politburo. Of the five Jews who have served on that body, only one is still a member. For the reason given previously, the Georgians are again overrepresented.

### Table 3
#### ETHNIC DISTRIBUTION OF POLITBURO MEMBERS

| | Number in Millions 1939* | Percentage of Population* | Number of Politburo Members | Percentage of Politburo Members |
|---|---|---|---|---|
| Great Russians | 99 | 58 | 11 | 40 |
| Jews | 3 | 2 | 6 | 22 |
| Ukrainians | 28 | 17 | 4 | 15 |
| Georgians | 2 | 1 | 3 | 11 |
| Poles | 0.6 | 1 | 1 | 4 |
| Armenians | 2 | 1 | 1 | 4 |
| Latvians | 0.1 | 0.05 | 1 | 4 |
| White Russians | 5 | 3 | 0 | 0 |
| Uzbeks | 5 | 3 | 0 | 0 |
| Tartars | 4 | 3 | 0 | 0 |
| Kazakhs | 3 | 2 | 0 | 0 |
| Azerbaijanians | 2 | 1 | 0 | 0 |
| Mordvinians | 1 | 1 | 0 | 0 |
| Germans | 1 | 1 | 0 | 0 |
| Chuvash | 1 | 1 | 0 | 0 |
| Tajiks | 1 | 1 | 0 | 0 |

*Cressey, op. cit., p. 43. The figures for the nationalities in this table are given for all those of one million or more. The figures are from the year 1939 and do not include the Baltic States, Moldavia, or the later-acquired Polish territories.

A word should be said about the problem of Russification. The sole fact that a man was born in the Ukraine, for instance, or is a Ukrainian by birth, is no assurance either that he is a Ukrainian or that he has Ukrainian interests at heart. Much too little is known about the personal opinions of the Politburo members to be certain on this point. There is evidence, however, that the Politburo does not favor national leaders or heroes in the Soviet Union. This seems to be particularly true in regard to the Ukraine, which for a long time has been a trouble spot for the Soviet leaders. Those members of the Politburo who were Ukrainians and had been especially identified with the Ukraine have been eliminated.[12] It seems likely that the remaining Politburo members of other than Great Russian background have become fairly well Russified, but the type of data used in this study does not enable us to shed light on that surmise.

*Urban-Rural Distribution*

The urban-rural make-up of the Soviet Union is such that there are only two cities of a truly metropolitan character. These are Moscow and Leningrad, and they are distinctly different from the other towns in the Soviet Union. For this reason the following breakdown has been used on this point: Village, Town, Moscow, and Leningrad. Another reason for selecting Moscow and Leningrad as a special and distinct category is their immense importance in the political life and the political direction of the country.

The definition of a "town" is difficult because of the great population changes in the Soviet Union during the last forty years. An attempt was made to determine the number of inhabitants of the birthplaces of the Politburo members during the 1890's. According to our data, the following nine Politburo members came from the towns listed, given with their approximate population in 1890:[13]

| | | |
|---|---|---|
| Krestinsky | Wilna | 159,568 |
| Rykov | Saratov | 123,230 |
| Kuibyshev | Omsk | 84,012 |
| Sverdlov | Nizhni-Novgorod | 70,412 |
| Zinoviev | Elizavetgrad | 60,217 |
| Malenkov | Orenburg | 56,000 |
| Lenin | Simbirsk | 39,048 |
| Kaganovich | Gomel | 29,438 |
| Zhdanov | Mariupol | 18,607 |

[12] Chubar and Kossior, both Ukrainians, had held high party and government positions in the Ukraine before they disappeared in 1938. In later years, Ukrainian affairs seem to have been handled largely by Kaganovich and Khrushchev, neither of whom is Ukrainian.

[13] Meyers, *Konversations-Lexikon* (5th ed.; Leipzig: Bibliographisches Institut, 1895–1897).

The next-largest community in which a Politburo member may have been born was Gori, with a population in 1890 of only about 5,000. Stalin according to some biographies, was born in Gori; according to others, "near Gori." Here he is counted as having been born in a village. Whenever a biography said a Politburo member "was born in the province of . . .," it was assumed he had been born in a village. On this basis, the breakdown for the Politburo members is as follows:

| | |
|---|---|
| Village | 13 |
| Town | 9 |
| Moscow and Leningrad | 3 |
| Unknown | 2 |
| | —— |
| | 27 |

The great majority of the members came from villages and smaller towns. (See Appendix B for data on birthplace.) Since the vast majority of the Russian population lives in the country or in small towns, this is not surprising.

A breakdown of the Politburo into these three categories in some years selected at random gives an interesting picture. The breakdown shows that in 1923, shortly after the revolution and before Lenin's death, the members from the towns and from Moscow and Leningrad had a majority of the seats on the Politburo. In 1925, after the death of Lenin, they occupied only one third of the seats. In 1930 and after — with the commencement of the Stalin period — no further Politburocrats from Moscow and Leningrad appeared. The relative number of urban-born Politburocrats has been reduced throughout the Stalin period.

| Year | Village | Town | Moscow and Leningrad | Un- known |
|---|---|---|---|---|
| 1923 | 3 | 2 | 3 | 0 |
| 1925 | 6 | 1 | 2 | 0 |
| 1930 | 6 | 3 | 0 | 0 |
| 1939 | 7 | 2 | 0 | 0 |
| 1949 | 7 | 2 | 0 | 0 |

This information furnishes at least supporting evidence for the thesis that the revolution was made, in the first instance, by the urban-born intellectuals and was later taken over by the rural-born organizers. This appears to indicate that as the revolution had been accomplished and settled down to routine, the need of the party for the flashy intellectual of the revolution-making period lessened, and the need for the patient, professional administrator grew in proportion. The unglamorous period of the 1930's could not accommodate such city-bred fire-brands as Zinoviev and Bukharin.[14] This is all the more significant because the general population trend in the Soviet Union was exactly the reverse: namely, from the country to the city. The relation between urban and rural population in the Soviet Union was:[15]

| Year | Urban | Rural |
|------|-------|-------|
| 1917 | 20% | 80% |
| 1926 | 18% | 82% |
| 1929 | 33% | 67% |

From these figures we can see that while the proportion of urban population was slightly diminished between 1917 and 1926, it almost doubled between 1926 and 1939. It should also be mentioned that all three members of the Politburo who came from Moscow and Leningrad are today regarded as traitors. Two of them (Bukharin and Kamenev) were executed, and the third one (Tomsky) committed suicide just before he was to be tried as a traitor.

In general, therefore, it can be stated that today a town or metropolitan background seems to be more of a hindrance than an advantage, at least as far as membership in the Politburo is concerned.

### Movement to a Large City

An effort was made to determine whether there was any regularity in the movement of the Politburocrats from their places of birth to larger places. Three of the twenty-seven were born in a metropolis and hence made no such move. Twenty moved to larger places between the ages of nine and twenty-one. Information is not available on four members; however, there is fairly good evidence to support the assumption that three out of four also moved to a city at an early age. The reasons for this assumption are the following:

Chubar    At the age of sixteen he was a "strike leader." Since a strike is probably associated with a factory, which in turn is associated with a city, it is probable that at the age of sixteen he was already in a city.

Kossior    At the age of twenty-five he was a party organizer in Kiev. Because he had this higher type of job, it can be assumed that he had been in Kiev for some time.

[14] For a discussion of this particular point, see Sigmund Neumann, "The International Civil War," *World Politics*, I (1949), pp. 341 ff.

[15] The figures for 1917 come from *Soviet Union Yearbook*, 1930 (London: G. Allen & Unwin, Ltd., 1930), p. 21. The figures for 1926 and 1939 come from Cressey, *op. cit.*, p. 44.

Zhdanov    He was born in a town (Mariupol) and at the age of
           twenty-one headed the Bolshevik organizations in Shad-
           rinsk. It is probable that he moved to another town before
           that.

It appears, therefore, that twenty-three members moved to the
city at a very early age; three were born in a metropolis; and on one
(Khrushchev) there is no reliable information to show that he moved
to a city before the age of thirty-five.

Since the city affords greater opportunities for the development of
an individual's possibilities, and for the attainment of a political education, it is indispensable for the aspiring political leader to get to the
city at an early age. Also, it has been pointed out that people in urban
areas tend to have a more effective claim upon social values and relatively more skill in asserting their claims. This has been found to be
true in the United States;[16] it is probably equally true in Russia.

## IV. PERSONAL HISTORY

### Age and Death

The material obtained on birth and death dates was used to determine the age composition of the Politburo as a whole. Appendix A is a
graph showing the average age, together with the mean ages of those
older and younger than average, year by year from 1917 to 1949.

The most striking thing about the average age curve is its general
upward trend. The rise in the average age has been steady and un-
checked, with only three exceptions. The first of these three downward
movements occurred in 1924, when Lenin, the oldest member of the
Politburo, died. The second occurred in 1930, when one of the older
members (Rykov) was removed, and three younger men (Kirov, Kossior, and Ordjonikidze) were admitted. The third took place in 1946,
when Kalinin, who by this time was the oldest member, died and two
younger men (Beria and Malenkov) joined the Politburo.

In the thirty-two years covered in this study, the average age of the
Politburo rose from a low of thirty-nine in 1917 to a high of fifty-seven
in 1949, or a total of eighteen years. The mean age of those older than
average started at forty-seven in 1917, went to a low of forty-four in
1924, and reached sixty-six in 1949. There are two definite breaks in
this curve: in 1924, when Lenin died, and in 1946, when Kalinin died.
The mean age of those younger than average started in 1917 with a

[16] See Warren S. Thompson, "Urbanization," in the *Encyclopedia of Social
Sciences;* and H. D. Lasswell, *The Analysis of Political Behavior* (New York:
Oxford University Press, 1949), p. 275.

low of thirty-six and reached a high of fifty-three in 1949. There are two downward movements in this curve: one in 1932 and the other in 1947, when younger men were taken into the Politburo. The general upward trend of all three curves, however, shows that the core of the Politburo has been unaltered for a long time, and therefore the body as a whole is growing older.

Only two of the members were born after the turn of the century (Malenkov and Voznesensky); but they, too, were born early enough (1901 and 1903) so that the revolution of 1917 is a living memory with them.

In 1948 the Politburo had eleven members. One of them (Zhdanov) died in 1948, and another (Voznesensky) was ousted in 1949. The number of members of the Politburo was therefore reduced to nine. Naturally, speculation has centered about who, if anybody, will replace these two men. First it might be pointed out that for most of its existence the Politburo has consisted of nine members; it is therefore entirely possible that no new members will be appointed at the moment. If, however, replacements are going to be appointed, and if the general pattern is followed, the two who have been alternates for the longest time will move up to fill the vacancies left by Zhdanov and Voznesensky. This would mean that Shvernik and Bulganin would become members. Since Shvernik is sixty-one and Bulganin is fifty-four, the average age certainly would not be lowered by their inclusion.

The possibility that some younger men might be taken into the ranks of the Politburo, however, should not be discounted completely. Among these possibilities is Kosygin, the third of the present alternate members, who at forty-four would be the youngest member of the Politburo. Some of the other rising stars seem to be Ponomarenko, Suslov, and Shkiryatov. Let us take, as an example, Ponomarenko, who is now forty-seven and seems to have had a very remarkable career. He comes from a worker's family, became an engineer, and wrote an authoritative book on the construction of locomotives. During the war he served in the Red Army and in 1943 was made a Lieutenant General. Since then he has worked in Byelo-Russia and in 1947–1948 held the job of chairman of the Council of Ministers of the Byelo-Russian S.S.R. After Zhdanov's death, in August 1948, Ponomarenko was relieved of this job and transferred to Moscow for "central work."[17] Since then it has been reported (December 1948) that he was appointed to the Secretariat in succession to Zhdanov.[18] As will be shown later, the Secretariat is one of the most important steppingstones before reaching membership in the Politburo.

[17] *Facts on File,* 1948, p. 310 K.
[18] *Ibid.,* p. 423 P.

Another indication of the ascendancy of Ponomarenko is that at the occasion of Zhdanov's funeral, Ponomarenko was standing on the platform with all the members of the Politburo. Since then, he has been photographed in this company many times. At the particular occasion of Zhdanov's funeral, the platform seems to have been reserved for the members and alternates of the Politburo and a very few high dignitaries of the Soviet State; and it does not seem that the mere job of chairman of the Council of Ministers of the Byelo-Russian S.S.R. would ordinarily have qualified a man to take part in this ceremony. At the last meeting of the Supreme Soviet in April of 1951, Ponomarenko as well as Shkiryatov and Suslov were photographed with the Politburo and were referred to in the news dispatches in such a way as to cause wide speculation as to whether they have been added to the Politburo.[19] It must be said, however, that Ponomarenko, if he is being groomed for the Politburo, would probably become an alternate member first and a full-fledged member at a later date. From the above data the following inferences can be drawn:

a. The revolution itself was led by comparatively young men, but the stabilization of the situation, after the large-scale political and physical elimination of opposing Politburo members, has tended to solidify the ruling elite and to make the Politburo a very stable body.

b. The leadership of the party seems to put more trust in the "old comrade" — the one who has fought in, or at least witnessed, the revolution of 1917.

c. The period required for a man to reach the top has increased.

d. Under stress the Politburo seems to become less fluid than ever. This is suggested by the rigidity of the Politburo between 1939 and 1945, the period just before and during World War II. During this period no changes in the composition of the Politburo took place at all.

If the last hypothesis is true, it may be assumed that as long as the present strained international situation continues, the Politburo will take replacements from the ranks of its candidates rather than bring in young and untried people. It may therefore seem likely that Zhdanov's place will be taken by Shvernik, and Voznesensky's by Bulganin. The list of alternates may well be replenished by the inclusion of Ponomarenko. On the other hand, it may be that no new members will be taken in, and that the membership will be kept at the present nine members.

### Cause of Death

Of the total membership of the Politburo, eighteen are no longer members. Fourteen of them died, three (Chubar, Kossior, and Rudzu-

---

[19] *Christ und Welt*, IV, No. 19 (May 10, 1951), p. 3.

tak), disappeared in the purge of 1938, and one (Voznesensky) was dropped in 1949. If we assume that the three who disappeared in the purge of 1938 were in fact executed, the causes of death for the seventeen are as follows:

|  |  |
|---|---|
| Executed | 8 |
| Natural causes | 6 |
| Murdered | 2 |
| Suicide | 1 |
|  | — |
|  | 17 |

Of the six who died of natural causes, one (Sverdlov) died in 1919, before the Soviet state had a chance to consolidate, and another (Lenin) died in 1924, before Stalin took over the leadership of the state. Since 1924, therefore, only four have died of natural causes. The specific causes for the natural deaths were:

|  |  |
|---|---|
| Sverdlov | Pneumonia |
| Lenin | Paralysis of the brain |
| Kuibyshev | Heart disease |
| Ordjonikidze | Heart disease |
| Kalinin | Old age |
| Zhdanov | Heart disease |

Those executed were:

|  |  |
|---|---|
| Kamenev and Zinoviev | 1936 |
| Bukharin, Krestinsky, and Rykov | 1938 |
| Chubar, Kossior, and Rudzutak | 1938 (disappeared) |

Zinoviev and Kamenev were tried in 1936 by the Military Collegium of the Supreme Court of the U.S.S.R. They were charged with counterrevolutionary activities, the murder of Kirov, attempts on the lives of other Soviet leaders, terrorism, and treasonable connections with Trotsky. The prosecutor was the present Foreign Minister, Andrei Vishinsky. It is interesting to note that one of the judges was I. Nikitchenko, who later was to be the Soviet Union's representative on the Nürnberg War Crimes Tribunal. The trial lasted from August 19 to 24, 1936, and ended in the sentencing of all the defendants to be shot.

Bukharin, Krestinsky, and Rykov were tried by the same court and also prosecuted by Vishinsky. Nikitchenko at this time was not a member of the court. They were charged with treason, espionage, committing acts of diversion, terrorism, wrecking, undermining the military power of the U.S.S.R., and provoking a military attack of foreign states upon the U.S.S.R. The trial lasted from March 2 to 13, 1938, and ended in the death penalty for all the accused, with the exception of three.[20]

Chubar, Kossior, and Rudzutak, who were lesser figures in the Soviet state, were not given a public trial, but simply disappeared in 1938. Kossior was officially expelled from the Politburo, but no reason was given.

The two members who were murdered were Kirov and Trotsky. Kirov was shot to death in his office in Leningrad by a young student. Officially this student was accused of being a tool of Trotsky, Zinoviev, and Kamenev; but there does not seem to be much evidence for this. Another version says that Stalin engineered or at least condoned the assassination. Still another version of the story is that Kirov had an affair with the wife of the student. The true cause for the murder will probably never be known. It must be noted here that of all those members who died a violent death, Kirov is the only one who did not die by government action. Trotsky was killed in his house in Mexico City by an assailant who was described as an agent of the GPU.

The only member of the Politburo to commit suicide was Tomsky, who took his own life in 1936, just before he was to be tried.

Almost all of the members of the Politburo who were expelled were dismissed after disagreement with Stalin, on either a theoretical or practical political question.

For these reasons, it seems clear that this body is a true "insecurity elite." On the other hand, those executed or murdered were, for the most part, the old Bolsheviks, who had regarded Stalin with suspicion from the days of the revolution, despite the fact that he had been allied with one or another faction many times. Perhaps Politburo members will be more secure in the future, since most of the implacable opposition has been eliminated, and the appropriate lessons, presumably, have been learned.[21] Besides Stalin, only two (Voroshilov and Molotov) are left who took a leading part in the revolution. Since those two have at all times been loyal supporters of Stalin, there seems to be no reason to be concerned about their fate.

In an elite body as insecure as the Politburo, a natural death always gives vent to a mass of rumors, accusations, and intimations of possible foul play. Such indications are to be found about all the ones who died a natural death, except in the case of Kalinin, who died at the ripe

[20] For details on these two trials see: People's Commissariat of Justice of the U.S.S.R., *Report of Court Proceedings in the Case of the Trotskyite-Zinovievite Terrorist Centre* (Moscow, 1936); and *Report of Court Proceedings in the Case of the Anti-Soviet "Bloc of Rights and Trotskyites"* (Moscow, 1938).

[21] Note that Andreyev, even after having been criticized, was not dropped from the Politburo. See footnote 28.

old age of seventy-one. Of all these stories, only two seem worth discussing in any detail.

The first is the case of Kuibyshev. He died in 1935 at the age of forty-seven. The doctors' verdict at the time was heart disease. In 1938 at the great purge trials, the doctor who had signed the death certificate was arrested and accused of being in complicity with the "Bloc of Rights and Trotskyites." The specific charge was that he had medically murdered Kuibyshev and Alexei Peshkov, the son of Maxim Gorky. The doctor "admitted" in the trial that he had given Kuibyshev treatments that aggravated, rather than cured, his heart disease.[22] Since it is generally agreed that the "confessions" at the purge trials must be taken with a grain of salt, and since the charge was never actually proved or particularly stressed, it might be better to continue to treat Kuibyshev's death as natural.

The second is the case of Zhdanov. Zhdanov died in August 1948, and again the doctors' verdict was heart disease. There have been only unsubstantiated rumors to the effect that Zhdanov might have been murdered. It might be worth while to mention here the possible relationship between Zhdanov's death and the failure of the Politburo's policy toward Yugoslavia. While there is no noncircumstantial evidence at the moment to support this point of view, there is evidence showing that members of Zhdanov's clique in the Politburo and in other branches of the Soviet government were removed from their posts after his death. Among those who were removed are:

| | |
|---|---|
| Voznesensky | He was dropped from membership in the Politburo. He was known as a protégé of Zhdanov mainly because Zhdanov selected him to head the Economic Planning Commission of Leningrad in 1935, when Voznesensky was only thirty-two years old. From then on, Voznesensky's rise to power was rapid. In quick succession he became a member of the Central Committee, alternate member of the Politburo, head of the Gosplan, and finally a member of the Politburo in 1947.[23] |
| Popkov | He was a close associate of Zhdanov and his second in command as party boss, as well as mayor of Leningrad and secretary of the party there. He was released from membership in the Presidium of the Supreme Soviet in March 1949 because "he is no longer working in Leningrad."[24] |

[22] See testimony of the accused Dr. Levin in People's Commissariat of Justice of the U.S.S.R., *Report of Court Proceedings in the Case of the Anti-Soviet "Bloc of Rights and Trotskyites"* (Moscow, 1938), pp. 536–537.

[23] Walter Duranty, *Stalin and Company* (New York: W. Sloane Associates, 1949), pp. 190–191.

[24] *Facts on File*, 1949, p. 91 J.

*Marriage*

Soviet leaders notoriously shun any kind of publicity regarding their private lives. There are never any articles in the Soviet press about the family life of the Soviet leaders. Consequently, it is very difficult to find information regarding the wives and children of the Politburo members. Twenty of the Politburo members are known to have been married. Through incidental information found in many different, mostly secondary sources, this has been established for fourteen of them. They are:

|  |  |
|---|---|
| Bukharin | Mikoyan |
| Chubar | Molotov |
| Kaganovich | Ordjonikidze |
| Kalinin | Stalin |
| Kamenev | Trotsky |
| Krestinsky | Zhdanov |
| Lenin | Zinoviev |

Boris Nicolaevsky adds from personal knowledge that the following six Politburo members also are or were married, but nothing more is known about their families:

|  |  |
|---|---|
| Rykov | Kirov |
| Voroshilov | Khrushchev |
| Andreyev | Tomsky |

There is available very little more than the mere fact that these twenty are or were married. The following list gives the information available regarding the marriages and the children of the fourteen on whom written sources have been found:

| | |
|---|---|
| Bukharin | Married. Nothing more is known. |
| Chubar | Married. Nothing more is known. |
| Kalinin | His wife managed a state farm. |
| Kaganovich | His wife is Jewish and is chairman of the Soviet Textile Workers Trade Union. |
| Kamenev | Married Trotsky's sister, Olga, in Paris. She was active in revolutionary work before the outbreak of the revolution. She also was editor and founder of the propaganda periodical *V.O.K.S.* |
| Krestinsky | His wife was an eminent physician and a revolutionary from the early days. |
| Lenin | His wife is the only one about whom there is ample information. She came from a family of poor nobility in Russian Poland and had some German ancestry. She first worked as a teacher and later became a revolutionary. After Lenin's death she had much prestige but very little influence in the Soviet Union. |

| | |
|---|---|
| Mikoyan | Nothing is known about his wife, but it is known that he has two grown sons. The sons do not seem to occupy any position of importance. |
| Molotov | His wife seems to be one at least who has been very active in politics. She has been a candidate to the Central Committee and held the positions of Commissar of the Cosmetic Industry, Commissar for Fisheries, and Assistant Commissar for the Food Industry. Since 1941 she has not held any office. They have two daughters. |
| Ordjonikidze | His wife supposedly was an Eskimo, whom he met while he was exiled in Siberia. |
| Stalin | His first wife was Catherine Svanidze, a Georgian who died before the revolution. He then married his secretary, Nadezhda Allilueva, the daughter of Sergo Alliluev, a blacksmith and old revolutionary, in whose house Stalin had once been hidden from the police in prerevolutionary days.[25] Nadezhda died in 1932, and there are many rumors to the effect that she committed suicide. According to most reports, Stalin is now living with Kaganovich's sister, Rosa. Whether he is married to her is not known. He has a son by his first wife, who has not distinguished himself; during the war he was captured by the Germans, who tried to use him for propaganda purposes — apparently without success. By his second wife Stalin has a daughter, Svetlana, who was married in 1944, and a son Vasily, who is now a Major General in the Air Force and receives a certain amount of publicity, even in the Soviet press. He was the one, for instance, who led a formation of jet bombers in a flight over Red Square at the last anniversary of the revolution. As far as can be ascertained, the press does not connect him with his father. |
| Trotsky | He was twice married. He divorced his first wife, whom he had married in prison and with whom he was later exiled. By his first wife he had two daughters. One died in 1928 in Moscow. The other daughter committed suicide in Berlin because she was deprived of her citizenship and was not allowed to go back to Russia to join her husband and child.[26] Both daughters were married and had children. By his second wife he had two sons. One was accused and exiled with him and later died in Paris; the other was arrested in Russia as a "poisoner of workers," and nothing about his fate was ever heard.[27] Both of Trotsky's wives were minor party workers. |
| Zhdanov | Nothing is known about his wife. He had one son who was supposed to be a brilliant student and a journalist. |

[25] Souvarine, *op. cit.*, p. 135.
[26] Preliminary Commission of Inquiry, *The Case of Leon Trotsky* (Coyoacán, Mexico, 1937), p. 41.
[27] *Ibid.*, pp. 40 ff.

Zinoviev          His wife, Lilina, was an intimate friend of Lenin and
                  Krupskaya (Lenin's wife). He had a son, called Stepa, of
                  whom Lenin was very fond. His wife died in 1929.

It is quite apparent that the personal family life of Politburo members is little publicized. Nepotism seems to be largely absent among
the Soviet elite. None of the wives and children of the members of the
Politburo appear to have any kind of political power that has been
gained through their husbands or fathers. On the other hand, quite
often wives have done responsible political work as party members.
This probably can be explained by the fact that a woman in the Soviet
Union, just like a man, is supposed to have some kind of political
activity. Since most activities in the Soviet Union are political activities
or have political connotations, this is not difficult to accomplish. In this
respect the wives of the Politburo members differ somewhat from their
counterparts in the Western elites.

## V. OCCUPATIONAL HISTORY

### Education

The educational breakdown for the members of the Politburo is as
follows:

| | |
|---|---|
| University | 9 |
| High school | 3 |
| Other higher schools | 3 |
| Trade schools | 3 |
| Religious schools | 2 |
| Elementary | 5 |
| Unknown | 2 |
| | 27 |

Comparable studies of the American, British, and French elites
show that a high proportion of the cabinet members in the Western
countries were university-educated. Similarly, a high proportion of
Politburo members attended a university. The future member of the
Politburo, usually for political reasons, often did not complete his
university education.

The university-educated members played different roles at different
times in Soviet Russia. Six of those who attended a university were
active and prominent in the years preceding Lenin's death. They were:

| | |
|---|---|
| Bukharin | Lenin |
| Kamenev | Rykov |
| Krestinsky | Zinoviev |

Of these six, only Lenin was not executed as a traitor. Three members received part of their university education abroad, and this cosmopolitan trait identifies them with the deviationists. They are Bukharin, Kamenev, and Zinoviev.

Three university-educated members were active at a later period. They are Kuibyshev, Molotov, and Voznesensky. Molotov actually was active in the first period but did not achieve prominence until the second.

From this we can see that while in the beginning the number of university-educated members was relatively high, there is now only one (Molotov) who received at least a partial university education. Thus, the Politburo exhibits a powerful trend away from the characteristics of a middle-class background, a higher education, and a town or metropolitan birthplace. This contention is supported by the fact that of the group that received the least amount of education — namely, the five who received only elementary education — there are four still in good standing:

| | |
|---|---|
| Andreyev[28] | Kalinin |
| Kaganovich | Voroshilov |

All of these, with the exception of Kalinin, who died, still occupy positions on the Politburo. Only one of this lowly educated group (Tomsky) has been a deviationist.

Only four of the members received all or part of their education in party-supported schools. Understandably, they all belong to the younger group in the Politburo — the oldest of this group, Khrushchev, now being fifty-five. Voznesensky, one of the four, went to an advanced university (Institute of Red Professors) and was the only member of the Politburo who ever got a Ph.D. Khrushchev went to an adult-education school, and Beria and Malenkov went to higher technical schools, which in Russia have university rank although they are more specialized.

It must be noted that those who went to party-supported schools, with the exception of Voznesensky, are all still members of the Politburo. Beria and Malenkov, moreover, seem to be two of the most powerful members aside from Stalin himself. Beria was the head and

---

28 Andreyev was attacked in *Pravda* for his farm policy in February 1950. Several days later he wrote a letter to *Pravda* confessing his errors. Following this, Andreyev apparently was relieved of his responsibility for agriculture, since a few months later Khrushchev made the principal speech concerning the new agricultural policy. Apparently, however, Andreyev is still a member of the Politburo. He was not included in the very latest picture of the Politburo taken in April 1951, but as late as March 1951, over a year after his reprimand, he was still appearing with the Politburo. See André Pierre, "Spekulationen um Andrejew," *Ost Probleme* (Infor. Services Division H.I.C.O.G.), III, No. 18 (May 1951), pp. 567–568.

is still supervisor of the MVD (NKVD); and Malenkov is the only member of the Politburo, besides Stalin, who at the same time is also a member of the Orgburo and the Secretariat.

Thus it can be concluded that in the period dominated by Lenin, a university education was of some help to the Politburocrat, while in the Stalin epoch this value declined and is now a neglible, if not a positive detriment to a successful career and continued good health.

### Nonpolitical Career

It would be illuminating to discover the first gainful job held by each of the members of the Politburo; however, it has not been possible to get these data in enough cases to warrant any conclusions. Nevertheless, it is useful to identify the main occupation of the members. In the case of the older Politburo members, their main occupations before the advent of Soviet power are used; and for the younger ones, their main occupations before becoming full-fledged politicians. The picture thus obtained is as follows:

| | |
|---|---|
| Industrial workers | 10 |
| Propagandists | 5 |
| Organizers and administrators | 2 |
| White-collar workers | 2 |
| Lawyers | 2 |
| University professor | 1 |
| Shepherd | 1 |
| Unknown | 4 |
| | 27 |

Under the category "Organizers and administrators" we placed those men who never held any regular job other than active party work. The "Propagandists" are the ones who were spokesmen of the revolution — those who prepared the revolution mainly by the printed word.

If one looks at the five "Propagandists," the same pattern emerges as in the previous indices. Four out of the five are "deviationists": Bukharin, Kamenev, Trotsky, and Zinoviev. The fifth is Molotov. This is the third time Molotov appears in the same group with the deviationists (see the earlier sections entitled "Social Class of Family" and "Education").

The conclusion might be drawn that Molotov, like the Trotskyites, in many ways does not fit into the group as a whole. It would indeed be rash to conclude from this that Molotov's days in the Politburo are numbered. However, one cannot help but wonder whether this is likely to have any influence upon Molotov's chances as "heir apparent" to

Stalin. He became an alternate member in 1921 and a full member of the Politburo in 1925. His road to power and success has been long and arduous and sometimes perhaps humiliating.[29]

On the other hand, such comparative upstarts as Malenkov (who has been an alternate only since 1941 and a member since 1946) have had much smoother sailing. It must be kept in mind, however, that Molotov, unlike the deviationists, has always been an unquestioning follower of Stalin. For this reason alone, his position may be judged fairly secure.

The only thing which the above is intended to suggest is that by reason of the information discovered, it would seem somewhat unlikely that Molotov would be chosen as the sole successor to Stalin.

In contrast to the category "Propagandists," there is the category of the men of action — those who fall under the heading "Organizers and administrators." The two men who come under this heading are Beria and Mikoyan, two trusted members of the Politburo and also of a somewhat younger generation. They were in their early twenties when World War I broke out, followed by the revolution in 1917, and they did not have much chance to pick up a vocation. They were much too young and inexperienced at that time to qualify as writers or propagandists. Their careers in the Politburo have been much more successful. Mikoyan is a close friend of Stalin's, and Beria is the official historian of Stalin's activities during his youth in the Caucasus.

It is not surprising that industrial workers should occupy the first place in the occupational breakdown; but it is strange that peasants — in a government of "workers and peasants" — should be totally missing. It is a striking fact that the peasant class, which at least in the beginning apparently welcomed the revolution, never was included in the most important governing body, the Politburo. To be sure, some of the members were the sons of peasants, but not one of them was at any time himself a peasant. The real engineers of the revolution were the propagandists and organizers, but they later lost their power and had to make way for the workers; or, as we have said before, the theoreticians had to make way for the administrators.

A word should be said about the two lawyers in the group. The other RADIR elite studies show that in the "Western democracies" the profession of law is a most important step in the ladder leading to political success. As expected, this does not hold true for revolutionary Russia, whose goal it was to remake the laws that governed the coun-

---

[29] Lenin called him "mediocre" and "the best filing clerk" in Russia. Cf. Duranty, *op. cit.*, p. 93.

try and the society itself.[30] One of the two lawyers was Lenin himself, who, it must be remembered, occupied a very special position in the hierarchy, and even his career was short and undistinguished. The other lawyer was Krestinsky, who was executed as a Trotskyite and a spy.

The one and only university professor is Voznesensky, who taught at a Soviet university and was dropped from the Politburo after a very short tenure.

The fact that the intellectuals often make the revolution but later drop out and give way to the workers or administrators has also been stated by Franz Mehring, who said about the intellectuals:

> If they wish to be practical fighters and not theorists, they become altogether insignificant as adherents to the labour movement. . . . The task of the intellectual consists in maintaining the freshness and vigour of the workers in their movement towards their great goal and in elucidating for them the social relationships which make the approaching victory of the proletariat a certainty.[31]

*Military Experience*

The military background of the Politburo is fairly diversified:

| | |
|---|---|
| No service | 11 |
| Czarist army | 3 |
| Revolution and Civil War | 13 |
| Unknown | 3 |

Since some of the members served in the Czarist Army as well as in the revolution and in the Civil War, the above figures add up to more than twenty-seven.

The eleven who did not see any military service at all have to be divided into three groups. First, there were those who were in exile abroad: Bukharin, Lenin, and Zinoviev. Then there are those who were in exile in Siberia or other places within Russia: Kalinin, Kamenev, Molotov, Rudzutak, Rykov, Sverdlov, and Tomsky. And finally, there are those who were too young to participate in either the revolution or the Civil War. The only man in this group is Voznesensky.

Only three, a very small percentage, saw some service in the Czarist Army: Chubar, Kaganovich, and Zhdanov. Zhdanov, who later became a Colonel General in the Red Army, was even promoted to ser-

---

[30] In this respect the Russian revolution was different from the French one, in which lawyers played a prominent part.

[31] Franz Mehring, *Akademiker und Proletarier*, II, "Leipziger Volkszeitung," xi, No. 95, as quoted in Robert Michels, *Political Parties* (Glencoe, Ill.: The Free Press, 1949), p. 327.

124    G. K. SCHUELLER

geant in the Czarist Army. Chubar and Kaganovich were also enlisted men; so we can say that no member of the Politburo was an officer in the Czarist Army.

There is no published information available as to the military service of Andreyev, Kossior, or Krestinsky.[32]

The thirteen members who participated in the revolution and the Civil War all held rather high posts in connection with those military events. Most of them were political commissars. In the whole group, however, there is only one man who could possibly be described as a professional soldier, and that is Voroshilov. Even he became a soldier only during the revolution, but he then continued in the Red Army. Voroshilov's father served for a long time in the Czarist Army, and this may have influenced his son toward a military career.

In World War II there were three Politburo members who saw active service. Zhdanov directed the defense of Leningrad and was promoted to the rank of Colonel General. Voroshilov was a Marshal, who at the beginning of the war had the over-all direction of Russian troops. He was later deposed as Commander-in-Chief and toward the end of the war directed what operations there were against the Japanese in the Far East. Khrushchev was a political Commissar during World War II and is said to have fought on the Stalingrad front. Whether or not Beria actively participated in the war could not be determined. He was made a Marshal of the Red Army in 1946, probably in recognition of the services he rendered in connection with the reorganization of the NKVD and also as Commanding Officer of the NKVD and other security troops. Those listed above include only those who fought actively in the war and not those who performed other duties.

It should be noted that in the Soviet Union the purely technical performance of military duties, however excellently carried out, does not lead to political rewards (as in Western countries). None of the Marshals of the Red Army who fought brilliantly during the war seem to have received any political reward.[33] It could be that this is an aftermath of the 1937 treason trials against some of the highest officers of the Soviet Union, but it seems that the military, as such, never played a very great political role in the Soviet Union. Such high military

[32] However, Boris Nicolaevsky, in a personal communication to the author, stated that these men were never in the service.

[33] The exceptions to this are Konev and Zhukov, who after the war were Military Governors of the Russian Zones of Austria and Germany, respectively; but after a comparatively short time they were recalled and replaced by relatively unknown figures.

leaders as Budjenny, Timoshenko, Bluecher, and others never reached high political positions.

It has happened, on the other hand, that some men like Frunze, Trotsky, and Stalin rose to high military ranks, although they were primarily politicians, and not soldiers. Frunze did have some military experience but only as the leader of guerrillas at the age of thirty-two.

In conclusion, it can be said that the Politburo as a body, now more so than previously, is fairly rich in military experience. The degree of leadership ascribed to some members during the revolution and the Civil War is probably somewhat exaggerated. There seems to be no stigma attached to service as an enlisted man in the Czarist Army, which is not surprising inasmuch as service was based on conscription.

### Communication and Propaganda Jobs

Since all members of the Politburo became propagandists after the revolution, we shall note here only activity in underground propaganda work before the revolution. With the exception of four of the younger members (Beria, Khrushchev, Malenkov, and Voznesensky), who were really too young to have engaged in any important work, all the Politburocrats spoke and wrote extensively before the revolution. Some were more active than others in this kind of work.

The following members of the Politburo were editors, or leading contributors, or both, to party and labor periodicals and newspapers: Bukharin, Kamenev, Kirov, Krestinsky, Lenin, Mikoyan, Molotov, Stalin, Tomsky, Trotsky, and Zinoviev.

Of the above list only Mikoyan, Molotov, and Stalin are still alive and active. Undoubtedly, the chief reason so many of the old Bolsheviks engaged in written propaganda is that this was the only prerevolutionary propaganda open to them, since they could not deliver public speeches, and an open party organization was impossible.

## VI. POLITICAL HISTORY

### Age of Affiliation with the Bolsheviks

Before the Bolshevik faction of the RSDLP (Russian Social Democratic Labor Party) constituted itself a party in 1912, all of the older members of the Politburo had belonged to the RSDLP. For that reason, in this section, we give the age at which they joined either the RSDLP or the Bolshevik Party, depending on the age of the man.

Appendix B includes information on the age of each Politburo member at joining one of the two parties mentioned. All of them joined at a very early age, the youngest at sixteen and the oldest at twenty-four. On an average, they joined the party at the age of nineteen. The present Politburo conforms to the general pattern inasmuch as the average age at which its members joined the party was nineteen. The ones who joined when they were over twenty are usually the oldest members of the group. This means that in the beginning of the pre-revolutionary and revolutionary period, the members seemed to join the party at a slightly more advanced age than in the postrevolution-ary period.

Probably the only inference to be drawn here is that it seems to be indispensable for success in the Politburo to have a long record of Bolshevik activity from an early age.

### Record of Imprisonment

The record of imprisonments and arrests of the members of the Politburo looks very large indeed. Of the twenty-seven, only six seem never to have been arrested. As could be expected, these six com-prise the youngest age group. They are:

| | |
|---|---|
| Andreyev | Malenkov |
| Beria | Voznesensky |
| Khrushchev | Zhdanov |

All the others have been in and out of jail, exiled, and banished many times. During the Czarist regime the Politburo members were almost always able to escape after being exiled, in most cases only to be arrested again shortly afterwards, but then to escape again. Rudzu-tak was the only one who served his sentence in full. He was arrested in 1907 and completed his sentence of ten years at hard labor. He was released in 1917 shortly before the revolution began.

The above information applies only to imprisonment under the Czarist regime. Under the Soviet regime, seven members of the Polit-buro were arrested:

| | |
|---|---|
| Bukharin | Trotsky |
| Kamenev | Tomsky |
| Krestinsky | Zinoviev |
| Rykov | |

In contrast to conditions that prevailed under the Czarist regime, those arrested by the Bolsheviks did not escape, with the exception of Trotsky. All were executed except Tomsky, who committed suicide. Even Trotsky was murdered later on. The three members who dis-appeared in 1938 (Chubar, Kossior, and Rudzutak) probably were arrested, too; but since there is no definite information available, they have not been included in the figures.

It can be seen that imprisonment by the Czarist police was something like a badge of honor for the Bolshevik leadership, but imprisonment by the Soviet regime was a badge of disgrace invariably ending in violent death.

### Government and Party Career

One difficulty in interpreting available information on governmental and party careers is the lack of clear-cut distinctions between governmental and party functions in the Soviet Union. For instance, the Politburo itself, while being strictly a party organization in reality, exercises governmental and managerial functions and might be described as the effective government of the Soviet Union. This lack of distinction between governmental and party functions is one of the peculiarities that the Soviet Union shares, to some extent, with all other dictatorships. The most strikingly similar example is Nazi Germany, where there also was a fusion of government and party offices.

In many instances there is also a duplication of functions. A case in point was the Central Control Commission and the Commissariat of Workers' and Peasants' Inspection. Both had essentially the same functions. The one watched over the conscience of the party members; the other watched over the conscience of the workers and peasants. Quite often, naturally, there was considerable overlapping. These two organizations were later changed to the Commission of Party Control and the Commission of Soviet Control. The latter subsequently became the Ministry of State Control. Their functions, however, remained the same.[34]

In order to give a clear picture of the political careers of these twenty-seven men, the career of each one must be traced separately and an attempt made to differentiate between governmental, party, and other political jobs. These career lines are not all-inclusive, since the information has been pieced together from many sources, and quite conceivably some jobs might have been missed, although it is hoped that all the important jobs are included. The career lines of the twenty-seven Politburo members are shown in Appendix C.

In looking at the career lines of these twenty-seven men, it becomes apparent that a seat on the Politburo, at least as far as the party career is concerned, is really the highest post which can be attained—with the exception of the position of Secretary-General of the Central Committee of the Communist Party, a post which has been held by Stalin since April 3, 1922. Very few men got other important party jobs after being elected to the Politburo. Andreyev and Kirov became members

[34] For the development of these bodies, see Towster, *op. cit.*, pp. 171 ff.

of the Secretariat after they joined the Politburo; and Kaganovich held
several temporary, more or less important, party jobs after joining the
Politburo. None of the others held other party jobs after they reached
membership in the Politburo.

It has not been possible in all instances to get data on when they
became alternates in the Politburo, but the usual waiting period between becoming an alternate and reaching full membership appears to
be between four and nine years. Only Khrushchev was an alternate for
less than four years, while the upper limit has been stretched at times.

Before the great purge trials of 1936 and 1938, members of the Politburo could be expelled while continuing to hold other jobs. Examples
are Bukharin, Kamenev, Rudzutak, and Tomsky. The careers of these
men after their expulsion from the Politburo will be discussed in the
following section.

There seem to be certain kinds of jobs that more readily than others
lead to membership in the Politburo. One is a certain amount of police
work or work in the secret police organizations (OGPU, NKVD, MVD,
and MGB). Work in the Commissariat for Workers' and Peasants'
Inspection and the two Control Commissions can also be considered
as a sort of police work. The following ten members of the Politburo
held such jobs before becoming members:

| | |
|---|---|
| Andreyev | Ordjonikidze |
| Beria | Rudzutak |
| Kaganovich | Stalin[35] |
| Kuibyshev | Voroshilov |
| Kossior | Voznesensky |

It will be noted that these jobs were never held by any of those
members who were openly charged with treason and deviationism and
who were later tried and executed. Of those who held these jobs, all
but three are still in good repute, and five are still on the Politburo.

Another job that often seems to be a step on the ladder to membership in the Politburo is "Secretary to the Central Committee." The
following eleven men held this position before achieving membership
in the Politburo, and all but three are still in good repute:

| | |
|---|---|
| Andreyev | Malenkov |
| Kaganovich | Molotov |
| Kirov | Rudzutak |
| Kossior | Stalin (Secretary-General) |
| Krestinsky | Zhdanov |
| Kuibyshev | |

Kirov was the only one of these men who was appointed Secretary of
the Central Committee after he had become a member of the Politburo.

[35] Stalin actually held such a job after becoming a member of the Politburo.

A further, rather curious, feature is that party work in one or more of three specific regions seems to have been regarded as a stepping-stone to more important jobs. These three regions are the Ukraine, the Caucasus, and Nizhni-Novgorod. The following seventeen members did party work in one or more of these regions:

| | |
|---|---|
| Andreyev | Mikoyan |
| Beria | Molotov |
| Chubar | Ordjonikidze |
| Kaganovich | Stalin |
| Kalinin | Sverdlov |
| Kamenev | Voroshilov |
| Khrushchev | Voznesensky |
| Kirov | Zhdanov |
| Kossior | |

For each of these regions, the breakdown is:

| | |
|---|---|
| Caucasus | 9 |
| Ukraine | 8 |
| Nizhni-Novgorod | 5 |

We can see from this that more than half the members did party work in one or more of these three regions.

Why do these three types of jobs, more than any others, seem to be a factor in political advancement? The following hypotheses are suggested as possible answers:

1. The emergence of the policeman or the "specialist on violence" (i.e., GPU, NKVD, MVD, Central Control Commission, and Commissariat for Workers' and Peasants' Inspection) has been described and forecast by some social scientists as a sign of the "revolution of our time."[36] Another reason why police work seems to be a steppingstone to the highest positions in the party might be that the leader (Stalin) tries to find out whether the prospective member of the Politburo can carry out distasteful orders loyally and unquestioningly. Furthermore, it might be that the leader gives the future members of the Politburo these police assignments in order to make them hated and feared by the population at large. Consequently, it becomes unlikely that these men will become either popular leaders in a revolt or potential counterelites able to deal effectively with foreign powers in case of war (unconditional surrender policy).[37]

2. The Secretariat (i.e., Secretary to the Central Committee) is the organization that controls almost every internal aspect of party life,

[36] See Lasswell, op. cit., pp. 146 ff.

[37] For a description of the impact of the secret police on the people, see Ernst Kohn-Bramstedt, Dictatorship and Political Police: The Technique of Control by Fear (London: Kegan, Paul, 1945), pp. 176 ff.

and it is probable that it is considered as a training ground for the even higher position on the Politburo. In the Secretariat a man is trained for the administrative work he will do later on in the Politburo. It is an institution that came into being when the symbol specialist declined and the administrator and organizer came to the fore (see the section entitled "Publications"). It also trains the bureaucratic element in the Politburo.[38]

3. The reason why party work in the Ukraine and in the Caucasus appears to be important may be that these areas have been trouble spots for the Bolsheviks for a long time. In the Ukraine this still seems to be the case. Recall that during the German advance in the Ukraine, many inhabitants were apparently glad to see the Soviets defeated, and greeted the Germans as liberators. No adequate reason could be found as to why Nizhni-Novgorod seemed to be of such importance. This may be set down as chance.[39]

There has been a noticeable trend lately toward freeing members of the Politburo from other duties. In earlier times all members of the Politburo held one job or another in the executive branch of the government, and many times were even Commissars for a particular department; but in 1949 this policy apparently was changed. Previously the members of the Politburo held many different jobs in the executive departments, even disregarding such semiexecutive jobs as membership in the Central Executive Committee of the Presidium of the Supreme Soviet. In 1923 four out of eight held such jobs; in 1928, five out of nine; in 1935, eight out of ten; and in 1943, six out of nine. In 1949 not one of the members of the Politburo was directly responsible for any department as such. The last two who held such jobs were Molotov and Mikoyan, and they were relieved as Ministers early in 1949. When Molotov and Mikoyan relinquished their posts as Foreign Minister and Minister for Food Supply, respectively, the Western press generally called this a "purge" and tried to give the impression that Molotov and Mikoyan were "removed" from their posts. Actually, since they were made Vice-Premiers at the same time, it apparently was of a promotion than demotion. Now all members of the Politburo, with the exception of Khrushchev, are Vice-Premiers; but they do not have individual departments to administer. Instead, they each have the supervision of a cluster of ministries. This means they are not so burdened with detail, and are able to oversee large segments of the government.

[38] In regard to the bureaucratic aspects of the elite in a dictatorship, see Neumann, *op. cit.*, pp. 77 ff.

[39] Boris Nicolaevsky suggests the reason for this might be that Kaganovich, who was secretary of the party there, recruited people from the local party machinery.

In the power structure of the Soviet Union, the party stands above the government. It appears, in looking over the career lines of the twenty-seven members, that almost all of them entered the most important government jobs only after becoming at least candidates to the Politburo. The road to the most conspicuous government jobs such as Vice-Premier, member of the Presidium of the Central Executive Committee or the Supreme Soviet, etc., is through prior success in the party. Some less important commissariats have never been held by members of the Politburo. Of the present nine members of the Politburo, only Molotov and Stalin held fairly high jobs in the party before 1917; while Beria, Khrushchev, Malenkov, and Mikoyan did not have any party jobs before the revolution. These last four constitute the youngest group, and they could hardly have held any such jobs before 1917.

In summary, it can be said that the ladder of success today in the Soviet Union, as far as membership in the Politburo is concerned, looks something like this:

> Member of the Politburo
> High government job
> Candidate to the Politburo
> Becomes a member of the Secretariat
> Becomes a member of the Central Committee
> Has no higher education
> Does party work in one of the three regions men-
>    tioned above; also does some police work
> Joins party before the age of twenty
> Of low social origin
> Born in a village

In the pre-Stalinist period the same ladder of success would have looked something like this:

> Member of the Politburo
> Becomes a member of the government
> Becomes a member of the Central Committee
> Goes abroad and studies there; also
>    publishes paper there.
> Is arrested and jailed several times
> Does propaganda work for the party
> Has probably attended a university
> Joins party at an early age, but probably
>    after the age of twenty
> Of middle-class origin
> Born in a town or metropolis

### Post-Politburo Career

Of the eighteen former members of the Politburo who are no longer in that body, seven died while holding the job of Politburo member.

The remaining eleven, who continued to live after being dropped from the Politburo, had the following careers:

Krestinsky    1921  Left Politburo to become Ambassador to Germany; held this job until 1930.
1930–1938  Vice-Commissar for Foreign Affairs.
Member of the Central Executive Committee of the U.S.S.R.
1938  Tried and executed.

Trotsky    1926  Expelled from Politburo; did not hold any jobs later.

Zinoviev    1926  Expelled from Politburo.
1927  Expelled from Communist Party.
1928  Readmitted to party membership.
1932  Expelled again.
1935  Arrested and tried; sentenced to ten years in jail.
1936  Retried and executed.

Kamenev    1926  Dropped from Politburo.
1926  Appointed Ambassador to Italy.
1927  Expelled from party.
1928  Readmitted to Communist Party.
Director of Supreme Council of National Economy.
1932  Expelled from party; readmitted the same year.
1935  Expelled from party; tried and sentenced to ten years.
1936  Tried and executed.

Bukharin    1929  Expelled from Politburo and also from Central Committee.
1933  Member of Collegium of People's Commissariat for Heavy Industry.
1934  Editor of *Izvestia* of the CEC of the Union.
1934  Candidate to the CC.
President of the Association of Research Institutes.
Member of the Academy of Sciences.
1937  Expelled from the party.
1938  Tried and executed.

Rykov    1929  Expelled from Politburo and Communist Party.
1931  Readmitted to party membership.
1931–1937  People's Commissar for Communications.
1938  Tried and executed.

Tomsky    1929  Expelled from Politburo, but remained a member of Supreme Council of National Economy and a member of the CEC.
1935  Head of the State Literary Publishing House.
1936  Arrested; committed suicide before trial.

Rudzutak    1931   Left Politburo.
                   Remained as People's Commissar for Workers' and
                   Peasants' Inspection, and Vice-President of the
                   Council of People's Commissars.
            1934   Became an alternate member of the Politburo again
                   and remained as such until 1936.
            1938   Reported missing.

Chubar      1938   Was still a member of the Politburo, but has not
                   been heard from since.

Kossior     1938   Relieved from his post in the Politburo. Has not
                   been heard from since.

Voznesensky 1949   Removed from Politburo. No information as to his
                   present job is available.

Three of the eleven held no jobs after being dropped from the Politburo. They are Chubar, Kossior, and Trotsky. One (Voznesensky) was
dismissed from the Politburo such a short time ago that nothing can be
said about his subsequent career at the moment. Zinoviev did not hold
any jobs after 1926, but he was once readmitted to membership in the
Communist Party. There remain six who have held different jobs after
being expelled from the Politburo. Two of them seem to occupy a special position, since they were not actually expelled, but left the Politburo in order to take up other duties. These two are Krestinsky and
Rudzutak.

*Krestinsky* left the Politburo at a very early date (1921) in order to
take over the job as Ambassador to Germany, which at that time, in
view of the recent revolution in Germany, was considered to be of
special importance. In 1930 he was recalled from Berlin and promoted
to Vice-Commissar of Foreign Affairs under Litvinov. At the same time
he was a member of the Central Executive Committee of the U.S.S.R.
In 1938, when he still held both jobs, he was arrested and tried for
conspiracy with Trotsky, and was also accused of having plotted with
the German General Staff while serving as Ambassador in Berlin. He
was executed in 1938.

*Rudzutak*, who had been a member of the Politburo since 1926, was
appointed chairman of the Central Control Commission and Commissar for Workers' and Peasants' Inspection in 1931. At this time Rudzutak apparently gave up his position on the Politburo because one of
the organizational rules of the Central Control Commission says that
the members, in order to fulfill their tasks, should not be burdened
with other work.[40] Rudzutak held both jobs until 1934. In February

---

[40] VKP(b) *XI s"ezd Rossiiskoi kommunisticheskoi partii (bol'shevikov).* Steno-

1934 he was relieved of both jobs; and he again became an alternate member of the Politburo. From this day on he remained in the background, and in 1936 he was no longer listed as an alternate member. Apparently he did not hold any other job. In 1938 he was reported missing and was probably a victim of the purge.

The remaining four are Bukharin, Kamenev, Rykov, and Tomsky. *Kamenev* was expelled from the Politburo in 1926; the others, in 1929. All four of them held jobs of varying importance after being expelled.

*Bukharin*, who probably was among the most respected Bolsheviks after Lenin's death, held a job in a People's Commissariat and was editor of the official government newspaper *Izvestia*, and also, in 1934, was again made a candidate to the Central Committee of the Communist Party.

*Rykov* was made People's Commissar for Communications in 1931, and at the same time was readmitted into the Communist Party. He held his job as People's Commissar until 1937, shortly before his arrest and subsequent execution.

*Tomsky* after his dismissal remained a member of the Supreme Council of National Economy and a member of the Central Executive Committee. In 1935 he was made head of the State Publishing House. One observer reports that Tomsky was in good spirits while working at this job and did not seem very much affected by his removal from the Politburo.[41] However, he held this job only for a short time, because in 1936 he was arrested and committed suicide while in jail.

The picture as a whole shows the same pattern which emerges in other parts of this study. At the time of the expulsion of the deviationists, between 1926 and 1929, Stalin's power and prestige was not yet sufficiently great to enable him to do away with such old and famous Bolsheviks as Bukharin, Rykov, Kamenev, and Zinoviev. It was still necessary to keep them at least nominally on the scene and give them some kind of job. Bukharin, the widely known old Bolshevik, was even made a candidate to the Central Committee again. The others, however, never reached any important posts in the party hierarchy after once being expelled from the Politburo.

Those who came into opposition to Stalin at a later date (Chubar, Kossior, and Rudzutak), when Stalin's power was definitely established, were removed without much fanfare, never received another job, and disappeared completely from the scene. If it is admissible to

---

grafcheskii otchet (Kiev: Gos. izd-vo, 1922), p. 326. Later this rule was not strictly applied. Rudzutak was relieved by Kaganovich, who was already, at this time, a member of the Politburo.

[41] Sir Walter Citrine, *I Search for Truth in Russia* (London: G. Routledge & Sons, Ltd., 1936), pp. 132 ff.

judge from this past experience, it would seem unlikely that Vozne-sensky will get any other important job in the future.

### Death (Recapitulation)

Table 4 gives a clearer picture of the causes of violent death among the Politburocrats. It is clear urban, cosmopolitan, middle-class intel-lectuals have been Stalin's main targets of internecine violence among the Soviet elite.

## VII. MISCELLANEOUS CHARACTERISTICS

### Publications

In the writings of the members of the Politburo, there is a definite dividing line. The old-time Bolsheviks, mostly the ones who were later purged, were quite prolific in their writings. Clearly, before the revolu-tion, they depended to a great extent on the printed word to get their message across to the people. And in the period immediately following the revolution, theoretical discussion and controversy were still prac-ticed and encouraged. But with the ascendancy of Stalin, the amount of writing done by members of the Politburo declined considerably, and their printed works were usually restricted to reports and speeches given before Soviet gatherings.

Also, before the revolution and up to the time Stalin's leadership was established, the leading members of the Politburo wrote books and treatises on theoretical aspects of Marxism and Bolshevism, while in later years the theoretical treatment of such subjects was entirely missing. To illustrate this point one has only to look, for instance, at the works of Lenin and Trotsky, which have become classics in their field. Of the others, one could mention such works as:

| | |
|---|---|
| Zinoviev | *Istoriia Rossiiskoi Kommunistichestoi partii (bolshevikov)* (*The History of the Russian Communist Party* [Bol-shevik]). |
| | *Voina i krizis sotsializma* (*The War and the Crisis of Socialism*). |
| | *Protiv techeniia* (*Against the Current*). |
| Kamenev | *Mezhdu dvumia revoliutsiiami; sbornik statei* (*Between Two Revolutions*). |
| | *Ekonomicheskaia sistema imperializma i zadachi sotsializma* (*The Economic System of Imperialism and the Tasks of Socialism*). |
| Bukharin | *Historical Materialism: A System of Sociology. The ABC of Communism and World Economy. The Economic Theory of the Leisure Class.* |

*Table 4*

VIOLENT DEATHS AMONG POLITBURO MEMBERS*

| Politburo Member | Bukharin | Kamenev | Krestinsky | Rykov | Tomsky | Trotsky | Zinoviev |
|---|---|---|---|---|---|---|---|
| Date of Death | 1938 | 1936 | 1938 | 1938 | 1936 | 1940 | 1936 |
| Cause of Death | Executed | Executed | Executed | Executed | Suicide | Murdered | Executed |
| Social Class | Middle | Middle | Middle | Low | Low | Middle | Middle |
| Higher Education | Yes | Yes | Yes | Yes | No | Yes | Yes |
| Urban Background | Yes | Yes | Yes | Yes | Yes | No | Yes |
| Cosmopolitan Background** | Yes | Yes | Yes | Yes | No | Yes | Yes |
| Religious Background | Orthodox | Jewish | ? | Orthodox | Orthodox | Jewish | Jewish |
| Theoretician | Yes | Yes | No | Yes | Yes | Yes | Yes |

* Kirov was murdered in 1934, in Leningrad. His was the only violent death not brought about by government action. He was a faithful Bolshevik and not involved in any deviationist activities. Also, interesting to note, he does not exhibit any of the positive traits described in rows 3 to 8. Chubar, Kossior, and Rudzutak disappeared in the purge of 1938 and can be presumed executed. They also do not exhibit any of the positive traits described in rows 3 to 8.

** Those who spent part of their life abroad.

None of the later members of the Politburo has written any works of such breadth and scope. The only one who still writes an occasional article on theoretical questions is Stalin, and he has not written any big works in many years.

Of the present nine members of the Politburo, only the following have done any kind of writing at all:

| | |
|---|---|
| Beria | Wrote a book on the history of the Bolshevik organization in the Caucasus. |
| Molotov | Wrote a few small pamphlets. The rest of his published works are reprints of speeches and reports made to either Soviet organs or international gatherings. |
| Stalin | Wrote several early books, among them *Problems of Leninism, Foundations of Leninism,* and *On the Nationality Question.* The rest of his works again are collections of articles and speeches. |
| Voroshilov | Wrote a few small pamphlets. |

Voznesensky, too, should be mentioned, although he has left the Politburo. In 1947 he wrote a book entitled *War Economy of the U.S.S.R. During the War of Liberation,* which was awarded the Stalin prize.

If one compares this meager output with the earlier days, a striking difference appears. Leading the list of the early Bolsheviks are Lenin and Trotsky, whose works fill many volumes. Then comes Bukharin, who wrote at least five books, mostly on Bolshevik theory; Kamenev, who wrote four books, including a biography of Lenin; and Zinoviev, who wrote six. Tomsky wrote a few pamphlets on trade-union questions. In addition to books, all of the above members wrote innumerable articles for Soviet newspapers — a practice that today has all but disappeared. Those who were members of the Politburo in the 1930's also confined themselves mostly to reports, speeches, and a very few small pamphlets. Kirov, in 1912, wrote a little book called *The Simplicity of Manners.* He continued to write more than the others, but he never wrote an important book.

It is interesting to note that not one of the members except Trotsky has written an autobiography, and that only two of them (Lenin and Stalin) have had official biographers. Trotsky also had some biographers, but since the biographies were not written in Soviet Russia, they are not considered official. In fact, with the exception of Lenin, Stalin, and Trotsky, no full-scale biography of any member has been written by non-Russians.

Undoubtedly this is because there is available insufficient material to write such a biography. If the written output of the Politburo members is considered as a whole, one can see again that the trend in the Politburo has been away from the theoretician (who writes a lot) and toward the organizer (who writes little or nothing).

The private lives, habits, and opinions of the Politburo members are probably as unknown to the ordinary Russian as they are to the foreigner. Edgar Snow stated that he once wanted to do a story about the members of the Politburo and sent a questionnaire to the NKVD. He asked questions similar to those which were asked in this study. The answer he got was, "Things like that can't possibly be of any interest to foreigners."[42]

### Foreign Contacts

There is a widespread impression that the members of the Politburo have had very few foreign contacts, and it is therefore surprising to find that twenty-two out of the twenty-seven have had some kind of contact with foreign countries. The only five who have not — or about whom no information is available — are: Andreyev, Chubar, Kuibyshev, and Voznesensky. It must be made clear, however, that foreign contacts, particularly with the Western world, for the most part took place before 1930; since then the foreign contacts of the Politburo have been few and far between. The contacts Politburocrats have had with the West (excluding Eastern Europe and the Balkans) since 1935 are the following:

| | |
|---|---|
| Beria | 1946 — Berlin, for an operation. |
| Kaganovich | 1935 — Vienna, to see a doctor. |
| Mikoyan | 1936 — Inspected the food industry in the United States. |
| Molotov | Many international conferences. |
| Stalin | 1945 — Potsdam Conference. |
| Tomsky | 1935 — Breslau, to see a doctor. |

As we can see, three out of the six went for medical reasons; and with the exception of Molotov and Mikoyan, all the contacts were with Germany or Austria. While in the Western countries it is a well-established custom that statesmen occasionally go on trips abroad, either for diplomatic or other reasons, in the Soviet Union this apparently was not a popular custom in the Stalin period.

The contacts with Eastern Europe, the East, and the Balkans since 1930 seem not to have been much more numerous:

| | |
|---|---|
| Khrushchev | 1945 — Poland, to negotiate with new government. |
| Malenkov | 1947 — Warsaw, and several trips to the Balkans. |
| Molotov | Many conferences. |
| Stalin | 1944 — Teheran Conference. |

[42] Edgar Snow, *The Pattern of Soviet Power* (New York: Random House, Inc., 1945), p. 168.

| Voroshilov | 1945 — Head of Allied Control Commission for Hungary. |
| Zhdanov | 1944 — Finland and several trips to the Balkans. |

While there was not much more contact with Eastern Europe than with Western Europe and the rest of the world, there has been an increase in contact with the eastern part of Europe since World War II and the establishment of what are today called the satellite states.

Before 1930 the picture was decidedly different. Then many of the Politburo members went abroad for long periods of time and traveled extensively through various countries. There also was a time when a member who had been dismissed from the Politburo could get an appointment as a Soviet Ambassador abroad (Kamenev in Italy and Krestinsky in Germany). Now, however, members of the Politburo do not hold diplomatic jobs either before or after becoming members. The only exception to this seems to be Molotov.

Before the revolution, when passports were little used in Europe, Bolshevik conferences took place in many of the capitals of Europe and were attended by the exiles as well as by the Bolsheviks from Russia itself. Since the revolution, however, these conferences invariably take place in the Soviet Union, and there is no longer any need to travel to a foreign country in order to participate. Before the revolution, also, some went abroad for their education — some by choice and others because they were barred from the educational institutions of Russia. Since the revolution none of the members of the Politburo have ever studied abroad.

### Honors

Information regarding honors is not always complete in the available biographical dictionaries. According to Article 49 of the 1936 Constitution, it is one of the prerogatives of the Presidium of the Supreme Soviet to award titles, medals, and other decorations. The practice was frowned upon in the young Soviet Republic and was only revived in the 1930's. For this reason, only Politburocrats who have held office since then have been highly decorated.

All of the present nine members of the Politburo have the highest order of the Soviet Union — the Order of Lenin. Kalinin, Voznesensky, and Zhdanov, who were members until recently, also had this decoration.

Aside from these twelve, however, this high order has not been given to any member of the Politburo. Most of those who became members of the Politburo during and after the 1930's also hold either the title "Hero of Socialist Labor" or the "Hammer and Sickle Gold Medal" or both.

## VIII. CONCLUSIONS

### Review of Results

The most important results obtained in this study can be summarized as follows:

1. The revolution of 1917 was led and organized by brilliant young intellectuals from a middle-class background. In the course of the establishment of the Soviet state, the need for such people diminished, and they were gradually replaced by less colorful but efficient administrators and organizers. This shift is illustrated, at the top, by the change in leadership from Lenin to Stalin.

2. In many ways the Politburo is not at all representative of the population of the Soviet Union. Some areas and nationalities are over-represented (the most noteworthy example being Georgia and the Georgians), while some vast areas are not represented at all. It has been suggested in the body of the paper that this might be a factor on which national discontent might focus. This point might well be considered by the "Voice of America" in its propaganda broadcasts to the Soviet Union.

3. The Politburo, like the leadership body of most other dictatorships, is in many respects self-perpetuating, and replacements are slow and few. For this reason the average age of the Politburo member has risen markedly in the last thirty-two years. This must be a factor of great concern to the Soviet leaders, who have to think of the future and of the possibilities of finding able and young replacements. Whether they are going to succeed, only the future will show. A beginning has been made with the inclusion of Malenkov and the grooming of Ponomarenko for this important post.

4. It has always been the impression in Western countries that members of the Politburo live under a tremendous strain and that another purge is always just around the corner. Contrary to this prevalent opinion, it rather seems that Stalin has picked his men carefully enough that he can now trust them to a greater degree; and unless some internal or external upheaval occurs, another purge is quite unlikely — at least so long as Stalin continues to hold the reins of leadership firmly in his hands.

5. There are no clear signs as to who will be Stalin's successor, in the event of his death. Some signs point to the possibility of a sort of triumvirate which would take over the leadership. However, Stalin probably remembers the days when a triumvirate — consisting of himself, Kamenev, and Zinoviev — ruled Russia; and undoubtedly his memories in this respect are not very favorable. Other signs point to

Molotov; but, as has been pointed out in the paper, it is unlikely that he would be the sole successor to Stalin. It is almost impossible to see what single personality would be able to replace Stalin and — what is more important — keep the other Politburocrats in line.

6. Although the government of the Soviet Union advertises itself as a "Government of Workers and Peasants," it is a curious fact that the peasant class is not represented on the Politburo.

7. The steps a young Bolshevik has to take in order to climb up the ladder of success have become fairly well standardized, and the apprenticeship is usually long and arduous. Since almost no young people educated under the Soviet regime have become members of the Politburo, one must conclude that the Soviet system has not as yet turned out the kind of leader whom Stalin would consider for a post on the Politburo.

8. Despite the Soviet emphasis on the emancipation of women, there are no women in the highest ranks of the Soviet elite.

### Comparison with Other Countries

A comparison of the Politburo with the leadership of [democratic] countries, especially with the British and the American leadership, shows the great difference between the two systems. Some of the difference is to be found in the fact that the Politburo, while in reality the government of the country, is not so in theory. It is accountable only to the Central Committee of the Communist Party, and that, too, is more of a formality than anything else. The Politburo, unlike the governments of the Western countries, is not dependent on popular elections and therefore does not have to seek public favor. This may account for the facts that Politburo members lead an almost anonymous life, and that only meager information is available about the private lives of themselves and their families, with the possible exception of Stalin. Indeed, they seem to shun publicity.

As in other countries, a job on the Politburo is won mostly through devotion to the leader and through long and faithful service to the party. In this respect, the Politburo does not differ materially from the cabinets of other countries. In Western countries, however, cabinet posts are won not only by party wheelhorses, but also by outstanding national figures who have distinguished themselves in other fields, such as diplomacy or the armed services. As has been shown in this study, this never happens in the Politburo. In part, this difference can be accounted for by the fact that the Soviet Union has a one-party system, and therefore those who have been "outs," and have made their reputation in other fields, never come "in."

Much has been made of the fact that the members of the Politburo owe allegiance to the leader — Stalin — and that their political life is dependent upon their loyalty to him. While this is certainly true, it is not a characteristic unique with the Soviet system, since it would be impossible for a British or American cabinet minister to rebel seriously against the Prime Minister or the President and expect to keep his job. The possible further consequences following loss of job, however, are another matter.

While the job of member of the Politburo is far more important than a comparable job on the British or American cabinet, it is not connected with as much outward prestige. It would be interesting to know how many Russians could not identify Khrushchev, for example; one suspects there are many. The members of the Politburo prefer to work in almost complete anonymity, in marked contrast to their counterparts in the West. An important difference is to be found in the security status of the respective officeholder. The security enjoyed by the member of the Politburo lasts only as long as he remains a loyal follower of Stalin and so long as he remains on the Politburo. There are no known cases where a man stepped out from the post of Politburo member and continued to pursue a normal career for any length of time. In the Western countries almost the opposite is true. Once a man has reached the high level of a cabinet post, he can look forward with much certainty to a rewarding career in or out of the government. He might leave the government of his own accord, or he might be forced to leave the government by his chief; nevertheless, his respect status remains almost unchanged, and, with rare exceptions, he can always take up his career again where he left it before entering the cabinet, or he can get an even more rewarding post in private industry.

In the matter of foreign contacts and experience, the difference is also great. In the Western countries, it is virtually indispensable for a cabinet officer to have a certain amount of experience outside his own country (this, however, is more true in Britain and France than it is in the United States); while in the Soviet Union, foreign contacts are not only of no particular help to the Politburo member, but they might even render him suspect in the eyes of the leader.

In general, it may be said that while there are some similarities between the leadership of Soviet Russia and that of the Western world, the dissimilarities are much greater and more important.

# APPENDIX

## APPENDIX A

AVERAGE AGE OF POLITBURO MEMBERS, BY YEARS
PLUS AND MINUS DEVIATIONS, BY YEARS

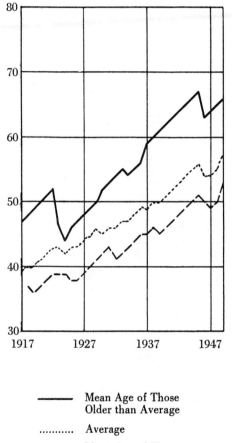

——————  Mean Age of Those
Older than Average

............  Average

— — — —  Mean Age of Those
Younger than Average

APPENDIX B

VITAL STATISTICS OF POLITBURO MEMBERS

| Member | | Province of Birth | Nationality | Age Joined Bolshevik Party or RSDLP* | Cause of Death |
|---|---|---|---|---|---|
| Andreyev | R.S.F.S.R. | Near Smolensk | Russian | 19 | |
| Beria | Georgia | Merkheul | Georgian | 18 | |
| Bukharin | R.S.F.S.R. | Moscow | Russian | 18 | Executed |
| Chubar | Ukraine | Ekaterinoslav | Ukrainian | 16 | Disappeared |
| Kaganovich | Byelo-Russia | Gomel | Jewish | 18 | |
| Kalinin | R.S.F.S.R. | Tver Province | Russian | 23 | Natural |
| Kamenev | R.S.F.S.R. | Moscow | Jewish | 18 | Executed |
| Khrushchev | R.S.F.S.R. | Near Kursk | Russian | 24 | |
| Kirov | R.S.F.S.R. | Urzhum (Viatka Province) | Russian | 18 | Murdered |
| Kossior | Ukraine | Unknown | Ukrainian | 18 | Disappeared |
| Krestinsky | Byelo-Russia | Wilna | Russian | 20 | Executed |
| Kuibyshev | R.S.F.S.R. | Omsk | Russian | 16 | Natural |
| Lenin | R.S.F.S.R. | Simbirsk | Russian | 29 | Natural |
| Malenkov | R.S.F.S.R. | Orenburg | Russian | 19 | |
| Mikoyan | Georgia | Tiflis Province | Armenian | 20 | |
| Molotov | R.S.F.S.R. | Viatka Province | Russian | 16 | |
| Ordjonikidze | Georgia | Goreska | Georgian | 17 | Natural |
| Rudzutak | Latvia | Near Riga | Latvian | 18 | Disappeared |
| Rykov | R.S.F.S.R. | Saratov | Russian | 19 | Executed |
| Stalin | Georgia | Gori | Georgian | 20 | |
| Sverdlov | R.S.F.S.R. | Nizhni-Novgorod | Jewish | 16 | Natural |
| Tomsky | R.S.F.S.R. | St. Petersburg | Russian | 24 | Suicide |
| Trotsky | Ukraine | Near Elizavetgrad | Jewish | 23 | Murdered |
| Voroshilov | Ukraine | Near Ekaterinoslav | Ukrainian | 22 | |
| Voznesensky | R.S.F.S.R. | Near Tula | Russian | 16 | |
| Zhdanov | Ukraine | Mariupol | Ukrainian | 19 | Natural |
| Zinoviev | Ukraine | Elisavetgrad | Jewish | 20 | Executed |

* Average age, nineteen.

## CAREER LINES OF POLITBURO MEMBERS*

### Andreyev

| Party | | Government | | Other | |
|---|---|---|---|---|---|
| 1914 | Joined party | | | | |
| 1915–1916 | Member, Petrograd Committee | | | 1919–1920 | Member, CC of Metal Workers' Union of Ukraine |
| 1920 | Member, CC | | | | |
| 1924–1925 | Secretary, CC | 1927 | Member, CEC; member, Presidium of Soviet of Nationalities | 1919 | Member, Presidium of All-Russian CC of Trade-Unions |
| 1926 | Candidate, Politburo | | | | |
| 1928–1929 | Secretary, North Caucasian District Committee | 1930–1931 | Commissar for Workers' and Peasants' Inspection | 1920–1928 | President of Railroad Union |
| 1930–1931 | Chairman of Central Control Commission | 1931–1935 | Commissar for Transport | | |
| | | 1940–1944 | President, Soviet of the Union | | |
| 1932 | Member, Politburo | 1943–1946 | Minister for Agriculture | 1943 | Member, Committee for Economic Rehabilitation of Liberated Areas |
| 1935–1946 | Member of Secretariat | 1946 | Chairman, Farm Council; deputy chairman and acting chairman, Council of Ministers | | |
| 1940–1946 | Chairman, Commission of Party Control | | | | |

* Appendix C is designed to outline the career pattern of the Politburo, not to give full biographical data. It should be kept in mind that active Bolshevik leaders have typically held a great number of concurrent posts. Some of these, both in the period of illegality and also recently, are not even publicly announced. [See Appendix E for a key to the abbreviations used.]

## Beria

| Party | | Government | | Other | |
|---|---|---|---|---|---|
| 1917 | Joined party | | | | |
| | | | | 1921–1931 | Commissar for Public Security in the Caucasus |
| 1931 | General Secretary, CC of CP of Georgia | | | | |
| 1932 | General Secretary, Trans-Caucasian Regional Committee | | | | |
| 1934 | Member, CC | | | | |
| | | 1938–1946 | Commissar for Internal Affairs and Public Security | | |
| 1939 | Candidate for Politburo | 1941 | Vice-Chairman, Council of People's Commissars. Member, Committee of State Defense | | |
| | | | | 1943 | Member, Committee for Economic Rehabilitation of Liberated Areas |
| 1946 | Member, Politburo | 1946 | Member, Presidium of Supreme Soviet | | |

## Bukharin

| Party | | Government | | Other | |
|---|---|---|---|---|---|
| 1906 | Joined party | | | | |
| 1908 | Member, Moscow Committee | | | | |
| 1917 | Member, CC | | | | |
| 1918 | Member, Politburo | | | 1917–1929 | Editor of *Pravda* |

## Bukharin (*Continued*)

| Party | | Government | | Other | |
|---|---|---|---|---|---|
| | | | | 1919–1929 | Member, Executive Committee of the CI |
| 1929 | Expelled from Politburo and CC | | | | |
| | | 1933 | Member, Collegium of People's Commissariat of Heavy Industry | | |
| 1934 | Candidate to CC | | | 1934–1937 | Editor, *Izvestia* |
| 1937 | Expelled | | | | |
| | | | | 1938 | Tried and executed |

## Chubar

| Party | | Government | | Other | |
|---|---|---|---|---|---|
| 1907 | Joined party | | | | |
| | | 1917 | Commissar of Main Artillery Administration | | |
| 1920 | Member, CC of Ukraine | | | | |
| 1921 | Candidate for CC | | | | |
| 1922 | Member, CC | | | 1922–1923 | Manager of Coal Industry in Donbasin |
| 1923 | Member, Politburo of Ukraine | 1923–1927 | Chairman, Council of People's Commissars of the Ukraine; member, Committee on Financial Policy | | |
| 1927 | Candidate for Politburo | | | | |
| | | 1934–1938 | Vice-Chairman, Council of People's Commissars | | |
| 1935 | Member, Politburo | 1935 | Member, Committee for Constitutional Reform | | |

## Chubar (Continued)

| | Party | | Government | Other |
|---|---|---|---|---|
| | | 1937 | Member, Supreme Soviet of U.S.S.R.; Commissar for Finance | |
| 1938 | Dropped from Politburo and disappeared | | | |

## Kaganovich

| | Party | Government | | Other |
|---|---|---|---|---|
| 1911 | Joined party | | | |
| | | | 1916 | Head of Leather Workers' Union in Dnjepropetrovsk |
| 1917 | Chairman, Polessie Committee; member, All-Russian Bureau of Military Organizations | | | |
| 1919 | Chairman, Nizhni-Novgorod Gubernia Committee | | | |
| | | | 1920 | Mayor of Tashkent |
| 1921 | Member, CC | | 1921 | Member, CC of Leather Workers' Union |
| 1922 | Member, Turkestan Bureau of CC; head of Organizational Instruction Department of CC | | | |
| 1924–1925 | Secretary, CC | | | |
| 1925–1928 | General Secretary, CC of Ukrainian CP | | | |

## Kaganovich (*Continued*)

| | Party | | Government | Other |
|---|---|---|---|---|
| 1926 | Candidate for Politburo | | | |
| 1928 | Secretary, CC; member, Orgburo | | | |
| 1930 | Member, Politburo | | | |
| 1930–1935 | Secretary, Moscow City and Regional Committee | | | |
| 1934–1935 | Head of CCC | 1935–1937 | Commissar for Transport | |
| | | 1937–1941 | Commissar for Heavy Industry and Fuel Industries | |
| | | 1938 | Vice-Chairman, Council of People's Commissars | |
| | | 1942 | Member, State Defense Committee | |
| | | 1942–1944 | Vice-Chairman, Committee for Coordination of Transport | |
| | | 1944 | Vice-Chairman, Council of Ministers | |

## Kaganovich (Continued)

| Party | | Government | | Other |
|---|---|---|---|---|
| | | 1945 | Deputy Minister for Foreign Trade | |
| | | 1946 | Minister for Building Material Industry | |
| 1947 | First Secretary, CC of Ukrainian CP | | | |
| | | 1947 | Vice-Premier | |

## Kalinin

| Party | | Government | | Other |
|---|---|---|---|---|
| 1898 | Joined party | | | |
| 1905 | Joined Bolsheviks. Member, Petersburg Committee | | | |
| 1906 | Delegate, Stockholm Congress | | | |
| 1912 | Alternate member, CC | | | |
| 1919 | Member, CC | 1919 | Chairman, CEC | |
| 1926–1946 | Member, Politburo | 1938–1946 | Chairman, Presidium of the Supreme Soviet | |

## Kamenev

| Party | | Government | Other |
|---|---|---|---|
| 1901 | Joined party | | |
| 1903 | Joined Bolsheviks; sent to Caucasus by Lenin | | |

## Kamenev (Continued)

| Party | | Government | | Other | |
|---|---|---|---|---|---|
| 1905 | Delegate from Caucasian Bolsheviks, Third Party Congress, London | | | | |
| 1907 | Delegate, Fifth Party Congress, London | | | | |
| 1908 | Delegate, Fifth Party Conference, Paris | | | | |
| 1914 | Finland Conference | | | | |
| 1917 | Member, CC | 1917 | Member, Presidium of Petrograd Soviet | | |
| | | 1918–1926 | Chairman, Moscow Soviet | | |
| 1919–1926 | Member, Politburo | | | | |
| | | 1922 | Vice-Chairman, Council of People's Commissars | | |
| | | 1924 | Chairman, Labor and Defense Council | 1924 | Director, Lenin Institute |
| | | 1926 | People's Commissar for Trade | | |
| 1927 | Expelled from party | | | 1926–1927 | Ambassador to Italy |

## Kamenev (Continued)

| | Party | | Government | Other |
|---|---|---|---|---|
| 1928 | Readmitted | 1928 | Director, Supreme Council of National Economy | |
| 1932 | Expelled and readmitted | | | |
| 1935 | Finally expelled | | | |

## Khrushchev

| | Party | | Government | Other |
|---|---|---|---|---|
| 1918 | Joined party. Held minor party jobs in Kiev and Stalino. | | | |
| 1931 | Party boss of two Moscow districts | | | |
| 1932 | Secretary, Moscow Committee | | | |
| 1934 | Member, CC | | | |
| 1935 | First Secretary of Moscow City and District Committee | 1937 | Deputy, Supreme Soviet | |
| 1938 | Secretary, CC of CP of Ukraine. Candidate, Politburo | 1938–1946 | Member of Presidium, Supreme Soviet | |
| 1939 | Member, Politburo | 1944–1947 | Chairman, Council of Ministers of Ukraine | |

## Khrushchev (Continued)

| Party | Government | | Other |
|---|---|---|---|
| | 1946 | Member of Presidium, Council on Collective Farm Affairs | |

## Kirov

| Party | | Government | Other | |
|---|---|---|---|---|
| 1904 | Joined party | | | |
| 1905 | Member, Tomsk Committee | | | |
| 1917 | Delegate from Caucasus to All-Russian Soviet | | | |
| 1919 | Chairman, Astrakhan Military Revolutionary Committee | | | |
| 1920 | Member, Caucasian CC | | 1920 | Plenipotentiary of R.S.F.S.R. to Georgia. Delegate to Polish Peace Negotiations |
| 1921 | Member, CC; delegate, CC to North Caucasus; member, Presidium of Caucasian Bureau of CP; Secretary, CC of Azerbaijan CP | | | |

## Kirov (*Continued*)

| | Party | Government | Other |
|---|---|---|---|
| 1926 | Secretary, N.W. Bureau of CC; First Secretary, Leningrad District Committee. Candidate, Politburo | | |
| 1930 | Member, Politburo | | |
| 1934 | Secretary, CC | | |

## Kossior

| | Party | Government | Other |
|---|---|---|---|
| 1907 | Joined party | | |
| 1914 | Party organizer in Kiev | | |
| 1917 | Member, Petrograd Committee | | |
| 1918 | Member, CC | | |
| 1919 | Secretary, CC of Ukraine | | |
| 1922–1925 | Secretary, Siberian Bureau of CC | | |
| 1923 | Candidate, Politburo | | |
| 1925–1928 | Secretary, CC | | |
| 1928 | Secretary, CC of Ukraine | 1928 Candidate, Presidium of CEC | |

## Kossior (Continued)

| | Party | | Government | Other |
|---|---|---|---|---|
| 1930 | Member, Politburo | | | |
| 1938 | Chief, CCC. Expelled from Politburo | 1938 | Vice-Chairman, Council of Commissars | |

## Krestinsky

| | Party | | Government | Other |
|---|---|---|---|---|
| 1903 | Joined party. Member, Ural and Ekaterinburg Regional Committee | | | |
| 1917–1921 | Member, CC | 1917 | Commissar of Justice | |
| | | 1918–1922 | Commissar of Finance | |
| 1919–1921 | Secretary, CC. Member, Politburo | 1921–1930 | Ambassador to Germany | |
| | | 1930–1936 | Member, CEC | |
| | | 1930–1938 | Vice-Commissar for Foreign Affairs | |

## Kuibyshev

| | Party | Government | Other |
|---|---|---|---|
| 1905 | Joined party | | |
| 1906 | Member of Omsk Committee | | |
| 1907 | Member of Tomsk Committee | | |

## Kuibyshev (Continued)

| | Party | | Government | | Other |
|---|---|---|---|---|---|
| 1917 | Chairman of Samara Committee | | | | |
| | | | | 1920 | Member, Presidium of All-Russian Trade Union Council; member, Presidium of large Soviet encyclopedia |
| 1921 | Candidate, CC | | | | |
| 1922 | Member, CC | | | | |
| 1922–1923 | Secretary, CC | | | | |
| 1923–1926 | Chairman, CCC | 1923–1926 | Commissar for Workers' and Peasants' Inspection | | |
| 1927 | Member, Politburo | 1926–1930 | Chairman, Supreme Council of National Economy | | |
| | | 1930 | Vice-Chairman, Council of People's Commissars | | |
| | | 1930–1934 | Chairman, State Planning Committee; member, Labor and Defense Council | | |

## Lenin

| | Party | | Government | Other |
|---|---|---|---|---|
| 1889 | Joined Marxist circle | | | |
| 1895 | Organized "Union for the Liberation of Working Class." Delegate of RSDLP to 2nd International | | | |
| 1912 | Member, CC | | | |
| 1917–1924 | Member, Politburo | 1917 | Chairman, Council of People's Commissars. Chairman, CEC | |
| 1919 | Organized Communist International | | | |

## Malenkov

| | Party | Government | Other |
|---|---|---|---|
| 1920 | Joined party | | |
| 1925–1930 | Worked for CC (probably as Stalin's secretary) | | |
| 1930–1934 | Organizational secretary, Moscow Committee of CP | | |
| 1934–1939 | Head, Personnel Department, CC of CP | | |

## Malenkov (Continued)

| | Party | | Government | | Other |
|---|---|---|---|---|---|
| 1939 | Member and Secretary of CC. Member, Orgburo | | | | |
| 1941 | Candidate, Politburo | 1941 | Member, Committee for State Defense; deputy to Supreme Soviet | | |
| | | | | 1943 | Member, Committee for Economic Rehabilitation of Liberated Areas |
| 1946 | Member, Politburo | 1946 | Vice-Premier | | |

## Mikoyan

| | Party | | Government | | Other |
|---|---|---|---|---|---|
| 1915 | Joined party | | | | |
| 1918–1919 | Head of Baku Committee | | | | |
| 1920–1922 | Secretary, Nizhni-Novgorod Gubernia Committee | | | | |
| 1922–1926 | Secretary, North Caucasian District Committee | | | | |
| 1923 | Member, CC | | | | |
| 1926 | Candidate, Politburo | 1926 | People's Commissar for Trade; member, Labor and Defense Council | | |

## Mikoyan (Continued)

| Party | | Government | | Other |
|---|---|---|---|---|
| | | 1930–1938 | People's Commissar for Supplies | |
| 1935 | Member, Politburo | 1935 | Member, CEC | |
| | | 1935–1939 | People's Commissar for Food Industry | |
| | | 1937 | Vice-Chairman, Council of People's Commissars; deputy, Supreme Soviet | |
| | | 1942 | Member, State Committee on Defense | |
| | | 1939–1949 | Minister for Foreign Trade | |

## Molotov

| Party | | Government | Other | |
|---|---|---|---|---|
| 1906 | Joined party | | | |
| | | | 1912 | Secretary, editorial board of *Pravda* |
| 1916 | Member, CC; member, Russian Bureau of CC | | | |

## Molotov (Continued)

| Party | | Government | | Other | |
|---|---|---|---|---|---|
| 1917 | Member, Petrograd Soviet EC. Member, Petrograd Military Revolutionary Committee | | | | |
| 1920 | Secretary, CC of Ukrainian CP | | | | |
| 1921 | Candidate, Politburo; secretary, CC. Member, Orgburo | | | | |
| 1925 | Member, Politburo | 1927 | Member, CEC | | |
| | | | | 1928–1934 | Member, Presidium of EC of CI |
| | | 1930–1941 | Chairman, Council of People's Commissars | | |
| | | 1935–1949 | Commissar for Foreign Affairs | | |
| | | 1941 | Deputy Chairman, State Committee for Defense. Vice-Chairman, Council of PC | | |

## Ordjonikidze

| Party | | Government | | Other |
|---|---|---|---|---|
| 1903 | Joined party | | | |
| 1912 | Member, CC | | | |
| 1917 | Member, CC; member, Petrograd Committee | 1917 | Special Commissar for Ukraine, Southern Russia, and North Caucasus | |
| 1920–1926 | Many jobs in Caucasus | | | |
| 1926–1930 | Chairman, CCC; candidate, Politburo | 1926–1930 | People's Commissar for Workers' and Peasants' Inspection | |
| 1930–1937 | Member, Politburo | 1930 | Chairman, Supreme Council of National Economy | |
| | | 1932–1936 | People's Commissar for Heavy Industry; member, CEC | |

## Rudzutak

| Party | | Government | | Other |
|---|---|---|---|---|
| 1905 | Joined party | | | |
| | | 1918 | Member, Presidium of Supreme Council of National Economy | 1918 | Member, Presidium of Textile Workers' Union |

## Rudzutak (Continued)

| | Party | | Government | | Other |
|---|---|---|---|---|---|
| 1920 | Member, CC | | | 1920 | Member of Presidium and Geneneral secretary, All-Russian CC of Trade Unions |
| | | | | 1921 | Member, Committee for Turkestan Affairs |
| 1923–1924 | Secretary, CC | | | 1923–1924 | Chairman, CEC of Railway and Waterway Workers |
| | | 1924–1930 | Commissar for Transport; Vice-Chairman, Labor and Defense Council | | |
| 1926 | Candidate, Politburo | 1926–1934 | People's Commissar for Workers' Inspection; Vice-Chairman, Council of People's Commissars | | |
| 1927–1931 | Member, Politburo | | | | |
| 1931–1934 | Head of CCC | | | | |
| 1934 | Candidate, Politburo | | | | |

## Rykov

| | Party | | Government | | Other |
|---|---|---|---|---|---|
| 1901 | Joined party | | | | |
| 1905 | Delegate, London Congress | | | | |

# Rykov (Continued)

| Party | | Government | | Other |
|---|---|---|---|---|
| 1906 | Member, CC | | | |
| | | 1917 | Commissar of Interior | |
| | | 1918 | Chairman, Supreme Council of National Economy | |
| 1919–1929 | Member, Politburo | | | |
| | | 1924–1929 | Chairman, Council of People's Commissars of U.S.S.R. and R.S.F.S.R.; member, Presidium of CEC | |
| 1929 | Expelled from party | | | |
| 1931 | Rejoined | 1931–1937 | People's Commissar of Communications | |
| 1937 | Expelled | | | |

# Stalin

| Party | | Government | | Other |
|---|---|---|---|---|
| 1899 | Joined party | | | |
| 1900 | Leader of Tiflis Committee | | | |
| 1905 | Delegate to Tammerfors Conference | | | |
| 1907 | London Congress | | | |
| 1912 | Member, CC | | | |

## Stalin (Continued)

| | Party | | Government | Other |
|---|---|---|---|---|
| 1917 | Member, Politburo | 1917–1923 | People's Commissar for Nationalities | |
| | | 1919–1922 | People's Commissar for Workers' and Peasants' Inspection | |
| 1922 | Secretary-General, CP | 1920–1923 | Member, Revolutionary Council | |
| | | 1924 | Member, Presidium of CEC | |
| | | 1941 | Chairman, Council of Ministers; Minister for National Defense; First Delegate to Supreme Soviet | |
| | | 1941–1946 | Commander-in-Chief; chairman, State Committee for Defense | |

## Sverdlov

| | Party | Government | Other |
|---|---|---|---|
| 1902 | Joined party. Established Bolshevik organization in Nizhni-Novgorod | | |

## Sverdlov (Continued)

| | Party | | Government | | Other |
|---|---|---|---|---|---|
| 1906 | Organized in Urals | | | | |
| 1909 | Organized Moscow organization | | | | |
| 1913 | Nominated to CC | | | | |
| 1917 | Member, CC and Politburo; worked in Petersburg Secretariat of CC | 1917 | Chairman, of CEC | | |

## Tomsky

| | Party | | Government | | Other |
|---|---|---|---|---|---|
| 1904 | Joined party | | | | |
| 1906 | Member, Petersburg Committee | | | | |
| 1907 | Delegate, London Congress. Member, CC | | | | |
| 1909 | Sent by CC to Moscow | | | | (Before revolution) Trade-union organizer |
| 1917 | Member, Petrograd EC | | | 1917 | Chairman, Moscow Council of Trade Unions |
| 1919 | Member, Politburo until 1929 | | | 1918–1928 | Chairman, All-Russian CC of Trade Unions |

## Tomsky (Continued)

| Party | Government | | Other | |
|---|---|---|---|---|
| | | 1920 | | Secretary-General, Trade-Union International |
| | 1929 | Member, Supreme Council of National Economy; member, Presidium of CEC | 1921 | Chairman, Committee on Turkestan Affairs |
| | 1935 | Head of State Publishing House | | |

## Trotsky

| Party | | Government | | Other | |
|---|---|---|---|---|---|
| 1902 | Joined party | | | | |
| 1904–1917 | Led his own faction | | | | |
| 1905 | Member and later chairman, Petersburg Soviet | | | | |
| 1917 | Joined party. Member, CC | 1917 | Chairman, Soviet of Workers' Deputies; People's Commissar for Foreign Affairs | 1918 | Concluded Peace of Brest-Litovsk with Germany |
| 1917–1926 | Member, Politburo | 1918–1924 | Commissar of War; chairman, Revolutionary War Council | | |

## Trotsky (Continued)

| Party | Government | Other |
|---|---|---|
| | 1920–1921 Commissar for Transport | |
| | 1925 Head, Control Committee for Concessions, and Committee for Development of Electric Power | |
| 1927 Expelled from party | | |

## Voroshilov

| Party | Government | Other |
|---|---|---|
| 1903 Joined party | | |
| 1906 Delegate, Fourth Party Congress | | |
| 1907 South Russian Party Conference in Kiev; member of Baku Committee | | |
| 1917 Chairman of Lugansk town Duma | 1917 Commissar of Petrograd Soviet; organized Cheka | |
| | 1918 Commissar for Foreign Affairs of Ukraine | |
| 1919 Member, CC of Ukraine | | |

## Voroshilov (Continued)

| Party | | Government | | Other | |
|---|---|---|---|---|---|
| 1921 | Member, CC | 1921 | Member, CEC of R.F.S.F.R. and U.S.S.R. | | |
| 1921–1924 | Member, South-eastern Bureau of CC | | | | |
| | | 1924–1941 | Commissar for War and Navy | | |
| 1925 | Member, Politburo | 1940 | Assistant chairman, Council of People's Commis-sars and chairman of its Defense Commit-tee; mem-ber, Su-preme Soviet | | |
| | | 1941 | Member, State Committee for Defense | 1945 | Head of Al-lied Con-trol Com-mission for Hungary |

## Voznesensky

| Party | | Government | | Other | |
|---|---|---|---|---|---|
| 1919 | Joined party | | | | |
| 1919–1921 | Leader of Young Commu-nist League in Chernskii County | | | | |
| 1924 | For several years party official in Donets region | | | | |

## Voznesensky (Continued)

| | Party | | Government | Other |
|---|---|---|---|---|
| | | 1934 | Member, mission of Soviet Control | |
| 1935 | Vice-chairman, Leningrad | | | |
| | | 1938 | Chairman, State Planning Commission; member, Executive Bureau Commission of Soviet Control | |
| 1939 | Member, CC | 1939 | Vice-chairman, Council of People's Commissars | |
| 1941 | Candidate, Politburo | 1941 | Vice-Premier for Economic Affairs | |
| | | 1942 | Member, State Committee for Defense | |
| 1947 | Member, Politburo | | | |
| 1949 | Dropped from Politburo | | | |

## Zhdanov

| | Party | Government | Other |
|---|---|---|---|
| 1915 | Joined party | | |
| 1917 | Head of Bolshevik organization in Shadrinsk | | |

## Zhdanov *(Continued)*

| Party | | Government | Other | |
|---|---|---|---|---|
| 1918–1922 | Chairman, Provincial EC in Tver | | | |
| 1924–1934 | Secretary, Nizhni-Novgorod Gubernia Committee and Gorki Territorial Committee | | | |
| 1924 | Member, CC | Member, CEC of R.S.F.S.R. and of U.S.S.R.; deputy, Supreme Soviet; member, Presidium of Supreme Soviet; chairman, Committee on Foreign Affairs; chairman, Supreme Soviet of R.S.F.S.R. | | |
| 1934–1940 | Secretary, CC; head of party in Leningrad | | To 1943 | Member, EC of CI |
| 1935 | Candidate, Politburo | | 1944 | Head, Control Commission in Finland; member, Soviet Commission on Nazi Crimes |
| 1939–1948 | Member, Politburo | | | |

## Zinoviev

| Party | | Government | Other | |
|---|---|---|---|---|
| 1901 | Joined party | | | |
| 1907 | London Congress. Elected to CC | | | |
| 1917 | President, Petersburg Soviet. Resigned from and rejoined CC | | 1919–1926 | Chairman, EC of CI |

## Zinoviev (Continued)

| Party | Government | Other |
|---|---|---|
| 1923    Member, Politburo | | |
| 1926    Expelled from Politburo | | |
| 1927    Expelled from party | | |
| 1928    Readmitted | | |
| 1935    Tried and convicted; sentenced to ten years in jail | | |
| 1936    Tried again and shot | | |

Additional notes, 1965, on various leaders:

### Andreyev

| | |
|---|---|
| 1946–1953 | Deputy chairman and acting chairman, Council of Ministers; chairman, Farm Council |
| 1954 | Elected member of Presidium of Supreme Soviet |
| 1958 | Re-elected to same position |
| 1957–? | Chairman, Sino-Soviet Friendship Society |

### Beria

L. P. Beria is the second former member of the Politburo to have died since 1951. Beria, who had emerged as one of the most powerful figures after Stalin's death, was executed and shot a little more than three months later.

At the occasion of Stalin's funeral, Khrushchev had given the main oration. At his invitation, only three other members of the Politburo had spoken. These three were Malenkov, Beria, and Molotov. In the immediate period following Stalin's death, this triumvirate emerged as the most powerful group in the Soviet Union.

Before Stalin's death, Beria's star had been steadily declining. In April of 1952, Beria was selected by Stalin to be in charge of a purge in Georgia and the other Caucasian republics. Since Beria was a Georgian himself and had been considered to be in charge of Caucasus affairs inside the Politburo, this was hardly a flattering assignment. In early 1953, when the so-called "doctors' plot" burst on the scene, there were many indications in the Soviet press that Beria and his secret police were being blamed for laxity. When the Politburo was dissolved at the Nineteenth Party Congress and reconstituted as the Presidium, Beria continued to hold his membership. Soon thereafter, however, signs of his decline began to reappear. On November 7, 1952, the anniversary of the October Revolution, Beria's portrait in Red Square for the first time was preceded by that of Voroshilov and Bulganin. His protégé Abakumov, who had headed the Ministry of State Security, was removed, and it became apparent that Beria's control of the secret police was slipping. At this point, probably fortunately for Beria, Stalin died.

After the emergence of Malenkov, Beria, and Molotov, these three proceeded to divide up the most important state and party offices. Beria nominated Malenkov for the post of Premier and First Secretary. Malenkov, in turn, nominated Beria to become First Deputy Prime Minister. Molotov became Second First Deputy Prime Minister and Minister of Foreign Affairs. Beria in his new post immediately took control of the State Security Forces but was able to hold this control only for about three months.

On June 29, 1953, he was arrested. Within twenty-four hours after his arrest and "trial," he was executed. His picture and the article about his career were removed from the *Great Soviet Encyclopedia*, and after having been accused of being an imperialist agent, he ceased to exist.

In 1956, talking to a French senator, Khrushchev gave an account of Beria's arrest, "trial," and execution, in which he states that soon after Stalin's death it became apparent that Beria was preparing a conspiracy against the Presidium. A special session of the Presidium was called, to which, of course, the unsuspecting Beria was also invited. Right there he was accused and cross-examined for about four hours. After that, the other members of the Presidium left the room and deliberated among themselves about Beria's fate. All of them, according to Khrushchev, were convinced of Beria's guilt, but they were also in agreement that not enough judicial evidence was available for a trial. The unanimous decision was to shoot him immediately. This decision was carried out on the spot.

SOURCES: Bertram Wolfe, *Khrushchev and Stalin's Ghost* (New York: Frederick A. Praeger, 1956); G. D. Embree, *The Soviet Union Between the 19th and the 20th Party Congresses 1952–56* (The Hague: Martinus Nijhoff, 1959); Merle Fainsod, *How Russia Is Ruled* (Cambridge, Mass.: Harvard University Press, 1954).

### Kaganovich

1953–1957  Member of Presidium of Central Committee
1953–1957  Deputy chairman of Council of Ministers

1955–1956    Chairman, Advisory Committee to Council of Ministers on Labor Problems
1956–1957    Minister for Building Materials and Industry in the Urals
1957         Loses his posts as member of the hostile opposition

According to some reports, Kaganovich lives on a pension in Moscow. According to other reports, he manages a factory in Magnitogorsk.

## Khrushchev

1949–1953    Secretary of Central Committee and First Secretary of Moscow Regional Committee
1952–        Member of Presidium of Central Committee
1953–        First Secretary of Central Committee
1958–1964    Chairman, Council of Ministers
1964         Relieved of his post as chairman of the Council of Ministers and as First Secretary of the Central Committee. It is unclear what posts, if any, he still occupies.

## Malenkov

1953         Chairman of the Council of Ministers
1953–1957    Member of Presidium of Central Committee
1955         Resigns his post as chairman of the Council of Ministers
1955–1957    Deputy chairman of the Council of Ministers and Minister for Hydro-electric Power
1957         As a member of the "opposition" loses his posts in the Presidium and the Central Committee
1957–        Chief of a hydroelectric plant at Ust Kamenogorsk in the Kazakh, U.S.S.R.

## Mikoyan

1952–1953    Member of Presidium of Central Committee
1942–1955    Member of State Committee on Defense
1953–1955    Minister of Commerce
1953–        Minister for Internal and External Trade
1955–1964    First Deputy Chairman of Council of Ministers
1956–        Member of Presidium of Central Committee
1964–        Chairman of Presidium of Supreme Soviet

## Molotov

1952–1956    Minister for Foreign Affairs
1952–1957    Member of Presidium of Central Committee; First Deputy Chairman, Council of Ministers
1956–1957    Minister for State Control
1957         As a member of the "opposition" loses all posts
1957–1960    Ambassador to the People's Republic of Mongolia
1960–1961    Permanent representative of the U.S.S.R. at the International Atomic Energy Agency in Vienna, Austria

## Stalin

Stalin died of a brain hemorrhage on March 5, 1953. Since at this time he was seventy-four years old, the most natural assumption is, of course, that his death was indeed due to natural causes. As in almost all cases of the death of Politburo members there are the inevitable rumors of violent death, but actually there is no real evidence to substantiate these rumors.

One of the several versions of Stalin's death is the one reported in the International Edition of the *New York Times* of June 8, 1957. This version, which is attributed to Ponomarenko, states that Stalin suffered his fatal stroke at a Presidium meeting in late February 1953, after Voroshilov had violently opposed his plan to deport all Soviet Jews to Birobidzhan, the autonomous Jewish area in Siberia. From there on, until his death in March, Stalin was reported to have remained virtually unconscious.

Perhaps the most important event between 1951 and the time of Stalin's death was the long-awaited Nineteenth Party Congress, which finally took place in October 1952. It had been expected by some that the question of Stalin's successor would be settled at this congress. Those expectations remained unfulfilled, although Malenkov, who was thought to be one of the main contenders, gave the major speech at the congress.

Of particular interest to this study is the fact that at the Nineteenth Party Congress the Politburo itself was dissolved and replaced by a rather amorphous Presidium of twenty-five members and eleven candidates. The new Presidium contained all the old Politburo members, with the exception of Andreyev, who had been dropped earlier. Added were the members of the Secretariat who had not been members of the Politburo before and also thirteen deputy chairmen of the U.S.S.R. Council of Ministers. Other members of the new Presidium included the head of the trade unions, the former First Secretary of the Komsomols, two representatives from the Ukraine, the First Secretary of the Byelo-Russian Party, some regional party leaders, and lesser figures. The result was a complete merging of party and state administration.

Stalin's last years were characterized by growing terror and anti-Semitism within the Soviet Union. Most of the information concerning these events has been revealed in Khrushchev's so-called "secret speech" before the Twentieth Party Congress in February 1956.

### Voroshilov

1953–1960   Chairman of Presidium of Supreme Soviet
1960        Asks to be relieved of his post for reasons of health and age; continues as a member of the Presidium of the Supreme Soviet
1960        On his retirement Khrushchev proposes that Voroshilov be given the title of "Hero of Socialist Labor," the Order of Lenin, and the Hammer and Sickle Medal.

SOURCES: *Portraits der UdSSR Prominenz* (Munich: Institut zur Erforschung der UdSSR, 1960); *The International Who's Who 1964–65* (London: London Europa Publications Ltd., 1964).

# Appendix D
## Length of Service

APPENDIX E

ABBREVIATIONS USED IN TEXT

| | |
|---|---|
| CC | Central Committee (of the Communist Party) |
| CCC | Central Control Commission |
| CEC | Central Executive Committee |
| CI | Communist International |
| CP | Communist Party |
| EC | Executive Council |
| MGB | Ministry of State Security |
| MVD | Ministry of Internal Affairs |
| NKVD | People's Commissariat for Internal Affairs |
| OGPU | Unified State Political Administration |
| PC | People's Commissar |
| RSDLP | Russian Social Democratic Labor Party |
| R.S.F.S.R. | Russian Socialist Federated Soviet Republic |
| SD | Social Democrats |
| S.S.R. | Soviet Socialist Republic |
| U.S.S.R. | Union of Soviet Socialist Republics |

# BIBLIOGRAPHY

*Encyclopedias and Biographical Dictionaries*

*Biographical Encyclopedia of the World.* New York, 1946.
*Bolshaia Sovetskaia Entsiklopediia.* Moscow, 1932–1940.
*International Who's Who.* London, 1937 and 1944–1945.
*Malaia Sovetskaia Entsiklopediia.* Moscow, 1935.
*Politicheskii Slovar.* Moscow, 1940.
*Soviet Union Yearbook,* 1930. London, 1930.

*Official Documents and Reports*

People's Commissariat of Justice of the U.S.S.R., *Report of Court Proceedings in the Case of the Anti-Soviet Trotskyite Center.* Moscow, 1937.

———. *Report of Court Proceedings in the Case of the Anti-Soviet Bloc of Rights and Trotskyites.* Moscow, 1938.

*Prezidium Revvoensoveta S.S.S.R. Biografii t.t. M.V. Frunze, I.S. Unshlikhta, A.S. Bubnova, K.E. Voroshilova, S.S. Kameneva.* Moscow: Gos. izd-vo, 1925.

VKP (b) *XI s"ezd Rossiiskoi Kommunisticheskoi partii* (b) *Stenograficheskii ochet po biulleteniam s"ezda.* Kiev: Gos. izd-vo, 1922.

———. *Deviatyi s"ezd Rossiiskoi Kommunisticheskoi partii. Stenograficheskii otchet (29 marta–4 aprelia 1920 g.).* Moscow: Gos. izd-vo, 1920.

*Vsesoiuznaia Kommunisticheskaia Partiia (b) v rezoliutsiiakh i resheniiakh s"ezdov, konferentsii i plenumov TsK (1898–1932)*, Part I, *1898–1924*, (4th ed.; Moscow, MEL Institute publication, 1932), p. 315.

## Books and Articles

Barmine, Alexander. *Memoirs of a Soviet Diplomat*. London: L. Dickson Ltd., 1938.

Batsell, Walter R. *Soviet Rule in Russia*. New York: The Macmillan Company, 1929.

Chamberlain, W. H. *Russia's Iron Age*. Boston: Little, Brown & Company, 1934.

Citrine, Sir Walter. *I Search for Truth in Russia*. London: G. Routledge & Sons, Ltd., 1936.

Cressey, George B. *The Basis of Soviet Strength*. New York: McGraw-Hill Book Company, Inc., 1945.

Deutscher, I. *Stalin: A Political Biography*. New York: Oxford University Press, 1949.

Duranty, Walter. *Stalin and Co.* New York: W. Sloane Associates, 1949.

Essad, bey. *Stalin: The Career of a Fanatic*. New York: The Viking Press, 1932.

Eudin, Xenia; Fisher, Helen D.; and Fisher, Harold H. *The Life of a Chemist: Memoirs of V. N. Ipatieff*. Stanford, Calif.: Stanford University Press, 1946.

Kohn-Bramstedt, Ernst. *Dictatorship and Political Police: The Technique of Control by Fear*. London: Kegan, Paul, 1945.

Kravchenko, V. *I Chose Freedom*. New York: Charles Scribner's Sons, 1946.

Lasswell, Harold D. *The Analysis of Political Behavior*. New York: Oxford University Press, 1949.

Lenin, V. I. *Sochineniia*. 3 izd. Moscow: Gos. izd-vo polit. lit-ry, 1926–1937.

Michels, Robert. *Political Parties*. Glencoe, Ill.: The Free Press, 1949.

Neumann, Sigmund. *Permanent Revolution*. New York: Harper & Brothers, 1942.

————. "The International Civil War," *World Politics*, I (1949), pp. 341 ff.

Pierre, André, "Spekulationen um Andrejew," *Ost Probleme* (Information Services Division, H.I.C.O.G.), III, No. 18 (May 1951), pp. 567–568.

Preliminary Commission of Inquiry. *The Case of Leon Trotsky*. Coyoacán, Mexico, 1937.

Reed, John. *Ten Days That Shook the World.* New York: Boni & Liveright, 1919.

Schuman, F. L. *Soviet Politics at Home and Abroad.* New York: Alfred A. Knopf, 1946.

Shchadenko, E. (ed.). *Na Sluzhbe proletarskoi revoluitsii.* Moscow: Gos. voennoe izd-vo, 1931.

Shub, David. *Lenin.* New York: Doubleday & Company, Inc., 1948.

Snow, Edgar. *The Pattern of Soviet Power.* New York: Random House, Inc., 1945.

Souvarine, Boris. *Stalin: A Critical Survey of Bolshevism.* New York: Longmans, Green and Co., Inc., 1939.

Towster, Julian. *Political Power in the U.S.S.R., 1917–1947.* New York: Oxford University Press, 1948.

Trotsky, L. *My Life.* New York: Charles Scribner's Sons, 1930.

Voline, Boris. *12 Militants Russes.* Paris: Librairie de l'Humanité, 1925.

Williams, A. R. *The Soviets.* New York: Harcourt, Brace and Company, 1937.

Wolfe, Bertram D. *Three Who Made a Revolution.* New York: Dial Press, 1948.

Yaroslavsky, E. *Istoriia VKP (b).* Moscow: izd-vo, 1933.

―――. *Landmarks in the Life of Stalin.* Moscow: Foreign Languages Publishing House, 1940.

Ypsilon (pseud. of Johann Rindl and Julian Gumperz). *Pattern for World Revolution.* New York: Ziff-Davis Publishing Co., 1947.

## CHAPTER FOUR

HAROLD D. LASSWELL with RENZO SERENO

# The Fascists:
# The Changing Italian Elite*

STUDY of the governmental and party leaders of prewar Fascist Italy
may contribute to our understanding of the Fascist state, whether we
are concerned with public law, comparative government, or comparative politics. The application of the rules of law by any public law
agency is affected by the characteristics of those who constitute the
agency. Whatever affects the social position or the relative strength of
the groups with which an agency is affiliated affects the relative
strength of the agency. Hence it is important to ascertain the class,
skill, personality, and attitude characteristics of officials in relation to
the composition of the community as a whole.

The present analysis therefore begins by classifying the agencies of
the Fascist Italian state into those which, when examined from the
viewpoint of public law, are "rising" and those which are "falling" (or
at all events not rising). We shall eliminate from consideration those
agencies consisting of a single individual, like the king and the chief of
the government. Among the pre-Fascist organs of government, two
have risen: the cabinet and the prefects. The cabinet has attained
more freedom from the control of Parliament, and widened its legislative scope. The prefects have more authority, including direct control
over local government. The following organs of pre-Fascist Italy have
fallen (or not risen): Senate, Chamber, ministers of state, and *podestà*.

* Originally published in the *American Political Science Review*, XXXI, (October 1937), pp. 914–929. Reprinted with permission of the authors and publisher.
Minor editorial changes have been made.

All of the new agencies introduced by the Fascists are obviously "rising" (when compared with pre-Fascist institutions).[1]

# I

Much of the material assembled in this study of governmental and party elites[2] is on public record. The communiqués of the *Ufficio Stampa* (later the Under-Ministry and finally Ministry for the Press and Propaganda) are usually short and matter-of-fact. The editorial comment that follows a biography often yields more information than the biography, because the official news stresses the relationship between the individual and his new job, and the editorial eulogy often provides more intimate details. The Italian *Who's Who* (*Chi è? Dizionario degli Italiani d'oggi*) is devoted more to literary than to political figures. A special dictionary concerned wholly with politicians (*La Nazione Operante*, Edoardo Savinio, Milan, 1934) contains three thousand biographies and is indispensable for the minor hierarchies. Supplementary details have been gleaned from local publications and interviews.

Critical comparison of sources has been relied upon to reduce the distortions arising from tendencies to reconstruct biography to fit the values of the new order of things. How far this revision may go is shown by some sporadic cases of politicians who moved their birthplace closer to the cradle of fascism and copied the encomiums appropriate to Romagna. No biography of Mussolini forgets to play on the Romagna and the Romagnolo, for popular tradition has it that Romagna is the country of sunshine, wheat, and wine, and the Romagnoli are bloody, fierce, and picturesque.[3]

Table 1 shows the number of cases reported in this investigation, and the data relating to class and skill. The number of cases tabulated does not necessarily correspond to the number of offices, since no person has been counted twice. He has been assigned to his most important office. *Il Duce* has not been included. In order to emphasize the more active elements in Parliament, the whole membership has not been studied. The 190 senators who have taken the most active part in

[1] For basic distinctions, reference may be made to Santi Romano, *Corso di Diritto amministrativo* (Milan, 1931), and Oreste Ranelletti, *Elementi di Diritto Pubblico Italiano* (Milan, 1933).

[2] The term "elite" is used in no invidious or romantic sense. It designates those who exercise the most influence in a given situation in which influence is appraised, for purposes of analysis, in a determinate way.

[3] A representative biography in this vein is *L'Uomo Nuovo*, by Antonio Beltramelli (Milan, 1923).

## Table 1
### CLASS ANALYSIS

| | Number of Cases | Proletariat | | Lesser Bourgeoisie | Plutocracy | Aristocracy |
|---|---|---|---|---|---|---|
| **Rising Agencies:** | | | | | | |
| Cabinet | 24 | O | 3 | 12 | 7 | 2 |
| | | P | 0 | 0 | 20 | 4 |
| Grand Council | 9 | O | 0 | 7 | 1 | 1 |
| | | P | 0 | 0 | 7 | 2 |
| Party Executive Committee | 7 | O | 0 | 6 | 0 | 1 |
| | | P | 0 | 2 | 4 | 1 |
| Provincial Party Secretaries | 66 | O | 3 | 50 | 9 | 4 |
| | | P | 0 | 20 | 42 | 4 |
| Chief Executives National Unions and Associations | 12 | O | 0 | 10 | 1 | 1 |
| | | P | 0 | 0 | 11 | 1 |
| Provincial Secretaries Union Agricultural Workers | 53 | O | 0 | 53 | 0 | 0 |
| | | P | 0 | 53 | 0 | 0 |
| Provincial Secretaries Union Industrial Workers | 51 | O | 0 | 51 | 0 | 0 |
| | | P | 0 | 46 | 5 | 0 |
| Provincial Secretaries Union Commercial Workers | 43 | O | 4 | 39 | 0 | 0 |
| | | P | 0 | 43 | 0 | 0 |
| Provincial Secretaries Employers' Associations | 43 | O | 0 | 26 | 12 | 5 |
| | | P | 0 | 4 | 34 | 5 |
| **Declining Agencies:** | | | | | | |
| Senate | 190 | O | 3 | 87 | 54 | 46 |
| | | P | 0 | 60 | 78 | 52 |
| Chamber | 187 | O | 16 | 93 | 50 | 28 |
| | | P | 0 | 95 | 64 | 28 |
| Ministers of State | 16 | O | 0 | 6 | 3 | 7 |
| | | P | 0 | 1 | 7 | 8 |
| Podestà | 38 | O | 3 | 5 | 18 | 12 |
| | | P | 0 | 3 | 23 | 12 |

O = origin.          P = present status.

the senatorial sessions since 1929 are included, and the 187 deputies ratified in the plebiscites of 1929 and 1934 are reported. In general, the data depict the situation prior to the Ethiopian War.

For purposes of this investigation, four terms have been used to designate class origins and present status. Aristocracy includes persons from families with titles of nobility and persons who have acquired titles in their own right (Fascist and pre-Fascist). Plutocracy covers persons enjoying high incomes. When the individual is among the wealthy few in his region, he is included among the plutocracy, although he may not qualify from the standpoint of the nation as a whole. About 15 per cent of those called plutocratic in this list would be excluded if we were to classify them according to the national income pyramid. The lesser bourgeoisie takes in everyone who falls short of inclusion in the plutocracy, but who stands outside the proletariat. Skilled workers, professional persons of middle or low income, independent businessmen, and executives of middle or low income are thus considered lesser bourgeoisie. The proletariat includes unskilled workers in industry and agriculture. At least 95 per cent of the aristocracy are sufficiently wealthy to be classified with the plutocracy, although double classification is not used in this report.

Table 2 exhibits the data about skills, which are defined as teachable and learnable operations. Skills are classified into those acquired and exercised before entry into politics, skills bringing the individual into politics, and present skills. In each of these subcategories, the principal skill is recorded, and other skills are omitted. Skill in ceremony is perhaps the most novel. It includes persons who are masters of etiquette, e.g., aristocrats or retired army officers and high officials. It also includes individuals who have high symbolic value because they stand for some traditional distinction with which the new regime desires to associate itself (like descendants of illustrious personages). A third and smaller subcategory refers to individuals who, having attained eminence (like a famous scientist or engineer), are attached to some official agency as a symbolic gesture. Bargaining is a distinctive skill of those engaged in business; organizing refers to the coordination of non-profit-making activities, public or private. Propaganda specialists include newspaper men, personnel of information offices, and teachers of controversial subjects. The term "attorneys" includes bar and bench.

## II

The outstanding contrast between rising and declining agencies is the lesser bourgeois origin of the personnel of the rising agencies. Three fourths of the provincial party secretaries, and an overwhelming proportion of all other Fascist Party agencies, come from the lesser bourgeoisie. Half the cabinet is from this social formation. Less than a seventh of the *podestà*, a declining agency, spring from the lesser bourgeoisie, and only a little over a third of the ministers of state. Half of the Senate and Chamber cases derive from this class.

## Table 2
### SKILL ANALYSIS

| | | 1 | 2 | 3 | 4 | 5 | 6 | 7 | 8 | 9 | 10 | 11 |
|---|---|---|---|---|---|---|---|---|---|---|---|---|
| **Rising Agencies:** | | | | | | | | | | | | |
| Cabinet | O | 2 | 1 | — | — | 4 | 2 | 1 | 5 | 4 | 5 | — |
| | E | — | 1 | — | — | 7 | 2 | — | 5 | 4 | 5 | — |
| | P | — | — | — | — | 3 | 2 | 2 | 8 | 4 | 5 | — |
| Grand Council | O | 1 | 1 | — | — | — | — | — | — | 2 | 3 | 2 |
| | E | — | — | — | — | 2 | 1 | — | 3 | 2 | 2 | — |
| | P | — | — | — | — | — | 1 | 1 | 3 | 2 | 2 | — |
| Party Executive | O | 1 | 1 | — | 1 | — | — | — | 1 | 1 | 2 | — |
| | E | — | — | — | — | — | — | 1 | 3 | 1 | 2 | — |
| | P | — | — | — | — | — | — | 1 | 3 | 1 | 2 | — |
| Provincial Party | O | 1 | 3 | 4 | 4 | — | 4 | 1 | 12 | 10 | 13 | 13 |
| Secretaries | E | — | 3 | 2 | 2 | 29 | 4 | — | 12 | 8 | 6 | — |
| | P | (all exercise 5, 8, 9) | | | — | — | — | — | — | — | — | — |
| Chief Executives Na- | O | 1 | — | 1 | — | — | — | 3 | 2 | 3 | 2 | — |
| tional Unions and | E | — | — | — | — | — | — | 3 | 4 | 3 | 2 | — |
| Associations | P | (all exercise 7, 8) | | | — | — | — | — | — | — | — | — |
| Provincial Secretaries | O | — | — | 4 | — | 2 | — | 24 | — | — | 5 | 18 |
| Agricultural | E | — | — | — | — | 7 | — | — | 37 | 8 | 5 | — |
| Workers | P | (all exercise 7, 8, 9) | | | — | — | — | — | — | — | — | — |
| Provincial Secretaries | O | — | 2 | 1 | — | 1 | — | — | 26 | 7 | 14 | — |
| Industrial | E | — | — | 1 | — | 8 | — | — | 37 | — | 5 | — |
| Workers | P | (all exercise 7, 8, 9) | | | — | — | — | — | — | — | — | — |
| Provincial Secretaries | O | 6 | — | — | — | 3 | — | 13 | 2 | 2 | 5 | 12 |
| Commercial | E | — | — | — | — | 7 | — | — | 31 | — | 5 | — |
| Workers | P | (all exercise 7, 8, 9) | | | — | — | — | — | — | — | — | — |
| Provincial Secretaries | O | — | 4 | 3 | — | 2 | — | 19 | — | 5 | 10 | — |
| Employers' | E | — | — | — | — | 2 | 2 | 19 | 7 | 3 | 10 | — |
| Associations | P | (all exercise 7, 8, 10) | | | — | — | — | — | — | — | — | — |
| **Declining Agencies:** | | | | | | | | | | | | |
| Senate | O | — | 8 | 4 | 10 | 20 | 32 | 10 | 15 | 18 | 73 | — |
| | E | (Same) | | — | — | — | — | — | — | — | — | — |
| | P | (Same) | | — | — | — | — | — | — | — | — | — |
| Chamber | O | (Missing) | | — | — | — | — | — | — | — | — | — |
| | E | 12 | 17 | 2 | 8 | 27 | 20 | 19 | 18 | 23 | 41 | — |
| | P | (Same) | | — | — | — | — | — | — | — | — | — |
| Ministers of State | O | — | 1 | — | — | 3 | 7 | — | 1 | 9 | 3 | — |
| | E | — | — | — | — | 3 | 7 | — | 1 | 2 | 3 | — |
| | P | (Same) | | — | — | — | — | — | — | — | — | — |
| Podestà | O | — | 3 | 1 | 2 | 5 | 14 | 3 | 3 | 1 | 6 | — |
| | E | (Same) | | — | — | — | — | — | — | — | — | — |
| | P | (Same) | | — | — | — | — | — | — | — | — | — |

O = original skill.
E = skill by which entry was made into politics.
P = present skill.
1 = manual and semiskill.
2 = engineering.
3 = physical science.
4 = medicine.

5 = violence.
6 = ceremony.
7 = bargaining.
8 = organizing.
9 = propaganda.
10 = attorneys.
11 = no skill.

There is evidence of a slight recovery of aristocracy under Fascism. Table 3 gives the percentage of deputies in the Chamber who were aristocrats.

### Table 3
#### ARISTOCRATS IN THE CHAMBER OF DEPUTIES*

| Year | Percentage | Year | Percentage |
|------|-----------|------|-----------|
| 1861 | 37.6 | 1919 | 5.7 |
| 1904 | 19.5 | 1921 | 5.4 |
| 1909 | 18.1 | 1924 | 7.5† |
| 1913 | 15.3 | 1929 | 9.0‡ |

* Ubaldo Baldi-Papini, "Le condizioni presenti della Nobiltà italiana," *La Nobiltà della Stirpe*, II, Vol. 1 (1932), p. 141.
† First election after the March on Rome.
‡ First plebiscite.

Fifteen per cent of our sample of the Chamber elected in the plebiscite of 1934 are aristocrats. The new regime has conferred titles of nobility sparingly, although somewhat more freely than under the Liberal order. Biographers carefully point out (particularly when the aristocracy is old or the title ranks high) that the subject is a nobleman who, "instead of . . ." pursuing a life of leisure and sport, has devoted himself to public service.

Leaders of proletarian origin are sporadically found, which continues the situation under the pre-Fascist regimes.[4] The extent to which the lesser bourgeoisie contributes to the present plutocracy exhibits the opportunities for climbing which have been afforded by the rising agencies.

To choose, almost at random, typical careers of those who have risen from the lesser bourgeoisie to the new plutocracy:

Renato Ricci, born in 1896 in Carrara; war volunteer; member of Fascist Party since 1919; organized a local of the party and rose to be Vice-Secretary of the national party; initiator and organizer of the Fascist youth movement; leader of governmentalized sport activities; became Under-Secretary of Education, thus controlling physical education all over Italy; member of the cabinet.

Rino Parenti, born in 1895, in Milan; noncommissioned officer during the war; became Fascist in 1919, participating in local squadrist action; constantly held local party jobs; federal secretary for Milan.

[4] Roberto Michels, *Storia critica del movimento socialista italiano* (Florence, 1921), Ch. 6.

Cases typical of other careers:

Ugo Cavallero comes from a very modest family and was made a count in 1928; born in 1880 in Casale, province of Asti; entered military academy and fought during the war; in 1918, became General; after war, became director of the Ansaldo of Genoa, an iron and steel concern manufacturing armaments; appointed Senator in 1926, and then called to the Ministry of War. When in 1928 he left the ministry, he was named count.

Pompeo Cattaneo, born in 1885 into a wealthy family of Pavia; decorated with a war cross; joined party in 1921, and remained in local politics; cheese manufacturer and secretary of the provincial employers' association for commerce.

Marquis Mario Laureati, born in Ascoli-Piceno in 1867, of the most outstanding noble family of the province; entered military school and fought in the first Ethiopian, Turkish, and First World Wars, retiring as General; joined party in 1921; became secretary of employers' association for agriculture.

Edmondo Rossoni, born in 1882 in Ferrara into proletarian family; emigrated to United States, where he worked as a track laborer for railroads in Pittsburgh, Chicago, and New York; prominent in the radical labor movement among Italians in America, he later became an exponent of socialism with nationalistic coloring; organized the labor unions on a national scale under the Fascist regime; an exponent of the syndicalist versus the corporative tendencies; was the leader of the labor unions and publisher of *Lavoro Fascista;* later Under-Secretary of the Interior and then Secretary of Agriculture; draws salaries from the *Banca del Lavoro,* from several social insurance institutions, and from the sea salt corporation of Italian Somaliland.

### III

Possibly the outstanding revelation of the skill analysis is the relatively narrow recruiting base of the rising agencies. The personnel either has no original skill or wields a skill very closely connected with the functions performed in the party or governmental hierarchy. The older agencies, in addition to skill in organization, are recruited from a wider variety of specialties. In a sense, the new personnel made their own jobs through the organization of the party and the seizure of governmental authority. The new agencies are thus staffed by a highly specialized governing group.

Conspicuous, of course, is the importance of informal violence as a means of entering politics. Observe, for a striking instance, the provincial party secretaries, twenty-nine of whom particularly distinguished themselves in the squadrist phase of Fascism. Most of these had served in the First World War, 1915–1918, and many of them had become officers, rising to a social status higher than they had enjoyed before. After the War, they were unable to live up to the new standard of life that they had come to demand — hence the bitter resentment, from which direct action sprang.

As the internal organization of the centralized regime has consolidated, careers have become more regularized (which is to say, bureaucratized). There is a growing tendency for persons to be appointed federal secretary in provinces where they have never been active in politics, thus gradually transforming the party itself into a true bureaucracy. Under such conditions, there is less possibility that the central party leadership can be challenged effectively by local party machines. The future of this privileged group is determined chiefly by the central party figures.

There are now few examples to be found of new men who enter party or governmental positions without an original skill of some kind. A university degree has become increasingly necessary for the corporative appointments. Some of the agencies conduct rigid competitive examinations. These offices are not civil service positions, though the distinction has little practical significance. Somewhat less certainty of tenure is compensated by higher emoluments and prospects of more rapid advancement.

It should not be ignored that the older bureaucratic agencies have been infiltrated by persons who owe their careers to Fascist Party service. In 1928, the diplomatic and consular services were flooded with party men (the *ventottisti*), such as Cantalupo, Bastianini, Mazzolini, and several consuls-general. Among the first-class prefects, we find twenty-two (of forty-nine) appointed from outside the administration. Nine of these have records of vigorous squadristic action (Foschi, Tamburini, and Uccelli, for example). Most of the high bureaucracy in the Ministry of Corporations originated outside the government service.

Skill in ceremony is very prominent in the case of the *podestà*. The decline of local government in Italy has meant an enlarging sphere for the prefects and the provincial party secretaries. As a compensation for the loss of effective local control, the *podestà* have been chosen from individuals of local eminence. Both the Senate and the ministers of state show a substantial proportion of ceremonial personages. It will be noticed that the Chamber has seventeen engineers. No doubt it would be consistent with our analysis of ceremony to include all of these in the ceremonial category. They owe their preferment to their symbolic significance in the ideology of Fascism, which has glorified the technical man at the expense of the "windbags" of the democratic parliament. Despite all the emphasis, however, it is interesting to notice that the engineers are few and far between in the most effective agencies. They are still footmen of the chariot of state, not chauffeurs.

Despite the diatribes that have frequently been directed against attorneys, their number has not declined, and their role in the state appears to be about what it was before. The number of lawyers is now restricted, but the number of students taking the bar examinations is very large. The law schools actually train most of their men, not for private practice of law, but for posts in the government. In this connection, it may be observed also that the professors of law, philosophy, and social science have been reduced to their pedagogical function. Before the Fascist revolution, the professors contributed a very high proportion of political leaders to Italy; indeed, 85 per cent of all of the prime ministers were professors. Thus far, professors (of law and education, for example) have been named only to specialized ministries.

Although journalists have been frequently and fervently praised, they have been practically bureaucratized by the establishment of the Ministry of Propaganda and the Syndicate of Journalists. Editorships of important newspapers have occasionally been treated as party spoils.

The importance of skill in bargaining has declined with the general decline in the amount of business left in private hands. The manual and the semiskills contribute infinitesimally to the leadership of government and party. The twelve members of the Chamber who fall in this category are chiefly of ceremonial significance.

Representative careers include the following:

Renzo Chierici, born in 1895 in Reggio, Emilia; lesser bourgeois family; lieutenant during the war; joined party in 1919; went to Fiume with D'Annunzio, later identifying himself with the Balbo group; perhaps the best-known squadrist in Italy; established himself in Ferrara, becoming provincial party secretary.

Giuseppe Avenanti, born in 1898 at Arcevia, province of Ancona, of modest bourgeois parents; volunteered in the war and became lieutenant; joined party in 1919, engaging in local squadrist and journalistic activity; became provincial party secretary for Ancona; transferred as party secretary to Zara (apparently on account of shady activities); later transferred as federal secretary to Gorizia.

Renzo Morigi, born in Ravenna in 1895; corporal during the war; comes from fairly wealthy landowning family; joined party in 1919, and led squadrist action throughout region of Emilia; very proud of his Romagnolo descent; world's pistol-shooting champion, Los Angeles Olympic Games, 1932; provincial secretary of Ravenna and actual boss (*ras*); several times connected with central committee of the national party.

Paolo Boldrin, born in Padua in 1906 of lesser bourgeois family; joined party in 1922; shared squadrist activity and organized students; took Ph.D. later and became provincial party secretary for Padua; docent in public law, University of Padua, and author of scholarly publications.

Epaminonda Pasella, born in 1875 in Pombino; modest family origins; engineer in royal navy, serving in this capacity during the war; joined party in 1919, organizing seamen's union, cooperating with Costanzo Ciano; provincial party secretary for the island of Elba.

Nino Vicari, born in Pesaro in 1894, of lesser bourgeois family; captain in the army during the war; later employed in postal service; active in propaganda and newspaper work, and made honorary member of the party in 1923; provincial party secretary for Parma.

Rodolfo Vagliasindi, baron of Randazzo, born in 1887 at family seat at Randazzo, province of Catania; served as captain in the war; as Nationalist, took part in local politics; joined Fascist Party in 1921; comes from family of wealthy landowners and is himself actively engaged in agriculture; took a doctorate in chemistry and has published scientific contributions; provincial party secretary for Catania.

Count Pier-Ludovico Occhini, born in 1874 in Arezzo; wealthy landowning and noble family; served in war as officer attached to propaganda services; Nationalist until 1919, when he joined Fascist Party; holds doctorate in literature; contributor to and editor of several art reviews; aesthete and poet of the D'Annunzio school; interested in local history and art; *podestà* of Arezzo.

Gugielmo Marconi, born in Bologna in 1874; father, Giuseppe Marconi, mother *née* Annie Jameson; family wealthy; passed early life in Italy and England; early experiments worked out on his family estate, Pontecchio, and in England, where first successful results were obtained; aided by both Italian and English governments; recipient of several honorary degrees and Nobel Prize, 1909; Senator, 1914; delegate to Versailles Peace Conference, 1919; 1928, named president of National Research Council; 1929, named Marquis; September 1930, president of the Royal Academy and member of Fascist Grand Council.

Alessandro Mazzucotelli, born of poor parents in Lodi in 1865; began as a blacksmith's helper; became independent iron worker; established himself in a country house near Milan; interested in popular education and inaugurated the biennial exposition of decorative arts in Monza; has been appointed commissar of the arts for Milan and elected a member of the Chamber of Deputies; has attained international renown in his craft.

Among the less readily defined skills that have been the basis of successful careers in the Fascist state is skill in "fixing." The fixer is a negotiator who enhances his private income by exercising, or seeming to exercise, governmental and party influence. He may be put on the board of directors of a corporation in the expectation that he will prevent the government or the party from making trouble for the corporation; he may be put on the board at the direct initiative of the political leaders themselves.

The fixer is prominent in Italy because monopoly has almost, but not quite, supplanted competition, and all organized hierarchies are not quite coordinated in a totalitarian unity. The fixer is not a simple broker who brings persons of equal bargaining power together to make a deal according to publicly understood rules. He is the go-between when the parties to an arrangement must consider many other matters than simple profit. He plays a part when a resort to violence or to coercive pressure may occur at different stages of the transaction.

Fixers tend to stabilize the existing state of tension between private and public hierarchies by building up vested interests in existing ambiguities. Owing to the confidential nature of the transactions mediated by the fixers, it is impossible to arrive at a satisfactory objective estimate of the relative importance of this skill. It is plain, however, that politicians of the second and third rank very commonly trade on their supposed power. This applies particularly to the members of the rather innocuous Chamber of Deputies and of some of the unions and associations. Owing to the great centralization of the party and government, the fixer functions as a go-between who seeks to adjust local to central interests. The growth of the newly rich members of the Fascist Party is often to be attributed to income derived from fixing.

Here are two examples:

A. was a modest lawyer in an important industrial center; a brother occupies a high position in the party and the government; hence, he has been generally assumed to exercise a considerable degree of influence; by using the name of his brother, he has been able to settle controversies, often very delicate and important, between unions and associations, industrial firms, and banks.

B. was a fairly prominent industrialist who felt apprehensive for the security of his business; at the beginning he was not sympathetic with Fascism, but joined the party after 1925 in order to protect himself; became very active in politics, financing his own campaigns; having attained some prestige in politics, he used his position not only to protect his business but to extend his connections; corporations appointed him to their boards of directors, and he extended the range of his operations on a national scale.

## IV

Another important aspect of governmental and party leadership is the degree of ideological incorporation in Fascism. To some extent, this can be shown by studying the length of time that the members of different agencies have been identified with the Fascist Party, and the nature of their previous party affiliations. By Fascists *della prima ora* (from the first hour), we mean those who joined the party before the March on Rome in October 1922 and had no previous party connections. The Nationalists supplied many members of the Fascist Party before March 1923, when the older party officially amalgamated with the Fascists. Some Liberals enlisted under the emblem of Fascism before October 1922. (The date, August 1922, is taken for the northern provinces; this marks the successful breaking up of the general strike in these provinces.) The Liberals were the right wing of the old Parliament (Monarchists, Constitutionalists, Liberals, Conservatives, and Democrats). Some of them passed over to Fascism between the March on Rome and the establishment of the dictatorship, January 3, 1925, which followed the Matteoti crisis. Some joined afterwards, when adherence to the Fascist Party had become practically compulsory.

The members of the Popular (Socialist-Catholic) Party who went over to Fascism can be grouped into the three periods used for the Liberals. The same subdivisions likewise apply to the Socialistic groups (Syndicalists, Official Socialists, Reformists, Maximalists, and Communists).

Table 4 is constructed to show these differences.

## Table 4
### PARTY ATTITUDES

1. *Fascisti della prima ora,* no previous affiliations.
2. Nationalists
   (*a*) Fascist before March 1923.
   (*b*) Fascist after March 1923.
3. Liberals
   (*a*) Fascist before October 1922.
   (*b*) Fascist between October 1922 and January 3, 1925.
   (*c*) Fascist after January 3, 1925.
4. Popular
   (Same subdivisions as above)
5. Socialistic groups
   (Same subdivisions as above)

| | 1 | 2a | 2b | 3a | 3b | 3c | 4a | 4b | 4c | 5a | 5b | 5c |
|---|---|---|---|---|---|---|---|---|---|---|---|---|
| *Rising Agencies:* | | | | | | | | | | | | |
| Cabinet | 6 | 1 | 3 | 3 | — | — | — | — | — | 6 | — | — |
| Grand Council | 6 | — | 1 | 1 | — | — | — | — | — | — | — | — |
| Party Executive | 6 | — | — | — | — | — | — | — | — | 1 | — | — |
| Provincial Party Secretaries | 46 | 2 | 4 | — | 1 | — | — | — | — | — | — | — |
| Chief Executives National Unions and Associations | 3 | 1 | 2 | 1 | — | 1 | — | — | — | 4 | — | — |
| *Declining Agencies:* | | | | | | | | | | | | |
| Chamber | 113 | 3 | 9 | 5 | 13 | 33 | — | 2 | 3 | 6 | — | — |
| Ministers | 1 | 1 | 1 | — | 3 | 6 | — | — | — | — | — | — |
| *Podestà* | 7 | 4 | 2 | — | 12 | 3 | — | 5 | — | — | — | — |

*Note:* Unaccounted for: Cabinet, 5; Provincial Party Secretaries, 13; Ministers of State, 4; *Podestà*, 5, with possible Popular affiliations.

The declining agencies show the most laggards in affiliating themselves with the new and ultimately successful party. In rising as well as declining agencies, there are some examples of former Socialists who went through the same transition as Mussolini himself. In all cases, the change was made before the March on Rome. Ex-Socialist members of the cabinet include Razza, Rossoni, Benni, Tassinari, Cobolli, and Lantini. An ex-Socialist member of the executive committee of the party is Marinelli, who was a bookkeeper on the *Popolo d'Italia* from its founding in 1914. Chief executives of national unions and associations include Barni, Ciardi, Pala (socialistic leanings), and Racheli. These four were trade-union organizers. Members of the Chamber of Deputies include Bolzon, Ciarlantini, Lanfranconi, Malusardi, Orano, and Paoloni.

The Italian Senate had practically no members of socialistic groups even before Fascism. More than half of the Senate was changed in 1922, and the new senators, if not party members, are at least in agreement with the regime. At least twenty-three of the 190 senators in our sample were formerly connected with the *Partito Popolare,* or were prominently identified with proclerical organizations. Five senators are ex-Socialists (Rossini was a trade-union organizer; Professor Achille Loria introduced historical materialism into academic circles). No more than ten senators can be identified as *Fascisti della prima ora.* Fascism glorifies youth, and the widespread recognition that the Senate is a declining, decorative post for old men means that appointment to it has been more resented than sought after by active leaders.

In considering the ideological charcteristics of Fascism, it is of interest to discover the extent to which the party is recruited from the nation as a whole, or from particular regions. The higher party councils give extraordinary prominence to persons from Bologna and nearby provinces: Grandi, Manaresi, Biagi, Oviglio (Bologna); Balbo, Rossoni (Ferrara); and the *Duce* (Forlì). During the formative years of Fascism, this region was the most active scene. The social structure of the area reveals some significant features. Some cities provided employment for urban proletarians; these cities were situated close to agricultural regions that depended upon city factories to process their products (sugar beets, hemp). In the production of these commodities, use was made of a large body of unskilled casual laborers (*braccianti*). Workers, both urban and rural, were organized, and the postwar years saw the high-water mark of union activity. The lesser bourgeoisie, except the section directly connected with the unions, were alienated by the dislocation of public services through frequent strikes, and by the improving status of the manual toilers. Small tradesmen were exposed to the ever-sharpening competition of the cooperatives, which were supported by the unions. Some degree of social disorganization was endemic in this region; illegitimacy rates, for example, were higher than anywhere else in Italy. The refineries in Ferrara were operated by corporations that were not locally owned; the city was constantly losing members of the rising bourgeoisie to other centers.

The further down one goes in the party and governmental hierarchy, the more completely does the personnel become representative of the nation as a whole. Indeed, many persons are advanced chiefly because they are identified with localities rather than for conspicuous party service. The most striking cases are from Sardinia or southern Italy in general.

V

The data assembled here about the governmental and party leaders of Italy refine in some degree our picture of Italian, and indeed of world, developments. By comparing the rising and the declining agencies of Italian public law, we have ascertained the degree to which certain social formations are becoming more or less influential. Outstanding is the extensive contribution made by the lesser bourgeoisie to leadership in the state. Equally plain, however, is the extent to which a section of the lesser bourgeoisie rises to a plutocratic level of income, thus establishing vested interests that are in many respects contradictory to the logical development of a lesser bourgeois polity.

In terms of skill, the rising agencies exhibit the relative predominance of those who are devoted to the arts of government and politics in the narrowest possible sense. There are found many who owe their entire career to skill in violence and who had no antecedent skill before their entry into politics. Party organization and party propaganda, with no previous skill acquisition, were the foundation of other careers. With the consolidation of the new regime, preliminary technical training assumes greater importance as the bureaucratizing tendencies of party and government manifest themselves. Among the less formalized skills, skill in fixing plays a prominent role. Totalitarian patterns of organization are not yet crystallized; hence, private and public hierarchies continue in unstable relationship to one another. The fixers capitalize existing insecurities and develop strong vested interests in preserving present ambiguities.

The ideological integration of the state around the symbols of a single party has gone forward with the broadening local basis of party and government. The association of the older aristocratic and plutocratic formations with the activistic section of the lesser bourgeoisie has tended to conserve older values, and to militate against the emergence of distinctive practices.

The data here summarized are but a fraction of all that one might desire for developmental interpretation of political events. The facts given have not been related to many facts about the circumstances in which transformations occurred in Italy. Nor have they been presented in relation to an explicit description of the social structure of Italy. They do, however, constitute a step on the way toward relating public law agencies organized in particular ways to the social contexts in which they operate.

## CHAPTER FIVE

*DANIEL LERNER* with the collaboration of *ITHIEL DE SOLA POOL*
and *GEORGE K. SCHUELLER*

# The Nazi Elite[*]

## I. PERSPECTIVE AND PROCEDURES

THE NAZI rise to power ranks as a great triumph of mass organization, persuasion, and coercion, perhaps the most impressive victory
in modern political history for the planned manipulation of men and
symbols. Like their Bolshevik and Fascist precursors, the Nazis developed a tiny "lunatic fringe" into a monolithic party claiming — and
receiving — a monopoly of state power. But the Nazis accomplished
this in a great modern industrial nation, and in one decade of activity.
From fugitive meetings in Munich beer halls in 1923, they planned,
talked, and punched their way into the Reich Chancellory by 1933.

The politics of parliament went down, in a decade of crisis, under
the aggressive politics of the street. This distinctive feature of Nazi
politics is explicitly recognized in the triumphant memoirs which
Nazi leaders brought out to celebrate their victory — e.g., *Auf den
Strassen des Sieges* and *Vom Kaiserhof zur Reichskanzlei.*[1] Both
Dietrich and Goebbels were masters of the politics of the street — the
organized use of voice and violence to gain power.

A study of the Nazi elite thus interests us as a way of clarifying
the process of power transference in one important historical situation.
When we notice that successful revolutionary elites in such varied
societies as Russia, Italy, and China reveal striking similarities to the

---

[*] Originally published in 1951 by the Stanford University Press, as Series B:
Elite Studies, No. 3, of the Hoover Institute Studies. Reprinted with permission
of the author and publisher. Minor editorial changes have been made in the text.
   [1] Otto Dietrich, *Auf den Strassen des Sieges* (München: Zentral-verlag der
NSDAP, F. Ehrer nachf., 1939); and Joseph Goebbels, *Vom Kaiserhof zur Reichskanzlei* (München: Zentral-verlag der NSDAP, F. Ehrer nachf., 1934).

Nazi elite, we may be on the track of some basic propositions about the "world revolution of our time." Some of the most pertinent data will be found in the study of the German cabinets from 1890 to 1945 by Max Knight, entitled *The German Executive* (Monograph No. 4 in the Hoover Institute Elite Series). Some of his findings for the later years reinforce the findings of this study, which is confined to the presentation of data on the members of the Nazi elite.

## Purpose and Method of the Inquiry

The *Fuehrerlexikon* published in 1934 is a *Who's Who* of Nazism. It gives biographical sketches of about 1,600 persons, nominally those who most helped the Nazi movement to achieve total victory but also many who were prestigious figures without being particularly vigorous Nazis. From this population we drew a systematic random sample of 10 per cent — i.e., drawing every tenth name as it occurred in the alphabetical listing of the *Fuehrerlexikon*. This procedure gave us an adequate sample (159 persons) to determine the salient biographical characteristics of this elite.

Next we drew three additional samples from this population — each exhausting a subcategory of the Nazi elite. One of these subclasses contains all the persons in the book who were classifiable as Nazi *propagandists* (128); the second contains all the persons classifiable as Nazi *administrators* (151); the third contains all the persons classifiable as Nazi *coercers* (139). Individual biographies were sorted into the categories on the basis of explicit criteria. Our criteria of classification are detailed in Appendix A, where they may be consulted by interested readers.

The purpose of drawing these independent subsamples (each approximately a tenth of the total population) was to accumulate data that would enable us to do the following things:

1. To find the *common* characteristics of the four groups together. Since together they number 577 persons (or approximately 36 per cent of the total population of the *Fuehrerlexikon*), from this sample we can gain reliable evidence on the characteristics of the Nazi elite as a whole.

2. To find the *variant* characteristics of each subclass. From these data we can determine which, if any, sociopsychological characteristics differentiate Nazi propagandists from Nazi administrators and Nazi coercers, and each of these three groups from the Nazi elite as a whole.

This second purpose requires further comment. A basic proposition concerning the "world revolution of our time" — elaborated notably in the works of H. D. Lasswell — asserts that it is being engineered by counterelites specializing in the use of organization, propaganda, and violence to gain power. The Nazi *Machtergreifung* was a clear victory for a political strategy based on the organized use of voice and violence to gain power. This suggests the question: What are the distinctive characteristics of persons who successfully use these weapons for the achievement of power? An answer to this question would help to clarify the nature of the world revolution — which so many diverse observers agree is occurring — by distinguishing the special attributes of persons who activate, and profit from, this revolutionary process.

At several points it seemed useful to make two additional comparisons. The purpose of these was to enable us to answer the following questions:

3. How does the Nazi elite compare with the Nazi Party membership — i.e., what attributes, besides those common to all Nazis, distinguish elite from mass within the movement?

4. How does the Nazi movement compare with the German population as a whole — i.e., what attributes, besides those common to all Germans, distinguish Nazis (both elite and mass)?

To answer the third question we drew from *Parteistatistik* (1935) comparable data on the Nazi Party as a whole. To answer the fourth question we drew comparable data on the whole German population from the *Statistisches Jahrbuch fuer das deutsche Reich.*

Finally, at several points we found ourselves interested in raising a fifth question:

5. How does the Nazi elite compare with the traditional German elite — i.e., what attributes distinguish the top Nazis from the top power groups of Imperial and Weimar Germany?

For this comparison we drew available data from the study mentioned earlier — the elite analysis of the German cabinet from 1890 to 1945, by Max Knight. The technical difficulties of comparing our two samples suggested that a more complex and satisfactory answer to our fifth question might be obtained by drawing from the standard *Wer Ist's* a sample directly comparable to ours from the *Fuehrerlexikon.* This research we have left for the future.

Two technical points concerning the method of this study should be noted here. First, we have applied to all the samples mentioned above a common check list of attributes, explicitly defined. Thus, the categories in which we have recorded data on age, education, and other attributes have been held constant throughout the analysis. Second, we have tried to keep our subsamples comparable both statistically (e.g., with respect to sample size) and functionally (e.g., with respect to social function). This is a rather complex problem, for social function does not yield easily to unidimensional definitions. The procedures used are described in Appendix A. Where we have had reason to believe that our data are not strictly comparable, we have indicated this in the text at appropriate places, with some explanation of the reasons for our belief.

The data are organized into five main parts, dealing in turn with the key propositions that these data are designed to test: (1) the *middle-income skill groups* as an independent operating force in modern politics, acquiring relatively high deference-values both in stable societies and in the counterelites which revolutionize these societies; (2) the *role of the alienated intellectuals* who, having acquired their distinctive skills as symbol specialists through high status in the old elite, maintain their high positions by applying these skills in the service of the counterelite; (3) the *rise of the plebeian* who vastly increases his status in the counterelite when, becoming disaffected from his lowly role in the old scheme of things, he comes early into the revolutionary party and rises high through taking control of its administrative apparatus; (4) the special *role of the coercers* who, while exercising the top coercive function of the counterelite as its valued specialists in violence, must subordinate themselves completely to its policy decisions made elsewhere (or, unless they can successfully defy their political rivals for policy control within the counterelite, go down to ignominy in the attempt); (5) *marginality* as the common attribute of the various types and groups that compose the revolutionary counterelite. Before turning to these data, we briefly restate these propositions in a form suitable for testing.

### The Key Propositions

Our data bear on key propositions concerning the sociological character of the Nazi revolution. We designate them as "key" propositions because we expect that they will interpret not only our data on the Nazis but also comparable data on other successful revolutionary elites of our time. We state these propositions initially in simple and general form; we shall qualify them later as the data require. They are:

1. The middle-income skill groups that acquired elite status in

traditional business civilization (e.g., engineers, lawyers, and managers) form a relatively independent force in the fluctuations of modern political life — and therefore they appear with relatively high frequency among the revolutionary elite.

2. The political function, and hence the social role, of the "alienated intellectual" (e.g., teachers, journalists, and artists) is greatly enhanced by revolutionary activities — and therefore they appear with relatively high frequency in the revolutionary elite.

## II. THE MIDDLE-INCOME SKILL GROUPS

The middle-income groups include those persons whose incomes lie in the middle ranges of the over-all scale of income distribution in any given society at any given time. For example, President Truman defined the minimum income for the middle ranges in 1950 America as $6,000 per annum. Several years before, President Roosevelt attempted to define, by implication, the maximum income for the middle ranges as $25,000 per annum. While there would no doubt be disagreement about any precise figures used to codify legally the minima and maxima for the middle ranges, there would surely be large agreement among Americans today that the middle ranges do lie between approximately these limits *in fact* (without regard to whether they should be compelled to observe these limits *in law*).

The exact figures defining the middle-income group fluctuate, then, within any society from time to time and between different societies at the same time. A fair approximation, however, can be achieved for any given society at any given time by establishing ratios between "real income" and "cost of living" indexes. One fixes a lower limit on this continuum: above this point a substantial middle-income group can provide themselves with the same goods and services; below this point a substantial lower-income group cannot. The same procedure enables us, by fixing an upper cutting point, to distinguish the middle-income group from the high-income range on the same continuum.

We are interested in the middle-income group in contemporary societies because a number of major constructs about the "world revolution of our time" assign a crucial role to this class. Their roles differ, and sometimes are even contradictory, as between these constructs. The Jeffersonian construct, for example, which in various reformulations serves as an ideology for many Americans (and democrats elsewhere) today, postulates that the "good society" will be attained through a constant process of enlarging the middle-income group — i.e., by making it possible for an even larger number of persons to provide themselves with the goods and services that are generally desired. The Marxian construct, in its current Leninist-Stalinist version, postulates the contrary, that the "good society" will be attained through elimination of the middle-income group (as well as the higher-income group).

The ultimate goals postulated as desirable by these two conflicting constructs obviously are compatible. In fact, they can be formulated as identical: i.e., wider sharing of economic abundance. The crucial difference is the intervening postulate of what must be done with the present middle-income group in order to attain this ultimate goal. The Jeffersonian postulates the necessity of wider sharing of power among all the people who are to obtain for themselves wider shares of wealth. The Marxian (Stalinist) postulates the necessity of narrower concentration of *power* among the few people who are to direct the wider distribution of wealth among all the others. Thus, the two main historical views of our future in terms of our past differ crucially with respect to the social role of the middle-income group.

Among the middle-income population, the present study differentiates those who are members by virtue of a distinctive skill-function. These are: the corporate entrepreneurs and managers, skilled in industrial production and administration; the bureaucrats, skilled in organizing and administering controls over social behavior; the lawyers, skilled in interpreting the codified rules of the game and applying them to concrete situations; the industrial engineers and other technologists, skilled in applying knowledge to specified social goals.

Our proposition is that this segment of the new "middle classes" — i.e., the middle-income *skill* groups — exhibits a relatively high rate of survival in the contemporary revolutionary process, at least in its initial phases. Other middle-class elements do not survive the revolutionary process which installs a new elite in the seats of power. The independent businessman, for example, whose distinctive success-trait is effective bargaining for private gains, tends not to survive because this trait is not readily adaptable to the goal of maximizing gains for others through a central decision-making apparatus. The skills of managers, bureaucrats, lawyers, and technologists, as enumerated above, *are* adaptable to the revolutionary goal just stated.

We turn first, then, to an examination of data on the "primary lifework" among the members of our samples of the Nazi elite. By primary lifework we refer, throughout this discussion, to the occupation in which a person spent the largest number of years in his reported career. The data accumulated are as shown in Table 1.

## Table 1
### PRIMARY LIFEWORK

| Class | Propagandists | Administrators | Random |
|---|---|---|---|
| Civil servant | 9.0% | 13.2% | 27.7% |
| Professions | 9.0 | 17.2 | 27.0 |
| Business (corporate) | 8.0 | 23.2 | 18.9 |
| NS Party official | 16.0 | 15.9 | 6.9 |
| Military | 1.0 | 14.6 | 3.1 |
| Communications | 51.0 | 2.6 | 7.5 |
| Artisan | 1.0 | 2.0 | 0.0 |
| Farmer | 1.0 | 7.3 | 5.0 |
| Others | 3.0 | 2.0 | 3.8 |
| Unknown | 1.0 | 2.0 | 0.0 |
| Total | 100.0% | 100.0% | 99.9% |
| (Number) | (100) * | (151) | (159) |

* Our original sample of propagandists numbered 128. A question was raised about the validity of including certain types in this category. We thereupon eliminated these types and were left with a sample of 100 propagandists. Matching of distributions showed that there was no appreciable difference between the smaller and larger samples — few deviations appeared, and all differences were in the same direction. We have used the sample of 100 through most of the study. However, to save the labor of complete recomputation, we used the sample of 128 in several cases where inspection showed no deviation. Such cases are noted when they occur.

These figures offer a confirmation of the proposition that the middle-income skill groups show a considerable survival value in the revolutionary elite — at least in its early stages (the *Fuehrerlexikon* from which our data are drawn appeared in 1934). The typical middle-income skill occupations are those in the first three categories in the table. These are the occupations that, in the prerevolutionary period, were stabilized through a skill component and rewarded in the middle-income ranges. The most important figures in this connection are those for the random sample, which is the subgroup most representative of the elite as a whole. Adding these three categories together, we find 73.6 per cent of this sample clustered in these middle-income skill occupations. While it is quite possible that these numbers were reduced in the decade following the Nazi *Machtergreifung*, the fact that three out of every four members of a random sample fell into these categories demonstrates the high initial survival value of these "stable" occupations in revolutionary changes.

Further confirmation is supplied by the data on Nazi propagandists and administrators. Our chief propositions about these subgroups will be: first, that they deviate in various ways from the attributes of the Nazi elite as a whole (as revealed in the attributes of the random sample); second, that they deviate, respectively, in propagandist affiliations with "higher" strata (intellectuals) and in administrator affiliations with "lower" strata (plebeians) than the Nazi elite as a whole.

We shall make the accuracy of these propositions the subject of more detailed documentation later. If one assumes their accuracy at this point, then it becomes the more significant that even these subgroups, which are deviant in most other respects, should conform roughly to the data for the random subgroup. The Nazi administrators, for example, locate 53 per cent of their total in the three categories of civil service, professions, and business. This gives a concentration of about 2 out of every 4 administrators, as compared with 3 out of 4 for the Nazis selected at random. The propagandists place somewhat better than 1 out of every 4 — or a total of 26 per cent — in these three categories.

We notice, in Table 1, that the propagandists cluster very heavily (51 per cent) in the "communications" category, the administrators fairly heavily (14.6 per cent) in the "military" category, and both in the "NS Party official" category. The latter suggests that many administrators and propagandists started but did not go very far in the occupations for which they were trained before they devoted themselves mainly to Nazi Party or proto-Nazi occupations. Therefore we also tabulated data on the "subsidiary lifework" of our samples, including here the occupations at which they spent the second-longest periods of their careers. In Table 2 we present the combined percentages of those in each sample who made each of the three "stable" occupations their primary *or* subsidiary lifework.

*Table 2*
REPRESENTATION OF "STABLE" OCCUPATIONS

| Class | Propagandists | Administrators | Random |
|-------|---------------|----------------|--------|
| Civil service | 21.0% | 15.1% | 40.1% |
| Professions | 12.0 | 17.4 | 46.1 |
| Corporate business | 10.0 | 26.2 | 20.7 |
| Total | 43.0% | 58.7% | 106.9% |
| (Number) | (100) | (151) | (159) |

No man was counted twice in the same category — i.e., no man with civil service as his primary lifework was again assigned civil service as his subsidiary lifework. (Where no clear subsidiary occupation was given, the person was classified in "None.") Thus, the explanation for the total of 106 per cent random Nazis in the three "stable" occupations is that several of them moved from one of these occupations as his primary lifework to another of these three occupations as his subsidiary lifework.

Since the number of persons who did this was not large, it is fair to conclude that nearly every member of the Nazi elite sampled at random made one or more of these stable categories, as his first or second most prolonged occupation, the basis of his career. This is true, also, of approximately 1 out of every 2 propagandists and administrators in our samples of the Nazi elite.

These data document the proposition that the middle-income skill groups tend to survive the revolutionary process, as demonstrated by the relatively high frequency of their appearance in the revolutionary Nazi elite. Survival is facilitated by their readiness, when rewards for their skills are reduced in the disintegrating old society, to affiliate with the revolutionary counterelite. Whereas other segments of the middle class are unacceptable, these skill groups are permitted (even encouraged, by high rewards) to affiliate with the new elite, precisely because their skills are needed for "consolidating" revolutionary control over the new society. This would appear to suggest that the "liquidation of the middle classes" — which various revolutionary constructs of our time postulate as a condition for attaining the ultimate revolutionary goal — may be more useful as a propaganda slogan than as an analysis of the contemporary political process. The *rentier*, the private entrepreneur, and the independent farmer do seem highly liable to liquidation; but the investment analyst, the corporate manager, and the agronomist are more likely to be "reorganized" into the revolutionary elite. This is probably the significant distinction that is brought to our attention by the proposition that the middle-income skill groups show a high survival value in the contemporary revolutionary process.

## III. ALIENATED INTELLECTUALS (THE NAZI PROPAGANDISTS)

The middle-income skill groups supply some of the administrative and technical abilities required to operate revolutionary movements that aim to subvert the current symbols and sanctions of power and thereby to undermine the ruling elite. Three important specialties are required for efficient operation of a revolutionary movement: organization, coercion, and persuasion.

Effective persuasion is a necessary (but not sufficient) condition of revolutionary success. No small revolutionary core in a modern mass state can expect to seize and organize power without winning to its side substantial numbers of the population. These are needed to make and applaud the speeches, to address and stamp the envelopes, to carry messages, to fight in the streets, to convince their neighbors, to harass the ruling elite and its defenders, and in every way to heighten the morale (i.e., expectations of success) among the revolutionary movement. To win these lieutenants, sergeants, and privates of party action to the movement, great initial efforts must be made by the captains of persuasion who "spearhead" the movement. Prominent among the revolutionary elite, therefore, we expect to find the propagandists.

Who are these propagandists? Where do they come from in the old society? What sorts of men are they?

Our central answer to these questions is that the propagandists of revolutionary elites are, most characteristically, the "alienated intellectuals" of the old society. By *intellectuals* we mean those persons who are predisposed — through temperament, family, education, occupation, etc. — to manipulate the symbolic rather than the material environment. By *alienated* intellectuals we mean those who do not identify themselves with the prevailing structure of symbols and sanctions in the societies that nurture them. In particular, such alienated intellectuals are likely to respond negatively to the prevailing structure of deference values in the old society.

We shall leave to Part VI of this study the exposition of several clues that our data provide on the question: What sorts of men are these propagandists? Here we shall attempt to answer the question: Where do they come from in the old society?

No answer to this question can be given in general terms. Where the propagandists of any revolutionary movement are drawn from depends mainly upon the structure of the old society that is to be revolutionized. A revolutionary movement in a highly developed industrial and urban mass society probably will recruit its captains of persuasion from different social ranks than will such a movement in an underdeveloped agrarian society. The latter, to illustrate with an extreme case, will have no need for — and also no candidates from — high-pressure advertising specialists. What will be common to both, then, is not the social group that produces the "alienated intellectuals" but the fact that — in their respective societies — they *are* the alienated intellectuals.

## Age

Our first clue to the social sources of Nazi propagandists comes from the comparative data on the age distributions within our samples, as shown in Table 3.

*Table 3*

AGE DISTRIBUTION (5-YEAR PERIODS)

| Class | Propagandists | Administrators | Random |
|-------|---------------|----------------|--------|
| Under 25 | 3.0% | 0.0% | 0.0% |
| 26–30 | 13.0 | 11.2 | 5.6 |
| 31–35 | 19.0 | 15.3 | 8.1 |
| 36–40 | 26.0 | 21.2 | 13.3 |
| 41–45 | 20.0 | 15.3 | 14.5 |
| 46–50 | 12.0 | 16.6 | 15.1 |
| 51–55 | 3.0 | 11.2 | 12.6 |
| 56–60 | 3.0 | 6.6 | 14.5 |
| 61–65 | 0.0 | 2.0 | 10.0 |
| 66–70 | 0.0 | 0.6 | 4.4 |
| Over 70 | 1.0 | 0.0 | 1.8 |
| Total | 100.0% | 100.0% | 99.9% |
| (Number) | (100) | (151) | (159) |

The ages of the random sample are most evenly distributed over the categories. If plotted on coordinate axes, this distribution would approximate a normal curve. Plotted on the same axes, the age distribution of the propagandists would give us a sharply left-skewed curve. Nearly 2 out of every 3 of the propagandists are under forty, and more than 3 out of every 4 are under forty-three. Their differences from the random sample are brought out even more pointedly when the figures are arranged cumulatively, as in Table 4.

*Table 4*

AGE DISTRIBUTION (CUMULATIVE PERCENTAGES)

| Class | Propagandists | Administrators | Random |
|-------|---------------|----------------|--------|
| Under 25 | 3.0% | 0.0% | 0.0% |
| Under 30 | 16.0 | 11.2 | 5.6 |
| Under 35 | 35.0 | 26.4 | 13.7 |
| Under 40 | 61.0 | 47.5 | 26.9 |
| Under 45 | 81.0 | 62.7 | 41.3 |
| Under 50 | 93.0 | 79.2 | 56.3 |

All but 7 of our 100 propagandists thus are under fifty, i.e., 93 per cent of this sample, as compared with three fourths of the administrators and only one half of the random sample of Nazis. The disproportionate youth of the propagandists increases as one goes from fifty down through the younger age-categories. The only three persons under twenty-five in all the samples turn out, indeed, to be propagandists.

The average age of propagandists is 38.9 years, running about five years younger than the administrators and about ten years younger than the Nazi elite as a whole (as reflected in our random sample). The comparative mean ages for the three groups are shown in Table 5, which also shows the mean deviations above and below the median age for each group. Since these are the ages as of 1934, the average age of the propagandists when World War I broke out in 1914 was 18.9. The propagandists thus appear as predominantly a postwar generation.

### Table 5
#### AGE DISTRIBUTION (MEAN)

|  | *Propagandists* | *Administrators* | *Random* |
|---|---|---|---|
| Plus mean deviation | 47.2 (+ 8.3) | 52.5 (+ 10.3) | 59.4 (+ 10.9) |
| Mean age | 38.9 | 42.2 | 48.5 |
| Minus mean deviation | 33.5 (− 5.4) | 34.0 (− 8.2) | 37.4 (− 11.1) |

The youthfulness of the propagandists in 1934 suggests that they must have commenced their Nazi activities at an early age, and that is indeed the case, as one can see by Table 6. The median age at which propagandists joined the Nazi Party is considerably lower than

### Table 6
#### MEDIAN AGE OF JOINING NSDAP*

|  | *Through 1928* | *After 1928* |
|---|---|---|
| Propagandists | 22 | 34 |
| Administrators | 30 | 37 |
| Random sample | 27 | 40 |

* It is probably true that the rise in median age at time of joining the NDSAP [German National Socialist Labor Party] reflects a real aging of the party, but the data at hand cannot support this hypothesis since the nature of the sample tends to produce the same result. To attain the elite, even in so young an elite as that of the Nazis, takes a certain number of adult years. Thus a man who became a Nazi at twenty is much more likely to be in the *Fuehrerlexikon* in 1934 if he joined in 1923 than if he joined in 1933. A man who joined in 1933 if included is probably older and is probably included for achievements outside the party. The years 1928-1929 represent a sharp breaking point in this set of data. The results for those who joined in 1923 or before are almost exactly the same as those reported for 1928 and before.

that at which administrators or random Nazis did. The propagandists were young men in a hurry. The administrators too were undoubtedly discontented persons, but they were slower and less impetuous than the precocious propagandists. Age is a factor of more than usual importance in differentiating segments of modern German society. Two wars and two revolutions have broken the continuity of German life, and so each generation has been molded by different sets of experiences. Growing up in the *Kaiserreich*, growing up in the years of inflation, or growing up in the *Hitlerjugend* were experiences that stamped their differences on the succeeding generations. The significance of the differential in age between propagandists, administrators, and random Nazis may be seen if we look at the data on military service.

### Military Service

Since the propagandists were mainly of the postwar generation and became men in a "demilitarized" Germany, they had less military service than the administrators or random sample: 83 per cent of the propagandists saw no service before World War I, as compared with 66 per cent of the administrators and 70 per cent of the random sample. This means that in the Nazi elite as a whole, approximately 1 out of every 4 saw some service prior to World War I, and among the administrators 1 out of every 3 saw some service, whereas among the propagandists less than 1 out of every 5 saw service.

In World War I, 40 per cent of the propagandists report no service, as compared with 23 per cent of the administrators and 35 per cent of the random Nazis. In other words, nearly 1 out of every 2 propagandists saw no service in the Great War, as contrasted with 1 out of 3 random Nazis and only 1 out of 4 administrators.

Age was thus the primary factor in determining the military experience of members of the Nazi elite. It was, however, not the only factor. Even when we hold age constant, we find that the administrators had more military experience than the propagandists or random sample.

In Table 7 the ages are grouped so as to separate persons at ages for which military service was possible, but not normal, from those at ages for which military service was a normal experience. (The ages are given as of 1934.) Almost without exception, more administrators from every age group had military experience than did propagandists or random Nazis.

The Nazi administrators were clearly recruited not only from age levels wherein military service was common but also from among individuals who had an inclination toward military life. The Nazi Party in turn provided these individuals with a substitute for the Army. The propagandists, on the other hand, were not only generally too young to have acquired much military experience but also were types not prone to the ordered bureaucratic life of the barracks. Two points are of special interest on the propagandists — first, their biog-

## Table 7
### INDIVIDUALS IN EACH CELL WHO HAD MILITARY SERVICE

|  | Service before W. W. I | | | Service in W. W. I | | | |
|---|---|---|---|---|---|---|---|
|  | 36–40 | 41–45 | 46–70 | 31–36 | 36–50 | 51–55 | 56–70 |
| Propagandists | 7.4% | 30.4% | 38.1% | 15.0% | 90.1% | 77.8% | 80.0% |
| Administrators | 9.4 | 43.5 | 67.9 | 39.1 | 96.2 | 88.2 | 100.0 |
| Random | 0.0 | 21.8 | 45.2 | 33.0 | 92.6 | 65.0 | 50.0 |

|  | Service in Reichswehr | | |
|---|---|---|---|
|  | 26–30* | 31–35 | 36–70 |
| Propagandists | 15.4% | 35.0% | 6.8% |
| Administrators | 6.5 | 43.5 | 11.7 |
| Random | 11.1 | 38.5 | 1.5 |

*Only four individuals.

raphies show no disposition toward military service; second, those who did serve received high ranks for their age. Table 8 provides data relevant to the first point.

We have, then, represented in the Nazi propagandists a generation

## Table 8
### RANK IN WORLD WAR I

| Class | Propagandists | | Administrators | | Random | |
|---|---|---|---|---|---|---|
| General | 0.0% | | 0.7% | | 1.9% | |
| Field grades | 0.0 | | 3.3 | | 4.4 | |
| Company grades | 25.0 | | 40.4 | | 28.9 | |
| Captains | | 5.0% | | 13.9% | | 10.7% |
| 1st Lieuts. | | 7.0 | | 5.3 | | 5.0 |
| 2nd Lieuts. | | 13.0 | | 19.2 | | 12.6 |
| Unspecified | | 0.0 | | 2.0 | | 0.6 |
| N.C.O.'s | 7.0 | | 4.6 | | 1.3 | |
| Soldiers | 8.0 | | 23.2 | | 16.4 | |
| Rank unknown | 20.0 | | 4.0 | | 11.9 | |
| No service | 40.0 | | 23.8 | | 35.2 | |
| Total | 100.0% | | 100.0% | | 100.0% | |
| (Number) | (100) | | (151) | | (159) | |

that, just over eighteen when World War I started, reached maturity during the war and immediate postwar years. These were the historic years of political and economic crisis in Germany — military occupation and national subordination, street fighting and political instability, fantastic inflation and widespread unemployment, self-pity and self-hatred and the "Shame of Versailles." Yet, not all the young men of this generation became Nazis — or Nazi propagandists. To answer our question about whence, in the old German society, these men came, we shall have to differentiate the Nazis from other young men of their generation.

A clue is provided by a closer look at the data in Table 8. It is very striking, for example, that only 8 per cent of this younger group should have served as common soldiers — as compared with the older groups of administrators (23.1 per cent) and random Nazis (16.3 per cent). One possible explanation is that these propagandists-to-be uniformly demonstrated skills that rated higher ranks, despite fewer years, in the old *Reichswehr*. Another is that they uniformly demonstrated a talent for military self-advancement (regardless of special skills). Neither of these interesting hypotheses is inherently implausible. But we wish to offer instead an explanation, not incompatible with either of the others, which is more readily documented by our data: namely, that the propagandists characteristically came from the upper middle class of Imperial (and Weimar) Germany; and further, that they represent the "alienated intellectuals" that characteristically emerge from this class in times of troubles.

*Status*

The data on World War I military ranks are revealing on this point — that the Nazi propagandists were recruited from the higher social strata of Imperial and Republican Germany. The documentation of this point becomes clearer if we present the data on ranks as a percentage of those who served in known ranks (dropping the last two categories in Table 8 — those whose rank is not known and those who saw no service). The results are shown in Table 9.

Military rank is normally a function of specialized skill, of civilian status, and of age. Since the sample of professional military men is excluded from this tabulation, there seems no reason to assume that the three subsamples in the table differed markedly in military skill. If skill is excluded as a variable, age and civilian status remain. And a cross tabulation reveals that both factors were operative. The older the individual, the higher his military rank was apt to be. Also, however, at most age levels fewer propagandists than administrators or random Nazis were found at lower ranks, indicating that the propagandists came from a higher social status.

The absence of propagandists among generals and field grades reflects the fact that they are a considerably younger group than the others. All the men who achieved these grades were over fifty-one in

1934, or over thirty-one in 1914. There were only 8 such propagandists who saw service and on whom we have data. Since only about one of every four of the administrators or random sample over fifty-one who served achieved field or general officer rank in the First World War, it is of doubtful significance that no propagandists out of eight did. If it is not pure chance, it may reflect the irregular and undisciplined character of the typical propagandist career.

The group over fifty-one (thirty-one in 1914) includes few enlisted men or N.C.O.'s (7 altogether). Similarly at the other end of the age scale, the men from thirty-one to thirty-five in 1934 (or fifteen to nineteen in 1918) were overwhelmingly common soldiers and included but one officer. In the middle ranges of the age scale, however, a real possibility existed for a man to be either a common soldier or an officer, and age within this range made but a small difference. It is in this range, therefore, that we can see the effects of social class operating. It is precisely here that we find by far the smallest proportion of enlisted men among the propagandists. Furthermore, despite their greater youthfulness, there are as many officers among the propagandists as among the administrators. In other words, holding age constant only reinforces the conclusions that stand out from Table 9. For, whatever influence is attributable to age only would lead us to expect that the younger propagandists would be found predominantly in the *lower* ranks — as compared with the older groups. Yet our data show precisely the opposite finding: they actually are found predominantly in the *higher* ranks.

*Table 9*
WORLD WAR RANKS (OF THOSE WHO SERVED)

| Class | Propagandists | | Administrators | | Random | |
|---|---|---|---|---|---|---|
| Generals | 0.0% | | 0.9% | | 3.6% | |
| Field grades | 0.0 | | 4.6 | | 8.3 | |
| Company grades | 62.5 | | 60.0 | | 54.8 | |
| Captains | | 12.5% | | 22.0% | | 21.4% |
| 1st Lieuts. | | 17.5 | | 7.3 | | 9.5 |
| 2nd Lieuts. | | 32.5 | | 26.6 | | 23.8 |
| N.C.O.'s | 17.5 | | 6.4 | | 2.4 | |
| Unteroffiziere | | 10.0 | | 5.5 | | 1.1 |
| Feldwebel | | 7.5 | | 0.9 | | 1.1 |
| Soldiers | 20.0 | | 32.1 | | 31.0 | |
| Total | 100.0% | | 100.0% | | 100.1% | |
| (Number) | (40) | | (109) | | (84) | |

*Table 10*

WORLD WAR RANKS (FOR MIDDLE AGE-GROUPS)

|  | 36–40 | | | 41–45 | | | 46–50 | | | 36–50 | | |
|  | Number | | | | | | | | | Percentage | | |
|  | P | A | R | P | A | R | P | A | R | P | A | R |
|---|---|---|---|---|---|---|---|---|---|---|---|---|
| Officers | 12 | 10 | 8 | 5 | 15 | 8 | 8 | 14 | 12 | 64.1 | 13.9 | 57.2 |
| N.C.O.'s | 4 | 1 | 1 | 4 | 1 | 1 | — | 2 | 1 | 20.5 | 6.6 | 6.1 |
| Soldiers | 2 | 7 | 6 | 2 | 7 | 6 | 2 | 4 | 6 | 15.4 | 29.5 | 36.7 |
| Total | 18 | 18 | 15 | 11 | 23 | 15 | 10 | 20 | 19 | 100 | 100 | 100 |
| (Number) | | | | | | | | | | (39) | (61) | (49) |

We have already mentioned the extraordinarily small number of propagandists who were common soldiers — only 1 out of every 5, as compared with 1 out of every 3 administrators and random Nazis. This is brought out even more sharply in the N.C.O. grades, which were attained by about 1 out of every 2 propagandists who did not attain the status of commissioned officer, as compared with 1 out of 6 administrators and 1 out of 16 random Nazis who did not become officers.

For a satisfactory explanation of the small number of enlisted men among the propagandists, we must look to the distinctive special skill and civilian rank of those young men in the postwar generation of Weimar Germany who made their way into the Nazi elite as propagandists. We have already mentioned two skill-hypotheses that are plausible and that, if our data on skills were fuller, might provide an adequate explanation of the results we have reported. Here, we adduce the finding that the propagandists, despite their youth, attained a higher proportionate representation as junior officers for themselves than did the older administrators and random Nazis as evidence that they were recruited from a *higher civilian rank in German society.*

Apart from the comparison with our other samples, the simple finding that two thirds of the propagandists became officers is quite remarkable unless we assume that they came from higher social classes. To see this, we need only imagine the probability that two thirds of all German youths who were eighteen years old in 1914 became officers before the end of World War I. We have computed the actual mathematical probability from available statistics on the German Army. The question is this: How many individuals would any sample of 100 men drawn at random from the total population of the German Army have placed in junior officer grades? The simplest way to answer this question is to give the ratio between junior officers and total army strength which actually existed in the German Army. In 1914, just before the outbreak of war, the Army numbered 800,000 men, of whom 22,000 were junior officers.[2] The ratio of officers to total is therefore 1 to 36. In other words, a true random sample of 100 men would have only 3 chances of becoming officers. The probability coefficient for any individual drawn at random from this sample thus is 2.7, or success for only 1 individual out of 36. The sample of 100 propagandists, on the other hand, shows a probability coefficient of 62.5 to each individual, or success for better than 1 out of every 2 propagandists. (This is a very striking difference even if we assume, as seems likely, that after war broke out, the ratio of officers to enlisted men increased.)

The propagandists attained their prevalence in junior officer ranks, *despite* obstacles of youth and brief service because of some "other factor." This other factor was, we have indicated, higher civilian status in prewar German society. Data on our other indicators provide further evidence by which this assertion can be documented somewhat more directly.

### Occupations

The Chicago sociologist Robert E. Park once said that what a man works at occupies most of his lifetime and all of his obituary. Business civilization has made a man's occupation the definition of his status as well as the source of his income. We have already shown in Tables 1 and 2 that our samples provide uniformly high representations in the "stable occupations" of business societies — i.e., those occupations which continue to provide high rewards in deference and income despite fluctuations of political life. These are the characteristic occupations of the middle-income skill groups in modern life.

To distinguish the variant social status of our three samples, it is useful to look at the distribution of occupations among the *fathers* of persons in these samples. The Nazi elite, as we have seen, matured mainly in the post–World War I period. They found their jobs (when they found them) under a republic that, legally, operated on the democratic basis of reward for individual merit. But they were oriented and trained for their lifework in pre-Weimar days. They came from families rooted in the social climate of Imperial Germany, and their fathers located themselves in occupations according to the predemocratic conventions of the *Kaiserreich*, which rewarded status along with (and

[2] War Department, General Staff, *Strength and Organization of the Armies of France, Germany, Austria, Russia, England, Italy, Mexico, and Japan*, No. 22 (Washington, 1916).

often ahead of) merit. To examine the occupations of these fathers thus gives us some insight into the social status from which came these members of the Nazi elite. The data, with the categories roughly ranked according to status, from high to low, are given in Table 11.

### Table 11
#### OCCUPATION OF FATHER

| Class | Propagandists | Administrators | Random |
|---|---|---|---|
| Landowner | 3.0% | 2.0% | 1.9% |
| Military | 7.0 | 5.3 | 1.3 |
| Ecclesiastic | 5.0 | 1.3 | 1.3 |
| Professions | 17.0 | 11.9 | 18.9 |
| Civil service | 14.0 | 7.9 | 14.5 |
| Business | 16.0 | 9.9 | 19.5 |
| Communication | 1.0 | 0.0 | 1.3 |
| Artisan | 3.0 | 6.0 | 2.5 |
| Peasant | 1.0 | 7.3 | 3.1 |
| Others | 2.0 | 5.3 | 1.9 |
| Unknown | 31.0 | 43.0 | 34.0 |
| Total | 100.0% | 99.9% | 100.2% |
| (Number) | (100) | (151) | (159) |

The propagandists clearly outnumber the others in the first three categories, whose top status in Imperial Germany there is little reason to doubt. The cumulative totals for these top three occupations are:

| Propagandists | Administrators | Random |
|---|---|---|
| 15.0% | 8.6% | 4.5% |

These results become even clearer when we learn that of the propagandists' fathers classified as "military," 100 per cent were reported as officers; whereas only 62.5 per cent of the administrators' fathers were officers.

The propagandists continue to lead the others down the ladder of deference, although naturally less clearly as we get into the categories where specific rank may be as important as general occupation type. When we compute the cumulative totals down through category 7 (communications), the propagandists are still ahead:

| Propagandists | Administrators | Random |
|---|---|---|
| 63.0% | 38.3% | 58.7% |

This finding is confirmed when we consider the figures for the two categories of occupation which were definitely low-status in Imperial Germany — i.e., artisan and peasant. The propagandists are lower than both of the others in each of these categories, and the combined figures show the relative absence of propagandists' fathers from low-prestige occupations:

| Propagandists | Administrators | Random |
|---|---|---|
| 4.0% | 13.1% | 5.6% |

Further evidence of the higher status of propagandists is provided by our data on ancestral background. The manner in which these data are presented requires brief explanation. We began by sorting the occupational data on his forebears given by each biographee into two separate tabulations: one on "patriarchal background" (giving the lineage on the father's side), the other on "matriarchal background" (giving the lineage on the mother's side). That enough relevant data should regularly be given in a "who's who" type of biographical dictionary is itself a remarkable demonstration of the Nazi elite's emphasis on the respectability of its roots in the German past. (Contrast this, for example, with the autobiographical reporting in *Who's Who in America*). Further, we were interested to learn whether Nazi great-grandpapas, lacking sufficient social status by birth, tended to acquire it by marriage — and vice versa. The reverse, but equally valuable, conclusion is supported by our data: there is practically no significant variation between the social stratification represented in the patriarchal and matriarchal lineage of the Nazi elite. Men and women who "had class," in the older Germany, tended to marry each other. Since there is no important difference between them, we have averaged the two (and dropped the "unknowns") to make a single tabulation on "ancestral background" (see Table 12).

*Table 12*
ANCESTRAL BACKGROUND (OCCUPATIONS)

| Class | Propagandists | Administrators | Random |
|---|---|---|---|
| Landowner | 10.2% | 1.5% | 13.6% |
| Military | 6.1 | 6.1 | 4.5 |
| Ecclesiastic | 4.1 | 3.0 | 7.6 |
| Professions | 10.2 | 3.0 | 7.6 |
| Civil service | 6.1 | 0.0 | 4.5 |
| Business | 6.1 | 7.6 | 13.6 |
| Communication | 0.0 | 0.0 | 0.0 |
| Artisan | 12.2 | 18.2 | 10.6 |
| Peasant | 44.9 | 56.1 | 37.9 |
| Others | 0.0 | 4.5 | 0.0 |
| Total | 99.9% | 100.0% | 99.9% |
| (Number) | (49) | (66) | (66) |

The most striking result in this tabulation is the enormous increase of "peasants" among ancestors over the number of peasants among the biographees themselves and their parents. In part, of course, this reflects the transition from rural agriculture to urban industry which has taken place in Germany as in all Western societies in modern times. There is good reason to assume, however, that partly this reflects also the German myth as promoted by the Nazis. Under the dispensation of this "city slicker" movement, while it was silly to be a farmer oneself and perhaps even a little degrading to have a peasant father, it was a mark of the highest respectability to have one's ancestry "rooted in the German soil." (Contrast this with the American myth, for example, that has glorified, probably since Jackson and certainly since Lincoln, the farmer in the present man — namely the continual reappearance of the barefoot boy from Wall Street as a political candidate, and the intimate connection between political ambitions and the front porch of one's country birthplace.) We emphasize the Nazi myth, rather than the possible facts regarding differential mobility, because reporting of data is a key variable in this study.

The German myth probably figures, too, in the large increase of ancestral artisans. Hans Sachs, the musical and happy cobbler, is an important German myth-figure. While the master craftsman represented by Sachs is substantially higher than the farmer in his own epoch, artisans in the Nazi epoch rank quite low in the social scale. Thus, Nazi hypersensitivity to questions of their own current social status (shown in their persistent efforts to give themselves "class" by claiming as adherents high-status Germans whose actual Nazi affiliations were minimal) coexisted comfortably with the admiration for earthier origins in the more remote ancestral past. This is clear from a comparison of the artisan and peasant categories for the Nazis themselves, for their parents, and for their remoter ancestors. The figures in Table 13 are based on the combined data for artisans and peasants, expressed as a percentage of the known data in each case.

### Table 13
#### Low-Status Occupations (by Generations)

| Class | Propagandists | Administrators | Random |
|-------|---------------|----------------|--------|
| Nazis | 2.0% | 7.1% | 3.1% |
| Parents | 4.0 | 13.1 | 5.6 |
| Ancestors | 57.0 | 74.1 | 48.4 |

The progression is exponential. Among the propagandists, for example, almost 1 out of 2 ancestors were peasants-artisans, as compared with 1 out of 25 parents, and only 1 out of 50 in the current Nazi generation. A similar trend, though somewhat less extreme, holds for the random Nazis. Even the administrators who, as we shall demonstrate later, form the plebeian element in the Nazi elite exhibit a similar pattern: 3 out of 4 ancestors are peasants-artisans, but only 3 out of 25 parents, and only 3 out of 40 current Nazis.

An interesting sidelight is provided by our data on the occupations of fathers-in-law of the Nazi subgroups. Such data, because marriage in Germany (as elsewhere) is an act of social affiliation as well as ego-involvement, are particularly useful as a reflection of self-images among the Nazis and, therefore, even as a clue to their expectations and demands, with respect to social status. Many of the sampled Nazis do not report on this particular item of their life history (a fact which we shall discuss in Part VI). But of those 26 who do report, *only one* gives the occupation of his father-in-law as a peasant. Otherwise, both categories, peasant and artisan, are, for all three samples, completely empty.

## Education

Another important indicator of family social status is the level of education attained by the children. In Imperial and Weimar Germany, even more than in other Western societies, it was a particular point of pride with "good families" that their children should go well beyond the average in formal education. This desire also became widespread among families that may have been virtuous, but were not sufficiently well-heeled to activate their aspirations. The attainment of collegiate levels of education remained largely confined to the business, professional, and higher social strata, while children of the lower orders were compelled to leave school earlier. This effect of parental status on education attained may be documented from our data. Table 14

*Table 14*
FATHER'S OCCUPATION AND OWN EDUCATION

|  | Propagandists | | Administrators | | Random | |
|---|---|---|---|---|---|---|
|  | Peasants and Artisans | Other Occupations | Peasants and Artisans | Other Occupations | Peasants and Artisans | Other Occupations |
| University | 25.0% | 60.7% | 15.0% | 29.2% | 25.0% | 63.5% |
| Higher schools | 25.0 | 11.1 | 10.0 | 20.8 | — | 11.5 |
| Trade or high grade schools | 50.0 | 28.2 | 75.0 | 50.0 | 75.0 | 25.0 |
| (Number) | (8) | (117) | (20) | (120) | (8) | (148) |

shows that a smaller proportion of those from plebeian backgrounds attended universities and a larger proportion never got beyond trade schools, high schools, or grade schools.

The data on highest educational level attended, presented in Table 15, provide a good indicator of the relative social status of our three samples.

### Table 15
#### EDUCATION (HIGHEST LEVEL ATTENDED)

| Class | Propagandists | Administrators | Random |
|---|---|---|---|
| University | 59.0% | 25.2% | 60.4% |
| Technical Hochschule | 6.0 | 6.6 | 7.6 |
| Other higher schools | 5.0 | 11.3 | 3.0 |
| Trade schools | 11.0 | 25.2 | 11.3 |
| High school | 15.0 | 27.8 | 12.6 |
| Grade school | 1.0 | 3.3 | 5.0 |
| Unknown | 3.0 | 0.7 | 0.0 |
| Total | 100.0% | 100.1% | 99.9% |
| (Number) | (100) | (151) | (159) |

There appears to be no significant difference between the educational levels attained by the propagandists and the random Nazis. The differences between these subgroups and the administrators, however, provide clear evidence that the propagandists were recruited from higher social strata than the administrators. For example, better than 1 out of every 2 propagandists attended a university, as contrasted with 1 out of 4 administrators. On the other hand, 1 out of 4 administrators finished his educational career in high school or trade school (categories 4 and 5), whereas only about 1 out of 10 propagandists stopped at these levels instead of going on to the higher levels. The higher social status of the propagandists, as compared with the administrators, is brought out most clearly by comparing categories 1 and 4: more than twice as many administrators went to *trade* schools (and no further) as did propagandists; conversely, more than twice as many propagandists reached the highest educational level at universities as did administrators (of whom 3 out of 4 had been left behind far below the university level).

Interesting data relevant to social status come from comparing the courses of study followed by university men among our three samples. The full tabulation shows the distribution through ten major fields. We shall summarize these data in three categories: (1) culture-oriented (which includes humanities, foreign language, and culture, and *Germanistik*); (2) skill-oriented (which includes business, journalism, agriculture, social sciences, and natural sciences); and (3) professional studies (which includes all courses leading to licensed professional degrees). The figures, as presented in Table 16, express the percentage in each category of those who report on their major studies at universities (i.e., eliminating both those who did not attend universities and those who attended but did not report on their major studies).

*Table 16*
MAJOR UNIVERSITY STUDIES

| Class | Propagandists | Administrators | Random |
|---|---|---|---|
| Culture-oriented | 33.7% | 9.8% | 12.4% |
| Skill-oriented | 6.7 | 23.2 | 9.7 |
| Professional studies | 59.6 | 67.1 | 77.9 |
| Total | 100.0% | 100.1% | 100.0% |
| (Number) | (89) | (82) | (113) |

It should be mentioned that these categories might be less significant if our samples included a large number of teachers. Since German teachers had to go through the program of studies we have called "culture-oriented" in order to get their teaching certificates, for them such studies would be skill-oriented. However, our data show that a large proportion of Nazis in this category never completed their courses and hence that these courses did not become a significant career-component at all. Further, few of these top leaders became teachers, so that their humanistic studies did not form a specific skill-component. While it is true that teachers were numerous in the lesser ranks of the Nazi hierarchy,[3] they clearly were not at the top. The combined data for lifework (Table 2) show that only 12 per cent of the propagandists were "professionals," a category including lawyers, doctors, engineers, and others, in addition to teachers. In this case, therefore, the categories of culture-oriented and skill-oriented are mutually exclusive in fact and may be treated as dichotomous.

The propagandists greatly outnumber the others in the culture-oriented studies. These studies — generally classified as the humanities — seem to have carried, for this group, higher prestige and lower career-utility than the other fields of study. They were not used as skill training for a teachers' certificate, since very many propagandists never completed their courses at all, and very few became teachers. They were affiliated rather with aestheticism of a sort particularly emphasized in Germany — Kant called it enjoyment "apart from the

[3] See Hans Gerth, "The Nazi Party: Its Leadership and Composition," *American Journal of Sociology*, XLV, No. 4 (1940), p. 525.

idea of an end" — and were very rich in "snob appeal." Such studies were more likely to attract either students whose families were better able to afford to pay for this strictly nonutilitarian type of education, or students who yearned for *Kultur* affiliations regardless of their families' ability to pay. These reflect, respectively, an actually high socioeconomic family status and a desire to share values commonly associated with such high status (whether one has it or not). Both are important indicators of the role of social status in career histories, and it is likely that both occur among the propagandists in this category, who outnumber the administrators and random Nazis by approximately 3 to 1.

This finding is strengthened by the figures on skill-oriented studies. Here, the administrators outnumber the two other subgroups by about 3 to 1. And this, in the analysis we have been presenting, is what we should have expected. The skill-oriented studies are utilitarian in the sense that they prepare students for postcollegiate careers, but enjoy less prestige among the higher social strata whose careers are assured more by familial status than by formal training. Students who major in agriculture acquire tools that will help them make a living as farmers, but they do not — in campus social life and later — attain the same lustrous levels of prestige as those who discuss Ranke and Rilke. Our proposition that the propagandists have characteristically higher social status, and administrators lower status, thus is further documented by the findings that 1 out of every 3 propagandists majored in culture-oriented studies as compared with 1 out of 10 administrators; whereas, conversely, 1 out of 4 administrators concentrated on skill-oriented studies as compared with 1 out of 15 propagandists.

Interesting additional evidence is provided by the figures on professional studies. These comprise the group of studies that lead to the "stable occupations" characteristic of the middle-income skill groups. As we showed earlier, these occupations combine in optimum degree the values of income, deference, and safety (the latter shown, as indicated earlier in this study, by the high survival value of the middle-income skill groups through revolutionary crises). The skill-oriented studies — leading mainly to such occupations as laboratory and research technicians, agricultural and business specialists, middle-to-lower-status bureaucrats — yield very high safety, moderate-to-low income, and low prestige. The culture-oriented studies — leading to such occupations as artist, critic, lecturer, and professor — yield, conversely, high prestige, moderate-to-low income, and low safety. It is the professional studies that distinctively enable persons to maximize all these values simultaneously and yield optimum combinations. This would explain the high representation of all three subgroups in this category. It is by comparing this category with the others — or, by combining professional with either of the other two to emphasize the distinctive skill or culture character of the third — that we see most clearly the higher social affiliations of the propagandists (or the random Nazis, who also compose a high-status subgroup) as compared with the administrators.

### Marriage

Other data seem to confirm our main proposition. Age at marriage, for example, is a particularly interesting indicator of socioeconomic status in Weimar Germany. Recall the prevailing circumstances recorded in Hans Fallada's *Kleiner Mann, was nun?*[4] which dramatized the troubles of young Germans who wanted to get married during this period. The depression, inflation, and unemployment that undermined the Weimar Republic also undermined the marriage institution. Young people could not, economically, afford marriage; yet they could not, psychically, afford celibacy. The result was that "companionate marriage" became an established practice, postponing formal marriage for several years, particularly among those in the less solvent social classes.

Under these conditions, one may regard the age at which people married, during this postwar period, as one indicator of their familial (and personal) socioeconomic status. Since the majority of our sampled Nazis married during this period of fifteen years (1918–1933), we have tabulated the data on their age at marriage. These data are expressed in Table 17 as the average age, with mean deviations above and below the arithmetic mean, of those whose age at marriage is reported in their autobiographical sketches.

### Table 17
#### AGE AT MARRIAGE (MEAN)

| Class | Propagandists (39) | Administrators (17) | Random (44) |
|---|---|---|---|
| Minus deviation | 25 (− 3) | 26 (− 7) | 27 (− 3) |
| Mean age | 28 | 33 | 30 |
| Plus deviation | 31 (+ 3) | 40 (+ 7) | 34 (+ 4) |

This test again confirms our analysis of comparative social status among these three subgroups. The propagandists married younger — on the average five years younger than the administrators — and with

[4] Hans Fallada [pseud., Rudolf Ditzen], *Kleiner Mann, was nun?* (Berlin: Rowohlt, 1932). English translation, *Little Man, What Now?* (New York: Simon and Schuster, Inc., 1933).

a much smaller scatter of age-distribution. Their deviations are contained within a six-year period, as compared with a fourteen-year spread of mean deviations for the administrators. Even their older range (thirty-one years) is still lower than the mean age thirty-three for the administrators. The random Nazis, as the analysis would lead us to expect (since they are older but also higher-status), run slightly older at marriage but conform almost perfectly to the pattern of mean and deviations exhibited by the propagandists.

## Foreign Contacts

A final indicator of social status that we shall introduce here is that of foreign contacts. Such activities as travel abroad and education abroad are regarded as marks of superior social status in most Western societies, and this seems to have been particularly pronounced in pre-Nazi Germany. In Table 18 we give the figures, on five categories of foreign contact, as percentages of the total number of persons sampled.

### Table 18
#### FOREIGN CONTACTS (BY SPECIFIC INDICATORS)

| Class | Propagandists | Administrators | Random |
|---|---|---|---|
| Born abroad | 7.0% | 4.6% | 2.5% |
| Foreign marriage | 3.9 | 0.0 | 1.8 |
| Higher education abroad | 7.8 | 1.9 | 5.6 |
| Travel abroad | 26.5 | 17.2 | 21.3 |
| International organizations | 5.4 | 1.9 | 2.5 |
| Total | 50.6% | 25.6% | 33.7% |
| (Number) | (128) | (151) | (159) |

Categories 3 and 4 may be taken as relatively unambiguous indicators of familial status, for reasons already mentioned, while the other categories taken separately would be less adequate. Foreign birth is included because persons in this category were born abroad mainly by reason of high family status — e.g., fathers represented the German government or important business interests in the place of birth. Foreign marriage was included because it appears that in many cases such marriages maintained (or increased) the social status of the persons in these categories. Membership in international organizations, as here defined, is an indicator of status in the careers followed by the persons in these categories. No data on "occupation abroad" are given, because this item seems to reflect skill rather than status (i.e., men normally are offered employment abroad on account of some special ability in the field of employment).

The possibility was investigated that our high figures for the propagandists might be biased by close association among all these categories in actual life. Such association might mean that the probability of appearing in any one category was not independent of the probability of appearing in any of the others, and consequently that the same propagandists recurred in several categories because they appeared in one category. To satisfy ourselves that this distortion (if present) only emphasized the prevailing tendency in the data, without altering its direction, we recomputed the data to get the number of individual persons who had at least one of the foreign contacts specified above. The results are presented in Table 19.

### Table 19
#### FOREIGN CONTACTS (BY INDIVIDUAL NAZIS)

| Propagandists (128) | Administrators (151) | Random (159) |
|---|---|---|
| 35.1% (45) | 19.8% (30) | 25.1% (40) |

These figures indicate that there is practically no distortion whatsoever in the totals presented for the combined index in Table 18. Comparing the totals given in the two tables as proportions of their sample sizes, we arrive at the following coefficients of independence:

| Propagandists | Administrators | Random |
|---|---|---|
| .714 | .769 | .740 |

Thus, while there obviously is a "dependence factor" (of the magnitude .25–.30) among the items in the combined index, this factor remains fairly constant for all three samples. It differs by .055 or less between any of the three possible paired comparisons. With only this insignificant range of deviations, then, the probability of appearing in any one category *can be treated as independent* of the probability of appearing in any other category. And therefore, joint occurrences (totals) can be expressed as the sum, or product, of separate occurrences in all the categories severally — for purposes of comparing totals as between the three samples.

Thus, we are justified in using either a combined index on all kinds of foreign contact or the separate figures on individual indicators. Both give us the same results. Since we have postulated that degree of foreign contact, as defined above, is a simple function of socioeconomic status, these tests again confirm our hypothesis that the propagandists are characteristically recruited from the higher social strata of pre-Nazi German society, the administrators from the lower social strata.

Conceived as a "battery of tests," the data already presented con-

stitute sufficient evidence that this proposition is true. It is important
to note, as we have pointed out at appropriate places, that several of
our indicators are possibly ambiguous — i.e., they are not demon-
strably unidimensional, and therefore, particularly when combined as
"indices," they may in fact document other possible assertions as well
as they do the propositions we intend them to confirm. Since methodological rigor has not been possible in all cases, we do not assert that
our central proposition is confirmed by any one of these items — but
that it is confirmed by the prevailing tendency uniformly exhibited in
the *whole battery* of items, conceived as tests of the same central
proposition.

### Process: From Elite to Alienated Intellectuals of Counterelite

With the proposition that the propagandists are drawn from higher
social strata confirmed, we may now turn to the propositions that
indicate the significance of this finding: (1) The propagandists are
intellectuals; (2) they are alienated intellectuals. When these two
statements are confirmed, we shall have documented the key proposition of this part of the study: that the Nazi propagandists were,
characteristically, a class of intellectuals born and raised within the
*elite* of Imperial and Weimar Germany who became *alienated* from
the prevailing structure of symbols and sanctions of the elite that
nurtured them.

Once the accuracy of this key proposition is accepted, we shall be in
a position to present the argument (which, since it concerns a process
rather than a class of characteristics, we shall have to make plausible
by reasoning rather than probable by data) that *alienated intellectuals*
are both an index and agent of the modern revolutionary process. We
view the history of the Nazi movement as a single instance of the process, and a test case of the general proposition. The main line of the
argument is this: Intellectuals are, by definition, those distinctively
occupied in manipulating the symbolic environment of the institutional structure of any society. As such, they expect — and receive —
high deference among the elite of any society whose symbols and
sanctions (i.e., institutional structure) of persuasion and coercion are
in a continuous and reciprocal stable relationship. Any decline in the
deference position of intellectuals from their previous level among a
particular elite is a "sign," or indicator, that the relationship between
symbols and sanctions has become unstabilized and that disintegrative
changes are occurring in that society. Decline in their deference position is thus an *index* of "alienation" among the intellectuals and hence
of social instability. As a corollary, such "alienation" is also an agent of

further disintegrative changes in the society. Intellectuals declining in deference position among a ruling elite are no longer producing the symbols that justify the sanctions institutionalized by that elite. Instead they are producing symbols that justify a rival structure of sanctions proposed by a counterelite. By withdrawing their support of the "myth" (the ruling symbols) in favor of a competing "ideology" (the rival symbols) — to use these terms in Mannheim's sense — alienated intellectuals thus contribute to the displacement of elite by counterelite that we designate as the revolutionary process of our time.[5]

With this much of our context in mind, we now turn to documenting our proposition that the Nazi propagandists are in fact "alienated intellectuals" of the former German elite. That they were drawn from the former elite has been demonstrated, and that they were intellectuals among this elite has already been indicated by the same data. The fact that they attended universities in very great number (1 out of every 2), and even when their family background discouraged such attendance, is one such indication (see Table 15); the fact that, among those who attended universities, they outnumbered the other subgroups by 3 to 1 in study of the humanities is another such indication (see Table 16). What we have called the culture-oriented studies are typically concerned with the symbolic environment of a society — both with the prevailing system of values and goals that constitute the "myth," and, particularly in times of troubles, with the literature of protest that accompanies the formation of contending values and goals into rival "ideology." The skill-oriented studies, *per contra*, are typically concerned with manipulation of the material rather than the symbolic environment. Students of business, agriculture, and engineering are trained to manipulate commodities rather than values. (Professional studies — medicine, law, engineering, etc. — usually involve facility with specialized sets of both symbols and commodities.) Our Table 16, then, which shows the administrators solidly clustered in the skill-oriented studies and the propagandists in the culture-oriented studies, can be adduced here as evidence that the latter are the intellectuals.

Besides his education, a man's occupation is an important indicator of his status as an intellectual — i.e., as a *professional* intellectual. This test, too, provides evidence that the propagandists were drawn

[5] The equilibrium metaphor is here used for expository purposes only. As formulated by Pareto, and as implied by Toynbee and others, the equilibrium metaphor has been used for purposes irrelevant to this discussion. Our data could be accounted for by other metaphors, e.g. the developmental metaphor, with equal plausibility but less facility of exposition.

predominantly from the intellectuals of the pre-Nazi German elite. Table 1 shows that the primary lifework of over half the propagandists in our sample falls into the category designated as "communications." Conceiving intellectuals as symbol manipulators (and there seems to be no more general way of defining the social function of professional intellectuals), we find that this information confirms the validity of our sample. It also presents us with an interesting tautology requiring that we elaborate our original conception as follows.

Three occupations in which the professional manipulation of symbols has become institutionalized are those of preacher, teacher, and writer. Each of these occupations is regarded as having a certain psychic sanctity about it, closely connected with the heavy burden of social responsibility (e.g., for the prevailing myth) laid upon its practitioners. It is regarded as important that any man who enters these occupations should exhibit a predispositional structure appropriate to these responsibilities — e.g., common parlance revealingly speaks of "having a call" in connection with the decision to enter one of these occupations. (It is possible that this view of medicine, sometimes heard nowadays, developed during the centuries when this profession consisted of magic and incantation, and was therefore more directly responsible for the social myth than at present.)

The appropriate predispositions, whatever they may be, are clearly encouraged or hindered by the childhood, and particularly family, environment of any individual. Such items in the childhood environment as the presence of a library in the home, the characteristic topics of discussion among dinner guests, the foci of interest of the parents, intellectual relations between parents and children — all these are involved in encouraging predispositions toward symbol manipulation among the children. We have not accumulated data on such items, but a fairly reliable index to their presence or absence is provided by the occupation of the father. A father who is a preacher or teacher or lawyer will be more likely than one who is a farmer or businessman or worker to own a private library, discuss general principles of life with his friends, analyze politics on a high level, select readings for his children with an eye to their literary merit, encourage and aid his children in their schooling.

We therefore look back to the data on father's occupations presented earlier in this study (see Table 11). Combining the three categories of ecclesiastic, professional, and communications, we find the totals shown in Table 20. As we should have expected, the propagandists outnumber both the others — the administrators by a very wide margin, the random Nazis by a narrow margin. The results are even

## Table 20
### INTELLECTUALS AMONG FATHERS

| Propagandists | Administrators | Random |
|:---:|:---:|:---:|
| 23.0% | 13.1% | 21.2% |

more pointed when we re-examine Table 11 and its sequels from this perspective. The propagandists outnumber the others in all categories of paternal occupation — e.g., landowners, higher civil service, high military office — that are likely to provide the characteristics we mentioned above as encouraging predispositions among the children to become intellectuals.

The same pattern emerges from the data we have accumulated on one direct indicator of professional intellectualism — the production of printed matter. Professional intellectuals live, occupationally, by their output of symbols in spoken and written form. Since we are here interested in demonstrating only the degree of professionalism as intellectuals, not the quality of thought, we adduce as a relevant indicator the amount of printed symbolic output among the groups shown in Table 21.

## Table 21
### NUMBER OF PUBLICATIONS

| Class | Propagandists | Administrators | Random |
|---|:---:|:---:|:---:|
| Occasional pamphlets | 4.0% | 0.0% | 0.0% |
| Regular pamphlets | 0.0 | 0.0 | 0.0 |
| Occasional articles | 12.0 | 8.6 | 12.6 |
| Regular articles | 26.0 | 24.5 | 18.2 |
| 1 Book | 1.0 | 0.6 | 3.8 |
| 2 Books | 6.0 | 3.3 | 1.3 |
| 3 Books | 7.0 | 2.6 | 1.9 |
| 4 Books | 0.0 | 1.3 | 2.5 |
| 5 Books | 0.0 | 0.0 | 2.5 |
| 6 Books | 0.0 | 0.7 | 1.3 |
| More than 6 books | 13.0 | 2.0 | 5.0 |
| Unknown | 8.0 | 3.3 | 0.6 |
| None | 23.0 | 53.0 | 52.2 |
| Total | 100.0% | 99.9% | 100.0% |
| (Number) | (100) | (151) | (159) |

The first set of figures which engages our attention in Table 21 is that for the category "none." Less than one fourth of the propagandists reported *no* publications, whereas more than one half of the administrators and random Nazis had none to report. Of those who did produce, the propagandists exceeded the others in every category of publication — books, pamphlets, and even articles (which were a habitual form of expression for important Nazi officials, regardless of their literacy). The second set of figures which strikes us is that for the producers of "more than 6 books." These are the real professionals, and here the gap between propagandists and others is most distinct: better than 1 out of every 10 propagandists published more than six books, as compared with 1 out of 20 random Nazis and 1 out of 50 administrators. (This gap is even wider when one counts our larger sample of 128 propagandists — which gives us the figure of 21.1 per cent, or better than 1 out of 5 propagandists who produced more than six books.) Since these categories in Table 21 are cumulative — no person is counted in more than one category — we may compute the number of persons in each sample who did *some* writing for publication. Even this figure, which minimizes the importance of the amount of publication, shows the propagandists to be distinctively the professional intellectuals among the Nazi elite (see Table 22).

*Table 22*

NUMBER OF WRITERS

| Propagandists | Administrators | Random |
|---------------|----------------|--------|
| 69.0% | 43.4% | 46.7% |

The type of writing done by these subgroups is also of interest here. The writer "by calling" tends to produce works of a more general nature than the person whose distinctive skill in some other field leads him to write a book about his specialty. The professional intellectual thus produces fewer technical books, more general and belle-lettristic books, and far more books that present arguments for which he is the spokesman (though the ideas on which they rest may have originated with another person, group, or party). The propagandists, as one would expect, outnumber the other Nazis in the production of writings on current history and politics (*Zeitgeschichte*) — which is the main area in which all three groups of Nazis do their writing. Conversely as expected, the propagandists lag behind the others in production of technical writings. The pattern of contrast is shown in Table 23.

It seems clear that our sample of propagandists are, characteristically, the intellectuals of the pre-Nazi German elite. Our next problem is to show that they are the "alienated" members of this intelligentsia. That this must be so seems obvious. For professional intellectuals of high status to affiliate with a revolutionary counterelite

*Table 23*
FIELD OF PUBLICATION

| Class | Propagandists | Administrators | Random |
|---|---|---|---|
| Belles-lettres | 10.2% | 0.7% | 3.1% |
| Philosophy and history | 0.8 | 0.7 | 3.8 |
| Zeitgeschichte | 42.2 | 34.4 | 13.8 |
| Natural sciences | 0.0 | 0.0 | 0.6 |
| Technical | 4.0 | 4.6 | 13.2 |
| Social science | 0.0 | 0.7 | 5.7 |
| Communication and propaganda | 7.0 | 0.0 | 0.0 |
| Racial themes | 0.8 | 0.0 | 0.6 |
| Administrative | 2.3 | 4.0 | 2.5 |
| Other | 0.8 | 0.0 | 3.1 |
| None | 22.7 | 53.0 | 52.8 |
| Don't know | 9.4 | 2.0 | 0.6 |
| Total | 100.2% | 100.1% | 99.8% |
| (Number) | (128) | (151) | (159) |

means that they must disaffiliate with the prevailing elite. This act of disaffiliation must be based on disaffection — i.e., "alienation" — due either to the decline of the elite as a whole, or to the decline in status of these intellectuals within the elite, or to both.

Our data, unfortunately, are rather meager at this point — but they do provide some indications that both of the factors just mentioned were operative in the alienation of young German intellectuals from the old elite and into affiliation with the rising Nazi counterelite. The crucial period, of course, was that of the Weimar Republic (1918–1933).

One very important indicator of the stability of any elite is the rate of unemployment in the society that it governs. Unemployment was, in fact, the rock upon which the Weimar Republic foundered and went down. The effects of unemployment upon young German intellectuals in the immediate postwar years were particularly poignant and catastrophic. We shall see, in a moment, the reflection of this unemployment on our propagandists: the data do not show that these men were totally unemployed following the war; they do show, more importantly, that they were not employed in jobs that made them proud or content with their lot, i.e., jobs that they were willing to report in the *Fuehrerlexikon.* The data bear upon the postwar phenomenon among young German intellectuals that they themselves designated as *Seelische Arbeitslosigkeit* (spiritual unemployment). The alienating effects of this prevailing situation, leading to aggressive hostility toward Weimar, among precisely the group we are discussing — whom we earlier showed to be the junior officers of the *Reichswehr* in World War I — has been depicted by Konrad Heiden:

> When the German Republic disbanded the army, more generals retained their posts than the English army has in peacetime; those who were discharged received pensions they could live on. The well-paid generals became easily reconciled to the republic. But the lieutenants and captains saw no place for advancement in the tiny army of a hundred thousand men; they saw themselves reduced to the level of armed elite proletarians. . . .
>
> This seemed the end of the lordly life to which the German intellectual youth had grown accustomed during the war. Their school course had been broken off ahead of time; their examinations had been made easy for them. After a short period of active service, they were sent to an officers' training course and soon they were lieutenants with a monthly salary of three hundred gold marks. It was a dangerous existence, but one full of pride and pleasure. The material level of life was high enough to permit of a hard fall, when, as Roehm put it, 'peace broke out.' . . .
>
> These armed intellectuals were the German army, they preserved its spirit, upheld its tradition. Even before the First World War, it had ceased to be the army of Prussian junkers, which foreigners held it to be. . . . Since the broad mass of the lower officers gives an army its character, the German Army of the World War could be called an army of armed students. And since these intellectuals in uniform found no career and no bread in the breakdown after the peace, their officer days remained for many the high point of their existence; the hope for a return of the golden days remained their secret consolation.[6]

Heiden's commentary dramatizes the process of alienation in terms of several indicators that we have been using in this study. We have already shown that the propagandists were, distinctively, the scions of those upper-middle-class strata that sent their sons to the universities in great numbers. They were, again distinctively, the junior officers in the "army of armed students" whom Heiden emphasizes. They were, finally, also the "armed intellectuals." Finding no provision for the maintenance of their high deference-status in the plans and operations of the Weimar "elite" (whom they regarded contemptuously as trade-union *Bonzen* and domesticated bureaucrats, when they did not despise them as *Verraeter* of the people and traitorous tools of foreign interests), they became the disaffected and alienated elements who shifted their allegiance to the Nazi movement, which offered them the promise of a brighter place in the sun. The terrific rate of postwar unemployment among these "armed intellectuals" is shown in Table 24.

[6] Konrad Heiden, *Der Fuehrer* (Boston: Houghton Mifflin Company, 1944), pp. 28–29.

*Table 24*
POSTWAR UNEMPLOYMENT (MORE THAN ONE FULL YEAR)

|                | Propagandists | Random |
|----------------|:-------------:|:------:|
| No job reported | 20.0%        | 13.8%  |
| Only Nazi jobs  | 25.0         | 7.5    |
| Vagueness       | 31.0         | 18.2   |
| Total           | 76.0%        | 39.5%  |
| (Number)        | (100)        | (159)  |

These comparative figures for propagandists and random Nazis (no data on this indicator were accumulated for the administrators) show quite striking differences. Since we counted only the employment date after age eighteen, the fact that propagandists are a younger group does not bias the results. (If anything, the bias is adverse to our hypothesis, since more random Nazis stayed in universities, as we showed in Table 15, past the age of eighteen.)

Nevertheless, the propagandists clearly outnumber the random Nazis in each category. For the Weimar period, 1 out of 5 propagandists reports no job at some point, as compared with somewhat less than 1 out of 7 random Nazis. The unemployment of these people came in the immediate postwar years — 16 per cent of the propagandists (and 13.2 per cent of the random Nazis) reporting no jobs for the years 1919–1923. The average duration of lack of *reported* employment for the propagandists was slightly over 4½ years, less for the others.

To these figures must be added those who report *only* Nazi jobs, i.e., employment in the NSDAP, which appears to have precluded the reporting of unemployment elsewhere. In this category propagandists outnumber random Nazis by 3 to 1. To these should be added also the category of "vagueness" — in which are included those whose failure to specify any particular jobs or dates indicates that they were in fact unemployed during part, at least, of the Weimar period. A typical example of vagueness so classified is Heinrich Salzmann, whose *Berufsgang* (occupational history) for the postwar years reads as follows:

> . . . 1920 aus dem Heer ausgeschieden und fuer das Propagandafach ausgebildet; spaeter in diesem Fach in grossen Firmen taetig; selbstaendiger Propagandafachmann.
>
> (1920 demobilized from the Army and trained for propaganda field; later active in this field in big firms; free-lance propaganda specialist.)

When all three categories are combined, we find that the rate of unemployment — which we should call, more exactly, unreported and unsatisfactory years of occupational history — we find that the propagandists out-number the random Nazis by approximately 2 to 1. Among the propagandists, nearly 4 out of every 5 fall into these categories, as compared with only 2 out of 5 random Nazis.

The data in Table 24 are based on the autobiographical data for *Berufsgang* supplied in the *Fuehrerlexikon*. The fact that a man does not report a specific job for a given period cannot be taken to mean that he had no job at all. It can, however, be taken to mean that during this period he held no job *of which he was proud* (since the main point of the *Berufsgang* in these autobiographical sketches is to report those occupations in each man's past of which he feels proud). This is, of course, the basis of our argument that "spiritual unemployment" (*Seelische Arbeitslosigkeit*) is a key indicator of the alienation of our group from the upper-middle-class German elite that nurtured them, into the Nazi counterelite that promised them the rewards to which they felt themselves entitled. Their autobiographical occupational histories illustrate the various ways in which they found a spiritual home, as professional intellectuals, in the Nazi movement.

## IV. RISE OF THE PLEBEIAN (THE NAZI ADMINISTRATORS)

The distinctive character of the Nazi propagandists, as we have seen, was its recruitment from among the alienated young intellectuals of the upper middle classes who had formed the elite of pre-Nazi Germany. The men who rose to prominence in the Nazi elite as administrators, rather than propagandists, present us with quite a different typical social status in the background of their careers (though, as we shall see later, they exhibit several interesting characteristics in common with the propagandists and with the Nazi elite in general).

### Nazi Administrators as German Plebeians

The administrators, to put the matter sharply, represent the rise of the plebeian — men born and raised in the lower social strata — to positions of high deference by means of the revolutionary process. Many of the indicators that produce evidence of their lower origins were discussed in the preceding section, where the pre-Nazi social status of administrators was compared with that of propagandists. These can be summarily recapitulated and several additional indicators can be adduced here to clarify the point still further.

We have seen that the ancestral background of administrators shows lower status than that of propagandists and random Nazis (Table 12). We have seen, too, that their parental background was also of lower status (Table 11). Particularly in those parental occupations likely to provide a home atmosphere conducive to intellectuality did we find administrators significantly outclassed by the others (Table 20). Their own education stopped at considerably lower levels (Table 15). Even among those who acquired education, its prevailing direction was in the lower-status types of learning — e.g., trade school instead of high school; skill-oriented studies (among the much smaller number who went to college) instead of culture-oriented studies (Table 16). The administrator wrote least (Table 21) and married latest (Table 17). He remained more often in enlisted status in the Army (Table 9). Where he achieved successes at all, outside of the Nazi movement, he did this less often in the high-prestige occupations and more often in the "open" field of business manipulation (Table 1).

These and other findings have already been presented to document our assertion that the Nazi administrator was recruited from the lower strata of pre-Nazi German society. What is the significance of this proposition? What does its documentation add to our understanding of the revolutionary process of our time, as illustrated by the success story of the Nazi movement in Germany? These are difficult questions, and we shall present here only the main lines of the argument needed to clarify our analysis.

We have already presented the view that the Nazi movement was the political instrument of a counterelite determined to undermine the governing elite of Weimar Germany and install itself in the seats of power. We have indicated why this movement scorned and despised the prevailing structure of symbols and sanctions upon which rested the power of the Weimar elite, and how they proposed to undermine this structure. We have indicated, finally, how the decade of crisis — inflation, unemployment, and national shame on the internal scene; isolationism, unstable international relations, and catastrophic economic depression in the world arena — facilitated the conquest of the Weimar politics of parliament by the Nazi politics of the street.

Politics of the street is a complex process. It involves a number and variety of skills, which we earlier characterized simply as "the organized use of voice and violence to gain power." The coordinated use of mass persuasion and coercion to gain power through the streets requires certain types of behavior that are not permissible to representatives of a modern governing elite that operates under a democratic structure of symbols and sanctions. Elite representatives who have become routinized in the behavioral restraints of a democratic process may no longer be capable, temperamentally, of behaving in such ways. This is illustrated by the complete failure of the German Social-Democratic Party — the newest comer to the German elite under Weimar and the only group within this elite whose official ideology gave formal sanction to such tactics — when it attempted to compete with the Nazi Party in the politics of the streets.[7]

We have already enumerated some of the tasks which must be accomplished in the Nazi type of street politics: make and applaud speeches, write and deliver messages, fight in the streets, etc. Such activities become the province of skill specialists: the propagandists handle the politics of voice; the coercers (whom we shall discuss in the next section of this study) handle the politics of violence. As the movement grows, such activities multiply, and their effective coordination becomes a major task. The key to success thus moves into the hands of those men who organize such special skills and separate activities so that they make maximum contributions to the movement's objective — gaining power. These men are the administrators.

The administrators are those who come early and stay late in the movement. In the early days, they use voice and violence themselves, as well as organizing its use by others. As the movement grows, they move up its ladder of deference status; as the number and variety of the movement's activities increase, they become those who direct the behavior of others on a full-time basis. They are the operating arm of the movement's policy directorate, which is usually composed of individuals who have come from their own ranks. They are the *echt-Nazi* corps of the Nazi elite, the embodiment of the new structure of symbols and sanctions that is to prevail when "the revolution" succeeds.

It is of great importance, therefore, to notice what manner of men these are and where they came from. The fact that the Nazi administrators were drawn from the lower social strata contributes to our understanding of German society, and particularly its ills in the Weimar period. It contributes to our understanding of the role of the Nazi movement, and particularly its appeal to those men who became its administrators. It contributes to our general understanding of the characteristic behavior of these administrators as a social formation in a time of prolonged crisis.

Among the ills of German society in the Weimar period was, centrally, the absence of a unified elite operating a homogeneous structure of symbols and sanctions that commanded a consensus of loyalty

---

[7] See Serge Chakhotin, *Rape of the Masses* (London: Routledge, 1940). The other party whose official dogma sanctioned such tactics, the Communist, was not included among the Weimar elite.

among the citizens. The social process fluctuated without central purpose and governing direction in its movements. With each fluctuation, one or another segment of the population was alienated. Hardest hit, perhaps, was the numerically most important segment — the plebeian masses. The plebeian is not identical with the proletarian. He is, rather, the "unorganized" worker, the unemployed worker (*Lumpenproletariat*), the peasant, the small peddler and shopkeeper — all those variants of the "*kleiner Mann*," the little man without strong and dignified interest-group affiliations, with whom so many Germans identify themselves. The life pattern of the plebeian, historically, has been the brutish life of incessant toil whose purpose was supplied by the sense of direction elaborated by the elite that governed him.

The movement of Western history had been, in other countries, directed toward ameliorating the lot of the plebeian — by lightening his daily toil and by giving him a share in the shaping of its purpose. This movement in history had achieved few conspicuous successes in Imperial Germany, but the elite of the *Kaiserreich* remained fairly homogeneous and in possession of a fairly stable structure of symbols and sanctions.[8] The heterogeneous elite of the Weimar Republic, whose avowed purpose was to give the lagging democratic process in Germany a push forward, failed miserably to provide its plebeian masses with either the toil to keep them busy or the sense of direction to keep them happy. It failed even — and this is the bitter paradox — to increase their share in the articulation of a governing code to their own choosing. The trade-union *Bonzen* and others who drew the scorn and contempt of the Nazis drew also the scorn and contempt of the plebeian masses, whom they sometimes claimed to represent. It was the Nazi movement, during these high-tension years of Weimar frustration and failure, which increasingly became the sole spokesman that said to the plebeian German: Come with us to seize the seats of power, throw out these contemptible "representatives" who speak for no German interest or ideal, and thereafter we German people shall be our own spokesmen.

### Role of the NSDAP

The plebeian was naturally drawn to such a movement, even if the proletarian (the urban worker with a movement of his own) was not. For such a goal, he saw purpose in licking stamps and envelopes, in chalking swastikas on walls, in courting injuries from "their" security

---

[8] Still the most brilliant exposition of this process in the *Kaiserreich* is Thorstein Veblen's *Imperial Germany and the Industrial Revolution* (New York: The Viking Press, 1946).

police. The Nazi movement gave him work to fill his hours and a sense of purpose to fill his days. The *Bewegung* would bring into being the plebeian republic of which the *Bonzen* only talked and despaired. To the *Bewegung*, then, the plebeian came — first only the hardy and convinced ones; then as success began to succeed, the desirous many. The administrators-to-be were the first to come, as is shown in Table 25.

*Table 25*
DATE OF JOINING NSDAP

| Class | Propagandists | Administrators | Random |
|---|---|---|---|
| Pre-1923 | 20.3% | 27.2% | 9.4% |
| 1924 | 0.8 | 3.3 | 0.0 |
| 1925 | 2.3 | 5.3 | 1.9 |
| 1926 | 0.8 | 5.3 | 0.6 |
| 1927 | 1.6 | 4.0 | 3.1 |
| 1928 | 2.3 | 4.6 | 1.9 |
| 1929 | 7.8 | 9.9 | 5.0 |
| 1930 | 3.1 | 9.9 | 1.9 |
| 1931 | 0.8 | 9.3 | 5.0 |
| 1932 | 1.6 | 1.3 | 0.0 |
| 1933 and after | 1.6 | 2.0 | 0.0 |
| Unknown | 57.0 | 17.9 | 71.1 |
| Total | 100.0% | 100.0% | 99.9% |
| (Number) | (128) | (151) | (159) |

The priority of the administrators over the random Nazis, and even over the propagandists, is quite striking. More than 1 out of 4 administrators who reached elite status (through inclusion in the *Fuehrerlexikon*) was already affiliated with the infant NSDAP in its birth pangs of the pre-1923 years — as compared with 1 out of 5 propagandists and 1 out of 10 random Nazis. The results are even clearer when presented cumulatively, as in Table 26. By 1930 — that is, before

*Table 26*
DATE OF JOINING NSDAP (CUMULATIVE)

| Class | Propagandists | Administrators | Random |
|---|---|---|---|
| Through 1923 | 20.3% | 27.1% | 9.4% |
| Through 1925 | 23.4 | 35.6 | 11.2 |
| Through 1930 | 39.0 | 69.1 | 23.5 |

the Nazis achieved their first great public victory — two thirds of the administrators were already members of the party, as compared with only one third of the propagandists and one fourth of the random Nazis. (The interesting category of "unknown," which we shall later analyze in some detail, here as elsewhere is quite revealing. The exact inverse correspondence between the size of the unknowns and the priority of known dates in the three samples is a strong indication of what we would anyhow expect: that the dates not given were those that came late, or not at all, rather than early.)

The administrators not only came early and stayed late, but they also went higher in the Nazi movement. Evidence of the central role of the administrators is the data on status in the NSDAP (as reported in the *Fuehrerlexikon*) shown in Table 27.

### Table 27
#### NSDAP Status

| Class | Propagandists | Administrators | Random |
|---|---|---|---|
| High officer | 28.1% | 51.7% | 14.5% |
| Middle officer | 12.5 | 24.5 | 13.2 |
| Low officer | 0.0 | 3.3 | 0.0 |
| Officer (no rank given) | 1.6 | 0.7 | 0.0 |
| No officer (membership given) | 5.5 | 0.0 | 0.6 |
| Don't know | 52.3 | 19.9 | 71.7 |
| Total | 100.0% | 100.1% | 100.0% |
| (Number) | (128) | (151) | (159) |

Administrators outnumbered propagandists in the higher ranks of the NSDAP by 2 to 1, and again outnumbered them by 2 to 1 in the middle ranks. They outnumbered the random Nazis by nearly 4 to 1 in the higher ranks, and by 2 to 1 in the middle ranks. Again, the "don't know" category may be taken as approximately the number of those who held no high or middle rank (or else, in the *Fuehrerlexikon*, they would surely have volunteered this information). And here, the other two samples overwhelmingly outnumber the administrators.

The same result appears uniformly in our survey of the major organizations affiliated to the Nazi movement. This is shown in Tables 28

### Table 28
#### Status in NSDAP Action Organs (S.A., S.S., N.S.K.K.)

| Class | Propagandists | Administrators | Random |
|---|---|---|---|
| High officer | 3.9% | 14.6% | 4.4% |
| Middle officer | 6.2 | 7.9 | 3.8 |
| Low officer | 3.1 | 2.0 | 1.3 |
| Don't know | 86.7 | 75.5 | 90.6 |
| Total | 99.9% | 100.0% | 100.1% |
| (Number) | (128) | (151) | (159) |

*Table 29*
STATUS IN NSDAP CULTURAL-PROFESSIONAL ORGANS

| Class | Propagandists | Administrators | Random |
|---|---|---|---|
| High officer | 33.6% | 59.6% | 22.0% |
| Middle officer | 1.6 | 2.6 | 3.1 |
| Low officer | 0.8 | 0.0 | 0.0 |
| Don't know | 64.0 | 37.7 | 74.8 |
| Total | 100.0% | 99.9% | 99.9% |
| (Number) | (128) | (151) | (159) |

and 29. These data are very striking. It is perhaps natural that administrators should greatly outnumber the others in the top status of "action organs" such as the S.A., S.S., and N.S.K.K. That administrators should outnumber propagandists by 2 to 1, and random Nazis by 3 to 1, in the direction of the "cultural-professional organs" for those fields of interest in which these other Nazi subgroups were predominantly specialized can only be accounted for by the proposition that the administrators came early *and took over* the direction of the Nazi movement as a whole — a proposition documented by all the available data.

That the administrators, who were the ones that came earliest, took the highest positions in the Nazi movement is in line with a heavy emphasis in the Nazi Party on seniority. Early membership was one of the most important distinctions a Nazi could claim. Not only among the administrators, but in each sample, the oldest members predominate in the highest ranks, as shown in Table 30. The conclusion we draw is that in the Nazi Party, despite its being a revolutionary movement, leadership came chiefly, not to those of propagandist brilliance or charismatic qualities, but to those with the more bureaucratic qualities of loyalty and seniority — traits the administrators showed. While the administrators had joined early and remained steadfast long, it should not be assumed that they joined young. It will be recalled that both in the early years of the Nazi movement and later on, the administrators joined at a later age than did the propagandists (see Table 6). They had "knocked around" longer. They were not student Bohemians like the propagandists, but disappointed men from the lower ranks who had tried to make a middle-class career, and had failed.

### Origins

Where did these plebeian administrators, who took over the movement, come from? Our data on their region of birth, as shown in Table 31, give some interesting comparisons with the other groups.

Table 30

RANK IN NSDAP BY DATE OF JOINING

| Date Joined NSDAP | Propagandists | | | | Administrators | | | | Random | | | |
|---|---|---|---|---|---|---|---|---|---|---|---|---|
| | High Office | Mid. Office | Low Office | Mem-ber* | High Office | Mid. Office | Low Office | Mem-ber* | High Office | Mid. Office | Low Office | Mem-ber* |
| 1923 or before | 20 | 4 | 1 | 1 | 29 | 10 | 1 | 1 | 8 | 7 | — | — |
| 1924–1926 | 3 | 2 | — | — | 12 | 5 | — | 4 | 2 | 2 | — | — |
| 1927–1929 | 4 | 5 | 1 | 5 | 18 | 6 | 2 | 2 | 5 | 4 | — | 7 |
| 1930 and after | 3 | 3 | — | 3 | 8 | 12 | 2 | 11 | 2 | 4 | — | 5 |
| Total | 30 | 14 | 2 | 9 | 67 | 33 | 5 | 18 | 17 | 17 | — | 12 |

* Holding of office not mentioned in biography.

*Table 31*
PROVINCE OF BIRTH

|  | Propagandists | Administrators | Random |
|---|---|---|---|
| Prussia, North of Berlin (incl. Berlin) | 14.1% | 8.6% | 17.0% |
| Prussia, East of Berlin (incl. Silesia) | 13.3 | 11.9 | 11.3 |
| Prussia, West of Berlin | 10.9 | 15.2 | 22.6 |
| Saxony (State) | 7.0 | 4.6 | 5.0 |
| Thuringia | 3.9 | 3.3 | 3.1 |
| Bavaria | 10.2 | 20.5 | 9.4 |
| Wuerttemberg-Baden | 9.4 | 8.6 | 10.1 |
| Alsace-Lorraine and Saar | 1.6 | 6.0 | 1.3 |
| Hessen-Nassau | 4.7 | 6.0 | 8.2 |
| Rhineland | 7.8 | 6.0 | 3.1 |
| Ruhr | 3.9 | 0.7 | 4.4 |
| Other | 2.3 | 2.0 | 1.9 |
| Abroad | 7.0 | 4.6 | 2.5 |
| No data | 3.9 | 2.0 | 0.0 |
| Total | 100.0% | 100.0% | 99.9% |
| (Number) | (128) | (151) | (159) |

We shall return to this table later, in our discussion of "marginality" among the Nazi elite (Part VI), when the preponderance of random Nazis in the central provinces of Germany will be contrasted with the preponderance of propagandists and administrators in the outlying, border, and foreign areas. Here we wish to note especially only the very heavy concentration of administrators in Bavaria — 1 out of every 5 was born there, as contrasted with 1 out of every 10 propagandists and random Nazis. These figures show a clear deviation: the population of Bavaria in 1890 — which is approximately the median date of birth for these samples — was 5,594,982.[9] This is approximately one tenth of the total population of Germany at that time (49,428,470), which corresponds to the 10 per cent of propagandists and random Nazis born there. The fact that twice as many administrators were born there as were Germans as a whole, or even other samples of the Nazi elite, probably must be accounted for by the fact that the Nazi movement originated and grew to power in Bavaria (with its chief command posts at Munich and Nuremberg). The administrators, who, as we have seen, came earliest and rose highest fastest, were predominantly recruited from the local talent available in Bavaria.

The finding that the administrators born in Bavaria outnumber the

[9] All figures from *Statistisches Jahrbuch fuer das deutsche Reich*, 1892 ed.

others by 2 to 1 takes on added meaning, with reference to the "rise of the plebeian," when we examine the comparative data on size of birthplace, as presented in Table 32.

That none of these Nazis reports himself as born on a farm is probably due to the habit of reporting birthplace in terms of the nearest *Gemeinde* (civil administration unit). The administrators substan-

### Table 32
#### SIZE OF BIRTHPLACE

| Class | Propagandists | Administrators | Random |
|---|---|---|---|
| Farm | 0.0% | 0.0% | 0.0% |
| Village (under 2,000) | 18.0 | 25.8 | 21.4 |
| Rural town (2,000–5,000) | 2.0 | 9.3 | 6.3 |
| Small city (5,000–20,000) | 11.0 | 9.3 | 13.8 |
| Middle city (20,000–100,000) | 14.0 | 19.2 | 17.0 |
| Large city (over 100,000) | 13.0 | 16.6 | 17.6 |
| Metropolis* | 24.0 | 13.2 | 14.5 |
| University city | 2.0 | 0.0 | 0.0 |
| Abroad (metropolis) | 6.0 | 4.6 | 2.5 |
| No data | 10.0 | 2.0 | 6.9 |
| Total | 100.0% | 100.0% | 100.0% |
| (Number) | (100) | (151) | (159) |

* Metropolis includes Berlin, Munich, Breslau, Dresden, Hamburg, Koeln, Koenigsberg, Leipzig, and Stuttgart.

tially outnumber the others in villages and in rural towns. The comparative pattern of birthplaces become clearer when the figures are presented grouped, as in Table 33. This shows, quite clearly, that the

### Table 33
#### SIZE OF BIRTHPLACE (GROUPED)

| Class | Propagandists | Administrators | Random |
|---|---|---|---|
| Rural (under 5,000) | 20.0% | 35.0% | 27.5% |
| Urban (5,000– 100,000 plus) | 38.0 | 44.9 | 48.3 |
| Metropolitan (Categories 7 and 9) | 32.0 | 17.7 | 16.9 |

random Nazis conform most closely to the normal distribution of the German population — heaviest in the middle-sized cities, with the next-greatest concentration in rural places, outnumbering the density in metropolitan places by about 1½ to 1. The propagandists are the "big city slickers": they deviate by reversing the pattern in favor of the metropolitan (communication centers — showing 1 out of 3 born in a metropolis as compared with only 1 out of 5 born in a rural area. The administrators precisely reverse this pattern of the propagandists showing more than 1 out of 3 born in rural places and less than 1 out of 5 born in metropolitan centers. The administrators characteristically differ from the other Nazis in their origins as peasants and sons of peasants — and, to a marked degree, Bavarian peasants.

### Movements and Career

We shall not undertake here any commentary on the psychology of the German peasant, and particularly the Bavarian peasant. Our interest here is to show that, whatever this German peasantry was like, the men who became our sample of Nazi administrators moved away from it and into greener pastures fairly early in life. The autobiographies in the *Fuehrerlexikon* show a remarkable rate of movement from smaller birthplaces to larger cities. We therefore computed the percentage of those within each sample who made such a move, and noted the age at which the move was made. The results are shown in Table 34. The most interesting categories here are the first two. Of the

*Table 34*
AGE AT MOVE TO METROPOLIS (ENTIRE SAMPLE)

| Class | Propagandists | Administrators | Random |
|---|---|---|---|
| Under 18 | 17.2% | 25.2% | 13.8% |
| 18–25 | 8.6 | 20.5 | 47.8 |
| Over 25 | 1.6 | 2.0 | 4.4 |
| No move | 3.1 | 0.0 | 3.8 |
| Born in metropolis | 25.0 | 15.2 | 13.8 |
| No date | 44.5 | 37.1 | 16.4 |
| Total | 100.0% | 100.0% | 100.0% |
| (Number) | (128) | (151) | (159) |

administrators, 1 out of every 4 moved to the big city before he was eighteen years old; 1 out of every 5 who stayed home longer made his move before he was twenty-five. Since these percentages somewhat obscure the factor of birth in metropolis (which obviates the need for a move), and since the importance of this factor varies considerably between the three samples (as does the size of the "no data" category), we have recomputed the data and express them in Table 35 as percentages of those whose moves are reported.

This presentation gives us a somewhat better perspective on the

*Table 35*

AGE AT MOVE TO METROPOLIS (MOVES REPORTED)

| Class | Propagandists | Administrators | Random |
|---|---|---|---|
| Under 18 | 56.4% | 52.8% | 19.8% |
| 18–25 | 28.2 | 43.1 | 68.4 |
| Over 25 | 5.1 | 4.2 | 6.3 |
| No move | 10.2 | 0.0 | 5.4 |
| Total | 99.9% | 100.1% | 99.9% |
| (Number) | (39) | (72) | (111) |

propagandists as young-men-in-a-hurry. The administrators, however, clearly lead the procession when one cumulates the first two rows, to get the percentages of those who moved to the big city before they were twenty-five years old, namely:

| | Propagandists | Administrators | Random |
|---|---|---|---|
| Under 25 | 84.6% | 95.9% | 88.2% |

Not only did the administrators go younger, but apparently more of them went. No administrator born in a smaller place reports that he did not move to a metropolis, whereas 1 out of 10 propagandists and 1 out of 20 random Nazis report no such move.

The questions which then arise are: What did these young men go to the big city for? What did they do after they got there? Data bearing on these questions were gathered by tabulating the main occupations of these persons after their move to the metropolis. The results are expressed in Table 36 as percentages in each category of those who did move.

So, though the administrator-to-be hurried to the big city at a tender

*Table 36*

MAIN OCCUPATION AFTER MOVE TO METROPOLIS

| Class | Propagandists | Administrators | Random |
|---|---|---|---|
| Schooling | 64.2% | 48.5% | 70.5% |
| Nazi Party official | 0.0 | 3.1 | 0.8 |
| Civil service | 0.0 | 2.3 | 2.3 |
| Military | 3.2 | 3.1 | 0.8 |
| Business | 2.1 | 3.9 | 4.5 |
| Professions | 0.0 | 0.0 | 0.8 |
| Communications | 6.3 | 0.0 | 0.8 |
| Other | 0.0 | 0.0 | 0.0 |
| No data | 24.2 | 39.1 | 19.7 |
| Total | 100.0% | 100.0% | 100.2% |
| (Number) | (95) | (128) | (132) |

age, and got there before the other Nazis, he did not go for an education, as Table 36 indicates. Whereas two thirds of the propagandists and random Nazis went to school after their arrival in the metropolis, less than one half of the younger administrators occupied their time in this way. Nor were the administrators more significantly employed in gainful occupations. (The null category of "other" employment is shown in Table 36 merely to demonstrate that all reported employment is exhausted within our categories.) If we omit schooling and NSDAP affiliation, neither of which was an income-producing occupation, we find the following figures for gainful employment after moving to the metropolis:

|  | *Propagandists* | *Administrators* | *Random* |
|---|---|---|---|
| Gainful employment | 11.6% | 9.3% | 9.2% |

The one place where the administrators, who lag behind in both schooling and gainful employment, got something of a head start over the others by rushing to the city was in the officialdom of the Nazi Party. But the most important category in Table 36, as in so many other cases, is that of "no data." It is here that the administrators make up their lag behind the others: 39 per cent of them report no data on this important period in their life histories. That is, 15 per cent more administrators than propagandists, and 20 per cent more administrators than random Nazis, chose to remain silent about how they occupied their time after they moved to the big city. It seems highly probable that, here as elsewhere, "no data" can be taken as roughly equivalent to a statement, "no worthwhile activities to report," by the autobiographees.

Valuable evidence that "no data" is, in this particular case, an important equivalent of "no worthwhile activity" comes from the figures we have gathered on the age at which these men held their first career jobs. To define the categories used in Table 37, we considered as the "first career job" that in which the person first worked in the field of *his own* primary (or secondary) lifework.

Table 37, in the light of the data already presented, provides us with some of our most valuable material on all of these three samples. We shall take space here to draw only the main conclusions that bear on the key propositions we have formulated, particularly with respect to the administrators.

One striking pattern is that exhibited by the random Nazis. Practically all of these persons are launched in their careers before they are thirty-five; only three of them lag into the next decade of their

*Table 37*
AGE AT FIRST CAREER JOB

| Class | Propagandists | Administrators | Random* |
|---|---|---|---|
| Under 18 | 3.9% | 2.0% | 1.4% |
| 18–25 | 32.8 | 27.8 | 37.1 |
| 26–30 | 18.0 | 21.9 | 37.1 |
| 31–35 | 10.9 | 16.6 | 10.1 |
| 36–40 | 3.1 | 3.3 | 1.4 |
| 41–45 | 3.1 | 4.6 | 0.6 |
| 46–50 | 1.6 | 1.3 | 0.0 |
| 51–55 | 1.6 | 0.7 | 0.0 |
| 56–60 | 0.8 | 1.3 | 0.0 |
| 61–65 | 1.6 | 2.6 | 0.0 |
| Over 65 | 0.0 | 0.0 | 0.0 |
| No data | 22.6 | 17.9 | 12.2 |
| Total | 100.0% | 99.9% | 99.9% |
| (Number) | (128) | (151) | (159) |

* In the case of the random sample the first responsible job was coded. This is not necessarily the same career that they later followed.

lives; after forty-five, all of them are "settled." This contrasts greatly with the two other Nazi subgroups, many of whom continue to find their first career jobs after thirty-five and up to sixty-five. The distinctive patterns are brought out more clearly by separating the groups under and over age thirty-five, where the natural division in Table 37 seems to come for all three samples, namely:

| Class | Propagandists | Administrators | Random |
|---|---|---|---|
| Under 35 | 84.8% | 83.0% | 97.8% |
| Over 35 | 15.1 | 16.9 | 2.1 |
| Totals | 99.9% | 99.9% | 99.9% |
| (Number) | (128) | (151) | (159) |

The picture is clarified still further when, again presenting the figures as percentages of known data, the division is made at age thirty, namely:

| Class | Propagandists | Administrators | Random |
|---|---|---|---|
| Under 30 | 70.7% | 62.9% | 86.3% |
| Over 30 | 29.2 | 37.0 | 13.6 |
| Totals | 99.9% | 99.9% | 99.9% |
| (Number) | (128) | (151) | (159) |

By age thirty, then, only 2 out of 3 administrators had settled in some career job — as compared with 3 out of 4 propagandists and 9 out of 10 random Nazis. By age thirty-five, the random Nazis were practically all "settled," but the administrators — with 1 out of 6 still unsettled — had nearly caught up on the propagandists. This lag of five years behind the propagandists is characteristic of the broken and halting character of the careers of the administrators. They started with a handicap, coming from provincial backgrounds, poorer families, and lesser schooling. More often they served time in the Army. Then they came out into an economy where unemployment was widespread. Lacking the skills of the other groups, they were unemployed longer and held more transitory and menial jobs. This was true of those administrators who joined the Nazis in the early years. It was even more strikingly true for those who joined later on, as shown in Table 38.

## Table 38
### Party Members without First Responsible Job by Twenty-Five

|  | Propagandists | Administrators | Random |
|---|---|---|---|
| Joined by 1928 | 34.2% | 46.0% | 28.5% |
| Joined after 1929 | 42.9 | 79.5 | 56.3 |

Despite their shorter schooling and therefore earlier job availability, the administrators were slower in getting responsible jobs. The most striking fact, however, is the great increase in the number without early responsible jobs. Those who joined the party earlier were older, for one thing. They may have held responsible jobs in the more stable days before the First World War, or they may have held responsible military posts during the war. Furthermore, those who joined the party early acquired party jobs. Those who stayed out until later postponed the possibility of acquiring such positions. Those, however, were a minority. The majority of administrators had joined by 1928.

This we have already seen from the data on their comparative dates of joining the NSDAP (see Table 25). The point is clear from comparing the numbers who joined in the five years between 1918 and 1923. These were the years when the NSDAP was merely a gleam in the eyes of a Munich "lunatic fringe" and the act of joining it was mainly significant as a symbolic rite of alienation from existing German society. It is therefore useful to look here at the figures on those who performed this rite prior to 1923:

|  | Propagandists | Administrators | Random |
|---|---|---|---|
| Joined NSDAP before 1923 | 20.3% | 27.2% | 9.4% |

It is clear that the "alienated intellectuals," the propagandists, also found their way early into the Nazi movement. But it is the "alienated plebeians," the administrators, who outnumber the others — with almost as many members in the NSDAP prior to 1923 as the two other samples combined.

### Education, Occupation, and Career

What careers did these men make for themselves, these men who joined the party early and settled in their careers late? Let us look first at the group that, after moving to the big city, attended school for a time. We have already seen that comparatively few of the administrators reached the university level of education, namely (from Table 15):

|  | Propagandists | Administrators | Random |
|---|---|---|---|
| University education | 59.0% | 25.2% | 60.4% |

Whereas better than 1 out of 2 propagandists and random Nazis attended universities, only 1 out of 4 (or half as many) administrators attained this level. Of those who did attend, the great majority concentrated on professional studies leading to licensed occupations — in this case even a higher proportion of administrators than propagandists — namely (from Table 16):

|  | Propagandists | Administrators | Random |
|---|---|---|---|
| Professional studies | 59.6% | 67.1% | 77.9% |

Comparatively few of the administrators actually received professional degrees — only 29 per cent of the administrators, as compared with 38 per cent of the propagandists and 48 per cent of the random Nazis. The numbers, and the fields to which they received academic certification, are shown in Table 39. In this table the categories are arranged according to a rough ranking of their deference status in postwar Germany, and the figures are expressed as percentages in each category of those who actually received degrees.

Our data do not permit us to make all the precise distinctions we would wish to have, for example, as between those law and education degrees which bore the title of *Referendar* or *Assessor*. The information given, however, is adequate for accurate distinctions between high, middle, and low status in these professions. In the civil service category, indeed, we have included only those whose status entitled them to the "professional" label. Hence, we may discuss the meaning of this table for deference status with some confidence.

Deference includes, in addition to the rewards in income and prestige that are attached to an occupation, the opportunity to gain these

*Table 39*
PROFESSIONAL DEGREES RECEIVED

| Class | Propagandists | Administrators | Random |
|---|---|---|---|
| Law | 57.9% | 17.3% | 56.0% |
| Civil service | 0.0 | 1.9 | 1.2 |
| Theology | 2.6 | 1.9 | 6.0 |
| Medical sciences | 10.5 | 13.5 | 15.5 |
| Education | 10.5 | 15.4 | 6.0 |
| Engineering | 5.3 | 7.7 | 13.1 |
| Architecture | 7.9 | 9.6 | 0.0 |
| Business (*Diplomkaufmann*) | 0.0 | 3.8 | 1.2 |
| Military | 5.3 | 28.8 | 1.2 |
| Total | 100.0% | 99.9% | 100.1% |
| (Number) | (38) | (52) | (84) |

rewards by actually working at these occupations. For this reason we have placed law and civil service in the two top categories; and the building, business, and military professions in the bottom four categories.[10] There can be little doubt that the postwar years in Germany offered persons in these last four professions fewer opportunities to gain through actual practice the rewards which traditionally were accorded to them. Yet it is precisely in these lower categories that the administrators, who lag behind at the top, begin to outnumber the other Nazis. Because expectations among these professionals were high, such deprivations were felt all the more keenly. (We can mention here Hitler's disappointment in an abortive architectural career, and also Rosenberg's, not as impressive evidence but merely as illustrative cases.)

The point we wish to make is shown most clearly by comparing the top category with the bottom category. The lawyers, who enjoyed high prestige, had fair opportunities for employment even under Weimar: with a new type of government to operate (Republican rather than Imperial), with a brand-new constitution to expound and interpret, with many and varied claims arising from the war to be presented for legal adjudication. At the bottom, we have placed the military professionals, who were surely among the most frustrated Germans under Weimar — with a profession traditionally entitled to

---

[10] Cf. the ranking of professions at this period given in Hans L. Menzel, *Wirtschaftliche Grundlagen des Studiums vor und nach dem Kriege* (Inaug. dissertation, University of Berlin, 1931), pp. 19–20.

high deference, but with no opportunities to acquire its rewards through practice. At the top, the administrators are outnumbered 3 to 1 by the others; at the frustrating bottom, the administrators outnumber the others by even wider margins.

The unimpressive careers of the administrators are further evidenced by the jobs they actually took. This was shown in Table 1. We might add, however, that even when an administrator went into the higher-ranking categories of profession it was often at a lower level. Thus, we noted that the civil service was the primary lifework of 9.0 per cent of the propagandists, 13.2 per cent of the administrators, and 27.7 per cent of the random sample. The civil service jobs that the administrators took, however, were ones open to persons with less education than the jobs taken by the propagandists and administrators. German civil service examinations were closely geared to the educational system. The propagandists and random Nazis took them when they were equipped for the better jobs. The administrators took them when they were prepared only for lower jobs. Table 40 makes this clear.

*Table 40*

INDIVIDUALS IN EACH CELL WHOSE PRIMARY LIFEWORK WAS CIVIL SERVICE

| Education Attained | Propagandists | Administrators | Random |
|---|---|---|---|
| University | 12.3% | 7.8% | 37.5% |
| Higher schools | 6.7 | 14.8 | 29.4 |
| Trade, high, or grade school | 2.7 | 14.1 | 4.7 |

How about that large group of administrators who did not go to school, but also did not find jobs? It is difficult to trace their history through the usual criteria, for they chose not to report on these postwar years when little that they did by way of "normal" occupation gave them satisfaction and pride. Some evidence of how these persons spent their time can be gleaned, however, from our data on their participation in "abnormal" occupations — such as the *Reichswehr*, the *Freikorps*, and the NSDAP. For these were activities that — from the perspective of the *Fuehrerlexikon* in 1934–1935, at least — did give them satisfaction and pride. On such activities, accordingly, those who did participate report without reserve.

The comparative figures on service in the *Reichswehr*, expressed as percentages of all who report service within each sample, are shown in Table 41.

*Table 41*
SERVICE IN REICHSWEHR

| Propagandists | Administrators | Random |
|---------------|---------------|--------|
| 7.8% | 14.7% | 4.3% |

The average length of service for those who served is as shown in Table 42. These figures indicate that administrators outnumbered

*Table 42*
LENGTH OF SERVICE IN REICHSWEHR

| Propagandists | Administrators | Random |
|---------------|---------------|--------|
| 2.4 years | 4.1 years | 2.0 years |

propagandists by about 2 to 1, and outnumbered random Nazis by well over 3 to 1, in *Reichswehr* service. Those more numerous administrators who served, we notice, also served twice as long as the others.

The autobiographical information reported on service in the *Freikorps*, which sprang up throughout Germany as the most extreme form of protest against Weimar and particularly against its acquiescent posture toward the "shame of Versailles," shows the same pattern even more clearly. (Figures for average length of service all are insignificant owing to the brief life of the *Freikorps*.) The comparative percentages of each subgroup for service in the *Freikorps* are as shown in Table 43. The *Freikorps* drew into its ranks 1 out of 4

*Table 43*
SERVICE IN FREIKORPS

| Propagandists | Administrators | Random |
|---------------|---------------|--------|
| 9.2% | 23.5% | 14.3% |

administrators, as compared with 1 out of 7 random Nazis and 1 out of 11 propagandists. These *Freikorps*, which began the work of undermining the Weimar elite, became the main recruiting ground of the Nazis who finished that job. They were also the training ground of those *echt*-Nazi German plebeians who came early to the party, rose highest in its ranks, and gave it the distinctive character that brought it to triumph in one decade, and then to ruin in the next decade.

The last set of data we shall present on the administrators, to complete this portrait of their life histories during the postwar and pre-Nazi Weimar decade, shows what happened to the vast majority of them — those who went to school and those who did not, those who joined the

*Reichswehr-Freikorps* and those who did not. These data bear on what we have called the subsidiary lifework of the Nazis. Our interest in this class of data arose when we noted the extraordinary amount of shift and discontinuity in the occupational histories reported by these persons. We noted that primary lifework was, in very many cases, an inadequate indicator of the career line because so many men who wanted to receive professional degrees never received them, those who did receive them practiced their professions for only a limited period, and so on through the run of items in the *"Berufsgänge"* of these Nazis. Accordingly, we began to supplement our data on education and occupation with other indicators, such as we have been reporting on above — *Reichswehr, Freikorps*, etc. We found that these data accounted for most of the years of the Weimar period (1918–1933) for most of the individuals sampled. But they most distinctly failed to account satisfactorily for the activities of the administrators, until we began to collect information about those activities at which these men spent the second-longest period of time in their *"Berufsgänge."* These data provide the thread of continuity through the decade when the Nazis were moving from obscurity to total power, and they show most clearly why the administrators are distinct from the others in the way they spent their time during these years.

### Table 44
#### SUBSIDIARY LIFEWORK

| Class | Propagandists | Administrators | Random |
|---|---|---|---|
| NSDAP official | 21.9% | 81.5% | 24.5% |
| Civil service | 11.7 | 2.0 | 12.6 |
| Professions | 5.5 | 0.7 | 19.5 |
| Communications | 36.7 | 2.6 | 6.3 |
| Military | 1.6 | 1.3 | 2.5 |
| Business | 3.1 | 3.3 | 1.9 |
| Artisans | 0.8 | 0.7 | 0.0 |
| Farmers | 0.8 | 2.0 | 1.3 |
| Others | 2.4 | 0.0 | 1.9 |
| No subsidiary lifework | 15.6 | 6.0 | 29.6 |
| Total | 100.1% | 100.1% | 100.0% |
| (Number) | (128) | (151) | (159) |

Many important points are brought to light by Table 44. Starting from the bottom, we notice first that more than 1 out of 4 random Nazis and 1 out of 6 propagandists report no subsidiary lifework — thus indicating that they stayed put, relatively, and thereby explaining why their years were pretty adequately accounted for by adding education to primary lifework and comparing the sum with their average age. The administrators, however, for whom this procedure left us with a gap of years unaccounted for, report that only 1 out of 20 had no subsidiary lifework. In other words, more than 9 out of 10 administrators did make significant career-shifts outside of the normal occupational categories during this period.

Coming up the table, we notice other useful bits of evidence concerning the administrators. Their absence from the category of "other" indicates, for example, that all their subsidiary lifework activities are contained in the categories enumerated above. The next two categories of farmers-artisans indicate that relatively few administrators — but still more than double the other samples — stuck to their plebeian lasts for a protracted period during the Weimar years. The next two categories of business-military, the very categories of educational specialization in which the administrators consistently outnumbered the others (see Table 16), show that even these fields did not hold them any more than they did the other Nazis.

The crux of the story lies in the first four categories. Here the distinctive role of the administrators in the Nazi movement is most clearly demonstrated. Notice Categories 2 through 4: these together account for the great majority of the other two subgroups — 54 per cent of the propagandists and 38 per cent of the random Nazis — but account for only 5 per cent of the administrators. What is the significance of this? We see this by looking at the three categories separately: the propagandists cluster in *their* distinctive skill-status role as communicators; the random Nazis cluster in *their* distinctive skill-status role as professional men; both score high in the skill-status category of civil service.

The administrators are conspicuous by their absence from these categories. These, we recall, are distinctively the plebeians — the men without distinctive skill and without distinctive status. When their primary lifework fails them, they have no place to go in the framework of deference established by the ruling elite. To find deference for themselves, they must go outside of this established framework. And outside of it these administrators-to-be, these men without distinctive skill or status, in fact did go. As compared with 1 out of 5 of the other Nazis, 4 out of every 5 of these *echt*-Nazis devoted his subsidiary lifework to the Nazi Party.

### Composite Portrait

The portrait of our administrators, as sketched by our data thus far, seems to run something like this (we are speaking now in terms of the *special* characteristics of this *group* — i.e., the pattern of its deviations from the two other samples representing the Nazi propagandists and the Nazi elite as a whole): Born largely in rural places and smaller towns, of parents with little income and less prestige, they acquired little formal education and, after military service, found themselves confronting a life filled with hard and unrewarding labor in jobs that offered them, like their fathers, little income and less prestige.

The shame and instability of the Weimar years deprived them of even one more ingredient of a satisfying life — that ingredient which, perhaps, was what made their lot satisfying or at least bearable to their fathers — a sense of purpose. Cut off from their roots by the world war (in which some of them had risen to become N.C.O.'s and even junior officers), and by the bitter sequel of the postwar years (in which the opportunities to maintain themselves even in their lowly inherited status had become severely restricted), these men of plebeian origins rebelled at the prospect of a miserable life devoted to the maintenance of a governing elite that they despised. These feelings of rootlessness, repugnance, and rebellion carried over to younger brothers and neighbors. Thus they spread even among those youths of plebeian Germany who had not served in the world war, but whose received version of it gave them the same perspective on the postwar situation under Weimar.

These young men, confronting prospects for the future that seemed to them intolerable, cut their roots and early left the village for the metropolis. Some went to school, but afterward their careers did not bring them successes and satisfactions (inflation was still rampant and unemployment still high). A very few found employment, but these, too, moved from job to job with a frequency and discontinuity that indicated discontent. A substantial, and very significant, number wandered about the big cities neither at school nor at work. Rootless, restless, unoccupied, with nothing but time in hand and ambition in heart — these plebeians on the loose gradually found their destiny.

Some of them discovered the Nazi "movement" early and became its "alte Kaempfer." Here was vitality and a mission; here was lots of work (even if unpaid, at first) for idle heads and hands; here was a fraternity that offered status and reward to the brethren — a place in the sun for them and the fatherland. As these first young men moved in and happily began to take and give orders, as the orders began to take shape in effectual action, the Bewegung began to grow. Other young men, and older men, too, came to join the movement. No longer did administrators-to-be wander the streets with useless diplomas and no work, or shift from one unrewarding job to another, or wonder what to do next. The Bewegung showed them how to make these streets come alive with action and purpose, how to take over these streets as a prelude to taking over the houses and shops and banks and bureaus. The streets became theirs, and the plebeian revolution had conquered.

## V. SPECIALISTS ON VIOLENCE (THE NAZI COERCERS)

In the preceding sections, after discussing the general class role of the middle-income skill groups, we have dealt in turn with two of our subsamples — the propagandists and the administrators. Each of these was compared with the other; and both were compared with our subsample of random Nazis, who represent most closely the salient attributes of the Nazi elite as a whole. It was largely in terms of their characteristic deviations from the random subsample that we characterized the propagandists and administrators. In turning to the subsample of coercers, we confront a special problem. They include two rather distinct groups, reflecting the fact that the use of violence is specialized in two quite different ways — for external purposes and for internal purposes.

### Coercers: Soldiers and Police

The external use of violence, through war and the threat of war, is primary among the traditional instruments of social policy. Defense of the tribe, as well as attack upon its enemies, is a function honored by time and usage. The warrior caste has rated high in the deference scale of most societies in recorded history. So, in most modern nations, the soldier high in his profession has also been high in his society. In Germany, more securely than in most other societies of the Western world, professional soldiery retained the extreme deference once accorded to military castes. The soldier was conceived as the hero *in posse*, and his rewards were those of the hero *in esse*.

The internal use of violence was in rather different condition. With the spread of civilization, the use of violence by the governors against the governed became increasingly disapproved. The process of civilization may even be defined as the substitution of rational persuasion for violent coercion as a mode of social control. Not that coercion has ever been completely eliminated from government, but the fairly steady trend of modern history has been toward reduction of coercion and elimination of its violent techniques. Most modern societies have made corporal punishment illegal, and many have eliminated capital punishment.[11] Policemen who do unsanctioned violence to citizens are

---

[11] It is of some interest that corporal punishment of schoolchildren was reinstituted in Bavaria at the end of World War II.

themselves subject to very extreme penalties. The most respected police in the Western world undoubtedly are the British "bobbies," who (by law) carry no instruments of violence.

With the decline of internal coercion, the status of those specialized to such coercion also declined. The dazzling "palace guard" of earlier centuries has become a symbol of mockery, rather than might, in our days. "Flic" and "flatfoot" are not symbols of high deference. Rewards in income and power have declined along with prestige. The attempt to assassinate President Truman brought to light the fact that the would-be assassin received a higher wage than the Secret Service man killed by his bullet. In a democratic business society, the productive worker receives higher rewards than members of the "palace guard." It was not without justice that W. S. Gilbert's protagonist complained, perhaps wistful over past glory, that in nineteenth-century England "a policeman's lot is not a happy one."

Whereas the soldier has maintained his high status in recent history, and seems in fact to have elevated it in several ways, the policeman's status has steadily declined. The profession specialized to internal violence had become so unrewarding that it attracted only those whose aspirations, affiliations, and abilities could take them no higher. A study of "New York's finest," or the uniformed police force of any important city in the Western world, probably would reveal lower- or lower-middle-class origins.

In Germany, the difference between *Junker* and *Schupo* (*Schutzpolizei*) is the distance between the very top of the deference scale and an area rather close to the bottom. This, however, would be a misleading comparison — for the soldier status comparable to *Schupo* is *Landser* (common uniformed soldier); the police status to be compared with *Junker* is *Polizeipraesident* (the top officials of the police hierarchy). Even these two pairs of terms, however, suggest important differences of deference status familiar to all who knew Germany. The *Junker* belongs to a caste with fairly definite homogeneous characteristics: whose landed families possessed traditional prestige, including many titles of nobility; whose members were raised on manorial private estates, frequently located in East and North Prussia; whose sons were educated to succeed their fathers as officers of the German Army and in fact devoted their careers to this end. The *Polizeipraesident* suggests a quite different set of heterogeneous characteristics: First of all, his role is not inherited but acquired, and thus is presumably (in Weimar Germany) based not on status but on merit. Second, his office usually represents a "step up," or several steps up, in a career composed of such steps. Third, his office is civil service and therefore falls within the German stereotype of bureaucratic *Bonzen* (as contrasted with the "English gentleman" stereotype with which many Germans identified their caste of generals).

### Soldiers versus Police in "Fuehrerlexikon"

These differences show up in our comparative data on soldiers and police selected for inclusion in the *Fuehrerlexikon*. It is interesting, to begin with, that the book contains only 35 police of the top grades (since no lower grades appeared in the book), as compared with 104 soldiers (this excludes a few individuals counted as propagandists or administrators; see Appendix A). This is particularly revealing when we point out that of these 35 police, at least a dozen were soldiers of career who had to be mustered out when the *Reichswehr* was cut after the Versailles Treaty. The police simply do not rate, as compared with the soldiers. The differences between them stand out clearly, despite the elevating bias introduced by the dozen soldiers counted as police. We shall later discuss this point more fully. Here we wish to present, in summary fashion, a few tables which compare the data on these two groups, using the same categories of status as throughout this study. We shall try not to repeat excessively the evaluations of these indicators, which were presented in the preceding sections and with which the reader is presumably familiar. We note that the soldiers are an older group — average age fifty-two years as compared with average age forty-seven years for the police — and proceed to the data on birthplace, as shown in Table 45. The soldiers

### Table 45
#### BIRTHPLACE

| Class | Soldiers | Police |
|-------|----------|--------|
| North and East Prussia | 37.5% | 25.7% |
| Status places | 6.7 | 0.0 |
| Large cities (over 100,000) | 7.7 | 20.0 |

originate in birthplaces of smaller size, while the police are more heavily clustered in the large cities. The fact that better than 1 out of 3 soldiers comes from Northeast Prussia is reported here as an item relevant to the *Junker* stereotype mentioned above. We have classified as "status" birthplaces: family estates (3.8 per cent of these soldiers mention that they were born on a *Rittergut*); university towns and foreign capitals (for reasons we elaborated earlier which indicated both these birthplaces to be associated with higher status of father).

The data on careers also yield patterns of considerable interest.

*Table 46*
CAREER PATTERNS

| Class | Soldiers | Police |
|---|---|---|
| Sustained military contact under 18 | 44.2% | 20.0% |
| First career job under 25 | 94.2 | 68.6 |
| First job in military | 99.0 | 60.0 |
| First job in police | 0.0 | 14.3 |
| First job in all other fields | 1.0 | 25.8 |
| Primary lifework in career | 72.7 | 42.8 |

Some clarification of the categories used in Table 46 is necessary to discuss the meaning of these figures. "Sustained military contact" was defined to mean continuous contact with the military service over a period longer than five years (to eliminate those who might have served in World War I from start to end but had no continuous service before or after the war). The percentages show how many of each group began such sustained service before they were eighteen years old. The soldiers outnumber the others by 2 to 1. This unusual figure is explained by the very large number who acquired their education at the *Kadettenanstalt* (military academy) before they were eighteen, at which time they became junior officers. For this group, then, it would appear that the career decision was made for them, by family tradition or preference, and that this first decision settled their careers in fact.

The second category shows what percentage of each group was launched on its final career before the age of twenty-five. Here again the soldiers vastly outnumber the others, by a ratio of approximately 3 to 2. The significance of this item comes out more clearly in connection with the next three categories, which indicate several interesting points about the respective career patterns of these groups. The soldiers, of whom 94 per cent were started in their careers before they were twenty-five years old, began these careers in the military to the extraordinary figure of 99 per cent. (We shall explain in a moment why this is surprising, rather than a mere validation of our sample.) None of them began his career in the police, and only one (actually a fraction less than 1 per cent) began his career in any occupation other than military.

Now obviously, this indicates that our sample is a good one — i.e., those we are calling soldiers are professional soldiers in fact. But it also indicates more than that. In sorting biographees in the *Fuehrerlexikon* into our categories, our chief criterion was the occupation or title each man gave himself at the head of his sketch. Thus a man who labeled himself *General der Infanterie* or *Stabsoffizier* was automatically classified as a soldier in our tabulations. To increase the size of the sample, we later added those biographees who had served over five years as officers. However, it is possible, indeed likely, that many men who chose to label themselves in this way, or who served five years as officers, had spent only the last five or ten or twenty years of their lives in military service. It was not at all required by our sampling procedure that: all but one of them should have begun his career in the military; that all but six should have begun this career before they were twenty-five years old; and that over four out of five should have worked longer in the military service than in any other occupation.

This latter fact is shown by our final category. Whereas "career" was defined by the occupational label each biographee chose for himself, "primary lifework" was defined as the occupation in which he spent the greatest number of his working years. Hence, it was far from certain that over 81 per cent of the soldiers would have their primary lifework in their occupations of career. Particularly was this uncertain because these men lived a substantial portion of their working life through the fifteen years of Weimar — when the *Reichswehr* was cut to the bone and the vast majority of career soldiers had to find other occupations whether they wanted to or not.

These facts indicate that the occupational pattern of these soldiers conforms rather well to the stereotype of the *Junker*, which we sketched earlier: they started their military contact very early, by registration in the *Kadettenanstalt* upon graduation from elementary school. Since this was regarded as a great privilege (during one period even requiring the permission of the Kaiser), it was regarded as a special prerogative of "the better German families." It shows, too, the strong family influence on predispositions and decisions to enter the military service. Further, all but one of these young men tried no other occupation as a start, but went straight to the military for his first work (again indicating family influence). The vast majority remained within military service for the greatest part of their lives, even during a long period when professional unemployment and absence of traditional rewards were the rule for soldiers. Such fidelity to the shadow of a profession indicates disdain for other types of work, and a refusal to "lower oneself" by trying it, which is caste behavior of a degree rare in the Western world.

The occupational pattern of our police sample stands in sharp contrast to the above at every crucial point. Less than half as many police as soldiers were in military contact (via the *Kadettenanstalt*) before they were eighteen, and one third fewer had gotten a start in their career jobs before they were twenty-five. The following categories are even more revealing. As compared with 99 per cent of the soldiers whose first job was military, only 42 per cent of the police started out in the police field which was to become their career. Some 25 per cent of the police started out in other miscellaneous fields, as compared with 1 per cent of the soldiers — a unique stray from the military fold. Most interesting of all, perhaps, whereas not a single man who called himself soldier started out in the police, 60 per cent of the police started out in the military. This extremely high figure is due to two main sequences of events in the careers of these police: (1) A large number of temporary younger officers who served through World War I, perhaps a years or two before or after, were mustered out into civilian life. (2) A somewhat smaller number of professional senior officers who, as the *Reichswehr* was compelled to reduce its officer corps, were assigned to high-ranking posts in the police.

### Military Career

These sequences are documented by our data on the military careers of these two groups. The importance of military career to these men, whose working lives were very largely spanned by World War I and its aftermath in Germany, has been discussed at some length with respect to the personal histories of the propagandists and administrators. It should be kept in mind as we pass rather quickly over the data that follow.

*Table 47*
PRE-WORLD WAR I RANKS

| Class | Soldiers | Police |
|---|---|---|
| Generals | 2.0% | 0.0% |
| Senior officers | 7.0 | 0.0 |
| Junior officers | 88.0 | 100.0 |
| Soldiers | 3.0 | 0.0 |
| Total | 100.0% | 100.0% |
| (Number) | (101) | (17) |

Before World War I, then, as shown in Table 47, some 9.0 per cent of the soldiers had already attained senior and general officer ranks. None of the police had attained such ranks. In fact, only half of the police had served at all pre–World War I, as compared with practically all the soldiers (101 out of 104). Of those police who served, about one third had served less than five years. This is not to be explained simply in terms of age. The average ages of the groups in 1934 were fifty-two years for the soldiers and forty-seven years for the police. These five years would have made some difference before 1914, but not so much as appears in our data. After all, in 1914 the police were average age twenty-seven — which means they had ten working years already behind them. Further, the differences remain constant through World War I and after, though the five-year age differential faded in importance, as shown in Table 48.

### Table 48
#### WORLD WAR I RANKS

| Class | Soldiers | Police |
|-------|----------|--------|
| General | 17.3% | 0.0% |
| Field grade | 27.2 | 21.4 |
| Captain | 42.0 | 28.6 |
| Lieutenant | 9.9 | 39.3 |
| Soldier | 3.7 | 10.7 |
| Total | 100.1% | 100.0% |
| (Number) | (81) | (28) |

By this time two thirds of our police sample are in the picture. The soldiers vastly outnumber them in the top three categories, which are the distinctive status-categories of the military occupation. The combined score for these three top categories is: 86.5 per cent soldiers, 50.0 per cent police. Half of the police (very likely the half which does *not* include the Versailles-displaced soldiers who were forced into the police) are still in the lower-status positions. (The 13.6 per cent of the soldiers who are still lieutenants or under at this point probably introduce a converse bias in our sample of soldiers — including men of the type of Sepp Dietrich and Ramcke, who became ranking generals of the *Wehrmacht* through identification with the Nazi counterelite rather than the *Junker* caste). The point of Tables 47 and 48 has not been merely to document the obvious point that the soldiers ranked higher in the military than did the police. It has been, rather, to show that our police group was heavily military in character during its early years (half served in the prewar army, and *all* who served were junior officers) and that this military connection weakened during the postwar years. The latter point is documented by the data on separation from military service, by years, given in Table 49.

These figures express percentages of those who left the military service. Of those who were separated, 20 per cent of the soldiers remained in the army after 1920 — when the demilitarization provi-

## Table 49
### Separation from Military Service

| Class | Soldiers | Police |
|---|---|---|
| Before 1918 | 3.9% | 6.9% |
| 1918–1920 | 75.3 | 89.7 |
| 1921–1926 | 7.8 | 3.4 |
| After 1926 | 13.0 | 0.0 |
| Total | 100.0% | 100.0% |
| (Number) | (77) | (29) |

sions of the Versailles Treaty went into effect — whereas only 3.4 per cent of the police remained. It is noteworthy, however, that the 89.4 per cent of the police separated in 1918–1920 show the following figures on a year-by-year basis:

| Year of Separation | Percentage of Police Separated |
|---|---|
| 1918 | 34.4% |
| 1919 | 13.7 |
| 1920 | 41.3 |

After the initial flood of separations, following the Armistice in 1918, those in service tended to stay in during the treaty negotiations which continued through 1919. With the signing of the treaty, and the activation of its disarmament clauses in 1920, the largest number of police were separated — twice as large a percentage (41.3 per cent) for police as for soldiers (22 per cent) separated in 1920.

It seems reasonable to attribute this to the fact that the General Staff, forced to cut its officer corps somewhere, naturally was more inclined to cut first those not of the military caste. The "genuine" soldiers, as we see from Table 49, were separated in small numbers during the decade that followed. What happened to those who were separated — and in some measure to those who remained — is the subject to which we now turn.

### Postwar Careers

Our analysis of the postwar careers is limited by the paucity of reporting on these years among both soldiers and police in the *Fuehrerlexikon*. For this reason, we present much of our data as averages (arithmetic mean) on those who report in the various categories. In a few places, where it seems to clarify the data, we have also given extrapolations from figures on those reporting to the group as a whole. We have done this only where the procedure seemed appropriate. The reader will judge for himself, in each case, the validity of the assumption of continuity from the sample to the whole group.

Of those who spent some (or all) of the postwar years in the *Reichswehr*, respectively 50 per cent of the soldiers and 30 per cent of the police, the average length of service in years was as shown in Table 50.

### Table 50
#### AVERAGE LENGTH OF REICHSWEHR SERVICE

| Class | Soldiers | Police |
|---|---|---|
| Arithmetic mean (in years) | 8.5 (57) | 1.9 (11) |

The *Reichswehr* thus accounts for a fairly substantial proportion of the postwar lives of the soldiers. If we consider the postwar period as the decade 1920–1930 and multiply our sample of 104 soldiers by 10 years, we get 1,040 postwar man-years to be accounted for by this sample. Table 50 indicates that if we multiply the 57 soldiers who served in the *Reichswehr* by the 8.5 years of service that they averaged, we get as our product 484.5 man-years. Thus, the *Reichswehr* accounts for almost half the postwar man-years of the soldiers. Performing the same operations for the police, we get 350 man-years to be accounted for and only 20.9 actually accounted for — or 6 per cent of the police man-years as compared with 47 per cent of the soldier man-years.

Our problem, therefore, is how to account for the postwar years of 53 per cent of the soldiers and 94 per cent of the police. We shall not be able to do this conclusively, for some activities are not reported and some are reported but may have been contemporaneous with others. We do have some indications, however, of the direction taken by these respective postwar careers. One suggestive indicator is the data on *Freikorps* service. The average length of service, by years, is 1.2 for the soldiers and 1.6 for the police. The difference here is not great in length of service, but is quite noteworthy in two other respects: (1) It is the only military category in which police exceed soldiers in length of service (2) It is the only such category where police proportionately outnumber soldiers. This is brought out in striking fashion if we compare the percentages with "no service" in the various categories already discussed.

Table 51 indicates several points of contrast: The soldiers in our sample are a professional military group, practically all with service prior to World War I. (Although their younger age cannot account for this, only half the police saw prewar service; and it is likely that even this figure would have been less without the former professional

*Table 51*
"No Service" in Military Categories

| Class | Soldiers | Police |
|-------|----------|--------|
| Pre–World War I | 2.9% | 48.6% |
| World War I | 1.0 | 11.4 |
| Reichswehr | 44.2 | 68.6 |
| Freikorps | 82.7 | 77.1 |

soldier forced out of service under Weimar and into the police.) Through World War I and the postwar *Reichswehr*, the police with "no service" continue to outnumber the military by very considerable margins. It is in the *Freikorps*, for the first time, that more police than soldiers see service (and, as noted above, somewhat longer average service).

The explanation for this is to be sought in the character of the *Freikorps*. The Free Corps was made up of veterans and violent nationalists, with no legal status. In fact, they maintained their illegal existence despite the general provisions of Versailles and the specific interdictions of Weimar. These units were officered by *Reichswehr* men and attracted to their flag (the Imperial black-white-red, not the new Republican black-red-gold), a hard core of the "armed bohemia," which Konrad Heiden has described as the backbone of the Nazi movement — the spiritually homeless, jobless, and restless. Without income, without status, without power, their only hope was to win these things for themselves and the only method open to them was violence.

The big push came in March 1920 — with the first concerted effort to overthrow the Republican government by violence. The "Kapp Putsch," led jointly by the Nationalist politician Kapp and the *Reichswehr* General von Luettwitz, was carried out by the *Freikorps* from the Baltic states. It drove the government out of Berlin all the way to Stuttgart and installed Kapp as Chancellor. While this lasted only four days, it frightened the Republican coalition enough to put new vigor into dismemberment of the illegal *Freikorps*.[12]

This accounts for the brief duration of average service in the *Freikorps*: 1.2 years for the soldiers and 1.6 years for the police. It also helps to explain why the victorious counterrevolution ultimately was made under the NSDAP rather than the *Friekorps*. The short life of the putsch made it evident to interested observers — among whom, as his autobiography makes clear, Hitler must be reckoned a very intense

[12] See Arthur Rosenberg, *A History of the German Republic* (London: Methuen, 1936), Chapter 5.

member — that "the necessary political preparation was lacking to Kapp's enterprise." The leading historian of the period, a member of the Reichstag and an official of both the Communist and left-Socialist parties, has written the following estimate:

> The venture might easily have succeeded if it had been proclaimed as the movement of an influential section of the German middle classes. If the leading politicians of the middle classes, or at all events of the Nationalist Party and the People's Party, had headed the revolt, the workers would not have been able to put up any resistance worth speaking of. The Army and the Police, the Home Defence Service, and the short-service Volunteers, in addition to the Civil Service, would have put themselves at the disposal of the new rulers.[13]

The lesson learned by this observer was not lost on Hitler and others with counterrevolutionary goals and a predisposition to violence. The Nazi movement gained power by carefully making "the necessary political preparation," which had been found "lacking to Kapp's enterprise." These preparations consumed the decade 1920–1930 of Nazi activity, and our sample of coercers participated in this activity — particularly the police, whose emergent inclination toward counterrevolutionary violence became apparent with the above data on their affiliation to the *Freikorps*. Republican disbandment of the Free Corps thus robbed those men only of a transient institutional vehicle for their counterrevolutionary aspirations, and one which had already shown its inadequacy for their purpose. Their aspirations were not changed; a new instrument for fulfilling them had to be forged. The instrument was the Nazi movement.

How can we get a measure of the activities of these groups of men during the decade 1920–1930 when this new instrument was being forged? Perhaps the most enlightening indicator would be a direct measure of unemployment. However, for obvious reasons, these stars of the Nazi firmament did not choose to report their years of unemployment in the *Fuehrerlexikon*. Our best clue is the absence of reporting. As we observed at several points in the preceding sections of the study, the biographees were careful to mention only those past activities of which (at their ascendancy in 1934) they were proud. They were equally careful not to mention those past activities of which they were not proud. We have therefore computed the figures on years for which no occupation is reported in their biographical sketches (Table 52). While this is not a direct measure of unemployment — since unsatisfactory unemployment also is not reported — it does help

[13] *Ibid.*, pp. 135–136.

*Table 52*
NO REPORTED OCCUPATION

| Class | Soldiers | Police |
|---|---|---|
| At least 1 year | 37.5% | 27.2% |
| At least 2 years | 25.0 | 18.1 |
| At least 3 years | 18.7 | 18.1 |
| At least 4 years | 6.2 | 9.0 |
| At least 5 years | 12.5 | 18.0 |

us to account for the way these men spent their lives in the 1920–1930 decade.

These percentages refer only to those who do not report employment — which includes about one third of the police as compared to about one sixth of the soldiers. Also the soldiers decline more steadily and rapidly than the police as the number of nonreported years increases. (The last category includes also those with over five years not reported.) The average duration of nonreported years is therefore also larger for the police — 3.7 years as compared with 2.3 years for the soldiers. Using the accounting procedure outlined above, we find that nonreporting covers 11.6 per cent of police man-years, as compared with only 3.7 per cent of soldier man-years, for the whole decade.

Where else can we look for information on how the coercers spent these years? After unemployment, or nonreporting, an obvious place to look is the Nazi Party. In Table 53 we give the year of joining the NSDAP, with figures expressed as percentages of those who report their date of joining. The pattern here is quite clear. The police came

*Table 53*
DATE OF JOINING NSDAP

| Class | Soldiers | Police |
|---|---|---|
| Before 1923 | 31.2% | 50.0% |
| 1924–1929 | 18.7 | 30.0 |
| After 1930 | 49.9 | 20.0 |

to the NSDAP considerably earlier, half of them before 1923. By 1930, when the party was on its feet and marching to power, 80 per cent of the police were already members as compared with only half of the soldiers. These two figures show that the average duration of membership for the police was considerably longer during the decade we are discussing. Applying the procedure we have been using to account for man-years in 1920–1930, we find the following results: average duration of 6 years of NSDAP membership for the police who joined, as compared with 3.9 years for the soldiers. This accounts for 60 police man-years (or 17.6 per cent of their total), as against 62.4 soldier man-years (or 6 per cent of their total).

The more intimate connection of the police with the NSDAP is shown also by the comparative figures on status in the party and its affiliated organizations. In Table 54 are the percentages of both groups who held office (the organizations and categories are precisely the

### Table 54
#### NAZI STATUS

| Class | Soldiers | Police |
|---|---|---|
| High officer | 19.3% | 37.5% |
| Middle officer | 10.6 | 22.8 |
| Low officer | 1.0 | 0.0 |

same as were described in preceding sections). Particularly noteworthy is that police considerably outnumbered soldiers as high officers of the NSDAP itself (approximately 3 to 1) and of its action organs (approximately 4 to 1). Only in the culture organizations of the NSDAP did the soldiers outnumber the police, which reflects both their greater distance from the Nazi core and their higher social status. The latter point is documented also by our data on comparative status in non-Nazi cultural and political organizations, shown in Table 55.

### Table 55
#### NON-NAZI ORGANIZATIONS

| Class | Soldiers | Police |
|---|---|---|
| Officer | 30.8% | 17.2% |
| Member | 27.9 | 22.9 |

### Social Status

The discussion thus far has turned on three main propositions: (1) The soldiers come from the upper strata of German society (the *Junker* caste, those who shared its pretensions if not its history), the police from the lower-middle strata (civil service). (2) The careers of both groups were disturbed by World War I and its aftermath, but the soldiers stuck closer to the military profession of their caste, while those who were to become the police were much more seriously uprooted and displaced. (3) Displacement, and the alienation from

Republican Weimar that this entailed, led these policemen quicker and closer to the Nazi movement.

In an important sense, the life histories of these men in the Weimar and Nazi decades can be viewed as a function of the social status in which they were born. The higher social orders of Imperial Germany regarded Weimar as a threat to the values ingrained in them during the rather loudmouthed prewar years under the late Kaiser. Some among the top social groups regarded even the Wilhelm era as a vulgarization of the Imperial tradition shaped in the preceding generation by Bismarck. Such people never could be reconciled to Weimar, nor could their children be expected to love either the democratic Republic or the plebeian dictatorship which followed. Of the group of soldiers, many came from this aristocratic tradition.

For the middle orders of German society, the position was quite different. Wilhelm's Germany — with its emphasis on industrial expansion and its glorification of production technique — had already, before World War I, become a business society. The *"Danker und Dichter"* were still honored, but in the past. In the present, German artists and thinkers sought ever more extravagant modes of expression, imported like impressionism and indigenous like expressionism, but they attracted little attention outside the narrow circles of the faithful in Berlin and Munich cafés. The heroes of the present Germany were those who made and used the steel of the Ruhr. The businessman was, if not king, then surely the king's most favored subject.

The postwar aftermath changed all this. The government of Weimar was not antibusiness, but the circumstances under which it governed clearly were. The German businessman, after the war, found his factories intact, a labor force clamoring for work, markets available almost as before, and productive energies high. All that stood in his way, it seemed to him, were the horrible provisions of the Versailles Treaty and the contemptible Weimar government (with its unspeakable little *heraufgekommene* trade-union *Bonzen*) which showed no backbone except in enforcing this treaty. Small wonder, then, that the Nazi movement claimed his attention and increasingly — as his own middle-class parties went down in coalition after coalition with the Socialists — claimed his affection. Here was a movement which denounced the shame of Versailles, which dedicated itself to the release of German *Tüchtigkeit* rather than its repression, which promised to restore the great nation that Germany had become under the Kaiser. True, there were some disorderly, even ruffian, elements in the NSDAP. But even Wilhelm had said: *"Gegen Demokraten helfen nur Soldaten!"* Besides, the movement was only feeling its oats. Once in positions of responsibility, the good German sense of *Ordnung* would put things right. Certainly they can't be worse than what we have. Let's give them a chance and see.

These sequences of interplay between social class and attitude from prewar through postwar Germany have been dramatized by German novelists of the period. Perhaps the most perceptive and vivid is the series of novels by Ernest Glaeser. The first of these, *Jahrgang 1902*, portrays these prewar and wartime years to the Armistice through the lives of two German lads who just missed the war.[14] Born in military class 1902, they were twelve at its start and sixteen at its end. Their perspective on these years is poignant and plausible — and particularly so is the view seen through the eyes of their fathers. One boy is the son of an aristocratic soldier, whose contempt for the new bourgeois Germany and consequent belief that a war against England is suicide for his class earns him the appellation *"Der rote Major."* The other boy's father is a higher civil servant with business affiliations, whose view of German greatness reflects the goals of Wilhelm II, and who has learned to keep his mouth shut on public questions in public places. These two men and their sons illustrate the sequences we have been discussing. In the pages that follow we wish to show the distribution of these attributes in the Nazi movement during the postwar decade.

One indicator of top status in Germany was the presence of "von" in the family name. Although cases are known where this distinctive preposition was misappropriated, the indicator is fairly reliable — particularly when used in conjunction with a battery of indicators. In Table 56 we give the percentage in each subgroup whose family name includes the "von." The soldiers rather clearly score high above the

*Table 56*
"VON" IN FAMILY NAME

| Soldiers | Police |
|---|---|
| 34.6% (36) | 8.5% (3) |

police in top-status affiliation. The gap is widened even further when we observe that of the 3 police with "von," 2 are professional soldiers of career who were assigned to high police posts late in the Weimar period. The only titled civilian among the police is Count von Helldorf, *Polizeipraesident* of Berlin. Since he acted in concert with the soldiers,

[14] Available in translation as *Class 1902* (London: Secker, 1929). The postwar sequel is entitled *Frieden [Peace]* (Berlin: Kiepenheuer, 1930).

as we shall see in discussing the July 20 putsch against Hitler, it is probably fair to say that no police of career were in this category of patronymic "von," that about half the soldiers were, and that all but one in this category were soldiers.

A second indicator is the occupation of fathers among the *Fuehrer-lexikon* elite. We have discussed the significance of this indicator in preceding sections and here need only recapitulate that the father's occupation sets the tone of home and family life, conditions the level of aspiration among the children, and even affects the level of achievement. The latter point is particularly important with regard to prewar Germany, when family wealth and status largely determined the kind and degree of education received by the children. In this context, the distribution of paternal occupations among those who report provides a quite useful indicator. It is shown in Table 57.

*Table 57*
OCCUPATION OF FATHER

| Class | Soldiers | Police |
|-------|----------|--------|
| Military | 40.8% | 19.0% |
| Landowner | 6.6 | 0.0 |
| Professions | 25.0 | 23.8 |
| Civil service | 13.2 | 33.3 |
| Business | 13.2 | 19.0 |
| Peasants | 1.3 | 4.8 |
| Total | 100.1% | 99.9% |
| (Number) | (76) | (21) |

The caste character of the German Officers' Corps is again indicated by the figure for military fathers. If we add the figures for the first three categories, which represent top status, we get these results: 72.4 per cent soldiers and 42.8 per cent police. Categories 4 and 5 combined, representing the middle status, give us: 26.4 per cent soldiers and 52.3 per cent police. With an adjusted sample, therefore, soldiers would outnumber police by at least 2 to 1 in the top categories, police would outnumber soldiers at least 2 to 1 in the middle categories. No person reported a worker or artisan father, and the one soldier who reported a peasant father is clearly among the "Nazi generals," whom we shall discuss later.

A supplementary indicator of familial social status is ancestral background. Here, as on paternal occupation, the police report far less than the soldiers. This factor of nonreporting we have already seen to occur most frequently when the *Fuehrerlexikon* elite have nothing they are proud to report. The sparse data which are available confirm this

### Table 58
#### ANCESTRAL BACKGROUND

| Class | Soldiers | Police |
|---|---|---|
| Military | 21.9% (7) | 9.1% (1) |
| Landowner | 34.4 (11) | 0.0 (0) |
| Professions | 6.3 (2) | 36.4 (4) |
| Civil service | 3.1 (1) | 27.3 (3) |
| Others | 34.4 (11) | 27.3 (3) |
| Total | 100.1% (32) | 100.1% (11) |
| (Number) | (32) | (11) |

impression regarding ancestral background (which combines patri-archal and matriarchal figures) in Table 58.

A fourth indicator, and a rather crucial one because it provides the channel from inherited status to the acquired skills by which status is maintained, is the level of education attained. We have already seen that a very large number of the soldiers acquired their education in the *Kadettenanstalt*, whence, at eighteen, they graduated into their officer's commissions in the Army. It is very striking, therefore, that a higher proportion of soldiers than police graduated from universities. The figures in Table 59 are particularly interesting. Of the 26 per cent of

### Table 59
#### UNIVERSITY EDUCATION

| Class | Soldiers | Police |
|---|---|---|
| Graduated from university | 11.5% | 8.5% |
| Attended, but did not graduate | 15.3 | 31.4 |
| Total | 26.8% | 39.9% |
| (Number) | (28) | (14) |

the soldiers who attended universities, about half graduated; of the 40 per cent of the police who attended, about one fifth graduated. This higher casualty rate among the police is to be explained partly by the aid that the Weimar Republic gave to veterans who wished to try higher education. The state of Prussia alone gave these increasing sums for the support of students in three postwar years:

| 1924 | RM 182,600 |
|---|---|
| 1925 | RM 527,600 |
| 1926 | RM 558,000 |

These were the years immediately following the imprisonment of Hitler and the illegalization of the NSDAP. Such events, plus the earlier reduction of the *Reichswehr* and disbandment of the *Freikorps*, may have decided many unemployed veterans to try college. There, at least, one could get a subsidy and live cheaply: e.g., in 1923 the student *Wirtschaftshilfe* sold 40,000 meals daily at a cost of 5–10 pfennigs.[15] In inflationary Germany, this was worth a good deal more to an unemployed veteran than some bare-subsistence job or no job at at all. Besides, it left more time free for other things.

That they put in a good deal of time on "other things" is indicated by comparing the figures for those students in each group who specialized in professional (certificated) fields and those who actually received their certificates in these fields, as shown in Table 60.

*Table 60*

PROFESSIONAL STUDIES AND CERTIFICATES

| | Soldiers | | Police | |
| Class | Studied | Certified | Studied | Certified |
|---|---|---|---|---|
| Law | 6.7% | 1.9% | 28.6% | 8.5% |
| All others | 40.4 | 4.7 | 25.7 | 2.8 |

These data have been selected because students in professional fields presumably have their eyes on a definite goal and are therefore more likely to carry through till finished. It is therefore enlightening that these data resemble the outcome on the other studies: most never finished. Some went into the NSDAP; some worked at various jobs; some drifted without work. We have already examined the data on these various sequences in the 1920–1930 decade. Some were married, and the data here contain several points of interest. A greater number of soldiers apparently could afford, despite the hard times for the

*Table 61*

AGE AT MARRIAGE

| | Soldiers | Police |
|---|---|---|
| Under 30 | 15.4% | 8.6% |
| Over 30 | 15.4 | 11.4 |
| No data | 68.3 | 80.0 |
| Total | 99.1% | 100.0% |
| (Number) | (104)* | (35) |

* One unmarried.

military caste, to marry younger. Even more interesting, in Table 61, is the discrepancy on nonreporting and the high level of nonreporting for both.

[15] These figures are taken from Menzel, *op. cit.*, p. 2.

Of those who report on their marriages, two items are suggestive. The data on father-in-law's occupation are distributed as shown in Table 62.

### Table 62
#### FATHER-IN-LAW'S OCCUPATION

| Class | Soldiers | Police |
|---|---|---|
| Military | 29.0% | 12.5% |
| Landowner | 13.0 | 12.5 |
| Professional | 16.0 | 25.0 |
| Civil service | 13.0 | 12.5 |
| Business | 29.0 | 37.5 |
| Total | 100.0% | 100.0% |
| (Number) | (31) | (8) |

Our second item of interest concerns the sex of their children. Both groups raise families of exactly the same average size — 1.7 children per family. On dividing the children by number in each sex, however, the figures shown in Table 63 appear for the 89 cases reported. It

### Table 63
#### CHILDREN (BY SEX)

| Class | Soldiers (73) | | Police (16) | |
|---|---|---|---|---|
| | Boys | Girls | Boys | Girls |
| None | 4.8% | 9.6% | 0.0% | 14.3% |
| 1 | 14.4 | 15.4 | 8.6 | 5.7 |
| 2 | 11.5 | 3.8 | 8.6 | 2.9 |
| 3 | 4.8 | 2.8 | 5.7 | 0.0 |
| 4 | 0.0 | 1.9 | 0.0 | 0.0 |
| 5 | 0.0 | 1.0 | 0.0 | 0.0 |

would appear that both groups curtailed their procreative activities with the appearance of three male children. The police also stopped with two females, while several soldiers continued to produce female children up to five in number. The close correspondence between the number of soldiers without sons and the number with more than two daughters suggests that this added effort may have been expended in search of a son and heir. Such activity is common in male-oriented societies. We merely call attention to its apparent intensity among the these soldiers.

The superior social level of the soldiers is indicated again in Table 64 by our combined index of foreign contact (see Table 18 for items in the index). The figure for the police is considerably overweighted by the item on "occupation abroad" — the only item on which they scored

*Table 64*
FOREIGN CONTACTS (COMBINED INDEX)

| Soldiers | Police |
|:---:|:---:|
| 6.3% | 4.3% |

significantly, and the one which must be attributed to former soldiers counted as police. Although both groups rate low in this index, the soldiers clearly outnumber the police.

On the indicator of publication, the soldiers outdistance the police by a very wide margin. Only 2 police produced books as compared with 20 soldiers, and the average production per author was about 3 books for the soldiers as against 1.5 books for the police. The writing of these soldiers also fell into a wide range of content categories. In addition to the usual technical and strategic (*Wahrpolitik*) books and the inevitable memoirs, they produced books in philosophy and history, social and economic studies, and several books on *Zeitgeschichte* (current history).

*Postlude: The Nazi Decade*

The preceding sections make it quite clear that the soldiers were of considerably higher social status than the police (or any other sub-sample examined in this study). What is the significance of this finding? Its significance lies in the whole matrix of relationships between Nazis and *Junkers* — relationships that helped the Nazis to win power, and to consolidate their victory, but which eventually contributed to their downfall.

How does our data contribute to an understanding of this relationship? Consider, first of all, the indicators of family background. The figures on region and size of birthplace, on paternal and ancestral occupations, all show that the soldiers were born into a different social world from those in which our other subsamples saw the light of day. Consider next the data on their early training in *Kadettenanstalten*, their superior status in World War I (the deep traumatic events for this generation of Germans), their persistence in the debilitated *Reichswehr*, their marriage to girls of or near their own social class, their production of books in various fields, their foreign contacts, and so forth. All these indicate that they were living the life patterns marked out for them at birth.

But Germany was becoming different, and the soldiers did not like the changes as they saw them. Where the Kaiser and his advisors ruled firmly over a rich and expanding Germany, now a pusillanimous coali-

tion of Socialists and "traitors" (whose boldest act was to try to substitute a new flag for the Imperial black-white-red) presided by endless
bickering over the liquidation of the Reich according to the dictate of
Versailles. The Eastern Territories were gone (not to mention the
colonies), the *Reichswehr* was enfeebled and under the Weimar treaty
would ultimately become a farce, the nation had lost its *Stimmung* and
listened to wild-haired Red agitators while nobody acted.

Some of the so-called Nationalists seemed to the soldiers no better —
forming endless coalitions with the civil service bureaucrats and
laborite *Bonzen*, acquiescing in the liquidation of the *Freikorps*, and
appearing more concerned about staying in office than saving the
nation. What the Army needed, it was clear, was some energetic new
force that would put vitality into a real German program, that would
devote itself to winning German rights rather than meeting Allied
demands, that would tell the Frenchmen what they could do with their
ridiculous claims for reparations. These Nazis, for example, had the
passion needed. True, they seemed a bit coarse and undisciplined. But
perhaps their mass appeal could be made to serve military purposes
without the *Reichswehr* becoming involved in their excesses!

How to do this? Indications are provided by our data on the number
and date of soldier affiliations with the NSDAP. The affiliations were
few in number, and they came late. This documents the assertion
that the military did not work either by infiltration or coalition — two
important techniques commonly used by counterrevoluntary organizations. That is, they neither sent in picked officers to take over control
of the NSDAP nor encouraged soldiers to join the NSDAP as individuals (which would have required them to blink at the law prohibiting
political affiliation among *Reichswehr* men).

Instead they used the technique of liaison on high levels — a technique favored by any hierarchy that prizes its organizational independence and possesses an indispensable skill-function. Such liaison,
indeed, with civilians at home (and military men abroad) had been
for decades the traditional mode of operation in the German Officers'
Corps. In this case, the liaison was performed mainly by "ex" *Reichswehr* men who had left the service officially but whose heart belonged
to the Officers' Corps and who maintained intimate channels with its
desires and decisions. Such "ex" *Reichswehr* officers as General Erich
Ludendorff, General von Luettwitz (of the Kapp Putsch), and General
Franz von Epp kept the General Staff informed of NSDAP activities —
and made the NSDAP aware of military attitudes through younger
"ex-officers" like Captain Roehm (who had been von Epp's aide-de-
camp in postwar Munich). Another was Captain Goering, whose

World War I career as squadron leader in the famed Richthofen Circus had won him the *Pour le Mérite*, highest military honor in Germany, and entry into high circles — including the private study of Marshal Hindenburg.[16] Through such channels of liaison, the *Reichswehr* was able to maintain its respectable facade of observing the law against political affiliation and the traditional German legend of the Officers' Corps as *unpolitische Fachleute* (nonpolitical specialists).

The case of General von Epp is particularly instructive. While still in active service, as commander of the *Reichswehr* in Bavaria, he was inept enough to allow his name to be associated publicly and continuously with the beer-hall conspirators in Munich. A flood of complaints from Socialists and others came to the Social Democratic President of the Reich, who complained to the *Reichswehr* Minister. Reluctantly, the *Reichswehr* Minister, a former major, called his generals to account. In the end the Berlin generals conducted a hasty and inadequate investigation in Munich.[17] General von Epp was transferred. A year later, in 1923, he resigned. His next important job was as head of the *Wehrpolitisches Amt* (Military-Political Bureau) of the NSDAP.

Through such liaison the *Reichswehr* maintained all the connection it wanted with the NSDAP, and at the same time its superiority, its independence — and its distance. It was no part of the General Staff's purpose to work for the great power and glory of the NSDAP. Their purpose was to use the NSDAP as an instrument for achieving the kind of Germany they wanted — unfettered from Versailles, treated as a first-class power in the world arena, and able to maintain a *Reichswehr* appropriate for such a power.

The Nazi leaders understood this relationship quite well and had their own ideas about how to use it. They courted the top-prestige generals incessantly before 1933, and even afterward for a time. The *Fuehrerlexikon*, for example, includes all the most respected generals — whether field commanders like Rundstedt and Bock, or General Staff officers like Fritsch and Witzleben. Every one of these has the "von" in his name. (On the other hand, none of these who were later to rise to fame as "Nazi generals" — e.g., Rommel, Jodl, Model, Dietrich, Guderian, Ramcke — appears in the *Fuehrerlexikon*.) The Nazis, clearly, were playing for the top rank of *Reichswehr* officers.

These they never got. For these men cooperated only on their own terms. Their terms, however, were not terms the Nazis would grant. A monolithic party-state does not grant independence and autonomy to

16 Heiden, *op. cit.*, p. 510.
17 *Ibid.*, p. 153.

any social formation — and particularly not the military. As the *Reichswehr* Chiefs of Staff continued after 1933 to work toward autonomy as their price, they were dismissed — first von Brauchitsch, then von Fritsch. The Nazis continued to insist on their own supremacy and installed a weaker, more amenable general, Halder, though even he was characterized by Hitler as an *"ewiger Besserwisser"* (chronic know-it-all) and had to be dismissed ultimately.[18] Then began the ominous withdrawal of support by the military caste that led to the attempted assassination of Hitler in 1944. This was, with Goerdeler and other civilians figuring mainly through the same sort of liaison that is the traditional *Reichswehr* technique of counterrevolutionary activity, predominantly a military operation. It was their final effort to stop the man and government that wished to rule the Officers' Corps. They failed; but they carefully underwrote the failure of their adversary as well. At Nuremberg, two years later, the Nazis and some puppet generals lost their heads. The Officers' Corps, having made its sacrifice on July 20, 1944, survived.

Many lessons are contained in this relationship of over 25 years, between *Reichswehr* and NSDAP. The point we wish to notice here, since it is the Nazi organism we are studying, is that as his final effort to break the soldiers to his power Hitler turned to the police. Himmler, the former *Kadettenanstalt* student and *Faehnrich* (standard-bearer), the schoolteacher who had become supreme policeman of the Reich, took over control of the Army as well.

To understand this strange phenomenon, we must recall something of the structural and functional development of the German police under the Nazis. The NSDAP made its start, in Munich, with a beerhall putsch. This was the token of its entire career — violence and the threat of violence as the method of social control. It ran up an impressive record of murder and assassination — Kurt Eisner, Matthias Erzberger, Walther Rathenau, General Kurt von Schleicher. These men were, respectively, an Independent Socialist leader (because he was a leftist leader), a Reich Finance Minister (because he had signed the Armistice of Compiègne), a Reich Foreign Minister (because he was Jewish), a pro-Nazi general who had developed the *Freikorps* system (because he had become too close with Roehm and Gregor Strasser). The variety of these four cases illustrates the widespread of purpose for which the NSDAP found murder their best weapon. Although some of the above four were murdered before the NSDAP was officially organized, all of these assassinations were sanctioned by the NSDAP

---

[18] Quoted from Walter Goerlitz, *Der deutsche Generalstab* (Frankfurt: Verlag der Frankfurter Hefte, 1951), p. 546.

and the murderers heroized. The precise number of assassinations instigated, performed, or endorsed by the Nazis has never been established. The *Fehme* and *Stahlhelm* and *Kyffhaeuserbund* were rival units, but with interlocking memberships, in the politics of violence. It took only a few years, however, for the Nazis to establish their undisputed mastery in this field of operations.

The Nazis integrated individual assassination with mass violence and terror. Mass violence dominates NSDAP history from their first putsch through the "blood purge" of their own membership (the Roehm-Strasser factions) after the seizure of power. The two episodes just mentioned, in fact, provide a key to the history of the Nazi movement and the sociology of the Nazi police. The beer-hall putsch in Munich was the traumatic birth-event of the S.A. (*Sturm-Abteilung*) in the form it was to maintain through the next decade. The blood purge in 1934 symbolized (and accomplished) the liquidation of the S.A. in this form by the S.S. (*Schutz-Staffel*) and the rise of a new police concept embodied in the S.S. A brief glance at these two police instruments of Nazi policy clarifies the crucial difference between them.

The S.A., organized mainly from students by Rudolf Hess in 1921 (and later briefly commanded by Goering), came into its own with the beer-hall putsch of 1923. Of some 2,000 S.A. participating, 14 were killed. The blood-soaked banner carried in that fight immediately became the symbol of the NSDAP and the proudest possession of the S.A. — the *Blutfahne*, which every subsequent party banner had to be hallowed by touching. The symbol glorified the S.A. weapon — violence; and the S.A. motto shouted their goal — "today Germany, tomorrow the world." The combination was their ultimate undoing. Violence in German streets designed to gain the NSDAP total power was highly approved. But when the Nazis gained total power, the S.A. claim to manage external violence for the state proved embarrassing, and the claimants had to be removed. The reason: they compromised the party's continuing, and after 1933 intensified, efforts to win over the General Staff of the *Reichswehr*.

The post-1923 conception of the S.A. had been that it should form the nucleus of the future German Army. Point 22 of the original party program stated: "We demand the suppression of the army of mercenaries [the *Reichswehr* was a professional army] and the founding of a national army." During the decade that followed, this view, spread among and beyond the S.A. by its Chief of Staff, Captain Roehm, was a good morale builder and a useful threat in Nazi negotiations with the *Reichswehr*. But when the Nazis took power, and Roehm, installed as a Secretary of State and War Minister of the *party*, persisted in behaving as though he were War Minister of the *government* (a post toward which he obviously was conniving), the old concept became embarrassing. When Roehm, in April 1934, told the diplomatic corps at Berlin, fearful of this paramilitary force, that "the Storm Troops are a guarantee for the peace of Central Europe," he joined his issue with the *Reichswehr* in public: "A clash became unavoidable between the brown army and the *Reichswehr* over the function of the 'supreme arms bearer' in the Third Reich."[19]

But Hitler could no longer afford to back Roehm's "political soldiers" against the professionals. As responsible chief of state he needed the General Staff. Joint *Reichswehr-S.A.* maneuvers along the Polish frontier, later that spring, demonstrated conclusively the incompetence of the amateurs against the professionals, even after the long restrictive diet on which the *Reichswehr* had labored while the S.A. was fattening itself on party funds and loot. The *Reichswehr* won, the S.A. was sent on a month's furlough. On June 30, 1934, Roehm was murdered, and the S.A. top command was decimated (a process defined by Hess as follows: "every tenth man, without any investigation, whether innocent or guilty, was struck by a bullet").

The reason given in public was the widespread sexual depravity of the S.A. leadership (which Hitler had known and tolerated for over ten years); in party circles the rumor of a counterrevoluntary conspiracy was spread (which meant that Roehm would not acquiesce in subordinating the S.A. to the *Reichswehr*). In truth, Hitler in power no longer needed the S.A. of pre-1933 days. For external violence he needed a professional army; for internal violence a disciplined police corps that would question no decision of his. The S.A. now embarrassed him. He therefore "decimated" its leadership (including some of the oldest "*Alte Kaempfer*"), deputized the *Reichswehr* for external violence, and turned over to Himmler's S.S. the management of internal violence. On July 13, Hitler piously told the *Reichstag*:

> For fourteen years I have stated consistently that the fighting organizations of the party are political institutions and that they have nothing to do with the Army. . . . In the State there is only one arms bearer, and that is the Army; there is only one bearer of political will, and that is the NSDAP.[20]

The S.A. mass was permitted to survive. Its ranks reduced from 3 to 1 million (drawn from the "better elements"), stripped of all weapons

[19] Alfred Vagts, *Hitler's Second Army* (Washington: Infantry Journal, 1943), p. 17.
[20] *Ibid.*, p. 18.

(aside from its daggers), the S.A. was reorganized in January 1936 with Viktor Lutze, servant of Hitler and friend of the *Reichswehr*, as Chief of Staff. Only once again was its flair for mass bloodletting mobilized — in the Jewish massacre of 1938 known as *"Die Nacht der langen Messer"* (Night of the Long Knives).[21] Lutze gave the new orientation as follows: "Our task as S.A. is to take care that the German people *remain* National Socialists." To the diplomatic corps in Berlin, he tried to repair Roehm's indiscretion of 1934 as follows:

> The tasks of the S.A. are the tasks of the party. They are consequently in the field of home policies. When the S.A. was set up, there was for the first time in history created a soldier type with functions of an exclusively *weltanschaulich* kind, the political soldier! And even today, after we have obtained the power in the State, this political soldierdom still survives. For there is a sharp difference between the soldier who is the carrier of the National Socialist worldview and the soldier who is the arms bearer of the nation.[22]

Thus did Hitler make his peace with the generals. His bid for the minor virtue of consistency (patently false to all familiar with Point 22 of his original program of 1923) could not, however, obscure the major change of policy, occasioned by the passage from ambitious pretension to actual power, and expressed through a basic redefinition of the police function. No longer was there any need for "street soldiers," for the Nazis now ruled the streets. The need was for "loyalty soldiers," to ensure the streets against any new pretenders. The job, as Lutze put it, was to make sure "the German people *remain* National Socialists." But for this purpose Lutze's shadow of the once-omnipotent S.A. was ill suited. For systematic surveillance, and liquidation, of potential opposition, a Grand Inquisitor with modern methods was needed. Himmler and his elite S.S. were obviously the ideal instruments. Thus began the extraordinary second act in the career of the most remarkable chief and corps of police in recent history.

The new conception of the police role was epitomized in the phrase invented by Himmler himself: *"Kriegsschauplatz Inner-Deutschland"*

---

[21] A well-known verse favored by the S.A. ran as follows:

Wetzt die langen Messer an dem Buergersteig,
  dass sie besser flutschen in der Pfaffen Leib . . .
Und kommt die Stunde der Vergeltung,
stehn wir zu jedem Massenmord bereit!

(Sharpen the long knives on the sidewalks,
  so that they cut better into the clergy's flesh . . .
Comes the hour of revenge and
we stand ready for any mass murder.)

[22] Vagts, *op. cit.*, p. 22.

(Theater-of-War Inner Germany). The role was to come downstage center during the third act of the Nazi drama after 1940 (when Hitler decided to invade Russia and finally alienated the top men of the General Staff). In the second act, 1934–1939, Himmler put his machinery for policing Germany as a theater of war into order for the great scenes to come. His first attention, as a good administrator, was to his own personnel. The police, naturally, had already been "purified" and "coordinated" several times. Goering, in his exhibitionist way, early disclosed his operations as Prussian Prime Minister (and head of its Gestapo):

> To begin with it seemed to me of the first importance to get the weapon of the criminal and political police firmly into my own hands. Here it was that I made my first sweeping changes of personnel. Out of thirty-two police chiefs I removed twenty-two. Hundreds of instructors and thousands of police-sergeants followed in the course of the next months. New men were brought in and in every case these men came from the great reservoir of the Storm Troopers and Guards.[23]

Criteria that might satisfy Goering, however, would not satisfy Himmler. He sometimes behaved as though he were the only top Nazi who genuinely believed in the Aryan myth as his leading article of faith. The measures he took to ensure "racial purity" among his political soldiers seemed to many, including other top Nazis, fantastic. But the eugenic screen through which S.S. aspirants had to pass, the battery of tests designed to ensure that only those incapable of disloyalty to Hitler-Himmler would survive their S.S. novitiate, were fantastic mainly in the sense that never in modern history has a myth been so creatively sustained by industrious (even ingenious) application of personnel procedures.

Along with this went continuous refinement of functional techniques. As the Grand Inquisitor of the epoch, Himmler knew the supreme importance, for the loyalty police of a "total state" run by clique, of the "man with the dossiers." Accordingly, he expanded the "intelligence function" of the S.S. to a point of efficiency perhaps never before attained by a modern police force. Compared with the reports of his S.D. (*Sicherheitsdienst*), the Gestapo produced mainly sycophantic nonsense, Goebbels's apparatus was powerless, and even Bormann's formidable card files on top leaders (his strongest point) were feeble.[24]

[23] Hermann Goering, *Germany Reborn* (London: E. Mathews & Marrot, 1934), p. 121.

[24] See: Daniel Lerner, *Sykewar: Psychological Warfare Against Germany* (New York: George W. Stewart, 1949), pp. 294 ff. Also: Ernst Kohn-Bramstedt, *Dictatorship and Political Police: The Technique of Control by Fear* (London: Kegan Paul, 1945).

With each succeeding year, Himmler extended and strengthened the police function performed by him and his organization. With the disaffection of the generals in 1940, he began to bring the Army as well under his official surveillance (it was an open secret that they had been there unofficially all the while), and finally under his control. Already head of the S.S., Waffen-S.S., Gestapo, and KRIPO (criminal police), in 1943 he became Minister of the Interior and thereby united under his command the entire police system of Germany. In 1944, he made his first major inroad on the *Wehrmacht* by taking over from Admiral Canaris the *Abwehr* (Foreign Intelligence Service) which hitherto had operated under the Combined General Staff (*Oberkommando der Wehrmacht*). With the failure of the July 20 plot, Himmler opened the throttle to full speed ahead. On that very day he succeeded Fromm as Commander-in-Chief of the Reserve Army (*Ersatzheer*). Next he took over from the *Wehrmacht* command of all prisoner-of-war camps. Next this former *Faehnrich* (roughly equivalent to warrant officer), who had acquired in the Army mainly his skill for keeping orderly card files, was himself in command of an Army Group on the Vistula Front, vainly resisting the Russians — whose destruction was the key goal of his entire career.

But all this came too late. The policemen had conquered the soldiers, but the victory was indeed Pyrrhic. The triumph came in the last scene of the last act, just as the curtain was going down on both.[25]

## VI. THE NAZI ELITE: CONCLUSIONS

We have presented comparative data on five groups within the Nazi elite: administrators, propagandists, soldiers, police, and a random subsample. We have examined similarities and differences in the biographical characteristics of these groups, with a view to gaining insight into the process of social change which produced the Nazi movement. The propositions we have sought to document and test, while specific to the Nazis, we believe to hold for other revolutionary movements of the present century.

As we have said before, the RADIR Project conceives revolution as "rapid and extensive change in the composition and the vocabulary of the ruling few." The Symbol Series of the Hoover Institute Studies was focused on changes in the vocabulary of various ruling groups. The

[25] The sequence of these relationships between party-soldiers-police can be traced through three lucid books: for the period to 1933, see Konrad Heiden, *op. cit.*; for the decade 1933–1943, see Vagts, *op. cit.*; for the final scene analyzed with great clarity, see H. R. Trevor-Roper, *The Last Days of Hitler* (London: Macmillan, 1947).

Elite Series studied changes in the composition of ruling groups in diverse societies. These studies show the "pattern of differences and similarities that we regard as the social process characterizing the "world revolution of our time."

To demonstrate the more general relevance of the propositions considered in this study will require comparative analysis of our data on various elites. To see how radical were the changes made by the Nazis in the composition of preceding elites in their society, the data in this research should be compared with those on the German elites of the Imperial and Weimar epochs. To see how closely the Nazis approximate trends in other revolutionary movements of our century that have made rapid and extensive changes in the composition of the ruling few, we can compare the data in this study with those on the Politburo in Russia and those on the Kuomintang and Communist Party elites in China. The results of such a comparison would enable us to go a step further and compare data on the revolutionary counterelites with trends in the relatively stable (or nonrevolutionary) elites of Britain, France, and the United States.

In concluding this study, we wish to recapitulate our findings with sufficient generality to indicate how they might serve for the different sorts of comparative analysis mentioned earlier. To do this, we first evaluate the method we have used. Next, we summarize the differences between subsamples that have occupied most of our attention in this study. Next, we discuss the similarities between the groups, somewhat more fully since we have paid less attention to these points in the running analysis of our data. In discussing similarities among the Nazis, we make extensive use of the category "marginality." As will be seen, we use this term as shorthand for a quite general proposition about the role of "marginal men" in the process of social change. We conclude with a brief statement on the policy significance of our findings.

### Evaluation of the Method

Our analysis of "differences" used three main standards of measurement: (1) direct comparison between two subsamples (as in the section on soldiers and police); (2) comparison between one subsample and another with respect to a third (as in comparing propagandists and administrators with respect to their deviations from figures on the random Nazis); (3) comparison of one or more subsamples with the population of the NSDAP or of Germany as a whole.

Our samples are small (the sample of 35 police being conspicuously weak in this respect), and our indicators are subject to some of the ambiguities that bedevil most "operational indexes." In some cases we have reduced or eliminated such ambiguities by technical means, e.g., use of a fourfold contingency table and a "coefficient of independence." For the most part, however, we have relied on a procedure more open to commonsense evaluation. We have foregone tests for "significant difference" — which can be very misleading when applied to differences between small samples on qualitative variates — and thereby cut ourselves off from conclusions based on any one indicator. Instead, we have grouped our indicators so that they form a "battery of tests," rather than a single-indicator "crucial test," of our various propositions. That is, we have based none of our conclusions on the fact that differences between subsamples on any one indicator are "statistically significant." Our conclusions disregard the size of differences on individual indicators and base themselves on the *number* of indicators on which differences (however large or small) tend in the same *direction* as between subsamples.

To illustrate: We do not conclude that propagandists came from a higher social class than administrators simply because their fathers appeared in the high-status occupations in much greater numbers. Rather, we base this conclusion on the fact that the propagandists outnumber (sometimes by a wide margin, sometimes by a small margin) administrators in the higher-status categories of practically all our indicators. Not only in their fathers' occupations — but in their own occupations, their own level of education, their fields of educational and other interest, their Army ranks, their ancestral background, their age at marriage, etc. — the propagandists consistently "outrank" the administrators with respect to status in social origins. (Conversely, administrators clearly outrank propagandists with respect to status in the party machinery.)

One pitfall lurks in such a method, which we believe we have avoided, but to which the reader should be alerted. When the differences are consistently small, in a group of indicators, even though they tend consistently in the same direction, the possibility must be considered that these differences are all due to the same individuals in the sample. This is particularly true when the samples are small and when the indicators are validly grouped. Both of these conditions obtain in our data. Valid grouping of such indicators as we have used tends to reduce their independence of each other — e.g., it is reasonable to suppose that high-status occupations among both fathers and sons, if these are validly grouped as indicators of high social class, will be more highly correlated than high-status fathers and low-status sons. Hence, occupational status of fathers and sons cannot be regarded as

completely independent indicators in research because they are associated (to some undetermined but significant degree) in actual life.

We have avoided the pitfall of assuming independence of indicators,
where interdependence may in fact exist, in three ways: first, by using
a "coefficient of independence," which gives us an approximation of
the actual degree of independence between two indicators; second, we
have run a fairly extensive series of cross tabulations, which enable us
to determine which pairs of indicators in fact reflect the characteristics
of the same individuals (e.g., to what degree the number of Catholics
merely duplicates the number of Bavarians); third, we have formulated our conclusions in terms of characteristic *deviations* as between
subsamples rather than characteristics of the subsamples as wholly
homogeneous groups.

That is, we recognize that none of our subsamples is completely
homogeneous with respect to any characteristic — other than that by
which they were defined. All are persons honored by the Nazis through
inclusion in the *Fuehrerlexikon*. This gives them the one common
characteristic needed to define them as a sample of the Nazi elite,
from which subsamples may be drawn and compared with each other.
Each of these subsamples is constituted by sorting persons into categories defined by another single common characteristic — their distinctive function with respect to the Nazi movement.

We demand, therefore, that they be homogeneous with respect to
their defining characteristic — that the propagandists be propagandists, the administrators be administrators, etc. We do not demand —
nor do we even expect — that they will be homogeneous with respect
to other attributes. Homogeneity of this sort could be expected only in
a caste system with a degree of rigidity that probably has never existed
in recorded history. Certainly, common knowledge of Nazi history
leads us to expect considerable heterogeneity on other attributes
among individuals classifiable as propagandists, administrators, etc.

On the central attribute of social status, certainly, it is clear that
each of our subsamples includes some individuals who rank very high
and some who rank quite low. Our conclusions, therefore, are not that
any subsample is wholly high or low but that its characteristic *deviation* from other subsamples, or from some other population, is in the
direction of "higher" or "lower." This may mean only that, while a
large number (perhaps a majority) in one subsample have the same
status as a large number in another subsample, those who do deviate,
deviate upward in the one sample, while in the other sample they
deviate downward. It was to make this point clear that we began our
presentation of data with a section on the "middle-income skill

groups." We believe that the data adduced there and later show a considerable, perhaps predominant, representation of these groups throughout the Nazi movement as a whole and through each of the subsamples. When we speak of the propagandists as exhibiting higher social status than administrators, we refer to the characteristic deviants among these subsamples. We do not repeat this point in every possible place, to avoid making a paper already very lengthy even more tiresome. Occasionally, some stylistic ineptitude may suggest that we have disregarded our own self-imposed limitation. At such places, the alert reader will translate our words into the terms of reference just outlined. We turn now to a summary recapitulation of the actual deviations detailed in the body of the study.

### Characteristic Differences: Recapitulation

In the next section we summarize certain similarities among the various groups of Nazis. Such similarities become significant when they distinguish Nazis from other Germans. In this section we concentrate upon differences between groups of Nazis, and these become significant when they distinguish components within the Nazi movement.

Our random subsample we have taken as fairly representative of the distribution of certain definite attributes among the Nazi elite as a whole, at the time when it culminated its career as a counterrevolutionary movement by taking over total power in the state. This subsample seems to reflect the Nazi elite fairly well, even to its foibles, according to our common knowledge of Nazi beliefs and behavior. For example, the random subsample includes many individuals who were not members of the NSDAP — and some who were known (to the Nazis at that time) to be hostile to one or another aspect of the Nazi program. Such individuals were often included because of their national prestige, which the Nazis wished to identify with themselves. Included in the *Fuehrerlexikon*, for example, were Hermann Oncken, noted historian whose cordiality to the Nazis was dubious, and Karl Goerdeler, the Lord Mayor of Leipzig whose anti-Nazism early led him to become a key figure in the July 20 conspiracy against Hitler.

Both in its central tendencies and its peculiar deviations, the random subsample appears to represent adequately the distribution of relevant attributes in the German elite under the Nazis. We have therefore used data on this subsample as a standard against which to evaluate deviations in the other subsamples. It is largely by this procedure that we reached several of our conclusions concerning the propagandists and administrators.

Our group of administrators we characterized as "plebeians on the make." Though a substantial number of middle-status individuals appear in this subsample, and even a few high-status individuals (mainly professional soldiers trained in military administration), the prevailing direction of its deviations is downward with respect to social origins. The administrators consistently outnumber all other sub-samples in the low-status categories on indicators of social origins — ancestral and parental background, university attendance and speciali-zation, career history, military rank, etc. On the other hand, the admin-istrators rather consistently outnumber the others of Nazi prominence — e.g., rank within the party and its affiliated organs. When the party came to power, consequently, they rode with it into the higher cate-gories of elite status in German society as a whole. The career of Martin Bormann, head of the Party Chancellory and Nazi adminis-trator *par excellence*, indicates this sequence from plebeian origins to top social status by means of increasing deference position within the counterelite NSDAP. Others are: Fritz Sauckel, who left grammar school to be a common sailor, and later became *Gauleiter* of Thuringia and *Reichstatthalter*; Robert Ley, son of a peasant, who became head of the D.A.F. (*Deutsche Arbeitsfront*) and thereby chief ruler over Germany's civilian manpower. We have called this process, illustrated most clearly by the Nazi administrators, the "rise of the plebeian."

A special case of this sequence is the Nazi police. This is our poorest subsample because it is small and impure (only 35 individuals, of whom eight are professional soldiers sorted into this category as an artifact of our definition). We are able to use these data despite impurity of the subsample because we can account for its bias with precision and because the bias throws the advantage of every doubt against the conclusion we reach. That is, these eight soldiers bias every indicator in the direction of high-status social origins, whereas our conclusion is that the police deviate characteristically toward lower-middle status in their social origins. We speak here of the police proper. That is, we exclude top Nazi administrators of the police, like Himmler and Lutze, whose plebeian origins conform to those of Nazi administrators generally; and we exclude the eight professional sol-diers, whose origins are top-status like the others of the military caste. The police proper seem to originate uniformly in the middle classes. These men did not rise from the bottom to the top via the NSDAP as their career. They tended to rise rather from lower-middle to the upper-middle ranges of deference via the civil service as their career, combined with Nazi-receptive attitudes. They tended to come from families in the middle (probably somewhat lower-middle) ranges of civil service, business, and professional activity. An illustrative case is Johannes Lieff, who became *Polizeipraesident* of Braunschweig. Lieff characterizes his social origins thus: *"stammt aus einer alten braun-schweigischen Beamtenfamilie arischen Ursprungs"* (stems from an old Braunschweig family of officials, of Aryan ancestry). Without this family background, but with this inclination to mention his Aryan ancestry (which many biographees omit), he might have become a party rather than civil service police administrator; with the family background, but without this inclination, he might have stayed where he was (or been thrown out in the successive purges of Prussian police initiated by Goering and continued by others). With both the background and the inclination, he was most likely to rise just as he did.

The subsample next highest on the status ladder of social origins is the propagandists. Considerably higher than the plebeian adminis-trators and discernibly higher than the lower-middle-class police, the propagandists cross the imaginary line drawn along the averages for the random Nazis on our various indicators. Whereas the adminis-trators and police outnumber random Nazis in low-status categories (and are outnumbered by them in high-status categories), the propa-gandists reverse this pattern. We are, therefore, led to conclude that the propagandists not only come from higher social strata than the other subsamples discussed, but that they are drawn from the upper-middle strata of German society as a whole.

In this, naturally, we are referring to the tendency of their devia-tions. The subsample is heterogeneous, including such individuals as Max Amann, who, as director of Franz Eher Verlag (main Nazi pub-lishing organ), was an important administrator of propaganda and shows the plebeian origins common to Nazi administrators. The operating propagandists — those who made their careers via their skill in manipulating symbols for Nazi purposes — mainly deviate toward the upper-middle ranges of German society. An illustrative case is Alfred Berndt, chief writer of D.N.B. (*Deutsches Nachrichtenbureau*), who reports his ancestry thus:

> . . . Enstammt mütterlicherseits einer jahrhundertealten ostdeutschen Kolonisten-und Bauernfamilie, väterlicherseits einer pommerschen und schwedischen Landwirts-und Beamtenfamilie.
>
> (. . . Stems on mother's side from a centuries-old East German family of colonizers and farmers, on father's side from a Pomeranian and Swedish family of landowners and officials.)

Other cases are abundant. Walter Funk, press chief of the Reich government, gives his ancestry as follows:

> . . . Father was royal architect, grandfather a great merchant (wholesale)

of Koenigsberg; lineage certified to 16th century; forefathers played an important role in the Lutheran wars of religion.

The propagandists, though they come from higher origins than the others just reviewed, do not tend to attain higher positions in the NSDAP or the Nazi state. They are specialists with the "correct" orientation (somewhat like the police), and they go only as high in the Nazi movement as the function served by their skills. This was quite high indeed in some cases, for the skilled propagandist is an important voice in the councils of those who seek power. So long as he continues to function *qua* propagandist, however, his importance is limited by his skill; and his skill is primarily as adviser and executor, not decision maker and leader. This is indicated by our data on the comparative distribution of the subsamples in the higher offices of the Nazi movement. The propagandists are considerably outnumbered by the administrators in these offices; they are outnumbered, too, in such offices as *Gauleiter*, which enabled Nazis to amass private fortunes and private armies (or, at least, private courts) to guard their power and status. Whereas the propagandists tended to maintain status of origin by means of their skill, or to recover Imperial status lost under Weimar, top honors of the counterelite went to the administrators. The administrators were not specialists *with* the correct orientation but generalists *in* the correct orientation.

The group whose origins are indisputably top-status are the soldiers. While our subsample has a slight "impurity" — notably the Nazi soldiers in the *Fuehrerlexikon* who would probably never have made the grade apart from their Nazi affiliations — it must be recognized that the *Junker* caste had been infiltrated even before Weimar by strong bourgeois elements. Such elements, however, tended to rise in field commands, and sometimes, when they rose sufficiently high, were "integrated" into the caste by the bestowal of a title. The General Staff remained firmly under *Junker* control. The caste features of this group are well known, and our data merely confirm their presence in the Nazi period. Since the caste could not run the Nazis, and would not be run by them, they went down in official disgrace and physical destruction. Here was the reverse of the Nazi plebeian — the aristocrat who originated at the top level of social deference, but was broken by the counterelite which could not absorb him along with his skill.

If we were to portray graphically the beginning and end of these four groups (omitting the random), showing their level of origin and level of attainment on a scale of social deference, we might get a suggestive picture of their characteristic deviations like that shown on the chart.

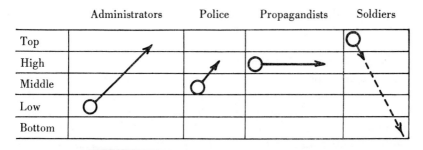

The administrators, low and touching bottom in some cases, go to (or very close to) the top. The police move up in a more restricted range — from middle to high (or lower-middle to upper-middle). The propagandists, starting fairly high and obviously gaining personal power, do not appear to have increased their status as a group over that which was held by their fathers a generation earlier. Their accomplishment seems to have been that, faced with a sharp decline in status, they disaffiliated from a foundering elite and, by using their acquired skills, maintained or regained high status through affiliation with a counter-elite by whom such skills were prized and rewarded. The soldiers, equipped with skills less plastic than those of the propagandist (or the generalized talents of the administrator), came from a background that ingrained the identification of skill with class — i.e., caste. The Nazis, though they needed the skills, could not tolerate its caste context. Their counterelite required places for themselves at the top in every agency of social policy. For the sake of these — which meant their freedom to control external violence through Rommel, Jodl, Guderian, and ultimately Himmler, rather than be shackled by von Brauchitsch, von Fritsch, and even Halder — they were prepared to destroy the caste that had been the pride of Prussia and Germany for centuries.

In these ways do our subsamples of the Nazi counterelite differ from each other. Other, deeper individual differences are also discernible that we have not studied here. Our focus has been upon status differences on the view that, in a status-ridden society, "class will tell." The differences spotlighted by our data are sufficient evidence that the *Fuehrerlexikon* is not really a handbook of "the Nazi elite" in any strict sense. From this we infer that there was in fact no Nazi elite that spanned and integrated the whole German society. There was, rather, a more limited set of changes in "the composition of the ruling few" that produced a Nazi variant of the German elite. The character of this variant is clarified by study of the common attributes of its two most distinctive groups — administrators and propagandists. As we have seen, these differ from each other in very significant ways. Their similarities, too, are significant.

### Marginality: The Common Attributes

In a society predominantly Moslem, Christians are marginal with respect to religion. In a Catholic society, Protestants are marginal on this characteristic. "Predominant" attributes are those most frequent in the elite and most preferred by all. A man who deviates from a substantial number and variety of predominant attributes in his society may be regarded as a "marginal man." In this sense, the Nazi movement was led and followed by marginal men. The groups at the core of the movement — administrators and propagandists — exhibit marginality as their strongest common bond.

We have suggested this similarity underlying their differences by speaking of them as "alienated intellectuals" and "disaffected plebeians." Their differences, as intellectuals and plebeians, are quite clear. Their alienation and disaffection is their common link in the "armed bohemia" of the NSDAP. Such attitudes are consequences; here we wish to look at some of the common characteristics associated with disaffection and alienation.

Our conception of marginality concentrates on the number and variety of indicators on which we found deviations among our subsamples. As we explained earlier, it is the deviant cases that give each group its special character. To test our general proposition, that *echt*-Nazi elite were the "marginal men" of Weimar Germany, we formed a combined index based on thirteen of our indicators (the complete list is given in Appendix A). Computing the number of individuals marginal on one or more of these thirteen indicators, we arrived at the totals shown in Table 65.

*Table 65*
### THE NAZIS AS MARGINAL MEN

| Class | Propagandists | Administrators | Police | Military | Random |
|---|---|---|---|---|---|
| Marginal | 77.4% | 82.1% | 77.1% | 51.0% | 56.6% |
| Nonmarginal | 22.6 | 17.9 | 29.9 | 49.0 | 43.4 |
| Total | 100.0% | 100.0% | 100.0% | 100.0% | 100.0% |
| (Number) | (128) | (151) | (35) | (104) | (159) |

We turn now to the data on several single indicators, to illustrate the influence of marginality in shaping the career line of these Nazis. Rather consistently the random Nazis and the soldiers are heavily concentrated in the categories of centrality (nonmarginal), while the propagandists and the police deviate strongly, and the administrators even more strongly, into the marginal categories.

Perhaps the most striking characteristic is the marginality of the Nazis with respect to birthplace. This has been noted by several commentators. Hitler himself was born in Austria, and not in Germany at all. Several extreme nationalistic and counterrevolutionary movements against Weimar, particularly in the early postwar years, originated in marginal eastern areas. People in or near the "lost eastern territories," lost through the Versailles Treaty and the acquiescence of Weimar, resorted to violence against the government whose passivity threatened them with loss of their "*Deutschtum*" and submergence in the "Slavic hordes" for all time. The Kapp Putsch was conceived and executed from these marginal territories. Alfred Rosenberg, the racial "philosopher" of the Nazi movement, was a Balt, whose fears of eternal marginality or intolerable Slavization probably were associated with his great contribution to Nazi political folklore — the categories of *Reichsdeutsch* and *Volksdeutsch*. The NSDAP itself was born and raised in the marginal area of Bavaria — whose marginality, indeed, had been a major problem since the triumph of Hohenzollern over Wittelsbach and the integration of *Grossdeutschland* under predominant Prussia.

The core Nazis are considerably overrepresented in marginal areas, as the figures in Table 66 make clear. We have included the fragmentary data on NSDAP and total population (statistics on other areas were so organized as to be noncomparable with our data) to indicate the close correspondence between NSDAP and general populations for the marginal areas of Germany — interesting because these areas were always underrepresented in the pre-Nazi elites, which exhibited the predominant, rather than marginal, attributes. The random sample, too, corresponds rather closely. Their total for Bavaria-Rhineland is 3 per cent less than those for NSDAP and total population; this margin is probably filled by the non-Nazi but high-prestige Germans brought into the *Fuehrerlexikon* for reasons we have discussed.

What mainly interests us here is the common marginality of the core Nazis on this indicator. The administrators, whom we have described as the *echt*-Nazis incarnate, are the most marginal — exceeding the propagandists by 10 per cent (the extra 10 per cent who originated in the Bavarian homeland of the NSDAP). It is also interesting that the plebeian administrators predominate in Bavaria, Alsace, and Saar — rural and peasant areas; whereas the propagandists are more numerous in the Rhineland and foreign capitals, centers of commerce and

Table 66

MARGINAL BIRTHPLACE

| | Propagandists | Administrators | Military | Police | Random | NSDAP | Total Population |
|---|---|---|---|---|---|---|---|
| Bavaria | 10.2% | 20.5% | 9.6% | 2.9% | 9.5% | 9.8% | 10.1% |
| Rhineland | 7.8 | 5.9 | 4.8 | 2.9 | 3.1 | 5.7 | 5.5 |
| Alsace and Saar | 1.6 | 5.9 | 1.0 | 0.0 | 1.2 | 0.0 | 0.0 |
| Foreign | 7.0 | 4.6 | 1.9 | 0.0 | 2.5 | 0.0 | 0.0 |
| Total | 26.6% | 36.9% | 17.3% | 5.8% | 16.2% | | |

culture (i.e., universities). The totals indicate that both core groups considerably outnumber the random subsample in marginality on birthplace.

Another indicator of interest is age. The Nazi movement has frequently been characterized as one of bitter young men. To see how closely the facts bear out this view, we computed in Table 67 the mean ages for all German men over twenty-five.

### Table 67
#### Mean Ages (German)

|  | Propa- gandists | Admin- istrators | Military | Police | Random | NSDAP | Total Population |
|---|---|---|---|---|---|---|---|
| In 1934 | 38.9 | 42.2 | 52.0 | 47.0 | 48.5 | 37.6 | 44.9 |

The figures for 1934 indicate rather clearly what, on the analysis we have made, was to be expected. The NSDAP male membership averages more than seven years younger than the male population (over twenty-five) as a whole. The core of the NSDAP elite are naturally somewhat older than the NSDAP mass — the propagandists about one year older, the administrators about four years older. The Nazi core is exactly eight years younger on the average (the combined propagandist-administrator average being 40.5 years) than the random sample. (That the random group and the soldiers are the oldest was to be expected, owing to its heavy admixture of non-Nazis with high status attained through career prominence.) The Nazi core is also about five years younger than the German male population as a whole. With respect to age, then, the Nazi elite may be considered "marginal" in the sense that it is dominated by a generation that took power in the state a decade or so younger than was the rule for German and other elites in Western societies. Note the comparison with mean ages for cabinet members in the other elite studies of this series, shown in Table 68.

### Table 68
#### Mean Ages (Cross-National)

| | |
|---|---|
| United States | 56 |
| United Kingdom | 56 |
| France | 53 |
| Germany | 53 |
| Nazi core–elite | 40 |

The figures for mean age in 1920, which are merely those for 1934 subtracted by fourteen years, are given in Table 68 simply to

Table 69
AGE DATA (IN YEARS)

|  | Propa-gandists | Admin-istrators | Military | Police | Random | NSDAP | Total Population |
|---|---|---|---|---|---|---|---|
| Mean age in 1920 | 24.9 | 28.2 | 38.0 | 33.0 | 37.5 | 23.6 | 30.9 |
| Mean age at marriage | 28.0 | 33.0 | 31.3 | 30.4 | 30.0 | — | 30.0 |

make more vivid the position of these core Nazis when demobilized at the end of World War I, i.e., when they began their careers in the Nazi movement. A significant detail is added when we view mean age in 1918 alongside of the data on mean age at marriage, as shown in Table 69.

The adult male population of Germany, in 1920, married at age thirty on the average. Thus, this population had already been married about one year in 1920. The random Nazis had already been married about seven and one-half years, on the average, at this time. The position of the core Nazis in 1920 was quite different: Not only were they unmarried in the main, but the propagandists were to put in another three years as "lone wolves," while another five years were to elapse before the administrators married. These men, as our data have shown, were joining themselves to the NSDAP rather than to wives. The figures for those who joined the party before 1923 (see Table 25) are:

| Propa-gandists | Admin-istrators | Military | Police | Random |
|---|---|---|---|---|
| 20.3% | 27.1% | 4.8% | 14.3% | 9.4% |

In this respect, too, the core Nazis are marginal. At the ages, and during the years, when most German males were already married, these core Nazis were hanging around beer halls plotting murders and planning a future for Germany in which they would figure prominently. While their contemporaries were adjusting to the wife-home-family sequence of behavior, these core Nazis were prowling the streets in the company of other ex-heroes in fact or fantasy.

The restlessness of these men is further displayed in their occupational histories. Our earlier data on these indicators showed that the core Nazis took their first career jobs (i.e., as denoted in their own *Fuehrerlexikon* sketches) much later than the random sample and much later than the soldiers and the police.

The figures for those who were in their first career jobs by age thirty are as follows (see Table 37):

| Propa-gandists | Admin-istrators | Military | Police | Random |
|---|---|---|---|---|
| 54.7% | 51.3% | 95.2% | 91.4% | 75.4% |

In the case of the police the first responsible job was coded. This was not necessarily police work.

Our earlier data showed, too, that these core Nazis did not stay settled after they once were settled. At age thirty, about half of the propagandists and administrators had not yet found jobs in the fields that they were to consider their career. But most of these did not stay put even when they had taken these first jobs, as is shown by the figures for those who report no subsidiary lifework (see Table 44):

| Propa-<br>gandists | Admin-<br>istrators | Military | Police | Random |
|---|---|---|---|---|
| 15% | 5% | 37.5% | 5.7% | 30% |

About two thirds (70 per cent) of the random Nazis changed their primary occupation long enough to be counted under some subsidiary lifework. This is a fairly large proportion, and reflects the instability of employment in postwar Germany. The high number of professional soldiers who changed their job (62.5 per cent) can probably be attributed to the demilitarization of Germany after World War I. But twice as many propagandists, and six times as many administrators, and police, made such shifts in employment. This is clearly quite excessive job-instability, even for Weimar Germany, by available measures. It would seem appropriate to consider the core Nazis "marginal" with respect to the search for stability in personal life — a trait we here designate simply as "restlessness."

With such an expanded concept of marginality, however, we move onto different terrain than that covered by our study. Our indicators have been concerned exclusively with objective measures of public behavior. To some degree, we have dealt even with objective measures beyond the control of the *Fuehrerlexikon* biographees — e.g., family status, birthplace, and religion. The main control biographees could exercise over such indicators was suppressing information — i.e., the factor of "no data." (Outright falsification was probably infrequent in the data, because verification by one's friends — or, more important in Nazi circles, one's enemies — was fairly easy.) We have, at several places in the study, called attention to the significance of over- and underreporting on various indicators. And we shall return to this factor once more by way of illustrating a general point in the concluding section.

Here we wish to point out that such objective indicators as we have reported in this study may provide useful clues to personality attributes common to a group of individuals. We have not permitted ourselves to formulate explicit conclusions regarding "the Nazi personality" but have confined ourselves rather to conclusions about the interaction of our quite formal indicators with the sequence of public events familiar to all who know Nazi history. We suggest here an inference from our data to such a personality concept as "restlessness," to indicate a point of general methodological interest and of specific substantive bearing on the Nazis.

To wit: political analysts have frequently alluded to ambition or power seeking as a common trait of Nazi personality; clinical psychologists have long been familiar with job instability as an indicator for diagnosing case histories; sociologists (and economists) have accumulated masses of data on the distribution of job instability with reference to various social institutions. Few studies, however, have used the methods of the sociologist to test the indicators of the psychologist with respect to the propositions of the political analyst. In consequence the "political personality" is, from the standpoint of systematic research, very largely *terra incognita*.

We have not explored this unknown territory either, but we wish to suggest that reanalysis of the data here presented could make a substantial contribution to our understanding of the Nazi psyche. Other data would be needed, certainly, but those already reported would serve rather well as a starter. A person interested in analyzing (in addition to naming) "restlessness" as a common characteristic of core Nazis — or more specific characteristics like "ambition" or "power seeking" — would find useful data by comparing our data on education. He would find the discrepancies between university attendance and attainment, as shown in Table 70, quite revealing. He would prob-

*Table 70*
UNIVERSITY ATTENDANCE AND ATTAINMENT

|  | Propagandists | Administrators | Military | Police | Random |
|---|---|---|---|---|---|
| Attended university | 59.0% | 25.1% | 26.8% | 39.9% | 60.3% |
| Graduated from university | 32.8 | 13.9 | 11.5 | 8.5 | 52.2 |

ably be struck by the extremely high proportion of Nazis who attended universities. By consulting a statistical handbook, he would learn that in the academic year 1922–1923 (which is probably the median year of attendance for many of the core Nazis tabulated above) 82,213 students were registered at German universities. Discounting slightly for foreign students, this is around 4.2 per cent of the total male population over twenty-five (the group that includes our subsamples). The administrators exceed this figure, despite their plebeian origins, probably owing to the generous state aid to students during these years. The low figure for the soldiers can be traced back to the fact that most of them went to military schools rather than universities. The propagandists and random Nazis more than double the attendance of the administrators, probably owing to their higher family status, since home orientation and family pressure undoubtedly are major factors in the decision whether a person goes to college.

Thus far, we are still on the familiar terrain of interaction between sets of objective data. But, how shall we account for the failure of so many core Nazis to complete their university courses? Of those who attended universities, only slightly over one half of the propagandists and administrators graduated, as compared with over 80 per cent of the random Nazis.

The difference becomes even more striking if we examine the data on academic completion by certain kinds of primary lifework. We have described civil service, business, and the professions as the stable occupations. To these we can contrast the typically Nazi occupations of party official or communications. Table 71 shows what proportion of those persons in each of these occupations who attended a university or *Technische Hochschule* failed to complete the course of studies.

*Table 71*
PERSONS WHO FAILED TO COMPLETE STUDIES

|  | Propa-gandists | Admin-istrators | Random |
|---|---|---|---|
| Stable occupations | 20.6% | 20.0% | 9.5% |
| Nazi occupations | 60.4 | 80.0 | 25.0 |

This result does not simply reflect the fact that completion of education is a *sine qua non* for some stable occupations, for the businessmen, who required no degrees, left school in no more than 25 per cent of the cases in any sample. This result seems to reflect an important fact which our other sets of objective data do not account for. The data most closely associated would seem to be those mentioned above, which indicate that the core Nazis also failed to complete their career-job activities. However, neither of these can "explain" the other (as higher family status *could* partly account for higher university attendance). Failure to complete educational activities and failure to complete occupational activities seem to stem from the same source — and hence both need be accounted for by some common trait of these individuals which would explain a *pattern* of "uncompleted life activities." In this way, reanalysis of the present data could lead to refinement of such a gross category as "restlessness" (or even "power seeking") and to documentation of basic propositions about "the Nazi personality."

Other items that call for reanalysis from this perspective suggest themselves throughout the study. Our treatment of the category "no data" has been merely illustrative. Re-examination of the figures appearing in this category under the various indicators would probably lead to fruitful conclusions concerning the characteristic "focus of attention" among ex-Nazis. Reanalysis would probably note such an indicator as religion, which gives us the data shown in Table 72. Many questions are raised by these data: Why is the proportion of Catholics so low, particularly since the core Nazis come so heavily from "marginal areas" predominantly Catholic (Bavaria, Rhineland). We are particularly struck by the figure of 9 per cent Catholic administrators, since we already know that 20 per cent of this subsample was born in Catholic Bavaria. Why, then, does cross tabulation show that of 31 administrators born in Bavaria only 6 report themselves Catholics, while 5 say Protestant, 1 *Deutschglaeubig*, and 19 give "no data"? If we choose simple explanations — e.g., that Nazism was an antireligious movement — how can we account for the large differential in the "no data" category? Why, particularly, do the more sophisticated propagandists (the specialists on what to say and what not to say in public), who on most other points tend to withhold most data, give exactly 20 per cent more answers on this item of religion? To answer such questions, systematic reanalysis of the "no data" categories would be enlightening.

An extremely suggestive set of figures, for such a purpose, appear in the "no data" categories with respect to women. Starting with the glaring absence of women from the *Fuehrerlexikon*, the researcher would notice that some of the most numerous "no data" categories are those which concern women — whether the core Nazis are married at all, whom they married, etc. Reanalysis of these "no data" items in the light of personality theory might suggest answers to the above questions concerning "no data" on religion. In any case it would surely add an important dimension to our conception of "marginality" among the core Nazis.

Such reanalysis would also throw light on some key propositions advanced by political analysts. An outstanding writer on Nazi military politics (*Wehrpolitik*), Alfred Vagts, was so struck by the consequences of this Nazi attitude toward women that he concluded his main work on the subject with this final sentence:

. . . It would be supreme historical irony, if, in the final balance of this

Table 72
RELIGION

| | Propagandists | Administrators | Military | Police | Random |
|---|---|---|---|---|---|
| Protestant | 45.0% | 27.1% | 36.5% | 40.0% | 35.2% |
| Roman Catholic | 8.0 | 9.2 | 3.8 | 2.9 | 5.6 |
| Deutschglaeubig | 4.0 | 0.6 | — | — | 0.0 |
| No data | 43.0 | 63.0 | 59.6 | 57.1 | 59.1 |
| Total | 100.0% | 99.9% | 99.9% | 100.0% | 99.9% |
| (Number) | (100) | (151) | (104) | (35) | (159) |

war, the eugenic principles of these warriors, standing in the way of making timely use of women in war work, should cause them to lose the war![26]

Our data, reanalyzed, would give a clearer conception of the typical Nazi attitudes toward women by clarifying the causes and correlates of these "eugenic principles." Reanalysis would also give us a better measure of the importance of these attitudes, by showing their frequency and distribution among various groups in the Nazi elite. Such information could be of considerable value for the policy scientist. We turn, in conclusion, to a few brief suggestions concerning the utility of our findings for students of the contemporary political process.

### Some Conclusions for Policy Scientists

We consider as "policy scientists" those who are concerned with bringing the findings of systematic research to bear upon current issues and processes of policy. One persistent issue of democratic policy in the past three decades has been how to cope successfully with aggressive totalitarianisms.

An essential step is to clarify one's own goals. Aside from its psychic value in reducing ambivalence and indecision on important matters, such clarification puts us in a position to evaluate how effectively these goals are being realized in theory and practice. Another essential step is to clarify the goals of others with whom we are related by conjunction or conflict of interests, needs, and desires. In this way we "know our neighbors," a wise and ancient injunction, at least well enough to distinguish our friends from our adversaries. With such information in hand, we are in a better position to make rational decisions on how to behave with respect to recurrent issues.

How to cope with aggressive totalitarianism is such a recurrent issue. To take the clarifying steps mentioned on such an issue requires a perspective that eschews parochialism. The Soviet Union, which is currently the chief protagonist of this issue, has always operated on a world stage. If we study its challenge on the same scale, we are more likely to detect essential similarities and differences that will clarify our situation than if we forsake inquiry in favor of some *a priori* and parochial dogma like "Soviet Russia and World Communism are one and the same thing." Perhaps research will lead to this conclusion — which hardly seems likely — but if it does, the proposition will be more solidly founded. The point is that we are better served by accurate information than dogmatic affirmation — and that the information we require for our most crucial issues is global in scope.

[26] Vagts, *op. cit.*, p. 241.

Since we *are* concerned with the aggressiveness of a centralized revolutionary force that is global in scope like world communism, and with dispersed totalitarian forces that nevertheless exhibit striking similarities like Italian Fascism and Japanese Imperialism and German Nazism, then we are surely well advised to study the "world revolution of our time." Comparative data on such movements will reveal the patterns of similar and dissimilar behavior underlying the movements that have constituted the persistent problem of democratic policy. By studying ourselves and our friends — Britain, France, etc. — on the same scale of behavior, we clarify the similarities and differences among ourselves, and between us and others. Such information enables us to decide more rationally — i.e., with a higher probability of accomplishing our purpose — what to do on current issues.

This series of elite studies is designed to provide comparative information of this sort about the men who make top decisions in various societies of the world community. We study ourselves and our adversaries. The executive branches of Britain, France, and the United States are investigated; so is the Soviet Politburo. So are cases where the issue is still being fought, where there is not one government but two parties — e.g., Kuomintang and Communists in China. So are aggressive totalitarianisms that have been overthrown, but which have contributed ideas and practices still current in the world political arena — e.g., the Nazi elite.

The present study has presented our data on the Nazis in terms of several propositions concerning the personnel and personalities who have been engaged in engineering the "world revolution of our time." These data will become more significant when subjected to comparative analysis alongside our data on other revolutionary counterelites of our epoch.

# APPENDIX

## APPENDIX A: DESCRIPTION OF PROCEDURES

### SOURCE: THE "FUEHRERLEXIKON"

The *Fuehrerlexikon* was published in 1934 by the publishing house of Otto Stollberg, Berlin. It was not an official publication of the NSDAP, but the fact that it had the approval of the party is indicated by a sentence on the title page which reads:

> The NSDAP has no objection against the publication of this book.
>
> Munich June 15, 1934

In the Preface to the book the publishers state their purpose as
follows:

> The German *Fuehrerlexikon* attempts to show the realization of the
> Fuehrer principle in the public life of Germany.

The publishers state that they are not compiling a social register, but
that their sole criterion for inclusion of a man was whether he was
officially charged with a leadership function. The book does not include
a single woman.

No information is given on how the biographies were secured. Since
most of the biographies follow a standard pattern, it is reasonable to
assume that a standard questionnaire was used. Although not explicitly
stated, it appears that each biographee was sent a questionnaire and
filled it in himself. The material was then checked by the organization
to which the biographee belonged. A list of organizations that helped
to check the material is given at the beginning of the book.

The Preface also states that the book contains more than 1,700
biographies. Actually, however, it contains only about 1,600 biographies and over 100 blank spaces. These blank spaces represent biographies originally included, but later dropped — between typesetting
and publication. This strange fact can be explained by the date of
publication. The book was published toward the middle of 1934, just
about the time of the "blood purge" of Roehm and the decimation of
S.A. leadership discussed earlier in this study. It is clear that about 100
persons involved in the purge were originally included in the *Fuehrerlexikon* but were no longer current when the book went to press. Evidence that this assumption is correct is provided by a postscript to the
publisher's Preface, which reads as follows:

> Because of a series of political events we have corrected the already
> finished volume in all important places, taking into account the events up
> to August 2nd of this year. The further influence of these occurrences on
> party, state and people will be taken into account in a special supple-
> ment or in the second edition.

August 2, 1934                                 The Publishers

## THE SAMPLES

### The Propagandists

The following groups of persons were selected for inclusion in the
sample of propagandists:

High officers of the Propaganda Ministry
Officials of the Reichs Culture Chamber or one of its subsidiaries
Managers of radio stations
Newspaper editors
Journalists
Writers
Officers of the *Reichspropagandaleitung der NSDAP*
Press and propaganda officers of other Nazi organizations.

In this, as in all the other samples, the main criterion for inclusion was the title given at the head of each man's biography. Second, the biographies were read to search out those who had spent a major part of their active life as propagandists, even if they were not in such a position when the *Fuehrerlexikon* appeared.

A careful perusal of the *Fuehrerlexikon* yielded 128 individuals who could be classified under the heading of "propagandists." A question was later raised whether it was proper to include some of the officials of the Propaganda Ministry (those who were primarily civil servants), officials of the Culture Chamber and its subsidiaries (those who were primarily party administrators), and some of the literary artists (those who wrote only in nonpolitical fields). It was felt that the inclusion of such individuals, who were only indirectly concerned with propaganda, might prejudice the validity of our sample. To guard against bias in the sample, all 28 individuals in the above three groups were eliminated. Later, however, it was found that the smaller sample of 100 men exhibited essentially the same characteristics as the full sample of 128. The differences *in all cases* were small and in the same direction. In the presentation of the data both subsamples have been used. In no case, however, would the subsample that was not used show a significantly different result from the one that was used (see footnote to Table 1).

## The Administrators

Under this category we included those who held an administrative job in the NSDAP or one of its subsidiaries. The *Fuehrerlexikon* includes more administrators than there are in our sample. Since it was important to keep the samples comparable in size, we excluded the lower-ranking group of administrators, taking only the higher ranks for our sample. According to these standards, 151 individuals were selected, consisting of the following groups:

Officials of the *Reichsleitung der NSDAP*
Officials of the *Reichsleitung* of subsidiary NS organizations

*Gauleiters* (because of the special importance of Berlin, the **Deputy** *Gauleiter* of that city is also included)
*Gauarbeitsfuehrer*
*Landesbauernfuehrer*
High officers (down to the *Land* level) of Nazi-sponsored organizations

In order to avoid duplication, individuals already counted as propagandists were not included, even if they had an administrative function along with their propaganda function.

### The Random Sample

The procedure used in the selection of the random sample was to take every tenth name out of the *Fuehrerlexikon*. Since we required a systematic random sample, no tenth name was skipped, even if the man was already included in one of the other samples. Because of this characteristic of the sample, it includes: 16 propagandists, 18 administrators, and 5 coercers. In the light of this known bias, the differences between the random sample and our samples assume added significance. For, were we to eliminate the 39 individuals specified above, the differences now apparent in the data would be increased to that extent in every case.

### The Coercers

Two groups are included under this heading: the soldiers and the police. Individuals already counted as either propagandists or administrators were not included again in this sample. All members of the police were included. By the very nature of the book, these were only police officers of high rank such as police presidents and police generals. The total number in this subgroup came to 35.

Under soldiers we included those who listed a military rank in the title line of their biography, and we also added those who had served in the Army or the Navy for a period of more than five years. There were two reasons for this:

*a.* The professional soldier, in whom we were interested, would be the one who stayed in the service for more than five years.
*b.* It was our aim to eliminate those who served only through the First World War from 1914 to 1918.

Again because of the nature of the book, this sample contains mainly higher-ranking officers. Their number came to 104. Hence, the size of the whole sample of coercers, combining soldiers and police, amounted to 139.

## TECHNIQUES

After the sample had been selected, we proceeded to code every biography, to attain data on the 43 indicators in our check list. Almost all of the indicators yielded a sufficient number of answers to be used in the interpretation of the data. After the coding was completed, the information gathered was punched on IBM cards. All tabulations and cross tabulations were made from these cards.

Some of the standards according to which the coding was done are described in the list that follows.

a. *Primary Lifework:* Under this index we chose the kind of work in which the biographee spent the most years of his reported *Berufsgang* (occupational history).

b. *Subsidiary Lifework:* Here we included the kind of work that occupied the second-largest number of years of his reported *Berufsgang*.

c. *Education:* The highest grade of education attained was coded regardless of whether or not the man finished the school in question. Military schools and *Kadettenanstalt* were coded under "trade school."

d. *Special Educational Interests:* Since many mentioned more than one subject, the one listed first was taken as the field of primary interest.

e. *Military Career in World War I:* Only the highest rank attained was coded.

f. *Number of Publications:* Several men wrote articles as well as books. Since we could not conveniently count both (to avoid "double-punching" on the IBM code-cards), we ranked these and gave books precedence over articles. Hence, if a man wrote two books and many articles, for instance, he was coded as having written two books. Only those who wrote no books were counted in the category of articles.

g. *Subject of Publications:* If a man wrote on more than one subject, the one in which he did most of his writing was coded.

It is believed that the coding of all other indices is self-explanatory.

## MARGINALITY

In compiling Table 65, the following items were treated as indicating a marginal status. Those individuals having any one of these traits were considered marginal for the purposes of the table. These criteria were selected as deviations from the stereotype of the ideally preferred background and career of a nationalist elite German.

*Province of Birth*

Alsace-Lorraine and Saar
Rhineland
Abroad

*Religion*

Catholic
*Deutschglaeubig*
Atheist

*Primary Lifework*

Peasant
Artisan

*Occupation of Father*

Peasant
Artisan

*Education*

Attended university but did not graduate
Attended *Technische Hochschule* but did not graduate
Attended other higher schools but did not graduate
Attended trade school but did not graduate
Attended grade school but did not graduate
Graduated from grade school

*Age at Marriage*

18–21
35 and over

*Father-in-Law's Occupation*

Peasant
Artisan

*Military Career pre-World War I and World War I*

Enlisted man

*Date of Joining NSDAP*

Pre-1923 to 1925

*Foreign Marriage*

*Foreign Parentage*

*Higher Education Abroad*

*Occupation Abroad*

## APPENDIX B: NAZIS AND THEIR ALLIES IN THE CABINET

The object of this appendix was to find out how far our findings from the *Fuehrerlexikon* held for the very top of the elite, both the top of the Nazi hierarchy and those Germans who were sought by the Nazis as allies. To study this problem we took the German cabinet at the end of 1934 and divided it into two groups: (1) the Nazi leaders, and (2) the other members of the cabinet who were not Nazi leaders.[27] The latter group contained two men who joined the NSDAP before 1933: Guertner and Rust. These two, however, did not belong to the top of the Nazi hierarchy. Their inclusion in the second group, which we call non-Nazis for short, seems justified by their actual status. The cabinet thus had fifteen members, divided into six Nazis and nine non-Nazis.

| *Nazis* | *Non-Nazis* |
|---|---|
| Hitler | von Neurath |
| Goebbels | Schwerin von Krosigk |
| Goering | Schmitt |
| Frick | Seldte |
| Darre | Guertner |
| Hess | von Blomberg |
| | von Eltz-Ruebenach |
| | Rust |
| | Kerrl |

In order to increase the size of the Nazi sample, we added several other top Nazis who were not in the cabinet at this time. They were:

| | |
|---|---|
| Himmler | Streicher |
| Rosenberg | Funk |
| Ley | Schirach |
| von Ribbentrop | |

This gave us a sample of thirteen top Nazis and nine non-Nazis. Information on these men was compiled for the same indices as in our study of the *Fuehrerlexikon*. Since the numbers are very small, proper

[27] This study supplements the study of the German cabinet from 1890 to 1945; see Max Knight, *The German Executive, 1890–1933* (Stanford, Calif.: Stanford University Press, 1952). This supplement is designed to secure more intensive data for the Nazi period on certain points dealt with in the present study. Knight's monograph places the Nazi cabinets in the perspective of the previous ones. Unlike this study it deals with all Nazi ministers, not just the cabinet as of 1934, and with cabinet ministers only. The results of the two studies, however, generally confirm each other.

comparisons and valid conclusions were not possible in every case. We therefore confine ourselves here to showing similarities and dissimilarities on a few selected indices.

## MARGINALITY

In the main body of the study (Table 65) it has already been shown that the majority of all our samples were marginal to German society as a whole. The administrators were the most marginal, followed by the propagandists and the random sample. Using the same indicators of marginality that are described in Appendix A, we find that, of the 22 men included in both the Nazi and the non-Nazi sample, only one (among the non-Nazis) did not have at least one attribute of marginality. All the rest had one or more of these attributes. Hitler himself led the field with seven counts of marginality. For the total counts of marginality we get the following figures:

|  | Non-Nazis | Nazis |
|---|---|---|
| Total marginality counts | 15.0 | 44.0 |
| Average per individual | 1.7 | 3.4 |

We see that the Nazis are exactly twice as marginal as the non-Nazis. Since the Nazi leaders were always fond of describing themselves as true German men of the people, these figures throw an interesting light on this claim.

The comparison between Nazis and non-Nazis can be illustrated by one specific marginality — place of birth. This is shown in Table 73.

### Table 73
#### PLACE OF BIRTH

|  | Non-Nazis | Nazis |
|---|---|---|
| Bavaria | 1 | 4 |
| Rhineland | 1 | 3 |
| Abroad | — | 4 |
| Total marginal | 2 | 11 |
| Total nonmarginal | 7 | 2 |

Here we find an important difference between Nazis and non-Nazis. Among the Nazis, 11 out of 13 were born in three marginal areas. If we look at the figures given in Table 66, we see that only 15 per cent of the population came from these areas, whereas all but two of the top

Nazis came from there. The Nazis are therefore marginal on birthplace by a ratio of about five to one. The non-Nazis in the cabinet, on the other hand, conform roughly to the random sample and to the German population as a whole (two out of nine being about 22 per cent rather than 15 per cent).

The above sets of figures indicate that the top Nazi leadership is even more marginal than all of our other samples, while the non-Nazis in the cabinet are roughly similar to the random sample (which, as we have pointed out, also includes many important Germans who were included in the *Fuehrerlexikon* elite even though they were not particularly devoted Nazis).

## CAREER

In the pursuit of their careers, the two groups again show interesting differences. In general, the non-Nazis stayed in the stable occupations and received more education, while the Nazis in most cases worked only in the party administration itself or in "communication" jobs. Table 74 illustrates this point.

*Table 74*

FIELD OF FIRST JOB

|  | Non-Nazis | Nazis |
|---|---|---|
| Stable occupations (law and civil service) | 6 | 1 |
| Party administration and communication | — | 8 |

The non-Nazis show themselves fairly similar to the random sample and very different from the top Nazi leadership. They illustrate the survival value of the middle-income skills, despite only casual affiliation with the NSDAP. For the Nazi group in the cabinet, however, the NSDAP *was* their career. Any skills these men possessed they brought to the party at an early age and developed in its service. While the non-Nazis were getting their education in schools, the Nazi group was going to the party young and making careers in its service. This is shown by the data concerning the age at which they held their first responsible jobs.

As Table 75 indicates, the top Nazis started on their main career, which was mainly party administration, at a fairly young age. These were the men who, as the body of this study has shown, came early and rose high in NSDAP officialdom.

*Table 75*
AGE AT WHICH FIRST RESPONSIBLE JOB WAS HELD

|  | Non-Nazis | Nazis |
|---|---|---|
| 18–25 | 2 | 7 |
| 26–30 | 5 | — |
| 31–35 | 1 | 2 |
| 36–40 | 1 | — |
| Don't know | 1 | 4 |

The non-Nazis also concentrated their educational careers mostly on professional studies, whereas the Nazis went in for party administration. This is illustrated by the figures for primary lifework, shown in Table 76.[28]

*Table 76*
PRIMARY LIFEWORK

|  | Non-Nazis | Nazis |
|---|---|---|
| Farmer | — | 1 |
| NS official | — | 10 |
| Civil service | 4 | 1 |
| Professions | 2 | — |
| Business | 1 | 1 |
| Military | 1 | — |
| Other | 1 | — |
| Total | 9 | 13 |

The figures in Table 77, showing subsidiary lifework, confirm the same conclusions.

These figures show why the Nazis started out on their first job at an earlier age than the non-Nazis. The Nazis are heavily concentrated in party administration and communication, whereas the non-Nazis are concentrated in the stable occupations, which require more time for preparation and study. These figures also show again that the non-Nazis conform most closely to the random sample, while the Nazis are closely related to the propagandists and administrators.

The information on primary and subsidiary lifework is summarized in Table 78.

[28] There is a rather wide discrepancy between these figures and those reported in Knight's *The German Executive*. The discrepancy arises from the method of computation. This study of the Nazi elite includes political occupations and reports the predominance of party leadership among the professions of Nazi ministers. The Knight study reports only nonpolitical occupations that were usually not the main occupations of the Nazis, but were the occupations to which they might have devoted their lives in quieter times.

*Table 77*
SUBSIDIARY LIFEWORK

|  | Non-Nazis | Nazis |
|---|---|---|
| NS official | 2 | 2 |
| Civil servant | 5 | 1 |
| Professions | — | 1 |
| Military | — | 2 |
| Communication | — | 5 |
| None | 2 | 2 |
| Total | 9 | 13 |

*Table 78*
FIELD OF LIFEWORK

|  | Non-Nazis | Nazis |
|---|---|---|
| Stable occupations (professions, civil service) | 11 | 4 |
| Party administration and communication | 2 | 17 |

## EDUCATION

On the indicator of university attendance, both groups are strikingly similar. This suggests that both groups came from the higher social strata. Among the non-Nazis, 6 out of 9 attended a university; among the Nazis, 8 out of 13 did. An interesting difference appears, however, if we consider the fields of study of the two groups. Using the same groupings as were used in Table 16, we see the comparison shown in Table 79. Since the Nazis predominate in both the culture-oriented

*Table 79*
FIELD OF STUDY

|  | Non-Nazis | Nazis |
|---|---|---|
| Culture-oriented | 1 | 5 |
| Skill-oriented | 1 | 3 |
| Professional studies | 6 | 3 |

and skill-oriented studies, it would appear that they have the characteristics of both the propagandists and the administrators. In fact, men of these two kinds were what the leadership of the Nazi Party consisted of, as has been shown by previous figures.

## PUBLICATIONS

As would be expected, the top Nazis are the more verbal Nazis. On the indicator of publications, the Nazis lead by far. Although 8 out of

9 non-Nazis did *not* report any publications, 11 out of 13 Nazis did. Since the main profession of the Nazi leadership was politics, it is reasonable that this should be the principal field in which they published. Indeed, it is the only one; all eleven Nazis in our group published their books or articles in this field.

## FOREIGN CONTACT

In the main text of this study we discussed foreign contacts as an indicator of social status. The result was that the three groups were ranked in the following order in descending frequency of foreign contacts: propagandists, random, and administrators. Using the same indices on the two groups at hand, we arrive at the results shown in Table 80.

*Table 80*
FOREIGN CONTACT

|  | Non-Nazis | Nazis |
|---|---|---|
| Born abroad | — | 4 |
| Foreign marriage | — | 1 |
| Higher education abroad | 1 | 3 |
| Travel abroad | 5 | 6 |

Since, among the Nazis, several of the indicators apply to the same person, two groups actually contain about the same proportion of persons who have had foreign contacts. If these figures are compared with those in Table 18, it appears that both groups have had far more foreign contacts than any of the other subgroups. This indicates not only the high status from which they come but also their marginality, which we have discussed earlier.

## OCCUPATION OF FATHER

Arranging the data in the same way as in Table 11, we get the results shown in Table 81.

*Table 81*
OCCUPATION OF FATHER

|  | Non-Nazis | Nazis |
|---|---|---|
| Landowner | 2 | — |
| Military | 1 | 2 |
| Professions | 2 | 4 |
| Civil service | 1 | 2 |
| Business | 1 | 3 |
| Peasant | — | 1 |
| Worker | 1 | — |
| Unknown | 1 | 1 |
| Total | 9 | 13 |

These figures indicate that the non-Nazis as well as the Nazis came from the upper social stratum of German society, with the non-Nazis having a slightly higher background than the Nazis. In this instance, again, both groups are more similar to the propagandists and to the administrators than to the random sample.

## MISCELLANEOUS

In their age distribution, the Nazis, with a mean age in 1934 of 41.4, are located between the propagandists (38.9) and the administrators (42.2), while the non-Nazis, with a mean age of 53.6, are far older than all the other groups.

It has been suggested earlier in this study that the Nazis tend to report less on all indices that have to do with women. Although some of these figures are probably connected also with social status and age, they seem, nevertheless, to suggest the validity of this assertion.

|  | Non-Nazis | Nazis |
|---|---|---|
| Don't know if married | 1 | 4 |
| Father-in-law's occupation unknown | 4 | 10 |
| No report on children | 1 | 6 |

## CONCLUSION

It was pointed out in the beginning of this Appendix that the figures used in this survey are too small to permit firm conclusions. Nevertheless, if all indicators are taken together, a few points seem reasonably clear:

1. Both groups are more marginal to German society than any of the other groups sampled.

2. Both groups come from a high social stratum, the non-Nazis from an even higher one than the Nazis.

3. The Nazis reveal a mixture of the attributes which we found previously in the propagandists and the administrators. In general, they seem to conform more to the propagandists, but they contain strong elements of both.

4. The non-Nazis had the skill-oriented professional education and careers that helped them to survive the revolution the Nazis had achieved with their politics of the street. They served the Nazis in this capacity until the Nazis themselves were secure enough, and versed

enough in the processes of government, to be able to dispense with the services of the non-Nazis.

5. The first Hitler cabinet, as a test case, indicates that the top German elite of the Nazi period exhibits the general characteristics that we found for the *Fuehrerlexikon* elite. Indeed, the top Nazis exhibit these characteristics even more pointedly.

## APPENDIX C: WHO ROSE HIGHEST IN THE NAZI PARTY

In the text we have noted the distinctive traits of certain subsamples of the Nazi elite. In the course of collecting these data, there emerged a few additional facts of interest that, although they do not differentiate between the subsamples, throw light on the traits of different strata within all of them. Specifically, we note that the persons who rose highest in the Nazi Party (whether propagandist, administrator, or random) had less education and less military experience and status than the rest. In a way, this is remarkable, since in most movements of a simliar sort the leaders have been better educated than the people they have led, and in most nationalist political movements military stature is an asset.

The key facts on education are presented in Table 82, which shows that the highest officers of the party had less education than the less exalted officers and still less than the ordinary members. This cannot be accounted for by any tendency of more active Nazis to disrupt their schooling by political activities. Like the Russian revolutionaries of the Czarist era, the Nazis did sometimes fail to complete their academic courses because they became involved in political activities. But in Table 82 we do not differentiate completed from incompleted courses. If we were to do so, we would find that the higher Nazis not only attempted less schooling but also, to a limited extent, failed more often in their attempt.

A more adequate explanation of the lesser education of the higher Nazis would be that the men without education faced greater frustrations and had fewer opportunities to make an acceptable career for themselves along normal lines. For the others, education facilitated an extraparty career, as indicated by the fact that the more educated subsamples (propagandists and administrators) got their first responsible jobs earlier than administrators.

Especially in the early years, educated people avoided the Nazi movement. Education is here an index of social status. The Nazi movement started as a plebeian movement of low respectability. In its later years, when it had grown strong, rich, and more conservative, people

Table 82

EDUCATION BY PARTY RANK

| Highest School Attended | Propagandists | | | Administrators | | | Random | | |
|---|---|---|---|---|---|---|---|---|---|
| | High Officer | Middle Officer* | Non-Officer | High Officer | Middle Officer* | Non-Officer | High Officer | Middle Officer* | Non-Officer |
| University | 48.6% | 37.5% | 64.7% | 19.2% | 32.4% | 33.3% | 47.8% | 42.9% | 70.4% |
| Other higher school | 5.7 | 25.0 | 11.8 | 20.5 | 21.6 | 7.4 | 8.7 | 9.5 | 7.4 |
| Trade, high, or grade school | 54.7 | 37.5 | 23.5 | 60.3 | 45.9 | 59.3 | 43.5 | 47.6 | 22.2 |
| Total | 100.0% | 100.0% | 100.0% | 100.0% | 99.9% | 100.0% | 100.0% | 100.0% | 100.0% |
| (Number) | (35) | (16) | (17) | (78) | (37) | (27) | (23) | (21) | (27) |

* There are too few low officers to include them.

with more education — that is to say, people with better nonpolitical jobs and higher status — joined it in increasing numbers. On the other hand, the people who joined the party early and became the *alter Kaempfer* and high officers were people without much status or good job prospects. These facts are shown in Table 83.

*Table 83*

PERCENTAGE OF PERSONS IN EACH GROUP WHO HAD ATTENDED UNIVERSITY

|  | Propagandists | Administrators | Random |
|---|---|---|---|
| Joined 1923 or before | 38.5 | 17.1 | 26.7 |
| Joined 1924–1928 | 50.0 | 20.6 | 72.8 |
| Joined 1929 on | 72.3 | 26.5 | 63.2 |

Thus we find that in the Nazi movement the uneducated were leading the educated. In the same way, although it was a militaristic movement, the nonveterans were leading the veterans. Table 84 shows that in each case those without military service tended to be found in larger numbers in the higher ranks than in the lower ranks.

Furthermore, there is some tendency, although a less clear-cut one, for party rank to be negatively correlated with military rank. Except among the propagandists, the proportion of enlisted men and N.C.O.'s among the party officers is greater than among the party nonofficers. The higher *military* rank of the propagandists is due to their recruitment from higher social strata. The higher *party* rank of the administrators, on the contrary, is due largely to their recruitment from lower social strata. They were the plebeians who, having least to lose in the old order, came earliest into the new movement and took control over its party apparatus. The negative correlation between military and party rank thus is accounted for by the differential *social* ranks which competed for top power in the complicated power-structure of the Nazi period. Behind this correlation, therefore, lie those differences of social position and perspective which led to the internal dissension between the party and military hierarchies that we have discussed in Parts V and VI of this study. In the focusing of such conflicts, the Nazi movement was indeed a "social revolution" characteristic of our times.

*Table 84*
RANK IN NAZI PARTY BY MILITARY SERVICE

| | Propagandists | | | Administrators | | | Random | | |
|---|---|---|---|---|---|---|---|---|---|
| | *High Officer* | *Middle Officer* | *Non-Officer* | *High Officer* | *Middle Officer* | *Non-Officer* | *High Officer* | *Middle Officer* | *Non-Officer* |
| Those with no service | 66.7% | 37.5% | 15.0% | 20.7% | 33.3% | 14.8% | 43.5% | 28.6% | 19.2% |
| Those with service | 33.3 | 62.5 | 85.0 | 79.3 | 66.7 | 85.2 | 56.5 | 71.4 | 80.8 |
| Total | 100.0% | 100.0% | 100.0% | 100.0% | 100.0% | 100.0% | 100.0% | 100.0% | 100.0% |
| (Number) | (36) | (16) | (20) | (77) | (36) | (27) | (23) | (21) | (26) |

## SELECTED REFERENCES*

Chakhotin, Serge. *Rape of the Masses*. London: Routledge, 1940.

*Das deutsche Fuehrerlexikon 1934–35*. Berlin: Stollberg, 1934.

*Die Wirtschaftshilfe der deutschen Studentenschaft 1923–25*. Leipzig: Quelle-Meyer, 1925.

Dietrich, Otto. *Auf den Strassen des Sieges*. Munich: Zentral-verlag der NSDAP., F. Ehrer nachf., 1939.

Fallada, Hans [pseud., Rudolf Ditzen]. *Kleiner Mann, was nun?* Berlin: Rowohlt, 1932. English translation, *Little Man, What Now?* New York: Simon & Schuster, Inc., 1933.

Gerth, Hans. "The Nazi Party: Its Leadership and Composition." *American Journal of Sociology*, XLV (1940), pp. 517 ff.

Gilbert, G. M. *Nuremberg Diary*. New York: Farrar, Straus & Co., Inc., 1947.

Glaeser, Ernst. *Frieden*. Berlin: Kiepenheuer, 1930.

————. *Jahrgang 1902*. Available in translation as *Class 1902*. London: Secker, 1929.

Goebbels, Joseph. *Vom Kaiserhof zur Reichskanzlei*. Munich: Zentral-verlag der NSDAP., F. Ehrer nachf., 1934.

Goering, Hermann. *Germany Reborn*. London: E. Mathews & Marrot, 1934.

Goerlitz, Walter. "Wallensteins Lager 1920–1938. Das Verhaeltnis der deutschen Generalitaet zur Republik und zum National-Sozialismus." *Frankfurter Hefte*, 3d year, Nos. 5 and 6 (May and June 1948), 4th year, No. 3 (March 1949).

————. *Der deutsche Generalstab*. Frankfurt: Verlag der Frankfurter Hefte, 1951.

Heiden, Konrad. *Der Fuehrer*. Boston: Houghton Mifflin Co., 1944.

Hossbach, Friedrich. *Zwischen Wehrmacht und Hitler*. Wolfenbuettel & Hanover: Wolfenbuettler Verlagsanstalt, 1949.

Kohn-Bramstedt, Ernst. *Dictatorship and Political Police: The Technique of Control by Fear*. London: Kegan Paul, 1945.

Kris, Ernst, and Speier, Hans. *German Radio Propaganda*. London: Oxford University Press, 1944.

Menzel, Hans L. *Wirtschaftliche Grundlagen des Studiums vor und nach dem Kriege*. Inaugural dissertation, University of Berlin, 1931.

---

*\* Note:* These references include only those titles cited by the authors, plus a few titles containing data supplementary to those presented in this study. It is not a checklist of relevant titles, which would number several hundred items.

Neumann, Franz. *Behemoth: The Structure and Practice of National Social-ism.* New York: Oxford University Press, 1944.

Neumann, Sigmund. *Permanent Revolution.* New York: Harper & Bros., 1942.

*NSDAP—Partei Statistik 1935.* 4 vols. NSDAP, 1935.

Peak, Helen. "Observations of the Characteristics and Distribution of German Nazis." *Psychological Monographs* No. 276 (1945).

Rees, J. R. (ed.). *The Case of Rudolf Hess.* New York: W. W. Norton & Co., 1948.

Rosenberg, Arthur. *A History of the German Republic.* London: Methuen, 1936.

*Statistisches Jahrbuch für das deutsche Reich.* Berlin: Statistisches Reichsamt, Annual Publication.

Trevor-Roper, H. R. *The Last Days of Hitler.* London: Macmillan & Co., Ltd., 1947.

Vagts, Alfred. *Hitler's Second Army.* Washington: Infantry Journal, 1943.

Veblen, Thorstein. *Imperial Germany and the Industrial Revolution.* New York: The Viking Press, 1946.

War Department, General Staff. *Strength and Organization of the Armies of France, Germany, Austria, Russia, England, Italy, Mexico and Japan.* No. 22 (Washington, 1916).

*Wer Ist's.* 10th ed. Berlin: Degener, 1935.

CHAPTER SIX

ROBERT C. NORTH, with the collaboration of ITHIEL DE SOLA POOL

# Kuomintang and Chinese Communist Elites *

## I. THE COLLAPSE OF THE IMPERIAL ELITE

Since the fall of the Manchu Empire in 1911, the Chinese Revolution has seen the development of two highly organized elite bodies — the Kuomintang and the Chinese Communist Party — that have interacted in such a complicated fashion that it is almost impossible to isolate the growth and decay of one from the development of the other.

Each emerged from the political, social, and economic chaos that came with the impact of Western culture upon Chinese society and with the breakdown of the Ch'ing dynasty. Each was a blend of indigenous impulse and foreign political theory and organization. Each cooperated with the other when its interests required. Each sought the other's annihilation once political circumstances changed.

Thus, within the course of a single lifetime, early members of the Kuomintang have developed from a counterelite (under the Empire) to a ruling elite, have cooperated with and have sought to destroy the Chinese Communists, have enjoyed enormous prestige and power, have suffered military defeats, and have now been pushed from the mainland of China. During the space of an even shorter lifetime, the Communists have grown from a few disorganized left-wing intellectual discussion groups into a thoroughly organized and tightly disciplined conspiratorial organization, have allied themselves with and have

* Originally published in 1952 by the Stanford University Press as Series B: Elite Studies, No. 8, of the Hoover Institute Studies. Reprinted with permission of the authors and publisher. Minor editorial changes have been made in the text.

sought to destroy the Kuomintang, have been forced underground and nearly exterminated, have risen again, and have now become the *de facto* rulers of China.

The revolutionary pattern, as developed first by the Kuomintang and later by the Communists, displayed a number of distinctive features. To a notable extent, both leadership elites were composed of culturally alienated intellectuals — men and women of well-to-do families who had removed themselves from the orthodox stream of their society's traditional culture. In both, this peculiar trend resulted from powerful influences on the economy of China and on its intellectual leaders. In both cases, most members of this displaced intellectual elite rose to revolutionary power by devoting their lives to political organization and action and by using their inherited high social status to change the directions of Chinese cultural trends.

This new elite scheme presented a sharp contrast to the imperial pattern of the Ch'ing dynasty. The political leadership of the Chinese Empire functioned within a system that has been described as "an autocracy superimposed upon a democracy." The Emperor was the balance between heaven and earth, but in return for his divine right to rule, he assumed a large responsibility for the maintenance of order, peace, and prosperity within his realm. If he should fail in this, it was assumed that his subjects would rebel against him.

Yet the Emperor ruled, an absolute and legally unlimited monarch, with various of the Imperial clan clustered about him. Directly below him in the administrative hierarchy came the Grand Council and the Grand Secretariat, and below these came six (eventually increased to twelve) departments or boards roughly comparable to ministries. Under the central government came the provincial administrations headed in each case by a Governor-General (Viceroy) and/or a Governor. In addition to these officials, the Ch'ing dynasty established in eleven provinces the post of Tartar-General, who ranked "with, but before," the Viceroy.

Each province was divided into smaller units designated as *tao* or circuits over which an intendant presided. Each *tao* was made up of *fu* (overseen by a prefect), and the *fu*, in turn, were subdivided into departments (under departmental magistrates) and *hsien* (under magistrates). These officials secured their appointments from above, all commissions being issued by the Emperor. But within the departments and *hsien* were also town and village officials who secured their mandates from popular support.

Throughout the whole governmental system, the securing of public office depended to a considerable extent upon the possession of one of three literary degrees — *hsiu ts'ai, chü jen,* and *chin shih.*

Examinations for the *hsiu ts'ai* were held in prefectural cities for students who had first been screened by tests given by the magistrates in their *hsien* (districts). Provincial examinations for the *chü jen* were usually held triennially in the autumn at the various provincial capitals. Normally, out of some ten to twelve thousand competitors, in each province, only about three hundred were passed.[1]

Theoretically, these examinations, which anyone, with few exceptions, was privileged to take, served as the gateways to public life, but how the system actually functioned is still a subject for investigation. Writing in 1938, Dr. Karl A. Wittfogel came to the tentative conclusion that whereas some "fresh blood" from lower strata of society may have been absorbed through the examination system, the prevailing tendency was for the ruling elite to reproduce itself socially by recruiting from its own ranks. Wittfogel's material, drawn largely from the *Dynastic Histories,* included two dynasties, Han (206 B.C.–A.D. 22) and Chin (265–420), falling prior to the establishment of the examination system, together with the T'ang (618–906), Sung (906–1279), Yuan (1280–1368), and Ming (1368–1644) eras.[2] In recent years, these data have been found to contrast with material gathered by Dr. Edward A. Kracke, Jr., from early lists of civil service examination graduates.[3]

On the evidence of two lists (A.D. 1148 and 1256), a majority of candidates who passed the examinations seem to have emerged from nonofficial families. It is Dr. Kracke's conclusion, then, that although the topmost elite of Chinese officialdom, as represented by biographies in the *Dynastic Histories,* was recruited, for the most part, from official families, the entire body of candidates passing through the examination system was notably more representative of lower strata of Chinese society.

An examination of twenty-three late nineteenth-century and early twentieth-century Empire careers, drawn for illustrative purposes from a definitive biographical source,[4] reveals a number of diverse patterns, as shown in Table 1.

[1] Richard Wilhelm, *A Short History of Chinese Civilization,* translated by Joan Joshua (New York: Viking Press, 1929), pp. 215, 240, 258.

[2] Karl August Wittfogel, *New Light on Chinese Society* (New York: International Secretariat, Institute of Pacific Relations, 1938), pp. 11–12.

[3] E. A. Kracke, Jr., "Family vs. Merit in Chinese Civil Service Examinations under the Empire," *Harvard Journal of Asiatic Studies,* X (1947), pp. 103–123. Cf. Wittfogel, *op. cit.,* "Public Office in the Liao Dynasty and the Chinese Examination System," pp. 13–40.

[4] Arthur W. Hummel (ed.), *Eminent Chinese of the Ch'ing Period* (2 vols.;

*Table 1*

STATISTICS ON THE LIVES OF TWENTY-THREE LEADERS
OF THE CH'ING DYNASTY BETWEEN 1890 AND 1911

| Background | Number |
|---|---|
| Scholar-official family | 7 |
| Minor government official (father) | 3 |
| Imperial family (father) | 3 |
| Merchant (father) | 2 |
| Army officer (father) | 1 |
| Peasant (father) | 1 |
| Outlaw | 1 |
| Don't know | 5 |
| Prerequisite for office: | |
| *Chin Shih* degree | 8 |
| *Chü Jen* degree | 2 |
| *Hsiu Ts'ai* degree | 1 |
| Among those who did not pass through the examination system: | |
| Purchase | 2 |
| Royal birth | 3 |
| Knowledge of English language | 1 |
| Military service (officer) | 2 |
| Military service (promotion from ranks) | 1 |
| Royal concubine | 1 |
| Royal eunuch | 1 |
| Private education | 1 |

Of this illustrative (but not necessarily statistically representative) sample, the large majority came from official families. Indeed, only four out of the eighteen on whom we have information had fathers in private occupations. A very thin stratum of the millions of Chinese families actually constituted the ruling elite despite the nominally democratic character of the examination system. The father of only one of the leaders came from among the hundreds of millions of peasants. The much smaller merchant class contributed two sons to our sample of the Imperial elite, which was not disproportionate to their numbers in the population but contrasts with the many sons of officials. The business classes had not yet gained easy access to the

Washington, D.C.: Government Printing Office, 1943). These twenty-three, as selected by the author for illustrative purposes, are: Chang Chih-tung, Chang Yin-huan, Jung Hung, Kuang-hsü, Tuan-fang, Li Wen-t'ien, Liu K'un-i, Yuan Shih-k'ai, Prince Ch'un, I-hsin, Feng Tzu-ts'ai, Tz'u-hsi, T'ang Chiung, Sun Chia-nai, Wu Ta-ch'eng, Jung-lu, Li Lien-ying, Sung Ch'ing, Hsü Ching-ch'eng, Liu K'un-i, Chih-jui, Ch'iu Feng-chia, T'an Ssu-t'ung.

centers of governmental prestige, although education provided a possible portal for men of business background.[5]

Of the twenty-three leaders not quite half entered their careers through the portals of the examination system. Twelve, however, managed to reach office through other channels. In general the scholars, officials, and merchants, the counterparts of the middle classes in the West, sent their sons through the regular examination process more often than did the others. Those sons who entered public careers without the advantage of Imperial ancestry or who struggled into public careers from less-favored backgrounds were the ones who made their way into public office through irregular channels.

Of the seven sons of scholar-officials, five took examinations.

Of the three sons of minor officials, two took examinations.

Of the two sons of merchants, both took examinations.

The remaining two leaders who entered public office through the examination system are among those whose fathers' occupations we do not know. Thus the examination system was part of a pattern by which persons from scholar-official-merchant backgrounds entered public life. How the other half of our sample entered reveals some alternative patterns.

Of the two sons of scholar-officials who did not take examinations, one had studied under a private tutor, and one purchased his first position. The one leader whose father was a minor government official and who did not take examinations was a girl who acquired her position by becoming a royal concubine — and eventually Empress Dowager of China.

Among members of the Imperial family, I-huan, the seventh son of the Kuang-hsü Emperor by a concubine, was created a Prince of the Second Degree during his tenth year and Lieutenant General of the Banner during his twenty-first year; his elder brother, I-hsin, was made Grand Councillor at the age of twenty; and the Kuang-hsü Emperor, the second son of I-huan, was adopted during his childhood by the Empress Dowager in violation of the laws of succession and ascended the throne at the age of four years.

A Brigadier General's son helped to organize the first army corps in China to be equipped with modern arms and to be drilled in the Western manner. At twenty-eight the son made brigade rank, and two years later he was promoted to the grade of Lieutenant General. Concurrently he held civilian positions and rose to a Grand Secretaryship.

---

[5] The sons of two merchants advanced through the examination system, obtained *chin shih* degrees, and served for brief periods at Hanlin Academy, the highest institution of learning within the Empire.

The son of a peasant entered a missionary school, then studied in Macao, Hong Kong, and Monson Academy in Massachusetts, and eventually graduated from Yale. Later his knowledge of English yielded him a position in the Imperial Customs Service and started him on a career that led into diplomacy.

Feng Tzu-ts'ai, brought up as an outlaw, was head of a band by the time he reached his early thirties. Later he entered the Imperial Army and won rapid promotions.

One man of influence — Li Lien-ying, a eunuch — scarcely fits into any conventional classification. Born of "humble parents," he was apprenticed to a cobbler at an early age. He appears to have had no schooling, no money to buy rank, and no military power or experience, but through extreme self-sacrifice — suffered during his sixteenth year — he was able to enter the Imperial Service, whereupon, by the crafty use of remaining talents, he in time became one of the most powerful persons in the Empire.

### The Western Impact

By the middle of the nineteenth century the whole body of Empire leadership (of which these individuals were but a small segment) was struggling to meet the threat of foreign conquest.

Invasion, of course, was nothing new to the Chinese people. But twentieth-century conquest was something of a different sort, for the modern invader won his ground less by force of arms than by technology and Western finance; the great campaigns were not military expeditions but construction jobs; and the columns that began pushing their way across China were railroads rather than regiments of infantry.

Chinese leaders were discovering themselves to be nearly helpless against this onslaught. The country had no effective weapons — no powerful finance, no modern technology — for resisting, nor could they be obtained except from foreign sources.

During the nineteenth century, various European states had induced the Manchu Empire to open a number of ports to foreign trade, and then, with this foothold, they had pushed inland, leasing, building railroads, buying up concessions, and lending money. The dilemma was inescapable, for if China was to build its economic defenses, it needed both money and railroads, but each new acquisition of this sort brought a deeper entrenchment of foreign influence. Among the results were further indebtedness and balances of trade unfavorable to China.

China's leadership could not agree upon proper measures. During the nineteenth century, sincere and able efforts had been made to adjust the governmental structure for coping not only with the direct foreign impact but also with the internal dislocations that soon resulted from the invasion of an alien culture. But the framework and machinery and functions of the Empire remained inadequate.

There was undoubtedly a complex variety of reasons for this inadequacy. This most recent invasion — in contrast to earlier ones — depended upon a more complex system of commercial and mechanical techniques than Chinese culture had so far produced. Its transportation system was more highly developed than those of previous invasions and of China itself. Its warfare was more highly mechanized and mobilized. Its trade lines, its communications, its whole cultural pattern had spread out over continents and seas and had, in a sense, nearly surrounded China before the invasion began.

In addition, there were uncommon weaknesses in the Imperial structure itself. The ruling Manchu dynasty, which was still not completely assimilated, was perhaps less adaptable, less resilient, and less sensitive to moods of the Chinese people than a thoroughly indigenous dynasty might have been. Corruption had been spreading within the hierarchy. The Empress Dowager was self-willed, stubborn, and intolerant of opposition on the part of her subordinates.

Individual leaders ranged themselves according to their attitudes toward the foreign impact. Some, like the Empress Dowager, hoped to resist through rigid preservation of the structure as it was; others wanted to modify structure, machinery, and functions to cope with foreign influences and new conditions; and still others saw no solution short of tearing down the old framework and rebuilding according to Western models.

### The Communist Influence

Such was the background against which liberal and conservative elements struggled for influence during the last two decades of Manchu rule and from which both the Kuomintang and Chinese Communist leaderships gradually emerged. But it was Russian communism that godfathered both new parties.

Prior to 1924 Dr. Sun Yat-sen's Kuomintang remained weak, disorganized, and floundering. Comprising a peculiar mixture of idealistic intellectuals and treaty port merchants, the movement had no army or unified party structure. In his later years Dr. Sun was in poor health; rank-and-file membership was scattered; and party headquarters in Canton depended upon the whimsical good will of local war lords for its security.[6]

[6] For a concise account of events during this period, consult Harley Farnsworth MacNair, *China in Revolution* (Chicago: University of Chicago Press, 1931), pp. 34–64.

Leaders of world communism became interested in the Kuomintang when they convinced themselves that this party, which stressed national equality and unity as its main reason for being, could be turned to Communist purposes. In 1920 the Second Congress of the Communist International developed a strategy for harnessing Asian revolutions that were already under way and for bringing them to bear against the forces of world capitalism. In this plan, however, there were two mutually contradictory concepts that plagued Bolshevik leaders through early phases of Chinese Communist history and which were not satisfactorily resolved until the rise of Mao Tse-tung to leadership.

At the Second Congress, M. N. Roy, an Indian delegate who later separated himself from the Communist movement, stressed the belief that Western capitalism was drawing its chief strength from colonial possessions and dependencies. Without this control of raw materials and markets, he said, the capitalist powers of the world could not maintain their existence. "Super-profit gained in the colonies," he said, "is the mainstay of modern capitalism, and so long as the latter is not deprived of this source of super-profit, it will not be easy for the European working class to overthrow the capitalist order."[7]

Lenin accepted this principle, maintaining that it was implicit in his own earlier writings, but he criticized the emphasis Roy placed on class conflict in Asia. Roy, he felt, went too far in declaring that the destiny of the West would depend exclusively upon the development and strength of peasant and working-class revolts in Asian countries. On the contrary, Lenin considered it necessary for all Communist parties to enlarge their influence by rendering assistance to existing "bourgeois-democratic liberation movements" in economically backward areas where, he said, working-class revolutions were not as yet sufficiently matured to be effective.

In seeking to resolve this contradiction between class conflict and the concept of cooperation with nationalist revolutions, the Second Congress accepted both, in what amounted to a policy of cooperation combined with opposition. While extending support to middle-class nationalist movements such as the Kuomintang, Communist leaders

---

[7] The rough outlines of this controversy can be pieced together from *The Communist International, Executive Committee: The Second Congress* (no place, no date), pp. 108–158, 475–479, 570–579, and from *The Second Congress of the Communist International: As Reported and Interpreted by the Official Newspapers of Soviet Russia* (Washington, D.C.: Government Printing Office, 1920), pp. 38–46. For the interpretation presented in this paper, the author has given considerable weight to a statement given him by M. N. Roy in Dehra Dun, India, October 15, 1950.

were expected to arouse and organize the working masses and to penetrate and gain leadership over the revolutionary groups they were aiding.

The reasoning behind this strategy was expressed by a Chinese Communist delegate to the Fourth Congress of the Communist International in 1922:

> If we do not join this party [the Kuomintang] we shall remain isolated and we shall preach a communism which consists of a great and noble ideal, but one which the masses do not follow. The masses certainly would follow the bourgeois party, and this party would use the masses for its purposes. If we join the party, we shall be able to show the masses that we too are for a revolutionary democracy, but that for us revolutionary democracy is only a means to an end. Furthermore, we shall be able to point out that although we are for this distant goal, we nevertheless do not forget the daily needs of the masses. We shall be able to gather the masses around us and split the Kuomintang party.[8]

Bolshevik success in regard to cooperation with the Kuomintang was not immediate, but in January 1923 Adolph Joffe, the Soviet Ambassador in Peking, met Sun in Shanghai and concluded an agreement that became the basis for closer relations before the year was out. During the late summer, Michael Borodin arrived in Canton as advisor to Dr. Sun, and a complete reorganization of the Kuomintang was undertaken.

In China the tradition of professional military and political classes was strong, but under Russian influence the Kuomintang and the Chinese Communist parties both developed special kinds of military and political elites. These were leadership groups that devoted themselves to military service and to political organization and administration with special party frameworks. A vast majority of Kuomintang and Chinese Communist leaders have risen to power and influence through these specialized activities.

There are other initial similarities between Kuomintang and Chinese Communist elites. Both emerged from the political, social, and economic chaos that came with the impact of Western culture upon Chinese society and with the breakdown of the Ch'ing dynasty. Both came from similar socioeconomic groups — from landlord, scholar, or bureaucratic families, from merchant or moneylender circles, or from the newly developed capitalist class of large cities along the coast.

In the early stages of their developments, both elites tended to receive their educations in Japan, Europe, or the United States. In the beginning, both sought to break away from the main flow of traditional

8 *Protokoll des IV Kongresses der Kommunistischen Internationale* (Hamburg, 1923), p. 615.

Chinese culture and practice, although, with the passage of time, the Kuomintang, at best, moved closer to the older current. Both bodies developed schisms and conducted purges, but neither tended to take drastic action against its own disobedients. Both relied heavily on military force.

The divergencies between the two elites are equally noteworthy. The Kuomintang, which began as a Western-oriented, middle-class revolutionary movement with undisciplined organization and ill-defined goals, became increasingly radical with the introduction of Russian influence — but only up to the point where revolution threatened the security of members springing from the landowning and merchant classes. At that contingency the Kuomintang leadership, seeking to preserve both power and property, swung over into a course — increasingly militaristic and counterrevolutionary — which severed their contact with, and brought them into opposition to, a large section of the population, especially the peasantry. The Communists, although shifting their strategy, never abandoned their central plan for capturing the Chinese Revolution and using it for their own special purposes.

In moving closer to the flow of traditional Chinese culture, the Kuomintang, which had emerged as an embodiment of Chinese nationalism, tried to adapt a kind of neo-Confucianism to problems of the twentieth century. The Chinese Communists, on the other hand, took the concepts of nationalism, democracy, and the people's livelihood which Sun Yat-sen and his followers had developed, set them in a Marxist-Leninist framework, and gave them a totally new meaning.

Although Kuomintang organization and principles of party discipline were superficially similar to those of the Chinese Communists, the actual functioning of the two parties was different. Chiang Kai-shek rose to power largely through military alliances, police force, quickly executed coups, and the weaving of antagonistic factions — to which he himself did not belong — into an interlacing political system. The Communists succeeded through skillful adaptation of Leninist strategy and tactics to Chinese conditions. Mao and his followers, while championing the cause of the peasant, made what use they could of calculated alliances with the Kuomintang. Supporting Chiang when Chiang was useful, they trained peasant armies to turn against him when the proper moment came. Chiang, though fully aware of Communist purposes, never devised an effective counterprogram nor succeeded in eradicating the Kuomintang's inefficiency, corruption, and complacency, which Communist leadership continually exploited.

## II. THE DEVELOPMENT OF THE KUOMINTANG LEADERSHIP

Since 1924 there have been six National Congresses of the KMT (Kuomintang) Party and six Central Executive Committees. We take the members of these CEC's as our sample of the leadership of the Kuomintang. Through the years the relative power of these bodies has varied, but their structure and their position within the party framework has remained essentially as fixed by Borodin and Sun Yat-sen.

When Borodin reached China in the latter part of 1923, he found Sun Yat-sen's revolutionary movement disunited and floundering. Among seamen of the port cities, among coolies, among workers in British and Japanese textile factories, among students and intellectuals, there existed a powerful revolutionary potential. But Sun and his Kuomintang had not yet been able to harness this dynamic or to drive it in any consistent direction.

It was clear that the Kuomintang needed advice, material aid, and disciplined leadership — all of which Borodin was in a position to offer.

Sun Yat-sen was not unaware of Kuomintang weaknesses, and consequently Borodin found the Chinese leader in a receptive frame of mind. For a number of years Sun had been trying to secure European and American aid for the support of a Republic of China, but without tangible result. Now, through Borodin, the Soviet Union was offering arms, ammunition, and technical advice — the very support that Sun had felt in need of.

### The First Central Executive Committee

Under Borodin's supervision the Kuomintang was rebuilt along the Communist Party pattern, with a series of organizational units pyramiding upward through subdistrict, district, and provincial levels to an annual National Congress, designed as the final authority on both party and governmental policy, and a Central Executive Committee to direct party affairs between meetings of the National Congress.

In theory, at least, this system (like that of Communist parties) was tied together by democratic centralism. The usual interpretation of this principle is that free discussion must be allowed within all party organs until the moment a decision has been reached, at which point unconditional obedience is required of all members regardless of private disagreement. In other terms, party membership elected authorities to higher echelons, either directly or through intervening congresses, whereupon such authorities were endowed with powers of command and the right to be obeyed. Theoretically, then, the mandate of power flowed upward through the party pyramid, while control fanned downward. In practice, it has usually come about under democratic centralism that whatever authorities control the central organization of a party actually control the party. In this respect the Kuomintang has not proved itself an exception.

Within the Kuomintang there have been four structural levels pyramiding upward from *Ch'ü* through *Hsien*, Provincial, and Central Organizations. Each of these tiers has maintained executive and supervising committees. These are elected at the *Ch'ü* level by party members, but in higher echelons they are elected by congresses of party delegates who, in turn, are elected by the congress of a lower level. Each level has maintained a party secretary and a series of commissions and departments appointed by and responsible to the appropriate executive committee. Among these various units, the Organizational Department, controlling the organization of party branches beneath it, has enjoyed exceptional power.[9]

The Kuomintang Constitution (Article 29) left to the discretion of the Central Executive Committee the actual drafting of regulations concerning the  organization of the National Congress, the election of delegates, and the appointment of representatives to the Convention. Thereupon, on the grounds that only the province of Kwangtung (i.e., the area around Canton) was under Kuomintang jurisdiction at the time of the First and Second Congresses in 1924 and 1926, the Central Executive Committee felt justified in instituting the practice of designating delegates from relatively inaccessible areas, a circumvention of democratic process that established something of a precedent and subsequently evoked considerable criticism from opponents of Kuomintang policy.[10]

The duties of the National Congress included the adoption and approving of national government reports, the revision of the party platform and constitution, the formulation of new policies and programs for the national government, and the election of members to the Central Executive and Central Supervisory Committees. Between sessions of the National Congress, the Central Executive Committee constituted the highest authority of the party (Article 10). To it was entrusted the political authority of the national government whenever the National Kuomintang Congress was not in session.

[9] Ch'ien Tuan-sheng, *The Government and Politics of China* (Cambridge; Harvard University Press, 1950), pp. 119, 120, 124. See also Min-ch'ien T. Z. Tyau, *Two Years of Nationalist China* (Shanghai, 1930), p. 26. The Kuomintang Constitution appears in Arthur N. Holcombe, *The Chinese Revolution* (Cambridge: Harvard University Press, 1930), Appendix C, pp. 356–370.
[10] *The China Year Book, 1931* (Peking and Tientsin, 1931), p. 556.

It was stipulated that the Central Executive Committee should hold plenary sessions at least once each six months and should elect a Standing Committee of five to nine members to transact business between plenary sessions of the parent organization. Directly beneath the Standing Committee of the Central Executive Committee were ranged a secretariat, an organizational department, a publicity department, a training department, a bureau for statistics, and four special committees dealing with finance, the affairs of overseas Chinese, the drafting of documents, and the compilation of party history.[11]

In theory, all political sanction was supposed to flow from the bottom of the party pyramid toward the top. However, the party constitution (Article 21) designated Dr. Sun as President of the party throughout his lifetime, and stated that "the members should follow the direction of the President and work for the advancement of the Party" (Article 22), that the President should have the power to disapprove resolutions of the party congress (Article 25), and that his voice should be the decisive one in the Central Executive Committee (Article 26). Sun could, if he chose, exercise complete dictatorial authority over both party and government. As long as Dr. Sun lived, there was a degree of cohesion within Kuomintang membership, but after his death existing factions began a struggle for power that continued for more than a decade. In a rough fashion these cliques formed themselves initially into three main groups: the extreme right, or Western Hills faction, which opposed the Communist alliance from the very beginning; a middle group that formed itself around Chiang Kai-shek; and a left wing under the leadership of Wang Ching-wei, Eugene Chen, Mme. Sun Yat-sen, and others.[12]

From the time of its election, the First Central Executive Committee of the Kuomintang suffered spasms of internal strife, but it was not until Dr. Sun's death on March 12, 1925, that these conflicts became severe enough to threaten the party's existence. During Dr. Sun's final illness, Kuomintang leaders were in almost continual session, in various parts of China, in an effort to decide upon a new leadership. There was dissension in all sections of the party, but those most bitterly opposed to the Communist alliance, known later as the Western Hills group, were the only ones to take precipitate action. These went so far

[11] Chih-fang Wu (W. F. Wu), *Chinese Government and Politics* (Shanghai, 1935), p. 286.
[12] There is some confusion in regard to the precise Communist membership of this committee. All sources agree that T'an P'ing-shan and Yu Shu-te had seats, but it cannot be stated for certain whether or not Li Ta-chao and Kan Shu-te were also members. If they were, then their names must have been eliminated from lists published after the Kuomintang-Communist break in 1927.

as to form a separate club with headquarters at 44 Route Vallon,[13] in Shanghai, from which they watched political developments with increasing apprehension, especially as Borodin and Chiang Kai-shek (then a young military officer only beginning to win notice in Kuomintang circles) built up the Whampoa Cadet School and consolidated their military power.[14]

This split, together with increasing Communist influence within the party, constituted a prime factor in shaping the nature of the Second National Congress and in bringing about a sharp upheaval in Central Executive Committee membership.

### The Second Central Executive Committee

Elections for the Second CEC, in January 1926, brought defeat for those who had identified themselves with the Western Hills viewpoint (Chü Cheng, Tsou Lu, Hsiung K'e-wu, Lin Shen, Shih Ching-yang, T'an Cheng, Yang Hsi-min, and Yeh Ch'u-ts'ang), and victory for those who favored continued cooperation with the Soviet Union and close working relations with the Communist Party of China. Among the thirteen committeemen re-elected from the 1924 Committee were a number of prominent Communist sympathizers, two Communists, and Hu Han-min, who had accepted many favors from the Russians in the first days of the alliance, but who, through the years, moved more and more toward the Western Hills group. To these incumbents were added at least four new Communist members and several pro-Communists, among whom the two widows, Mme. Sun Yat-sen and Mme. Liao Chung-k'ai, were especially notable (see Appendix B, Table 2).

Between the Second National Congress of January 1926 and the Third National Congress of March 1929, Kuomintang history was shaped to a remarkable degree by Chiang Kai-shek's increasing power and by his antagonism to the Communists. This conflict resulted in a party split, with a Kuomintang left wing maintaining a short-lived Communist alliance in opposition to Chiang.[15]

[13] "Protest of the Chungkuo Kuomintang Tungchi Club," *The China Year Book, 1928*, p. 1329.

[14] Holcombe, *op. cit.*, p. 229.

[15] For differing viewpoints in regard to this complex struggle for power, consult Harold R. Isaacs, *The Tragedy of the Chinese Revolution* (Stanford, Calif.: Stanford University Press, 1951), pp. 74–252; T'ang Leang-li, *The Inner History of the Chinese Revolution* (London, 1930), pp. 242–244; Louis Fischer, *The Soviets in World Affairs* (New York: J. Cape &. H. Smith, 1930), XI, p. 652; T. C. Woo, *The Kuomintang and the Future of the Chinese Revolution* (London: G. Allen & Unwin, 1928), pp. 167–174; George Sokolsky, *The Tinder Box in Asia* (Garden City, N.Y.: Doubleday, Doran & Co. Inc., 1933), and *The China Year Book, 1928*, p. 1326.

## The Third Central Executive Committee

Chiang Kai-shek effected two coups against the Communists, one in March 1926 and a second in April 1927. His preparations for the seizure of power followed two courses. Militarily, he established relations or working alliances with various individual officers, army cliques, and independent or semi-independent war lords. Politically, he encouraged the organization, under Ch'en Kuo-fu and Ch'en Li-fu, of an intraparty faction that later, complete with police and intelligence arms, became the well-known Organization Group, or CC Clique. For a time the Kuomintang left wing continued its alliance with the Reds, but by the beginning of 1928 thousands of Communists had been killed and the leaders had been driven underground.

The Third National Congress, which was opened on March 15, 1929, by Hu Han-min as provisional chairman and which remained in session thirteen days, elected a Central Executive Committee of thirty-six members whose political complexion was remarkably different from that of the 1926 membership. Certainly, there were no Communists on the 1929 committee, and there were not many who could be accused of sympathizing with communism. At least one prominent Western Hills supporter, Yeh Ch'u-ts'ang, was reinstated with full membership (Appendix B, Table 3). Wang Ching-wei, opposing Chiang Kai-shek, allied himself first with T'ang Sheng-chih, a minor militarist, and later (1930) with Feng Yü-hsiang and Yen Hsi-shan.

At the time of this congress, Chiang Kai-shek was probably the most powerful political and military leader in China, with tight control over Central Kuomintang Headquarters. For the next few years, however, he was to find himself unable to control his party and govern the country without allying himself with either Hu Han-min or Wang Ching-wei. It is significant, moreover, that the Standing Committee of the Central Executive Committee had decided as early as October 25, 1928, that the Central Party Headquarters should have power to name one half of the delegates sent to the Third Congress by district Kuomintang organs.[16]

The six known Communists on the 1926 committee had long since lost their seats on the Central Executive Committee, most of them disappearing — for the time being — without trace, and every effort was made by Chiang Kai-shek and his supporters (Ch'en Li-fu headed the intelligence section of the Kuomintang) to exclude other suspected Reds and their sympathizers from all positions of influence in the

[16] Yen Hsi-shan's telegram to Chiang Kai-shek, February 24, 1931, as reprinted in *The China Year Book, 1931*, p. 556.

party. Ch'en Kuo-fu, who with his brother, Ch'en Li-fu, was shaping the powerful anti-Communist CC Clique, was an important member of this committee.

These factional conflicts, rather than preference changes on the part of any sort of Kuomintang electorate, determined the character of the Third Central Executive Committee. The period between the Third National Congress (March 1929) and the Fourth National Congress (November 1931) was marked by a long and complicated series of intraparty intrigues, rebellions (such as those of Feng Yü-hsiang, Yen Hsi-shan, the Wang Ching-wei clique, and the Kwangsi militarists), and Communist uprisings, which somewhat weakened the power of Chiang Kai-shek.

A basic cause of these various conflicts was the fact that Chiang and the Nanking government were able to maintain direct control over only those provinces near the mouth of the Yangtze River. In other areas, Nationalist authority rested upon a series of alliances with military men such as Feng Yü-hsiang in the Northwest, Yen Hsi-shan (who had extended his forces eastward from Shansi), and generals of the Kwangsi clique (such as Li Tsung-jen) who controlled the Hankow region.

Aggravating this fundamental instability were two other opposition groups with which Chiang Kai-shek was forced to cope: the Communists who, under Mao Tse-tung and Chu Te, were building soviets and a peasant Red Army in mountain districts of Hunan and Kiangsi; and the Reorganizationalists, or Kuomintang left-wingers grouped around Wang Ching-wei, who periodically accused Chiang of abandoning the revolutionary principles of Dr. Sun in favor of a personal military dictatorship.

### The Fourth Central Executive Committee

To unify the Kuomintang in the face of Japanese aggression, it was decided during the autumn of 1931 that all members of the First, Second, and Third Central Executive Committees, with the exception of Communists, would automatically become members of the Fourth Central Executive Committee. To this group Chiang's Nanking party would add four new members, and the Canton branch, five new members (Appendix B, Table 5.).

At this point Chiang Kai-shek, who had alienated both Wang Ching-wei and Hu Han-min, did not enjoy the power, either within the party or throughout China, which he had commanded at the time of the Third Congress. Of the seventy-two members of the CEC, about 15 per cent seem to have been associated with the Ch'en brothers' CC

Clique, or Organization Group, which came to control the Organization Department of the party; about 9 per cent (almost wholly military men) were considered personal affiliates of Chiang; and 4 per cent were Whampoa graduates or allied military officers upon whom Chiang could count. In addition to these, there were a number of small factions consisting of former Western Hills leaders and other conservatives inclined toward Chiang. There was no certain unity, but possibly these groupings displayed more cohesion than was achieved by the feuding opposition of Hu Han-min and Wang Ching-wei.

It is fairly certain that the nature of this CEC, as in the case of the 1929 committee, was determined to a large degree by conflicts of military force. Although both periods were marked by personal competition for power, the notable difference is that the 1926–1929 struggles emphasized disagreements over the Communist question, whereas the 1929–1931 antagonisms emphasized disagreements over problems which were largely of an intra-Kuomintang nature.

During the years between the Fourth and Fifth Congresses, an external factor — Japanese aggression — contributed to an increase in Chiang Kai-shek's power.

The compromise government of January 1932, hailed by many observers as a "progressive" one, included Sun Fo as Premier, Eugene Chen as Foreign Minister, and Ch'en Kung-po as Minister of Labor. Various Liberal and left-wing circles expressed considerable approval of the fact that a change had been brought about by political, rather than military, action.[17] But the subsequent records of some of its leaders, especially Ch'en Kung-po, who became a Japanese puppet, cast considerable doubt over their potentialities. In any case, the new combination was short-lived. With the departure of T. V. Soong from the government, the flow of financial support from Shanghai banking circles diminished. Chiang Kai-shek, who had resigned from his office as President of the national government, retired to his native village of Fenghua, and Wang Ching-wei and Hu Han-min refused to go to Nanking because of "ill-health." Under these circumstances, the government under Sun Fo remained nearly helpless. Further, the Standing Committee never met, and the Canton leaders quickly formed three new organizations — the Southwest Executive Committee of the Kuomintang, the Southwest Political Council, and the Southwest Military Council — through which to channel their dissensions.

During this period Eugene Chen tried to initiate a policy of vigorous opposition to Japanese aggression, but both Chiang Kai-shek and

[17] T. A. Bisson, "The Years of the Kuomintang: Revolution vs. Reaction," *Foreign Policy Reports*, VIII, No. 25 (February 15, 1933), p. 301.

Wang Ching-wei blocked these efforts, and since Ho Ying-ch'in, Chiang's appointee as Minister of War, remained in control over most of Nanking's military forces, the new administration (already short of funds) found itself unable to act against Japan.

Failing to achieve a change in Chinese policy toward Japan, Eugene Chen tendered his resignation. Thereupon Sun Fo went to Shanghai for the purpose of urging Chen to reconsider. But in the course of their conversations, Chen persuaded Sun to send in his own resignation.[18] This brought an end to the coalition movement. The fact was that the achievement of a unified government remained all but impossible without the participation of Chiang Kai-shek, who controlled the armed forces and had access to sources of finance.

Supported now by Wang Ching-wei, his former antagonist, and by the financial wizardry of T. V. Soong, Chiang regained power. To the government were also added several members of an older generation of Chinese diplomats who had previously served under the northern militarists in Peking. V. K. Wellington Koo was perhaps representative of these men.

During the spring of 1932 a disagreement developed between Wang Ching-wei and Chang Hsüeh-liang, the young "Marshal of Manchuria," over the latter's conduct of operations against the Japanese. Wang, who later defected to the Japanese, maintained at this time that his opponent ought either to put up stubborn resistance against the invader or to resign in favor of a more able commander. Chang, on the other hand, argued that his troops were not sufficiently armed or adequately paid and that if Nanking wanted more fighting, they should be willing to underwrite a campaign with arms and money. In the midst of this situation, both men resigned their Nanking posts, and Wang set off for another of his health trips to Europe. For the next three years, the various factions in the Kuomintang were in continual conflict — often debates, sometimes abortive rebellions. Among the armed struggles was the Fukien revolt. Three military leaders organized a People's Government with a program for tariff autonomy, abolition of unequal treaties, freedom of strikes, religious liberty, state ownership of lands, forests, and mines, and militant resistance against the Japanese. Among the members of the new government were Eugene Chen, Li Chi-shen, and Ts'ai T'ing-kai. Fukien leaders had hoped for support from Kwangtung and Kwangsi militarists, but this aid was not forthcoming, and after a brief engagement with Nationalist forces the rebellion died. In the meantime, Japanese troops cap-

---

[18] Sun Fo's telegram of resignation, *The China Year Book, 1934*, p. 348.

tured Shanhaikwan and, in February 1933, opened an attack on Jehol.

The Fifth National Congress of the Kuomintang suffered two more postponements before it was finally set for November 12, 1935. During the twelve months preceding its convocation, the Japanese restored the Imperial dynasty in Manchuria with P'u Yi upon the throne; Chiang Kai-shek inaugurated the New Life Movement, devoted to the rejuvenation of Confucian teachings, and the Standing Committee of the Central Executive Committee set August 27 as a national holiday in honor of Confucius. These three separate events are in a sense symbolic of later developments important to the growing power of Chiang, namely, the advancing threat of Japanese domination, the organization of extraparty movements under the leadership of Chiang and his affiliates, and the emphasizing of Confucianism as a dynamic in economic, political, and social phases of party and government.

### The Fifth Central Executive Committee

The Fifth National Congress of the Kuomintang, meeting between November 12 and November 23, 1935, comprised a total of 405 delegates from various parts of China, including southern areas which at one time or another had supported the Canton separatist movement. Thus there was at least an appearance of unity, with Chiang Kai-shek, Wang Ching-wei, Sun Fo, Hu Han-min, and various of their supporters, all appearing on the new Central Executive Committee of 120 members. However, the new body could not claim even the impression of "progressiveness" which the 1931 committee had offered.

The proportion of membership claimed by the Ch'en brothers' CC Clique, by Chiang's personal affiliates, and by the Whampoa and related military factions had probably increased over 1931, while the percentage of Wang, Sun Fo, and Eugene Chen supporters and allies seems to have diminished. It is perhaps especially notable that Mme. Sun Yat-sen was shifted from regular to reserve membership in the 1935 committee.

Japanese expansion and the resultant years of war dominated developments within the Kuomintang during the period between the Fifth Congress in 1935 and the Sixth in 1945. This pressure of foreign aggression brought about two critical developments within the Chinese nation. The first of these was a new Kuomintang-Communist alliance; the second consisted of intraparty unification within the Kuomintang itself.

In general, the Chinese Communists, rather than Chiang, were responsible for united-front action against Japan. For years — ever since April 1927 — both Russian and Chinese Communists had been denouncing Chiang as a reactionary, a tool of Western imperialists, a traitor deserving execution. Yet in the face of Japanese aggression, the Communist Party of China was forced to the conclusion that only Chiang could serve as a symbol for Chinese unity. By 1937, therefore, the Chinese Communist Party, developing a program begun in 1932, was demanding cessation of civil wars, the establishment of an anti-Japanese united front, and militant preparation for resistance against the invader.[19]

During the early years after the Japanese occupation of Mukden, Chiang, reluctant to take action against the aggressors while the Communists opposed him, had evoked bitter criticism from men like Hu Han-min (who, almost until the hour of his death in 1936, had called insistently for organized opposition to Tokyo). Finally, in December 1936, Chang Hsüeh-liang and other officers in command of troops charged with fighting Communists kidnaped Chiang at Sian and demanded military resistance against Japan.

Among Kuomintang leaders there had been no unity of opinion in regard to a Japanese policy, and the subsequent defection of Wang Ching-wei, Chou Fo-hai, and Ch'en Kung-po to the enemy camp makes a purely ideological analysis of various Chinese viewpoints nearly impossible.[20] But the Sian kidnaping incident, together with various related developments, convinced Chiang that leadership in China depended upon militant opposition to the invaders. The resulting Communist-Kuomintang alliance was an uneasy one at best, but it did allow Chiang respite in which to unify both party and government and to strengthen his power in China.

The CC Clique and army factions loyal to Chiang steadily tightened their discipline over Kuomintang leadership. Of minor influence in the party, but important in provincial echelons of the government, were members of the Political Science group who tended to represent business and financial interests and who were, on the whole, more moderate in their political attitudes and more clearly oriented toward the West than were members of the other two cliques.

During the Fifth National Congress a resolution had been passed to the effect that all civil servants should be required to study party doctrine. Emphasis was placed upon the twelve rules of conduct set forth

---

[19] *China Weekly Review* (Shanghai), February 20, 1937, p. 408.
[20] Wang died of diabetes in a Japanese hospital November 10, 1944; Chou died of a heart attack in a Chinese prison in February 1948; and Ch'en was executed for treason in June 1946. For a discussion of Wang and his motives see Travers E. Durkee, "Wang Ching-wei and Japan, 1937–1940" (Master's thesis, Stanford University, 1949).

by the New Life Movement, which included loyalty, faithfulness, sincerity, obedience, and similar steadying virtues. Then, in July 1936, the Second Plenary Session of the Central Executive Committee had successfully abolished the Southwest Executive and the Southwest Political Council through which Hu Han-min and his followers had formerly expressed their opposition.

Next, in 1938, an Extraordinary Kuomintang National Congress elected Chiang Kai-shek *Tsung-tsai*, or Director-General, and endowed him with all the powers that Dr. Sun had enjoyed, including chairmanship of the Party Congress and of the Central Executive Committee, absolute right of veto over decisions of the Central Executive Committee, and suspensive veto over decisions of the congress.

Further, in January 1939, the Fifth Plenary Session of the Central Executive Committee reorganized the Supreme National Defense Conference (which for more than a year had, in effect, directed all party, political, and military affairs) into a Supreme National Defense Council under the chairmanship of the *Tsung-tsai*. In this new capacity, Chiang enjoyed emergency powers that exempted him from traditional party procedures in handling both political and military affairs, and enabled him to issue such decrees as changing conditions might warrant.[21] Moreover, the principle of permitting the national government to appoint representatives to the National Party Congress had been formalized in 1937 by the act of the Legislative Yuan. Chiang now enjoyed virtual control over both party and government. In accordance with this law, 240 of the 1,440 representatives (16.7 per cent) constituting National Congress membership were to be designated by the national government itself.[22]

The formation of auxiliary Kuomintang organizations served further to strengthen Chiang's position within the party. Of these, the San Min Chu I Youth Corps is perhaps the best example. Founded for the expressed purposes of uniting and training young people, enforcing the San Min Chu I, defending the nation, and bringing about a national "rebirth," this organization was open to Chinese between sixteen and twenty-five years of age. Based on the principles of the New Life Movement, the corps strove for rigid discipline. The corps leader, according to its constitution, was the "Party Chief of the Kuo-

[21] *China Hand Book, 1937–1945* (rev. ed.; New York: Chinese Ministry of Information, 1947), p. 96. See also Ch'ien Tuan-sheng, *op. cit.*, p. 122.

[22] Act of the Legislative Yuan, April 31, XXVI (1937), governing the election of representatives to the National Congress. Paul M. Linebarger, *The China of Chiang Kai-shek* (Boston: World Peace Foundation, 1941), Appendix G, p. 302.

mintang" (Chiang Kai-shek) with unrestricted powers of sanction and veto.[23] Chapter XIII of its 1938 constitution laid down the following rules:[24]

66. All members should obey the following commandments:
   a. All questions may be freely discussed. But no dispute is allowed once the resolution is passed.
   b. It is not allowed to rebel against the principles of the New Life Movement.
   c. It is prohibited to reveal the secrets of the corps.
   d. It is prohibited for members to join other organizations.
   e. It is prohibited to criticize unfavorably the Kuomintang and the corps, or to plot against other members.
   f. It is prohibited to express one's ideas too freely upon current events, especially those that are against the resolved plans or policies of the Kuomintang or the corps.
   g. It is prohibited to form other organizations within the corps.

67. Those who are proved to act against the above rules will be punished in the following ways:
   a. Warning
   b. Demerit
   c. Cross-questioning
   d. Expulsion
   e. Other appropriate punishments

Finally, as wartime measures, efforts were made to tighten Kuomintang Party controls. The first of these was the reintroduction of the Small Group, or Party Cell (*Hsiao-tsu*). The second consisted of the further development of party purging facilities through the Party Supervisor's Net (*Tang-jen Chien-ch'a Wang*).

All these measures — the organization of the New Life Movement, the abolition of the Southwest Political Conference, the granting of extraordinary powers to Chiang, the principle of designating a portion of the National Congress membership, the formation of auxiliary party organizations, the reintroduction of Party Cells, and the working out of new devices for purging party membership — are illustrative of the effect which the Japanese threat had upon the Kuomintang. They suggest, too, an inability on the part of party organs to meet the wartime needs of China, and they are clearly indicative of the grip which Chiang and his supporters were able to obtain on party machinery.

### The Sixth Central Executive Committee

The Sixth National Congress of the Kuomintang, meeting between May 5 and May 21, 1945, comprised a total of 600 delegates plus the

---

[23] *Ibid.*, Appendix II-B, pp. 331–340.
[24] *Ibid.*, p. 141; Appendix II-B, p. 339; and Appendix II-D, p. 354.

memberships of the Central Executive and Central Supervisory Committee. This body re-elected Chiang Kai-shek as *Tsung-tsai,* and selected 222 members for the Central Executive Committee.

It had long been evident that Chiang Kai-shek and his organization had achieved a virtual monopoly of power within the Kuomintang. Of the new Central Executive Committee, 64.2 per cent allegedly belonged to the CC Clique, which, with its own police and intelligence arms, had sought control over vast sections of party and government machinery. In addition to CC members, it is estimated that about 6.3 per cent of the Central Executive Committee membership were Chiang's personal affiliates, while a scattering of former Western Hills leaders, Whampoa graduates, and other military and political cliques lent further reliable support. These figures are by no means incontrovertible, since factional affiliation, based often on reports that are scarcely more than rumor, is difficult to fix. In this case it is significant, however, that a CC-sponsored resolution which required all delegates to sign their ballots in CEC elections was passed and put into effect during the Sixth Congress.

There was, then (and this will be indicated more graphically in Section IV), a power balance, presided over by Chiang Kai-shek, between civilian party organizers on the one hand and military men on the other. Neither had a monopoly of power, but Chiang Kai-shek, being in a position to use one group as a check on the activities of the other, enjoyed the loyalty — and the accumulated power — of both.

### Over-All Trends

In view of the long record of unrest in China during the period under consideration, in view of the professed revolutionary nature of the Kuomintang, and in view of the importance that military strength played in the struggle for power, party leadership seems to have been remarkably secure in office. Central Committeemen (with the exception of unwavering Communists) were re-elected by one congress after another, or, if dropped (as in the case of the Western Hills leaders in 1926), they almost invariably reappeared as the result of some later realignment or political truce. There was, moreover, a minimum of intraparty bloodshed (except for the numerous executions of Communists) resulting from the various struggles for power.

At the time of the Sixth National Congress nearly 90 per cent of the previous committee members were still alive, and almost all, with the exception of the Communists, held positions of leadership in the party. Of the seventeen deaths recorded, two resulted from assassination (neither case was satisfactorily accounted for), and two men were executed (one for deserting to Japan, one for "graft in office"). The rest died more or less peacefully of old age or from various diseases of the flesh.

In a narrow sense, the total of these trends, together with events of historical record, suggests that the development of the Central Executive Committee elite after 1926 cannot be separated from Chiang's personal rise to power. In this connection, there is good reason for believing that in 1929 his power was derived largely from victories of the Northern Expedition, but that in succeeding years the balance was more precarious, depending upon the juxtaposition of various independent or semi-independent political factions and military cliques in relation to power.

But the Japanese accumulation of power in northern China tended to redress this balance to Chiang's advantage. For the Japanese threat, more than any other single element, brought about a working, if uneasy, alliance between Kuomintang and Communist parties; secured emergency powers for Chiang; obtained foreign loans; and provided exactly the secret, wartime-emergency environment in which police and intelligence functions could most easily and properly be expanded. In short, it was to a considerable degree the Japanese threat which made Chiang Kai-shek the recognized leader of wartime China, from Yenan and Chungking to Washington and Moscow.

If this analysis is correct, then the size and composition of the Central Executive Committee (never a representative body in the Western, parliamentary sense) were, especially after 1931, symptomatic rather than critical political factors; had little to do with the true wishes of rank-and-file Kuomintang members; and bore almost no relationship whatsoever to the will of the general population of China. Increases in Chiang's power within the Kuomintang can be explained largely in terms of two factors: the Japanese threat, and the weakness of the Kuomintang in the face of the overwhelming needs of China.

## III. THE DEVELOPMENT OF THE CHINESE COMMUNIST PARTY LEADERSHIP

The current Chinese Communist leadership represents the culmination of thirty years of growth, a complex development which can be divided into four main phases: the leadership of Ch'en Tu-hsiu (1918–August 1927); the period of urban insurrection (August 1927–January 1931); the returned student leadership (January 1931–January 1935); and the rise of Mao Tse-tung from January 1935 until the present.

It is not easy to assemble precise information about the various leadership groups, or to determine exactly what changes took place. To date, the only full Central Committee membership rolls are those of recent years, and most Politburo lists are admittedly incomplete.[25] Because of this faulty documentation one can only assemble and piece together whatever data are available with the hope that future research may fill in present gaps and correct current misconceptions.

If it is difficult to document developments in leadership, it is nearly impossible to document adequately the revolution which these leaders succeeded in capturing. Many observers, Western as well as Chinese, have described phases of the agrarian unrest and agrarian uprisings which Mao and his followers gradually harnessed. Communist documents indicate that Red leaders — especially during the period 1928–1934 — were disturbed by the fact that other groups and other leaders (including Wang Ching-wei and even Chiang Kai-shek) were themselves trying to win over the peasantry with its spontaneous revolutionary dynamic. But these are indirect and loosely worded descriptions of an upheaval that could have been measured adequately only by specialized techniques in the hands of specialized investigators there at the time. Unfortunately, there were no teams of economists, sociologists, or anthropologists roaming the hills of Hunan and Kiangsi during the years when agrarian unrest broke into agrarian revolt. Because of this, we are now inclined all too often to confuse the sometimes mute, sometimes amorphous, but potentially dynamic masses of dissatisfied peasantry with the tightly organized, conspiratorial, often Moscow-trained leadership that gradually won control of them.

No attempt is made here to isolate causes of mass discontent or to analyze dynamic forces released by peasants in revolt against traditional social structures. Rather, this study seeks to investigate only the higher echelons of Communist leadership — the changes it has undergone, its interrelationships, and some of its contacts with central party headquarters in Moscow.

### The Leadership of Ch'en Tu-hsiu: 1918–August 1927

It was the impact of the Russian Revolution on China that opened the first phase by impressing upon certain Chinese radical leaders the promise of Marxism as a key to solving China's national problems and later the value of Leninist tactics for the exploitation of indigenous discontent. Within a year after the Russian Revolution of October 1917, Marxist circles had been organized among certain intellectual groups in China. At Peking University the dean of the College of

[25] The growth of cliques and their place in this balance is ably discussed by Ch'ien Tuan-sheng, *op. cit.*, pp. 128–132.

Literature, Ch'en Tu-hsiu, and the chief librarian, Li Ta-chao, founded such groups. A student named Mao Tse-tung organized a similar one at Changsha. Ch'en Tu-hsiu, in order to unify these tendencies, next gathered together a group of potential revolutionists and began publication of *Mei-chou P'ing-lun*, a periodical weekly newspaper dedicated to radical thinking. By the beginning of 1919, Soviet Russian leaders had begun expressing interest in the possibility of helping to organize an effective revolutionary government in southern China.

In the spring of 1920 the Comintern dispatched two agents, Voitinsky and an overseas Chinese named Yang Ming-chai, to help organize the Chinese Communist movement. On reaching Peking, Voitinsky made contact with Li Ta-chao, who then introduced him to a Shanghai literary group to which Ch'en Tu-hsiu belonged. In that city he set up his headquarters and began organizational work. Unable to gather together a group of true Communists, he assembled a number of leftists of varying shades and founded the Chinese Socialist Youth Club. This, as well as subsequent organizational work, was done with such secrecy that even the British Intelligence Service is said to have been unaware of the presence of Russian agents in China until nearly two years later.

This group consisted of about eight original members. As soon as it was set up, similar cells were established elsewhere. Chang Kuo-t'ao organized one in Peking, Mao Tse-tung started one in Hunan, and Tung Pi-wu formed one in Hupeh. At about the same time four Chinese students established a cell in Japan, while others, including Chou En-lai and Li Li-san, formed one in Paris.

In Shanghai Ch'en Tu-hsiu and his comrades started the Communist Youth Association with about a hundred members, began publishing two Bolshevik organs, and organized a so-called "School of Foreign Languages" in order to prepare the best revolutionaries for work in China and for study at the Communist University of the Far East in Soviet Russia. In 1920 the enrollment at this foreign language school consisted of about sixty students, most of whom belonged to the Communist Youth League.

Early in 1921 a war lord named Ch'en Chiung-ming seized control of Kwangtung Province and invited Dr. Sun Yat-sen to return to Canton. Somewhat previously Ch'en Tu-hsiu had attracted the attention of Ch'en Chiung-ming,[26] who now asked the Communist organizer to serve as chief of the Education Board in Canton. Ch'en Tu-hsiu

[26] Kanichi Hatano, "History of the Chinese Communist Party," *Asia Mondai Koza*, Vol. II (Toyko, 1938).

accepted with alacrity, explaining to Voitinsky that he would take the job and use it for purposes of Communist propaganda. Once installed in his new position, Ch'en Tu-hsiu oversaw the formation of a Communist cell in Canton and the setting up of a school for party organizers and propagandists. Later in the year he returned to Shanghai, where he joined forces with a prominent Kuomintang revolutionist named Tai Chi-t'ao. Shortly after his arrival there, however, he was imprisoned by German authorities. Subsequently, after his release had been effected, Ch'en Tu-hsiu cooperated with Tai Chi-t'ao in revolutionary activities. Working together, they organized trade-unions, published a number of different newspapers and periodicals of left-wing complexion, and gradually succeeded in assembling about them the nucleus of what was later to develop into the Communist Party of China.

During this first year of activity, a number of splits occurred in the new Communist movement. For the most part, this difficulty arose from the fact that many of the early members considered themselves anarchists, rather than Bolsheviks. The first break took place within the Peking cell while a provisional party statute was under discussion. One paragraph dealt with the dictatorship of the proletariat, a concept that the anarchists refused to accept, and many of them, therefore, left the movement.[27]

The Chinese Communists held their First Congress in Shanghai during the last week of July 1921 (Appendix C, Table 2). Thirteen representatives spoke for about fifty members of the Communist Party nuclei of Peking, Tientsin, Hunan, Hupeh, Shantung, and Kwangtung. Each area had elected two representatives, and one had been sent from the cell in Japan. The Comintern had at least one agent present, a Hollander named Maring.

The first acknowledged head of the Chinese Communist Party, Ch'en Tu-hsiu, was forty-one years old at the time of the First Congress. Born in Anhwei of a wealthy Mandarin family, he had studied naval architecture in Chekiang and had later continued his education in France. In 1915 he launched *Hsin ch'ing-nien* (*La Jeunesse*), a review demanding the introduction into China of Western ideas, the opposing of traditional Chinese ideas, and the elimination of Confucianism. Two years later he was appointed dean of the College of Literature at the University of Peking, and it was while serving in this position that he

---

[27] *Chung-kuo hsien-tai ko-ming yun-tung Shih* [*A History of the Contemporary Revolutionary Movement in China*] (4th ed.; no place, 1938), Vol. I, Chap. 5, Sec. 2; Kanichi-Hatano, *Gendai Shina no Seiji to Jimbutsu* (Toyko, 1937), from notes taken by John Paasche.

was first attracted by Leninist ideas. Ch'en was dismissed from the Chinese Communist Party after the Kuomintang-Communist alliance failed in 1927. Sentenced in 1932 to fifteen years' imprisonment by the Kuomintang, he was released during the Japanese war and died thereafter.

At least five of the thirteen delegates to the First Congress were alive in 1949, but only two — Mao Tse-tung and Tung Pi-wu — were still prominent in the Communist Party. Of the rest, Ho Shu-heng was shot by the Kuomintang in 1927; Chou Fo-hai left the Communist Party and, in February 1948, died of a heart attack in a Chinese prison; Ch'en Kung-po also left the Communist Party and, in June 1946, was executed for treason. Chang Kuo-t'ao, long a powerful figure in the Communist Party, was expelled in 1938 and was elected in 1945 to the Sixth Executive Committee of the Kuomintang. The remaining three disappeared from sight at one time or another, and no information concerning their fates is available.

This congress reflected the real composition of the Chinese Communist movement at the time. For despite recent upheavals in various cells, the delegates still included followers of what were called "biblical socialism, social democracy, anarchism and various shades of communism."[28]

Unable to attend the meeting, Ch'en Tu-hsiu sent a carefully drawn-up and relatively moderate program for consideration by the delegates. His proposals included plans for educating party members, for encouraging a "democratic" spirit, for developing party discipline, and for making cautious contacts with the masses. The time was not ripe, he maintained, for the party to consider a seizure of power, and consequently, the movement should confine itself to preparatory activities.[29]

The various delegations found themselves in immediate disagreement over Ch'en's proposals. Some thought them too radical, while others wanted more precipitate action. One delegate pointed out that in Germany and Russia there had been separate revolutionary movements — one pointing toward democracy, the other toward a dictatorship of the proletariat. Why not send representatives to study both situations and report back with their findings?

According to subsequent accounts, however, "a decisive resistance was shown to all these dangerous currents" and most of Ch'en's pro-

[28] Kisselev, "A History of Communism in China," *The China Illustrated Review*, January 28, 1928, p. 16.
[29] *Ibid.*

posals were accepted in a "positive sense."[30] It was determined that the movement should henceforth consider itself a Communist Party, that its work should follow Communist principles, and that the final aim of this work should be the organization of the proletariat and the seizure of power by the laboring masses under party guidance. The congress further decreed that thereafter all members of the movement who were holding non-Communist views were to be purged from the party.

Before the close of this congress, the delegates resolved to cooperate with Dr. Sun Yat-sen through extraparty support. There was some "ultra-leftist" opposition from those who maintained that Communists could not logically support middle-class revolutionary movements under any circumstance and who insisted that a dictatorship of the proletariat should be set up immediately. But support for Dr. Sun was entirely in line with tactics that Lenin had laid down at the Second Congress of the Communist International less than a year earlier, and the resolution was passed.[31]

### Early Communist Party Structure

The First Congress of the Chinese Communist Party erected the skeletal framework of what grew into a full-sized Communist Party structure. During the early years after the Bolshevik Revolution in Russia the Comintern and the Communist Party of the Soviet Union developed a system of party organization pyramiding upward from the factory (and street) nucleus and the party fraction. According to rules laid down by the Third International, all Communists working in a single factory or other place of labor must belong to the nucleus of that particular place. Members of this group were then required to elect an executive committee of between three and five members.

In cities where numerous factories existed, all nuclei were united into subsections, which, in turn, were welded into sections. All the sections in a given city constituted a local party organization, and thus the various organs pyramided upward through national and international levels. In each stratum membership was charged with electing the next-higher organ, except when the Communist Party was illegal, in which case the whole system might be streamlined for security

---

[30] Ibid.

[31] Chung-kuo hsien-tai ko-ming yun-tung Shih, op. cit.; South China Morning Post, February 3, 1928. Translation of a document by Chang Kuo-t'ao, seized in the Soviet Consulate in Canton in December 1927; The Second Congress of the Communist International (Moscow, 1920), p. 571.

purposes. In line with principles of "democratic centralism," no opposition to a majority opinion was tolerated once a decision had been reached.

The tasks of the factory nucleus were laid down precisely by the Comintern. Members were specifically held responsible for the conduct of Communist agitation and propaganda among workers; for the instruction of non-Communist laborers in order to draw them into Bolshevik ranks; for the discussion of factory problems with all the workers; for the issuance of a special factory newspaper; for participation in and leadership of demonstrations and strikes; for pointing out to fellow workers the political consequences of the labor struggle; and for carrying on an obstinate fight in all factories against other parties, especially non-Bolshevik socialists and other antagonistic labor groups.

The party fraction served a different purpose. Whereas the nucleus formed an organizational basis for the whole party structure, the fraction had a much more specialized function — namely, to infiltrate and, where necessary, to capture other already existing organizations such as labor unions, factory committees, strike committees, congresses, parliaments, and similar organizations.[32] According to Comintern regulations, it was mandatory, in any organization where there were three or more Communists, to form a fraction for the increase of "Party influence" and for the introduction of "Party policy into non-Party masses."[33]

The strength of the fraction depended upon two regulations. First, every question subject to the decision of a nonparty body or institution must be discussed and decided upon at an earlier meeting of the parasite fraction. And second, all fraction members must act and vote as a unit on all questions within meetings of the nonparty body or institution.

During 1921 the Chinese Communist Party structure did not progress beyond the formative stages, and existing accounts are so contradictory that it is nearly impossible to determine the exact nature of its leadership. There is, for example, considerable disagreement concerning the size and membership of the First Central Committee. It has been said that all delegates to the First Congress were included upon the First Committee. But Mao Tse-tung, in an interview with Edgar Snow a decade and a half later, presented a different membership list (Appendix C, Table 2).

---

[32] "The Organization of Factory Nuclei and Fractions," *International Press Correspondence* (Vienna, London), February 27, 1924, pp. 111–114.
[33] "Statutes of the Comintern," *International Press Correspondence*, June 5, 1924, p. 321.

## The Communist-Kuomintang Alliance

During the early months after the First Congress, the Chinese Communist Party carried on its activities independently and, in accordance with decisions reached at the congress, offered only extraparty support to Dr. Sun Yat-sen and the Kuomintang. But it soon became clear to certain Communist leaders both in Moscow and in China that neither the Chinese Communist Party nor the Kuomintang was acting with maximum effectiveness. Dr. Sun had a larger following than the Communists, but his party lacked the organization and discipline that Leninist advisors could presumably supply.[34] Therefore, at a Special Plenum of the Central Committee of the Chinese Communist Party in August 1922, Maring invoked the authority of the Comintern to persuade the Chinese Communists that their membership must infiltrate or invade the Kuomintang.

Ch'en Tu-hsiu may have opposed this Communist-Kuomintang alliance. "Myself and other Central Committee members . . . were opposed," he wrote later, "because the conglomeration of forces within the Kuomintang blurred class distinctions, thus checking our independent policy. Maring (representing the Comintern) countered by asking if we wanted to disobey a Comintern decision, so that the Central Committee gave in for the sake of party discipline and voted to join the Kuomintang."[35]

Maring had his way. But after Ch'en Chiung-ming had effected his rebellion against Dr. Sun, Red leaders decided that more active measures must be taken. The Communist Party consequently sent representatives to confer with Sun and to propose united-front action against enemies of the Kuomintang. Sun, discouraged by defeat and by weaknesses within the Kuomintang, accepted, and at that particular time, even some of his rightist followers approved.

A long series of negotiations was necessary, however, before the Communist Party and the Kuomintang were able to come to a working agreement. From the Red viewpoint, Dr. Sun's Kuomintang suffered two basic weaknesses. First, it was clear to Communist observers in Russia and China alike that the Kuomintang was dependent upon foreign help for the completion of its revolution. And second, the Kuomintang, considering military action the only means of

[34] Benjamin I. Schwartz, "Ch'en Tu-hsiu: Pre-Communist Phase," in *Papers on China*, Vol. II, from the Regional Studies Seminars (mimeographed for private distribution by the Committee on International and Regional Studies, Harvard University, May 1948), pp. 167–197.

[35] Hatano, "History of the Communist Party," *op. cit.* For a contrary statement in regard to Ch'en's viewpoint at this time, consult Isaacs, *op. cit.*, p. 58.

furthering the revolution, had concentrated all its efforts on military affairs, thus neglecting to reach the masses through propaganda.

Bolshevik leaders in Moscow decided, therefore, to negotiate directly with Sun in order to make the Kuomintang a more effective force. In January 1923, Adolph Joffe, who had been treating unsuccessfully with the Peking government, was directed to stop off in the course of a trip to Japan for conversations with Dr. Sun in Shanghai. The result of these discussions was the signing of a joint statement in which the Bolshevik representative agreed with the Kuomintang leader that neither the Communist order nor the soviet system could be introduced into China under existing conditions, but that the primary problem was one of national unification and independence.

Joffe reaffirmed earlier Soviet renunciations of all Czarist treaties, privileges, and exactions and expressed willingness to negotiate on a basis of equality. This understanding was followed by further negotiations, and in June 1923 the Manifesto of the Third Congress of the Chinese Communist Party recognized the Kuomintang as "the central force of the revolution" and urged "all revolutionary elements" to rally to the Kuomintang. The Communist mission was defined, however, in terms of "liberating" the Chinese people and advancing the world revolution.[36] Related to these policies was an understanding between Sun and the Soviet Union whereby Moscow sent arms, ammunition, and money to the Canton government, and subsequently an advisory mission under a veteran Bolshevik agent, Michael Borodin.

When Borodin arrived in Canton in September 1923, he found the Kuomintang disorganized, the workers divided, and the peasants apolitical. Sun himself was so short of military supplies as to be utterly helpless against neighboring war lords and without hope for immediate prosecution of a revolution. But now, with the aid of Russian funds and a cadre of Russian experts, Borodin reorganized the Kuomintang, established the Whampoa Military Academy to train officers for Sun's armies, negotiated an alliance between the Soviet Union and the Canton government, and made arrangements for the shipment of military supplies from the U.S.S.R. to China by way of Vladivostok.

At the same time the Chinese Communist Party worked not only within the Kuomintang but also within student, labor, and similar

---

[36] "The Manifesto of the Third Congress" (mimeographed for distribution by the Russian Research Center, Harvard University, 1950). For the position that Borodin held, see Great Britain, Foreign Office, Russia No. 2 (1927), *Documents Illustrating the Hostile Activities of the Soviet Union and the Third International Against Great Britain* (London, 1927). The Soviet Union protested that these documents were forgeries, but the indications concerning Borodin's position are entirely in line with other historical evidence.

movements with which it was now in legal contact. On paper, at least, the Chinese Communists and the Third International wove all these activities into a revolutionary network which extended over China from north to south. It included not only Borodin but also the Soviet ambassador to the Peking government, Karakhan, and the newly established Soviet diplomatic agencies, and was responsible to Comintern discipline and to Russian secret police surveillance.

To Communists — Chinese and Russian alike — the overthrow of the Peking government, the expulsion of foreign imperialists, and the victory of national revolutionary forces in China were inevitable developments within the dialectic struggle that Marx had prophesied and for which Lenin had systematized a whole manual of detailed strategies and tactics. Yet within the following three years quite the opposite came about: Borodin and his assistants were eliminated from the Kuomintang; the Third International's Chinese program failed; Chiang won control of the Kuomintang and killed or drove underground thousands of Chinese Communists; and topmost leaders of the world Communist movement found themselves groping for the reason. In many respects this unexpected failure was facilitated by the deaths of two men — Sun and Lenin.

The analysis of Kuomintang leadership has suggested the intraparty ferment and intrigue brought about by Sun's passing. The death of Lenin loosed a series of much more deadly conflicts. To a large degree, these conflicts resulted from the personal struggle for power between Stalin and Trotsky, a feud that opened a schism cutting all the way from Moscow to the nuclei and fractions in China.[37] With regard to Asia, however, serious conflicts also emerged from the essential contradiction between Roy's emphasis on the development of class conflict, and Lenin's concept of a Communist alliance with middle-class revolutionary movements like the Kuomintang. The Second Congress had tied these antagonistic concepts into a single policy, which Borodin, his colleagues and subordinates, and the Chinese Communist Party were now charged with carrying out.

In February 1926, Borodin left Canton for northern China, ostensibly to negotiate with the so-called "Christian general," Feng Yü-hsiang, but also, according to some observers, for the purpose of meeting with a Comintern investigating commission. Whether or not the

---

[37] N. Popov, *Outline History of the Communist Party of the Soviet Union*, Part II (New York: International Publishers, 1934), pp. 271–273; *International Press Correspondence*, January 27, 1926, p. 130; Isaacs, *op. cit.*; and J. Stalin, *Marxism and the National and Colonial Question* (New York: International Publishers, 1935), present the two viewpoints.

latter was his purpose, there is no question about the rift that had appeared in China between those like Borodin and Ch'en Tu-hsiu, who wanted to work slowly through the Kuomintang, and others who wanted to accelerate the development of a peasant and working-class revolution.

Conflict raged especially among those Communists who were working through Kuomintang army fractions and the peasant movement.[38] Jay Calvin Huston, an American consular official, reported subsequently that the chief of the Russian military group at Canton had complained to Karakhan that activities of Communist agitators in Nationalist armies were antagonizing Kuomintang officers.[39] The consular official supported this view with a report from another Soviet agent who charged that Communist organizers (Russian and Chinese) were centralizing their control over the armies with dangerous haste. The Reds were trying to spread Bolshevik ideas too fast, he said, by rooting out the Kuomintang "always and everywhere" and thus creating opposition that strengthened the position of Chiang and other Nationalist leaders.[40]

Many revolutionists denounced this viewpoint, asserting that Borodin and Ch'en Tu-hsiu had compromised with the bourgeoisie, had submitted to Chiang Kai-shek, and had betrayed the revolution. To paraphrase Harold R. Isaacs's much later criticism of Borodin's tactics: Chiang wrapped himself in radical phrases and presented himself to Borodin and to the masses as the Red hope of the revolutionary army. Borodin therefore employed every possible political stratagem to drive Chiang to the top of the heap. Chiang, in turn, quoted Sun that in taking Borodin's advice, he was taking Sun's advice. And Borodin said that no matter whether Communist or Kuomintang, all must obey Chiang.[41]

Huston, who was staunchly anti-Communist, but who respected Borodin as an individual, wrote, on the other hand, that the Comintern agent knew exactly what he was doing. "Borodin had dreamed of five

[38] "Letter from Shanghai," in Leon Trotsky, *Problems of the Chinese Revolution* (New York: Pioneer Publishers, 1932), presents the two viewpoints.

[39] Jay Calvin Huston in a dispatch *circa* spring 1928 entitled, "Sun Yat-sen, the Kuomintang, and the Chinese Russian Political Economic Alliance" (Huston Collection in the Hoover Library, Stanford, Calif.), p. 126, quotes a letter from Chief of the Russian Military Group Kissanka to Karakhan. This letter is one of many documents purportedly seized in a Chinese raid on the Soviet Embassy in Peking in April 1927.

[40] *Ibid.*, p. 127. Huston quotes a report from Soviet agent Stepanoff to his superiors in Peking. This is another document purportedly captured in the Peking raid.

[41] Isaacs, *op. cit.*, p. 84; cf. T'ang, *op. cit.*, pp. 234–247.

years in which he hoped to have the laborers and peasants of Kwangtung organized into a revolutionary force that would sweep over
China. But the impetuosity of Communist leaders in the Kuomintang
and their Russian confreres upset his plans and made it necessary to
compromise with a leader who had a growing ambition to dominate
the Chinese situation in a military way."

According to Huston, these "impetuous" Communist leaders were convinced that the time had come for seizing Canton as one objective in
an imminent world revolution, whereas Borodin (supported by Ch'en
Tu-hsiu) actually understood the realities of the situation, "his object
being to create a strong revolutionary base under Kuomintang rule."[42]

In retrospect it appears that, in terms of their own self-interests, both
groups erred. The former, by pushing for an immediate Bolshevik
revolution, probably strengthened Chiang and facilitated his coups
against the Chinese Communists and the Kuomintang. The latter —
especially Borodin and Ch'en Tu-hsiu — seem, on the other hand, to
have trusted in Chiang with unbelievable naïveté.

While Borodin was in the north treating with Feng Yü-hsiang (and
facing, perhaps, a Comintern investigating commission), Chiang Kai-
shek accomplished his coup of March 20, 1926. This should have been
warning enough to the Communists that the Kuomintang General was
not a docile ally. Yet Stalinist reactions seem to have been confined
largely to the issuance of denials that such a coup had ever taken place.

Although Chiang proceeded to disqualify Communists from serving
as the heads of departments under the Central Executive Committee
of the Kuomintang and from filling other posts of responsibility within
his party, Borodin, on his return from the north, accepted all restrictions upon himself and his fellow Communists and compromised his
position even further by "appointing" Chiang Commander in Chief of
the Northern Expedition with extraordinary powers over military,
political, and Kuomintang party organs and functions.[43] According to
the Comintern, this policy of further cooperation was undertaken in
order to "prevent unification between Chiang Kai-shek and the Right
wing" by making concessions to him.[44]

A year later Chiang's troops, aided by Russian supplies and by the
coordinated agitation and organizational activities of the Chinese
Communists, neared Shanghai; whereupon the Communist-controlled

[42] Huston, op. cit., pp. 134–139.
[43] The resolutions limiting Communist activities appear in T. C. Woo, op. cit.,
pp. 175–177.
[44] Report on the Activity of the Communist International, March–November
1926 (no place, no date), p. 119.

General Labor Union in the city called a strike, disarmed the garrison, and welcomed Kuomintang troops, who were thus able to enter without resistance from enemy forces.

At the time when Shanghai Communists were handing the city over to Chiang, the foreign quarter buzzed with rumors to the effect that the Kuomintang leader was preparing for a second coup. Reports indicated that he had organized an intraparty police force of his own and that he was negotiating with Shanghai banking circles for a loan.

Following their tactics of the preceding year, Russian Communists denied these stories. A split within the Kuomintang was absolutely out of the question, they said. A revolutionary like Chiang Kai-shek could not possibly cooperate with counterrevolutionists,[45] and in any case, the "revolutionary pressure from below" was so strong that Chiang was being compelled to swear allegiance to the principles of revolutionary loyalty and to "submit himself" to the leadership of the "mass party of the Kuomintang."[46]

Chiang, less than a month later, launched his "Purification Movement," which, within the first few days of its prosecution, wiped out the Communist-controlled labor movement in Shanghai and, according to Communist estimates, cost the lives of 600 Chinese "proletarians."[47] And concurrently Chiang negotiated a substantial loan from financiers in Shanghai, inaugurated in Nanking a new Kuomintang Central Executive Committee and a new national government, and prepared for a further extension of his power.

During the late spring of 1927, Stalinist theoreticians in Moscow were describing Chiang's coup as a foreseen and dialectically inevitable event marking the end of one phase of the Chinese conflict and the beginning of a new one that called for the confiscation and nationalization of land. This did not mean that the Chinese Communists should leave the Wuhan (or Hankow) Kuomintang under Wang Ching-wei and his colleagues. On the contrary, Chinese Reds were instructed "to take a leading role" within the Kuomintang left wing. They were to encourage the Wuhan government to release the agrarian revolt and change itself into an "organizational-political center of the workers and peasants revolution" and into an organ of the "democratic dictatorship of the proletariat and peasantry."[48]

A section of Chinese Communist leadership headed by Ch'en Tu-hsiu and T'an P'ing-shan opposed the vigorous prosecution of so radi-

[45] *International Press Correspondence*, March 31, 1927, p. 446.
[46] *Pravda*, March 16, 1927.
[47] *Pravda*, April 15, 1927.
[48] *International Press Correspondence*, June 16, 1927, pp. 731–741.

cal an agrarian program on the ground that, since many Kuomintang leaders, both left wing and right, and many officers in the Kuomintang army were landholders or the sons of landholders, a policy of widespread confiscation might drive a wedge between them and the Communist Party. Ch'en Tu-hsiu, while admitting that the Communist agrarian program had been "too peaceful," warned that the confiscation of large and middle-sized landed estates must await further development of the military situation. "The only correct solution at the present moment," he told the Fifth Congress of the Chinese Communist Party in April 1927, "is to deepen the revolution after it has first been spread."[49] In line with this viewpoint, Chinese Communist officials actively restrained a spontaneous peasant outbreak at Changsha in May 1927 and cooperated with Kuomintang leftists in attempts to eliminate other "anarchic" conditions in the villages.[50]

But Communist leaders in Moscow, despite the fact that their policies had been based upon continued cooperation with the Kuomintang Left, insisted that the time for peasant agitation had arrived. "Without an agrarian revolution, victory is impossible," Stalin wired his agents in China in late May 1927.[51] Certain old leaders of the Central Committee of the Kuomintang, he stated, were afraid of what was taking place. Consequently, the Communists must arrange for drawing a large number of peasant and working-class leaders into the Wuhan government to change the structure of the Kuomintang, for setting up a military tribunal to punish those maintaining contact with Chiang or attacking workers and peasants, and for raising a reliable army of about 20,000 Communists and 50,000 revolutionary workers and peasants before it was "too late."

On June 1, 1927, this telegram was brought to the attention of Wang Ching-wei, who, with expressions of extreme consternation,[52] took immediate action against Borodin and the Chinese Communists. Within a few weeks the former was on his way back to the Soviet

[49] Ch'en Tu-hsiu, "Political and Organizational Report of the Central Committee," *International Press Correspondence*, June 9, 1927, pp. 716–717.

[50] "Manifesto of the August 7 Conference of the Chinese Communist Party, August 7, 1927," and files of the *People's Tribune*, Hankow, for May 1927.

[51] Stalin, *op. cit.*, p. 249.

[52] According to one source, Wang Ching-wei, returning to China in the spring of 1927 *on the advice of the Russians*, had stopped over in Moscow long enough to agree to a program that included land confiscation and other points urged by Stalin. But Wang, influenced by such "known reactionaries" as Sun Fo, Eugene Chen, and T'an Yen-k'ai, who had "come to a secret understanding with Chiang Kai-shek," was no longer in a position to accept Stalin's advice—M. N. Roy, *Revolution and Counter-Revolution in China* (Calcutta, 1946), p. 519. It is entirely possible that Wang did agree to a general program without comprehending its full implications. The rest of this assertion is open to question.

Union, and Chinese Communists were hiding out wherever they could escape detection.

## The Period of Urban Insurrection: August 1927–January 1931

The second period in the development of Chinese Communist leadership began on August 7, 1927, with the calling of a Special Conference which, on advice from Moscow, censured the Chinese Central Committee for carrying out "an opportunistic policy of betrayal," deposed Ch'en Tu-hsiu, and reorganized the whole party hierarchy. A resolution adopted by the conference stated:

> We welcome the energetic intervention of the Comintern which enabled us to expose the mistakes of the previous Party leadership and thus save the Party. We emphatically condemn the opportunist, non-revolutionary policy pursued by our Central Committee and consider it necessary, on the basis of lessons of the past, radically to change the course of Party policy.[53]

An important reason for past mistakes, the conference decided, was that leadership had been generally in the hands of intelligentsia and bourgeoisie. Only upon the insistence of the Comintern, according to the August 7 Manifesto of the party, had a few workers been admitted to the central hierarchy, whereas the Central Committee had often discriminated against workers on the grounds that their culture standards were too low.

The Special Conference condemned Ch'en Tu-hsiu and T'an P'ingshan for stating that the revolution must be spread before it could be deepened, severely criticized the policy of restraining the peasants, and censured the leadership for "retreating temporarily in order to retain the alliance with the Kuomintang."

Concurrently, the Special Conference, in line with a policy initiated by Stalin, decided against a Communist withdrawal from the Left Kuomintang. Supporting a Moscow resolution to the effect that the Communist Party "must take all necessary measures to arouse the lower strata of the Left Kuomintang against the upper,"[54] the Chinese leadership promised to "fight this struggle [against militarists, imperialists, and feudalists] with the really revolutionary members of the Kuomintang and with the masses of the Kuomintang." In the words of a Chinese resolution, the Communists had "no reason to leave the Kuomintang or to refuse to cooperate with it."[55]

[53] P. Mif, *Heroic China: Fifteen Years of the Communist Party of China* (New York: Worker's Library Publishers, 1937), p. 53.
[54] Stalin, as reported in *Pravda*, July 28, 1927, "A Resolution on the International Situation," *International Press Correspondence*, August 18, 1927, p. 1076.
[55] *International Press Correspondence*, August 4, 1927, p. 1006.

Within a few weeks the error in this tactic became evident, as we shall see later. For if there had ever been any possibility of arousing the "lower strata" of the Kuomintang Left against the upper, that time had passed. The whole plan failed, whereupon, less than a year later, the Comintern (without criticizing Stalin, its own Executive Committee, or the Russian Communist Party) was exposing a serious error on the part of the Special Conference of the Chinese Communist Party: *It had raised false hopes for the emergence of a left revolutionary Kuomintang and had actually called for action under such a banner!*[56]

The fact was that after the failure of this tactic, no one wanted to take responsibility for it. Nearly a decade later Mao Tse-tung, who by then had risen to leadership of the Chinese Communist Party, told Edgar Snow that at the Special Conference "all hope of cooperation with the Kuomintang was given up for the present. . . ."[57]

There is no official Central Committee membership list available for the period, but the ruling clique is said to have consisted of Li Li-san, Hsiang Chung-fa, Ch'ü Ch'iu-pai, Chou En-lai, Li Wei-han, and Liu Shao-ch'i. Officially, Ch'ü Ch'iu-pai succeeded Ch'en Tu-hsiu as Secretary-General of the party,[58] but some sources indicate that activities were largely undertaken by Li Li-san, while actual power throughout the autumn of 1927 stemmed from two Comintern agents, Heinz Neumann and Besso Lominadze.[59]

The mood of the new leadership was for action to replace the caution which Ch'en Tu-hsiu had displayed. Six days prior to the opening of the Special Conference a Communist uprising "under the banner of the Kuomintang Left" had taken place at Nanchang when Red elements under Yeh Ting, Ho Lung (Commander in Chief of the Twentieth Kuomintang Army), and Chu Te carried out a successful mutiny within the "ironsides," the best army corps in Kuomintang service, and thus brought into Communist ranks a reported total of nearly 20,000 men.[60]

This victory was hailed as the beginning of a new revolutionary upsurge, whereupon a "drive to the sea" was initiated, and from Sep-

---

[56] *The Communist International: Between the Fifth and Sixth World Congresses, 1924–28* (London, 1928), pp. 451–452.

[57] Edgar Snow, *Red Star Over China* (rev. ed.; New York: Garden City Publishing Co., 1939), p. 149.

[58] The office of Secretary-General never regained the prestige lost when Ch'en Tu-hsiu was deposed.

[59] *Chinese Communist Party Yearbook* (Toyko: Japanese Foreign Ministry, 1935).

[60] Mif, *op. cit.*, p. 54. Listed as members of the "Revolutionary Committee" for the Nanchang Uprising were such Kuomintang leftists as Mme. Sun Yat-sen, Teng Yen-ta, and Eugene Chen, en route to European exile at the time, and General Chang Fa-kuei, who soon displayed remarkable efficiency at exterminating Communists.

tember 24 to October 20 the city of Swatow lay under Communist control. But before long the whole revolutionary army, because of "the superiority of reactionary militarists and its own wrong tactics," was in full retreat.[61] This was the beginning of the end for the "Kuomintang Left" line of the Comintern; yet two days before the retreat began, *Pravda* was still hailing temporary successes as a "new revolutionary upsurge." The Kuomintang Left had been successfully exploited, one editorial maintained, and had brought about the beginning of a new phase — the formation of soviets.[62] But as soon as it became clear that the rebellion had actually failed, responsibility was pinned — not on Stalin or his agents or the "ruling clique" — but on T'an P'ing-shan, who was denounced and expelled for his "Kuomintang Left illusions."[63]

Depending now on a strategy of urban insurrections, Lominadze and Neumann still hoped for quick revolutionary successes in China.

By November 1927, power in Canton was being shared by two rival Generals, Li Chi-shen and Chang Fa-kuei. The latter, with support from Wang Ching-wei, was now planning a coup for complete control of the city. It was this situation which Neumann and his associates were planning to exploit. Tactics were laid out on paper and arrangements made for setting up a Soviet of Workers', Soldiers', and Peasants' Deputies.

Two days before the insurrection, Canton police uncovered the plot and issued a directive for the arrest of all Communist leaders, whereupon Red forces, acting quickly, seized police headquarters, barracks, and post and telegraph offices, and set up a "Soviet regime." But fresh elements of Chang Fa-kuei's troops soon entered the city, while fleet units opened a bombardment, and before long the "Canton Commune" fell. Neumann and Lominadze were recalled to Moscow, where Stalin called them personally to task.[64]

Stalin now described the situation in China as a trough between two waves, but he, as well as the Chinese Communist Party leadership, claimed to foresee an imminent revolutionary upsurge that the Bolsheviks could exploit. During the latter months of 1928 the Sixth Congress of the Third International, while reaffirming Lenin's theses for revolution in backward countries, laid out for China a program of armed insurrection essentially similar to the plan which had failed at Canton as the "sole path to the completion of bourgeois democratic

---

[61] *Ibid.*

[62] *Pravda*, September 30, 1927.

[63] Mif, *op. cit.*, p. 55.

[64] A. Neuberg (Heinz Neumann), *L'Insurrection Armée* (Paris, 1931); *International Press Correspondence*, December 12, 1928, p. 1672.

revolution" and to the overthrow of the Kuomintang.[65] After a long series of preparatory directives addressed to the Central Committee of the Chinese Communist Party, the Comintern in October 1929 dispatched a letter calling for action under this program.

There were three primary premises for Moscow's decision to push a policy of armed insurrection at this time: an acceleration of peasant guerrilla warfare in widespread rural areas; an increase in the number and intensity of rebellions against Chiang Kai-shek (such as those of Feng Yü-hsiang, Yen Hsi-shan, the Wang Ching-wei clique, and the Kwangsi militarists); and an allegedly imminent and violent upsurge among labor masses.[66]

Moscow, in the same directive, issued decisive orders to the Chinese Communist Party for the carrying out of the insurrectionary program: consolidate and expand guerrilla warfare; develop political strikes; turn the "fratricidal war" (the Fukien Rebellion and others) into a class war; and transform peasant struggles into urban insurrections.

When this policy failed during the latter half of 1930, it was to Li Li-san that responsibility for defeat was assigned. And while it was undoubtedly true that Li Li-san did act precipitously, pushing ahead faster than Moscow's directives had intended and committing tactical errors within the framework of Comintern strategy, there is also strong evidence of three fundamental and critical misconceptions on the part of Moscow.

The first of these misconceptions pertained to the nature of peasant guerrilla warfare and its relation to the revolution in China. For Stalinists, despite their emphasis upon the necessity for building a peasant army, still viewed agrarian revolution as a subsidiary part of the total Chinese upheaval. If at any given time the urban workers needed an army, the peasantry could provide it. And if at any time the urban workers were too weakened by defeat to act, the peasantry might even be allowed to take *momentary initiative*. But according to Moscow, insurrections begun in villages must be transported to the cities, to the big industrial centers, for the establishment of an urban-based Soviet Government of Workers and Peasants.[67]

[65] "Theses and Resolutions of the VI World Congress of the Communist International," *International Press Correspondence*, December 12, 1928, p. 1672.

[66] "A Letter to the Central Committee of the Chinese Communist Party from the Executive Committee of the Comintern (approved by the Political Secretariat of the Comintern, October 26, 1929)," *Hung Ch'i* [*Red Flag*], No. 76, February 15, 1930.

[67] "Molotov's Report to the Sixteenth Congress of the Communist Party of the Soviet Union," *Vsesoiuznaia kommunisticheskaia partiia (bol'shevikov): XVI S"ezd Vsesoiuznoĭ kommunisticheskoĭ partii, Stenograficheskiĭ otchet* (Moscow, 1931), pp. 415–416.

The truth was, however (as Chinese Communist Party statistics admit), that the Chinese Communist mass movement was undergoing an acute transformation from primarily proletarian to primarily peasant composition. Near the end of 1926, according to Communist figures, at least 66 per cent of Chinese Communist Party membership could be classed as proletarian. Another 22 per cent were considered to be intellectuals. Only 5 per cent were peasants, and 2 per cent were soldiers.[68] But by the early months of 1930, elements that could possibly be labeled working class totaled only 8 per cent of Chinese Communist Party membership, while the number of industrial workers was "still smaller, accounting for only 2 per cent" of party membership.[69] The Chinese Red Army, which, more than any other Red organ, had been responsible for Chinese Communist victories and the establishment of soviets, was overwhelmingly peasant.

This was the party, and this was the military force, upon which Moscow depended for the transformation of the agrarian struggle into urban insurrection.

The second Stalinist misconception comprised a faulty evaluation of the Feng, Yen, Wang, and Kwangsi rebellions, which were factional struggles rather than deep-seated conflicts capable of being transformed into class wars.

The third misconception on the part of Stalin and his followers was twofold: an overestimation of the "revival of the labor movement" in China as the "most-important, ever-growing symbol of the revolutionary upsurge" and a faulty understanding of labor's relationship to the Chinese Communist Party. For, despite the numerous strikes that Communist officials had so carefully recorded, the Chinese proletariat was not then organized for, or (if subsequent events are a criterion) politically susceptible to, calls for armed rebellion. The Communist Party, furthermore, had much less influence over the labor movement than it had enjoyed during the peak of labor unrest that characterized the Borodin period. Party nuclei were few and scattered. Party fractions had lost their former power. Even trade-union organizations had "shrunk to almost nothing."[70]

During the summer of 1930, Li Li-san, translating Comintern policies into a plan for attacks on Changsha, Hankow, and other urban centers, compounded Stalinist strategical errors with tactical mistakes of his

[68] *Report on the Activity of the Communist International, March–November, 1926*, p. 118.

[69] "Letter from the Central Committee of the Chinese Communist Party to All Party Members," *Hung Ch'i*, No. 87, March 26, 1930.

[70] "Notice of the Central Committee of the Chinese Communist Party," *Hung Ch'i*, February 15, 1930.

own. Chinese Communist forces, enjoying momentary success, captured Changsha in late July and succeeded in holding the city for nearly a week. But with insufficient support from urban masses, Red units were forced to withdraw, and other cities, more heavily garrisoned than Changsha, could not be captured at all. Although Li Li-san pushed his insurrectionary policy throughout the summer, the campaign was a failure, whereupon the Comintern, disturbed by these defeats, dispatched Ch'ü Ch'iu-pai and Chou En-lai (who were in Moscow at the time) to China for the convening of the Third Plenum of the Central Committee of the Chinese Communist Party in Lushan.

The *Report to the Third Plenum*, drafted by Ch'ü Ch'iu-pai and Chou En-lai, rebuked Li Li-san for having "overestimated the tempo" and for having committed tactical mistakes; nevertheless, it stated that the general line was still "in complete harmony with the Comintern." The task of the Chinese Communist Party, according to the report, was to consolidate existing but scattered soviet districts, weld them together, strengthen and centralize the leadership of the Red Armies, set broader peasant masses in motion, and establish a Central Soviet Government to develop toward the industrial cities.[71]

Within a few weeks, however, the Comintern on the basis of further Chinese Communist defeats ordered a complete change of policy, the withdrawal of Li Li-san from active party policy making, and the substitution of a new party leadership.

Li Li-san's overthrow was directed by the Comintern representative in China, Pavel Mif, and by a group of recently returned graduates from Sun Yat-sen University in Moscow. Weeks later Li Li-san, answering for his failure before the Oriental Department of the Comintern in Moscow, admitted a long series of errors: He had thought that he could mobilize the working class "simply by raising the slogan of military insurrection"; he had attempted an insurrectionary policy without proper political preparation; he had thought that the revolutionary situation was spread evenly throughout China and that a revolutionary government could not be set up until he had occupied large industrial and administrative cities; he had overestimated the upsurge of the world revolutionary movement; he had maintained that the victory of the bourgeois democratic revolution would go directly over into a socialist revolution.

The Comintern, finding Li Li-san guilty of "non-Marxist and non-

---

[71] Chou En-lai, *Report to the Third Plenum* (no place, no date). Chou En-lai seems to have escaped the severe criticism suffered by Ch'ü. To date, the record of Chou's relationships with various leadership cliques and with Moscow is in need of clarification.

Leninist blind actionism," required him to remain in Moscow indefinitely for purposes of Bolshevik study. At the same time, while urging Li to "expose the whole clique situation" in the Chinese Communist Party, Russian Bolshevik leaders condemned Ch'ü Ch'iu-pai for his actions at the Third Plenum. Ch'ü Ch'iu-pai, according to Comintern officials, had repudiated the Li Li-san line before his departure from Moscow prior to the Third Plenum. Yet, upon his arrival in China, Ch'ü had "double-crossed" the Comintern by ignoring directives and softening his criticisms of Li Li-san in documents of the Third Plenum.[72]

Of further concern to the Comintern — and one of the more notable findings of the investigation — was the fact that Chinese Communist leaders had expressed keen resentment over Russian domination within the Red hierarchy. Chinese comrades, according to Li Li-san, felt that the Russians not only did not understand conditions in China, but also harbored narrow racial prejudices.[73]

### The "Returned Students": January 1931–January 1935

From January 1931 until January 1935, nominal leadership of the Chinese Communist Party — at least partly on Russian advice — rested in the hands of a group centering on Wang Ming (Ch'en Shao-yü). But this was, in fact, a critical transition period in the development of the Chinese Communist Party, a period during which the peasant composition of the Red movement achieved recognition and during which Mao Tse-tung gradually increased his power.

As early as 1927, Mao had recognized the peasants as the chief dynamic force in the Chinese Revolution. "If we allot ten points to the accomplishment of the democratic revolution," he wrote in a report on the Hunanese peasant movement, "then the achievements of the urban dwellers and the military units rate only three points, while the remaining seven points should go to the peasants in their rural revolution." In terms of recent Chinese Communist attempts at retailoring their ideology more nearly in conformity with that of the Soviet Union, it is significant that the 1951 Chinese version of Mao Tse-tung's Collected Works has omitted this statement. Whether or not it is ever allowed to reappear in official Communist doctrine, this concept remains fundamental to Mao's political strategy and tactics between 1927 and 1950. According to Mao in 1927, the millions of poor peasants had nothing to lose by revolt and everything to gain. "Sun Yat-sen devoted forty

---

[72] "The Report of the Oriental Department of the Comintern," *Pu-erh-sai-wei-ko* (Bolshevik), May 10, 1931. This issue contains various materials pertaining to Li Li-san's "trial in Moscow."
[73] "The Discussion of the Li Li-san Line by the Presidium of the Executive Committee of the Communist International," and Manuilsky's statement, *ibid.*

years to the national revolution," Mao stated in his report. "What he wanted but failed to achieve has been accomplished by the peasants in a few months."[74]

But Mao did not yet have control of the Chinese Communist movement. At the Fourth Plenum in January 1931, a group of recently returned students, centering on Wang Ming and supported by Pavel Mif, took over leadership of the Chinese Communist Party. Hsiang Chung-fa, surviving Li Li-san's dismissal, continued to serve as Secretary-General until his execution by the Kuomintang in June 1931, but Wang Ming and his followers enjoyed Comintern blessing and were considered to be the actual leaders of the Politburo. After Mao had secured his leadership, however, they were condemned as "dogmatists" by the Chinese Communists on the basis of what was called their "pure proletarian line" and for their failure to unite with the Fukien Rebellion against Chiang Kai-shek in 1934.[75]

Chinese Communist leadership remained young, the average age of four of these men being twenty-nine years, and in other respects their characteristics did not differ radically from those of previous leaderships. At least five had received a part of their education in the Soviet Union; one had studied in France, one in Japan, and one, Chang Wen-t'ien, in the United States. Three classified their fathers as "Mandarin," "provincial governor," and "boatman," respectively. Two here called their fathers "wealthy peasants."

After Hsiang Chung-fa's capture and execution by the Kuomintang in June 1931, Meng Ch'ing-shu (Mme. Ch'en Shao-yü) was elevated to the Politburo, and her husband, Wang Ming, was made Secretary-General.

So far Moscow, in centering its attention upon Central Committee headquarters in Shanghai, had tended to overlook developments that were taking place under Mao Tse-tung and Chu Te in mountain areas of Kiangsi and Hunan. But as the Red Army grew in strength and as soviets sprang up in more and more peasant villages, Comintern leaders began gradually to shift emphasis in the direction of rural areas.

In April 1931, Manuilsky laid down three objectives for the current

[74] Mao Tse-tung, "Report on an Investigation of the Peasant Movement in Hunan" (translated and mimeographed for private distribution by the Russian Research Center, Harvard University, 1950).

[75] Compare Mif, *op. cit.*, p. 68, with Anna Louise Strong, "The Thought of Mao Tse-tung," *Amerasia*, June 1947, p. 166. Mao's relationship to the "pure proletarian line" *at the time* is a matter for investigation. According to Composite Ypsilon, *Pattern for World Revolution* (New York: Ziff-Davis Publishing Co., 1947), p. 425, Mao was called to Moscow for instructions on at least two occasions (1931 and 1934), but convincing evidence of these journeys has yet to be presented.

stage of the Chinese Revolution: the Red Army must be converted into a regular workers' and peasants' Red Army with a sound territorial base; the economic and political struggles of the working class and peasantry in nonsoviet territories must be developed through trade-unions, peasant committees, and propaganda work in various militarist armies; and a central soviet government must be formed in China[76] in order to carry out a program of anti-imperialist and agrarian revolt.[77]

During November 1931, two months after Japanese action in Man-churia, the First All-China Congress of Soviets, meeting in Juichin, established a Chinese Soviet Republic with Mao Tse-tung as chairman and Chang Kuo-t'ao and Hsiang Ying as vice-chairmen. Before ad-journing, the congress accepted a government constitution, passed agrarian and labor laws, and elected a government Central Committee under Mao's chairmanship. In February 1932 the new government declared war on Japan and sent out a call to all classes and political groups in China to join in resisting Japanese aggression.[78] This was the beginning of what was called "a united front from below."

For another year the Central Committee of the Chinese Communist Party maintained its headquarters in Shanghai, while Mao and his followers devoted themselves to affairs of the Juichin Republic, to the building of the Red Army, and to resisting a series of Nationalist attacks that Chiang Kai-shek had initiated. But during the autumn of 1932, Wang Ming, Chang Wen-t'ien, Po Ku (Ch'in Pang-hsien), Shen Tse-min, and other Central Committeemen, under Kuomintang pres-sure, moved to Juichin. Shortly thereafter Wang Ming was relieved of his position as Secretary-General and recalled to the Soviet Union, where he served from 1932 to 1938 as a Chinese Communist represent-ative in Moscow. One is tempted to conclude that this may have been the result of some internal party conflict, but Chang Kuo-t'ao told the author in a personal interview that the Chinese Communist Party was having trouble with its underground apparatus at the time, that some-one had to be sent to Moscow, and that Wang Ming seemed the logical one.[79] He was replaced as Secretary-General by Po Ku (Ch'in Pang-hsien).[80]

[76] Mao actually, if not officially, had long since set up a rural soviet system, but Moscow had continued to think in urban terms.

[77] *International Press Correspondence*, June 10, 1931, p. 552.

[78] *Räte-China, Documente der Chinesichen Revolution* (Moscow-Leningrad, 1934); *International Press Correspondence*, January 23, 1933, p. 91.

[79] Chang Kuo-t'ao in an interview with the author, Hong Kong, November 3, 1950.

[80] O. Briere, "The Twenty-five Years of the Chinese Communist Party, 1921–1946," Aurora University *Bulletin*, VII, No. 3 (1946), p. 111. There is some doubt concerning the exact date of the Central Committee's transfer to Juichin

The necessity for meeting Chiang Kai-shek's attacks was undoubtedly a positive factor in the long-range growth and strengthening of the Red Army, in the consolidation of Mao's power within the party, and in the eventual expansion of the Communist Party itself. But the immediate effect of Chiang's campaigns was to weaken the Soviet Republic and to force it out of Kiangsi.

Chiang's first offensive, undertaken in December 1930, proved unsuccessful. Red leaders, with their forces centered in mountain areas, found the terrain well suited for guerrilla warfare. Basic to Communist tactics was the principle that Red troops should attack only when they enjoyed local superiority over the enemy and were certain to win a restricted engagement. In order to create such situations, therefore, Mao and Chu Te had trained their troops in tricks of decoy and ambush designed to isolate small Nationalist detachments from the main body. The theory was that, once this maneuver had been accomplished, it would be comparatively easy to surround and annihilate the enemy unit and make away with their weapons and supplies.[81]

During May and June 1931, Chiang Kai-shek pressed his second attack. This time he dispatched 200,000 men (nearly double the number employed in the first offensive) under Ho Ying-ch'in, while Communist leaders made what preparations they could with the aid of arms and equipment captured during the previous offensive.

Ho's plan was to advance slowly, consolidating his gains as he moved along. But Red troops, attacking the Nationalist rear, were able to repulse the Kuomintang attack in fifteen days and, according to Chu Te, to capture 30,000 rifles.

Chiang took personal command of the third campaign, which lasted from July to October 1931. This time, according to Chu Te, Red leaders miscalculated, being unaware that Chiang was so soon in a position to strike again. Nationalist troops advanced along four parallel

and about the relationship, at this time, between the Chinese Communist Party and Chinese Soviet power. Presumably Mao increased his power through his position in the Central Soviet. But it is not clear whether or not Mif's protégés had already lost their influence, nor is it certain whether Mao received Moscow's instructions directly or through Central Committee headquarters. There is also some question whether the "returned students" associated themselves with Mao voluntarily, through direction from Moscow, or by force of circumstances alone. Chang Kuo-t'ao expressed the opinion to the author that Mao's position was relatively unimportant until the Tsun-yi Conference and that all directives passed through regular channels.

[81] Accounts of Red Army actions against the Kuomintang are available in Snow, *op. cit.*, pp. 157–167; Nym Wales, *Inside Red China* (New York: Doubleday, Doran & Co., 1939), pp. 251–256; Victor A. Yakhontov, *The Chinese Soviets* (New York: Coward-McCann, Inc., 1934), pp. 100–121. There are also numerous scattered articles in the files of *International Press Correspondence*.

lines, concentrating their attack upon soviets in Kiangsi. To meet this offensive, Communist elements infiltrated the spaces between Chiang's lines and began harassing operations. Since the weather was hot, Nationalist troops, allegedly less accustomed to hard marching than the Reds, soon began to tire, and as a result, Communist tactics were momentarily successful. Neither side was able to register a decisive victory, however, and the campaign came to a conclusion only when Chiang, as a result of the Mukden incident, was forced to withdraw his troops. In order to avoid further stalemates, Chiang next made plans for coordinated military offensives and economic blockade. Nationalist leaders laid out a whole network of blockhouses and field fortifications to isolate Communist territories and began, at the same time, the mobilization of a million men.

The combined military and economic attack that Chiang subsequently loosed upon the Soviet areas was already endangering Juichin when the Second Congress of Chinese Soviets opened in January 1934. At the Fifth Plenum of the Chinese Communist Party, held concurrently, another of the "returned student" group, Chang Wen-t'ien, replaced Po Ku as Secretary-General of the party. Chang Kuo-t'ao reports that at the Fifth Plenum Po Ku attacked Mao for his "countryside policy" and "banditry doctrine" and used every effort to keep Mao's growing power in bounds.[82] But Mao seems to have dominated the Second Congress of Soviets. Admitting the serious effects of Chiang Kai-shek's blockade, Mao called for an aggressive program to save the Soviet Republic and to enlarge it in the face of the Nationalist offensive. He wanted to build Red Army strength to a million men, to increase the size of reserve units such as the Red Guards and the Communist Youth Guards, and to boost production, both agricultural and industrial.

But during the congress, Nationalist forces were already tightening their encirclement of soviet areas. Hard fighting took place during the spring and summer of 1934, and casualties mounted on both sides. According to Mao and Chu Te, the Nationalists maneuvered Red forces into abandoning their guerrilla tactics in favor of positional warfare and thus gained a further advantage.[83]

Before the year was up, Communist leaders found themselves compelled to organize a nearly complete evacuation of soviet areas and a retreat from their strongholds in Central China. By the date of the Juichin Republic's fall (November 10, 1934), they and their followers

[82] Chang interview.
[83] "Report of Mao Tse-tung to the Second Congress of Chinese Soviets," *International Press Correspondence*, June 29, 1934, p. 957; July 6, 1934, p. 977.

were already embarking upon the Long March, which, during the following twelve months, took them more than 6,000 miles across the face of China.

### The Fourth Period of Leadership

This stage, which began in August 1935, saw the completion of the Long March, the establishment of a united front against Japan, victory in the civil war against Chiang Kai-shek and the Kuomintang, the establishment of a nationwide, Communist-controlled People's Republic, and the concurrent maturing of present party leadership under Mao Tse-tung.

It is difficult to obtain details concerning Mao Tse-tung's actual achievement of power within the Chinese Communist Party. The following analysis depends rather heavily upon information given the author by Chang Kuo-t'ao, who, throughout the Long March and for two years thereafter, was Mao's chief rival for power. For the most part, Chang's statements are supported by the fragmentary documentary evidence, but he himself emphasized that he had no notes or documents for reference and was, furthermore, a party to the controversy he was describing.[84]

Chang Kuo-t'ao states that Mao's power dates from the Tsun-yi Conference in Kweichow during January 1935. Prior to that, Mao's position in the party was considered relatively unimportant, Chang insists, both because Moscow had favored the "returned students" and because of Po Ku's attacks on Mao's "countryside" policies.

Sometime in late October or November 1934, according to Chang, Communist authorities in Juichin received a radiogram from Moscow advising them to pull out and seek safety, perhaps as far away as Outer Mongolia. The local decision to begin the Long March was made by Po Ku and Chou En-lai. The evacuation began November 10, and, for a number of months thereafter, Communist leaders had no contact with Moscow.

At Tsun-yi various Communist leaders attacked Po Ku and succeeded in removing him from power. Mao and his supporters based their attack on the charges that Po Ku had used ineffective guerrilla tactics against the Kuomintang and had weakened the Communist position by refusing to cooperate with an anti-Kuomintang revolt in Fukien during 1933. Chang Kuo-t'ao, who was not present at the meeting, but who kept in touch by telegram, went further, attacking the whole principle of soviets for China.

[84] Chang interview.

The conference upheld the first two charges, but refused to support Chang's attack on the soviet principle. As a result of these debates, Mao achieved power, while Chang assumed the role of an oppositionist. In June 1935 the main column of the Long March made a junction in Szechwan Province with troops of Chang Kuo-t'ao and Hsu Hsiang-ch'ien, who had set up a soviet base in this area a short time previously. After proceeding to Mao-erh-kai, the two groups held a joint meeting where the differences between Mao and Chang broke into open debate.

The conflict arose over ratification of the decisions reached at Tsun-yi, Chang reopening his argument that the soviet principle was inapplicable to Chinese conditions. Beyond this, a further disagreement developed over the ultimate destination of the Long March. All admitted that a period of rest was necessary, but Mao wanted to settle somewhere near Inner Mongolia, perhaps in the vicinity of Ningsia, and as close as possible to the troops of Kao Kang, a peasant guerrilla leader who had participated in building a soviet in Shensi. Chang Kuo-t'ao, on the other hand, proposed to continue into Sinkiang.

At this point, according to Chang, contact was momentarily re-established with Moscow, whereupon the Comintern proposed the recognition of two independent bases, one under Mao, the other under Chang — a solution to which the Chinese could not agree. Thereupon, Moscow sent Lin Piao's uncle, Lin Yü-yin, to take over authority and seek some other way out; this attempt also failed to win Chinese support.

Chang maintains that Moscow then approved the journey to Sinkiang and that the two groups, having separated, made another juncture and began a crossing of the Yellow River. Kuomintang forces interposed, however, and nearly destroyed two Communist armies. A conflicting source maintains that, after the second juncture of the two forces, the old conflict broke out again, whereupon Chang and Hsu returned to Mao-erh-kai, whence they struck westward into Sinkiang, while Mao proceeded to Shensi.[85] In any case, the two groups both settled in Shensi eventually, for it was there that the final Mao-Chang clash took place.

Mao and his followers selected Pao An as their capital, remaining there until December 1936, when, after the Communist capture of Yenan, they transferred their headquarters to the latter town. The period from the termination of the Long March until the summer of 1937 was one of negotiations which were characteristic of a new tactical stage in Chinese Communist development.

[85] Briere, op. cit. See also Susumu Kinoshita, The Chinese Communist Party and Its Politics (Tokyo, 1948).

The Japanese invasion of Manchuria had been recognized by Russian and Chinese Communist leaders alike as a particularly critical development. In Moscow, Bolshevik strategists saw not only a new imperialist threat to the Chinese revolution, but also a new menace to the Soviet Union, which, during the progress of the Five-Year Plan, was especially anxious to preserve world peace. In China, Mao and his followers, beyond their awareness of these factors, may have seen the further probability that unified Chinese action against Japan would bring an end to the anti-Communist "extermination campaigns" of Chiang Kai-shek.

As early as April 1932 the Chinese Communists had "called upon the mass of Chinese people to join . . . in the fight against Japanese imperialism," and in January 1933 a Comintern publication carried a similar appeal on the part of the Chinese Soviet Government and the Revolutionary War Council of the Chinese Red Army signed by Mao, Chang Kuo-t'ao, Chu Te, and others:

> . . . We declare before the whole Chinese people: The Red Army is prepared to enter into a fighting alliance with any army or any body of troops against the Japanese invasion. Our conditions for such alliance are: (1) immediate cessation of the offensive against the Soviet districts; (2) immediate granting of democratic popular rights, the right of combination, freedom of speech and press, the right to hold meetings, etc.; (3) immediate arming of the people and formation of armed volunteer troops for the fight for the defense of the independence and unity of China. . . .[86]

On August 1, 1935, the Mao-erh-kai Conference in northwestern Szechwan decided on an anti-Japanese People's United Front and issued a proclamation urging all classes to fight against Japan. Calling on "all fellow countrymen, in spite of differences of political opinions, strivings, and interests" to "unite as one man," the convention made a special appeal to Chiang Kai-shek, promising to cooperate with the Kuomintang if Chiang would stop his fight "against his own people." At the same time the proclamation called also for the "formation of a United All-Chinese People's Government of National Defense jointly with the Soviet Government and the Anti-Japanese local authorities in Manchuria" and for the "organization of a united All-China Anti-Japanese Army jointly with the Red Army and the Anti-Japanese partisan units in Manchuria."[87]

[86] *International Press Correspondence*, January 26, 1933, p. 91.
[87] Shigeo Watanabe, *Sho Kaiseki to Mo Chitaku* [*Chiang Kai-shek and Mao Tse-tung*], (Tokyo, 1941), Harvard-Yenching Library. Cited by Chao Kuo-chun, "Thirty Years of the Communist Movement in China" (Russian Research Center, Harvard University, 1950); *International Press Correspondence*, December 21, 1935, p. 1728.

On the following day, August 2, Georgi Dimitrov, advocating a worldwide united-front policy to the Seventh Congress of the Communist International in Moscow, said:

> . . . We therefore approve the initiative taken by our courageous brother Party of China in the creation of a most extensive anti-imperialist united front against Japanese imperialism and its Chinese agents, jointly with all those organized forces existing on the territory of China who are ready to wage a real struggle for the salvation of their country and their people.[88]

Five days later Wang Ming told the same congress:

> In my opinion and in the opinion of the entire Central Committee of the Communist Party of China, the latter, together with the Soviet government of China should issue a joint appeal to the whole nation, to all parties, groups, troops, mass organizations, and all prominent political and social persons, to organize together with us an all-China united people's government of national defense.[89]

Chang Kuo-t'ao states that to his knowledge the Chinese Communists, prior to the Seventh Congress, had carried on no communications with Moscow in regard to a broad united-front policy as opposed to the old "united front from below."[90] It is also worth noting that at the Congress Chinese delegates other than Wang Ming were continuing to call for an anti-imperialist and *anti-Kuomintang* united front as late as August 11 — nine days after Dimitrov's speech.[91] Both Chinese and Russian leaders, according to Chang Kuo-t'ao, had been considering the problem of opposing Japanese expansion and, independently, had reached some of the same conclusions concerning a broad united front. There was no coordination, however, until Lin Yü-ying returned to China with a copy of the Seventh Congress Resolution dealing with the new united-front policy.[92]

This resolution, passed August 20, demanded a broad front in colonial and semicolonial countries, including China, "under the slogan of a national-revolutionary struggle of the armed people against the imperialist enslavers, in the first place against Japanese imperialism and its Chinese servitors."[93] In China the soviets were to be the rallying center of this movement, but by implication the road was left open for the Kuomintang if Chiang saw fit to call off his anti-Communist campaigns and join in the fight against Japan.

[88] *International Press Correspondence*, August 20, 1935, pp. 971–972.
[89] *Ibid.*, November 9, 1935, p. 1489.
[90] Chang interview.
[91] *International Press Correspondence*, December 2, 1935, p. 1666.
[92] Chang interview.
[93] *International Press Correspondence*, September 19, 1935, p. 1181.

Chiang showed no willingness to heed Communist appeals until his kidnaping at Sian in December 1936. At this time Chang Hsüeh-liang, whose forces had been driven out of Manchuria into Shensi, and Yang Hü-cheng, the Pacification Commissioner of Shensi, captured Chiang and pressed upon him the view that the main war was against the Japanese, rather than the Communists. In the negotiations which led to Chiang's eventual release, Chinese Communist leaders acted as mediators, a service that paved the way for effecting a Communist-Kuomintang truce. This took place shortly after Chiang's return to Nanking.

Six months later the Chinese Communists offered specifically to abolish soviets and the Red Army designation, to carry out "democracy," to abandon its policy of overthrowing the Kuomintang, and to discontinue land confiscations in return for a Kuomintang cessation of the civil war, a Kuomintang policy of "democracy and freedom," the convocation of a National Assembly, concrete preparations for a war against Japan, and an improvement in the people's livelihood.[94]

The Kuomintang took no action in regard to this offer, but negotiations continued between the two parties. In the meantime, Japanese expansion on the Asian mainland was giving rise to militant Chinese nationalism and widespread demands for unity. With the beginning of the Sino-Japanese War in July 1937, an agreement was finally reached. Communist leaders issued statements to the effect that the first step in preparation for a Marxist socialist state was now believed to be the attainment of national independence and of "democratic" institutions and that further Communist action toward the attainment of these goals would coincide with the Three Principles of Dr. Sun Yat-sen.[95]

Relations between Red Army and peasantry were necessarily revised. For whereas under the soviets Communist military forces had been expanded at the expense of landowning and similar sections of the populace, united-front policies forbade the antagonizing of gentry and related classes. During the uneasy Communist-Kuomintang alliance which resulted from the conclusion of these agreements, Mao's leadership was subjected to another internal crisis.

In translating Dimitrov's united-front policy into Chinese terms, Mao advanced the slogan, "Defeat for all!" meaning defeat for the

[94] Mao Tse-tung and others, *China: The March Toward Unity* (New York: Workers' Library, 1937), pp. 119–123, gives Communist releases concerning the Sian incident.

[95] "Communist Statement on Unity (1937)." For an English translation, see Lawrence K. Rosinger, *China's Wartime Politics 1937–1944* (Princeton, N.J., Princeton University Press, 1944), pp. 96–97.

Japanese and eventual defeat for non-Communist groups in the alliance, including the Kuomintang. Attacking this policy, Chang Kuo-t'ao proposed the slogan, "Victory for all!" with the hope that, through a sincere alliance, the Communists might be able to lead the Kuomintang and other non-Communist groups along a more progressive path than they had followed in the past. The two policies were debated at a conference at Lochuan, but when it became clear (according to Chang) that a majority of those present favored a "Victory for all!" policy, Mao cut off further discussion and closed the meeting.[96] The issue was then referred to the Comintern, which decided in favor of Mao. Moscow endorsed a Chinese Communist charge that Chang had "betrayed" Communism and "the cause of the anti-Japanese front" by being too friendly with the Kuomintang and confirmed his expulsion from the party.[97]

In prosecuting Mao's "defeat for all" united-front policy, Chinese Communist leaders, while championing the cause of the peasant, made what use they could of their uneasy alliance with the Kuomintang. Then, once the war was over, they proceeded to exploit Kuomintang weaknesses, leading armies of dissatisfied peasants against the Nationalist government. The results were military victories for Mao and the establishment in late September 1949 of a Chinese People's Republic.

During the Japanese War the Chinese Communist Party strengthened itself both organizationally and ideologically. Much of its organizational experience took place in the so-called liberated areas behind Japanese lines, and it was in these areas that Red leaders — especially the young ones — became expert in guerilla warfare, propaganda techniques, and civil organization.[98]

Ideologically, the chief development during the Japanese War was the completion of Mao Tse-tung's blueprint for the New Democracy. To a large extent, Mao's concept had been derived from Lenin's "Theses on the National and Colonial Questions," presented to the Second Congress of the Communist International in 1920, and from the "Theses on the Revolutionary Movement in the Colonies and Semi-Colonies," passed by the Sixth Congress in 1928. Mao, therefore, in adjusting these principles to his own revolutionary experiences and to social and economic peculiarities of the Chinese situation, produced a plan that

---

[96] Chang interview.

[97] *Communist International*, XV, No. 7 (July 1938), pp. 688-689.

[98] The differences between junior cadres who had been working in front line areas and those who had remained in various party headquarters have been noted by Michael Lindsay, "Post War Government and Politics of Communist China," *Post War Governments of the Far East* (Gainesville, Fla.: University of Florida, 1947).

differed in detail from programs of the past but which found a logical position within the dialectics of the Leninist-Stalinist revolutionary system.

> The thesis that the state form is the dictatorship of all revolutionary classes and the government form is the system of democratic centralism is the political foundation of the "new democracy." . . .[99]

In an economic sense, Mao's program amounts to a Communist elaboration of Dr. Sun Yat-sen's plan for state control of distribution, transportation, and production as a weapon against imperialism. For the present it contemplates a mixed economy undertaken partly by cooperatives, partly by private enterprise, and partly by the state. Being a Communist concept, however, the New Democracy must be considered as only one stage in a planned and, from the Communist standpoint, an inevitable advance into Marxist socialism and communism.

That Mao did not have any intention of ignoring Communist teachings or of breaching Communist discipline is suggested by the ideological training program which he set in motion during the first months of 1942.[100] Calling together several thousands of Red officials, Mao started them off on a rigorous course in Communist philosophy, strategy, and tactics based upon a textbook of twenty-two outstanding Communist documents. Both Chinese and Western Communist selections were included, but both proportion and sequence gave emphasis to Mao's writings and to those of other CCP (Chinese Communist Party) writers, rather than to the writings of Marx, Engels, Lenin, and Stalin. It should not be overlooked, however, that the Chinese writers developed their arguments within a Bolshevik framework and relied heavily upon Marx, Engels, Lenin, and Stalin for their supporting citations.

When these thousands of Red officials had completed this indoctrination, Mao dispersed them throughout Red areas of China in order to instruct the rank and file and, at the same time, to tighten up the Communist Party apparatus. Mao used this opportunity to expel undesirable elements from the party hierarchy, but certain men (like Wang Ming) who had been named as purge victims in National Central News Agency reports were as recently as 1948 occupying

[99] Mao Tse-tung, *China's New Democracy.* An English translation is available in U.S. Congress, House Foreign Affairs Committee Report, *Strategy and Tactics of World Communism,* Supplement No. C, Appendix (Washington, D.C.: U.S. Government Printing Office, 1948), p. 75.

[100] For party reform documents pertaining to this development, see *Mao's China,* with translation and introduction by Boyd Compton (Seattle, Wash.: University of Washington Press, 1952).

official, if somewhat subordinate, positions within the top hierarchy of the Chinese Communist Party.[101]

## Over-All Trends

From 1921 through 1931, Moscow was responsible for making and breaking top Chinese Communist leadership. In the beginning, it is true, Ch'en Tu-hsiu achieved leadership through his own initiative, prestige, and organizational efforts. But after the First Congress, he remained in office only through sufferance on the part of Moscow. This does not mean that the Chinese subordinated themselves gracefully. On the contrary, there is evidence that many of them resented Russian interference and were sometimes outspoken about it. But during these years they either submitted to discipline or were relieved of their responsibilities by the hierarchy.

Between 1928 and 1934, however, the composition of the Chinese Communist Party underwent a radical change. Proletarian membership nearly disappeared, while peasants flocked into the ranks. Mao sensed and made the most of this trend from the beginning, transforming theory into agrarian revolutionary practice (Mao has also won recognition as a theorist), but Moscow was slow to recognize what was taking place. As a result, Mao and his associates, blessed with an opportunity accorded by circumstances to few Communist leaders in recent years, rose to power largely through their own efforts, and this fact, combined with conditions pertaining to the Juichin Republic and the Long March, established new criteria for leadership.

Moscow's blessing continued, no doubt, to be desirable, but on-the-scene performance in China became increasingly more important than close relationships with Comintern agents such as Heinz Neumann and Pavel Mif. For during the Long March and the Japanese War a prospective Chinese Communist leader, even if approved by Moscow, had yet to win his position through endurance, personal magnetism, guerrilla leadership, administrative excellence, propaganda activities, or organizational work among the peasantry. He had to be tough; he had to command respect; he had to be able.

Yet the hierarchy in which he rose was by no means democratic in the Western sense. Behavior was governed by the principles of democratic centralism, a disciplinary system requiring rigid personal subordination to the will of the majority (or, in some cases, to the will of the superior hierarchy). At intervals there have been intensive cam-

[101] U.S. Congress, House Foreign Affairs Committee, National and International Movements, report: *The Strategy and Tactics of World Communism*, Supplement IV, p. iii.

paigns — some carried on through intervention from Moscow, others initiated by Chinese leadership, including Mao himself — to rid the party of deviationists, incompetents, and other elements considered undesirable by those in power.

At various points during the course of Chinese Communist Party history, internal conflicts have found expression in clique activities that were serious enough to cause concern in Moscow. Up to this writing, however, there is no reliable evidence that these personal struggles (or official campaigns for weeding out undesirables) have ever led to disappearances, assassinations, or executions on the scale common to the Soviet Union after 1934. In this respect, Chinese Communist practice is like that characteristic of Russia during the earlier years of the Soviet regime. Chinese Communist leaders have risen and fallen; some have been reprimanded; others have been expelled; thousands have been killed by Nationalist armies and Nationalist police, and thousands of non-Communists have been killed by Communist armies and police. But to date there is no authenticated record of a *prominent* Chinese Communist leader executed by his own party, no matter how serious the doctrinal deviation. On the contrary, there has been a strong tendency — best evidenced in the case of Li Li-san — to reform the fallen leader and even to give him limited opportunities for reconstructing his career.

The current internal political health of the Chinese Communist Party is uncertain. There have been reports of antagonistic clique alignments, both on the basis of personal conflicts and on the basis of individual attitudes toward the Soviet Union. But there is also a respectable body of contrary evidence which would suggest that high-level internal conflicts may be at a minimum, that discipline is strict, and that Mao's position is generally respected throughout the party.

With the development of the Korean War, and especially during the early months of 1952, the Chinese Communist Party has carried on an intensive campaign against "corruption, decay, and bureaucracy" in both party and nonparty ranks. There are evidences indicating that the purpose of this campaign is threefold: to ensure cleaner and more efficient government; to promote class struggle against groups considered inimicable to Bolshevik interests at this particular stage of the revolution; and to cleanse the party of undesirable personnel. The seriousness of Communist intent can be judged from remarks made by Kao Kang in a report at the Higher-Level Cadres Meeting of the Northeast Bureau of the Central Committee of the Chinese Communist Party, January 10, 1952:

The following should be accomplished during the present campaign:

(1) Purge all departments of corruption, waste and bureaucracy. The cases of corruption and waste should be given penalties ranging from dismissal, prison terms, labor reform to death sentence.[102]

## IV. THE SOCIAL CHARACTERISTICS OF CHINESE PARTY ELITES

For the greater part of three decades the Kuomintang and the Communist Party have fought each other with all the bitterness of a class war. On the surface the rival interests involved in this conflict seem clear, for here are all the superficial characteristics of a struggle between masses on the one hand and classes on the other. The policies of the Kuomintang and the way of life of its leaders have again and again lent credence to the picture that its enemies propagate, namely, that the Kuomintang is simply a landlord clique. Moreover, the utilization by the Communists of peasant discontent, together with their insistent profession of a Marxian ideology, has created the strong impression that their movement is a movement of the masses. But an examination of membership data raises the question: how far does the character of Kuomintang and Communist leaderships support or contradict these preconceptions?

It is certainly true that Communist Party leaders differ from Kuomintang leaders in social and economic background. Indeed, the leaders of the right, center, and left within the Kuomintang also differ in these respects. But before considering these differences, we ought to take into account a number of rather striking similarities. For despite all the detailed differences, we find ourselves forced to concede that a major portion of the elite of both movements came from quite similar high social strata, and responded to similar Western and native influences during their years of growth and education.

### Common Characteristics

In both parties, the leaders have been drawn most frequently from a relatively thin upper layer of the Chinese population. In both parties these men were often the sons of landlords, merchants, scholars, or officials, and they usually came from parts of China where Western influence had first penetrated and where the penetration itself was most vigorous. All of them had higher educations, and most of them had studied abroad. The leaders of both parties, despite a relatively high status in private life, showed a reluctance or perhaps an inability

[102] Kao Kang's report has been translated and mimeographed by the American Consulate General, Hong Kong, *Current Background*, No. 163, March 5, 1952.

to establish private careers. The majority were alienated intellectuals, men and women whose Western educations isolated them from the main currents of Chinese society. In the chaos of modern China, these persons became full-time professional politicians specializing, for the most part, in military violence or in party administration. Whichever party they belonged to, Communist or Kuomintang, they differed from the Imperial elite, which we described at the beginning of this study (cf. pp. 319–328, in that they were drawn from a much wider circle. It is true that the sons of scholar-officials continued to enter politics — and very successfully — but more noteworthy, perhaps, is the fact that recent revolutions in China have brought forward the sons of the *nouveau-riche* compradors, other business classes of coastal cities, the sons of landlords, and recently, even, the sons of wealthy peasants. On the other hand, despite plebeian protestations of the Communists, the relatively smaller mass of proletarians have continued to enjoy only limited access to the elite.

The basic similarity in social origins of the largest portion of both Kuomintang and Communist leaders is emphasized by figures on their fathers' occupations and social status (cf. Table 2). The 1945 Central Committee of the Chinese Communist Party contained eight sons of landlords, two sons of merchants, and one son of an official. Against these eleven men of high social status, there were also eleven sons of peasants, of whom six were wealthy peasants. There were also two sons of workers. And the composition of the Politburos from the beginning until 1945 was similar. For these ten leading bodies (including, as in all our Politburo tabulations, the First Congress in 1921 and the "ruling clique" of August 1927) contained, in all, five sons of landlords, two sons of merchants, four sons of officials, and one son of a scholar. Against these twelve men of upper-class origin, there were ten sons of peasants, of whom six were wealthy peasants. There were also two sons of workers. Thus we find about half of the Communist elite drawn from upper-class and middle-class families, and another quarter from the prosperous section of the peasantry.

In the Kuomintang elite all but three of the fifty-one members of the first three Central Executive Committees whose occupations we know were upper or upper-middle class. Aside from these three (all sons of medium or poor peasants), there were fourteen sons of landlords, three sons of officials, and three sons of scholars whose occupations we cannot further identify. In addition there were twenty-two sons of merchants who, although middle-class, enjoyed less prestige than would merchants in the West.

In this and some later tabulations we include only the first three

*Table 2*
FATHER'S GENERAL OCCUPATION*

| | Kuomintang CEC's 1924, 1926, 1929 | | Communist Politburo | | Communist CEC 1945 | |
|---|---|---|---|---|---|---|
| | No. | % | No. | % | No. | % |
| Wealthy landlord or scholar-landlord | 10 | 21.3 | 3 | 12.5 | 7 | 23.3 |
| Scholar-official | 3 | 6.4 | 4 | 16.7 | 3 | 10.0 |
| Scholar | 3 | 6.4 | 1 | 4.2 | — | — |
| Merchant-scholar or wealthy merchant | 7 | 14.9 | — | — | 1 | 3.3 |
| Upper class, indeterminate | — | — | — | — | 1 | 3.3 |
| | | 48.9 | | 33.3 | | 40.0 |
| Other landlords | 4 | 8.5 | 2 | 8.3 | 1 | 3.3 |
| Other merchants | 15 | 31.9 | 2 | 8.3 | 1 | 3.3 |
| Professional revolutionary | 2 | 4.3 | — | — | — | — |
| Wealthy peasant | — | — | 6 | 25.0 | 6 | 20.0 |
| Middle class, indeterminate | — | — | — | — | 3 | 10.0 |
| | | 44.7 | | 41.7 | | 36.7 |
| Other peasants | 3 | 6.4 | 4 | 16.7 | 5 | 16.7 |
| Workers | — | — | 2 | 8.3 | 2 | 6.7 |
| | | 6.4 | | 25.0 | | 23.3 |
| Total known | 47 | 100.0 | 24 | 100.0 | 30 | 100.0 |
| Don't know | 23 | | 18 | | 14 | |
| Total | 70 | | 42 | | 44 | |

* For full data see Appendix D.

committees because the informants who provided the data had enjoyed close contacts with earlier, rather than later, members of the Kuomintang.

It is not easy to secure material concerning the social and economic status of Chinese leaders. They have been traditionally reticent about revealing information on the source or level of an individual's income. Moreover, many leaders, especially among the Communists, lived underground for many years at a stretch, assumed revolutionary names, and covered their movements with utmost caution. Nevertheless, a few broad conclusions can be drawn from the reports of Western businessmen, missionaries, and travelers who succeeded in establishing close personal relationships with influential Chinese. Such informants have materially aided this study by reporting on Chinese leaders they have known, providing information on source of income and occupation of father, and offering subjective ratings of financial status. The resultant data on Politburo members have been relatively full, owing to the fact that members of this body are few in number.

On the basis of these data it is clear that both elites have drawn heavily from limited circles of the population. There may be support for the impression that the social origins of Kuomintang leaders were higher than those of the Communist elite, but three cautions must be observed. Note first that many of the middle-class Kuomintang leaders were merchants' sons, of limited social status. Second, note the large number of "don't knows." For about one third of the members of the first three Kuomintang CEC's and for over 40 per cent of the CCP Politburo members we do not know the fathers' occupations, and there is no ground for assuming that these men had the same backgrounds as did those whose status we know. Usually, leaders whose origins are unreported in biographical sources are those of lower-class origins; prominent parents are likely to be known. This generalization certainly applies to Kuomintang leaders, for their ideology is such that they normally prefer to publicize reputable origins. With Communists, however, the pattern is quite the opposite, both in China and elsewhere. They prefer to hide upper-class backgrounds and to feature or even fabricate proletarian origins. Thus, among the Communist "don't knows" there is probably a higher proportion of upper-class parents than among Kuomintang "don't knows." This is one reason for suspecting that the relatively small difference in the social status of fathers of Kuomintang and Communist leaders is not significant.

A third factor also tends to emphasize the fallacy in assuming that Kuomintang leaders came from higher social backgrounds than Communist leaders. Since our data ran out after 1929, we used

Kuomintang CEC's only through that date. If we limit our examination
to Politburos appointed up to and through that same year, we find
that only three of the Politburo members were sons of peasants and
that only one member was the son of a proletarian, while eight were
sons of upper-class or middle-class parents. Clearly, then, *in both the
Communist Party and the Kuomintang* the plebeians entered later. This
is not to deny the possibility, of course, that there may have been a
genuine difference between parties in the number of plebeians. The
point to be noted, however, is that both parties drew heavily on the
upper ranks of the population for recruiting their leadership (cf. Table

*Table 3*

STATUS OF FATHERS OF POLITBUROCRATS
(SHOWING ENTRY OF PLEBEIANS AFTER 1927)

| Politburo | Upper and Middle | Lower |
|---|---|---|
| 1921 | 4 | — |
| April 1, 1927 | 4 | 1 |
| July 13, 1927 | 4 | — |
| August 1927 | 3 | 2 |
| 1928 | 3 | 2 |
| January 1931 | 4 | 1 |
| June 1931 | 4 | — |
| 1934 | 7 | 3 |
| 1937 | 5 | 2 |
| 1945 | 9 | 3 |

3). It is not at all surprising that the Kuomintang included in its
leadership a number of persons born to wealth and prominence, but
it is worthy of note that among Communist leaders, too, we find, for
example, three fathers who were wealthy landlords, one who was
both a wealthy landlord and an official, and in addition to these, three
men who listed their fathers respectively as statesman, Mandarin,
and provincial governor.

So, too, members of the two elites are similar in the educations they
have received. Aside from two members of the Politburo and one other
member of the 1945 Central Committee of the Communist Party, all
the elite members on whom we have information enjoyed a higher
education (cf. Table 4). Some went to universities in China or abroad,
some had classical Chinese educations, some attended military
schools; but, with the rarest exceptions, they were trained men. Despite
the revolutionary character of recent Chinese history, political involvement did not truncate their education as it did in the cases of so many
Soviet and Nazi leaders. Despite the poverty of China and the very

small proportion of families able to afford higher educations for their sons, leaders simply did not arise by making their own way through channels outside normal educational patterns.

### Table 4
#### EDUCATION OF ELITE MEMBERS

|  | Kuomintang CEC | Politburo |
|---|---|---|
| No higher education | 2 | 2 |
| Chinese education only | 123 | 2 |
| Foreign education | 136 | 25 |
| Total known | 261 | 29 |
| Don't know | 26 | 13 |
| Total | 287 | 42 |

Once touched by an education, the hitherto fatalistic peasant boy who has looked forward to a life no different from that of his ancestors gradually achieves a consciousness of progress and an awareness of the good things that technology can provide. And whatever his local background, the man trained as an engineer is impressed by the fact that in his own country the number of factories, and hence of jobs, is limited, with foreign "imperialists" filling most of the top positions of a technical nature. Soon he concludes that, born in the West, he would have a job and command a factory, but that, short of a thoroughgoing revolution, he can look forward to no better prospect than unemployment in his own backward country. So, too, the man trained as a banker or chemist feels a similar lack of opportunities in his field. So it is for these and innumerable other reasons, some of them exceedingly subtle and complex, that students tended to provide the leadership for both Communist and "bourgeois nationalist" movements.

The impact of Western thought upon such people has provided fuel for anti-Western movements. This impact on both Kuomintang and Communist elites is indicated by figures showing the geographical distribution of institutions that have provided elite members with their educations. (cf. Table 5.) In the case of each elite the majority have been educated abroad. Out of 261 Kuomintang CEC members whose educational careers we know, 138 were educated abroad, and out of 29 Politburo members whose educational careers we know, 25 were educated abroad. Russian training accounts for the higher proportion of foreign training among Communist leaders, but if we leave Russian education aside, we still find that 38 per cent of the leaders of the Communist Party had been trained in advanced capitalist countries.

## Table 5
### Universities Attended*

| | Kuomintang CEC | | Politburo | | Communist CEC | |
|---|---|---|---|---|---|---|
| | No. | % | No. | % | No. | % |
| Chinese university | 86 | 33.0 | | | | |
| Chinese military school | 88 | 33.7 } China | 13 | 44.8 | 23 | 54.8 |
| Chinese classical education | 15 | 5.7 | | | | |
| Japanese university | 42 | 16.1 } Japan | 5 | 17.2 | 5 | 11.9 |
| Japanese military school | 26 | 10.0 | | | | |
| United States | 40 | 15.3 | 2 | 6.9 | 1 | 2.4 |
| France | 13 | 5.0 | 6 | 20.7 | 12 | 28.6 |
| Germany | 13 | 5.0 | 2 | 6.9 | 3 | 7.1 |
| Great Britain | 15 | 5.7 | — | — | — | — |
| Belgium | 2 | .8 | — | — | 1 | 2.4 |
| Soviet Union | 14 | 5.4 | 20 | 69.0 | 25 | 59.5 |
| Other | 3 | 1.1 | — | — | — | — |
| None | 2 | .8 | 2 | 6.9 | 3 | 7.1 |
| Total known | 261 | 100.0 | 29 | 100.0 | 42 | 100.0 |
| Don't know | 26 | | 13 | | 2 | |
| Total | 287 | | 42 | | 44 | |

* This table is nonadditive, since the same individual may go to several universities.

As awareness of the role of students might lead us to expect, the leaders of both the Kuomintang and the Communist Party were young. Not only did these revolutionists join the movements in their student years, but they rose to positions of leadership fast. Both elites tended to age over the years, but until 1945 no Kuomintang CEC had an average age of over forty-five, and no Politburo had an average age over forty (cf. Table 6 for full figures). From 1921 through 1931 in fact the average of each Politburo ranged between twenty-seven and thirty-three, while that of each Kuomintang CEC was either forty-two or forty-three. After that the average ages of both groups started to rise till in 1945 it was forty-nine for the Politburo and fifty-one for Kuomintang CEC. Even these figures are a little low as compared to those for other elites reported in the Hoover Institute Studies, but they are in the usual range. It is only in times of revolutionary change, however, that one finds an elite whose average age is in the thirties or early forties. In a stable society political leadership is likely to be a function of achieved status. "Notables" (to use Max Weber's term) from other fields of life are recruited to give prestige and standing to the political machines. A political elite of notables is necessarily of

*Table 6*
AVERAGE AGES OF PARTY ELITES

| Party Elites | Average Age of Members |
|---|---|
| *Kuomintang CEC* | |
| 1924 | 43.3 |
| 1926 | 44.6 |
| 1929 | 43.8 |
| 1931 | 42.6 |
| 1935 | 48.9 |
| 1945 | 54.9 |
| *Communist Politburo* | |
| 1921 | 29.4 |
| April 1927 | 33.4 |
| July 1927 | 27.3 |
| August 1927 | 29.0 |
| 1928 | 30.0 |
| January 1931 | 29.0 |
| June 1931 | 28.4 |
| 1934 | 35.2 |
| 1937 | 39.3 |
| 1945 | 48.9 |
| *Communist Party CC* | |
| 1945 | 46.8 |

reasonable advanced age — usually averaging in the fifties. An exception is the elite in an aristocratic society where a person may be a notable from birth. In such a society, however, he is likely to remain in politics till a fairly advanced age; so the average, although lower than in a democratic society where all must work their way up, is still apt to be well up in the forties. Modern China has certainly not been an aristocratic society in that sense. Neither the Kuomintang nor Communist elites have been born to their positions. They have achieved them by effort, but in the revolutionary conditions that existed they could achieve them rapidly by going directly into politics without establishing an outside reputation first.

As a matter of fact, we find that few of the leaders of either Kuomintang or Communist Party had extrapolitical careers. The overwhelming majority were professional politicians who devoted most of their adult life to party struggles. This we expect to be true of a Communist Politburo. A Politburo member must conform to the Leninist ideal of a professional revolutionary. Following the Politburo pattern in this respect, the 1945 Central Committee of the Communist Party consisted also of professional revolutionists. (cf. Table 7.) Forty-five per cent made their careers in party organization; another 39 per cent made careers of the army. Thus 84 per cent were professionally engaged in revolutionary struggle. Most of the remainder of the CC were presented as coming directly from the work benches. Any large Communist body is required to have some such proletarians as showpieces. How many of them in reality were primarily laborers and how many were primarily Communist functionaries is impossible to say, but even if all five were primarily laborers they were still but a sprinkling. In addition to these persons there were one educator and one journalist, and no persons with any other major career. Thus the Central Committee, like the Politburo, was clearly a body of professional party activists.

*Table 7*

CAREERS OF 1945 COMMUNIST CENTRAL COMMITTEE MEMBERS

|  | *Number* | *Percentage* |
|---|---|---|
| Party organization and administration | 20 | 45.5 |
| Military | 17 | 38.6 |
| Labor | 5 | 11.4 |
| Education | 1 | 2.3 |
| Journalism | 1 | 2.3 |
| Total | 44 | 100.0 |

What is surprising is that the situation was almost identical in the Kuomintang, as shown in Table 8. Fifty-one per cent of all Kuomintang CEC members made their careers in party organization. Thirty-six per cent had military careers. Thus 86 per cent were, above all, professional politicians. Of the residue we do not know the occupa-

*Table 8*

CAREERS OF KUOMINTANG EXECUTIVE COMMITTEEMEN ( IN PERCENTAGES )

|  | 1924 | 1926 | 1929 | 1931 | 1935 | 1945 | All CEC Members |
|---|---|---|---|---|---|---|---|
| Organization and administration | 58.3 | 55.6 | 55.6 | 63.9 | 45.4 | 50.2 | 50.5 |
| Military | 25.0 | 25.0 | 41.7 | 33.3 | 42.9 | 37.2 | 35.9 |
| Education | 4.2 | 5.6 | — | — | 5.0 | 6.3 | 5.6 |
| Journalism | 4.2 | 2.8 | 2.8 | 2.8 | 2.5 | 3.1 | 2.8 |
| Other | 4.2 | 2.8 | — | — | 1.7 | 1.8 | 2.1 |
| Don't know | 4.2 | 8.3 | — | — | 2.5 | 1.4 | 3.1 |
| Total | 100.0 | 100.0 | 100.0 | 100.0 | 100.0 | 100.0 | 100.0 |
| (Number) | (24) | (36) | (36) | (36) | (119) | (223) | (287) |

tions of 3 per cent; 6 per cent were in education, and 3 per cent in journalism. This leaves a total of 2 per cent, or six individuals, whose primary career was in any part of the entire remaining range of businesses and professions.

This does not imply that only these six individuals made money by business or professional activities. With the widespread corruption in the Kuomintang it goes without saying that a career in politics or the army was likely to be associated with extensive private business activity; but we may still distinguish between businessmen, few in number, who got into politics on the side, and the many politicians who seized upon the number of business opportunities that were made available by the very nature of a given political office. The picture may be clarified by looking at the main sources of income of the members of the first three CEC's. (Such data are not available for the other bodies in our sample.) The members of the CEC whose main income was from their party or government or army salary were outnumbered by more than two to one by those whose main source of income was nonpolitical (see Table 9). Yet, as we have seen, their main career activity was political. Most of their time was spent on politics, but most of their income came from private enterprise. This apparent contradiction is explained when we realize that very few (six out of forty-three) had a major source of private *earned* income.

*Table* 9

SOURCES OF INCOME OF KUOMINTANG CEC MEMBERS, 1924–1929

| | | |
|---|---:|---:|
| Salaries | | |
| Government | 2 | |
| Party | 8 | |
| Military | 4 | |
| Total political | | 14 |
| Land rents | 12 | |
| Interest on | | |
| investments | 11 | |
| Business | | |
| Large | — | |
| Medium | 2 | |
| Small | 1 | |
| Professional fees | 2 | |
| Wages | 1 | |
| Total private | | 29 |
| Don't know | | 27 |
| Total | | 70 |

Most of those with large private incomes lived on rent or interest. Their business dealings were not such as to conflict with the active pursuit of politics as a career.

Thus we see that the leaders of both the Kuomintang and the Communist Party were young, Western-educated, and Western-oriented professional politicians. (The term "Western" includes the U.S.S.R.) They were without roots in the normal enterprises of civilian life. Alienated and relatively hopeless of their futures in traditional careers, many found in revolutionary party politics new and appealing opportunities. Turning to the muddied waters of politics, they made their careers in the three main channels of political activity: organization, violence, and symbol manipulation.

In China the symbol specialists were relatively few as compared to their role in some other states. In the Hoover Institute Elite Studies we have found that the balance between these three kinds of political specialist is a highly significant index to the nature of the society. Among the stable cabinets in the West, for example, we found the role of army officers in Germany far greater than in Britain, France, or the United States, although even in Germany they were only about one third as frequent as in either party in China. In the Politburo we found that in the course of time the specialists on organization and domestic violence supplanted the specialists on persuasion. In the

Nazi elite we found that the specialists on organization dominated the specialists on persuasion. In the French Third Republic, however, the reverse was true: there the specialist on persuasion had the leading role.

In China, revolutionary chaos gave the specialist on violence (i.e., the military careerist) a larger role than anywhere else so far studied, and the role of the symbol specialists (lawyers, journalists, teachers) was considerably reduced. In both the Communist Party and the Kuomintang, persons with organizational and administrative careers constituted about half of the elite. Next most numerous were persons with military careers, who made up about one third and increased in number with the passage of time. The residue is small, but it is interesting to note that among all the remaining professions education and journalism were the only ones sufficiently frequent to be of note. The nonpersuasive professions — e.g., engineering — were completely out. Lawyers, the dominant symbol specialists in stable Western elites, were here completely absent. But then lawyers have never played the same role in China as in the West. The few ideologizers included in the elite were those who could make a mass appeal.

The dominance of men of violence is an index of the intensity of revolutionary struggles. The young elite in China, seeing no stable future for themselves in the backward economy of their homeland, were expressing a self-confirming expectation. In their hopelessness of stable careers they turned to violent politics, which, in fact, ultimately destroyed the chances for stable evolution. The career opportunities outside of politics gradually narrowed, and the standard of living gradually declined. This, plus the shattering of the old society, plus the slow spread of Western stimuli, and thus political activity, to ever wider circles of the population, gradually lowered the social status of the political elite.

It is easy to assume that the transfer of power from Kuomintang to Communists has been the key factor in the decline of upper-class and the rise of lower-class personnel in the elite. As already implied, this is not the whole story. A gradual decline in the status of elite members was taking place in both parties. The final triumph of the Communists symbolized (and perhaps was partly caused by, rather than caused) the rise of the plebeians.

A pair of related trends was in operation in both the Kuomintang and the Communist Party. In the first place, the circle from which the elite were being recruited was gradually widening to include broader sections of the population. In the second place, with the chaotic condition of the Chinese economy, the members of the elite were suffering downward social mobility more often than upward. They were less well off than their parents.

On these points our data on Kuomintang members cover only the members of the first three CEC's, but even in these early committees we can see these trends in operation. The widening of the circles from which elite members were recruited is brought out in Table 10. In it we find that (omitting the individuals on whom we do not have any information) the proportion of new members joining the CEC whose social status was lower-middle class or lower class went from 10.0 per cent in 1924 to 17.6 per cent in 1926 and to 31.3 per cent in 1929. Thus, in the course of five years, the plebeians who succeeded in reaching the CEC rose from one in ten to one in three.

*Table 10*

SOCIAL STATUS OF NEW MEMBERS OF KUOMINTANG CEC

|  | 1924 | | 1926 | | 1929 | |
|---|---|---|---|---|---|---|
|  | No. | % | No. | % | No. | % |
| Lower or lower-middle class | 2 | 10.0 | 3 | 17.6 | 5 | 31.3 |
| Upper, upper-middle, or middle-middle class | 18 | 90.0 | 14 | 82.4 | 11 | 68.7 |
| Total known | 20 | 100.0 | 17 | 100.0 | 16 | 100.0 |
| Don't know | 4 | | 6 | | 7 | |
| Total | 24 | | 23 | | 23 | |

On the whole these plebeians had plebeian fathers, and the men of higher social status had fathers of higher social status. However, the sons were having trouble maintaining their social status, or at least their income. More of them found that their incomes and statuses were declining rather than rising.

When we study an elite, we normally expect and assume that we are dealing with a group which has experienced upward social mobility. Our sample is a preselected sample of successful men. The incompetent, the lazy, the ineffectual are excluded from it. Except where status is strictly hereditary, we may take it for granted that some of those in the top positions have risen from lower ranks, and so we may assume that, among the elite, upward social mobility is more common than downward mobility. In some sense this must have been true in China, too. The men in our sample had reached the top political positions, while few of their fathers had such exalted status. But in another sense the political elite was not rising. As they rose politically, they were losing out by other standards of status. Whereas, normally, political advancement means economic and social advancement also, in the shattered economy and society of modern China the reverse has been the case. The men who turned to politics were men who were otherwise on the skids. Their rise even to the top positions in politics did not altogether check their financial decline. Of the members of the first three CEC's of the Kuomintang 57 per cent had the same general social status as their fathers (see Table 11). Of the remaining 43 per cent only 18 per cent had moved up, while 25 per cent had moved down.

*Table 11*
SOCIAL MOBILITY OF MEMBERS, 1924–1929 KUOMINTANG CEC

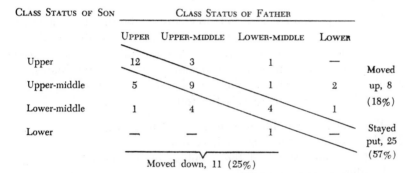

The Chinese political elite was a socially declining and discomfited elite. That this was true of the Communists is not surprising. Communist leaders are often recruited from deprived strata of the middle class. In China, however, what was true of the Communists was true of both major parties. We may follow the trend for Politburo members from 1921 right through to 1945. When we do so, the tendencies that we saw in operation in the Kuomintang CEC during the five years from 1924 to 1929 became much more apparent and may be seen to go further. In Table 12 we compare the men who joined the Politburo in 1929 and before with those who first joined after. Those whose fathers were peasants or proletarians rose from one third to two thirds of those on whom we have information. Specifically, what was taking place was a rise in peasant leadership. The rise of Mao to power and the emergence of Soviet areas in the hinterland were accompanied by the replacement of intellectuals of middle-class and upper-class backgrounds by sons of peasants. This trend we wish to explore further, but before we do so, let us note the role of the army in this change.

*Table 12*
OCCUPATIONS OF FATHERS OF POLITBUROCRATS

|  | Date First Joined Politburo | |
| --- | --- | --- |
| Father's Occupation | 1921–1928 | 1931–1945 |
| Peasant | 3 | 7 |
| Proletarian | 1 | 1 |
| Scholar, scholar-<br>official | 4 | 1 |
| Landlord | 3 | 2 |
| Merchant | 1 | 1 |
| Total known | 12 | 12 |
| Don't know | 15 | 3 |
| Total | 27 | 15 |

The army played a central role in changing the social characteristics of the political elite. The complex picture may be summarized in the statement that the decline of the manipulators and the rise of men of violence was simultaneously the decline of the old high-status, educated, governing class and the rise of new social strata. Spelled out more fully the picture reveals the following facts:

1. The number of military men in the elite grew.
2. The economic status of soldiers rose.
3. The economic status of the members of scholar-official governing families severely declined.
4. The army brought less educated men into the elite.
5. The army elite, although largely upper-class in origin, provided a channel by which even the son of a peasant could reach the top.
6. The army recruited in the more disorganized, less Westernized areas of China.

While we note each of these facts separately, let us keep in mind the central point which all of them illustrate: that the rise of the soldier broadened and democratized the recruitment of the Chinese elite. At the same time it helped undermine the traditional fabric of Chinese society and the potential for humane and stable development. These central facts may be seen in the development of both the Kuomintang and the Communist Party into military movements.

1. The increase in the number of soldiers in the Kuomintang CEC may be observed in Table 8. Ever since 1929 the proportion of military men in the CEC has remained above one third. Undoubtedly the 1929 peak in the percentage of committeemen with primarily military

backgrounds was closely related to the growing power of Chiang Kai-shek. In the earliest committees personal relations with Dr. Sun Yat-sen had been important. Thereafter, the characteristics of various committees seem to have been closely related to factors in the career of Chiang Kai-shek. By 1929 Chiang's military position was strong, but his apparatus for political control (both in party and government) had not yet been perfected. Military men, therefore, dominated the 1929 committee, and they continued to be a major force thereafter.

In similar fashion in the Communist Party the rise of military men may be tied to the rise of Mao and his policy of peasant revolt and guerrilla bases. In both parties the intellectuals (such as Sun Fo and Ch'en Tu-hsiu) came first, and the soldiers (such as Chiang and Chu Te) came later.

2. Through the army and the opportunities for economic exploitation which it yielded, many of the Kuomintang military elite succeeded in becoming wealthy. The troubled waters of China's economy may have been a bleak prospect for the ambitious young technician, but they yielded good fishing for the soldier. Needless to say, this source of income was not usually his military salary. Only four of seventeen soldiers on the CEC (about whom we have information) relied primarily on their military salaries. Two more depended on party salaries, while six lived mostly on rent and three more mostly on investments.

From these extracurricular activities they managed to obtain a higher income than their colleagues in the elite who were not soldiers (see Table 13). This was not because their fathers were richer. The

## Table 13
### FINANCIAL STATUS OF SOLDIERS AND OTHER MEMBERS OF KUOMINTANG CEC, 1924–1929

| Financial Status | Soldiers | Others |
|---|---|---|
| Upper | 7 | 8 |
| Upper-middle | 8 | 11 |
|  | 15 | 19 |
| Middle | 1 | 3 |
| Lower-middle | 2 | 8 |
| Lower | — | 4 |
|  | 3 | 15 |
| Total known | 18 | 34 |
| Don't know | 5 | 13 |
| Total | 23 | 47 |

wealth of their fathers was almost on a par with that of the rest of the elite. They became more prosperous than their nonmilitary colleagues who were suffering an economic decline. Only the soldiers did not suffer this decline.

3. We noted earlier the surprising fact that the Kuomintang CEC members were on the whole poorer than their fathers. Since this is not true for the military, it is even more strikingly true for party organizers —the other major segment of the elite. Table 14 suggests what was happening to the established elite strata of China, from among which the organizers were recruited. They were caught in a squeeze from which even the most successful were seldom able to escape.

### Table 14
MOBILITY OF SOLDIERS AND OTHER KUOMINTANG ELITE MEMBERS

| Son's Financial Status Compared with Father's | Soldiers | Other CEC Members |
| --- | --- | --- |
| Higher | 5 | 3 |
| Same | 10 | 15 |
| Lower | 2 | 9 |

4. This squeeze, as we have said, affected the educated scholarly groups from which China had long drawn her political leadership. The soldiers were educated, in that they had attended military schools and sometimes other schools too, but they did not have the liberal education of their colleagues. Sixty-five per cent of the soldiers on the Kuomintang CEC had studied only in China as compared with 30 per cent of the nonsoldiers. Furthermore, the soldiers did not come from the scholar-official families that had provided much of China's political leadership in the past. These carriers of Chinese culture scorned the military life. Ten Kuomintang CEC members had scholar fathers. Of these only one was a soldier. Similarly, in the Communist Party a number of the early intellectuals in the party came from families in the scholar-official tradition, but the later military leaders came from other — often peasant — backgrounds.

5. The peasants did not scorn the army. For them entry in the army represented not a comedown but a rise in social status.

Fei Hsiao-tung, on the basis of his experience in the study of communities in many different parts of China, remarked:
"In a village where farms are small and wealth is accumulated slowly, there are very few chances for a landless man to become a landowner or for a petty owner to become a large landowner. It takes generations to climb the ladder of success simply by frugality; and during these long

years the prospect of periodic upsets, from natural sources such as famine or from personal misfortunes such as illness and death must always be faced. . . . It is not going too far to say that in agriculture there is no way really to get ahead."

A major function of military roles in Chinese culture is the provision of alternative possibilities to individuals of ambition who desire to improve their social, political, and economic fortunes but who realize that humble tilling of the soil, thrift, and virtue do not often bring success.[103]

As we shall note later, the Chinese Communist Army certainly provided a channel of social mobility for the peasants. To some extent the Kuomintang army did too; all three members of the first three CEC's who came from peasant backgrounds were soldiers.

6. We have no later figures on fathers' occupations for the CEC, but all through, from 1924 to 1945, we find that the origin of the soldiers was the hinterland. This was also, we might add, the area of famine and disorganization in which the Communists recruited. (See Table 15.)

The coastal areas, where big cities, trade, commerce, and Western influence were dominant, led in providing the organizers for the Kuomintang. In particular this was true of the three provinces, Kwangtung, Chekiang, and Kiangsu. Canton is in Kwangtung (with Hong Kong near by); Shanghai is in Kiangsu with Chekiang close by. Even though Chekiang was the home of Chiang Kai-shek and a center of his machine, organizers rather than soldiers came from there, as they did from Kwangtung and Kiangsu too.

On the other hand, the Yangtze basin and the southern interior provinces of Yünnan and Kwangsi provided the soldiers.

The same ecological division between military leaders and others prevailed in the Communist leadership. As we shall see more fully later, the early intellectual leaders of the party tended to come from around Shanghai, but the soldiers who led the party in its later phase as a military movement tended to come from the Yangtze basin.

The ecology of the elite was thus more than a geographic matter. The geographic origins of the organizers and soldiers index their political character as cosmopolitans, on the one hand, or men of more limited backgrounds, on the other. The essential point to be noted is that in both parties civil war promoted the political soldier, and thereby a plebeianization of the elite. The scholar-politicians with a humanistic heritage — despite political skills that often kept them in office as

---

[103] Fei Hsiao-tung and Chang Chih-i, *Earthbound China* (Chicago: University of Chicago Press, 1945), p. 277, cited in Morton H. Fried, "Military Status in Chinese Society," *American Journal of Sociology*, LVII, No. 4 (1952), pp. 349-350.

individuals — were crushed as a social stratum marked by respect and a continuing tradition.

A gradual disintegration of Chinese society was taking place. The Imperial elite of scholar-officials who were sons of scholar-officials had given way by the early 1920's to a new elite of young, Western-educated, Western-oriented revolutionaries. Many of them were still sons of scholar-officials, although many were also sons of businessmen or landlords. But they themselves, although often educated for a business or professional career, became, above all, party politicians. Their incursion into revolutionary politics stemmed from frustration, the frustration of a disorganized colonial economy; but politics did nothing to check that frustration, and indeed made it worse. As time went on,

*Table 15*

BIRTHPLACES OF KUOMINTANG CENTRAL EXECUTIVE COMMITTEEMEN
(IN PERCENTAGES)

| Province of Birth | Soldiers | Others | All CEC Members |
|---|---|---|---|
| Coastal provinces | | | |
| Kwangtung | 14.6 | 15.2 | 15.0 |
| Chekiang | 10.7 | 14.1 | 12.9 |
| Kiangsu | 5.8 | 9.8 | 8.4 |
| Total from main centers of Western influence | 31.1 | 39.1 | 36.3 |
| Fukien | 2.9 | 2.7 | 2.8 |
| Shantung | 1.9 | 2.7 | 2.4 |
| Hopeh | 3.9 | 4.9 | 4.5 |
| Total from coastal provinces | 39.8 | 49.4 | 46.0 |
| Yangtze Basin | | | |
| Hunan | 9.7 | 8.2 | 8.7 |
| Szechwan | 9.7 | 3.8 | 5.9 |
| Hupeh | 5.8 | 3.3 | 4.2 |
| Anhwei | 6.8 | 1.6 | 3.5 |
| Total from Yangtze Basin | 32.0 | 16.9 | 22.3 |
| South interior | | | |
| Yunnan | 3.9 | .5 | 1.7 |
| Kwangsi | 4.9 | 2.2 | 3.1 |
| Total from south interior | 8.8 | 2.7 | 4.8 |
| Total from areas listed | 80.6 | 69.0 | 73.1 |

their personal lot became worse more often than it became better. At the same time, the movement they had started and the widening impact of Western thought began to stir new strata of the population. Lower-middle-class and peasant elements began to make their way into both Kuomintang and Communist Party leadership. This they did partly through their role as men of violence. With the deterioration of social order in China, the army became an increasingly important channel to leadership. (It was an extraordinarily important channel throughout the period.) The social composition of the highest ranks of the army excluded scholars and admitted a few peasants, and so its growing role facilitated the destruction of the old elite and the plebeianization of Chinese political leadership. In both parties the rootless but educated professional revolutionary became the dominant leadership type.

## Differences

Despite the common revolutionary character of both elites, some differences existed between the men who came to lead the Kuomintang and the men who came to lead the Communist Party. There were also differences between the major factions in the Kuomintang: left, right and followers of Chiang. And as we have already noted, there were differences between the earlier and later phases of the quarter century we are studying.

The most striking difference between the Kuomintang and the Communist Party elites was in their urban versus rural orientations. Both parties, as we noted, recruited at first among upper-class and middle-class circles and later also among lower-middle-class circles. However, the characteristic Communist leader was the son of a landlord or rich peasant, whereas the characteristic Kuomintang leader was the son of a merchant or other urban person.

The Marxian prognosis of proletarian revolution has never been confirmed. The revolt against the businessman has indeed occurred, but it has found its greatest strength, not in industrialized societies where proletarian masses were highly organized and strong, but in backward peasant economies. After the First World War backward Russia proved "the weakest link" of the capitalist chain. There a small coterie of petty bourgeois intellectuals led a revolution in a country where 80 per cent of the population was peasant. Since then the pattern has been repeated in other parts of the world.

In China, likewise, we find a Communist leadership that started out as a combination of rural rebels and urban professionals overthrowing a party whose leadership was distinctly business-class. In the

Communist Party leadership, there were few proletarians and also few sons of merchants. At first there was a goodly sprinkling of men from professional or intellectual families — men who gave the initial ideological impetus. Along with these, and increasingly dominant, however, was a group consisting of sons of peasants or sons of landlords. In this sense the Chinese Communist movement was indeed an agrarian revolution. It may have picked up and captured, or been captured by, the ideology of proletarian communism as interpreted in Moscow, but its social dynamic may be seen in the dominance of rural characters and urban intellectuals in the Communist Party; whereas business-class persons dominated the Kuomintang.

As we see in Table 16, merchants' sons were almost half of the

### Table 16
#### RURAL-URBAN DISTRIBUTION OF ELITES AS ESTIMATED
#### BY FATHER'S OCCUPATION

|  | Kuomintang CEC 1924–1929 | | Politburos | | Communist CC 1945 | |
|---|---|---|---|---|---|---|
|  | No. | % | No. | % | No. | % |
| Landlords | 14 |  | 5 |  | 8 |  |
| Peasants | 3 |  | 10 |  | 11 |  |
| Total rural | 17 | 38 | 15 | 65 | 19 | 73 |
| Scholars, officials* | 6 |  | 4 |  | 3 |  |
| Merchants | 22 |  | 2 |  | 2 |  |
| Proletarians | — |  | 2 |  | 2 |  |
| Total urban | 28 | 62 | 8 | 35 | 7 | 27 |
| Total known | 45 | 100 | 23 | 100 | 26 | 100 |
| Don't know | 25 |  | 19 |  | 18 |  |
| Total | 70 |  | 42 |  | 44 |  |

* Not elsewhere included.

identifiable members of the Kuomintang CEC's through 1929. (We lack later data on the Kuomintang.) In the same period they constitued 8 per cent of the Politburo members and remained at this low level later (cf. Table 11). Even if we add the proletarians to the businessmen, the entire group of those stemming from the capitalist economy was only one sixth of the Communist leaders.

Another group that can be classified as probably urban includes sons of fathers in professions, intellectual pursuits, or other nonbusiness-type middle-class activities. One third of the early Politburos consisted of such members of the intelligentsia (cf. Table 12). At that same period men of this character were but one sixth of the Kuomintang CEC. They were thus far more prominent in the Communist movement, but they did not stay so long. Just as in the Soviet Politburo, men of rural origins replaced these intellectuals, who had given the movement much of its original stimulus.

### Table 17
RURAL-URBAN DISTRIBUTION OF POLITBURO

|  | 1921–1928 | 1931–1945 |
|---|---|---|
| Rural | 6 | 9 |
| Urban | 5 | 3 |
| Total known | 11 | 12 |
| Don't know | 16 | 3 |
| Total | 27 | 15 |

Even from the beginning, however, half of the Communist leadership, as contrasted to only one third of that of the Kuomintang, was rural in origin. With the triumph of Mao and his peasant orientation, that half rose to three quarters. (See Table 17.)

We cannot trace trends in the Kuomintang as well as we have those in the Communist Party since our data run out after 1929. But if we look at the trends from 1924 through 1929, we find that, just as the Communist Party was growing more rural with time, the Kuomintang was becoming more urban and more of a business-class party. In the first three Kuomintang CEC's the members whose fathers were merchants went up from 31 per cent to 47 to 64 per cent of those on whom we have information (cf. Table 18). At the same time, although not quite so smoothly, the proportion of those whose own main sources of

### Table 18
RURAL-URBAN DISTRIBUTION: NEW MEMBERS
KUOMINTANG CEC, 1924–1929

|  | 1924 | 1926 | 1929 |
|---|---|---|---|
| Landlords' sons | 7 | 4 | 3 |
| Peasants' sons | — | 1 | 2 |
| Total rural | 7 | 5 | 5 |
| Scholars', officials' sons* | 4 | 2 | — |
| Merchants' sons | 5 | 8 | 9 |
| Proletarians' sons | — | — | — |
| Total urban | 9 | 10 | 9 |
| Total known | 16 | 15 | 14 |
| Don't know | 8 | 8 | 9 |
| Total | 24 | 23 | 23 |

* Not elsewhere included.

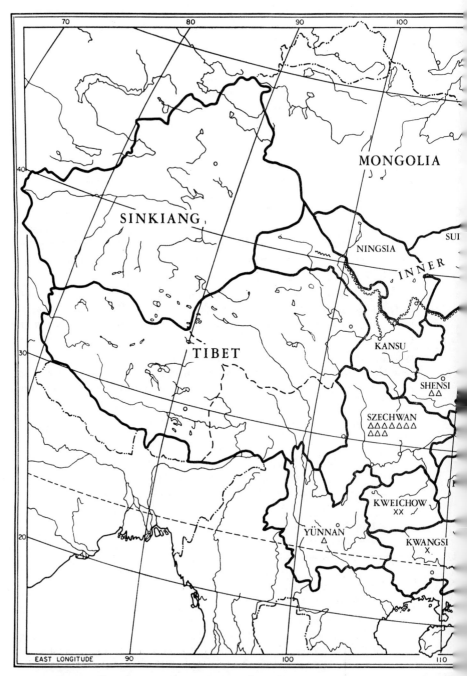

Fig. 1. *Distribution of Kuomintang Central Executive Committee compared with that of general population.*

DIFFERENCE BETWEEN PERCENTAGE OF TOTAL POPULATION
AND PERCENTAGE OF C. E. C. MEMBERS COMING FROM
EACH PROVINCE

△ = UNDERREPRESENTATION BY 1/2 PERCENTAGE
POINT OR 2.25 MILLION PEOPLE

X = OVERREPRESENTATION BY 1/2 PERCENTAGE
POINT OR 2.25 MILLION PEOPLE

SCALE

0   100   200   300   400   500 MILES

0      200     400     600   KILOMETERS
BONNE'S EQUAL-AREA PROJECTION

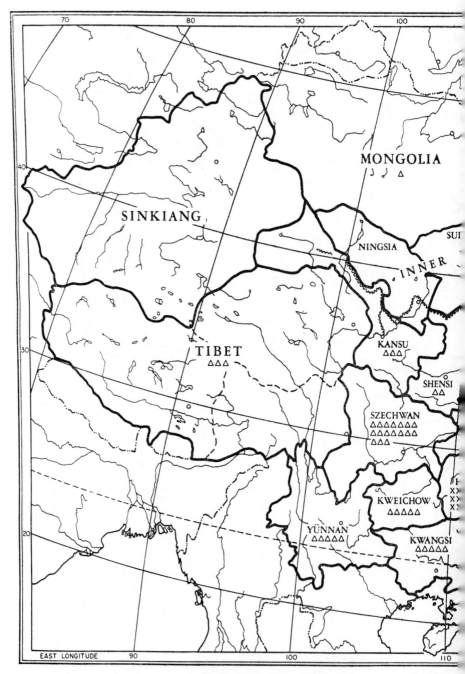

Fig. 2.  *Distribution of Politburo members compared with that of general population.*

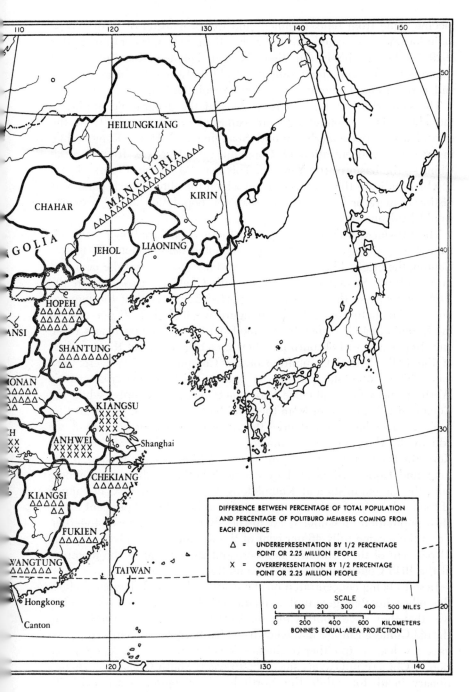

DIFFERENCE BETWEEN PERCENTAGE OF TOTAL POPULATION
AND PERCENTAGE OF POLITBURO MEMBERS COMING FROM
EACH PROVINCE

Δ  =  UNDERREPRESENTATION BY 1/2 PERCENTAGE
       POINT OR 2.25 MILLION PEOPLE

X  =  OVERREPRESENTATION BY 1/2 PERCENTAGE
       POINT OR 2.25 MILLION PEOPLE

SCALE

0    100   200   300   400   500 MILES

0      200      400      600   KILOMETERS

BONNE'S EQUAL-AREA PROJECTION

income came from rents declined, and the proportion of those whose main income was earned effected a rise. If these trends continued after 1929, as they probably did, then the split between Kuomintang and Communists became increasingly a split between business-oriented and rural-oriented young professional revolutionists.

The same thing stands out if we look at the geographic origins of the elites. The Kuomintang elite came more extensively from the coastal areas, particularly around Shanghai and Hong Kong, while the greatest concentration of Communist leaders was from Central China — the basin of the Yangtze. This may be seen in Figures 1 and 2, which indicate the provinces from which the elite of each party was distinctly more or less numerous than the population of the province would lead one to expect.

The provinces immediately around the main international ports are Kwangtung, Kiangsu, and Chekiang. As noted before, Hong Kong and Canton, the original home of the Kuomintang government, lie near and in Kwantung; Shanghai in Kiangsu with Chekiang close by. In the 1926 census these three provinces reported 22 per cent of the population of China. In contrast to that figure we find that 36 per cent of the Kuomintang CEC members came from those three provinces while only 19 per cent of Politburo members and 14 per cent of the members of the 1945 Central Committee of the Communist Party were born there. The Kuomintang drew its leaders from those areas where Western and urban influence had penetrated most deeply, while the Communists came rather from the rural hinterland. (See Table 19.)

To a somewhat lesser degree the same pattern may be seen if we add to the three provinces immediately around Shanghai and Hong Kong the three other coastal provinces of China proper: Fukien, Shantung, and Hopeh. Because these extend into the northern area, where both the Communists and Kuomintang were weak at first, not much of the leadership of either party came from them. Yet 40 per cent of the 1926 population of China lived in the six coastal provinces together. From them came fully 46 per cent of the Kuomintang leaders, but only 21 per cent of the Politburo members and 23 per cent of the members of the 1945 Communist Central Committee.

Besides being concentrated on the coast and around the major cities, the other notable geographic characteristic of Kuomintang leaders was that they were South Chinese. As the maps indicate, the heart of the old Chinese Empire in the north — Shantung, Honan, and Hopeh — gave few leaders to either of the new revolutionary elites. An examination of Chinese upheavals since 1850 reveals South China as a revolutionary incubator, while the North has been more conservative. To begin with, the southern regions, which were last conquered by the Manchus and which were furthest from the center of Manchu culture in Peking, were also the regions that had experienced longest contact with the West. Moreover, large numbers of southern Chinese had emigrated overseas, where they came directly under foreign influences.

*Table 19*

ECOLOGICAL DISTRIBUTION OF PARTY ELITES

| | Percent-age of China's Total Population of 1926* | Birthplaces | | |
| --- | --- | --- | --- | --- |
| | | of CEC Members (Percentage) | of Politburo Members (Percentage) | of Communist CC 1945 (Percentage) |
| South and Central Coast | | | | |
| Kwangtung | 7.6 | 15.0 | 4.8 | 2.3 |
| Fukien | 3.0 | 2.8 | — | 6.8 |
| Chekiang | 5.0 | 12.9 | 2.4 | — |
| Kiangsu | 7.1 | 8.4 | 11.9 | 11.4 |
| Central interior | | | | |
| Hunan | 8.4 | 8.7 | 19.0 | 27.3 |
| Szechwan | 10.7 | 5.9 | 2.4 | 13.6 |
| Hupeh | 5.9 | 4.2 | 11.9 | 11.4 |
| Anhwei | 4.2 | 3.5 | 9.5 | 2.3 |
| Kiangsi | 5.7 | 5.2 | 2.4 | 4.6 |
| South interior | | | | |
| Kwangsi | 2.5 | 3.1 | — | 2.3 |
| Kweichow | 2.3 | 3.5 | — | 2.3 |
| Yunnan | 2.3 | 1.7 | — | — |
| North | | | | |
| Shantung | 7.1 | 2.4 | 2.4 | 2.3 |
| Hopeh | 8.0 | 4.5 | — | — |
| Honan | 7.3 | .4 | — | — |
| Shansi | 2.5 | 3.1 | 2.4 | 6.8 |
| Shensi | 3.6 | 2.8 | 2.4 | 2.3 |
| Kansu | 1.5 | 1.4 | — | — |
| Tibet | 1.3 | 1.1 | — | — |
| Sinkiang | .5 | .4 | — | — |
| Mongolia | ‡ | 1.4 | — | — |
| Manchuria | 9.9 | 2.8 | — | 4.5 |
| Abroad | — | 1.1 | — | — |
| Don't know | — | 3.8 | 28.6 | — |
| Number | | (287) | (42) | (44) |

* Post office estimate. *The China Yearbook,* 1931, p. 2.
‡ Not included in estimate. In other estimates Mongolia's population is a little over 2 per cent of China's.

It was from this group, indeed, that Sun Yat-sen won his first revolutionary support. There is some coincidence of revolution and areas of flood and famine, notably in the Yangtze Valley, where a preponderance of the Communist elite originated. Thus there may be more than symbolism in the fact that Kuomintang centers of origin looked outward, while many leaders of communism rose from areas of misery. Yet the region of "China's sorrow" along the Yellow River yielded few Communist leaders.

The geographic distribution of elite members shows not only the influence of certain general regional differences, but also the impact of party organization. Disproportionate numbers of leaders come from certain specific provinces where well-developed machines took hold and assumed national importance. Just as there has been the Missouri factor in recent American politics, so there was a Chekiang factor in Kuomintang politics. Chekiang was the home of Chiang Kai-shek, and as his clique of military men gained power, the number of native sons of Chekiang entering the Kuomintang CEC gradually rose from one in 1924 — before Chiang became a CEC member — to nineteen in 1945, or the largest number from any one province. For similar reasons Kwangtung, the original home of the Kuomintang, was consistently overrepresented. Also the strong representation of Hunan and of Kiangsi on the Communist Party Politburos is in part the result of the development of strong Communist organizations (soviets) in those two areas.

Besides differences in geographic distribution and differences in rural-urban distribution, two other differences distinguish the Kuomintang and Communist leaderships. For one, the Politburocrats were somewhat younger than the Kuomintang CEC members. The former typically joined the Politburo at about age thirty or shortly thereafter, while the latter typically reached CEC membership in their early forties (cf. Table 6). Thus it took longer to reach recognition in the Kuomintang than in the Communist Party.

The elites of these parties also differed somewhat in their educational backgrounds. While it is not possible to make any flat generalization that one group was better or worse educated than the other, they did receive their educations in somewhat different places and types of institutions.

The Communist leadership contained a few more individuals with no formal higher education, though even among the Communists these were but a sprinkling. There were two such individuals on the Politburo (or 5 per cent) and three such individuals on the 1945 Central Committee of the Communist Party (or 7 per cent). In the

Kuomintang CEC's there were only two such individuals (or one per cent).

On the other hand, a larger proportion of the Communist leadership than the Kuomintang leadership had gone abroad for some of their higher education. The main reason for this is that much of the Communist leadership was Russian trained. Only 5 per cent of the Kuomintang CEC members had studied in Russia, while 48 per cent of the Politburo members and 57 per cent of the 1945 Communist Party Central Committee members had done so. (The Soviet universities that have specialized in training the Communist Far Eastern leadership are indicated in Table 20.)

*Table 20*
SOVIET UNIVERSITIES ATTENDED BY COMMUNIST CC MEMBERS

| University | Number |
|---|---|
| University of Moscow | 1 |
| Toilers of the Far East | 7 |
| Sun Yat-sen University | 6 |
| Red Army Academy | 4 |
| Lenin Institute | 2 |
| Don't know | 7 |

While Communist training in Russia was the most common kind of foreign education, it is not that type of training alone that accounts for the extensive foreign study of the Communist leaders. As can be seen from Table 5, many of the Communists, as well as many of the Kuomintang leaders, studied in universities in capitalist countries — many of them, in fact, in countries of the West.

There was, however, an interesting difference in the countries in which they studied. Those who studied in France, especially those under the worker-student plan, tended to go left, whereas those who studied in the United States or Japan seemed to go right. From the very beginning those who had been students in France formed an important core of the revolutionary movement in the Far East. The first leader of the Chinese Communist Party, Ch'en Tu-hsiu, was one of the group of French-trained intellectuals who gave an important start to the development of communism in the Far East. It might be noted that among this group are not only leaders of the Chinese Communist Party, but also such other Far Eastern Communist leaders as Ho Chi Minh. Obviously, mere familiarity and contact with the West did not assure acceptance of Western ideas.

Modernization and democratization were too far from the realities of the Chinese situation to instill in the Chinese students who met them abroad a placid acceptance of the status quo. The contrast between the aspirations imported from the West and the possibilities actually open in the Chinese situation was so glaring as to turn all of them revolutionary. Certain social determinants such as family background and educational experiences did apparently influence the brand of revolution the young uprooted politician turned to, but the social differences are so much smaller than the similarities that we may suggest that the crucial difference separating the Communist leaders from the Kuomintang leaders was not a social one so much as a personal psychological one. The Kuomintang, being established in power, got the careerists; the Communists got the ideologists. Few of the Communists had any careers or sources of income outside the movement. For a long time theirs was distinctly the harder lot. The corruption in the Kuomintang ultimately became notorious and was, perhaps, a major force in driving millions of Chinese into the arms of the Communists. It would be misleading to view the conflict as one between social stability and revolution, and certainly false to view it as a struggle between democracy and authoritarianism. Both movements were expressions of a prevailing malaise and disorganization. Both movements were ruthless, but the Communists were more successful in tapping the energies of those who sought moral justification for their activities, while the Kuomintang drew those with privatized attitudes.

We do not imply that in this respect the Kuomintang was a single undifferentiated whole. On the contrary, many conflicting tendencies within the Kuomintang may be differentiated. Specifically our data enable us to compare three tendencies: the left, the right, and the military faction around Chiang. The way in which the members of the various cliques were grouped into these three tendencies is indicated in Table 21. The definition of these tendencies changes with time. In 1924 "left" meant quite a radical orientation. By 1945 "left" meant anything left of Chiang. The definition of a tendency is in terms of the politics of that day, but allowing for this fact only strengthens and reinforces the conclusions which follow.

The shifts in power and composition of these three tendencies reveal how the Kuomintang gradually lost its popular touch. For one thing the left wing gradually lost out in the jockeying for power, as may be seen in Table 22. In the 1924, 1926, and 1929 Central Executive Committees combined, the left-wingers were almost half the total membership — thirty-four leftists, to thirty-six rightists and pro-Chiang members. Of the leftists, perhaps six were Communists, but even without those the leftists clearly played a major role in the early committees. By 1945 the three wings of the committee were fairly evenly divided, with the pro-Chiang members slightly more numerous than the others. By 1945 only a quarter of the left-wingers of the 1924, 1926, and 1929 committees were still on the committee, while 40 per cent of

### Table 21
#### GROUPING OF CLIQUES

*Left*
- (7) Kuomintang left
- (8) Sun Fo clique
- (11) Reorganization clique
- (16) The Middle Group
- (4) CP Rebels
- (28) European-American clique
- (106) Local cliques

*Pro-Chiang*
- (12) Party veterans—supporters of Chiang
- (33) Whampoa regeneration clique*
- (32) Direct affiliates*
- (9) Quasi-direct affiliates*
- (16) Officials (military)
- (2) Naval clique
- (14) Political science clique
- (10) Northeastern (Manchurian) Army clique
- (10) Overseas
- (9) Officials

*Right*
- (117) CC clique
- (10) Chu Chia-hua clique

* These military men were included under the Chiang group in spite of individual personal views (possibly more to the left) because at that time they supported Chiang as a group.

Except in a minority of individual cases the clique affiliation was used to determine political position.

### Table 22
#### POLITICAL COMPOSITION OF KUOMINTANG CEC's

|              | 1924–1929 | | 1945 | |
| --- | --- | --- | --- | --- |
|              | No. | % | No. | % |
| Left         | 34 | 48.6 | 71 | 31.9 |
| Pro-Chiang   | 21 | 30.0 | 79 | 35.4 |
| Right        | 15 | 21.4 | 73 | 32.7 |
| Total        | 70 | 100.0 | 223 | 100.0 |

## *Table 23*
### CONTINUATION IN OFFICE OF MEMBERS OF DIFFERENT TENDENCIES*

A.  PERCENTAGE OF 1924, 1926, 1929 CEC MEMBERS WHO HELD OFFICE IN EACH CEC

| Tendency | Number of Individuals | Percentage Holding Office in Each Committee | | | | | |
|---|---|---|---|---|---|---|---|
| | | 1924 | 1926 | 1929 | 1931 | 1935 | 1945 |
| Left | 34 | 32.4 | 85.3 | 29.4 | 14.7 | 35.3 | 26.5 |
| Pro-Chiang | 21 | 14.3 | 19.1 | 95.2 | 90.5 | 76.2 | 66.7 |
| Right | 15 | 66.7 | 20.0 | 40.0 | 40.0 | 60.0 | 40.0 |

B.  PERCENTAGE OF 1945 CEC MEMBERS WHO HELD OFFICE IN EACH EARLIER CEC

| Left | 71 | 5.6 | 9.9 | 9.9 | 8.5 | 40.9 | 100.0 |
|---|---|---|---|---|---|---|---|
| Pro-Chiang | 79 | 2.5 | 2.5 | 11.4 | 13.9 | 44.3 | 100.0 |
| Right | 73 | 1.4 | 1.4 | 9.6 | 9.6 | 32.9 | 100.0 |

* The political positions of individuals were not always the same in every committee, and also the criteria of Left and Right changed over the years. All Western Hills members were later either Left (4) or pro-Chiang (2). Seven of the earlier pro-Chiang group were later CC clique; of the pro-Chiang Right Wing in 1945, only one earlier Left was later listed as farther right, i.e., pro-Chiang. No earlier pro-Chiang men were later Left. To minimize the effect of these changes of classification and to demonstrate the general shift to the right independent of them, the classification of individuals is kept constant in Section A of the table, but not in Section B.

the rightists and two thirds of the Chiang supporters had retained their posts (cf. Table 23). Looking in the other direction — that is, from 1945 back — we find that the newer members were Chiang supporters or rightists, while the leftists were to some extent an "old guard." Thus 10 per cent of the leftists had been on the 1926 committee, as against only 3 per cent of the Chiang supporters and one per cent of the rightists. These old-guard leftists who retained their posts while their influence was gradually fading included such prominent individuals as Mme. Sun Yat-sen, Ku Meng-yü, Kan Nai-kuang, and Sun Fo.

The tendency of the left to become an old guard may also be seen in Table 24, which compares the ages of the members of the different factions. In 1929 the mean age of the leftists and rightists was about the same, although the Chiang supporters were somewhat younger, partly because they were largely soldiers (who can achieve prominence in youth) and partly because they were the rising revolutionary faction, many of whose members were just joining the committee. But in 1929 no left-right difference in age existed. By 1945, sixteen years later, a remarkable change had taken place. The leftists were largely fairly old men. The younger men who were just joining the committee were more often rightists. In sixteen years the average leftist had become seven years older than the average rightist.

### Table 24
#### AVERAGE AGE OF KUOMINTANG FACTION MEMBERS

|  | Members of 1924, 1926, and 1929 CEC's: Average Age in 1929 | Members of 1945 CEC: Average Age in 1945 |
|---|---|---|
| Left | 46.2 | 54.1 |
| Pro-Chiang | 41.2 | 51.7 |
| Right | 46.8 | 48.5 |

At the same time, as the new blood was going into the right rather than the left, the Chiang faction had moved further to the right, and the Communists and Communist sympathizers had been eliminated from the left. In other words, what was taking place between the Communist Party and the Kuomintang was a process of polarization. As so often happens when a new revolution approaches, the political and social lines grew sharper and sharper, and the middle disappeared. The individuals who strove to bridge the gap between the Kuomintang rightists at one end and the Communist leftists at the other declined in influence. Those in the center tended to move one way or the other, and — perhaps most important of all — the social characteristics of the Kuomintang and the Communist Party became more divergent.

We have already noted a growing tension between the rural and merchant groups as represented in the two parties. It remains to be noted that the struggle between left and right in the Kuomintang was a similar struggle in miniature, and that the decline of the left and the rise of the right was one of the factors that made of the Kuomintang increasingly a merchants' party and decreasingly a landlords' or rurally oriented one. Table 25 shows that on the first three Kuomintang

### Table 25
#### RURAL-URBAN DISTRIBUTION OF KUOMINTANG FACTIONS
(As ESTIMATED FROM FATHER'S OCCUPATION; 1924, 1926, 1929 CEC's)

| Origin | Left | Pro-Chiang | Right |
|---|---|---|---|
| Rural | 12 | 3 | 2 |
| Urban | 10 | 11 | 7 |
| Don't know | 12 | 7 | 6 |
| Total | 34 | 21 | 15 |

CEC's 35 per cent of the leftists were rural, as against 14 per cent of the Chiang supporters and 13 per cent of the rightists. In general, the CEC drew members of upper-class or at least middle-class origins (Table 26). Their fathers for the most part were wealthy landlords,

*Table 26*

OCCUPATIONS OF FATHERS OF CEC MEMBERS
IN DIFFERENT FACTIONS, 1924, 1926, 1929

|  | Left | Pro-Chiang | Right |
|---|---|---|---|
| Wealthy landlord, or scholar-landlord | 6 | 2 | 2 |
| Scholar-official | — | 1 | 2 |
| Scholar | 2 | — | 1 |
| Merchant-scholar or wealthy merchant | 3 | 3 | 1 |
| Other landlords | 3 | 1 | — |
| Other merchants | 5 | 7 | 3 |
| Professional revolutionary | 1 | — | 1 |
| Wealthy peasant | — | — | — |
| Other peasant | 3 | — | — |
| Don't know | 11 | 7 | 5 |
| Total | 34 | 21 | 15 |

scholars, or merchants. At the same time we see (in Table 27) that the rightists who, through the years, looked to Chiang for leadership, had a higher social status than either the leftists or Chiang's personal clique. Whereas one quarter of the Chiang clique on whom we have informa-

*Table 27*

SOCIAL STATUS, MEMBERS OF KUOMINTANG FACTIONS, 1924, 1926, 1929

| Status | Left | Right | Pro-Chiang |
|---|---|---|---|
| Upper | 12 | 9 | 7 |
| Upper-middle | 8 | 3 | 4 |
| Lower-middle | 4 | 3 | 1 |
| Lower | 1 | 1 | — |
| Total known | 25 | 16 | 12 |
| Don't know | 9 | 5 | 3 |
| Total | 34 | 21 | 15 |

tion had lower- or lower-middle-class parents, and whereas one fifth of the leftists on whom we have information came from such modest backgrounds, this was true for only one rightist out of twelve. Thus the right wing lacked the small popular leaven which the other factions had. In the early Kuomintang, and presumably later too, the left was the faction that gave expression to China's agrarian problems, and the right was the faction of urban vested interests. In the long run it was the right which came to lead the party.

The Chiang clique showed an interesting in-between tendency.

They were urban, but of lower status than the right, and of lower status, even, than the left. They were the faction of the newly politicized and disoriented urban middle class. They did not come from the professional strata that had provided the Imperial elite. It was, therefore, altogether appropriate that the main channel of social mobility that this group used was the army, which in China was traditionally scorned. The difference between the relatively stable vested interests represented by the right wing and the revolutionary upstarts of the Chiang factions shows up in table after table. The financial status of the Chiang clique was often lower than that of rightists and even of the leftists (Table 28). One quarter of them had

*Table 28*
FINANCIAL STATUS, MEMBERS OF KUOMINTANG FACTIONS, 1924, 1926, 1929

| Status | Left | Pro-Chiang | Right |
|---|---|---|---|
| Upper | 7 | 5 | 3 |
| Upper-middle | 9 | 6 | 4 |
| Middle | 1 | — | 3 |
| Lower-middle | 6 | 2 | 2 |
| Lower | 1 | 3 | — |
| Total known | 24 | 16 | 12 |
| Don't know | 10 | 5 | 3 |
| Total | 34 | 21 | 15 |

lower or lower-middle incomes as against one eighth of the rightists. The fathers of the rightists were often scholars or scholar-officials, that is, men with the highest prestige in old China. Only 10 per cent of the Chiang supporters had such honorable fathers as against one quarter of the rightists (cf. Table 29). The rightists, partly following in their fathers' footsteps, also became specialists in organization and administration. The Chiang clique were military specialists. They entered a

*Table 29*
SCHOLARS' SONS IN KUOMINTANG FACTIONS, 1924, 1926, 1929

| Father's Status | Left | Pro-Chiang | Right |
|---|---|---|---|
| Scholars | 4 | 2 | 4 |
| Others | 19 | 12 | 6 |
| Don't know | 11 | 7 | 5 |
| Total | 34 | 21 | 15 |

new profession for the Chinese elite; none of their fathers had followed it; they did not continue an established pattern of family prestige (cf. Table 30). Their departure from the established lines of prestige may

*Table 30*

CAREERS OF CENTRAL EXECUTIVE COMMITTEEMEN ACCORDING TO POLITICAL AFFILIATION

| | 1924, 1926, 1929 | | | | | | 1945 | | | | | |
| | Left | | Pro-Chiang | | Right | | Left | | Pro-Chiang | | Right | |
| | No. | % | No. | % | No. | % | No. | % | No. | % | No. | % |
|---|---|---|---|---|---|---|---|---|---|---|---|---|
| Organization and administration | 16 | 47.1 | 11 | 52.4 | 10 | 66.7 | 31 | 43.7 | 24 | 30.4 | 57 | 78.1 |
| Military | 11 | 32.4 | 10 | 47.6 | 2 | 13.3 | 26 | 36.6 | 51 | 64.6 | 6 | 8.2 |
| Education | 2 | 5.9 | — | | 1 | 6.7 | 8 | 11.3 | 1 | 1.3 | 5 | 6.9 |
| Journalism | 1 | 2.9 | — | | 1 | 6.7 | 2 | 2.8 | 1 | 1.3 | 4 | 5.5 |
| Other | 1 | 2.9 | — | | — | | 2 | 2.8 | 1 | 1.3 | 1 | 1.4 |
| Don't know | 3 | 8.8 | — | | 1 | 6.7 | 2 | 2.8 | 1 | 1.3 | — | |
| Total | 34 | 100.0 | 21 | 100.0 | 15 | 100.0 | 71 | 100.0 | 79 | 100.0 | 73 | 100.0 |

Table 31

EDUCATION OF CENTRAL EXECUTIVE COMMITTEEMEN ACCORDING TO POLITICAL AFFILIATION

| | 1924, 1926, 1929 | | | | | | 1945 | | | | | |
| | Left | | Pro-Chiang | | Right | | Left | | Pro-Chiang | | Right | |
| | No. | % | No. | % | No. | % | No. | % | No. | % | No. | % |
|---|---|---|---|---|---|---|---|---|---|---|---|---|
| Japanese university | 7 | 20.6 | 4 | 19.1 | 5 | 33.3 | 10 | 14.1 | 6 | 7.6 | 14 | 19.2 |
| Japanese military | 5 | 14.7 | 6 | 28.6 | 2 | 13.3 | 2 | 2.8 | 16 | 20.3 | — | |
| Chinese university | 9 | 26.5 | 4 | 19.1 | 2 | 13.3 | 19 | 26.8 | 11 | 13.9 | 46 | 63.0 |
| Chinese military | 8 | 23.5 | 7 | 33.3 | 1 | 6.7 | 24 | 33.8 | 49 | 62.0 | 5 | 6.9 |
| Chinese classical | 6 | 17.7 | 1 | 4.8 | 3 | 20.0 | 5 | 7.0 | 1 | 1.3 | 2 | 2.7 |
| United States | 4 | 11.8 | 3 | 14.3 | 3 | 20.0 | 15 | 21.1 | 4 | 5.1 | 15 | 20.6 |
| France | 2 | 5.9 | 1 | 4.8 | 1 | 6.7 | 4 | 5.6 | 2 | 2.5 | 3 | 4.1 |
| Germany | 1 | 2.9 | 1 | 4.8 | 1 | 6.7 | 3 | 4.2 | 2 | 2.5 | 8 | 15.1 |
| Great Britain | 2 | 5.9 | 2 | 9.5 | 1 | 6.7 | 2 | 2.8 | 5 | 6.3 | 4 | 5.5 |
| Belgium | | | | | 1 | 6.7 | 1 | 1.4 | | | | |
| Soviet Union | 2 | 5.9 | — | | — | | 2 | 2.8 | 8* | 10.1 | 1* | 1.4 |
| Other | | | | | | | 1 | 1.4 | | | 2 | 2.7 |
| None | | | | | | | | | 1 | 1.3 | — | |
| Don't know | 6 | 17.7 | — | | 3 | 20.0 | 5 | 7.0 | 1 | 1.3 | 3 | 4.1 |
| Total | 34 | | 21 | | 15 | | 71 | | 79 | | 73 | |
| Total military | 9 | 26.5 | 9 | 42.9 | 2 | 13.3 | 25 | 35.2 | 57 | 72.2 | 5 | 6.9 |
| China only | 10 | 29.4 | 5 | 23.8 | 2 | 13.3 | 33 | 46.5 | 40 | 50.6 | 33 | 45.2 |

* All these men except for two under Chiang had military education. The two under Left were nonmilitary.

be seen in their education, too. The number of CEC members with a Chinese classical education declined drastically for all factions between 1929 and 1945. But it was from among the Chiang supporters that persons with this traditional training for leadership disappeared first. The Chiang supporters started going to military schools instead of studying the Chinese classics (cf. Table 31). Thus in the Kuomintang the lines between the experts in pen and purse, on the one hand, and the experts in guns, on the other, grew over the years. The increasingly influential right wing became more and more exclusively a group of party organizers and administrators, while the Chiang faction continued to consist of the military (cf. Table 30).

These two groups lived in a fairly successful association; the organizers and the military men complemented each other without too much friction. This may be seen by comparing survival chances on the Executive Committee. On the whole, the followers of Chiang were the ones who managed to stay on most successfully from committee to committee. It will be recalled that two thirds of the Chiang clique who were on the first three committees were still on in 1945. Similarly, of the 1945 committee a larger proportion of the Chiang clique had been on the 1935, 1931, and 1929 committees than of either the rightists or leftists. But the rightists also managed to hold on to their posts fairly well. Their special qualification as administrators was of political value. Both organizers and military men averaged 1.7 incumbencies per individual. That is to say, the typical individual, whether army officer or party organizer, was on more than one, usually two, Central Executive Committees in the course of his career (cf. Table 32). Those whose main careers were nonpolitical served slightly less often, averaging 1.4 incumbencies per person. Thus the professionals had a somewhat better survival chance. It made no difference whether they played their part in the field of battle or in the field of party organization.

Success did depend, however, on coming from a major political center. Those who came from the provinces around Canton and Shanghai (Kiangsu and Kwangtung) tended to do well. They averaged 1.8 and 2.0 incumbencies each, respectively. For continued power, it was necessary to be part of a machine. The army was one. The party organizations in the two major centers were two others.

The type of education received also affected the individual's survival chance. The two individuals with no higher education served only once. Those with only a Chinese education had 1.6 incumbencies apiece. Those who studied in France or Russia were apt to be leftists, and so they enjoyed only 1.4 and 1.1 terms apiece on the average. On

*Table 32*

AVERAGE NUMBER OF INCUMBENCIES PER INDIVIDUAL FOR VARIOUS
CATEGORIES OF KUOMINTANG CEC MEMBERS

| Category | Number of Incumbencies | Number of Men | Incumbencies per Man |
|---|---|---|---|
| Total sample | 474 | 287 | 1.65 |
| By career: | | | |
| Organizers | 243 | 145 | 1.68 |
| Military | 176 | 103 | 1.71 |
| Other | 45 | 32 | 1.41 |
| Don't know | 10 | 9 | 1.11 |
| By education: | | | |
| Japanese university | 83 | 42 | 1.98 |
| Japanese military | 58 | 26 | 2.23 |
| Chinese university | 136 | 86 | 1.58 |
| Chinese military | 152 | 88 | 1.73 |
| Chinese classical | 41 | 15 | 2.73 |
| Chinese only | 193 | 123 | 1.57 |
| By place of birth: | | | |
| Kwangtung | 84 | 43 | 1.95 |
| Kiangsu | 44 | 24 | 1.83 |

the other hand, those who studied in Japanese universities (the main
schooling ground of the rightists) did very well. Those who went to
Japanese universities averaged two committee memberships apiece,
while those who went to Japanese military schools (which were also
extensively attended by Chiang followers) average 2.2 incumbencies
each. The most successful individuals of all, however, were those with
a Chinese classical education. They averaged 2.7 incumbencies apiece.
Men with this kind of education became rarer and rarer in the
Chinese elite, but apparently these few had been well trained for
political struggle. They came from families with a political tradition
and were brought up to play at the game of statecraft, which they did
with skill.

If there is any doubt as to the value of the political training received
by those who were brought up in families from the traditional political
classes of China, it is set at rest by the surprising discovery that these
same strata were not only the most successful in retaining power in
the Kuomintang CEC, but also the most successful in retaining power
in the Communist Party Politburo. Of forty-two members of the Politburo six served four or more times, seven served three times, and the
rest served once or twice. What sort of individuals were these six and
seven men who managed to hold office over various twists and turns

of the party line? Of the six who served four or more times, three were sons of scholar-officials. These three were all but one of the scholar-officials' sons who ever reached the Politburo. In other words, almost all these men were successful place holders, and they were also half of all the most successful place holders. The other half — that is, the other three individuals who served on four more committees — included one son of a wealthy landlord, and two sons of wealthy peasants. Thus the Politburo members with the best chance of survival were generally upper-class and correspondingly well educated. Specifically, they came from families with a tradition of governing.

When we turn to the seven individuals who served on three Politburos, we find a surprising paradox. They came from the lowest rungs of the Politburo social ladder. Five of them were sons of peasants, and of those, three were not wealthy peasants. In fact, those three were three out of the four Politburocrats who were sons of poor or middle peasants. Similarly, one of the two proletarians on the Politburo belonged to this group who served three times. Thus four of the seven men in this group were of lower-class origins.

What is the explanation of the strange phenomenon that the most successful Politburocrats were men of high-class origin and the next most successful men were of low-class origin, whereas the second rung in the Politburo was filled by men in between? The answer arises from the two phases of Communist development and the two groups of men — radical intellectuals and discontented agrarians — who came together to create the Chinese Communist movement. The first group were the radical intellectuals, sons of politicians themselves, most of whom (four out of six) came from Kiangsu, that is, Shanghai or its

*Table 33*

PERSISTENCE ON POLITBURO BY FATHER'S OCCUPATION

| Father's Occupation | Number of Times on Politburo | | |
|---|---|---|---|
| | 4 or more | 3 | 1 or 2 |
| Scholar-official | 3 | | 1 |
| Wealthy landlord | 1 | | 2 |
| Other landlord | | | 2 |
| Scholar-revolutionist | | | 1 |
| Merchant | | | 2 |
| Wealthy peasant | 2 | 2 | 2 |
| Other peasant | | 3 | 1 |
| Proletarian | | 1 | 1 |
| Don't know | — | 1 | 17 |
| Total | 6 | 7 | 29 |

vicinity. A little later they were joined by college-trained young men from the land. These were, for the most part, the sons of wealthy peasants or landlords, but those few who had the hardness and determination to rise to the very top and stay there were the poorest of the agrarian group. The sons of landlords and wealthy peasants filled the ranks of those who served on only one or two Politburos, and many of them ultimately broke from the Communist movement. Out of twelve Politburocrats, whose father's occupation we know, and who served on one or two committees, four were landlords, and two were wealthy peasants, making together one half. Thus it was clear that the top leadership of the Communist Party consisted of a team of scholar-politicians in the habit of ruling and were the more hard-bitten of the peasant leaders.

The former group, the members of scholar-official families, were successful in the Kuomintang. The latter group, sons of tillers of the soil, did not rise in the Kuomintang, and that was its fatal weakness.

The picture which emerges from this statistical analysis of the leadership of the two leading Chinese parties of the past quarter century has been summarized earlier in one word, "polarization." Both parties, as we have repeatedly noticed, broke away from the traditional Chinese values and forms of social organization. They were both revolutionary movements of rootless professional politicians feeding on disorganization and chaos. The Kuomintang, however, permitted itself to come increasingly under the control of backward-looking elements oriented toward securing personal economic advantage in business activities. Those factions and individuals with other orientations were gradually squeezed out. At the same time the Communist Party managed to transform itself from an intellectually oriented organization into a rural mass-oriented one. It made use of the ideological weapons which its early urban intellectual elements brought to it, but it also managed to give some kind of expression to the strivings of many young, Western-educated, discontented Chinese who were still sensitized to the problems of their home environment, the rural village. These problems were shared by most Chinese. In view of this polarization in the composition and orientation of the two major parties in China, and in view of the disorganization of Chinese society, it is not surprising that the struggle between parties eventually became civil war, nor is it surprising that the Communists won.

## V. DEVELOPMENTS UNDER THE PEOPLE'S GOVERNMENT

By the end of the Japanese War in August 1945, the relationship between the Kuomintang and Chinese Communist parties was such that civil war between them was almost inevitable. It was true that, during the first twelve months after the formation of the Kuomintang-Communist entente in September 1937, a series of concrete actions had been taken to bring about its implementation, and it was during this period that Chiang Kai-shek began to emerge as a symbol of Chinese unity. But as early as the closing months of 1938 Kuomintang-Communist relations had begun to deteriorate. In August of that year the Hankow-Wuchang Defense Headquarters outlawed three Communist-sponsored mass organizations on the basis that the Communists planned to use them for purposes of strengthening their positions in Nationalist territory. During succeeding months a number of similar Communist units were suppressed.

Considerable friction developed from the expansion of Communist military forces into areas outside the zones which had been assigned to them. This reached a climax in the New Fourth Army incident of January 1941, when Kuomintang forces attacked a Communist unit on the basis that the latter, wishing to expand its influence southward, had ignored a Nationalist order to engage the Japanese in the Yellow River area.

This and similar clashes led to periods of negotiation — with minor parties attempting to mediate — and to an American offer of good offices in 1944 by Major General Patrick J. Hurley, the personal representative of President Roosevelt. Despite long and tortuous negotiations, the two parties failed to reach a permanent understanding. It is true that Hurley reported an apparent readiness on the part of the Kuomintang and the Communists to cooperate. Moreover, Stalin personally assured him that the Soviet Union did not intend to recognize any government in China except that of the Nationalists with Chiang Kai-shek as its leader. But Chiang and Mao seemed more intent on furthering the interests of their respective parties than in cooperating, even in the face of Japanese aggression.

The United States, by force of circumstances, had been assuming increasingly heavy responsibility for prosecuting the war against Japan. Now it was clear that amphibious drives across the Central and South Pacific had taken a shocking toll in American lives, and estimates of the probable human cost of assaults on Japan were causing considerable apprehension. By the early months of 1945 both soldiers and civilians demanded to know why the Soviet Union had not accepted a share of the fighting in Asia.

It was through these circumstances and out of Allied relationships with the Soviet Union that the Yalta Agreement emerged. In signing this document, the United States and Great Britain paid a high price for Russian aid in a war that — although few outside Japan knew it — was all but won. The two Western powers, without consulting China, recognized a Soviet Russian claim to nearly all imperialist concessions on Chinese soil which Czarist Russia had lost to Japan through the Treaty of Portsmouth in 1905.

Essential aspects of this agreement served as a blueprint for the Sino-Soviet Treaty of Friendship and Alliance, August 14, 1945; however, the Soviet Union agreed in the latter document to give the national government of China both moral and material support and offered formal assurances that the Soviet Union would not interfere in China's affairs. Largely because of this guaranty, the Sino-Soviet Treaty was well received at first in China and in the United States. Many observers concluded that the Soviet Union was ignoring the Chinese Communists, and there were speculations that both Russian and Chinese Communists had reconciled themselves to Chiang Kai-shek and the Nationalist government. In retrospect it is clear that these observers did not understand the fundamental Communist tactic of cooperation combined with opposition. Within a few months Nationalist and Chinese Communist troops were engaged in a full-scale civil war.

Military, political, and economic conditions resulting from the abrupt capitulation of the Japanese, the advance of Soviet troops into Manchuria, the appearance of vacuums resulting from the surrender of Japanese forces in China, and the Russians' stripping of Manchurian industry — all these developments aggravated a situation that was already potentially dangerous.

After the Japanese surrender, Communist troops began racing Nationalist armies for control of areas occupied by the Japanese. The Nationalist government was estimated to hold a five-to-one advantage in troops and rifles and a near monopoly of transport, heavy equipment, and air strength. The Communists enjoyed a geographical advantage in being closer to many of the Japanese areas, including Manchuria.

The United States sought to help the Nationalists in their reoccupation of Japanese-held territory by transporting Nationalist armies by air to East and North China and more than 400,000 troops by water. United States Marines were detailed to hold key railroads and coal mines for the Nationalists. With this and other American assistance, Chiang Kai-shek's forces were able to accept the surrender of a great majority of the 1,200,000 Japanese troops in China proper. In Manchuria, however, the Nationalists did badly.

During the course of negotiations leading toward the Sino-Soviet

Treaty, the Soviet Union had assured the Nationalists that Russian forces would evacuate Manchuria within three weeks after the Japanese surrender and that the withdrawal would be completed within a three-month period. When Russian troops began pulling out, however, the Nationalists, with extended lines of communication and limited transportation facilities, were unable to take over evacuated areas ahead of the Chinese Communists. The Nationalist government found itself in the difficult position of having to ask the Russians to delay their departure.

When Soviet troops did evacuate Manchuria, they stripped the area of Japanese-built industrial equipment, but left behind for Chinese Communist forces valuable caches of Japanese rifles and a well-trained Communist army of local Chinese and former Japanese puppet troops. The Nationalists, risking the overextension of their lines, tried to reoccupy Manchuria through force of arms.

Incidents grew into open civil war, relieved, intermittently, by the uneasy truces that General Marshall's mission was able to achieve. President Truman had charged Marshall with the responsibility of bringing peace to China under conditions that would permit a stable government and progress along democratic lines and of assisting the Nationalist government in establishing its authority over the widest possible areas of China. The first objective was not realizable. The greatest obstacle to peace, General Marshall reported, was the complete, overwhelming suspicion with which the Chinese Communist Party and the Kuomintang regarded one another. Marshall was bitterly critical of irreconcilable groups within the Kuomintang, interested only in preserving their own feudal control of China, and of "dyed-in-the-wool" Communists who used abuse, lies, and any other drastic measures, even to wrecking the economy of the country, in order to achieve their ends. The only solution, he said, lay in the assumption of leadership by liberals in the government and in the minority parties. These men and women, however, were few in number, without influence or support, and entirely unable to act.

The second objective of the Marshall mission — to help the Nationalists extend their authority — seemed easier to realize, since by early 1947 Chiang's government had reached a peak of military successes and territorial expansion. Chinese Communist generals, however, brought superior forces to bear at points of greatest Nationalist extension — just as they had done during Chiang's "bandit suppression campaigns" in the days of the Juichin Republic — destroying isolated bodies of troops, cutting communications, and seizing arms. Through these tactics they were soon able to supplement Russian-donated

Japanese rifles with American weapons captured from American-trained and American-equipped Nationalist armies.

Chiang Kai-shek's troops rapidly lost their will to fight, and in October 1948 Nationalist defenders of Mukden defected to the Communists, taking with them valuable weapons and other equipment. Communist victories now followed one after the other: Tientsin fell on January 15, 1949; Peking surrendered without a fight; in April the Communists crossed the Yangtze; Shanghai fell in May, and on October 15 Canton, which had served as the Nationalist capital for the previous six months, capitulated without resistance. Chiang Kai-shek had already moved his headquarters to Formosa.

*Strengths and Weaknesses*

At this early point it is difficult to determine precisely which Kuomintang weaknesses and which Communists strengths, as well as what external factors, were critical in the overthrow of one elite and the coming to power of the other, but a number of factors are worth examining. It is clear that both leadership groups emerged from the political, social, and economic chaos accompanying the impact of Western culture upon Chinese society and the breakdown of the Ch'ing dynasty. Both began as relatively unorganized intellectual movements instigated by scholars and professional men, nearly all of whom had been educated abroad or had in one fashion or another been influenced by Western culture. Many individuals in both groups came from the same social and economic background — from landlord, scholar, or bureaucratic families, from merchant or moneylender circles, or from the newly developed capitalist class of large cities along the coast. These, of course, were the families who could afford to educate their sons in Japan or Europe and to provide them with incomes during long periods of exile or profitless political activity. Most leaders in both groups rose to prominence through organizational and administrative work within their respective parties, with a large majority attaining leadership through military service. Only a few built careers independent of government or party, and most of these served in professional fields, such as journalism and education, which were closely related to their Kuomintang or Communist activities. Both parties developed schisms and conducted purges, but neither tended to take drastic action against its own dissidents. The Kuomintang was quite ready to kill Communists, however, and vice versa.

The differences are equally noteworthy. The Kuomintang, which began as a Western-oriented, middle-class revolutionary movement with undisciplined organization and ill-defined goals, became increasingly radical with the introduction of Russian influence — but only up to the point where agrarian revolution threatened the security of members springing from the landowning classes. At that contingency the leaders of the Kuomintang, seeking to preserve both power and property, swung over into a course, increasingly militaristic and counterrevolutionary, that severed their contact with, and brought them into opposition to, a large section of the population, especially the peasant masses.

Once this turn had been made, it became clear that between so-called radical and conservative wings of the Kuomintang the struggle for power was more critical than disagreements over points of doctrine. Furthermore, since neither wing was willing to carry out a program that would appeal to peasant or labor masses, individual leaders found themselves compelled to depend upon political manipulation, factional maneuvering, and the juxtaposition of military force.

As Chiang Kai-shek consolidated his personal power, Kuomintang cliques became increasingly important as instruments of political expression. At the same time Kuomintang leadership grew older, and although the Central Executive Committee expanded more than nine times its original size, support for Chiang became more and more a prerequisite for election to that body.

The Communist Party, which began as a series of loosely organized intellectual discussion groups, accepted Russian Bolshevik organization and discipline at an early date, whereupon leaders who hitherto had owed their influence to literary or scholastic prestige came now to depend upon Moscow for their mandate. The party made no pretense to democracy in the Western sense; discipline was rigid; purges under Russian supervision at least as late as 1931 were conducted with every major shift in the tactical line. And when a policy failed, even though Stalin himself had made it, the most nearly responsible Chinese leader was commonly censured, whereupon he either recanted or suffered expulsion from the party.

The outstanding exception, the only group who not only disagreed with Stalin but also succeeded in holding to its course, was that composed of Mao Tse-tung and his followers. They strapped a readjusted Russo-Marxist bridle over the peasant movement (the central force in the Chinese Revolution) and put themselves astride while Stalin and his associates were still trying to team them to another horse.

Kuomintang military men, except for Whampoa graduates, were likely to be officers trained in the old style of military leadership. Beyond this, many were independent or semi-independent war lords whose loyalty to the Kuomintang could not always be counted on. In contrast to these, the quality and dedication of Communist generals, whose military duties were often superimposed upon a host of party responsibilities, may constitute one of the chief factors in the Communist Party success. Many of them had received in the Soviet Union specialized training in techniques of insurrection and perhaps also in twentieth-century mechanized warfare. Most had gained long experience as guerrilla leaders. Nearly all had submitted without qualification to Communist Party, as well as to military, discipline. Those who survived Chiang's "extermination campaigns," years of illegal underground activities, the vicissitudes of the Long March, and the battles of the Japanese War established long records of competence, loyalty, and dependability.

These various differences undoubtedly constitute some of the reasons for Communist successes and Kuomintang failures, but final evaluation must await a more thorough examination of the historical record than has yet been undertaken. To date it is almost impossible, for example, to determine the relationship, after the Long March, between the Chinese Communist Party and Stalinist leadership in Moscow. Chinese leaders, including Mao Tse-tung, have repeatedly acknowledged their acceptance of Bolshevik discipline and their sympathy with and loyalty to the Soviet Union. Recently Ch'en Po-ta, a Chinese Communist, in an effort to define the precise relationship between Mao and Stalin, stressed in glowing terms the Russian leader's insight and infallibility as a prophet of the Chinese revolution. Ch'en Po-ta wrote that because of language difficulties and "counterrevolutionary blockades," Chinese Communist leaders, including Mao, were not able to read the works of Stalin until comparatively recently. It happened, however, that Mao's ideas were "identical with those of Stalin, and consequently he was able to come to the same conclusions in regard to fundamental problems."[104]

But these are statements that cannot be accepted seriously. We know that from 1924 until 1932, at least, Moscow was in close touch with the Chinese Communist leadership. Many individual Chinese studied in Moscow, and Stalinist agents were nearly always attached to Communist headquarters in China, but Mao Tse-tung's ideas were not identical with Stalin's. Whatever the effect of these rationalizations in China, to the non-Communist Western critic they suggest that the true relationship between Mao and Stalin has been sufficiently unorthodox in the past to require — at the moment of China's emergence as a major Communist power — a degree of public readjustment.

[104] "New China News Agency in English Morse to North America, December 19, 1949."

It may be recognized that the advance of Soviet Russian troops into Manchuria and the Russian policy of turning over captured Japanese arms to the Chinese Communists speeded this emergence.[105] But the comparative histories of Russian on-the-spot direction of the Chinese revolution from 1924 until 1931, and of Mao Tse-tung's long agrarian struggle, suggest that it would be misleading, and from the American viewpoint dangerous, to underestimate the current strength of Chinese Communist leadership or to place it in the same general category with Communist elites in Eastern Europe, which have owed their existence almost entirely to the whims of Joseph Stalin.

## The Backgrounds and Characteristics of Various Individual Leaders*

When we have analyzed group characteristics and general trends in leadership, there remains a whole series of questions about the capabilities and inclinations of various individual Chinese Communist leaders of the present day. Which men hold actual power, and are they secure in their positions? Are the top leaders on good terms with one another, or does competition for power produce dangerous personal frictions? What are the attitudes of these men toward their own country and toward the Soviet Union? Are they Communists first, or would they turn against the Soviet Union in case of a severe conflict between Russian and Chinese interests? None of these questions is easily answered.

It remains extremely difficult to establish reliable criteria for judging the personal inclinations and relative standing, prestige, and power of various Chinese Communist leaders. Unofficial and semiofficial listings of top party officeholders often differ in important detail, and equally competent observers are often in disagreement. Even the biographical details of important leaders are controversial and subject to constant correction. The result is that interpretations of internal Chinese Communist Party politics remain highly subjective and should be considered with caution.

Central Committee members are believed to be listed in order according to the number of votes received in the elections, and in this

---

[105] The relative importance of Russian-supplied Japanese arms, and arms captured from Japanese and Kuomintang troops by the Chinese Communists themselves, is a subject of controversy which is not likely to be settled except through the perspective of history.

* The following section includes material drawn from Robert C. North, "The Chinese Communist Elite," in H. Arthur Steiner (ed.), "Report in China," *The Annals of the American Academy of Political and Social Science*, Vol. 227 (September 1951), pp. 70–74. Permission to reprint it here is gratefully acknowledged. A number of additions and corrections have been made on the basis of new data recently received [June 1952].

connection it is worth noting that membership in the Politburo does not seem necessarily to coincide with a high position on the Central Committee. As the roll is believed to stand at this writing, the first four — Mao Tse-tung, Chu Te, Liu Shao-ch'i, and Lin Tsu-han (in that order) — are Politburo members, but there is at least considerable skepticism about the reported Politburo membership of the fifth committeeman, Lin Piao. Politburo member Chou En-lai, on the other hand, stands nineteenth on the 1951 Central Committee listing (twenty-second on some earlier lists).

Investigations into the personal lives of Chinese Communist leaders generally fail to throw much light upon the internal politics of the Communist Party. Among those often listed by non-Communist sources as belonging to the Politburo are three "returned students" — Chang Wen-t'ien, Ch'en Shao-yü, and Wang Chia-hsiang. During the *Cheng Feng* or "ideological remolding movement" of 1942, Mao struck out fiercely at the "dogmatists" or "half-intellectuals" who had grounded themselves in Marxist-Leninist theory, but who remained incapable of wedding theory with practice. It is perhaps not certain that this attack was directed primarily against the "returned students," but it is true that these men dropped into temporary obscurity about that time. More recently the three have regained some prominence. Wang Chia-hsiang became the first new Chinese ambassador to Moscow late in 1949, returning from that post early in 1951 to become Vice-Minister of Foreign Affairs in the Central People's Government. Chang Wen-t'ien, in January 1950, was designated as the Central People's Republic permanent representative on the United Nations Security Council (still pending accreditation); in April 1951 he became ambassador to Moscow. Wang Ming (Ch'en Shao-yü) has, from the beginning of the new regime, been chairman of the Law Commission of the Central People's Government. All three are members of the Central Committee of the Party, but it is now seriously doubted that they belong currently to the Politburo.

In addition to the three "returned students" noted above, non-Communist sources often list Lin Piao, P'eng Te-huai, and K'ang Sheng as Politburo members, although there has been no confirmation of their current membership.

Widely recognized for his ability as a military strategist and technician, Lin Piao is reputed to inspire his officers and men with exceptional loyalty and *élan*. In 1949, for example, when his Fourth Field Army was moving into Central China, Western observers reported that his troops tended to identify themselves, not by unit or simply as Communists, but as "Lin Piao's boys." After years of active military service and a sojourn (1937–1942) in the Soviet Union, he led Chinese Communist troops into Manchuria in 1945, and was subsequently appointed commander of the Northeastern Democratic Army, which captured Tientsin in January 1949. Some months later his troops, redesignated as the Fourth Field Army, proceeded into Central China and captured Hankow. In late 1950 he led the same army into Korea.

P'eng Te-huai, who is also sometimes listed by non-Communist sources as a Politburo member, stands second in the Chinese Communist military hierarchy. It was he who was in command of troops that captured, and soon lost, Changsha in 1930, and later his First Red Army Corps figured prominently in the Long March. There are indications that in recent years he has taken over important duties from his chief, the veteran Chu Te. Communist sources do not currently confirm his Politburo membership.

A subject of considerable speculation is K'ang Sheng, who may possibly have achieved notable, but largely unmeasured, power as chief of the Chinese Communist secret police. In the thirties he spent six years in Moscow, where he became closely associated with Wang Ming. Reportedly raised to the Politburo in 1943, he became chief of the Social Affairs Department of the party Central Committee. In 1949 he assumed the post of Secretary to the Shantung Branch of the party's East China Bureau, a post that, on the face of it, seems oddly anti-climactical. During months prior to this writing, moreover, K'ang Sheng has not appeared publicly, being absent even from important government meetings, and there have been unconfirmed reports to the effect that his presence has not been noted either in Peking or Shantung. There are strong reasons for doubting that he serves currently on the Politburo.

At this writing, the most reliable analysis of the Central Organization of the Communist Party of China is *Current Background,* No. 137, issued by the American Consulate General, Hong Kong, November 15, 1951. This document lists Kao Kang and Tung Pi-wu as "probably" belonging to the Politburo. Kao Kang's background is exceptional in that he rose to prominence in a relatively independent fashion. Born of a poor peasant family, he received no formal education, but joined the Communist Party in 1926, and took part in a series of guerrilla uprisings that pushed him into a position of leadership in Shensi, a region then quite apart from the chief area of Communist development. When the main columns of Communist armies terminated the Long March in Shensi, Kao was one of two outstanding figures in a soviet that had already been established there. Upon its dissolution he was elected an official in the Shensi-Kansu-Ningsia Border Region.

At the close of World War II he was transferred to Manchuria, where he became head of the Northeast People's Government in August 1949. By some observers he is regarded as a figurehead who attained high office through his loyalty to Mao, while others consider him a strong man placed in the Northeast by Mao in order to keep that area securely under Chinese control. Again, there is no decisive evidence, although his activities and prominence in northeastern developments suggest the latter view.

Tung Pi-wu, a founder of the Chinese Communist Party, became known to Americans as a member of the Chinese delegation to the United Nations Conference on International Organization in 1945. Like Lin Tsu-han, he was active in Sun Yat-sen's revolutionary movement long before the formation of the Communist Party. After the Communist-Kuomintang split, he fled first to Japan and then to Moscow, where he studied until 1931. After completing the Long March, he became president of the Central Party School, a position he had held previously during the existence of the Kiangsi Soviet. At the present time he is one of the four Vice-Premiers of the State Administrative Council in the Central People's Government.

*Current Background,* No. 137, makes the following tentative listing of men who almost certainly serve on the current Politburo: Lin Tsu-han; P'eng Chen; Ch'en Yün; Chu Te; Chou En-lai; Liu Shao-ch'i, deputy chairman; and Mao Tse-tung, chairman.

Lin Tsu-han, like Tung Pi-wu, is a veteran revolutionist and former close associate of Sun Yat-sen. After the Communist-Kuomintang split in 1927, he studied in the Soviet Union and in other European countries and founded a Chinese workers' school in Khabarovsk. A participant in the Long March, he later served as Commissioner of Finance in the Shensi-Kansu-Ningsia Soviet and became chairman in 1937, when it was transformed into the Border Region Government. At the present time he is serving as Secretary-General of the Central People's Government.

P'eng Chen, after serving for three years as chairman of the Northeast Bureau of the Chinese Communist Party and political commissar to Lin Piao's United Democratic Army, became Secretary of the Peking Municipal Committee of the party in February 1949. A member of the Communist Party since 1926, P'eng devoted many of his early years to the organization of trade-union activities in North China.

A leading Communist economist and labor expert, Ch'en Yün was appointed chairman of the Mukden Military Central Commission and chairman of the All-China Federation of Labor. With a primary school education, he worked for the Commercial Press and later for the

Chung Hua Book Company in Shanghai. After joining the Communist Party in 1924, he participated in the Shanghai strikes of 1925 and 1927 and subsequently served as a labor union organizer under the Kiangsi Soviet. Between 1929 and about 1934 he served first as deputy chief and later as chief of the Department of Organization of the Communist Party. In 1949 he was reported as attending the Tenth All-Union Congress of Trade-Unions in Moscow.

Chu Te, Commander in Chief of the Chinese People's Liberation Army, was born in Szechwan in 1886, the son of a peasant father. After studying at the Yünnan Military Academy, he continued his education in Europe, where, with Chou En-lai, he founded a Berlin branch of the Chinese Communist Party. After being deported from Germany, he returned to China by way of Moscow and was one of the leaders of the Nanchang uprising in 1927. There was a time in the late thirties when the Chu-Mao combination was mistaken for one person by many Chinese, but despite Chu's twenty years as Commander in Chief of Chinese Communist armies, his political importance is believed to have remained secondary.

Among all Chinese Communist leaders, Chou En-lai is perhaps the most controversial. At one time or another, he has been described as "moderate," "Western-oriented," "orthodox," and "double-faced." While serving as negotiator at the time of Chiang Kai-shek's kidnaping at Sian in 1936, and later in Nanking, Chungking, and Peiping, he impressed many Westerners with his courtesy and apparent good will and "liberality." There are competent observers, on the other hand, who consider him powerful and crafty and who believe that his connections with Moscow are exceptionally close.

Born in 1898, of landlord antecedents, Chou En-lai has a notably cosmopolitan background. After attending middle school in China, he took training in Japan and then went to France under the worker-student plan. Together with Li Li-san and other Chinese students in Paris, he founded a French branch of the Chinese Communist Party in 1921, and later, while studying in Germany, joined with Chu Te in establishing a Berlin cell. After his return to China in 1924, he was appointed political instructor and acting chief of the Political Department of Whampoa Military Academy, where Lin Piao was one of his students.

Arrested during the Communist-Kuomintang schism, Chou En-lai escaped and subsequently went to Moscow for study. In September 1930, Chou was coauthor of the *Report of the Third Plenum*, which rebuked Li Li-san for overestimating the tempo of the Chinese revolution and for committing tactical mistakes, but which stated that the general line of urban insurrection was still "in complete harmony with the Comintern." During Li Li-san's subsequent trial before the Oriental Bureau of the Comintern, Russian Communist leaders condemned the other author, Ch'ü Ch'iu-pai, for his actions at the Third Plenum, but there is no evidence at hand that Chou En-lai was severely censured.

During the period of "returned student" leadership, Chou, according to one observer, was in charge of military affairs, superior to Chu Te, who was considered only a field commander. This same source states that Chou En-lai and Po Ku (Ch'in Pang-hsien), on the basis of a radiogram from Moscow, made the local decision to initiate the Long March. If these statements are true, it is noteworthy that Chou apparently survived Po Ku's fall from power and achieved added prominence during Mao's leadership.

After participating in the Long March, Chou served as the chief Communist representative in the negotiations leading to Chiang Kai-shek's release after the Sian kidnaping, and from that time forward he took part in nearly all important discussions between the Communists and the Kuomintang. More recently, he worked closely with Mao and Stalin in negotiating the Sino-Soviet Treaty of 1950.

It is extremely difficult to place Chou En-lai in any left-right spectrum of Chinese Communist politics. Through various shifts of the Communist line, he has been labeled leftist, rightist, and moderate, according to the stand he has taken toward the issues involved. It is said that he has great power, but prefers to exercise it through Mao, rather than in an independent fashion. Some observers consider him a likely successor to Mao, maintaining that he has a powerful personal following, including Chu Te, P'eng Te-huai, Chen Yi, and Liu Po-ch'eng on the military side, and men like Tung Pi-wu and Ch'en Yün on the political; but there is no incontrovertible evidence to support this view.

When non-Communist observers discuss top figures in the Chinese Communist hierarchy and suggest possible successors to Mao Tse-tung, the name of Liu Shao-ch'i is nearly always mentioned. Like Mao, this important leader was born in Hunan of well-to-do peasant stock, studied at Hunan Normal School, and attended Peking University. Unlike Mao, he studied economics in the Soviet Union. After joining the Chinese Communist Party in 1921, he worked with Li Li-san as a union organizer among Anyuan miners, and with Mao in Hunan. In 1927 he was elected to the Central Committee of the party. After the Communist-Kuomintang split of that year, he served at various times in the Manchurian labor movement and in the Shanghai underground.

Despite the fact that Liu Shao-ch'i reportedly supported Li Li-san during the period of urban insurrection, he was elected to the Polit-buro and the Secretariat in 1931, and is now believed to be loyal to Mao. After participating in the Long March, he was appointed Commissioner of Labor for the Shensi-Kansu-Ningsia Border Region Government in 1937. At the Seventh Congress of the Chinese Communist Party in 1945 he was elected vice-chairman of the Central Committee, and since then has been mentioned many times as number-two man in the hierarchy and as Mao's most likely successor.

A veteran Bolshevik with thirty years of party service, Liu is one of the more outstanding Communist scholars and Marxist-Leninist theoreticians that China has produced. In addition to such authoritative Chinese Communist works as *On Intra-Party Struggle*, *The Training of the Party Member*, and *Internationalism and Nationalism*, he is the author of *On the Party*, which possibly stands next to Mao's *On the New Democracy* as a guide for Chinese Communist theory and action. His prestige as a theoretician has spread throughout the Communist world, and in recent years certain of his pronouncements have been accepted as policy statements for the Communist line in Asia. It is entirely possible, however, that Liu Shao-ch'i will remain more a scholar than a man of action.

If this sketchy analysis of important individual Communists leaves unanswered all the leading questions about the capabilities, inclinations, and personal power relationships of party leadership, it is simply an indication of how little we actually know about the Chinese Communist elite. In general, it is safe only to reiterate conclusions reached in the quantitative sections of this study, namely, that the top ranks of the Chinese Communist elite consist almost wholly of experienced, disciplined men, nearly all of whom have had twenty years or more of active, varied, and rigorous experience within the Communist movement.

## The Chinese People's Republic

The Chinese Communist Party, by the middle of 1949, had won control over such vast areas of China that the decision was made to convene a new Political Consultative Conference. A Preparatory Committee composed of 134 delegates representing twenty-three organizations met in Peking on June 15–20, 1949. This committee elected a twenty-one-member Standing Committee, which, in turn, elected a chairman and five vice-chairmen. As an organizational forerunner of the Central People's Government of China inaugurated four months later, this Preparatory Committee is worthy of brief analysis.

Among the 133 delegates who actually attended (one did not

attend), only twenty-five — or 18 per cent — were known Communists. But since a sizable percentage of delegates about whom no information is available may also have been Communists, it is possible that the total may have been close to one third of the attendance. The Democratic League with thirty-eight members had the largest representation (27 per cent). The rest of the known membership consisted of eighteen members of the Kuomintang Revolutionary Committeemen, ten "nonpartisans," and five Chih-kung Tang.[106]

The Standing Committee was one-third Communist, and most of the key positions were held by Reds — the chairman, one out of five vice-chairmen, the chief secretary of the Standing Committee, and chairmen of three out of six subcommittees.

The average age of the Preparatory Committee was fifty-two years. The average for non-Communist members was fifty-five years; for Communist members the average was fifty years.

More committeemen were natives of Chekiang than any other province. Among Communists, however, Hunan (6 out of 25) and Kiangsu (5 out of 25) were the most common birthplaces. There is information concerning the educational backgrounds of 75 of the 133 Preparatory Committeemen: 28 were educated in China; 19 in Japan; 13 in the U.S.S.R.; 12 in France; 9 in the United States; and 5 in Germany. All but one of those educated in the Soviet Union and half of those who had received all or part of their training in France were members of the Communist Party.

The list of committeemen includes the names of most Kuomintang (and other non-Communist) "liberals" who had been prominent since the end of the Japanese War and one well-known ex-Communist (T'an P'ing-shan) who had been expelled from the party on the basis of Bolshevik discipline. When the State Administrative Council of the Central People's Government was announced on October 20, 1949, it was evident that the Chinese Communist Party had obtained an even stronger position in this body than it had enjoyed on the Preparatory Committee. This time out of 135 major posts,[107] more than half (70, or 51 per cent) were held by known Communists.

Of the 21 Portfolio Ministries, 11 were headed by Communists. Of

[106] According to the *People's Hand Book* (Hong Kong, 1950), Section F, p. 7, this party was organized by Chinese in the United States in 1925. During a conference in Hong Kong, May 1, 1947, the group adopted a platform calling for peace and political democracy and opposing dictatorship by a single party.

[107] These posts include the State Administrative Council officers, members, and Secretariat, as well as the heads and vice-heads of the 21 portfolio ministries, the four committees, the three commissions, the four administrations, the Academy of Science, and the People's Bank.

the 43 Vice-Ministers of the 21 Portfolios, 27 were Communist Party members. None of the Portfolio Ministries was staffed by non-Communists exclusively. Among 16 positions on the 4 committees, 8 were held by Communist Party members, and 2 of the committees were chaired by Communists. Of 16 commissions, 6 (out of 13) posts were held by Communists. Of the 4 administrations (Maritime Customs, News Agencies, Publications, and Information), 3 were headed by Communists, and among a total of 9 posts, 4 were held by Communists. The People's Bank had two responsible officers, a director and a vice-director. Both were Communists. The Academy of Sciences had a president and 4 vice-presidents. Two vice-presidents were Communists. In nearly every case where a responsible official was a non-Communist, his deputy was a recognized Communist, and many of the prominent non-Communist members of the Council (such as Mme. Liao Chung-k'ai, Mme. Feng Yü-hsiang, and Chang Po-chün) had long records of support of, or long association with, the Chinese Communist movement.

On lower bureaucratic levels the percentage of Communist, as compared with non-Communist, officials necessarily diminished. It is often said, in fact, that the Communist leadership, because its numbers are so small in relation to the size and population of China, has already "spread itself thin." The implication is, of course, that reliance upon untrained personnel and upon Kuomintang bureaucrats insensitive to Communist doctrine must seriously hamper governmental functioning. There is truth in this. But it is equally true that those absorbed by the new government include not only reluctant officials who had no other choice, but also many able men who, through dissatisfaction with the Nationalist regime, willingly transferred their allegiance. Many of these have been trained in the West, and in time they will be joined by younger men who are now attending institutions in the United States and Europe. Whether such persons render loyal service to the Communist regime or become dissidents and even revolutionaries depends not only upon the performance of the new government, but also upon the policy which the Chinese Communist Party follows in regard to nonparty personnel.

At the present time, increases in the ratio of Communist over non-Communist leaders holding high-level positions in the new government elite suggest that the power position of the non-Communists will not improve beyond the absolute requirements of governmental functioning, and an examination of the basic principles of Marxist-Leninist-Stalinist class warfare makes such a conclusion nearly mandatory.

By the establishment of pyramiding units of local government, moreover, the Chinese Communists have developed a pattern of military-political controls which places a near monopoly of local power in the hands of an exceedingly small group of senior leaders. At this writing (June 1952), the mainland of China is divided into seven principal administrative regions, with organs and functions subordinate, but similar, to those of the central government. It is noteworthy, then, that top administrative positions on regional and central government levels display a frequent overlapping of personnel, with key posts being held by senior party, government, and military personnel. "By virtue of this great concentration of control," according to reliable analysts, "a relatively small number of senior Communists, almost all of whom are members of the Central Committee of the party, do at the same time dominate the regional governmental and military hierarchies. This control, exercised through party organizations at the regional level, both discourages and prevents centrifugal tendencies from developing."[108] The same source estimates that a group numbering fewer than twenty individuals may control completely the political and military situation at the regional level in Communist China.

In view of this high degree of centralization, is there even a remote possibility that critically important contradictions or schisms can develop either within the People's Republic itself, or within the party, or between sections of the Chinese Communist Party and Bolshevik leaders in Moscow? At this point, no answer can be more than a speculation, but it is probably safe to say that the long-range future of the Chinese Communist movement is likely to depend upon at least four factors: the efficiency of Communist control techniques over the Chinese populace; the degree to which Red leadership remains sensitive to the needs of the country (especially the peasantry) and is reasonably able to meet them; the status of relations between China and the Soviet Union, on the one hand, and China and the United States, on the other; and the relations between the U.S.S.R. and the United States in a two-power world.

Chinese Communist leaders have stated their totalitarian intentions many times through the years, and the opening paragraph of the Constitution of the Chinese Communist Party makes clear that although the task of the party "in the present stage" is to struggle for the development of a "new democracy," the ultimate aim is the realization of communism in China. To date the Chinese Communists have published no precise timetable for the completion of their "present stage," but in June 1950 Mao Tse-tung estimated that about three years

[108] American Consulate General, Hong Kong, *Current Background*, No. 170, April 8, 1952.

would be needed to accomplish current phases of agrarian reform, to make a "readjustment" of commerce and industry, and to effect necessary government economies. Thereafter, at some unspecified future date, when the "test of war and the test of land reform" were passed, the only remaining task, the carrying out of Bolshevik socialist reform throughout the nation, would be passed easily.

Mao Tse-tung has indicated more than once that the Chinese Communist Party will not hesitate to use both calculated alliances with and armed struggle against the middle classes. During 1950 Chinese Communist leaders have published action programs defining principles and procedures for applying this kind of dual policy to industrial and agrarian problems. For this particular stage the Communist-controlled government will protect the interests of "all capitalists who benefit the nation's welfare and the people's livelihood" and for the time being will allow the rich peasants to maintain themselves. But the Chinese Communist radio, broadcasting about the trials and executions of "people's enemies," should remind us that "the existence and development of the Chinese Communist Party are inseparable from armed struggle."

Despite totalitarian methods, the Chinese Communist hierarchy, if it remains willing and able to adjust its doctrine to fundamental Chinese needs, may well remain in power a long time. If, on the other hand, it allows itself to become the mechanical instrument of Russo-Marxist dialectic and especially if it moves rapidly to force the peasant revolution into "higher" doctrinaire stages of Stalinist development, the Chinese Communist elite may run the risk of becoming a counter-revolutionary force in a new peasant upsurge.

Under either set of conditions, the record of Communist Party growth, of Russian misunderstandings and miscalculations in regard to the Chinese revolution, and of historic Chinese-Russian relations in and outside the Communist movement suggests that, in the long run, antagonisms between Chinese and Russian centers of communism are almost certain to appear, if they are not already developing. Whether such antagonisms become critically disruptive or not may depend as much upon Western skill at exploiting them as upon Moscow-Peiping relations. In the meantime, Russian Communists, while helping the Chinese to improve their economy and to strengthen their military and political power, are likely to use Leninist-Stalinist techniques for tightening Russian discipline over the Chinese Communist movement, for achieving a Soviet-style penetration of China's economy and politics, and for preventing antagonisms from developing toward a crisis.

# APPENDIX

## APPENDIX A. DEVELOPMENT OF THE KUOMINTANG

[Chih-fang Wu (T. F. Wu), *Chinese Government and Politics* (Shanghai, 1935), pp. 276–287]

Hsingchunghui, or Society for the Regeneration of China, 1893–1905
T'ungmenghui, or Alliance Society, 1905–1912
Kuomintang, or Nationalist Party, 1912–1914
Chunghua Ko-mintang, or China Revolutionary Party, 1914–1919
Chunghua Kuomintang, or Nationalist Party of China, 1920
Reorganization of the Chungkuo Kuomintang, 1924

## APPENDIX B. KUOMINTANG ELITE

### Table 1
### CEC OF THE KUOMINTANG,* 1924
[*China Year Book, 1931*, p. 544]

| | |
|---|---|
| 1. Chang Ching-chiang | 13. Shih Ying |
| 2. Chou Lu (Tsou Lu) | 14. Tai Chi-t'ao |
| 3. Chü Cheng | 15. T'an Cheng |
| 4. En-Ke-Pa-T'u | 16. T'an P'ing-shan |
| 5. Hsiung K'e-wu | 17. T'an Yen-k'ai |
| 6. Hu Han-min | 18. Ting Wei-fen |
| 7. Li Lieh-chün | 19. Wang Ching-wei |
| 8. Li Shou-chang | 20. Wang Fa-ch'in |
| 9. Liao Chung-k'ai | 21. Yang Hsi-min |
| 10. Lin Shen | 22. Yeh Ch'u-ts'ang |
| 11. Po Wen-wei | 23. Yu Shu-te |
| 12. Shih Ching-yang | 24. Yü Yu-jen |

* According to Chinese Communist Party histories, Li Ta-chao and Kan Shu-te, Communists, were among the twenty-four members of this Central Executive Committee.

### Table 2
### CEC OF THE KUOMINTANG, 1926
[*China Year Book, 1931*, p. 544]

| | |
|---|---|
| 1. Ch'en Kung-po* (Communist or former Communist) | 4. Chiang Kai-shek* (Chiang Chieh-shih) |
| 2. Ch'en Yu-jen* (Eugene Chen) | 5. Ching Heng-yi* |
| 3. Ch'eng Ch'ien* | 6. Chu Chi-hsün* |

* Newly elected in 1926.

*Table 2 (Continued)*

| | |
|---|---|
| 7. Chu P'ei-te* | 22. Sun Fo* (Sun K'o) |
| 8. En-Ke-Pa-T'u | 23. Sung Ch'ing-ling* (Mme. Sun |
| 9. Hsiao Fu-ch'eng* | Yat-sen) |
| 10. Hsü Chien* (George Hsu) | 24. Sung Tzu-wen* (T. V. |
| 11. Hu Han-min | Soong) |
| 12. Kan Nai-kuang* | 25. Tai Chi-t'ao |
| 13. Ku Meng-yü* | 26. T'an P'ing-shan (Communist) |
| 14. Li Chi-shen* | 27. T'an Yen-k'ai |
| 15. Li Lieh-chün | 28. Ting Wei-fen |
| 16. Li Shou-chang | 29. Wang Ching-wei |
| 17. Mme. Liao Chung-k'ai* | 30. Wang Fa-ch'in |
| (Ho Hsiang-ning) | 31. Wu Chao-shu* |
| 18. Lin Tsu-han* (Communist) | 32. Wu Yü-chang* (Communist) |
| 19. Liu Shou-chung* | 33. Yang Pan-an* (Communist) |
| 20. P'eng Che-ming* (Communist | 34. Yu Shu-te (Communist) |
| "allegiance") | 35. Yü Yu-jen |
| 21. Po Wen-wei | 36. Yün Tai-ying* (Communist) |

* Newly elected in 1926.

*Table 3*

CEC OF THE KUOMINTANG, 1929

[*The China Weekly Review*, XLVIII, No. 5 (March 30, 1929), p. 213]

| | |
|---|---|
| 1. Chang Ch'ün* | 20. Liu Lu-ying |
| 2. Chao Tai-wen* | 21. Shao Yüan-ch'ung* |
| 3. Ch'en Chao-ying* | 22. Sun Fo (Sun K'o) |
| 4. Ch'en Kuo-fu* | 23. Sung Ch'ing-ling (Mme. Sun |
| 5. Ch'en Li-fu* | Yat-sen) |
| 6. Ch'en Ming-shu* | 24. Sung Tzu-wen (T. V. Soong) |
| 7. Chiang Kai-shek (Chiang | 25. Tai Chi-t'ao |
| Chieh-shih) | 26. T'an Yen-k'ai |
| 8. Chou Ch'i-kang* | 27. Ting Wei-fen |
| 9. Chu Chia-hua* | 28. Tseng Yang-fu* |
| 10. Chu P'ei-te | 29. Wang Ching-wei |
| 11. Fang Chen-wu* | 30. Wang Po-ling* |
| 12. Fang Chiao-hui* | 31. Wu Ch'ao-shu |
| 13. Feng Yü-hsiang* | 32. Wu Te-chen* (Wu T'ieh- |
| 14. Ho Ch'eng-chün* | ch'eng) |
| 15. Ho Ying-ch'in* | 33. Yang Shu-chuang* |
| 16. Hu Han-min | 34. Yeh Ch'u-ts'ang |
| 17. Li Wen-fan* | 35. Yen Hsi-shan* |
| 18. Liu Chih* (Liu Shih) | 36. Yü Yu-jen |
| 19. Liu Chi-wen* | |

* Newly elected in 1929.

*Table 4*

CEC OF THE KUOMINTANG, 1931

[*China Year Book, 1931*, pp. 583–584]

| | |
|---|---|
| 1. Chang Chen* | 20. Liu Shih (Liu Chih) |
| 2. Chang Ch'ün | 21. Shao Yüan-ch'ung |
| 3. Ch'en Chao-ying | 22. Sun Fo (Sun K'o) |
| 4. Ch'en Kuo-fu | 23. Sung Ch'ing-ling (Mme. Sun |
| 5. Ch'en Li-fu | Yat-sen) |
| 6. Ch'en Ming-shu | 24. Sung Tzu-wen (T. V. Soong) |
| 7. Ch'en Yao-yuan* | 25. Tai Chi-t'ao |
| 8. Chiang Kai-shek (Chiang | 26. Ting Ch'ao-wu* |
| Chieh-shih) | 27. Ting Wei-fen |
| 9. Chou Ch'i-kang | 28. Tseng Yang-fu |
| 10. Chu Chia-hua | 29. Wang Cheng-t'ing* |
| 11. Chu P'ei-te | 30. Wang Po-ch'ün* |
| 12. Fang Chiao-hui | 31. Wang Po-ling |
| 13. Ho Ch'eng-chün | 32. Wu Ch'ao-shu |
| 14. Ho Ying-ch'in | 33. Wu T'ieh-ch'eng (Wu |
| 15. Hu Han-min | Te-chen) |
| 16. K'ung Hsiang-hsi* | 34. Yang Shu-chuang |
| 17. Li Wen-fan | 35. Yeh Ch'u-ts'ang |
| 18. Liu Chi-wen | 36. Yü Yu-jen |
| 19. Liu Lu-ying | |

* Newly elected in 1931.

*Table 5*

CEC OF THE KUOMINTANG, 1931

[*The Chinese Year Book, 1935–1936*, p. 147]

| | |
|---|---|
| 1. Chang Chen | 18. Chu Chia-hua |
| 2. Chang Chih-pen | 19. Chu P'ei-te |
| 3. Chang Ch'ün | 20. Fang Chiao-hui |
| 4. Chang Hui-chang | 21. Feng Yü-hsiang |
| 5. Chao Tai-wen | 22. Fu Ju-lin |
| 6. Ch'en Chao-ying | 23. Ho Ch'eng-chün |
| 7. Ch'en Chi-t'ang | 24. Ho Hsiang-ning (Mme. Liao |
| 8. Ch'en Kung-po | Chung-k'ai) |
| 9. Ch'en Kuo-fu | 25. Ho Yao-chu |
| 10. Ch'en Li-fu | 26. Ho Ying-ch'in |
| 11. Ch'en Ts'e | 27. Hsia Tou-yin |
| 12. Ch'eng Ch'ien | 28. Hsiung K'e-wu |
| 13. Chiang Kai-shek | 29. Hu Han-min |
| 14. Ching Heng-yi | 30. Kan Nai-kuang |
| 15. Chou Ch'i-kang | 31. Ku Chu-t'ung |
| 16. Chou Fo-hai | 32. Ku Meng-yü |
| 17. Chü Cheng | 33. Kuei Ch'ung-chi |

## Table 5 (Continued)

34. K'ung Hsiang-hsi
35. Li Lieh-chün
36. Li Tsung-huang
37. Li Wen-fan
38. Li Yang-ching
39. Lin Yi-chung
40. Liu Chih (Liu Shih)
41. Liu Chi-wen
42. Liu Lu-ying
43. Liu Shou-chung
44. Ma Ch'ao-chün
45. Mao Tsu-ch'üan
46. Po Ch'ung-hsi
47. Po Wen-wei
48. Po Yün-t'i
49. Shao Yüan-ch'ung
50. Shih Ching-yang
51. Shih Ying
52. Sun Fo (Sun K'o)
53. Sung Ch'ing-ling
54. Sung Tzu-wen
55. Tai Chi-t'ao
56. T'an Cheng
57. Teng Chia-yen
58. Ting Ch'ao-wu
59. Ting Wei-fen
60. Tseng Yang-fu
61. Wang Cheng-t'ing (C. T. Wang)
62. Wang Ching-wei
63. Wang Fa-ch'in
64. Wang Po-ch'ün
65. Wang Po-ling
66. Wo Te-chen (Wu T'ieh-ch'eng)
67. Yang Chieh
68. Yeh Ch'u-ts'ang
69. Yen Hsi-shan
70. Yü Han-mou
71. Yü Yu-jen

## Table 6

### CEC of the Kuomintang, 1935

[China Weekly Review, XXIV (November 30, 1934), p. 453]

1. Chang Chih-chung*
2. Chang Ch'ün
3. Chang Chung*
4. Chang Hsüeh-liang*
5. Chang Li-sheng*
6. Chang Tao-fan*
7. Chao Tai-wen
8. Ch'en Chao-ying
9. Ch'en Ch'eng*
10. Ch'en Chi-ch'eng*
11. Ch'en Chi-t'ang*
12. Ch'en Kung-po
13. Ch'en Kuo-fu
14. Ch'en Li-fu
15. Ch'en Pu-lei*
16. Ch'en Shao-k'uan*
17. Ch'en Ts'e*
18. Ch'en Yi* (Ch'en I)
19. Cheng Chan-nan*
20. Chiang Kai-shek (Chiang Chieh-shih)
21. Chiang Po-ch'eng*
22. Chiang Ting-wen*
23. Chiao I-t'ang*
24. Ch'ien Ta-chun*
25. Chou Ch'i-kang
26. Chou Fo-hai*
27. Chou Po-min*
28. Chü Cheng
29. Chu Chia-hua
30. Chu P'ei-te
31. Chu Shao-liang*
32. Fang Chiao-hui
33. Fang Chih*
34. Feng Yü-hsiang*
35. Fu Ping-ch'ang*

* Newly elected in 1935.

## Table 6 (Continued)

36. Fu Tso-yi*
37. Han Fu-ch'ü*
38. Ho Ch'eng-chün
39. Ho Chien*
40. Ho Chung-han*
41. Ho Ying-ch'in
42. Hsia Tou-yin*
43. Hsiao Chi-shan*
44. Hsiao T'ung-tz'u*
45. Hsiung Shih-hui*
46. Hsu En-tseng*
47. Hsü K'an*
48. Hsü Yüan-ch'üan*
49. Hu Han-min
50. Huang Hsü-ch'u*
51. Huang Mu-tung*
52. Hung Lan-yu*
53. Hung Lu-tung*
54. Kan Nai-kuang
55. Ku Cheng-kang*
56. Ku Cheng-lun*
57. Ku Chu-t'ung*
58. Ku Meng-yü
59. Kung-Chio-Chung-Ni*
60. K'ung Hsiang-hsi
61. Li Shen-ta*
62. Li Tsung-huang*
63. Li Wen-fan
64. Li Yang-ching*
65. Liang Han-ts'ao*
66. Lin Yi-chung*
67. Liu Chien-hsü*
68. Liu Chih (Liu Shih)
69. Liu Chi-wen
70. Liu Hsiang*
71. Liu Lu-ying
72. Liu Wei-chih*
73. Lo Ching-tao*
74. Lo-sang-chien-tsan*
75. Lu Chung-lin*
76. Ma Ch'ao-chün*
77. Mai-ssu-wu-te*
78. Mao Tsu-ch'üan*
79. Mei Kung-jen*
80. Miao P'ei-ch'eng*
81. Miao P'ei-nan*
82. P'an Kung-chan*
83. P'eng Hsüeh-p'ei*
84. Po Ch'ung-hsi*
85. Po Wen-wei
86. Shen Hung-lieh*
87. Shih Ying
88. Sun Fo (Sun K'o)
89. Sun Tzu-wen (T. V. Soong)
90. Tai Chi-t'ao
91. Tai Huai-sheng*
92. T'ang Yu-jen*
93. T'ien K'un-shan*
94. Ting Ch'ao-wu
95. Ting Wei-fen
96. Tseng K'uo-ch'ing*
97. Tseng Yang-fu
98. Tsou Lu    (Chou Lu)
99. Wang Chi*
100. Wang Ching-wei
101. Wang Chuan-sheng*
102. Wang Chun*
103. Wang Fa-ch'in
104. Wang I-che*
105. Wang Lu-yi*
106. Wang Po-ch'ün
107. Wang Po-ling
108. Wang Sou-fang*
109. Wei Li-huang*
110. Wu Hsing-ya*
111. Wu Te-chen (Wu T'ieh-ch'eng)
112. Yang Chieh*
113. Yeh Ch'u-ts'ang
114. Yen Hsi-shan
115. Yü Ching-t'ang*
116. Yü Han-mou*
117. Yu Hsi-shan*
118. Yü Hsüeh-chung*
119. Yü Yu-jen

* Newly elected in 1935.

## Table 7
### CEC OF THE KUOMINTANG, 1945
[*Biographies of Kuomintang Leaders*, Harvard University, 1948]

| | |
|---|---|
| 1. Chang Chen* | 46. Chü Cheng |
| 2. Chang Chia-ao* | 47. Chu Chi-ch'ing* |
| 3. Chang Ch'iang* | 48. Chu Chia-hua |
| 4. Chang Chih-chiang* | 49. Chu Huai-ping* |
| 5. Chang Chih-chung | 50. Chu Shao-liang |
| 6. Chang Ch'ün | 51. Fan Yü-sui* |
| 7. Chang Kuo-t'ao* | 52. Fang Chiao-hui |
| 8. Chang Li-sheng | 53. Fang Chih |
| 9. Chang Tao-fan | 54. Fang Ch'ing-ju* |
| 10. Chang T'ing-hsiu* | 55. Feng Ch'in-tsai* |
| 11. Chang Wei* | 56. Feng Yü-hsiang |
| 12. Chao Yün-yi* | 57. Fu Ju-lin* |
| 13. Ch'en Chao-ying | 58. Fu Ping-ch'ang |
| 14. Ch'en Ch'eng | 59. Fu Tso-yi |
| 15. Ch'en Chi-ch'eng | 60. Han Chen-sheng* |
| 16. Ch'en Chi-t'ang | 61. Ho Ch'eng-chün |
| 17. Ch'en Chien-ju* | 62. Ho Chien |
| 18. Ch'en Ch'ing-yün* | 63. Ho Chung-han |
| 19. Ch'en Fang-hsien* | 64. Ho Ying-ch'in |
| 20. Ch'en Hsi-hao* | 65. Hsia Tou-yin |
| 21. Ch'en Hsüeh-p'ing* | 66. Hsia Wei* |
| 22. Ch'en I (Ch'en Yi) | 67. Hsiang Chuan-yi* |
| 23. Ch'en Kuo-ch'u* | 68. Hsiang Ting-jung* |
| 24. Ch'en Kuo-fu | 69. Hsiao Cheng* |
| 25. Ch'en Li-fu | 70. Hsiao Chi-shan |
| 26. Ch'en Lien-fen* | 71. Hsiao T'ung-tz'u |
| 27. Ch'en Pu-lei | 72. Hsiung Shih-hui |
| 28. Ch'en Shao-k'uan | 73. Hsü Chen* |
| 29. Ch'en Shih-ch'üan* | 74. Hsü K'an |
| 30. Ch'en Shu-jen* | 75. Hsü Shao-ti* |
| 31. Ch'en Ts'e | 76. Hsü Yüan-ch'üan |
| 32. Cheng Chieh-min* | 77. Hsüeh Tu-pi* |
| 33. Ch'eng Ch'ien | 78. Hu Ch'ien-chung* |
| 34. Ch'eng Ssu-yüan* | 79. Hu Tsung-nan* |
| 35. Ch'eng T'ien-fang* | 80. Huang Chi-lu* |
| 36. Cheng Yen-fen* | 81. Huang Chung-hsiang* |
| 37. Ch'i Shih-ying* | 82. Huang Hsü-ch'u |
| 38. Chiang Po-ch'eng | 83. Huang Shih* |
| 39. Chiang Ting-wen | 84. Huang Yü-jen* |
| 40. Chiao I-t'ang | 85. Hung Lan-yu |
| 41. Ch'ien Ta-chün | 86. Hung Lu-tung |
| 42. Chou Ch'i-kang | 87. Jo Chen* |
| 43. Chou Chih-jou* | 88. Kan Chia-hsing* |
| 44. Chou Po-min | 89. Kan Nai-kuang |
| 45. Chou Yi-pin* | 90. K'ang Tse* |

* Newly elected in 1945.

*Table 7 (Continued)*

| | |
|---|---|
| 91. Ku Cheng-kang | 137. Lu Ch'ung-jen* |
| 92. Ku Cheng-lun | 138. Lu Chung-lin |
| 93. Ku Cheng-ting* | 139. Lu Fu-t'ing* |
| 94. Ku Chu-t'ung | 140. Lu Han* |
| 95. Ku Hsi-p'ing* | 141. Lü Yün-chang* |
| 96. Ku Meng-yü | 142. Ma Ch'ao-chün |
| 97. Ku Wei-chün* (V. K. | 143. Ma Hung-k'uei* |
|     Wellington Koo) | 144. Ma Yüan-fang* |
| 98. Kuan Lin-cheng* | 145. Mai-ssu-wu-te |
| 99. Kuei Yung-ch'ing* | 146. Mao Tsu-ch'üan |
| 100. K'ung Hsiang-hsi | 147. Mei Kung-jen |
| 101. Kung Tzu-chih* | 148. Mei Yi-ch'i* |
| 102. Kuo Hsien* | 149. Mei Yu-cho* |
| 103. Lai Lien* | 150. Miao P'ei-ch'eng |
| 104. Li Chung-hsiang* | 151. Miao P'ei-nan |
| 105. Li Han-hun* | 152. Ou-yang Chü* |
| 106. Li I-chung* | 153. P'an Kung-chan |
| 107. Li Jen-jen* | 154. P'an Kung-pi* |
| 108. Li Mo-an* | 155. P'ang Ching-t'ang* |
| 109. Li P'ei-chi* | 156. P'eng Chao-hsien* |
| 110. Li P'in-hsien* | 157. P'eng Hsüeh-p'ei |
| 111. Li Shu-hua* | 158. Po Ch'ung-hsi |
| 112. Li Ta-chao* | 159. Po Wen-wei |
| 113. Li Tsung-huang | 160. Po Yün-t'i* |
| 114. Li Wei-kuo* | 161. Shen Hui-lien* |
| 115. Li Wen-fan | 162. Shen Hung-lieh |
| 116. Li Yang-ching | 163. Shih Tzu-chou* |
| 117. Liang Han-ts'ao | 164. Sun Fo (Sun K'o) |
| 118. Lin Hsüeh-yüan* | 165. Sun Wei-ju* |
| 119. Lin Tieh* | 166. Sung Ch'ing-ling (Mme. Sun |
| 120. Lin Yi-chung |     Yat-sen) |
| 121. Liu Chien-ch'ün* | 167. Sung Hsi-lien* |
| 122. Liu Chien-hsü | 168. Sung Mei-ling* (Mme. Chiang |
| 123. Liu Chih (Liu Shih) |     Kai-shek) |
| 124. Liu Chi-hung* | 169. Sung Tzu-wen (T. V. Soong) |
| 125. Liu Chi-wen | 170. Ta-li-cha-ya* |
| 126. Liu Fei* | 171. Tai Ch'uan-hsien (Tai |
| 127. Liu K'o-shu* |     Chi-t'ao) |
| 128. Liu Wei-chih | 172. Tai Huai-sheng |
| 129. Liu Wen-hui* | 173. T'ang En-po* |
| 130. Liu Yao-chang* | 174. T'ang Sheng-chih* |
| 131. Lo Chia-lun* | 175. Teng Chia-yen* |
| 132. Lo Cho-ying* | 176. Teng Fei-huang* |
| 133. Lo Mei-huan* | 177. Teng Hsi-hou* |
| 134. Lo Sha-t'ien* | 178. Teng Pao-shan* |
| 135. Lo-sang-chien-tsan | 179. Teng Wen-yi* |
| 136. Lou T'ung-sun* | 180. Ti Ying* |

* Newly elected in 1945.

## Table 7 (Continued)

| | |
|---|---|
| 181. T'ien K'un-shan | 203. Wu K'ai-hsien* |
| 182. Ting Ch'ao-wu | 204. Wu Pao-feng* |
| 183. Ting Wei-fen | 205. Wu Shang-ying* |
| 184. Tseng K'uo-ch'ing | 206. Wu Shao-shu* |
| 185. Tseng Yang-fu | 207. Wu T'ieh-ch'eng (Wu |
| 186. Tsou Lu (Chou Lu) | Te-chen) |
| 187. Tuan Hsi-p'eng* | 208. Yang Ai-yüan*‡ |
| 188. Tung Hsien-kuang* | 209. Yang Chieh |
| (Hollington Tong) | 210. Yang Tuan-liu* |
| 189. Wan Fu-lin* | 211. Yeh Ch'u-ts'ang |
| 190. Wang Cheng-t'ing | 212. Yeh Hsiu-feng* |
| 191. Wang Ch'i-chiang* | 213. Yen Hsi-shan |
| 192. Wang Ling-chi* | 214. Yen Hua-t'ang* |
| 193. Wang Mou-kung* | 215. Yü Ching-t'ang |
| 194. Wang Tsan-hsü* | 216. Yü Chün-hsien* |
| 195. Wang Tsung-shan* | 217. Yü Fei-peng* |
| 196. Wang Tung-yüan* | 218. Yü Han-mou |
| 197. Wang Yao-wu* | 219. Yü Hsüeh-chung |
| 198. Wei Li-huang | 220. Yü Hung-chün* |
| 199. Wei Tao-ming* | 221. Yü Yu-jen |
| 200. Weng Wen-hao* | 222. Yüan Shou-ch'ien* |
| 201. Wu Chung-hsin* | 223. Yüan Yung (?)*‡ |
| 202. Wu I-feng* | |

* Newly elected in 1945.
‡ The *Chinese Year Book, 1945* names all but Yang Ai-yüan and Yüan Yung. Chiang Kai-shek as Tsungtsai is not included.

## Appendix C. Communist Party Elite

### Table 1
#### Congresses of the Chinese Communist Party

| Congress | Date | | Place | Number of Delegates | Reported Party Membership |
|---|---|---|---|---|---|
| First | July | 1921 | Shanghai | 13 | 50 |
| Second | May | 1922 | West Lake, Hangchow | 20 | 100 |
| Third | June | 1923 | Canton | 20 | 300 |
| Fourth | January | 1925 | Shanghai | — | 1,000 (at least) |
| Fifth | April | 1927 | Hankow | 100 | 60,000 |
| Special | August | 1927 | Kiukiang | 22 | |
| Sixth | August | 1928 | Moscow | 50 | 15,000 |
| Seventh | April | 1945 | Yenan | 485 | 1,000,000 (or more) |

### Table 2
### DELEGATES TO THE FIRST CHINESE COMMUNIST PARTY CONGRESS*
### (JULY 1921)

[The information in the following table was drawn from Kanichi Hatano, *History of the Chinese Communist Party, Asia Mondai Koza,* Vol. II, Tokyo, 1936; *History of the Chinese Communist Party,* Japanese Foreign Office, July 1931; *Chung-kuo hsien-tui ko-ming yun-tung shih,* 1941, Hsin-hua shu-tien, Chap. V, Sec. 2, "The Birth of the Communist Party"; Edgar Snow, *Red Star over China,* p. 157.]

| Name | Representing | Fate |
|------|------|------|
| 1. Chang Kuo-t'ao | Peking | Alive March 15, 1950 |
| 2. Ch'en Kung-po | Kwangtung | Executed June 4, 1948 |
| 3. Ch'en T'an-ch'iu | Wuhan | Alive January 1, 1950 |
| 4. Chou Fo-hai | Japan | Died in prison February 28, 1948 |
| 5. Ho Shu-heng | Changsha | Shot in May 1934 by KMT |
| 6. Li Han-chün | Shanghai | Killed by KMT in 1927 |
| 7. Li Ta | Shanghai | Uncertain. A "Li Ta" was alive January 15, 1949 |
| 8. Liu Jen-ch'ing | Peking | Uncertain |
| 9. Mao Tse-tung | Changsha | Alive March 15, 1950 |
| 10. Pao Hui-seng | Kwangtung | Alive March 15, 1950 |
| 11. T'ien En-min | | Uncertain |
| 12. Tung Pi-wu | Wuhan | Alive March 15, 1950 |
| 13. Wang Ch'iu-meng | | Uncertain |

* Tentative list.

It is probable that Comintern representatives Voitinsky and Maring were also present, although, according to some reports, Voitinsky was not there, but Maring and another agent named Nikorusky were.

### Table 3
### POLITBURO: CCP*
### (FIFTH CONGRESS, APRIL 1927)

| | |
|------|------|
| Chang Kuo-t'ao | Li Wei-han† |
| Ch'en Tu-hsiu† | T'an P'ing-shan† |
| Chou En-lai† | Su Chao-cheng† |
| Ch'ü Ch'iu-pai† | Ts'ai Ho-shen† |
| Li Li-san† | |

* Tentative list.
† New members.

*Table 4*
POLITBURO: CCP*
(REORGANIZED JULY 13, 1927)

| | |
|---|---|
| Chang T'ai-lei† | Li Wei-han |
| Ch'in Pang-hsien† | P'eng P'ai† |
| Chou En-lai | Su Chao-cheng |
| Ch'ü Ch'iu-pai | |

* Tentative list. Sources differ as to whether or not Mao was a full member of this Politburo.
† New members.

*Table 5*
"RULING CLIQUE": CCP*
(AUGUST 7, 1927)

| | |
|---|---|
| Chou En-lai | Li Li-san |
| Ch'ü Ch'iu-pai | Li Wei-han |
| Hsiang Chung-fa† | Liu Shao-ch'i† |

* Tentative list.
† New members.

*Table 6*
POLITBURO: CCP*
(SIXTH CONGRESS, JULY–SEPTEMBER 1928)

| | |
|---|---|
| Chang Kuo-t'ao | Hu Wen-chiang† |
| Chou En-lai | Li Li-san |
| Ch'ü Ch'iu-pai | Ts'ai Ho-shen |
| Hsiang Chung-fa (Sec.-Gen.) | |

* Tentative list. This list may or may not be complete.
† New member.

*Table 7*
POLITBURO: CCP*
(FOURTH PLENUM, JANUARY 8, 1931)

| | |
|---|---|
| Chang Wen-t'ien† | Chou En-lai |
| Ch'en Shao-yü† | Hsiang Chung-fa (Sec.-Gen.) |
| Ch'in Pang-hsien (?) | Shen Tse-min† |

* Tentative list. This list is probably incomplete.
† New members.

## Table 8
### POLITBURO: CCP*
### (JUNE 1931)

| | |
|---|---|
| Chang Wen-t'ien | Meng Ch'ing-shu (Mme. Ch'en |
| Ch'en Shao-yü (Sec.-Gen.) | Shao-yü)† |
| Ch'in Pang-hsien | Shen Tse-min |
| Chou En-lai | |

\* Tentative list. This list may or may not be complete.
† New member.

## Table 9
### POLITBURO: CCP*
### (JANUARY 1934)

| | |
|---|---|
| Chang Wen-t'ien | Liang Pai-tai† |
| Ch'en Shao-yü | Liu Shao-ch'i |
| Ch'in Pang-hsien | Mao Tse-tung |
| Chou En-lai | Wang Chia-hsiang† |
| Chu Te† | Wu Liang-ping† |
| Hsiang Ying† | |

\* Tentative list.
† New members.

## Table 10
### POLITBURO: CCP*
### (APRIL–JULY 1937)

| | |
|---|---|
| Chang Kuo-t'ao | Chu Te |
| Chang Wen-t'ien | Mao Tse-tung |
| Ch'in Pang-hsien | Wang Chia-hsiang |
| Chou En-lai | |

\* Tentative list. This list is probably incomplete.

## Table 11
### POLITBURO: CCP*
### (POST-1945)

| | |
|---|---|
| Chang Wen-t'ien | Lin Tsu-han† |
| Ch'en Yün† | Liu Shao-ch'i |
| Chou En-lai | Mao Tse-tung |
| Chu Te | P'eng Chen† |
| Jen Pi-shih† | Tung Pi-wu |
| K'ang Sheng† | Wang Chia-hsiang |
| Kao Kang† | |

\* Tentative list.
† New members.

*Table 12*
POLITBURO: CCP\*
(NOVEMBER 15, 1951)
[*Current Background*, No. 137, American Consulate General,
Hong Kong, p. 5]

| Ch'en Yün | Liu Shao-ch'i (Deputy Chair- |
|---|---|
| Chou En-lai | man) |
| Chu Te | Mao Tse-tung (Chairman) |
| Lin Tsu-han | P'eng Chen |

\* Tentative list.

*Table 13*
CENTRAL COMMITTEE OF THE CHINESE COMMUNIST PARTY (1945)\*
[*China Digest*, July 13, 1949, p. 17]

1. Chang Ting-ch'eng
2. Chang Yün-yi
3. Ch'en Shao-yü (Wang Ming)
4. Ch'en T'an-ch'iu
5. Ch'en Yi
6. Ch'en Yün
7. Cheng Wei-san
8. Ch'in Pang-hsien (Po Ku) (Wang Chia-hsiang, 2/15/50)†
9. Chou En-lai
10. Chu Te
11. Ho Lung
12. Hsu Hsiang-ch'ien
13. Hsü T'e-li
14. Jao Shu-shih
15. Jen Pi-shih
16. K'ang Sheng
17. Kao Kang
18. Kuan Hsiang-ying (Liao Ch'eng-chih, 2/15/50)†
19. Li Fu-ch'un
20. Li Hsien-nien
21. Li Li-san
22. Lin Feng
23. Lin Piao
24. Lin Po-ch'ü (Lin Tsu-han)
25. Liu Po-ch'eng
26. Liu Shao-ch'i
27. Lo Fu (Chang Wen-t'ien)
28. Lo Jung-huan
29. Lo Ting-yi (Lu Ting-yi)
30. Mao Tse-tung
31. Nieh Jung-chen
32. P'eng Chen
33. P'eng Te-huai
34. Po Yi-p'o
35. T'an Chen-lin
36. Teng Shiu-ping (Teng Hsiao-p'ing)
37. T'eng Tai-yüan
38. Teng Tzu-hui
39. Ts'ai Ch'ang (Miss)
40. Tseng Shan
41. Tung Pi-wu
42. Wang Jo-fei (Ch'en Po-ta, 2/15/50)†
43. Wu Yü-chang
44. Yeh Chien-ying

\* Tentative list.
† As of February 15, 1950, the Central Committee included the same members, except that Ch'in Pang-hsien, Kuan Hsiang-ying, and Wang Jo-fei, who have died since 1945, were replaced by Wang Chia-hsiang, Liao Ch'eng-chih, and Ch'en Po-ta.
In 1945 the top six alternates, in order, were Liao Ch'eng-chih, Wang Chia-hsiang, Ch'en Po-ta, Wang Shou-tao, Li Yu, and Teng Ying-ch'ao.

## Table 14
### CENTRAL COMMITTEE OF THE CHINESE COMMUNIST PARTY*
### (NOVEMBER 15, 1951)
[*Current Background*, No. 137, American Consulate General, Hong Kong, p. 3]

| | |
|---|---|
| 1. Mao Tse-tung | 22. Chang Wen-t'ien (Lo Fu) |
| 2. Chu Te | 23. Ts'ai Ch'ang (Mme. Li |
| 3. Liu Shao-ch'i | Fu-ch'un) |
| Jen Pi-shih (deceased) | 24. Teng Hsiao-p'ing |
| 4. Lin Tsu-han (Lin Po ch'ü) | 25. Lu Ting-yi |
| 5. Lin Piao | 26. Tseng Shan |
| 6. Tung Pi-wu | 27. Yeh Chien-ying |
| 7. Ch'en Yün | 28. Nieh Jung-chen |
| 8. Hsu Hsiang-ch'ien; Kuan | 29. P'eng Te-huai |
| Hsiang-ying (deceased), | 30. Teng Tzu-hui |
| Ch'en T'an-ch'iu (deceased) | 31. Wu Yü-chang |
| 9. Kao Kang | 32. Lin Feng |
| 10. Li Fu-ch'un | 33. T'eng Tai-yüan |
| 11. Jao Shu-shih | 34. Chang Ting-ch'eng |
| 12. Li Li-san | 35. Hsü T'e-li |
| 13. Lo Jung-huan | 36. T'an Chen-lin |
| 14. K'ang Sheng | 37. Li Hsien-nien |
| 15. P'eng Chen | 38. Po Yi-p'o |
| Wang Jo-fei (deceased) | 39. Ch'en Shao-yü |
| 16. Chang Yün-yi | Ch'in Pang-hsien (deceased) |
| 17. Ho Lung | 40. Liao Ch'eng-chih |
| 18. Ch'en Yi | 41. Wang Chia-hsiang |
| 19. Chou En-lai | 42. Ch'en Po-ta |
| 20. Liu Po-ch'eng | 43. Huang K'o-ch'eng† |
| 21. Cheng Wei-san | |

* Arranged in the order of votes received.

† Huang K'o-ch'eng is the only member not on the previous list.

## APPENDIX D. SUPPLEMENTARY STATISTICAL DATA

### Table 1

### BASIC DATA ON POLITBURO MEMBERS

| Group | Number of Members | Average Age | Birthplace | Education | Father's Status | Father's General Occupation | Class |
|---|---|---|---|---|---|---|---|
| Delegates 1st Congress (Ch'en incl.) July 1921 | 14 | 29.4 (Don't know, 5) | Hunan 3<br>Hupeh 3<br>Kiangsi 1<br>Anhwei 1<br>Kwangtung 1<br>(Don't know, 5) | China 4<br>Japan 4<br>S. U. 3<br>U. S. 1<br>(Don't know, 6) | Wealthy landlord 2<br>Wealthy peasant 1<br>Revolutionist 1<br>(Don't know, 10) | Landlord 2<br>Peasant 1<br>Scholar 1 | Upper, upper-middle 3<br>Middle 0<br>Lower-middle, lower 1 |
| Politburo April 1927 | 9 | 33.4 (Don't know, 2) | Hunan 3<br>Kiangsu 2<br>Kiangsi 1<br>Anhwei 1<br>Kwangtung 1<br>(Don't know, 1) | France 5<br>China 4<br>S. U. 4<br>Japan 2<br>Germany 1<br>(Don't know, 1) | Statesman 1<br>Mandarin 1<br>Wealthy landlord 1<br>Small merchant 1<br>Poor peasant 1<br>(Don't know, 4) | Landlord 1<br>Merchant 1<br>Peasant 1<br>Scholar-official 2 | Upper, upper-middle 3<br>Middle 0<br>Lower-middle, lower 2 |
| Politburo July 13, 1927 | 7 | 27.3 (Don't know, 3) | Kiangsu 3<br>Hunan 1<br>(Don't know, 3) | S. U. 3<br>France 1<br>China 1<br>Japan 1<br>Germany 1<br>(Don't know, 3) | Statesman 1<br>Mandarin 1<br>Provincial governor 1<br>Landlord 1<br>(Don't know, 3) | Landlord 1<br>Scholar-official 3 | Upper, upper-middle 4<br>Middle 0<br>Lower-middle, lower 0 |
| "Ruling Clique" August 7, 1927 | 6 | 29.0 (Don't know, 1) | Hunan 3<br>Kiangsu 2<br>Hupeh 1 | S. U. 5<br>France 3<br>China 3<br>Japan 1<br>Germany 1 | Statesman 1<br>Mandarin 1<br>Wealthy peasant 1<br>Poor peasant 1<br>Boatman 1<br>(Don't know, 1) | Scholar-official 2<br>Peasant 2<br>Proletarian 1 | Upper, upper-middle 2<br>Middle 0<br>Lower-middle, lower 3 |

*Table 1 (Continued)*

| Group | Number of Members | Average Age | Birthplace | Education | Father's Status | Father's General Occupation | Class |
|---|---|---|---|---|---|---|---|
| Politburo (may be complete), July–September 1928 | 7 | 30.0 (Don't know, 3) | Hunan 2<br>Kiangsu 2<br>Hupeh 1<br>Kiangsi 1<br>(Don't know, 1) | S. U. 5<br>France 3<br>China 3<br>Japan 1<br>Germany 1<br>(Don't know, 1) | Statesman 1<br>Mandarin 1<br>Wealthy land-lord 2<br>Poor peasant 1<br>Boatman 1<br>(Don't know, 2) | Landlord 1<br>Peasant 1<br>Scholar-official 2<br>Proletarian 1 | Upper, upper-middle 3<br>Middle 0<br>Lower-middle, lower 2 |
| Politburo (probably incomplete), January 8, 1931 | 6 | 29.0 (Don't know, 2) | Kiangsu 3<br>Anhwei 1<br>Hupeh 1<br>(Don't know, 1) | S. U. 5<br>France 1<br>Japan 1<br>Germany 1<br>U. S. 1<br>(Don't know, 1) | Mandarin 2<br>Provincial governor 1<br>Wealthy peasant 1<br>Boatman 2<br>(Don't know, 1) | Peasant 2<br>Scholar-official 2<br>Proletarian 1 | Upper, upper-middle 2<br>Middle 0<br>Lower-middle, lower 3 |
| Politburo (may be complete), June 1931 | 6 | 28.4 (Don't know, 1) | Kiangsu 3<br>Anhwei 2<br>(Don't know, 1) | S. U. 5<br>China 2<br>France 1<br>Japan 1<br>Germany 1<br>U. S. 1<br>(Don't know, 1) | Mandarin 1<br>Provincial governor 1<br>Wealthy peasant 2<br>(Don't know, 2) | Scholar-official 2<br>Peasant 1 | Upper, upper-middle 3<br>Middle 0<br>Lower-middle, lower 2<br>(Don't know, 1) |
| Politburo January 1934 | 11 | 35.2 (Don't know, 1) | Kiangsu 3<br>Hunan 2<br>Anhwei 2<br>Hupeh 1<br>Szechwan 1<br>Chekiang 1<br>(Don't know, 1) | S. U. 8<br>China 6<br>France 2<br>Germany 2<br>Japan 1<br>U. S. 1<br>No education 1<br>(Don't know, 1) | Mandarin 1<br>Provincial governor 1<br>Merchant 1<br>Wealthy peasant 4<br>Peasant 1<br>Landless peasant 1<br>Tailor 1<br>(Don't know, 1) | Merchant 1<br>Peasant 6<br>Scholar-official 2<br>Proletarian 1 | Upper, upper-middle 2<br>Middle 1<br>Lower-middle, lower 7 |

## Table 1 (Continued)

| Group | Number of Members | Average Age | Birthplace | Education | Father's Status | Father's General Occupation | Class |
|---|---|---|---|---|---|---|---|
| Politburo (probably incomplete), July 1937 | 7 | 39.3 | Kiangsu 3<br>Hunan 1<br>Anhwei 1<br>Szechwan 1<br>Kiangsi 1 | S. U. 6<br>China 5<br>France 2<br>Germany 2<br>Japan 1<br>U. S. 1 | Mandarin 1<br>Provincial governor 1<br>Wealthy landlord 1<br>Wealthy peasant 2<br>Peasant 1<br>Landless peasant 1 | Landlord 1<br>Peasant 4<br>Scholar-official 2 | Upper, upper-middle 3<br>Middle 0<br>Lower-middle, lower 4 |
| Politburo post-1945 | 13 | 48.9 (in 1945) | Hunan 4<br>Kiangsu 3<br>Anhwei 1<br>Hupeh 1<br>Szechwan 1<br>Shantung 1<br>Shensi 1<br>Shansi 1 | S. U. 11<br>China 8<br>Japan 4<br>France 3<br>Germany 2<br>U. S. 1<br>No education 1 | Mandarin 1<br>Wealthy landlord 2<br>Wealthy landlord official 1<br>Official 1<br>Wealthy peasant 4<br>Peasant 1<br>Landless peasant 2<br>(Don't know, 1) | Landlord 3<br>Peasant 7<br>Scholar-official 2 | Upper, upper-middle 5<br>Middle 0<br>Lower-middle, lower 7 |

## Table 1 (Continued)

| Group | Number of Members | Average Age | Birthplace | Education | Father's Status | Father's General Occupation | Father's Class |
|---|---|---|---|---|---|---|---|
| Total Politburo Members | 42 | 33.0* | Hunan (8) 19.1<br>Hupeh (5) 11.9<br>Kiangsu (5) 11.9<br>Anhwei (4) 9.5<br>Kwangtung (2) 4.8<br>Kiangsi (1) 2.4<br>Szechwan (1)<br>Chekiang (1) 2.4<br>Shantung (1) 2.4<br>Shensi (1) 2.4<br>Shansi (1) 2.4<br>Don't know (12) 28.6<br>100.0 | Soviet Union (20) 47.6<br>China (13) 31.0<br>France (6) 14.3<br>Japan (5) 11.9<br>United States (2) 4.8<br>Germany (2) 4.8<br>None (2) 4.8<br>Don't know (13) 31.0<br>China and Russia only (18) 42.9<br>China only (2)† 28.6<br>Military (2) 100.0 | Wealthy landlord (3) 7.1<br>Wealthy landlord official (1) 2.4<br>Landlord (1) 2.4<br>Mandarin (1) 2.4<br>Statesman (1) 2.4<br>Prov. Governor (1) 2.4<br>Official (1) 2.4<br>Revolutionist (1) 2.4<br>Merchant (1) 2.4<br>Small Merchant (1) 2.4<br>Wealthy peasant (6) 14.3<br>Peasant (1) 2.4<br>Poor peasant (1) 2.4<br>Landless peasant (2) 4.8<br>Boatman (1) 2.4<br>Tailor (1) 2.4<br>Don't know (18) 42.9<br>100.0 | Landlord (5) 11.9<br>Scholar-official (4) 9.5<br>Scholar (1) 2.4<br>Merchant (2) 4.8<br>Peasant (10) 23.8<br>Proletarian (2) 4.8<br>Don't know (18) 42.9<br>100.0 | Upper, upper-middle (11) 26.2<br>Middle (1) 2.4<br>Lower-middle, lower (13) 31.0<br>Don't know (17) 40.5<br>100.0 |

\* Average of the ten committees.
† Mao Tse-tung and T'an P'ing-shan.

*Table 2*
BASIC DATA ON CENTRAL COMMITTEE, CCP, 1945

| Age | | Father's Status | | |
|---|---|---|---|---|
| | | | No. | % |
| Average age | 46.8 | | | |
| Oldest | 68 | Aristocrat | 2 | 4.6 |
| Youngest | 36 | Upper class | 1 | 2.3 |
| 66–70 | 2 members | Wealthy landlord | 7 | 15.9 |
| 61–65 | 0 | Provincial governor | 1 | 2.3 |
| 56–60 | 3 | Wealthy merchant | 1 | 2.3 |
| 51–55 | 3 | Merchant | 1 | 2.3 |
| 46–50 | 14 | Small landlord | 1 | 2.3 |
| 41–45 | 14 | Middle class | 3 | 6.8 |
| 36–40 | 7 | Wealthy peasant | 6 | 13.6 |
| Don't know | 1 | Peasant | 1 | 2.3 |
| Total | 44 | Poor peasant | 4 | 9.1 |
| | | Proletariat | 2 | 4.6 |
| | | Don't know | 14 | 31.8 |

| Birthplace | | | | Long March | |
|---|---|---|---|---|---|
| | No. | % | | | |
| Hunan | (12) | 27.3 | | | |
| Szechwan | (6) | 13.6 | | Long March | |
| Kiangsu | (5) | 11.4 | | Yes | 24 |
| Hupeh | (5) | 11.4 | | No | 12 |
| Shansi | (3) | 6.8 | | Don't know | 8 |
| Fukien | (3) | 6.8 | | | |
| Kiangsi | (2) | 4.6 | | | |
| Anhwei | (1) | 2.3 | | | |
| Kwangtung | (1) | 2.3 | | | |
| Kwangsi | (1) | 2.3 | | | |
| Kweichow | (1) | 2.3 | | | |
| Heilungkiang | (1) | 2.3 | | | |
| Manchuria | (1) | 2.3 | | | |
| Shantung | (1) | 2.3 | | | |
| Shensi | (1) | 2.3 | | | |

## Table 3
FATHER'S STATUS: KUOMINTANG CENTRAL EXECUTIVE COMMITTEEMEN

|  | 1924 | | 1926 | | 1929 | | 1931 | |
|---|---|---|---|---|---|---|---|---|
|  | No. | % | No. | % | No. | % | No. | % |
| **Landlord** | | | | | | | | |
| Scholar | — | | (2) | 5.6 | — | | — | |
| Large | (3) | 12.5 | (3) | 8.3 | (4) | 11.1 | (2) | 5.6 |
| Medium | (3) | 12.5 | (3) | 8.3 | (1) | 2.8 | (2) | 5.6 |
| Small | (1) | 4.2 | (1) | 2.8 | — | | — | |
|  | | 29.2 | | 25.0 | | 13.9 | | 11.1 |
| **Merchant** | | | | | | | | |
| Scholar | (2) | 8.3 | (1) | 2.8 | (1) | 2.8 | (1) | 2.8 |
| Large | (1) | 4.2 | (4) | 11.1 | (3) | 8.3 | (4) | 11.1 |
| Medium | (1) | 4.2 | (5) | 13.9 | (5) | 13.9 | (4) | 11.1 |
| Small | (1) | 4.2 | (1) | 2.8 | (5) | 13.9 | (5) | 13.9 |
|  | | 20.8 | | 30.5 | | 38.9 | | 38.9 |
| **Peasant** | | | | | | | | |
| Large landed | — | | — | | — | | — | |
| Medium landed | — | | (1) | 2.8 | — | | — | |
| Small landed | — | | — | | (1) | 2.8 | (1) | 2.8 |
| Landless | — | | — | | (1) | 2.8 | — | |
|  | | 0.0 | | 2.8 | | 5.6 | | 2.8 |
| Scholar | (2) | 8.3 | (2) | 5.6 | — | | — | |
| Scholar-official | (2) | 8.3 | (2) | 5.6 | (2) | 5.6 | (2) | 5.6 |
| Artisan | | | | | | | | |
| Laborer | | | | | | | | |
| Military officer | | | | | | | | |
| Other—professional revolutionary | — | | (2) | 5.6 | (1) | 2.8 | (1) | 2.8 |
| Don't know | (8) | 33.3 | (9) | 25.0 | (12) | 33.3 | (14) | 38.9 |
|  | | 100.0 | | 100.0 | | 100.0 | | 100.0 |
| All scholars | (6) | 25.0 | (7) | 19.4 | (3) | 8.3 | (3) | 8.3 |

## Table 4
### BIRTHPLACES OF CENTRAL EXECUTIVE COMMITTEEMEN

| | 1924 | | | 1926 | | | 1929 | |
|---|---|---|---|---|---|---|---|---|
| | No. | % | | No. | % | | No. | % |
| Kwangtung | (4) | 16.7 | Kwangtung | (7) | 19.4 | Kwangtung | (9) | 25.0 |
| Hupeh | (4) | 16.7 | Hunan | (3) | 8.3 | Chekiang | (6) | 16.7 |
| Hunan | (2) | 8.3 | Hupeh | (3) | 8.3 | Kiangsu | (4) | 11.1 |
| Szechwan | (2) | 8.3 | Chekiang | (2) | 5.6 | Kiangsi | (3) | 8.3 |
| Chahar | (2) | 8.3 | Kiangsu | (2) | 5.6 | Szechwan | (2) | 5.6 |
| Chekiang | (1) | 4.2 | Szechwan | (2) | 5.6 | Anhwei | (2) | 5.6 |
| Kiangsu | (1) | 4.2 | Kiangsi | (2) | 5.6 | Shansi | (2) | 5.6 |
| Kiangsi | (1) | 4.2 | Hopeh | (2) | 5.6 | Hupeh | (2) | 5.6 |
| Hopeh | (1) | 4.2 | Kwangsi | (2) | 5.6 | Hunan | (1) | 2.8 |
| Anhwei | (1) | 4.2 | Shensi | (2) | 5.6 | Kweichow | (1) | 2.8 |
| Shantung | (1) | 4.2 | Chahar | (1) | 2.8 | Shantung | (1) | 2.8 |
| Shensi | (1) | 4.2 | Anhwei | (1) | 2.8 | Shensi | (1) | 2.8 |
| Fukien | (1) | 4.2 | Shantung | (1) | 2.8 | Fukien | (1) | 2.8 |
| | | | Yunnan | (1) | 2.8 | Yunnan | (1) | 2.8 |
| Don't know | (2) | 8.3 | Trinidad | (1) | 2.8 | | | |
| | | | Siam | (1) | 2.8 | Don't know | (0) | — |
| | | | | | | | | |
| | | | Don't know | (3) | 8.3 | | | |

| | 1931 | | | 1935 | | | 1945 | |
|---|---|---|---|---|---|---|---|---|
| | No. | % | | No. | % | | No. | % |
| Kwangtung | (9) | 25.0 | Kwangtung | (23) | 19.3 | Kwangtung | (32) | 14.4 |
| Chekiang | (7) | 19.4 | Chekiang | (14) | 11.8 | Chekiang | (31) | 13.9 |
| Kiangsu | (4) | 11.4 | Kiangsu | (9) | 7.6 | Kiangsu | (24) | 10.8 |
| Kiangsi | (3) | 8.3 | Hupeh | (9) | 7.6 | Hunan | (19) | 8.5 |
| Fukien | (3) | 8.3 | Hunan | (7) | 5.9 | Szechwan | (14) | 6.3 |
| Szechwan | (2) | 5.6 | Kweichow | (6) | 5.0 | Hopeh | (11) | 4.9 |
| Hupeh | (2) | 5.6 | Kiangsi | (6) | 5.0 | Kiangsi | (11) | 4.9 |
| Kweichow | (2) | 5.6 | Szechwan | (5) | 4.2 | Anhwei | (9) | 4.0 |
| Shansi | (1) | 2.8 | Anhwei | (5) | 4.2 | Kwangsi | (8) | 3.6 |
| Shantung | (1) | 2.8 | Shansi | (5) | 4.2 | Kweichow | (8) | 3.6 |
| Shensi | (1) | 2.8 | Hopeh | (4) | 3.4 | Shansi | (8) | 3.6 |
| Yunnan | (1) | 2.8 | Shensi | (4) | 3.4 | Shantung | (7) | 3.1 |
| | | | Kwangsi | (3) | 2.5 | Hupeh | (7) | 3.1 |
| Don't know | (0) | — | Fukien | (3) | 2.5 | Shensi | (6) | 2.7 |
| | | | Yunnan | (3) | 2.5 | Fukien | (5) | 2.2 |
| | | | Liaoning | (2) | 1.7 | Liaoning | (4) | 1.8 |
| | | | Tibet | (2) | 1.7 | Kansu | (4) | 1.8 |
| | | | Shantung | (2) | 1.7 | Yunnan | (4) | 1.8 |
| | | | Kansu | (1) | 0.8 | Tibet | (2) | 0.9 |
| | | | Sinkiang | (1) | 0.8 | Sinkiang | (1) | 0.5 |
| | | | Kirin | (1) | 0.8 | Kirin | (1) | 0.5 |
| | | | | | | Honan | (1) | 0.5 |
| | | | Don't know | (4) | 3.4 | Suiyuan | (1) | 0.5 |
| | | | | | | Heilungkiang | (1) | 0.5 |
| | | | | | | Inner Mongolia | (1) | 0.5 |
| | | | | | | Honolulu | (1) | 0.5 |
| | | | | | | | | |
| | | | | | | Don't know | (2) | 0.9 |

## Table 5
### Education of Central Executive Committeemen

|  | 1924 | | 1926 | | 1929 | | 1931 | | 1935 | | 1945 | |
|---|---|---|---|---|---|---|---|---|---|---|---|---|
|  | No. | % | No. | % | No. | % | No. | % | No. | % | No. | % |
| Japanese university | (9) | 37.5 | (10) | 27.8 | (8) | 22.2 | (8) | 22.2 | (18) | 15.1 | (30) | 13.5 |
| Japanese military | (3) | 12.5 | (4) | 11.1 | (9) | 25.0 | (7) | 19.4 | (17) | 14.3 | (18) | 8.1 |
| Chinese university | (6) | 25.0 | (11) | 30.6 | (7) | 19.4 | (8) | 22.2 | (28) | 23.5 | (76) | 34.1 |
| Chinese military | (2) | 8.3 | (6) | 16.7 | (12) | 33.3 | (11) | 30.6 | (43) | 36.1 | (78) | 35.0 |
| Chinese classical | (6) | 25.0 | (5) | 13.9 | (7) | 19.4 | (4) | 11.1 | (11) | 9.2 | (8) | 3.6 |
| China only | (5) | 20.8 | (9) | 25.0 | (10) | 27.8 | (9) | 25.0 | (54) | 45.4 | (106) | 47.5 |
| United States | (1) | 4.2 | (5) | 13.9 | (7) | 19.4 | (9) | 25.0 | (13) | 10.9 | (34) | 15.3 |
| France | (3) | 12.5 | (2) | 5.6 | (1) | 2.8 | (—) |  | (3) | 2.5 | (9) | 4.0 |
| Germany | (1) | 4.2 | (1) | 2.8 | (1) | 2.8 | (1) | 2.8 | (4) | 3.4 | (13) | 5.8 |
| Great Britain | (2) | 8.3 | (3) | 8.3 | (3) | 8.3 | (3) | 8.3 | (4) | 3.4 | (11) | 4.9 |
| Belgium | (1) | 4.2 | (—) |  | (—) |  | (—) |  | (2) | 1.7 | (1) | 0.5 |
| Soviet Union | (—) |  | (2) | 5.6 | (—) |  | (—) |  | (3) | 2.5 | (11) | 4.9 |
| Other | (—) |  | (—) |  | (—) |  | (—) |  | (1) | 0.8 | (3) | 1.4 |
| None | (—) |  | (—) |  | (—) |  | (—) |  | (1) | 0.8 | (1) | 0.5 |
| Don't know | (4) | 16.7 | (6) | 16.7 | (—) |  | (1) | 2.8 | (9) | 7.6 | (9) | 4.0 |
| Total military | (4) | 16.7 | (7) | 19.4 | (14) | 38.9 | (12) | 33.3 | (51) | 42.9 | (87) | 39.0 |

## CHAPTER SEVEN

*DANIEL LERNER*

# The Coercive Ideologists
# in Perspective

REVOLUTION means, literally, turnover. Political revolution involves the turnover of power—from one set of officeholders to another, usually by violent means. Social revolution involves the turnover of social relations—as between individuals, classes, and the values that previously patterned their interactions, not necessarily by violent means. The two sorts of revolution often occur separately and independently. When one *junta* of military men replaces another at the desks of government in Latin America or the Middle East, we designate this as a *coup*. When a segment of the populace attempts to overturn the elite by force, we call this a *rebellion*. The former is a political act, usually without direct or deep social concomitants. The latter is a sociological event, which may or may not produce significant political consequences.

Marxian theory alleges that a true revolution must be both political and social. This is the sort of definitional preference by which Marxism often prescribes history under the guise of describing it. Nonetheless, political and social revolution sometimes do go together. Europe, between the two world wars, produced a series of such revolutions. Probably no quarter-century in history has witnessed a parallel turnover of power relations associated with so comprehensive a turnover of social relations.

So rapid and complete was the political revolution that names which were household words to this writer and his contemporaries now sound like ancient history to his students. Within a few short years, the dynastic monarchies that had ruled Europe for centuries were gone or going — the Romanovs, Habsburgs, Hohenzollerns, Ottomans. Interwar turnovers consigned the imperial monarchs of Italy and Spain to history's dustbin, and World War II completed the process with the evacuation of the Balkan thrones. The long days of the kings were swiftly ended.[1]

The political violence that overturned the imperial dynasties also overturned the social relations that had been patterned upon the supremacy of crown and court. Out went the traditional elites of birth and blood; in came the new revolutionary elites of skill and will. The exiled aristocracy and decimated bourgeoisie were supplanted by professional revolutionaries and their populist cohorts. The new men of power brought with them new codes of conduct. In their hands, coercion served ideology, and both sustained power. The epithet "totalitarian" appeared in the world political lexicon to characterize these unprecedented regimes that founded new polities upon coercive ideological movements.

The pattern was set by the Bolsheviks in Russia. As opposed to Menshevik parliamentarism as to Czarist despotism, they activated the Leninist ideology of the "vanguard party" as the basis of Soviet polity.[2] The pattern spread swiftly in Eastern Europe — abortively after 1918, but triumphantly after 1945. In Western Europe, the ideology of Marxism produced a symbolic counterformation, but the methodology of Leninism served as an operational model. The eruption of Fascism in Italy, Nazism in Germany, Falangism in Spain — under the banner of anti-Communism — nicely illustrated Lasswell's concept of "restriction by partial incorporation." While restricting the Marxist ideology, they incorporated the Leninist strategy of the vanguard party. The regimes they installed were, like the Bolshevik, based upon coercive ideological movements.

These movements are the object of our studies in this volume. The differences among them are overt and obvious. Less systematically studied by social scientists — and more vigorously obscured by political propagandists — are the important characteristics that they have in common. Chief among the common characteristics is that each of these movements unleashed a social revolution in the course of executing its political revolution (caveat, pending discussion, Falangism in Spain). In the vanguard of each movement, and of the regime it founded, were men of a type never before seen at or near the ruling

[1] Edmond Taylor, The Fall of the Dynasties (Garden City, N.Y.: Doubleday, 1963).
[2] Philip Selznick, The Organizational Weapon (Glencoe, Ill.: The Free Press, 1959).

councils of European states. These were the "new men with new ideas" who led and staffed the interwar revolutions — which, in Lasswell's phrase, always involve a turnover in the "composition and vocabulary of the ruling few." The vocabulary of the coercive ideologues has been studied intensively elsewhere.[3] In this volume, we have focused upon the altered composition of the European elites wrought by the success of the revolutionary movements.

## RISE OF THE MIDDLE-INCOME SKILL GROUPS

The most obvious transformation of the European elites by the revolutionary movements was in terms of *social origins*. Under the imperial dynasties that ruled most of Europe during long centuries, people were defined as elite by *birth*. Status was inherited by the test of blood. The democratic transformations certified by the American and French revolutions at the end of the eighteenth century changed all this. Under the new democratic dispensation, status was earned by the test of merit. Birth was replaced by skill as the central criterion of elite membership.

Where the democratic code failed to take over the recruitment process, power remained in the hands of the traditional elites — as in the Czar's Russia, the Kaiser's Germany, the King's Italy. While the political elites of these countries remained immobile, however, social mobility was increasing in their economic, social, and cultural sectors. Individuals outside the aristocracy were everywhere acquiring wealth, education, and influence. In the democratic societies, such individuals were steadily gaining access to the offices of government. In the traditional dynasties, however, no political process operated to recruit these mobile individuals and groups, who were largely excluded from office and unrepresented in the councils of government.

With the fall of the dynasties, at the end of World War I, belated efforts to install a process of democratic representation were made — in Menshevik Russia and in Weimar Germany. But the ravages of war and inflation provided an uncongenial climate for bringing untutored peoples under the demanding discipline of democratic procedure. In short order the aspiring democracies succumbed to the politics of the street organized by the *Putsch* methods of the coercive ideologues, who took power to themselves under different banners and with different rules of political behavior.

Who were these violent men? Whence were they recruited? How

[3] Harold D. Lasswell *et al.*, *Language of Politics* (New York: George W. Stewart, 1949).

were their elites composed? In gross terms, they came from those middle and lower-middle classes that had been recruited into the political life of the democratic societies throughout the nineteenth century. In their own societies, however, these classes had been denied access to politics. The individuals from these classes who now came to the fore via the ideological movements brought with them the frustrations and resentments cumulated over a century of denial. Having failed to gain office by the pacific processes of representative democracy, they had committed themselves to the seizure of power via totalitarian ideology instrumented by political violence.

To say that the coercive ideologues were recruited from the "middle income" groups is to locate them in a diffuse, but significant, category. They were not the aristocrats who ruled the traditional societies of Europe for centuries — nor the plutocrats who acquired back-door influence as the dynasties faltered and failed. But neither were they the proletarians who, according to the Marxist ideology, were destined by history to take power in the new revolutionary society. It is important to register the historical fact that the "new men with new ideas" who revolutionized postwar Europe were not of the impoverished and brutalized proletariat — but of the frustrated and vengeful middle groups that had experienced some upward social mobility, gained some economic rewards, and wanted political power.

Because Marxist ideology canonized the proletariat as historical destiny, many Old Bolsheviks revised their biographies to claim or imply proletarian parentage. But it is clear, even from the sparse records which can be verified, that the early Politburo — the apex of Bolshevik power — was composed of individuals from quite different social backgrounds. Lenin's father was a school inspector, and three others were sired by teachers. Kamenev's father was an engineer, Trotsky's a landowner, and Molotov's a salesman! No proletarians these totalitarians!

A similar situation, *pari passu*, was exhibited by the Nazi elite. Since Nazi ideology glorified *Blut und Boden* (blood and soil), many of its spokesmen claimed ancestral descent from the German peasantry. But Nazi peasant origins were no more realistic than Bolshevik proletarian origins. As our study shows (see Tables 11 and 12 of *The Nazi Elite*), only a fraction of Nazi leaders — about 5 per cent in our sample — had peasant or artisan fathers. About half of them had fathers in solid middle-income occupations such as the professions, civil service, and business — whereas some 10 per cent were the scions of the higher social orders in the traditional society such as landowners, ecclesiastics, and military men.

We stress the middle-income origins of these elites because their respective mythologies — proletarian and peasant — have tended to obscure the historical facts and their concomitants. One important concomitant of middle-income status is education. The coercive ideologues, unlike most of their proletarian and peasant contemporaries, were educated men. Of our Politburo sample, over half had completed higher schools, and one third had completed university studies. Even those who did not, like Trotsky, were learned men and brilliant writers. The early Politburo, indeed, was an extraordinarily gifted group of political theorists. The works of Lenin and Trotsky are classics in their field, and no students of Russian history — or indeed of modern European history — can ignore the writings of Bukharin, Kamenev, Zinoviev.

The Nazi elite was also composed of men who had received formal education. Better than half of our sample had attended universities, and most of the others had been to high school — only a fractional 3 per cent having terminated their education with elementary schooling. This is an important key to understanding the recruitment process that operated among the revolutionary elites of the interwar generation. It was through their education that these individuals acquired the skills they used to articulate their political ideologies and organize their political movements. It is in this sense that we use the term middle-income skill groups to designate the social origins of the coercive ideologues. Their middle-income status gave them access to education, which taught them the skills they used for the seizure of power.

## DIFFERENTIATION OF SKILLS AND SHAPING OF REGIMES

The regimes installed by the coercive ideologues went through critical phases after the seizure of power. During the building of their revolutionary movements, prior to the big *Putsch,* those skilled in ideology worked tandem with those skilled in coercion. The propagandists formulated the slogans that the agitators spread among relevant sections of the population. The *agitprop* machinery of the Bolsheviks was justly famous for its effective mobilization of political action.

Through the seziure of power and its aftermath, however, there was no questioning the essential leadership of the ideologues. Without the symbol specialists to speak the words that caught the ears, touched the hearts, activated the behavior of the radicalized cohorts, the specialists in violence might have murdered and pillaged, but they could not have built a revolutionary movement capable of seizing state power. Each totalitarian regime began with its variant of an "intelligentsia" at or near the apex of the new elite. The Bolshevik elite comprised an intelligentsia of extremely high intellectual quality. Some of them, like Trotsky as War Commissar, exhibited considerable skill in the management of violence, but their primary task was to shape the images and teach the rites of the new ideology they dispensed.

Once power was seized, and its consolidation in process, an important shift occurred in the composition of the elite apex. The role of the intelligentsia, the specialists on persuasion, rapidly diminished; the power of the specialists on coercion rapidly increased. Our study of the Politburo shows this dramatic reversal of roles among the Bolsheviks. The regime of intellectuals in the Leninist Politburo was promptly subverted under the Stalinist regime. As our tables show, the Old Bolshevik intellectuals were executed, assassinated, or "disappeared" (in 1938). After Stalinization, only four members of the Politburo died of natural causes (three of "heart disease" and one of "old age"); all the rest were "removed" from office. In their place came the specialists skilled in violence rather than symbols, the administrators of coercion rather than persuasive ideology. The big change is well characterized by the transition from loquacious Lenin to silent Stalin.

Marxian theory had prepared the terrain for the prerevolutionary pre-eminence of the intelligentsia. The pre-Stalin theorist Franz Mehring, for example, had written: "The task of the intellectual consists in maintaining the freshness and vigour of the workers in their *movement towards* their great goal and in elucidating for them the social relationships which make the *approaching* victory of the proletariat a certainty."[4] (Italics supplied.) Marxian theorists were less well prepared, however, for the deadly fate that overtook them under the postrevolutionary regime. Even Lenin, whose doctrine of the "vanguard party" had assigned key roles to the intellectuals, did not foresee this turn of events — of which the first major example in current history occurred with his own death. Trotsky survived the assassin's axe just long enough to witness the process and reach back to the French Revolution for a historical parallel. The "Thermidorean Reaction" supplied the lesson.

With the decimation of the intelligentsia, the composition of the Soviet elite was transformed. Gone the theoreticians and specialists on persuasion; enthroned the administrators and specialists on

---

[4] This passage from Mehring's *Akademiker und Proletarier* is quoted in Robert Michels, *Political Parties* (Glencoe, Ill.: The Free Press, 1949), p. 327.

coercion. We are familiar with the bloody history of the U.S.S.R. under Stalin and the role of the secret police in this awesome blood-letting. Our point here is to recall that under Stalin a different manner of man rose to the apex of Soviet power. The one intellectual admitted to the Stalinist Politburo — Voznesensky, who had been a university professor — was dropped after a very short tenure. The one Old Bolshevik who displayed any longevity was Molotov, whom Lenin had called "the best filing clerk" in Russia[5] — a useful character in a regime that relied so heavily upon its filing system.

As the U.S.S.R. became an administrative state, ruled by a party cabal rather than led by a vanguard party, ideology was transmuted into theology, and persuasion was replaced by coercion. The violence legitimized by Bolshevik theorists was turned against them as it became a mode of governance under the Soviet administrators. Our study of the concomitant transformation in the composition of the Politburo moderately concludes:

> The revolution of 1917 was led and organized by brilliant young intel-lectuals from a middle-class background. In the course of the establish-ment of the Soviet state, the need for such people diminished, and they were replaced by less colorful but efficient administrators and organizers. The shift is illustrated, at the top, by the change in leadership from Lenin to Stalin.

A similar differentiation of skills appeared in the Nazi elite, whose short and abortive history compressed sociological processes. Our systematic comparison of Nazi leaders who performed ideological-persuasive functions with those who filled administrative-coercive roles shows the transition. Consistently the Nazi propagandists, im-portant while the NSDAP movement was being built, were sub-ordinated to the Nazi coercers after the *Machtergreifung*, which in-stalled the party in the seats of government.

While the Nazi propagandists of the early period were not in the same class intellectually with the early Bolshevik leaders, they were, nevertheless, intellectuals. They came from urban and well-to-do families, in which the fathers were mainly professionals and higher civil servants and businessmen (like the fathers of the early Polit-burocrats). They went to universities, were trained largely in the humanistic and culture-oriented studies, and became prolific pro-ducers of books and articles. These Nazi specialists on persuasion thus exhibited the biographical characteristics common to intellectuals in our times. Under the Weimar Republic, they were not forced into

[5] Walter Duranty, *Stalin and Company* (New York: W. Sloane Associates, 1949).

exile as the early Bolsheviks had been under Czarism, and thus were not exposed to those years of severe discipline which were intellectually so productive for the Bolsheviks. Instead, the "alienated intellectuals" of Weimar Germany withdrew into the self-indulgent bohemian subculture that flourished in Munich and other urban centers of postwar Germany. Bohemianism is the womb of irresponsibility in the guise of intellectuality, and the Nazi propagandists who issued from this matrix were intellectuals *manqués* by traditional standards. By Nazi standards, however, they were admirably equipped to function as the party intellectuals.

It was not long, however, before the specialists on coercion established their control over the specialists on persuasion along with the rest of the Nazi elite. Indeed, in the Nazi case, the intellectuals as a group were never permitted to rise to the top of the party apex (as they had done in the early Politburo). In the top offices of the NSDAP, the administrators outnumbered the propagandists by approximately two to one in 1934, immediately after the accession to power. Although we have no statistical data on the later period, it seems clear that as the decade of Nazi power wore on and the problems of popular persuasion receded before the problems of popular control, the specialists on administrative and police work broadened their domain over the entire party apparatus (including the propagandists).

Not only were the administrators less educated and more powerful than the propagandists, but in both groups the least educated men attained high party status in greater proportion than did the most educated men. The figures on education, with other data reported in the study, demonstrate a negative correlation between education and party status among the Nazi elite. Education is but one of a battery of tests that, in the study, indicate a more general negative correlation between Nazi status and previous social status; i.e., those rose highest among the Nazis who had been lowest in the pre-Nazi German society.

## POLITICAL PERSPECTIVE AND GLOBAL CONTEXT

The sociological focus of our elite studies has shown the mythologies created by the revolutionary elites to be seriously misleading in important respects. The Bolshevik elite was not proletarian; nor was the Nazi elite composed of sturdy German peasants. These interwar regimes of coercive ideology — along with their Fascist and Falangist counterparts — represented no "revolt of the masses." They were, rather, operated by and for frustrated segments of the middle classes who had been denied access to what they considered their proper place and organized violent action to gain what they had been denied. The striking historical feature is that this revolutionary process, once it erupted, spread so rapidly and so widely.

This is *not* to say that all the interwar "isms" were alike. Indeed, on the level of overt ideology, they were declared antagonists. The diffusion of coercive ideological movements throughout Europe (and elsewhere) was accomplished by the more subtle historical process of "restriction by partial incorporation." In the cause of restricting anti-Marxian ideology, the Fascists and Nazis incorporated political methodology learned from the Bolsheviks. Transformation of the European elites — and the social values represented by them — was its technique and its product.

Social change is but one aspect of any process of political sociology; the other aspect is political change. The sociological aspect was national in scope and aimed at reversing the roles between "have" and "have-not" classes. The political aspect was transnational in scope and aimed at reversing the roles between "have" and "have-not" nations. Each of the totalitarian regimes sought to make the nation an instrument of expansion in the world arena. The claim that Mussolini staked on the Mediterranean as an Italian lake — and Africa, presumably, as its farther shore — may seem absurd in retrospect, but it did not seem so when Haile Selassie addressed his vain plea for help to the League of Nations. Hitler's objective of unifying continental Europe under his *Herrenvolk* reposed upon an absurd theory, but it transposed a genocidal nightmare into a world-shaking political reality.

The most comprehensive conjunction of internal sociological processes with external political objectives was, of course, that made by Communist ideology. From the start Marxism operated with a global framework of exegesis and prescription. The *Communist Manifesto* addressed its counsel to a global audience: "Workers of the world, unite!" As the U.S.S.R. pronounced itself the "workers' fatherland," and took control of the world Communist movement via the Comintern, the identity between Soviet internal and external objectives was made complete.

The global context of Soviet policy is an essential datum for any analysis of the "world revolution of our time." It explains why the U.S.S.R., having survived the other interwar "isms" that were destroyed by World War II, emerged in the postwar period as *the* "eruptive center" of the world revolutionary process. Against the motive power generated in every part of the world by Soviet precept and practice, the non-Soviet world could operate only a defensive strategy of "containment." Perhaps no greater testimony to Soviet global prowess is needed than the nomenclature of the cold war. By the time of Stalin's death, the world arena had been effectively bi-polarized — between "the Soviet bloc" and the "non-Soviet world." Adherence or antagonism to Moscow thus became a defining principle of political action in the postwar world arena — a principle by which American policy was itself "contained."

During the two postwar decades, world politics was shaped largely by three components of the Soviet and American competition for world leadership: (1) the partition of Europe into Soviet and American spheres of influence; (2) the quest for larger spheres of influence in the rest of the world; (3) the "nuclear standoff" that obliged both superpowers to seek tacit agreement that the cold war would remain cold. The third factor has sometimes been called "nuclear stalemate" because bipolar parity rendered the nuclear power essential for mutual deterrence useless for unilateral expansion. The superpowers thus arrived at a reciprocally contained relationship. Among its apparently paradoxical effects was to broaden the scope of initiative among nations that disengaged from the bipolar deadlock. The Chinese case is of special interest.

## CHINA AND THE EMERGING NATIONS

Our study of the Chinese elites compared the top leadership of the Kuomintang and Communist movements. Again, the impression created by propaganda — that the Kuomintang was led by a landlord clique, while the Chinese Communist Party was a movement of the masses — turned out to be inaccurate and misleading. Our data showed that "a major portion of the elite of both movements came from quite similar high social strata, and responded to similar Western and native influences during their years of growth and education." The conclusion that there was a "basic similarity in social origins of the largest portion of both Kuomintang and Communist leaders" was based upon statistical tabulations summarized as follows:

> In both parties, the leaders have been drawn most frequently from a relatively thin upper layer of the Chinese population. In both parties these men were often the sons of landlords, merchants, scholars, or offi-cials, and they usually came from parts of China where Western influence had first penetrated and where the penetration itself was most vigorous. All of them had higher educations, and most of them had studied abroad. The leaders of both parties, despite a relatively high status in private life, showed a reluctance or perhaps an inability to establish private careers.

The majority were alienated intellectuals, men and women whose Western educations isolated them from the main currents of Chinese society. In the chaos of modern China, these persons became full-time professional politicians specializing, for the most part, in military violence or in party administration.

The similarities of both these revolutionary elites to those that disrupted interwar Europe are numerous and significant. Striking, too, is the later accession of plebeian individuals to the apex of party power. As among the European totalitarians, so among the coercive ideologues of China, intellectuals of higher social status founded the movements through which people of lesser status subsequently made their way to the top. This was particularly notable in the changing composition of the Chinese Communist Party Politburo, which exhibited on virtually all major aspects of social origin and life history a patterning that "conforms to the Leninist ideal of a professional revolutionary." The pattern recurred among the larger Central Committee, of whom only a half-dozen even claimed any occupation other than party work and military service — as our study concludes, "clearly a body of professional party activists."

The spread of the Bolshevik model to Asia was a stunning setback to Western, and particularly American, policy. The victory of communism in China vastly enlarged the Soviet camp and gave the Kremlin its clearest title to the global perspective and world leadership that its ideology had always claimed. It brought into doubt the historic Western claim to pre-eminence in Asia, and indeed brought Asia squarely into the sequence of cold war conflicts — from Korea, through Quemoy and Matsu, to South Viet Nam. Contained in Western Europe, Communist expansionism received a new impetus in all of South Asia via the Communization of China.

With the foundering of Western imperialism in Asia — the withdrawal of the British from India, Pakistan, Burma, Ceylon; the ejection of the French from Indochina and the Dutch from Indonesia — the emerging elites looked eagerly to the U.S.S.R. and China for support of their anti-Western purposes. They received support — and more, they received instructive guidance on how to shape their own regimes. As the first and major Asian nation to oust the imperialists and install its own regime, Communist China was a natural model for the new states.

The situation presented by Red China was characterized by John K. Fairbank, in an introduction to the Chinese elite study, in terms that are still applicable in Asia:

> Except in respect of the organization of political power, we may well claim that the West has fathered the Chinese revolution. . . . the influx

of Western ideas on all levels [has] contributed to the revolutionary process. Western contact has been subversive of the old order in China and
has inspired great new developments — not least, the rise of nationalism.
Yet in all this long and manifold process of intercultural contact, the non-
Communist West has not given China's leaders the secret of how to organize a modern political process.[6]

From this Professor Fairbank concluded: "We are here confronted
with a basic inadaptability of the Western European–American political system when applied to the agrarian-bureaucratic Chinese state."

This judgment raises major questions for science and policy in a
world arena that has produced several dozen new nations in the
past decade. Professor Fairbank's statement that "our type of Anglo-
Saxon parliamentary democracy has not been able to provide the
model for successful political organization" appears to be valid for
most of these nations. It is a matter of scientific interest to learn why
this has been so; it is a matter of policy concern to find ways of altering this situation in the future.

The Chinese challenge to the U.S.S.R. for leadership of the Communist world — certainly in Asia, and probably in Africa and Latin
America as well — has given new thrust to the process of Communization and new urgency to the problem of counteraction.[7] In those
Communist parties where the Chinese model is influential — where it
seems more relevant to political objectives than the restrained procedures of current Soviet operations — the recrudescence of coercive
ideology as a political methodology is imminent. This is an important
clue for diagnosis of the Communization process.

We have seen that the competing elites within China itself were
sociologically similar. Despite their deadly struggle for control of
state power, Kuomintang and Communist leaders were recruited
mainly from the same classes and through similar career patterns.
Even their political methods were similar, in the sense that the
Kuomintang relied as heavily upon coercion as the Communist regime.
As Fairbank points out, "the greatest difference would seem to lie in
the use of ideology as a factor in the exercise of political control."

It was just this factor of ideology as a mode of social control — and
specifically its coordination with systematic coercion — that produced
the distinctive political methodology of the European totalitarians
of the interwar period. It is this method that was introduced into

---

[6] Quoted from the Introduction to George K. Schueller, *The Politburo* (Stanford, Calif.: Stanford University Press, 1951), p. v.
[7] The global context of the Sino-Soviet dispute, and its political consequences
in selected countries, is being studied in a series of books under the general
editorship of William E. Griffith published by The M.I.T. Press.

Asia with the victory of the Communist Party in China, and it is this method that the Chinese Communists now seek to spread throughout the rest of the world. The policy sciences of democracy face no more important task than to produce an accurate diagnosis of the Communization process as a guide to effective — in this case, usually preventive — therapy.

# Index

469

Nazi elite (*continued*)
marginality of, 197, 238, 288–299, 304–305, 307–308
and method of study used, 195–198, 280–283
military service of, 206–208, 254–256
primary lifework of, 200–202, 308–310
publications of, 310–311
"restless personality" of, 295–297
Nazi Party
administrators' affiliation to, 242–245
and coercers, 262–264
and seniority, 236
*see also* German National Socialist Labor Party
Nazi police, 256–257, 258–263, 284
and NSDAP, 274–279
and *Schutz-Staffel*, 277–279
and *Sturm-Abteilung*, 236, 275–277
Nazi propagandists, 200–230, 285–286, 462
age distribution of, 203–206
education of, 215–219
foreign contacts of, 220–222
marriage of, 219–220
military service of, 206–208
occupations of, 211–215
postwar unemployment of, 229–230
publications of, 225–229
social status of, 208–211, 212
Nazi revolution, key propositions of, 197–198
Neumann, Heinz, 357, 358, 374
Neumann, John von, 35
Neumann, Sigmund, 102, 110
New Democracy, of Sun Yat-sen, 373
Nicholaevsky, Boris, 97, 117, 124, 130
"Night of the Long Knives," 277
Nikitchenko, I., 114
Nizhni-Novgorod, 129
NKVD, 121, 128, 138
Nomad, Max, 29, 86
Nonpolitical institutions, 52
North, Robert C., 424
NSDAP, *see* German National Socialist Labor Party; Nazi Party
Nuremberg, 238

Occhini, Pier-Ludovico, 188
Ogburn, W. F., 65
OGPU, 128
Oncken, Hermann, 283
Operational indexes, 44–45
Opler, Marvin K., 15
Order, public and civic, 11

Ordjonikidze, Grigorii K., 103, 111
career line of, 161
Organization Group, *see* CC Clique
Orgburo, 121

Parenti, Rino, 184
Pareto, Vilfredo, 3
Paris, center of bourgeois revolution, 80
Park, Robert E., 211
Parochialism
in bourgeois revolution, 80–81
in Moscow (1917), 75–76
in world politics, 64–68, 71–72
*Parteistatistik*, 196
Pasella, Epaminonda, 188
Pauker, Guy J., 93
Perception, pattern of, 76
Personality, role of
in elite composition, 15
of intellectual, 91
of Nazi elite, 295–297
and world politics, 68
Peshkov, Alexei, 116
Philip of Macedon, 24
Pierre, André, 120
Piggot, Stuart, 6
Plebeian, rise of, 78
Fascist, 182, 184, 193
Nazi, 197, 230–252
Russian, 104–105, 122
Plural-power pattern, 51
Politburo, *see* Chinese Politburo; Soviet Politburo
Political parties and pressure groups, 50
transnational, 6
Ponomarenko, P. K., 112–113
version of Stalin death, 174
Pool, Ithiel de Sola, 19
Popkov, P. S., 116
Popov, N., 351
Possony, Stefan T., 51
Postman, Leo, 77
Power, 8, 36
myth, 44–45, 46–47
representation and distribution of, 48
sharing of, 45–54
technique of, 47–48
unorganized arenas of, 51–52
Power elites, 12–28
continuity in, 26–27
decision process of, 10–12
definition of, 4–6
failures of British, 74–75
flexibility of British, 22
participants in, 20
social process of, 7–10